THE 1995 WORLD CHAMPION ATLANTA BRAVES

EDITED BY **TOM HUFFORD AND BILL NOWLIN**

ASSOCIATE EDITORS **LEN LEVIN AND CARL RIECHERS**

FOREWORD BY **JOHN SCHUERHOLZ**

Society for American Baseball Research, Inc.
Phoenix, AZ

"Braves Win! Braves Win! Braves Win!"
THE 1995 WORLD CHAMPION ATLANTA BRAVES
Edited by Tom Hufford and Bill Nowlin
Associate editors Len Levin and Carl Riechers
All photographs, except as noted, are courtesy of Atlanta National League Baseball Club LLC.
Major League Baseball trademarks and copyrights are used with permission of Major League Baseball. Visit MLB.com.
Front cover: On-field celebration October 28, 1995 at Atlanta-Fulton County
Stadium. Courtesy of Atlanta National League Baseball Club LLC.
Rear cover: Braves executives with the 1995 World Series trophy: Stan Kasten, John Schuerholz, Ted Turner, Bill
Bartholomay, Bobby Cox, and Terry McGuirk. Courtesy of Atlanta National League Baseball Club LLC.
1995 World Series uniform patch. Courtesy of Tom Hufford.
1995 World Championship ring. Courtesy of Tom Hufford.
Copyright © 2020 Society for American Baseball Research, Inc.
All rights reserved. Reproduction in whole or in part without permission is prohibited.
ISBN 978-1-970159-23-3
(Ebook ISBN 978-1-970159-22-6)
Book design: Rachael Sullivan
Society for American Baseball Research
Cronkite School at ASU
555 N. Central Ave. #416
Phoenix, AZ 85004
Phone: (602) 496-1460
Web: www.sabr.org
Facebook: Society for American Baseball Research
Twitter: @SABR

CONTENTS

Foreword 7
by JOHN SCHUERHOLZ

Introduction 10
by TOM HUFFORD

Players

1. *Steve Avery* 15
by TOM HUFFORD

2. *Steve Bedrosian* 24
by WYNN MONTGOMERY

3. *Rafael Belliard* 34
by JOE COX

4. *Jeff Blauser* 39
by CREG STEPHENSON

5. *Pedro Borbon Jr.* 46
by JUSTIN KRUEGER

6. *Terry Clark* 51
by TONY OLIVER

7. *Brad Clontz* 60
by JESSE ASBURY

8. *Mike Devereaux* 65
by GREG KING

9. *Ed Giovanola* 75
by CLAYTON TRUTOR

10. *Tom Glavine* 78
by JOSEPH WANCHO

11. *Marquis Grissom* 87
by ALAN MORRIS

12. *Chipper Jones* 93
by JACOB POMRENKE

13. *David Justice* 104
by SEAN TETERS

14. *Mike Kelly* 109
by JOEL RIPPEL

15. *Ryan Klesko* 116
by JOEL RIPPEL

16. *Brian Kowitz* 121
by JACK ZERBY

17. *Mark Lemke* 126
by PAUL HOFMANN

18. *Javy Lopez* 134
by KYLE EATON

19. *Greg Maddux* 141
by STEW THORNLEY

20. *Darrell May* 148
by DARIN WATSON

21. *Fred McGriff* 154
by PETER M. GORDON

22. *Greg McMichael* 160
by SCOTT BRIMER

23. *Kent Mercker* 164
by CLAYTON TRUTOR

24. *Mike Mordecai* 168
    by MARK S. STERNMAN
25. *Matt Murray* 173
    by BILL NOWLIN
26. *Rod Nichols* 179
    by MATTHEW BLOSS
27. *Charlie O'Brien* 182
    by STEVE WEST
28. *Jose Oliva* 188
    by NICK WADDELL
29. *Alejandro Pena* 192
    by ALAN COHEN
30. *Eddie Perez* 200
    by TONY OLIVER
31. *Luis Polonia* 211
    by JOHN STRUTH
32. *Jason Schmidt* 217
    by COSMO VIVANCO
33. *Mike Sharperson* 224
    by SAM GAZDZIAK
34. *Dwight Smith* 231
    by SAM GAZDZIAK
35. *John Smoltz* 237
    by WARREN CORBETT
36. *Mike Stanton* 243
    by NICK WADDELL
37. *Tom Thobe* 249
    by J. SCOTT SHAFFER
38. *Terrell Wade* 254
    by BILL JOHNSON
39. *Mark Wohlers* 258
    by TOM HUFFORD
40. *Brad Woodall* 266
    by CLAYTON TRUTOR

Manager, Coaches

41. *Bobby Cox* 271
    by TIM DEALE
42. *Jim Beauchamp* 284
    by C. PAUL ROGERS III
43. *Pat Corrales* 291
    by JAMES LINCOLN RAY
44. *Clarence Jones* 296
    by STEVE SCHMITT
45. *Leo Mazzone* 304
    by BILL PEARCH
46. *Jimy Williams* 310
    by BILL NOWLIN
47. *Ned Yost* 317
    by KEN CARRANO

Executives

48. *Ted Turner* 327
    by J. SCOTT SHAFFER AND MILLARD FISHER
49. *Stan Kasten* 332
    by BOB WEBSTER
50. *John Schuerholz* 337
    by DAN LEVITT & MARK ARMOUR
51. *Chuck LaMar* 343
    by JUSTIN KRUEGER

52. Paul Snyder 349
by LEE LOWENFISH

53. Bill Bartholomay 363
by ALAN MORRIS

Broadcasters

54. Skip Caray 369
by WYNN MONTGOMERY

55. Joe Simpson 383
by CURT SMITH

56. Don Sutton 394
by GREGORY H. WOLF

57. Pete Van Wieren 406
by BOB LEMOINE

58. Ernie Johnson Sr. 415
by DANA SPRAGUE

59. Ernie Johnson Jr. 421
by CURT SMITH

Ballpark

60. Atlanta-Fulton County Stadium 433
by SCOTT McLELLAN AND BOB BARRIER

Notable Games

61. Opening Day 441
APRIL 26, 1995: ATLANTA BRAVES 12, SAN FRANCISCO GIANTS 5, AT ATLANTA-FULTON COUNTY STADIUM, ATLANTA

by CHRIS JONES

62. Chipper Jones Belts First Career Home Run 443
MAY 9, 1995: ATLANTA BRAVES 3, NEW YORK METS 2, AT SHEA STADIUM, QUEENS, NEW YORK

by PAUL HOFMANN

63. Klesko and Jones Lead Braves' Biggest Offensive Show of the Season 446
JUNE 6, 1995: ATLANTA BRAVES 17, CHICAGO CUBS 3 AT ATLANTA-FULTON COUNTY STADIUM

by RICHARD CUICCHI

64. Braves Retake NL East Division Lead 449
JULY 4, 1995: ATLANTA BRAVES 3, LOS ANGELES DODGERS 2, AT ATLANTA-FULTON COUNTY STADIUM, ATLANTA

by JACK ZERBY

65. Braves Win Ninth Consecutive Game on McGriff's Home Run 452
JULY 9, 1995: ATLANTA BRAVES 3, SAN FRANCISCO GIANTS 2 AT ATLANTA-FULTON COUNTY STADIUM, ATLANTA

by THOMAS J. BROWN JR.

66. Maddux Tosses 2-hitter While Throwing Only 88 Pitches in 1-0 Win 455
AUGUST 20, 1995: ATLANTA BRAVES 1, ST. LOUIS CARDINALS 0, AT BUSCH STADIUM, ST. LOUIS

by MIKE HUBER

67. **Chipper Jones Hits Two Home Runs in 1995 NLDS Game One** 458

   OCTOBER 3, 1995: ATLANTA BRAVES 5, COLORADO ROCKIES 4, AT COORS FIELD, DENVER

   by LAURA H. PEEBLES

68. **Avery and Devereaux Shine as Braves Complete 1995 NLCS Sweep** 461

   OCTOBER 14, 1995: ATLANTA BRAVES 6, CINCINNATI REDS 0, AT ATLANTA-FULTON COUNTY STADIUM (GAME FOUR OF THE NATIONAL LEAGUE CHAMPIONSHIP SERIES)

   by RICHARD CUICCHI

69. **Greg Maddux's Gem Spoils Indians' Return to World Series** 464

   OCTOBER 21, 1995: ATLANTA BRAVES 3, CLEVELAND INDIANS 2, AT ATLANTA-FULTON

   by JACOB POMRENKE

70. **Glavine, Justice Win Back the Fans and Bring a World Series Championship to Atlanta**........467

   OCTOBER 28, 1995: ATLANTA BRAVES 1, CLEVELAND INDIANS 0, AT ATLANTA-FULTON COUNTY STADIUM, ATLANTA

   by JACOB POMRENKE

71. **Contributors** 473

Foreword

"BRAVES WIN! BRAVES WIN! BRAVES WIN!"
Those words from Skip Caray still ring loudly and sweetly in my ears.

When Marquis Grissom glided under the lazy fly ball in left-center field for the last out of the 1995 World Series, Skip, our play-by-play announcer, used his trademark exultation on that moment when the Atlanta Braves became the first world champion professional sports team in the city's history.

What a proud and thrilling moment that was for me, our entire organization, and our proud city.

That remarkable accomplishment, the crown jewel in an unprecedented and unbelievable run of 14 consecutive division championships, started for me when I decided to leave the Kansas City Royals and accept the executive VP/general manager position in Atlanta.

Not long after I joined the Braves, I attended the 1990 baseball winter meetings, and when I got there, I could sense what many of my longtime friends were thinking:

What a shame. Schuerholz was such a talented guy, but now he's lost his marbles.

I can excuse them for having such thoughts. I wrestled for weeks with this dramatic career move and I, too, often had moments of second-guessing. After all, what reasonably sane man would seriously consider leaving the revered Royals for a parallel move to join Ted Turner's Braves team. I knew the club's hidden potential and was aware of the fine job that then general manager Bobby Cox had started in rebuilding the farm system.

The Braves had been dead last three years in a row, four of the previous five.

In truth, I knew what I was getting into. I knew in my heart the potential of this Atlanta team, and I had confidence in its key core personnel and the organizational potential that went on to win 14 straight division titles, five National League championships, and one World Series. I felt for certain that the fan base was there, and we grew attendance to above three million from the embarrassment of being the only major-league team to draw fewer than a million fans in that just-ended 1990 season. Maybe it's my belief in the self-fulfilling prophecy that if you believe so strongly in something and you have the capabilities and a strong work ethic, you can achieve what you set out to do. I also believed in my ability to create a dedicated, committed staff, with the key personnel to work with me side by side in building a championship organization. I believed that very strongly then and I still do today.

Naturally, during my conversations with Stan Kasten and Terry McGuirk about possibly making the jump to Atlanta, we talked about Braves owner Ted Turner. Stan praised Ted for his dynamic, enthusiastic support of the sports franchises, and Ted's willingness to let good, capable people lead and do their jobs. Stan assured me that Ted was an owner who really would let us do what we felt was best and would stand behind us. He said Ted would do nothing but support, praise, and enjoy. And that was exactly what he did.

I was fortunate to join Bobby Cox in partnership when I came to Atlanta – he as the Braves manager and I as the general manager. Bobby had moved out of the front office and back into the dugout in the middle of the previous season, When Stan offered me the GM job in Atlanta, he said it was his intention to have Bobby continue as manager, and he asked if I was okay with that. Not only was I okay with it, I was delighted, since I always had great respect for Bobby.

When I first arrived in Atlanta, Bobby was in the hospital, recovering from double osteotomy knee surgery. Stan and I went to visit him, and when we walked into Bobby's room it was a jolting sight. Bobby was sort of groggy and pain-riddled and his cast-confined legs were stuck up in the air. Stan and I were with him trying to make small talk. In his typical, lighthearted style, Stan was laughing about the uniqueness of his new GM and manager having their first meeting in this strange setting.

I had never known anyone who had gone through two osteotomy surgeries at the same time. Usually they were done several months or even years apart, but not for Bobby. He wanted it over and done, so he could be ready for spring training, about four months away. That was foremost on his mind!

In my first week on the job, Skip Caray, the Braves' longtime play-by-play announcer, invited me to lunch. I couldn't have picked a better person to learn about the organization from than the guy who had been broadcasting them for decades. I saw it as a perfect opportunity to ask him about everything that had gone on in the organization, on the team, in the clubhouse, how people think, how people act – in general, just to get Skip's perspective of the organization.

He took me to a steakhouse, one of Atlanta's finest eateries. I learned a lot about the Braves personnel and practices that day. The picture he painted was not a pretty one. At the end of it, Skip said, "After all these things I've told you I want you to know also there's a flight back to Kansas City this afternoon. Or else I can drive you back to the stadium. Your choice."

I chose to return to my Braves office.

We slowly and meticulously went about the transformation of this organization. Changes in the baseball operation had begun years before under Stan and Bobby's leadership, with the commitment to rebuilding the farm system, through the draft and by getting young players back into the pipeline. All of a sudden, here's a club whose major-league team had been very bad, but unseen to most fans was a pipeline of talent making its way to The Show.

In my first year, 1991, we didn't have an opportunity to utilize many of those young guys yet. But we knew they were there. That talent was in place and on its way up.

What we really needed to accomplish was to improve our major-league club immediately – especially on the defensive side – and we did that with the signing of some key free agents – Terry Pendleton, Rafael Belliard, and Sid Bream, and the trade for Otis Nixon in spring training. And, as they say, the rest is history. A remarkable history.

It was one of the most thrilling and exciting seasons any team has ever experienced, going from worst to first in our league and into the World Series, coming within one run of a world championship that first year. To say that we were proud of this remarkable, unbelievable turnaround would be an understatement.

We continued our improvement and success over the next few seasons. The Braves returned to the World Series in 1992, and although we outscored the Toronto Blue Jays in the Series, we were defeated in yet another extra-inning, final-game heartbreaker. The next season, we reached a franchise high in wins, with 104, but were denied a return trip to the World Series by the Philadelphia Phillies' NLCS victory. And, of course, the 1994 season was truncated in August by an unfortunate work stoppage.

I've gone through this background as a prelude for our wonderful 1995 season, which you will read about in this book. For many of you, this will be a trip down memory lane, and for others it will be a history lesson. It is the story of a team, both on the field and other loyal staff behind the scenes, who worked tirelessly to reach the pinnacle of our profession. I am pleased to see that as well as the 40 player biographies, this book includes profiles of our coaches and many of the front-office and player development staff, people who were not household names to even the most ardent fan, but who played such vital roles in the success of the Atlanta Braves.

THE 1995 WORLD CHAMPION ATLANTA BRAVES

"Braves win!" encompasses so much more than just the 1995 World Series triumph, however. It signifies many of the various aspects of the organization during my time in Atlanta – the aspects that went into our annual quest for championship excellence and the successful hurdling of many barriers and challenges that the changing times erect in the path of any sports executive, especially those leading major-league baseball clubs.

"Braves win!" is a real signal cry that here is an organization that, during my years as GM, dedicated itself to the traditional principles of baseball, worked with those principles in a successful way, and consequently, ran off this remarkable, never-before-accomplished string of 14 consecutive division titles. I'm very proud of that.

"Braves win!" is about what I consider the most important element in my career and whatever success I have enjoyed, and that is *"Braves win!"* with GOOD PEOPLE. *"Braves win!"* occurred by recognizing and motivating those good people, continuing to educate them, celebrating the good work they did, and by acting upon the sound recommendations they made.

"Braves win!" is a message to our fans, who were properly skeptical at first in 1991, not knowing what this new general manager might do with their team. *"Braves win!"* was a cryout to our fans, saying, in effect, "This is for you. This is for your support. Because you came, because you supported us, because you began to believe in what we were doing, because you gave us your trust and allowed us the capability of being aggressive in our operations."

"Braves win! Braves win!" was a much appreciated validation of the principles and policies that I adopted, nurtured, and implemented both with the uniformed personnel and the club's administration throughout my tenure as general manager.

"Braves win! Braves win!" was a special legacy created by our clubhouse concept of team-oriented players who conducted and presented themselves in an appealing professional manner. It speaks volumes about the personal support and backing I have received from my family and from those who entrusted their baseball operations to a former junior high teacher with a dream.

I am both humbled and gratified beyond words to know that I was given the opportunity to play a key role in guiding, learning from, and working alongside all of those championship people in the adventure of this remarkable accomplishment.

And while Skip Caray's *"Braves win!"* exhortation on that 1995 October evening in old Atlanta-Fulton County Stadium heralded that we had achieved our ultimate goal, I often flash back to that first lunch we had together, when he filled me in about the ins and outs of the Braves organization. We won our division that first season and went to the World Series that year, so Skip and I had that lunch every winter after that. Our agreement was that he bought unless we won the World Series, then I would buy. The year we won the Series, the winter of 1995, I took him to one of the finest restaurants in Atlanta, credit card at the ready. We had a very elaborate lunch and had a good time. When I called for the check, the manager of the restaurant came over and said, "Oh, Mr. Schuerholz, thank you for what you've done in bringing us a World Series victory. The lunch is on me."

Skip was livid. And he's gone now. The one regret I have is that I never had the chance to buy a lot more of those lunches for him!

Braves win! Braves win! Braves win!"

John Schuerholz
Vice Chairman Emeritus
Atlanta Braves

Introduction

TOM HUFFORD

The first major-league game I ever saw in Atlanta was on Friday night, April 7, 1978. Don Sutton of the Los Angeles Dodgers faced off against the Atlanta Braves' best pitcher, Phil Niekro. It really wasn't much of a game, the Dodgers winning 13-4. And it wasn't a surprise – LA had won the National League pennant the year before, and the Braves had finished dead last, 37 games behind.

I did not live in Atlanta then. I was just in town that summer on a temporary assignment for the engineering company I worked for. What better way to fill my weekend than to start it by taking in Opening Night at the ballpark? I was somewhat impressed by the facilities. I had no problem getting a ticket and a good parking spot, and the crowd of nearly 43,000 was enthusiastic, at least in the early innings. I went back to the Sunday afternoon game, and found a crowd of about 11,500, and again on Tuesday night, where I had my choice of parking places adjacent to the main gate, as well as my choice of prime seats behind home plate. The announced attendance was only 2,616. I would come to learn that low attendance was pretty much the norm at Braves home games in those days. In 39 of the team's 75 home openings that season (there were six doubleheaders), the team failed to attract as many as 10,000 customers. Still, if you were a baseball fan, it was interesting to go to the ballpark – it wasn't crowded, there were no long lines for food or beverages, and if you got an aisle seat between home plate and the Braves' first-base dugout, you had a pretty good chance of team owner Ted Turner stopping to chat while on one of his several trips to the concession stand each night.

The Braves finished in last place again in 1978, but the gap was narrowed to only 26 games behind the Dodgers. So at least the team was showing a bit of improvement.

It wasn't until many years later that I realized that my first game at Atlanta-Fulton County Stadium, Opening Night 1978, was also Bobby Cox's first game as a major-league manager.

Atlanta had become a major-league city when the Milwaukee Braves moved south prior to the 1966 season. The Milwaukee Braves weren't a bad team – they never finished lower than third in the 1953-60 period and never had a losing team. But interest in the team dwindled to a league-low attendance of 555,584 patrons in 1965, and the team sought greener pastures in the South. The team finished pretty much in the middle of the pack for its first three seasons in Atlanta, before the major leagues went to a division format in 1969, and the Braves struck pay dirt, winning 93 games and taking the National League West championship. After losing the National League Championship Series, three games to none, to the upstart New York Mets, the team was fairly stagnant for most of the next decade.

Even though Bobby Cox compiled only one winning season during his 1978-81 tenure as Braves manager, the general feeling around the club was that progress was being made. Perhaps a harbinger of things to come occurred during the press conference in October 1981 when Ted Turner announced Bobby's dismissal. Asked by someone in the crowd who might be on the short list of managerial candidates, Turner replied, "It would be Bobby Cox if I hadn't just fired him. We need someone like him around here."

Bobby headed north to Toronto, leading the Blue Jays for four seasons – and the 1985 American League East Division championship. The Braves then brought Cox back to Atlanta as the general manager and he spent the next the next five seasons rebuilding the Braves' farm system, with an emphasis on pitching. When Braves manager Russ Nixon was dismissed in late June 1990, Cox came down from the front office to take over as manager. That opened the door for John Schuerholz to move from Kansas City and take over the GM position for the Braves. And the rest, as they say, is history.

I moved to Atlanta in 1979, and immediately became active in the Braves 400 Club, which was founded in 1965, not only as the team's booster club, but also to support baseball at all levels throughout the Atlanta area. In October 1990, shortly after taking the reins as GM, Schuerholz attended a 400 Club luncheon and gave a very impressive discourse about the importance of installing a winning attitude in the Braves organization. After John's talk, I was installed as president of the club, a position I held for two seasons. Aside from the obvious excitement about what was happening on the field those two seasons, what I enjoyed most was that John and I began meeting regularly for lunch at the Stadium Club, which we kept up for several seasons. Interestingly enough, we didn't just talk about baseball, but we covered myriad topics. It was easy for me to see why John would have been a success in any field he might have chosen, and that he was exactly the perfect choice to change the Braves' fortunes.

The Braves' meteoric and unexpected move from "Worst to First" in 1991 and a repeat trip to the World Series in 1992 only resulted in disappointing final-game, extra-inning losses each year. It was obvious that the Braves were not to be considered overnight sensations, but an unexpected loss to the Philadelphia Phillies in 1993 and an incomplete 1994 season due to a players strike left some fans wondering if the Atlanta team had lost their momentum, and perhaps a shot at a world championship.

They needn't have worried. The Braves came back stronger than ever, leading the National League with 90 victories, won the NL Division Series three games to one over the Colorado Rockies, and ran roughshod over the Cincinnati Reds in the NLCS, winning four straight games. They went on to meet the Cleveland Indians, who had led the major leagues with 100 regular-season wins, in the World Series. The Braves opened the Series on a high note, taking two games at home before heading to Cleveland, where the Indians took two out of three. When they returned home for Game Six, Tom Glavine and Mark Wohlers combined on a masterful one-hitter, and David Justice's solo sixth-inning home run gave the Braves the only run they needed to walk off the field as world champions!

It's now been 25 years since that magical night in Atlanta, October 28, 1995, when the Braves became the first team in any sport to give Atlanta a world championship.

In honor and in recognition of the 1995 Atlanta Braves' world championship season, *"Braves Win!, Braves Win!, Braves Win! – The 1995 World Champion Atlanta Braves* is the latest entry in SABR's publishing program.

There are exciting stories of the 10 most notable games of the 1995 season, and not all were in the postseason, as you might have thought. You will find behind-the-scenes stories of many of the Braves' front office personnel, who worked tirelessly, both at the major-league and the minor-league levels, to mold a championship organization. Not all are familiar names, but each played an integral part in making the Atlanta Braves the team they are today.

Biographies of each of the 40 players who took the field in a Braves uniform that season are included. Many had long and successful big-league careers, and for others their time in The Show was brief. But they all contributed to that championship season, and they all have interesting stories. Nine players made their major-league debuts with the 1995 Braves, and for three team members, that season marked the end of their big-league careers. One player, outfielder Brian Kowitz, fits in both categories – his 10-game stay with the Braves in June, while David Justice was out with an injury, was the only major-league service he saw during his eight-year professional career. Mike Devereaux spent only the last five weeks of the season with the Braves, but his MVP performance in the NLCS helped carry the team to the World Series. Sadly, two members of the team, Jose Oliva and Mike Sharperson, lost their lives in auto accidents not long after their stays with the Braves. Four members of the 1995 Atlanta Braves – Tom Glavine, Chipper Jones, Greg Maddux, and John Smoltz – along with manager Bobby Cox and general manager John Schuerholz have been enshrined in the National Baseball Hall of Fame and Museum, in Cooperstown, New York.

What this 1995 team accomplished was the pinnacle of a nearly 30-year run of excellence for the Braves, and that tradition continues. I am very pleased that SABR provided the opportunity for a dedicated group of over 50 members to contribute articles for this book, and am grateful to be able to work with Bill Nowlin as co-editors. Special thanks need to go out to members of the Magnolia (Georgia) Chapter of SABR for their support in this effort, and to Sam Wallace of the Atlanta Braves Ballpark Tours, Heritage and Hall of Fame for his diligent research in locating and providing the photos used in this book. And lastly, a heartfelt thanks goes to John Schuerholz for his Foreword and enthusiastic support of this book, and to Bobby Cox and John for their professional partnership, which made the 1995 Atlanta Braves world championship possible!

 PLAYERS

Steve Avery

BY TOM HUFFORD

Steve Avery

In the early 1990s, no major-league pitcher's nickname fit better than Steve Avery's – The Kid. Unfortunately for Steve and the teams he played with, the trials, tribulations, and disappointments that sometimes come with adulthood came much too fast.

Steven Thomas Avery was born in Trenton, Michigan, on April 14, 1970 to Kenneth W. and Constance "Connie" Marich Avery. Ken, a standout lefty pitcher from Michigan State, was signed by the Detroit Tigers to a contract with their Knoxville farm team in the summer of 1961, with orders to report to spring training the next season. Starting the year at Thomasville in the Georgia-Florida League, Ken posted a 6-2 record, earning him a promotion to Jamestown (NYP League), where he won nine more games, losing five. He and Connie were married that fall, and Ken returned to the mound the next year with the Duluth-Superior Dukes, in the Northern League. Ken fashioned a 13-4 record that season, on a mound staff that included future big leaguers Pete Craig, Pat Jarvis, Denny McLain, and Joe Sparma, as the Dukes won their pennant by 12 games. Rather than return to pro ball the next season, Ken decided to focus on family and a career outside of baseball, eventually retiring as athletic director of Taylor (Michigan) high schools. Ken and Connie Avery had four children – Ken Jr., Mike, Steve, and Jennifer.[1]

Steve had an outstanding prep career at Taylor's John F. Kennedy High School, where he participated in basketball and cross-country, as well as baseball. When he was 16, Avery led his American Legion baseball team to the state championship, and was awarded the KiKi Cuyler Award as the tournament's most valuable player.[2] In his senior year at JFK, Avery went 13-0 on the mound, with 196 strikeouts and an 0.51 ERA in 88 innings. He batted .511, with 8 home runs and 44 RBIs.[3]

There was not much doubt that Avery would be an early selection in the 1988 amateur draft; the only question was how high he would go. The San Diego Padres, choosing first and seeking more immediate help, decided to go the college route, selecting pitcher Andy Benes from the University of Evansville. The Cleveland Indians, who chose second, had their eyes on Avery, but instead went for high-school shortstop Mark Lewis, from Hamilton, Ohio. Next in line were the Atlanta Braves, who jumped at the chance to draft Avery, hoping to lure him away from his scholarship offer from Stanford University.

"Braves Win! Braves Win! Braves Win!"

The Braves had been doormats of the National League, having finished last or next to last each of the past five seasons. After a four-year managerial stint in Toronto, Bobby Cox had returned to Atlanta as the Braves' general manager in October 1985. He set out to rebuild the farm system as the road back to respectability, rather than trying to remake the team at the major-league level with trades and free agents. Steve Avery was exactly the type pitcher the team thought it could build around.

After nearly a month of negotiations, Avery finally signed with the Braves on June 30, 1988, for a reported bonus of $211,500. That was significant, because it was the highest bonus ever paid to a high-school pitcher. That "record" stood for five weeks, until the Montreal Expos signed Reid Cornelius, their 11th-round draft pick, for $225,000.[4]

Avery was assigned to the Braves' Appalachian (Rookie) League club in Pulaski, Virginia. After having his professional debut rained out the night before, he made his first appearance in the first game of a July 11 doubleheader against the Martinsville Phillies. The lefty pitched five innings, giving up four hits and a walk while striking out seven, to pick up the 5-0 victory. After the game, Pulaski manager Cloyd Boyer said, "I can see why they drafted him number one. He's definitely a big-league prospect." On the prospects of his club, Boyer continued, "I fully expect him to be with us the entire season, as all the rest of the players. Avery was sent here for me to work with. No longer than he's been here, it's obvious he's hard-working, dedicated, and has a good attitude. And the Lord blessed him with great ability."[5] (Incidentally, eighth-round draft pick Mark Wohlers closed out the doubleheader by hurling a 3-2 complete-game three-hitter, giving the Braves a hint that the future might be bright, indeed.)

In his debut pro season, Avery posted a 7-1 record and a 1.50 ERA in 10 games, with 80 strikeouts and only 19 walks in 66 innings. He was named to the Appalachian League All-Star team at the conclusion of the season.

Based on his showing in Pulaski, Avery jumped to the Durham Bulls, the Braves' high Class-A team in the Carolina League, for 1989. The team was loaded, with 10 players who would go on to see at least some major-league action, nine of them pitchers. The Bulls easily finished first in their division, but Avery wasn't around to see the finish. Based on a 6-4 record with a 1.45 ERA and 90 strikeouts against 20 walks, he was promoted in midseason to the Double-A Greenville Braves. Avery didn't miss a beat, going 6-3 in 13 starts. At age 19, he was the youngest player on the team, but had little trouble adjusting to his new surroundings.

Avery started the 1990 season at Richmond. He was only 20, and had reached Triple A much more quickly than anyone would have imagined. It was in Richmond that he first came under the guidance of pitching coach Leo Mazzone. "I didn't teach Steve Avery a pitch," said Mazzone. "He had them. So my job was to see that he kept them – and that worked out real well."[6] Avery's record was only 5-5 through the first two months of the season, but he was showing maturity and confidence beyond his years. "In Steve's case, he became a great pitcher at an early age because he trusted himself with a change of speeds," said Mazzone. "He was a power pitcher out of high school, and had always been a strikeout pitcher. Most times it's going to take a pitcher a long time to trust an offspeed pitch."

Come early June, the Braves found themselves in familiar territory – last place, but won six of their first 12 games for the month, including a doubleheader in Cincinnati on June 12. Marty Clary had already been dropped from the rotation, and so was Derek Lilliquist, after being on the short end of a 23-8 shellacking at the hands of the San Francisco Giants on June 8. Yet even though help was obviously needed on the pitching staff, Braves fans were surprised when Avery was summoned from Richmond to start the June 13 game against the Reds. He was still the youngest player on the roster, and most assumed the Braves would like him to get a full season under his belt there. Getting called up after only 13 Triple-A games to join the big-league club would be enough to make any rookie excited enough to leave all of his luggage in the taxi when he got to the Braves hotel, as Avery did, but he would be facing a team in first place in the NL West.[7]

Avery's nervousness may have lessened a bit when the Braves staked him to a 2-0 lead in the top of the first inning. He fared well in his initial major-league inning, allowing only a walk and a stolen base to Chris Sabo. Reality set in in the second, however, when the Reds tied the game at 2-2 on a leadoff triple by Glenn Braggs and singles by Todd Benzinger, Mariano Duncan, and Billy Hatcher. Things were no better in the third, when the Reds touched up Avery for two walks, a stolen base, three singles, and a double, driving him from the mound and taking a 6-2 lead. Reliever Marty Clary simply threw gasoline on the fire, allowing a wild pitch, two doubles, and a single without recording an out and leaving the game at 8-2.

Six days later, Avery again faced the Reds, this time in Atlanta, and fared a bit better. He pitched into the fifth inning, allowing only one run on six hits and two walks, leaving with the game tied 1-1.

Three days after Avery's first appearance before the home crowd, changes were made that affected Atlanta's baseball fortunes for the next two decades – Bobby Cox returned to the dugout as Braves manager (as well as keeping his general manager job, too), and he brought Leo Mazzone up from Richmond as his pitching coach. Cox decided to give The Kid a chance to stay in the rotation, and in Avery's next start, on June 26, he went seven innings, beating the Los Angeles Dodgers, 4-2, for his first major-league win.

The rest of the 1990 season was pretty much a learning experience for Avery. He started 20 games and had one more in relief, finishing the season with a 3-11 record. His best game, by far, was on August 24 in Atlanta, when he fashioned his first major-league complete game and shutout, 3-0, over Greg Maddux and the Chicago Cubs. Maddux also pitched a complete game, and at the plate both hurlers had success. Avery touched up Maddux for two singles, and Greg recorded one against Steve.

For the team as a whole, it was a disappointing year, with the Braves finishing in the cellar for the third straight year. At the end of the season, the pitching staff included Tom Glavine, John Smoltz, Charlie Leibrandt, Kent Mercker, and Paul Marak. All except Leibrandt were less than 25 years old, and only Smoltz had a winning record in 1990. Some in the press were starting to call Atlanta's staff the "Young Guns." The Young Guns were starting to mature in 1990, but few seemed to notice.

When spring training started in 1991, the Braves had a new general manager, John Schuerholz, who had come after a successful 23-year stay in Kansas City. The move allowed Bobby Cox to relinquish the general manager part of his job, and to focus exclusively on the team on the field. Schuerholz recognized the maturing of the pitching staff, but knew that to be effective, he needed to improve the defense behind them. So he did, importing first baseman Sid Bream, third baseman Terry Pendleton, shortstop Rafael Belliard, and center fielder Otis Nixon.

The revamped team got off to an 8-10 record in April, not great, but much improved over the 4-13 mark in 1990. By the end of May, the won-lost record stood at 25-19, and the team was in second place, only a half-game behind the Los Angeles Dodgers. Fans were starting to notice that there was a difference in this team. The Braves stayed within three games of the Dodgers until near the end of August, when consecutive wins by Leibrandt, Glavine, Smoltz, and Avery moved the Braves into first place.

The Braves held on through September, to win the NL West crown by one game over the Dodgers. Glavine's 20 wins garnered him the NL Cy Young Award at season's end, Smoltz won 14 and Leibrandt 15, and Avery seemingly matured overnight, posting an 18-8 mark, good to place him sixth in the Cy Young voting. The Young Guns had come through, and led the "Worst to First" Braves to their first postseason action since 1982.

Avery had atoned for his woes with the Cincinnati Reds in 1990 by beating them 7-5 to give the Braves their first win of the 1991 season. Down the stretch in September, he hurled two complete-game victories over the Dodgers, 9-1 in Atlanta on September 15, and a 3-0 shutout in Los Angeles five days later. In his last win of the season, he took a no-hitter into the seventh inning against Houston, settling for a three-hitter in a 5-2 victory.

Going into the National League Championship Series against the Pirates, the Braves dropped the first game in Pittsburgh, and Avery then drew the starting assignment for Game Two. He responded by twirling 8⅓ shutout innings before turning the game over to Alejandro Peña, in an eventual 1-0 Braves victory. Six days later, back in Atlanta, Pittsburgh had taken a 3-2 series lead over the Braves, when Avery went back out for Game Six. Following almost the same script as in Game Two, he threw eight scoreless innings of three-hit ball, with Peña coming in for the final inning of the 1-0 game. John Smoltz's 4-0 shutout the next night sent the Braves to their first World Series appearance since 1958. Avery's two 1-0 shutout victories and 16⅓ scoreless innings earned him the MVP honors for the NLCS.

In the 1991 World Series, against the Minnesota Twins, Avery pitched into the eighth inning in Game Three, leaving with a 4-2 lead in a contest the Braves eventually won 5-4, and left Game Six behind 3-2 in a game the Braves tied but finally lost 4-3 in the 11th inning. He didn't receive a decision in either game. The Braves ultimately lost the Series in an epic John Smoltz-Jack Morris pitching duel, which the Twins won 1-0 in 10 innings. Regardless of the outcome, Braves fans will never forget that magical "Worst to First" season!

Six days after the end of the World Series, Avery and Heather McMillan, his girlfriend since the seventh grade, were married. The ceremony was obviously planned well in advance, with a scheduling nod to the World Series – just in case. "It worked out," said Avery. "I got to miss all the planning. I didn't get stuck going to the shower and everything."[8]

When spring training 1992 came around, the excitement of the previous season subsided a bit while attention was paid to the work at hand – how to repeat what had happened in 1992, and take the next big step: winning the World Series. The team got off to a slow start, and found itself in a fourth-place tie on Memorial Day, five games behind the San Francisco Giants. The Braves didn't get back to the .500 level until June 7, and didn't find their way into first place until July 22. From then on, there was no stopping the team, and they finished the season winning their second consecutive National League West title by eight games over the Cincinnati Reds.

As for Avery, in some ways his 1992 season was better than 1991 – he led the league in games started with 35, pitched 23⅓ more innings, and lowered his ERA from 3.38 to 3.20. His won-lost record fell to 11-11, however, primarily because the team had trouble scoring when he was on the mound. Six of his 11 losses were by two or fewer runs.

When the postseason came along, Avery returned to his old ways against the NL East champion Pirates by extending his NLCS shutout streak to 22⅔ innings in Game Two and picking up the win. Up three games to one, Avery took the mound in Game Five, hoping to punch the Braves' ticket to the World Series. Nothing went as planned, and he experienced the worst start of his career, giving up four runs on a single and four doubles, while recording only one out, leading to a 7-1 Pirates victory. A 13-4 Pittsburgh blowout in Game Six brought on the decisive final game of the Series. Avery's early departure from Game Five made him available for work in Game Seven, and he made his first relief appearance of the season in the bottom of the seventh inning. Entering the game with two outs and the bases loaded, Avery induced a long fly out by Andy Van Slyke to end the inning, and then held the Pirates scoreless in the eighth, maintaining a 2-0 Pittsburgh lead. That kept the game close enough to set the stage for the heroics by Pendleton, Justice, Bream, Gant, Berryhill, Hunter, and, finally, Francisco Cabrera's bases-loaded two-run pinch-hit single in the bottom of the ninth, to send the Braves back to the World Series.

In the World Series against the Toronto Blue Jays, Avery pitched into the ninth inning of Game Three before giving up a leadoff single and leaving the game with the score tied 2-2. The trio of Mark Wohlers, Mike Stanton, and Jeff Reardon failed to get the job done, with Avery being charged with the 3-2 loss. In Game Six, he was pulled after the fourth inning, with the Blue Jays ahead 2-1. The Braves rallied to tie the game in the bottom of the ninth inning, but a two-run double by Dave Winfield in the top of the 11th put the Jays ahead 4-2, and they held on in the bottom of the inning to claim their first World Series ever. It was the Braves' second consecutive Series loss.

During the offseason, the Braves signed free-agent pitcher Greg Maddux, just off a Cy Young Award-winning season with the Cubs. The 1992 Braves pitching staff had given up the fewest runs in the league, and adding Maddux to the rotation that included Glavine, Smoltz, and Avery would only cement the expectation that the team would return to the World Series for a third straight year. To the dismay of the rest of the league, the Braves had added yet another star to their "Young Guns" staff, a rotation that is now considered to have been one of the best in baseball history.

Avery started 1993 with high hopes, and he didn't disappoint, posting the best year of his career to date. By the end of June, he sported a 9-2 record, with an eight-game winning streak, and was named to the National League All-Star team. He continued his fine work in the second half of the season, but ran into trouble on September 12 in San Diego. Leading 1-0 in the fourth inning, Avery suffered a muscle injury under his left (pitching) armpit, but kept pitching and gave up five runs on three hits, a walk, and an error before leaving the game. He pitched four more games in September, with two wins and a loss, to bring his season record to 18-4, with a 2.94 ERA.

The Braves won their division championship again in 1993, and took on the Philadelphia Phillies in the NLCS. Avery started Game One against the Phillies' Curt Schilling, but left after the sixth inning behind 3-2. The Braves rallied to tie the game in the ninth inning, but lost 4-3 in 10 innings. In Game Five Avery and Schilling faced off again. This time, he pitched through the seventh inning, but was behind 2-0 when he was replaced by Kent Mercker. The Braves came back in the ninth inning again, this time scoring three runs to tie the game, but the Phillies scored on a Lenny Dykstra home run off Mark Wohlers in the 10th to take the game. Two days later, back in Philadelphia, the Phillies prevailed in Game Six, to dash the Braves' hopes of a third straight World Series appearance.

The 1994 season opened with a cloud of uncertainty, with labor negotiations and the threat of a player strike having dragged through the winter. For the Averys, their lives were upheaved with the sudden and unexpected death of Heather's father, James McMillan, on March 29,[9] and the premature birth of Heather and Steve's first child, Evan Thomas, 12 days later. Evan was born nearly three months early, and weighed only 2 pounds, 13 ounces. "The doctors are amazed at how well he's doing," said Avery. "We're still worried, but now it's a different kind of worry. Before, we didn't even know if he was going to be born. At least now I can see him. That makes it a little easier."[10]

Evan stayed in the hospital until late July and underwent nine surgeries during his first year. Unbeknownst to the general public, Avery was a commuting pitcher for virtually the entire 1994 season. He made several trips back to Michigan during spring training, and after the season started, he flew back home after every start, rejoining the team in time for his next game.

"You could tell he was tense," said teammate John Smoltz. At times he had a shorter fuse, not as patient, because it was a continual roller-coaster. It was a difficult time, and we all felt for him."[11]

On the mound, Avery posted an 8-3 record, although the Braves actually won 15 of his 24 starts. His ERA jumped from 2.94 in 1993 to 4.04, even though his hits allowed per nine innings dropped and his strikeout total (122 compared with 125) was down by only three in about 72⅔ fewer innings compared with 1993. Through it all, Avery didn't miss a single start in 1994, but sometimes showed a lack of control – he walked 12 more batters in the abbreviated season than he did in all of 1993. Some thought he was just tired from the rigors of the season, but others wondered if he was concealing an injury, perhaps a carryover from his muscle injury the previous September.

When the strike eventually started on August 12, it cast a shadow over major-league baseball, but it couldn't have come at a better time for the Averys, letting them be together when Evan came home from the hospital.

Few remember that because the labor strike was not settled until April 2, the 1995 season opening was delayed until April 26. An abbreviated 144-game schedule was implemented, and the Braves started well, winning seven of their first eight games. The only loss in that span was a 9-1 drubbing by the Dodgers in Los Angeles. The loss was charged to Avery, who left the game after retiring only one out of five batters in the fourth, behind 3-0. After their first eight games, however, the team lost eight of their next 10, and didn't get back to first place until a July 4 win against the Dodgers.

Other than a 4-0 complete-game shutout against the Florida Marlins on May 19, Avery showed little of his previous dominance during the first half of the season. By August 1, he had pitched into the seventh inning in only nine of his 17 starts, and his 4.21 ERA at that point was his highest since his rookie season. He failed to find consistency through the rest of the season, dealing with mechanical issues and loss of confidence, and he ended the campaign with a 7-13 record.

Regardless, the Braves again led their division, and returned to the NLDS against the Colorado Rockies. Manager Bobby Cox decided to go with only three starters – Maddux, Glavine, and Smoltz, and took the series three games to one. Avery made only one appearance, in relief of Tom Glavine in the second game, and gave up a run while retiring only two batters.

In the NLCS against the Cincinnati Reds, Tom Glavine started Game One, and left after the seventh inning trailing 1-0. After the game was turned over to Alejandro Peña, the Braves tied the game in the ninth and took the lead in the 10th. Mark Wohlers worked the ninth and 10th for the Braves, and Brad Clontz took over in the 11th to protect the lead, but could record only one out before manager Cox called on Avery, who walked the only batter he faced. Thankfully, for the Braves, Greg McMichael came in and put out the fire, preserving the win.

After winning the first three games against the Reds, Cox made a very unpopular decision, in the fans' eyes. He decided to start Avery in Game Four, despite the fact that in two postseason relief outings he had retired only two batters. Perhaps Cox thought that since the Braves were already up three games to none, Avery might be able to give the other starters a bit of a rest. Whatever his thinking, he had to be pleased. The old Steve Avery showed up, pitched six innings of two-hit shutout ball, struck out six Reds, and was the winning pitcher as the Braves completed a four-game sweep of Cincinnati and headed back to the World Series. After two years of struggling, Avery felt he was back where he belonged.

Moving on to the World Series against Cleveland, the starters were rested and Maddux and Glavine each eked out one-run victories in the first two games. Smoltz was knocked around in Game Three and lasted less than three innings, but the Braves rebounded and the game went to overtime, the Indians pulling out a 7-6 win in 11 innings.

Come Game Four, manager Cox had no apprehension about giving the ball to Avery, and the lefty rewarded his trust with another six innings of three-hit, one-run baseball. The Braves won the game, 5-2, and moved to within one game of the championship.

What Avery remembered most about the game was that Bobby Cox gave him the ball when no one else wanted him to have it. "I pretty much stunk all year," said Avery. "He said, 'Ave, I've got confidence in you,' and that was it."[12]

Cleveland won Game Five, 5-4, and the Series moved back to Atlanta, where in Game Six Tom Glavine's eight innings of one-hit ball and Dave Justice's home run brought the Atlanta Braves their first World Series title.

Avery started out the 1996 season well, reaching the seventh inning in nine of his first 12 starts, and he sported a 6-4 record by the end of May. As the season progressed, however, ineffectiveness set in and he lost a bit of velocity on his fastball. He missed nearly two months due to injury near the end of the season, and he finished the season with only a 7-10 record.

The Braves reached the World Series again in 1996, this time against the New York Yankees. Avery's only appearance in the Series was in Game Four, when the Braves blew a 6-0 lead and eventually lost the game, 8-6. That game is remembered as the one where Mark Wohlers gave up a game-tying three-run home run to Yankees catcher Jim Leyritz, but Avery was actually the losing pitcher in that contest. Replacing Wohlers to start the 10th inning, Avery allowed a single and three walks in two-thirds of an inning, the last walk, to Wade Boggs, forcing in the go-ahead run. The Braves had entered that game having won two out of the first three games, but the Yankees then won this contest and the next two to claim their first championship since 1978.

In late October the Braves granted Steve Avery free agency. He had been through the highest of highs and the lowest of lows in his nine seasons in the Braves organization, and he is always mentioned when discussion comes up about his Hall of Fame rotation mates Tom Glavine, Greg Maddux, and John Smoltz. There are many in the Braves organization who think Avery was on the path to the Hall of Fame as well had injuries not taken their toll. He came up to the majors when the Braves had little pitching at all, and he left the Braves not because he really wanted to, but because the team now had too much talent for him to stay around.

Hoping that a change of scenery would help, Avery signed a one-year contract with the Boston Red Sox in January 1997. There, he was reunited with former Braves third-base coach Jimy Williams, who had just come over from Atlanta to replace Kevin Kennedy as the Red Sox manager. Williams was hoping Avery would benefit from the opportunity, and besides, he needed someone to fill the rotation vacancy created when Roger Clemens left Boston to sign with the Toronto Blue Jays.

Avery won two of his first four starts in Boston, but lost most of May and all of June to injury, and finished with only a 6-7 record for the season. He returned to the Red Sox for the 1998 season and pitched with a modicum of success, pitching to a 10-7 record, his first winning season since 1994. But he was still plagued by injuries that just weren't getting any better, and the Red Sox released Avery in October.

Hoping there was still a bit of magic left in Avery – after all, he was still just 29 years old – the Cincinnati Reds signed him in December, in an effort to bolster their staff. He added a bit, but not much, to the Reds' second-place finish in 1999, duplicating his 6-7 record with the Red Sox two years previously, but his season came to an end in late July, when he underwent season-ending surgery to repair a torn labrum. The Reds released him at the end of the season.

Avery tried to come back in 2000, signing with his original club, the Braves, in January. There was nothing the Braves would have liked more than for a healthy Steve Avery to be able to come back. Avery spent the season shuttling between the Braves' top four farm teams – Richmond, Greenville, Myrtle Beach, and Macon. He won 4 and lost 12 games in his minor-league stay, but the Braves weren't concerned about results, they just wanted to let him get his strength back and be healthy. Avery returned to spring training with the Braves in 2001, but things did not improve to the point where he would be able to pitch, and he was released just before the start of the season.

For a couple of years, Braves scouting director Paul Snyder tried to get Avery to come back with the club as a minor-league pitching coach, but he wasn't interested. "I understood that, he was home and had small children that he wanted to be with. But I still wanted him, he was smart, he had had successes and failures that he could relate to with young pitchers. I think he would have made a terrific coach," said Snyder.[13]

In late 2002, Avery started giving serious thought to making a comeback. He had gone two seasons without pitching, had continued his workouts, and was in shape. Also, 8-year-old Evan knew more about baseball now, but didn't remember ever seeing his dad pitch. Avery told his hometown Detroit Tigers he'd like to give it a try. On January 23, 2003, the Tigers signed him to a minor-league contract and invited him to spring training. Tigers manager Alan Trammell said that Avery was a long shot to make the team, but that he wasn't ruling it out.[14]

Avery was sent to Detroit's Toledo farm team at the end of spring training, but showed enough there that he was called up to the big-league club on May 9. He made his Tigers debut in Tampa Bay on May 11, when he entered the eighth inning with the Tigers leading the Devil Rays, 8-2. He gave up a leadoff single to Carl Crawford, who was erased on a double play, and Avery completed the inning unscathed. He made his home debut against the Oakland A's three days later when he came on with the score tied, the bases loaded, and two outs in the ninth inning. Avery struck out the only batter he faced, Scott Hatteberg, and picked up his first victory in almost four years when the Tigers rallied in the bottom of the ninth for the win. He recorded another relief win on May 26, and in all made 19 relief appearances for the Tigers before being sent back down on July 26. Only five of his 19 outings were in Tigers victories, which doesn't necessarily speak ill of Avery's performance – the team finished with a 43-119 record!

Avery finished with a 2-0 record for the Tigers, but an ERA of 5.63. He recorded only six strikeouts in 16 innings of work, a testament to his fastball no longer being effective.

Avery retired with a 96-83 major-league won-lost record, an All-Star Game appearance, an NLCS MVP award, three National League Championship rings, and one World Series trophy. His star rose quickly, shone brilliantly, but faded much too fast with injuries.

Said John Smoltz: "I'll give Steve credit, he came back and fulfilled the dream that every player has – playing for the home team. I grew up around Detroit and signed with the Tigers, but never got to play for them. Steve did. Tommy (Glavine) would love to have played for the Red Sox. He never got a chance, but Steve and I did. He was lucky in that way."[15]

As of 2020 Steve and Heather Avery lived in Dearborn, Michigan. Steve was inducted into the Taylor Sports Hall of Fame in 2004, and the baseball and softball fields at John F. Kennedy High School in Taylor are named for him. He coached the Detroit Bees Perfect Game 14U team to the Battle of Great Lakes championship in 2019. Evan pitched on the Adrian College baseball team. In 2020 he was an account executive in group and hospitality sales with the Braves. Daughter Emma Grace, born just after the close of the 1997 season, was a second-grade teacher in Detroit, and son Owen, born after Steve's career ended, was in high school.

THE 1995 WORLD CHAMPION ATLANTA BRAVES

Sources

In addition to the sources cited in the Notes, the author accessed Baseball-Reference.com, Retrosheet.org, and the online archives via Newspaper.com, NewspaperARCHIVE.com, and Ancestry.com.

Notes

1. The author's parents, Dean and Helen Hufford, served as a host family for Pulaski Braves players in the 1980s. Steve lived with them during his 1988 rookie season. Mrs. Hufford and Steve's mother, Connie, have maintained a correspondence of more than 30 years, and much of the family information in this biography is taken from Mrs. Avery's letters.
2. "Steve Avery – Inducted in 2004." ci.taylor.mi.us/605/Steve-Avery.
3. Allen Simpson, ed., Baseball America's Ultimate Draft Book 2016 (Durham, North Carolina: *Baseball America*, 2016), 350.
4. Simpson.
5. Tom Hawley, "Braves Take Twinbill, Avery Pitches Shutout," *Southwest Times* (Pulaski, Virginia), July 12, 1988: 6.
6. Leo Mazzone and Scott Freeman, Leo Mazzone's Tales From the Mound (Champaign, Illinois: *Sports Publishing,* 2006), 15.
7. bravesgeneralstore.com/brief-and-brilliant-steve-averys-time-in-atlanta-2/.
8. Steve Rushin, "Game Boy," *Sports Illustrated*, February 17, 1992.
9. Detroit News, April 1, 2004. genealogybank.com/doc/obituaries/obit/13BF267243875200-13BF267243875200.
10. *Augusta (Georgia) Chronicle*, April 13, 1994: 25.
11. Robes Patton, "Load Has Lightened for Avery as Son's Health Has Improved," *South Florida Sun-Sentinel* (Fort Lauderdale), April 22, 1995. sun-sentinel.com/news/fl-xpm-1995-04-22-9504214013-story.html#.
12. Steve Hummer, "Bobby Cox – The Players' Manager," *Atlanta Journal-Constitution*, August 29, 2010. ajc.com/sports/baseball/bobby-cox-the-players-manager/PdPc1Xf5vWf43F2t2mSBWN/.
13. Paul Snyder, telephone conversation with the author, January 10, 2020.
14. *Sunday Advocate* (Baton Rouge, Louisiana), February 16, 2003: 16C.
15. John Smoltz, personal conversation with the author, November 2014.

Steve Bedrosian

BY WYNN MONTGOMERY

Steve Bedrosian

Bedrock (n): *Unbroken solid rock; any firm foundation.*[1]

That dictionary definition explains why "Bedrock" was an apt nickname for Steve Bedrosian. In his prime, he was a rock-solid relief pitcher and the foundation on which his teams built a bullpen.

Stephen Wayne Bedrosian was born in Methuen, Massachusetts, on December 6, 1957, to Michael (a materials and inventory specialist for Western Electric) and Jean Bedrosian (office manager for W.T. Grant Company)[2] and is one of a handful of major leaguers of Armenian descent. He played baseball and soccer and wrestled for the Methuen High School Rangers, where his performance would (24 years later) earn him recognition by the *North Andover Eagle-Tribune* as the area's "Top Athlete of the 20th Century."[3] After graduation in 1975, he played baseball for the Knights of Northern Essex Community College in nearby Haverhill, Massachusetts, for two years before enrolling at the University of New Haven. In his only season there, he compiled a 13-3 record and three saves, helping Coach Frank "Porky" Viera's 1978 Chargers to a third-place finish in the Division II College World Series.[4] He was named to the Division II All-America First Team by ABCA/Rawlings and to *The Sporting News'* All-American Second Team.[5] He was one of only three Division II players (and the only pitcher) to be so recognized by *The Sporting News*.

Those All-American honors came on the heels of being selected by the Atlanta Braves in the third round of the 1978 amateur draft. He was the Braves' third pick – after future Atlanta teammates Bob Horner and Matt Sinatro – and the 53rd overall pick. He quickly signed with the Braves and was assigned to the Kingsport (Tennessee) Braves of the Appalachian (Rookie) League. After starting six games and compiling a 2-2 record and a 3.08 ERA, Bedrosian was promoted to the Class-A Greenwood (South Carolina) Braves, for whom he started eight games, went 5-1, and lowered his ERA to 2.13.

Bedrosian progressed steadily upward through the Braves farm system. He spent the next two seasons as a starter for the Savannah (Georgia) Braves in the Double-A Southern League. Although one reporter dubbed him perhaps the hardest thrower in the league, Bedrosian himself said it was "the first league I've been in where I can't just reach back and blow it by everyone."[6] He added: "I don't have a curve or a change-up. I'm going to have to learn them if I'm going to move up."[7] In 1980 he was a Southern League All-Star[8] and the workhorse of the Savannah staff, pitching 203 innings and completing nine of his 29 starts for a 14-10 record. That performance earned him a spot on Atlanta's 40-man roster.[9] After a season of winter baseball in the Dominican Republic,[10] Bedrosian joined the Richmond (Virginia) Braves in the Triple-A International League, where he started 25 games and made his first relief appearance. He had a 10-10 record and a 2.69 ERA when he was called up to Atlanta.

Bedrosian made his major-league debut on August 14, 1981, at Dodger Stadium. He relieved John Montefusco in the fourth inning with one out and the bases loaded after the Dodgers had scored two runs to break a scoreless tie. Bill Russell, the first batter Bedrosian faced, drove in a run with a sacrifice fly. Bedrosian then hit opposing pitcher Dave Goltz but got Davy Lopes to pop out to end the inning. He was lifted for a pinch-hitter in the bottom of the inning, but he was in the big leagues to stay. He earned his first major-league victory the following night when he struck out two of the three Dodgers he faced in the fifth inning to preserve a 1-1 tie before being removed for a pinch-hitter in the sixth, when the Braves scored an unearned run to take a lead they never relinquished.

One night later, the Dodgers avenged that loss with a 6-5 win, and Bedrosian was charged with the loss. He entered the game to start the seventh inning with the Braves leading 5-3 and walked two batters before yielding a two-out, two-RBI double to Steve Garvey and being replaced on the mound by Gene Garver, who allowed a RBI single that put the Dodgers ahead by the final score of 6-5.

Bedrosian's next appearance was on August 22 at Atlanta-Fulton County Stadium, when he made his home debut in his first major-league start in the first game of a doubleheader against the Montreal Expos. After five innings, he had yielded two hits and three walks, and the Braves led 3-0. He did not retire a batter in the sixth inning. He gave up an unearned run followed by John Milner's three-run homer and left the game trailing 4-3 with two runners aboard. One of those runners scored another unearned run, and when the Braves could muster only one more run, Bedrosian was charged with his second loss. After four games, his record was 1-2. He appeared in 11 more games (17 innings) in relief without another decision or another save opportunity and ended the 1981 season with an ERA of 4.44 – his highest until his final season. In December Bedrosian became the first Brave who did not have a long-term contract to agree to terms for the 1982 season ($37,000) and was dubbed one of the club's young pitchers "most difficult to pry away from the Braves."[11]

Bedrosian returned to the Dominican Republic for another season of winter baseball and was pitching well for the Estrellas[12] of San Pedro de Macoris (2.83 ERA) when he suffered minor injuries in an auto accident. At the time, he was called "one of the best pitching prospects since the Braves moved to Atlanta"[13] and one of eight candidates to join the Braves' starting rotation.[14] In March he exacerbated his injury-plagued offseason by breaking his finger. Fortunately for the lanky (6-feet-3, 200 pounds) right-hander, it was on his left hand. A month later, he was one of seven rookies on Atlanta's Opening Day roster.[15] He had arrived with two nicknames – Bedrock (the one that lasted throughout his career) and Mr. Smoke (later Kid Smoke)[16] – that attested to his two primary characteristics as a baseball player: a "fierce competitor" who "throws hard."[17]

The Braves got off to a record-breaking start in 1982, winning their first 13 games. Bedrosian was the starter on April 10 against Houston in the 3-0 Braves' second home game. The Braves staked him to an early 5-0 lead, but he gave up a walk and a two-run homer in the third inning and two more hits and a walk in the fourth before being lifted. Six days later, in Houston, he pitched three shutout innings to protect a 5-3 lead as the Braves improved to 9-0. Back in Atlanta on April 20, he relieved Tommy Boggs with two out in the second inning. The bases were loaded, and the Reds had a 2-0 lead. Bedrock got a quick out and followed with four more scoreless innings. When he left the game, the Braves led 4-2, and that was the final score, so Bedrosian was credited with the win in the game that gave "Hotlanta's Hotbraves"[18] their record-breaking 12th consecutive victory to start a season. The team increased that record to 13 straight wins (which was tied five years later by the AL Milwaukee Brewers). Bedrosian's fondest memory of that streak came at its end. After the Braves finally lost in Game 14, a fan displayed a sign that said: "161-1 Isn't Bad!"[19]

For the rest of that season, Bedrosian was used mainly in relief and did an "awesome" job.[20] Through July 27, his 1.46 ERA was the best on the team, and he had a 5-1 record and six saves in 34 games and was averaging 7.3 strikeouts per nine innings. He was deemed "among the hardest throwers ever to pitch for the Atlanta Braves." He acknowledged that he had loved striking batters out since his days in Little League and admitted that he didn't "try to nick corners."[21] Braves pitching coach Bob Gibson explained that Bedrosian was better suited for his relief role because starting gave him "too much time to think."[22]

Although he cooled off a bit in the latter part of the season, Bedrosian ended his first full season with a record of 8-6, 11 saves (in 17 opportunities), a 2.42 ERA, and 123 strikeouts (more than any other NL relief pitcher) in 64 games (only three starts). He did not fare well in the National League Championship Series when the Cardinals swept the Braves and went on to win the World Series. In Game One, Bedrosian replaced Pascual Perez in the sixth inning with no outs, the Braves down 2-0 and two runners aboard. He gave up a walk and three hits, allowing both inherited runners to score, and gave up two added runs, increasing the Cardinals lead to 6-0, while recording only two outs. He was also one of six pitchers the Braves used in the decisive Game Three, facing one batter (Keith Hernandez) and striking him out with the bases loaded in the eighth inning.

Postseason awards are based only on regular-season performance, and Bedrosian was named the National League Rookie Pitcher of the Year by *The Sporting News*. Pitching coach Gibson obviously had seen something others had missed; Steve Bedrosian, who had been a starter throughout his minor-league career (81 starts in 82 games), was now a reliever, and the Braves believed that their bullpen was set for 1983 with him paired with Gene Garber.[23] That duo plus Rick Camp, who contributed five saves, had been recognized by Rolaids as the "top team bullpen" in the majors.[24]

The Braves showed their confidence in Bedrosian with a pay raise from $37,000 to $155,000 – the highest percentage increase on the team[25] -- and he became the team's closer, finishing 52 of his 69 relief appearances. Bedrosian's work had him leading the race for the Rolaids Relief Pitcher Award in early August, but he struggled during the latter part of the season as his ERA rose from 3.00 to 3.74. At least one observer thought that these struggles were the result of his having been "shamefully overworked"[26] while Gene Garber was on the disabled list in July. His lone start that year came in the Braves' next-to-last game, on October 1 against the Padres in San Diego. He pitched seven strong innings and left the game in the eighth inning with a 2-1 lead, but lost the win when two relievers gave up two runs and the Braves then lost in the 10th. That game, his final appearance for the season, lowered his ERA to 3.60 but did not allow him to even his 9-10 record to .500. He did increase his strikeout rate to almost one per inning and his strikeout/walk ratio to 2.24, and recorded 19 saves (in 27 opportunities).

Early in 1984, there was some speculation that Bedrosian might move into the Braves' starting rotation because Phil Niekro had been released and Pascual Perez had been arrested in the Dominican Republic.[27] However, when the season started, Perez was a regular starter, and bullpen duties were distributed among Gene Garber (62 relief appearances/11 saves/42 closures), Donnie Moore (47/16/29), Jeff Dedmon (54/4/19), and Bedrosian (36/11/28).

Bedrosian got off to a fabulous start. By June 6, he had pitched 33⅓ innings in 19 games and had a 4-1 record plus eight saves with an ERA of 0.54. Then he struggled through a steak of four consecutive losses over an eight-day period in which he blew two ninth-inning leads on the road, gave up a 12th-inning walk-off single after walking the only other two batters he faced, and yielded back-to-back doubles to the first hitters he faced in the eighth inning of a tied home game. His ERA had tripled to 1.73. Those two blown-save opportunities were Bedrosian's first and last of the season; his overall success rate (84.8 percent) led the team.

Bedrosian was the only member of the bullpen quartet who logged any starting assignments. While his record in four starts was 3-1, he needed and received lots of run support (4.8 runs per game compared with the team's season average of 3.9); his ERA in those games was 3.86 (vs. 1.71 in his relief efforts). His overall ERA (2.37) was still lowest on the team among those who pitched in more than three games.

Bedrosian's fourth start, on August 15, was his last game of the 1984 season. The Braves had planned to move him into Craig McMurtry's slot in the rotation, but he was experiencing some pain in his right bicep that required attention and caution.[28] While his season ended early, there was much to be celebrated. He had improved his ERA, his winning percentage (9-6/.600), and his strikeout rate while lowering his WHIP to 1.171 (1.138 in relief). Talk of moving him into the starting rotation continued into the offseason.[29]

This time the talk resulted in a change. In 1985, the Braves had a new manager (Eddie Haas) and a new pitching coach (Johnny Sain). With Bruce Sutter now available as closer, Bedrock joined the starting rotation[30] -- for the first and only time in his major-league career. It was a less than stellar experience. He started 37 games (second only to Rick Mahler) and finished none of them – a record for most unfinished starts in a season.[31] He had the same number of losses (15) as Mahler, but 10 fewer wins (seven). Yet, compared to the rest of the starters, none of whom posted a winning record, his performance was admirable. His 3.83 ERA was second only to Mahler's, and his 5.8 strikeouts per nine innings led all starters. Not bad for a season when he pitched more innings than in his previous two seasons combined and was "supported" by a team that ranked 10th in the National League in runs scored (3.9 per game) and ninth in fielding percentage (.976), committing more errors (159) than all but one other team.

Yet, on December 10, 1985, the Braves traded Bedrosian and outfielder Milt Thompson to Philadelphia for catcher Ozzie Virgil and young pitcher Pete Smith. New general manager Bobby Cox wanted Virgil's power to "restore thunder"[32] to the Braves' anemic offense and risked giving up Bedrosian only after the Phillies turned down his offer of Jeff Dedmon. Phillies president Bill Giles made it clear that Bedrosian was the "plum" in the deal, seeing him as "the main short reliever in a really deep bullpen."[33]

After working his way through a sore arm during spring training,[34] Bedrosian started the 1986 season with his new team still trying to transition back into a reliever's role after a full year as a starter, and he struggled for a while.[35] He won in his Phillies debut, but it wasn't easy. He entered a 1-1 game in the top of the 10th in Cincinnati and got three quick outs. The Phillies scored four times in the 11th, but Bedrosian gave up two runs in the bottom of that inning before retiring a batter. The Reds had the tying runs on base before he struck out two batters to preserve the 5-3 win. His home debut was less stressful; he threw a 1-2-3 inning as the fifth of eight Philadelphia pitchers in a 9-8 win over the Mets. In his next game, he again took the mound in the 10th inning of a 1-1 tie, gave up two runs to the Pirates, and was the losing pitcher when the Phillies failed to rally.

By the end of April, Bedrosian had appeared in eight games, and his record was still 1-1. He ended the month with his first three saves, but gave up runs in two of them. His ERA was 7.27, and he had become a favorite target of the Phillies' notoriously noisy boo-birds.[36] The turnaround began in May with three solid relief appearances, and really took hold (perhaps appropriately) in Atlanta, when he earned a save on May 9 and a win two days later. Bedrosian gave Phillies pitching coach Claude Osteen credit for his improved mechanics.[37]

Bedrosian continued to improve and eventually earned the respect of those finicky fans, and the trade that brought him to Philadelphia was being praised as one of the best of the year as Bedrock gave the Phillies "the best right-handed relief in years."[38] His fastball was consistently timed at 95 mph and he was having one of the best seasons of any NL reliever.[39] He finished the season with 29 saves, tying the Phillies' team record. His ERA (3.39) and home-run rate (1.2 per 9 innings) were higher than in his last year as a Braves reliever, but his won-lost record (8-6) and walk and strikeout rates were remarkably similar to that year. He was back at home in the bullpen.

The reward was a two-year contract worth $1.75 million, ensuring that he would not become a free agent after the 1987 season, and Bedrosian declared himself to be "much more relaxed and ready to pitch well from the start."[40] Others expected him to be the anchor of the Philadelphia bullpen.[41] That optimism seemed unwarranted and certainly premature as Bedrock got off to another rocky start. In his first six games, he allowed 10 runs on 11 hits (including four home runs) and had an ERA of 11.05. Remarkably, he also had been credited with two victories and almost became the NL's first three-game winner on April 18 in the final game of that stretch. After Bedrosian gave up four runs to the Pirates in the eighth inning to blow a three-run lead, Mike Schmidt put the Phils ahead in the top of the ninth with his 500th career home run. The official scorer awarded the victory to Kent Tekulve, who shut down the Pirates in the bottom of that frame.

On April 26, in his eighth appearance, Bedrosian recorded his first save of the season, at home against the Pirates. On May 10 he started a streak in which he earned 19 saves in 20 appearances including a then-major-league record of 13 consecutive saves. He explained his success by saying, "I'm not aiming or trying to hit the corners. I'm just reaching back and letting it fly."[42] By the All-Star break, he had 24 saves and three wins for a team with only 42 victories, and he was named to the All-Star team for the first (and only) time in his career. In that game, he played a pivotal role with a fielding play that made him a hero instead of a potential "goat." He entered a scoreless game in the bottom of the ninth and sandwiched two walks around a successful sacrifice bunt, putting the potential winning run on second base. He then induced a grounder to first baseman Keith Hernandez, who threw to second for the force out. Hubie Brooks' return throw to Bedrosian, who was covering first, was wild and it looked as though the winning run would score, but he dove and snagged the errant throw, scrambled to his feet, and threw home where Ozzie Virgil (!) applied the tag that completed the double play and ended the inning.[43] The NL eventually won the game 2-0 in 13 innings.

Following his All-Star Game heroics, Bedrock continued to be rock-solid in relief. He eclipsed his previous season high in saves with his 30th on July 31 – the quickest in history to reach that milestone[44] -- and ended the season with a league-leading 40 saves, becoming the first Phillies pitcher to lead the league in that category since the save was adopted in 1969. That magical season was capped off when the BBWAA gave Bedrosian the Cy Young Award in the closest vote in the history of the award. Bedrosian (5-3; 2.83 ERA) edged Cubs starter Rick Sutcliffe (18-10; 3.68 ERA) by two points and Rick Reuschel (13-9; 3.09 ERA), who divided the season between the Giants and the Pirates, by three. Eight pitchers received votes, and no pitcher was named on all 24 ballots.[45]

Bedrosian's selection was controversial. No NL pitcher had been dominant, so each front-runner's fans could cite statistics that supported their man. His five wins and 40 saves meant that he had played a role in more than half of his fifth-place team's 80 victories. He observed: "I'm not going to say that I backed into it. I'm not looking at what starting pitchers did or didn't do this year. I'm looking at what I was able to accomplish."[46] The Phillies rewarded him with bonuses totaling $225,000 for his All-Star selection, Cy Young Award, and the Rolaids Relief Man of the Year Award. The latter, like *The Sporting News*'s designation as NL Fireman of the Year, was not controversial, and the Philadelphia Sportswriters Association named him the Pro Athlete of the Year.

There was understandable optimism heading into the 1988 season.[47] Then Bedrosian experienced chest pains while running sprints during spring training. The initial diagnosis was an acute strain,[48] but a later diagnosis was "walking pneumonia"[49] that put him out of action. He started the season on the 21-day disabled list after logging only one inning in spring training.[50] After a brief (five games) rehab assignment with the Triple-A Maine Phillies, Bedrock finally took the mound on May 20 in San Diego and retired the only batter he faced in the sixth inning to strand two runners and preserve a 3-2 lead. He then returned to his role as the Phillies' closer, finishing 49 games in 57 appearances and earning 28 saves. On September 25, his 95th career save for the Phillies broke Tug McGraw's team record.[51] After the season he was the only Phillies player offered a guaranteed multiyear contract, and he signed for three years at $1.45 million per year.[52]

The rumor mills went into overdrive in December when the Phillies traded for Jeff Parrett, who had appeared in 61 games for the Expos in 1988. GM Lee Thomas insisted that he had "no intention of trading" Bedrosian, whom he called "the best closer in baseball."[53] Bedrock, who had already expressed frustration over the limited number of save opportunities he had in 1988, explained: "I need work to stay sharp."[54] He had a strong spring training, allowing only six hits and a single run in nine games and started the regular season without allowing a run in his first five appearances.[55] By the end of April, however, he had been in 11 games and had a record of 1-2 with only two saves. On May 15 he earned his second win despite serving up two gopher balls and acknowledged: "I'm not throwing my slider the way I want. … I have to keep on battling."[56]

On June 16, Bedrosian gave up four runs in two innings and was the loser in a 15-11 slugfest won by the Mets. Two days later, he was traded to the San Francisco Giants, whose manager (Roger Craig) was sure that Bedrock would "get back on track with more work."[57] Bedrosian left the Phillies with a record of 2-3 and six more saves, raising his team record to 103 (since eclipsed). He was on the mound in Candlestick Park the day after the trade and earned a save. He then earned saves in his next four appearances, and finished the season with 17 saves and a 2.65 ERA for the Giants, who were champions of the NL West. Bedrosian appeared in four of the five NLCS games against the Cubs and got saves in the final three games, helping the Giants to win the NL pennant. He saw limited action (2⅔ innings in two appearances) in the "Earthquake" World Series that followed as Oakland swept the Giants in four games. Even though he had joined the team in midseason, Bedrock was voted a full share ($83,529.96) of the Giants' losing World Series earnings.[58]

Bedrosian entered the 1990 season as San Francisco's perceived "stopper." Craig Lefferts, who had lost his closer role when Bedrock joined the Giants, had been granted the free agency he requested[59] and had quickly signed with the Padres. Throughout spring training, Bedrosian had been worried about his 3-year-old son, Cody, who had been quite ill for several months. He reluctantly accompanied the team to Atlanta for Opening Day, but quickly went home to California when his wife, Tammy, called to say that Cody had gotten worse. The devastating diagnosis was leukemia, and Steve stayed with his son, missing the Giants' first five games. Tammy finally persuaded him to rejoin the team, and he went to Candlestick[60] on Sunday, April 15. He was sent to the mound in the ninth inning to protect a 3-2 lead over the Padres. He gave up four hits, including a two-run homer (on an 0-and-2 count) and lost the game, 4-3. He then showed his "leadership and character" by granting postgame interviews.[61] At the end of the season, those traits were officially acknowledged when Bedrosian received the Willie Mac "Spirit, Ability, and Leadership"[62] Award which annually recognizes the Giants' "most inspirational" player.

Bedrosian struggled off-and-on throughout 1990, but salvaged the season by finishing well.[63] In the three games after that disappointing first effort, he earned two saves. Then, on April 25, after holding the Pirates scoreless in the 10th and 11th innings, he was battered for four runs in the 12th and suffered another home loss. By June 1 he had earned seven saves, but did not get another until August 17. After earning two more August saves, he closed the season with seven saves and three wins (vs. one loss) in his last 11 appearances. His 1.46 ERA during that stretch lowered his season ERA by half a run to 4.20, still his highest since his call-up year. For the first time since that same year, Bedrosian walked more batters than he fanned. He had managed to equal his save total (17) from the previous year, and he had proved in the closing months of the season that he was still capable of closing games.

In December, the Giants traded Bedrosian to Minnesota for a player to be named later, and some pundits thought that he would become the Twins' closer, allowing Rick Aguilera to become a starter.[64] The pundits were wrong; Aguilera was still the closer, but Bedrosian got plenty of work, appearing in 56 games (but in only seven save situations). He finished the regular season with decent numbers (5-3, 4.42 ERA; six saves) and pitched briefly (1⅓ innings, two hits, no earned runs) in two ALCS games as the Twins beat the Blue Jays four games to one. Their World Series opponents were the Atlanta Braves.

Bedrosian appeared in three games against his former team – all played in Atlanta, all won by the Braves. His first two appearances were brief; he faced seven hitters and retired them all. His final appearance was less routine. He entered Game Five in the seventh inning with the Twins already trailing 7-3 and two runners on base. When he finally retired the side, he had given up two singles and a triple, allowing the two inherited runners to score, and was responsible for two more runs of his own. The Braves now led 11-3, and Bedrock was one of the five Twins pitchers whom the Braves "bent, folded, stapled, and mutilated"[65] that night. The Twins rebounded, winning the last two games at home, and Steve Bedrosian finally had earned a World Series ring.

Since June of that 1991 season, Bedrosian had been undergoing multiple medical examinations, tests, and treatments (including acupuncture) in an effort to determine why he was experiencing numbness in the index and middle fingers of his right (pitching) hand.[66] His once-dominant fastball now clocked only in the high 80s. He became a free agent at the end of the season and decided to take the next season off – a depressing "forced retirement" because his cold fingers had earned him a cold shoulder.[67] He later said: "I really thought I was done. Just out of the game for good."[68]

During his "retirement" on his 120-acre farm in Senoia, Georgia, while the 1992 season went on without him, the strange numbness subsided "suddenly and mysteriously."[69] Bedrosian contacted the Braves and was invited to spring training, where his comeback became "one of the best stories" of the spring.[70] Apparently, the numbness was related to tobacco and stress, so he gave up tobacco, and son Cody's leukemia was in remission. Bedrock was now "healthy and stress-free."[71]

When the 1993 season started, Steve Bedrosian was a Brave again, and now he was the second oldest pitcher on the team. He struggled in April, losing two games that were tied when he took the mound. He acknowledged that he no longer had manager Bobby Cox's confidence.[72] His performance improved as he adjusted to not being the closer. He appeared in 49 games (pitching only 49⅔ innings, none of them save opportunities). He did not lose another game, and earned five wins. His 1.63 ERA was lowest on the team and he struck out more than twice as many batters as he walked. He was no longer "Kid Smoke," but he could still be as solid as bedrock.

After the season the Braves avoided salary arbitration with Bedrosian by releasing him, but they signed him to a new contract two days later.[73] His role in the 1994 Braves bullpen was similar to the previous year. At 36, he was now the team's oldest pitcher. He pitched 46 innings in 46 games and was charged with two losses; he blew both of his save opportunities and earned no wins. His ERA rose to 3.33, but was second lowest on the team behind Greg Maddux's 1.56. Once again, he became a free agent at the end of the season, but was signed to a new contract within days.

Bedrock was back with the Braves to start the 1995 season. He announced that he had rediscovered his fastball thanks to acupuncture,[74] but that wasn't enough. In August, after appearing in only 29 of the Braves' 96 games, Bedrosian abruptly announced his retirement.[75] He left with a 1-2 record and a 6.11 ERA. He had blown his only two save opportunities, and in his final game had retired only one of the six batters he faced, giving up four hits and an intentional walk. He wasn't there when the Braves finally won a World Series later that year, but he did receive his second World Series ring and a partial share of the winning team's earnings.[76]

There was not another comeback. Steve Bedrosian's fine major-league playing career was over after 14 seasons in which he appeared in 732 regular-season games (only 46 as a starter), pitching 1,191 innings. He won 76 games, lost 79, saved 184 (representing a 76.3 percent success rate), and "held" 38 more. He struck out 921 batters (seven per nine innings) and walked approximately half that many (443) unintentionally. Only half of the 52 players drafted ahead of Bedrock in 1978 made it to "The Show," and only five (and just two pitchers) matched or exceeded his 14-year major-league career. One of those five was Hall of Famer Cal Ripken, who was drafted five slots before Bedrosian.

Bedrosian wasn't through with baseball or the Braves. He agreed to participate in 1996 spring training and then join the Appalachian (Rookie) League Danville Braves as pitching coach.[77]

Steve Bedrosian wasn't through with Georgia, either. The Massachusetts native stayed on the farm in Coweta County where he had settled during his first tour with the Braves. That's where he and Tammy raised their five children (Stephen Kyle, Cody, Carson, Cameron, and Katelyn); that was now home. Bedrosian had been a bachelor when he joined the Braves in 1981.[78] After he married singer[79] Tammy Raye Blackwell in 1984[80] and later became a father, he brought to that role the same strength and determination that he showed on the diamond. The importance of his family is reflected in Steve's choice of "the game of [his] life." He didn't choose a game in which he had excelled; he chose a game in which he gave up a tape-measure grand slam. He chose the May 10, 1994, game in which the Braves honored 6-year-old Cody Bedrosian, who was still battling leukemia. Cody got to throw out the first ball, and several Braves wore their pants knee-high and their sock stirrups high (Bedrosian style). Steve served up that homer and left the mound in the seventh inning with the Braves trailing 8-1 feeling that he "had let Cody down," but the Braves tied the game with a seven-run rally in the ninth and won 9-8 in the 15th for "a storybook ending."[81] Cody recovered (thanks in large part to a bone-marrow transplant with brother Cam as the donor)[82] and as of 2020 was doing well.

All four Bedrosian sons played baseball. Cody hung up his glove when he was 12.[83] Kyle, Cameron, and Carson all played for the East Coweta High Indians, where their father often served as assistant pitching coach. Kyle, a lefty, went on to play for four years at Mercer University. In 2010, Cameron (Cam), whose middle name is "Rock," was drafted out of high school in the first round by the Los Angeles Angels and made his major-league debut in 2014. He is a right-handed relief pitcher who averages more than a strikeout per inning and his nickname is "Bedrock." Does that sound familiar?

Steve served on the Coweta County (Georgia) Board of Education for several years and was elected to the Coweta Sports Hall of Fame in 2009. He was already enshrined in the University of New Haven's Athletics Hall of Fame (a 1996 inductee).

Sources

In addition to the sources cited in the Notes, the author consulted Baseball-Almanac, the Baseball Cube, Baseball-Reference.com, Retrosheet.org, and the Sports Illustrated Vault.

Notes

1. www.dictionary.com.
2. Email from Steve Bedrosian, November 11, 2019.
3. eagletribune.com/sports/local_sports/eagle-tribune-athletes-of-the-century/article_35307211-902c-5f80-b368-fe56d94d3f2a.html.
4. University of New Haven Athletics, newhavenchargers.com/hof.aspx?hof=69.
5. Lou Pavlovich, "Horner and Gibson Stand Out in Selections," *The Sporting News*, July 8, 1978: 42.
6. "Southern League Report," *The Sporting News*, June 2, 1979: 43.
7. "Southern League Report," *The Sporting News*, June 2, 1979: 43.
8. "Balboni Heads All-Stars," *The Sporting News*, July 12, 1980: 52.
9. Ken Picking, "Braves' Biggest Gain Was Down the Middle," *The Sporting News*, November 15, 1980: 53.
10. Picking, "Dayley Atlanta's Hill Prize," *The Sporting News*, December 13, 1980: 50.
11. Tim Tucker, "Braves Willing to Deal Pitcher," *The Sporting News*, December 12, 1981: 50.
12. Email from Steve Bedrosian, November 11, 2019.
13. Tucker, "Bedrosian's Injuries Believed to be Minor," *The Sporting News*, February 13, 1982: 39.
14. Tucker, "Eight Pitchers Battle for Braves Berths," *The Sporting News*, March 13, 1982: 40.
15. Tucker, "Braves Are Leaning on Horner, Murphy," *The Sporting News*, April 24, 1982: 21.
16. "Player Biographies: Steve Bedrosian," *Braves Illustrated: 1982 Yearbook*: 47.
17. *Fan: 1984 Atlanta Braves Official Program* (Vol. 19, No. 4), 27.
18. George Cunningham, "12-0! Hotlanta's Hotbraves Rewrite Record Book," *Atlanta Constitution*, April 21, 1982: 1.
19. Email from Steve Bedrosian, November 11, 2019.
20. Tucker, "Bedrosian Rates 'Awesome' Label," *The Sporting News*, August 9, 1982: 17.
21. Tucker, "Bedrosian Rates 'Awesome' Label."
22. Tucker, "Bedrosian Rates 'Awesome' Label."
23. Earl Lawson, "Reds Setting Sights on Atlanta Slugger," *The Sporting News*, December 13, 1982: 52.
24. Chris Mortensen, "Mr. Finesse and Kid Smoke," *Braves Illustrated: 1983 Yearbook*: 23.
25. Tucker, "Braves Face Huge Payroll," *The Sporting News*, March 28, 1983: 36.
26. Bill Conlin, "Phils Seek a Starting Pitcher," *The Sporting News*, November 14, 1983: 48.
27. Tucker, "Braves Seek Perez's Replacement," *The Sporting News*, February 6, 1984: 49, 52.
28. Gerry Fraley. "Barker. McMurtry Out of Rotation," *The Sporting News*, August 20, 1984: 19-20.
29. Fraley, "Do Braves Lead Chase of Sutter?" *The Sporting News*, December 10, 1984: 51.
30. Sandy Keenan, "10 Atlanta Braves," *Sports Illustrated*, April 15, 1985.
31. "Steve Bedrosian," Alchetron (alchetron.com/Steve-Bedrosian).
32. Fraley, "Braves Gear Up for Slugfests," *The Sporting News*, December 23, 1985: 44.
33. Peter Pascarelli, "Two Trades Have Ripple Effect," *The Sporting News*, December 23, 1985: 41.
34. Bill Conlin, "NL Beat," *The Sporting News*, March 10, 1986: 40.
35. Conlin, "NL East," *The Sporting News*, May 26, 1986: 18.
36. Pascarelli, "A Bullpen Bounce-Back by Phillies' Bedrosian," *The Sporting News*, September 8, 1986: 17.
37. Conlin, "NL East," *The Sporting News*, May 26, 1986: 18.
38. Murray Chass, "Baseball's Best Trades," *The Sporting News*, August 25, 1986: 14.
39. Pascarelli, "A Bullpen Bounce-Back."

40 "Notebook, NL East, Phils," *The Sporting News*, February 2, 1987: 42.

41 Pascarelli, "N.L. East: Phillies," *The Sporting News*, April 1, 1987: 24.

42 "N.L. East: Phillies," *The Sporting News*, July 13, 1987: 27.

43 Dave Nightingale, "A Relapse by the Rabbit?" *The Sporting News*, July 27, 1987: 45; YouTube video Alchetron.

44 "NL East," *The Sporting News*, August 17, 1987: 17.

45 Murray Chass, "Phillies' Bedrosian Cy Young Winner," *New York Times*, November 11, 1987.

46 Bill Brown, "Cy Young Award a Real Bonus," *The Sporting News*, November 23, 1987: 45.

47 Brown, "Bedrock Digs for Solid Start," *The Sporting News*, March 27, 1988: 24.

48 "Notebook: NL East: Phillies," *The Sporting News*, March 21, 1988: 37.

49 "Notebook: NL East: Phillies," *The Sporting News*, March 28, 1988: 33.

50 "Notebook: NL East: Phillies," *The Sporting News*, April 11, 1988: 49.

51 "Notebook: NL East: Phillies," *The Sporting News*, October 10, 1988: 23.

52 Chass, "Sax & Marshall Set Free," *The Sporting News*, November 14, 1988: 44.

53 "Notebook: NL East: Phillies," *The Sporting News*, March 6, 1989: 17.

54 "Notebook," *The Sporting News*, March 6, 1989: 19.

55 "Notebook: NL East: Phillies," *The Sporting News*, May 15, 1989: 21.

56 "Notebook: NL East: Phillies," *The Sporting News*, May 29, 1989: 23.

57 Brown, "Thomas Shakes Up Phillies," *The Sporting News*, June 26, 1989: 22.

58 Chass, "A's World Series Checks Set Record," *The Sporting News*, November 11, 1989: 61.

59 "Notebook: NL West: Giants," *The Sporting News*, January 1, 1990: 52.

60 Jack Wilkinson, "Steve Bedrosian," *The Game of My Life* (Champaign, Illinois: Sports Publishing, 2007), 64.

61 Art Spander. "Cody Bedrosian Can Be Proud of His Father," *The Sporting News*, May 7, 1990: 55.

62 "Willie Mac Award," baseball-almanac.com/awards/willie_mac_award.shtml.

63 "Bedrosian Salvages '90 with a Strong Finish," *The Sporting News*, October 15, 1990: 17.

64 "Notebook: AL West: Will Bedrosian Make Aguilera a Starter?" *The Sporting News*, December 17, 1990: 35.

65 Nightingale, "Twins Star in the Late Show," *The Sporting News*, November 4, 1991: 10.

66 Wilkinson, 62.

67 Sean Gavitan, "Life's Highways;" *Fan* (Atlanta Braves magazine), 1993: 56.

68 Wilkinson, 63.

69 Wilkinson, 63.

70 Pascarelli, "Baseball Report: Around the Bases," *The Sporting News*, March 15, 1993: 16.

71 Pascarelli, "Baseball Report: Around the Bases."

72 Bill Zach, "Baseball: NL East/West: Atlanta Braves," *The Sporting News*, May 31, 1993: 20.

73 Tim Luke, "AL/NL: Atlanta Braves: Bedrock's Back," *The Sporting News*, November 22, 1993: 43.

74 Zach, "NL East: Atlanta Braves," *The Sporting News*, May 8, 1995: 18.

75 Zach, "NL East: Atlanta Braves," *The Sporting News*, August 21, 1995: 16.

76 Telephone conversation with Steve Bedrosian. November 5, 2019.

77 Zach, "NL: Atlanta Braves," *The Sporting News*, December 18, 1995: 44.

78 "Career Statistics: Steve Bedrosian," *Braves Illustrated; 1981 Yearbook*: 66.

79 Email from Steve Bedrosian, November 11, 2019.

80 "Steve Bedrosian," *Atlanta Braves 1994 Team Yearbook*: 25.

81 Wilkinson, 65.

82 Telephone conversation with Steve Bedrosian, November 5, 2019.

83 Wilkinson, 66.

Rafael Belliard

BY JOE COX

Rafael Belliard

On the night of September 26, 1997, the Atlanta Braves and New York Mets were playing out the dregs of the regular season before a small crowd at Shea Stadium. But if part of baseball's appeal is that any trip to the ballpark can yield historic accomplishments, the partisans of New York were in for a treat.

In the seventh inning, Atlanta shortstop Rafael Belliard turned on a fastball from Mets lefty Brian Bohanon and hooked it over the left-field wall for a game-tying home run. The Braves dugout exploded, with many of Atlanta's biggest stars grinning like Little Leaguers as Belliard circled the bases and returned to the dugout amid an atmosphere of pandemonium. The celebration seemed to be of the type reserved for a pennant clincher or a ninth-inning grand slam. It was a long time coming.

"I've been looking for that for 10 years," Belliard exclaimed after the game. "Finally, I get it tonight. I'm dreaming."[1]

Rafael Belliard, 5-foot-6 shortstop extraordinaire, had hit his only previous big-league home run on May 5, 1987. After 10½ years and 1,869 major-league at-bats, Belliard finally managed his second – and final – big-league home run.

Belliard, as much as anyone, typified the good field/no hit shortstops who proliferated in the big leagues during his reign from the early 1980s to the late 1990s. He earned his way into the major leagues with his foot speed and fielding prowess and stayed there despite his lack of skill on offense, particularly power.

Belliard may be best remembered today for his 10½-year homerless drought. But instead of being memorialized as a ballplayer for what his career didn't include, Belliard could as easily be remembered for his decade and a half in the major leagues, for his slick glove, solid bunting, and for being a part of a Braves team that allowed him to appear in four World Series, and even star in one.

And then every 10 years or so, he'd add a home run.

*****

Rafael Leonidas Belliard Mattias was born on October 24, 1961, in Puerto Nuevo, Dominican Republic. Like many boys his age, Belliard spent a large part of his childhood refining his baseball skills, which in his case were largely defensive. "In Dominica, we play all year long, no matter where," he reflected in 1991. "There you practiced every day like spring training. You have like one month off, then you're back in practice."[2]

When Belliard was 17, he took a bus trip to Santo Domingo, where he tried out for a Dominican military team. When his slick fielding earned him a spot on the squad, his compensation was roughly $80 per month.[3] Belliard's big break likely was the 1979 Pan American Games, where his Dominican squad finished second, losing only to champion Cuba. Scouts may have watched the games to observe a lackluster 5-3 US squad, which failed to medal, but they couldn't fail to observe the pint-sized Dominican shortstop who not only caught everything hit to him, but managed to bat .375 in the eight games played.

Pittsburgh scout Pablo Cruz urged the Pirates to sign Belliard. When some questioned Cruz about the infielder's diminutive size, Cruz told them "not to worry about balls hit over his head, because there wouldn't be many hit through his legs."[4] Cruz also told other Pirates executives, "He has winning blood."[5]

Belliard signed with Pittsburgh in 1980, and that winning blood didn't manifest itself right away. In the summer of 1980, in 20 games split between the Gulf Coast League and the Pirates' South Atlantic League farm team in Shelby, he hit .182. He split time between second base, third base, and shortstop, and while his defensive skills were obvious, so were the limitations of his game. Few pegged Belliard as a long-term major leaguer.

The story essentially remained the same in 1981, when Pittsburgh made Belliard the everyday shortstop for the Class-A Alexandria Dukes. Belliard, who was just 19, played in 127 games and showed many of the skills that would define his career. He was part of 73 double plays at shortstop, which nearly led his league, had a dozen sacrifice bunts, and stole 42 bases. He also posted a batting line of .216/.264/.250 and fanned 92 times.

For many players, a promising career could have ended right there. But Belliard's destiny was shaped by the acts of the parent club, who were about to trade 1981 shortstop Tim Foli to the California Angels. Pittsburgh then planned to hand the everyday job to Dale Berra. The son of Yankee Hall of Famer Yogi Berra, Dale was a Pittsburgh first-round draft choice and had filled a utility role with the team for several seasons. He not only had the pedigree to be an everyday big leaguer, he had some of the necessary skills, but he struggled with consistency. In 1982 Berra would be the Pittsburgh shortstop, but he would need a backup, particularly somebody strong with the glove.

Meanwhile, Rafael Belliard spent most of the 1982 season with Double-A Buffalo. The starting job at shortstop there belonged to highly touted prospect Gregory Pastors. Pastors hit .193, and Belliard significantly outplayed him, batting .274 in 124 at-bats and posting a higher fielding percentage. Accordingly, on September 6, the Pirates called Belliard to the major leagues. He played in nine games, mostly as a pinch-runner and defensive replacement. He experienced his first major-league at-bat on September 25, pinch-hitting a single off Montreal's Scott Sanderson before stealing second base and scoring a run. Belliard ended the season 1-for-2 at the plate and handled four chances flawlessly in the field.

Belliard spent the next three seasons bouncing between the minor leagues, brief stints in Pittsburgh, and on one occasion, a lengthy trip to the disabled list. Most of 1983 was spent in Double-A Lynn (where he hit .262 in 431 at-bats). Most of 1984 was spent on the disabled list after Belliard fractured his left fibula on a bad landing from a difficult infield throw in Chicago. If there is any karma bounceback, surely it was 1985, when Belliard spent most of the season in Triple-A Hawaii (where he hit .246 in 341 at-bats). Altogether Belliard played in 41 big-league games from 1983 to 1985. He was 9-for-43 at the plate during those seasons.

Meanwhile, Pittsburgh had continued to rely on Dale Berra at shortstop, despite declining offensive returns and three consecutive 30-error seasons. Berra's performance issues may be somewhat explained by his appearance in the Pittsburgh Drug Trials of 1985. After the 1984 season, the

Pirates dealt Berra to the Yankees, where his father was the manager. Among the players they gained in return was Tim Foli. A March 1985 item in *The Sporting News* indicated that Belliard might split time with Foli,[6] but the latter retired after hitting .189 in 37 at-bats in Pittsburgh.

The Pirates went with Sam Khalifa at shortstop in 1985. He promptly hit .238 and made 16 errors, and after Pittsburgh went 57-104, manager Chuck Tanner was sent packing, to be followed by a career minor leaguer named Jim Leyland. It was one of the most fortunate moments of Rafael Belliard's career.

In the spring of 1986, Belliard was trying to play his way into a crowded shortstop rotation in Pittsburgh. The Pirates returned starter Khalifa and veteran Johnnie LeMaster. But Belliard made his mark. The Pirates released LeMaster before Opening Day, with Leyland telling a reporter, "Belliard played his way on the club. He has more versatility than LeMaster."[7]

Belliard spent his first full season in the big leagues under Leyland, who valued both youth and defense. As Belliard continued to improve, Khalifa struggled, and was ultimately sent down to the minors. The Pirates signed veteran U L Washington, but gave the majority of time at shortstop to Belliard. Rafael even provided some offensive punch early in the season, going 15-for-33 during one streak, and hitting .248 in the first half of the season, with 23 RBIs and 10 stolen bases.

He played in 117 games in 1986, mostly at shortstop, although he occasionally filled in at second base. His defense continued to be a highlight, as he finished fourth in the NL in range factor per nine innings as a shortstop, and fifth in the league in total zone runs among shortstops. Offensively, Belliard's 11 sacrifices were seventh most in the National League. That said, his .233/.298/.262 offensive line ensured that Belliard would continue to split time with more offensively capable middle infielders.

The 1987 season was something of a step back for Belliard. In spring training, Pirates GM Syd Thrift told a reporter, "You really need two (shortstops)."[8] Concern over Belliard's physical durability and his shy, quiet nature were cited as evidence in favor of the Pirates' search for another shortstop.[9] For the first half of the season, the concerns seemed unfounded. Belliard launched his first career home run on May 5, a three-run blast off the Padres' Eric Show. While Belliard had some struggles, Leyland spoke out in his favor, telling reporters that while Belliard was "not a .300 hitter," he also was "not a .200 hitter, either."[10] Leyland drew parallels between Belliard's defensive skills and those of Baltimore shortstop Mark Belanger, ultimately telling the media, "If the lineup just does what they can do, we feel we can play Belliard at shortstop and not worry about it."[11] It didn't work out that way in 1987.

Belliard was hitting .187 on July 8, when he was demoted to Double-A Harrisburg. He hit .338 there, and was recalled by the Pirates on August 16. Belliard promptly went 6-for-10 before ending his season by breaking his leg on August 26 while completing a double play against the Reds. The brief hot streak did allow Belliard to finish the season at .207, but he played in only 81 games, batting 203 times to post his .207/.286/.271 offensive line.

Over the next three years in Pittsburgh, the same basic pattern followed. The Pirates – particularly Leyland – appreciated Belliard's smooth glove and versatility. (Belliard even played a few games at third base for the Pirates in 1989 and 1990.) However, he simply didn't hit enough to be more than a part-time player. In 1988 Belliard played in 122 games, but was part of a three-headed Pittsburgh shortstop group (along with Felix Fermin and Al Pedrique) that combined to have more errors (20) than RBIs (17). Belliard played less in 1989 (67 games, 154 at-bats) and 1990 (47 games, 54 at-bats). Pittsburgh was increasingly playing shortstop Jay Bell at the position, and in 1990 Belliard's future was again in jeopardy after he was left off the Pirates' postseason roster when the team reached the 1990 NLCS.

In December 1990, a free agent, Belliard signed a two-year, $800,000 contract with the last-place Atlanta Braves. Braves GM John Schuerholz acted on some rave reviews from those close to Belliard. Former Pirate Sid Bream, who would play with Belliard in Atlanta, told Schuerholz, "He's as good a shortstop as Ozzie Smith."[12]

Veteran manager Bobby Cox used Belliard in tandem with good-hit, no-field shortstop Jeff Blauser, and the young Atlanta pitching staff, which included John Smoltz, Tom Glavine, and Steve Avery, provided many leads that justified keeping the light-hitting Belliard in games for defensive purposes. But Cox saw Belliard as his everyday shortstop, and told Rafael so. "I told him I hadn't really done that," recalled Belliard.[13]

Belliard played in 149 games in 1991, and batted 353 times, both career highs. He didn't lack for production, batting a career-best .249 and having some genuinely impressive hot streaks at the plate. On May 7 and 8, in a home series against the Cardinals, Belliard had five hits, including three doubles and a triple, to go with eight RBIs in the two games. Meanwhile, Belliard continued to impress Cox with his glove work. Late in the season, the skipper said, "Defense is a main part of the reason we are where we are and those two guys on the left side of our infield [Belliard and third baseman Terry Pendleton] are as good as there is."[14] When Atlanta played its way to a division title on the last weekend of the season, Belliard found himself taking on some familiar faces in his first playoff appearance. The Braves faced the Pirates in a seven-game NLCS, and Belliard started all seven games. He went 4-for-19 in the series, but also helped Braves pitchers rack up three shutouts over Pittsburgh, the final a 4-0 win in Game Seven.

From there, Belliard had a World Series to remember in the Braves' seven-game loss to the Twins. He again started every game, and went 6-for-16 at the plate, knocking in four runs. He also went errorless in 29 defensive chances, including four double plays, two of which helped preserve Game Seven as a scoreless tie until the 10th inning, when Minnesota broke the Braves' hearts. Despite the tough loss, Belliard had experienced his best season as a big leaguer and finished it with a superb World Series. "I knew I was playing for something important," Belliard said a quarter-century later, also admitting, "Hey, it did (surprise) me."[15]

In 1992 Belliard and the Braves played their way back to the Series again. This time, Rafael played in 144 games, earning 285 at-bats. But he hit only .211, and thus found himself filling in for defensive purposes by the time of the playoffs, batting once in the NLCS and contributing only a sacrifice bunt in the World Series against the Blue Jays. Still, observers cited Belliard for making "a sizeable contribution to the Braves' 1991 National League pennant" and being "just as important in 1992."[16]

From there, Belliard would serve Atlanta only as a reserve. Blauser had come into his own as an offensive threat, and while Rafael still appeared for defensive purposes at shortstop or occasionally at second base, he never again eclipsed 180 at-bats in a season.

The remaining highlight of Belliard's career was the 1995 season, when he did take those 180 at-bats, playing in 75 games for Atlanta, and finally winning the World Series that had eluded the squad. Belliard batted .222 in 1995, but Jeff Blauser was injured down the stretch run and Belliard again found himself an everyday shortstop in the World Series.

Belliard went 0-for-16 at the plate in the Series, but found ways to contribute, even during a hitting slump. His successful seventh-inning squeeze bunt in Game One was the winning margin of the Braves' 3-2 win over the Indians. He remained on the field to the end of the clinching Game Six, joining the dogpile on the pitching mound when Mark Wohlers retired the final batter of the Braves' title run.

From there, age and the continued improvement of other Braves shortstops spelled the gradual decline of Belliard's big-league career. He did manage his elusive second career home run in late 1997, but the following spring, after starting the season 5-for-20 and playing in seven of the Braves' first eight games, Belliard tore his left quadriceps muscle.[17] While he did rehabilitate himself from the injury, and the Braves had him on postseason standby if he was needed, Belliard never played in another major-league game after April 9, 1998.

In bits and pieces of 17 seasons in major-league baseball, Belliard finished his career as a .221 hitter. His 508 career hits included only two home runs, and he knocked in 142 total runs. Belliard's career OPS+ of 46 is a testimony to his struggles at bat, but he was a career .974 fielder at shortstop, and he ranks among the top 75 shortstops in total zone runs (since the stat can be tracked, which dates back to 1953).

Belliard transitioned from playing to coaching, spending several years with Atlanta as a roving minor-league instructor and then coaching for the Tigers.[18] During the offseason before 2013, Belliard was diagnosed with prostate cancer, but he underwent surgery with positive results.[19] In 2014 Belliard went to work for the Kansas City Royals, first as a special assistant to the general manager, and then, starting in 2015, as a roving infield coordinator. When not on the road, he lives in Boca Raton, Florida, with his wife of over three decades, Leonora. They have a son and two grandchildren.

While comic foibles of Belliard's decade-long chase after his second home run might be the biggest memory that casual fans have of his career, his four decades in Organized Baseball point to the incredible success of the undersized glove man. Perhaps instead of Belliard's inability to hit the long ball, future fans should know of his defensive skills, his positive attitude throughout his career's many twists and turns, and his surprising postseason heroics.

Notes

1. Buster Olney, "It's No Small Feat as Braves' Belliard Hits a Rare Homer," *New York Times*, September 27, 1997.
2. C. Ron Allen, "Touching Bases: Series Star for Braves Offers to Help Abused and Abandoned Children's Home in Boca," *South Florida Sun Sentinel* (Fort Lauderdale), November 13, 1991.
3. Steve Wulf, "Standing Tall at Short," *Sports Illustrated*, February 9, 1987. Interestingly, *Sports Illustrated* said it was a Navy team, while the *Atlanta Journal-Constitution* referred to it as an Army squad in a September 16, 2016, profile of Belliard, which is cited below.
4. Charles Feeney, "Belliard Has the Right Bloodlines," *The Sporting News*, June 30, 1986: 21.
5. Ibid.
6. Charles Feeney, "Foli May Share Short with Belliard," *The Sporting News*, March 25, 1985: 31.
7. Charles Feeney, "Pirates' Accent on Youth Added Khalifa, Belliard," *The Sporting News*, April 21, 1986: 26.
8. *The Sporting News*, February 16, 1987: 34.
9. Ibid.
10. Bob Hertzel, "He's Still a Glove Man," *The Sporting News*, May 25, 1987: 15.
11. Ibid.
12. Joel Bierig and Bruce Levine, "Brave New World," *The Sporting News*, May 27, 1991: 10.
13. I.J. Rosenberg, "Belliard Provided Defense, Clutch Play During Braves' Run," *Atlanta Journal-Constitution*, September 16, 2016.
14. Ross Newhan, "In Defense, Pendleton, Belliard are Fallible," *Los Angeles Times*, September 22, 1991.
15. Rosenberg, "Belliard Provided Defense."
16. Dave Nightengale, "Make a Deal, Face the Wheel," *The Sporting News*, November 23, 1992: 41.
17. *The Sporting News*, April 20, 1998: 38.
18. Rosenberg, "Belliard Provided Defense."
19. Jason Beck, "Following surgery, Belliard grateful for quick response," MLB.com, February 23, 2013, mlb.com/news/following-surgery-belliard-grateful-for-quick-response/c-41910186.

Jeff Blauser

BY GREG STEPHENSON

Jeff Blauser

After an early professional career filled with numerous false starts, position changes, injuries, and demotions, Jeff Blauser carved out 13 seasons in the major leagues, primarily as an offense-first shortstop. In 11 years with the Atlanta Braves (1987-97) and two with the Chicago Cubs (1998-99), he was a two-time All-Star and played on four World Series teams.

Blauser was a first-round pick by the Braves in 1984, when the team was about to begin a stretch of five 90-loss seasons in six years. By the time he left as a free agent more than a decade later, he'd helped transform Atlanta into one of baseball's model franchises.

Born on November 8, 1965, in Los Gatos, California, and raised just northeast of Sacramento in Auburn, Blauser first received baseball acclaim as a pitcher. He pitched two no-hitters in a three-week span for the Placer Savers Little League team when he was 12 years old,[1] then pitched another for the Value Giant Babe Ruth team two years later.[2]

At Placer High School, Blauser also excelled in football. He was a wide receiver, safety, kicker, and punter, once scoring 18 of his team's 24 points in a 1982 game against Woodland.[3] As a senior Blauser was named to the All-Capital Athletic League first-team as a kicker.[4]

Blauser also earned All-CAL honors as a shortstop in baseball the following spring, when he batted .347 with 33 hits, 8 doubles, 19 runs batted in, and 19 steals. He was chosen to play in the Optimist All-Star Game in Sacramento that summer.[5]

Blauser was not selected in the June 1983 draft, and signed a baseball scholarship with Sacramento City College. While playing in unofficial summer and winter games with the Sacramento City team, Blauser was able to improve his speed, which apparently impressed the St. Louis Cardinals enough for them to select him eighth overall in the January phase of the 1984 amateur draft.[6]

Draft rules at the time stipulated that Blauser had to finish his college season before he could turn pro, and he earned all-conference honors that spring, when he hit .383 with 26 RBIs. Two of his teammates at Sacramento City during that 1984 season were future major leaguers Greg Vaughn and Joe Bitker.[7]

Unable to come to terms with the Cardinals, Blauser re-entered the June draft, and the Braves selected him with the number-four overall pick in the secondary phase. At the time, the secondary phase was set aside for college players who had already been drafted at least once.

Blauser was being recruited by such NCAA baseball powers as Miami, Arizona State, and USC,[8] but this time elected to begin a professional career.[9] He was assigned to the Pulaski Braves of the rookie-level Appalachian League.

"He was our first choice all the way around," Braves scout Bill Wight said. "He's really come on in the last year and I think he'll make the big leagues within three or four years."[10]

Wight ended up being correct, as Blauser reached the majors with the Braves on July 5, 1987, a little more than three years after he was drafted. He spent the 1984 season at Pulaski, batting .249/.367/.327 in 62 games.

Blauser played the 1985 season at Low-A Sumter (South Atlantic League), batting .235/.367/.315 with 49 RBIs and 36 steals for a club that also included future Braves mainstays Tom Glavine, Ron Gant, and Mark Lemke. Blauser's defense was shaky, however; he made 24 errors in 58 games in 1984, 35 in 117 games in 1985, and 25 in 120 games in 1986.

By early 1986, Blauser began to catch the eye of the big-league Braves. An *Atlanta Journal Constitution* story that spring included him as the second baseman on a hypothetical "possible lineup: Opening Day 1990" along with Glavine, Bob Horner, and Dale Murphy.[11] Hank Aaron, then the Braves' director of player development, described Blauser as a "very intelligent player," adding, "You don't have to tell him anything twice."[12]

It was at High-A Durham in 1986 that Blauser started to develop his power stroke. He batted .286/.399/.447 with 27 doubles, 13 home runs, and 94 runs scored in a lineup that also featured Gant and David Justice.

Blauser was placed on the Braves' 40-man roster prior to the 1987 season,[13] and the club – then in the midst of five 90-loss seasons in six years – briefly toyed with the idea of elevating him straight to the major leagues after he hit .344 in spring training. "I love the kid," Braves manager Chuck Tanner told the *Atlanta Constitution*. "I don't care if he played in the North County League last year. He can play in the major leagues right now at second or short. There's no question about it."[14]

The Braves eventually reassigned Blauser to their minor-league camp. He began the 1987 season at Triple-A Richmond; there were plans to convert him to a second baseman.[15]

Blauser struggled at Richmond, however, batting .177/.244/.212 with only two extra-base hits in 33 games. By late May, he was demoted to Double-A Greenville and returned to shortstop.

On July 2 Blauser was hitting just .203 in 40 games at Greenville when he was summoned to Atlanta after starting shortstop Rafael Ramirez suffered a knee injury. (Ramirez's backup, Andres Thomas, was also hobbled by a sprained ankle.)[16] His stay in the big leagues was a short one; he was returned to Greenville after making just one pinch-hitting appearance.[17]

Blauser spent the next month at Double-A Greenville, raising his slash line to .249/.338/.366, and the Braves called him up again to replace the injured Thomas on August 10.[18] He started at shortstop the next night in San Diego, batting sixth and going 0-for-3 in a 7-6 Atlanta loss.

Blauser's first major-league hit came the next day, a third-inning infield single off the Padres' Eric Nolte. He hit his first big-league homer on August 16 in Houston, a solo shot against Jim Deshaies in the fourth inning of a 6-2 Braves loss.

Blauser got into 51 games for the Braves the remainder of the 1987 season, batting .242/.328/.352 with 2 home runs, 15 RBIs, and 7 stolen bases. But his big-league career didn't quite take off in 1988.

With Thomas back from injury the following spring to play shortstop, Blauser was sent back to Triple-A Richmond so he could play every day.[19] He batted .284/.340/.417 with 25 extra-base hits in 69 games, earning a call-up to Atlanta when rosters expanded in September.

Though he hit just .239/.268/.403 in 18 September games for the Braves, Blauser would never play in the minor leagues again. He made the big-league club out of spring training in 1989, playing in 142 games and posting a .735 OPS while seeing extensive time at third base and second base – and even one game in center field – in addition to shortstop. On August 26, 1989, Blauser began what would be a career-long habit of terrorizing the Chicago Cubs, homering twice in a 5-3 Braves victory at Wrigley Field.[20]

Blauser began the 1990 season as the Braves' starting shortstop, and on May 7 had another two-homer game in Chicago, including a two-run shot off Mitch Williams in the top of the ninth inning to give Atlanta a 9-8 victory. Blauser homered again the next day, a two-run blast in a 10-8 Braves loss.

Blauser missed nearly three weeks later that month with a thigh injury,[21] but finished the 1990 season batting .269/.338/.409 with 8 homers and 39 RBIs in 115 games for a last-place team. The Braves' fortunes soon improved dramatically.

Atlanta acquired third baseman Terry Pendleton and shortstop Rafael Belliard in free agency before the 1991 season, and had Lemke and Jeff Treadway set to platoon at second base. That relegated the 25-year-old Blauser to a utility role, and he hit .259/.358/.409 with 11 homers and 54 RBIs in 129 games while playing shortstop, second base, and third base.

Blauser homered in three consecutive games against the Phillies in early June, including a three-run shot off Terry Mulholland as part of a six-RBI day in the opener.[22] The Braves rolled to 94 victories and the National League pennant that season, losing the World Series to the Minnesota Twins in seven games.

Injuries – including a stiff shoulder, a fractured toe, and torn cartilage in his knee that required surgery – hampered Blauser in the second half, and he started just five games after September 3.[23] He totaled just nine plate appearances in the postseason, going 1-for-8 with a walk.

The light-hitting Belliard was again back to play shortstop in 1992, and Blauser was again a utility player. He started 72 games at shortstop and 18 at second base, but was often replaced by Belliard or Lemke for defensive purposes in the later innings.

Blauser had the only three-homer game of his career on July 12, 1992, the final game before the All-Star break. It happened, of course, in Chicago, as Blauser hit solo shots off Frank Castillo in the second and sixth innings, then a three-run blast against Paul Assenmacher in the top of the 10th to hand Atlanta a 7-4 victory.

"I guess I do well here because I love the atmosphere," Blauser said of his success at Wrigley. "It's a real ballpark."[24]

Blauser's three-homer game had helped the Braves cut their National League West deficit to two games behind Cincinnati at the break, and they eventually won the division by eight games. This time, Blauser started all 13 games for Atlanta in the postseason.

Blauser went 5-for-25 in the 1992 NLCS against Pittsburgh, including a home run off Doug Drabek in a 5-1 victory in Game One and an RBI triple against Danny Jackson in a 13-5 win in Game Two. He went 6-for-24, but did not have an extra-base hit or an RBI in the six-game World Series loss to Toronto.

Blauser enjoyed the best season of his career to that point in 1993, when the Braves won 104 games and edged out the San Francisco Giants by one game in the NL West. Blauser played in a career-high 161 games, batting .305/.401/.436 with 29 doubles, 15 homers, 73 RBIs, 16 steals, and 110 runs scored. He finished 16th in balloting for the National League Most Valuable Player Award.[25]

Blauser earned the first of two All-Star berths in 1993, but the game was not a memorable one for the Atlanta shortstop. He struck out in his only plate appearance and booted Carlos Baerga's grounder with two outs in the sixth inning, leading to a three-run inning as part of a 9-3 American League victory at Camden Yards in Baltimore.

Of Blauser's 15 home runs in 1993, four came against the Colorado Rockies and two more against the Cubs (the latter on back-to-back days in late August). He had his third career two-homer game on May 7 in Colorado, driving in four runs in a 13-5 Atlanta victory.

The Braves lost the NLCS in six games to Philadelphia, though Blauser hit well in the series. He batted .280 with three extra-base hits, including home runs in Games Two and Six.

Blauser got a major salary bump for 1994, his final season before he could become a free agent. He avoided arbitration by signing a one-year, $3.75 million deal.[26]

Blauser was slowed for much of May by an oblique injury,[27] and his stats suffered during that strike-shortened season. He played in 96 games, and batted .258/.329/.382 with 6 homers and 45 RBIs.

Blauser hit the only walk-off homer of his career on June 17, a two-run shot off Cincinnati's Jeff Brantley to give the Braves a 6-5 victory. The homer came after Atlanta's Greg McMichael had blown the save in the top of the inning, and handed manager Bobby Cox his 1,000th victory as a manager.[28]

The players strike ended the 1994 season on August 12 and left many potential free agents – Blauser included – in limbo that offseason. He was one of more than 200 veteran players who remained unsigned when the strike was finally settled the following April.[29]

"It's all new, nobody knows what to expect," Blauser said. "We'll have to get in contact with teams to see what their stance is, but time is of the essence."[30]

Blauser re-signed with the Braves on April 12, agreeing to a three-year, $10 million contract. The deal was sealed after more than seven hours of negotiating between Blauser's agent, Scott Boras, and Braves front-office officials.[31]

"It was hardball negotiating," Blauser said. "I got a first-hand picture of what it was like to be a general manager or agent, and I know now I belong in the locker room and not behind a desk."[32]

Though the Braves cruised to the NL East title and won their first World Series championship in Atlanta in 1995, Blauser suffered through a terrible season at the plate. He batted .211/.319/.341 with 12 homers and 31 RBIs, and his .660 OPS and 73 OPS+ were the lowest of his career to that point.

Blauser's troubles continued in the postseason, as a bruised thigh[33] limited him to just three games in the National League Division Series win over Colorado and just one game in the NLCS against Cincinnati (he went a combined 0-for-10). Blauser did not play at all in the World Series against Cleveland, with Belliard starting all six games at shortstop.

Blauser was again the Braves' primary shortstop to start 1996, but endured another injury-marred season. He injured his right knee on April 13 in San Diego, and went to the disabled list four days later with a slight tear of the posterior capsule.[34]

Blauser returned to the lineup on May 4, and drove in four runs with a homer and a double four days later vs. Colorado. He knocked in a career-best seven runs with two homers – including a first-inning grand slam – in an 11-3 victory over Philadelphia on May 11.

Blauser stayed in the lineup until July 15, when he suffered a broken left hand when he was hit by a pitch from Montreal's Jeff Juden.[35] He made a pinch-running appearance September 1, but did not start again until September 22.[36]

Blauser ended the 1996 season with serviceable numbers considering the injuries, batting .245/.356/.419 with 10 homers and 35 RBIs in 83 games. He started every game of the postseason at shortstop, but went a combined 7-for-44 with just three RBIs as Atlanta swept the Dodgers in the NLDS and beat the Cardinals in seven games in the NLCS before losing to the New York Yankees in the World Series.

Atlanta won the NL East again in 1997, and this time Blauser stayed healthy and productive. He played in 151 games and set numerous career highs, including batting average (.308), on-base percentage (.405), slugging percentage (.482), doubles (31), home runs (17), and RBIs (70), earning the National League's Silver Slugger Award at shortstop.

Blauser was an All-Star for the second and final time in 1997, starting the game at Jacobs Field in Cleveland when Barry Larkin sat out with an injury.[37] Blauser went 1-for-2 in the game, singling off Roger Clemens in the third inning of a 3-1 AL victory.

Atlanta swept Houston in three games in the NLDS before falling to the wild-card Florida Marlins in six games in the NLCS. Blauser hit .300 with one home run in each series, including a three-run shot against Mike Hampton in Game Two vs. the Astros.

Blauser singled and scored in the bottom of the ninth inning of the Braves' 7-4 loss to Florida in Game Six of the NLCS, which would be his last appearance in an Atlanta uniform. His contract expired, Blauser entered the free-agent market.

Even if Blauser wanted to return to the Braves, that door closed a few weeks later. On November 17, veteran shortstop Walt Weiss signed a three-year, $9 million deal with Atlanta.[38]

On December 9, 1997, Blauser signed with the club he'd been tormenting his entire career, agreeing with the Cubs on a two-year, $8.4 million deal[39] with an option for a third season. Cox, who'd managed Blauser for seven seasons, lamented the 32-year-old shortstop's departure.

"It's hard to part with guys like that because they've helped us so much and they can still play," Cox said. "But it's like everything else in baseball. You adjust. We're still going to have a good ballclub, period."[40]

Buoyed by MVP Sammy Sosa, the 1998 Cubs won 90 games and secured the NL wild card, their first postseason trip in nine years. However, Blauser had one of his worst seasons, batting .219/.340/.299 with 4 homers and 26 RBIs in 119 games, posting a career-low OPS+ of 69.

Blauser also began having trouble throwing the ball to second base. Skip Bayless of the *Chicago Tribune* wrote an especially scathing column on Blauser's struggles, alternately referring to him as "Jeff Blooper" and "Jeff Lousy."[41]

With the Cubs in a pennant race, Blauser was benched for much of September, with Jose Hernandez moving over from third base and Gary Gaetti stepping in for Hernandez.[42] Blauser did not play in Chicago's 5-3 victory over the San Francisco Giants in a one-game tiebreaker, then got just two at-bats as a pinch-hitter in a three-game NLDS sweep by his old team, the Braves.[43]

Entering 1999, Blauser was coming off elbow surgery[44] and was not guaranteed a starting job for the first time since 1992. With Gaetti back for a second season, Hernandez was penciled in to start at shortstop.[45]

Blauser started at second base in the Cubs' second game of the season, his first appearance at anywhere other than shortstop or designated hitter in seven years. He started only one other game for the remainder of April, and didn't hit his first home run until May 21.[46]

With the 40-year-old Gaetti finally starting to show his age, Blauser began receiving regular starts at third base in June. Hernandez was traded to Atlanta on July 31, but it was 24-year-old José Nieves – not Blauser – that the Cubs plugged in at shortstop down the stretch.[47]

Blauser played in 104 games for the Cubs in 1999, batting .240/.347/.420 with 9 homers and 26 RBIs. He started 14 games at second base, 14 at shortstop, and 12 at third base.[48]

The Cubs declined their $7 million option on Blauser at the end of the 1999 season, making him a free agent.[49] When no team signed him for the 2000 season, his playing career was over at age 34.

Blauser played in 1,407 major-league games, batting .262/.354/.406 with 122 home runs and 513 RBIs. He was worth 20.9 Wins Above Replacement according to Baseball Reference, 19.7 according to FanGraphs.[50]

Blauser remained in baseball for a time, working as a roving instructor in the Braves' minor-league system for three years before being hired as manager at Double-A Mississippi in 2006.[51] However, he lasted just one season as a manager, guiding the Mississippi Braves to a 58-80 record.[52]

By 2011, Blauser and his family – wife Andee, son Cooper, and daughter Abbie – had returned to live in the Atlanta area.[53] As of late 2019, Blauser held the position of senior partner at StaffMetrix HR,[54] a human resources firm.

In the spring of 2019, Cooper Blauser was a freshman on the baseball team at Wesleyan School in Peachtree Corners, Georgia. Also on the team was Druw Jones, the son of Andruw Jones, one of Jeff Blauser's teammates with the 1996 and 1997 Atlanta Braves.[55]

Sources

In addition to the sources mentioned in the notes, the author consulted baseball-reference.com, TheBaseballCube.com and Fangraphs.com.

Notes

1. "Auburn Little Leaguers Win First All-Star Tilt," *Auburn (California) Journal*, July 24, 1978: 8.
2. "Blauser Throws No-Hitter," *Auburn Journal*, May 28, 1980: 35.
3. Rob Knies, "Hillman Blauser Does It All," *Auburn Journal*, September 19, 1982: 27.
4. "Five Hillmen Named All-CAL," *Auburn Journal*, November 21, 1982: 37.
5. Jim Caster, "Beaver Named Top Player," *Auburn Journal*, May 26, 1983: 8.
6. Jim Caster, "Cards Pick Placers' Blauser in Draft," *Auburn Journal*, January 18, 1984: 15.
7. "Blauser Earns All-CNC Honors," *Auburn Journal*, May 20, 1984: 33.
8. Jim Caster, "Auburn's Blauser Picked by Braves," *Auburn Journal*, June 5, 1984: 7.
9. At some point during his minor-league career, Blauser switched from batting exclusively left-handed to his natural right-handed side. Numerous photos published in the *Auburn Journal* during his amateur career show him batting from the left side. In addition, the *Journal* story from after he was drafted by the Braves refers to him as a "left-handed hitting slugger."
10. "Auburn's Blauser Signs Braves Pact," *Auburn Journal*, June 14, 1984: 11.
11. Gerry Fraley, "Braves Find Northeast to Be Full of Prospects," *Atlanta Constitution*, April 6, 1986: 327.
12. Fraley, "Braves Find Northeast."
13. "Braves 40-Man Roster Going into Spring Training," *Atlanta Journal Constitution*, February 7, 1987: 35.
14. Gerry Fraley, "Blauser Forces His Way into Braves' Infield Plans Ahead of Schedule," *Atlanta Constitution*, March 12, 1987: 95.
15. Gerry Fraley, "Roster Moves Held Up by Garcia's Condition," *Atlanta Constitution*, March 29, 1987: 69. Second baseman Damaso Garcia, who had played for Braves general manager Bobby Cox in Toronto, missed all of 1987 with a knee injury.
16. Gerry Fraley, "Blauser May Be More than Backup Brave," *Atlanta Constitution*, July 3, 1987: 89-90.
17. Pinch-hitting for Doyle Alexander in the eighth inning of a 4-1 loss to St. Louis on July 5, Blauser grounded out to shortstop off Greg Mathews. Infielder Ken Oberkfell came off the disabled list two days later, prompting Blauser's demotion back to the minors.
18. Jeffery Weidel, "Braves Recall Blauser," *Auburn Journal*, August 11, 1987: 9.
19. Gerry Fraley, "Thomas, Garcia Will Start; Blauser, Gant Going to AAA," *Atlanta Constitution*, March 28, 1988: 41. After Garcia hit .117 in 21 games to start the 1988 season, he was released. Gant played second base for the Braves' big-league club the rest of the year, slugging 19 homers and finishing fourth in the National League Rookie of the Year voting.
20. Blauser batted .351/.413/.611 with 15 doubles, 15 home runs, and 48 RBIs in 78 career games vs. the Cubs. His OPS of 1.023 vs Chicago is the second highest against teams he faced in more than four games, just behind the 1.024 he posted in 57 games against the Colorado Rockies.
21. Joe Strauss, "Blauser Joins Disabled List," *Atlanta Constitution*, May 17, 1990: 80.
22. The opener of that series was Dale Murphy Night, as the Braves honored their former All-Star who was by then playing for the Phillies. The game was marred by a bench-clearing brawl in the eighth inning, when Otis Nixon charged the mound after being brushed back by Philadelphia reliever Wally Ritchie.
23. Joe Strauss, "Pendleton, Blauser Face Knee Operations Today," *Atlanta Constitution*, October 30, 1991: 34.
24. I.J. Rosenberg, "Blauser Has a 3-HR Bash," *Atlanta Constitution*, July 13, 1992: 52.

25 Blauser was also hit by pitch an NL-high 16 times in 1993. He ended his career with 91 HBPs, 122nd on the all-time list.

26 "Blauser, Braves Avoid Arbitration," *Tallahassee Democrat*, February 14, 1994: 36.

27 Thomas Stinson, "Blauser Feels Better but Still a Little Sore," *Atlanta Constitution*, May 8, 1994: 44.

28 I.J. Rosenberg, "Blauser's HR in 9th stems Reds rally," *Atlanta Constitution*, June 18, 1994: 49. Blauser's heroics were understandably overshadowed by a number of major events in the sports world that day, including Game 5 of the NBA Finals, Arnold Palmer's final US Open and the O.J. Simpson Bronco chase.

29 "End of Strike Doesn't Mean Quiet Return to Status Quo," *Louisville Courier-Journal*, April 3, 1995: 35.

30 "End of Strike."

31 Tim Tucker, "Braves' Deal with Blauser Worth Losing Sleep Over," *Atlanta Journal-Constitution*, April 13, 1995: D2.

32 Tucker.

33 I.J. Rosenberg, "Daughter Helps Cox in Scouting," *Atlanta Constitution*, October 17, 1995: 48.

34 Associated Press, "Braves 4, Marlins 2," *Louisville Courier-Journal*, April 18, 1996: 40.

35 I.J. Rosenberg, "Braves' Streak Grows, but Blauser Gets a Bad Break," *Atlanta Constitution*, July 16, 1996: 70.

36 Belliard, and later rookie Ed Giovanola, initially filled in at shortstop for Blauser. However, both hit so poorly that the Braves moved All-Star Chipper Jones from third to short for much of August and September.

37 I.J. Rosenberg, "Starters Pitching Tributes," *Atlanta Constitution*, July 8, 1997: 63.

38 Thomas Stinson, "Weiss In, Blauser Out for Braves," *Atlanta Constitution*, November 18, 1997: 57. Blauser was reportedly offered a deal similar to Weiss's, but did not immediately accept it and instead went pheasant hunting out of state. By the time he returned from his hunt, Weiss had signed with the Braves.

39 Associated Press, "Cubs Sign Shortstop Blauser, Eck to Red Sox," *Decatur* (Illinois) *Herald and Review*, December 10, 1997: 15.

40 Paul Newberry (Associated Press), "Braves Introduce New Shortstop Walt Weiss," *Anniston* (Alabama) *Star*, December 9, 1997: 13.

41 Skip Bayless, "Still a Cubs Killer: Blauser Eroding Before Our Eyes," *Chicago Tribune*, August 11, 1998.

42 The 39-year-old Gaetti began the season with the St. Louis Cardinals, but was released in mid-August before signing with the Cubs on August 19. He batted .320/.397/594 with 8 home runs in 37 games for Chicago the rest of the way.

43 Blauser did get revenge on the Braves at one point during the regular season, hitting a three-run homer off Denny Neagle in an 11-4 victory in Atlanta on July 20.

44 Associated Press, "Without Kerry Wood, Cubs Need Pitching," *Southern Illinoisan* (Carbondale, Illinois), April 4, 1999: 19.

45 Paul Sullivan "No Extra Protection for Sosa," *Chicago Tribune*, February 22, 1999: 29. Hernandez was also the top backup to center fielder Lance Johnson, meaning Blauser was set to start at shortstop when Hernandez was in the outfield.

46 Blauser again victimized his former team, hitting a two-run shot off the Braves' Justin Speier in the ninth inning of an 8-4 Chicago win in Atlanta.

47 Sosa hit 63 homers and drove in 141 runs in 1999, but the Cubs largely collapsed around him. Pitching phenom Kerry Wood missed the entire season with an elbow injury, and Chicago finished 67-95 and in last place in the NL Central.

48 Blauser also made his first appearance in the outfield since 1990, playing 2⅔ innings in center field on June 29 against Milwaukee.

49 Associated Press, "Diamondbacks Strike Out with Benes," *Southern Illinoisan*, October 30, 1999: 26.

50 According to FanGraphs, Blauser was worth 31.9 WAR on offense, but cost his teams 11.5 WAR on defense. The Baseball Reference numbers are 27.7 and 0.2, respectively.

51 Mike Christensen, "M-Braves Introduce Manager Blauser," *Jackson* (Mississippi) *Clarion-Ledger*, December 13, 2005: 19.

52 Guy Curtright, "Blauser Loses Job with Class AA Team," *Atlanta Constitution*, October 18, 2006: D5.

53 Amy Elbert, "Elegant and Family-Friendly Atlanta Home," TraditionalHome.com, September 2011.

54 Blauser's LinkedIn.com page, linkedin.com/in/jeff-blauser-32635ba8/.

55 David Friedlander, "Jones, Blauser Bring Major League Bloodlines to Wesleyan Baseball," GwinnettPrepSports.com, May 11, 2019.

Pedro Felix Borbón Jr.

BY JUSTIN KRUEGER

Pedro Felix Borbón Jr.

Pedro Felix Borbón Marte (also known as Pedro Borbón Jr.) was born on November 15, 1967, in the town of Valverde de Mao, Dominican Republic. He is the son of workhorse relief pitcher Pedro Borbón, a two-time World Series champion with the Big Red Machine and 2010 inductee into the Cincinnati Reds Hall of Fame. Of his father's time with the Reds, Borbón recalled, "I was really young, but even so you don't forget about a lot of the great players on those teams. That was always in my mind growing up when I knew I wanted to do the same thing my father did. It drove me."[1]

During his professional career he batted right-handed and threw left-handed. But he was not a natural born left-hander. As a youth Borbón decided to try his hand at it after seeing his younger brother throwing left-handed. Afterward, he noted, "I just switched."[2]

Borbón's parents divorced when he was 13 years old. At times the relationship with his father was tenuous with extended periods of silence. Of his father, Borbón Jr. iterated, "He was a competitor. That's one thing I inherited."[3] After his parents' divorce, he lived with his uncles in New York City, where he graduated from high school.

He was originally drafted by the Milwaukee Brewers in the 35th round of the 1985 June amateur draft from DeWitt Clinton High School in the Bronx. He decided not to sign because no signing bonus was offered, "just a plane ticket."[4] The following January he was drafted by the Los Angeles Dodgers in the third round of the January draft-secondary phase from Ranger College in Ranger, Texas. Again, he did not sign. Borbón eventually signed his first professional baseball contract as an amateur free agent with the Chicago White Sox on June 4, 1988, at the age of 20.

In his first season of rookie ball with the Gulf Coast League White Sox, Borbón went 5-3 with a 2.41 ERA in 74⅔ innings. In 16 appearances (11 of which were starts), he allowed 52 hits (one home run), and pitched a shutout. He also registered a save. But it was not enough. He was released by the White Sox organization in April 1989. Borbón later recalled that it was because, "They'd said I'd hit my peak."[5]

Returning to North Texas after his release, Borbón took a job installing home spas and working at a local chemical plant. When not at work, he took to pitching for a local independent semi-pro team. It was here that he was scouted by the Atlanta Braves organization. In late August 1989,

Borbón signed as a free agent with the Braves. He spent his next nine years in professional baseball with the organization.

The 1990 season was the best statistical year of his career. Posting a 15-8 record with a 3.00 ERA in 25 starts with two Class-A teams, Borbón had six complete games with two shutouts. He pitched in a career-high 159 innings, surrendering 146 hits. Pitching to contact, Bórbon recorded 113 strikeouts. The season, however, was a tale of opposite results. For the Low-A Burlington Braves, he went 11-3 with a 1.47 ERA, six complete games, and two shutouts. In 97⅔ innings pitched, he surrendered 73 hits. Called up to the High-A Durham Bulls, Borbón struggled to a 4-5 record with a 5.43 ERA in 61⅓ innings in 11 starts. He allowed more than a hit per inning (73).

During the 1991 season Borbón began his transition to the role of relief pitcher. His second season with the Bulls went much better than his first. Before earning an in-season promotion to Double-A Greenville (Southern League), Borbón logged a record of 4-3 with a 2.27 ERA in 91 innings and five saves. In his first taste at Double-A, Borbón made four starts and posted a 0-1 record with a 2.79 ERA.

Borbón pitched 94 innings in 39 games (10 starts) in 1992. His 10 starts were his last for more than a decade. It turned out to be a transitional year for Borbón, who was moving toward becoming a full-time relief pitcher. With a record of 8-2 and an ERA of 3.06, he earned a late-season call-up to Atlanta.

Jumping straight from Double-A, Borbón made his major-league debut with the Braves on October 2, 1992, in the second game of a doubleheader sweep of the San Diego Padres in Atlanta. Borbón stood 6-feet-1 and weighed 205 pounds. He was 24 years old. He entered the game with two outs in the ninth inning and got Fred McGriff out on a foul pop fly into short left field. Two days later he faced the Padres again in the 12th inning of a 3-3 game and gave up the winning run.

Borbón spent most of the 1993 season pitching with the Triple-A Richmond Braves, working exclusively as a reliever. He put together a 5-5 record with a 4.23 ERA in 52 games. While he averaged over a strikeout per inning (95 in 76⅔ innings), he also developed what would become a recurring trend of walking a high volume of batters (42). Once again he earned a September call-up, pitching 1⅔ innings in three games.

After one more season (1994) with Triple-A Richmond (59 games, 80⅔ innings, 2.79 ERA),

1995 was Borbón's first full season at the major-league level. Pitching in 41 games, he went 2-2 with a 3.09 ERA and two saves. During the 1995 playoffs he experienced ultimate professional success at both an individual and team level.

During the shortened regular season after the players strike was settled, the Braves posted a record of 90-54 and won the National League East by 21 games over the New York Mets and Philadelphia Phillies, who both finished at 69-75. Borbón pitched one scoreless inning of relief for the Braves in the Division Series against the Colorado Rockies. It was in the eighth inning of the extra-inning Game Three loss. He did not pitch in the four-game sweep of the Cincinnati Reds in the National League Championship Series.

Each of the first three games of the 1995 World Series had been close. All the games had been decided by one run as the Braves held a two-games-to-one lead over the Cleveland Indians.

Game Four in Cleveland was a career-defining moment for Borbón. Starting pitcher Steve Avery had pitched six innings of three-hit, one-run ball. Heading to the bottom of the ninth inning, the Braves were up 5-1 and poised to take a three-games-to-one Series lead. Closer Mark Wohlers came into the game to close out the Indians. Manny Ramirez led off the inning with a home run and Paul Sorrento followed with a double. Manager Bobby Cox turned to Borbón to save the game. It had been 19 days since he last pitched in the postseason. In the regular season, left-handed batters hit .171 against Borbón. Up first for the Indians was left-handed slugger Jim Thome.[6]

Two decades later, Borbón commented, "I remember running out to the mound and trying to not think about the crowd. I kept my head down and realized I was about to face some really good hitters. I had my best stuff that night."[7]

Future Hall of Famer Thome struck out looking. Next, Sandy Alomar Jr. struck out swinging. Leadoff man Kenny Lofton lined out to deep right field to end the game. Borbón had quashed the Indians' budding momentum and helped put the Braves up three games to one. Later, he admitted, "I'd be lying if I said I wasn't nervous."[8] Reflecting upon his defining inning, Borbón said, "I was going to get people out by throwing my best pitch and that's what I had on my mind. Just throw fastballs and if they hit it out, well at least I tried my best."[9] It just happened that that day Borbón was at his best. After the game Indians manager Mike Hargrove lamented, "We knew that Borbón had a reputation for being a little wild. We tried to allow him to do that, but he made the pitches."[10]

Reminiscing about it, Borbón said, "It's something you'll keep with you the rest of your life."[11] Three days later in Game Six, Tom Glavine pitched Atlanta to its first World Series championship with a dominating eight innings of one-hit ball for a 1-0 victory. The two games pitched were Borbón's only postseason experience.

The best statistical season of Borbón's major-league career came the following year. In 1996 he went 3-0 with an ERA of 2.75. In 43 games, he pitched 36 innings and allowed only 26 hits and 7 walks. It was the only year in which Borbón finished with a WHIP (Walks/Hits Per innings pitched) under 1.0 (.917). He missed the end of the 1996 season with an elbow injury.

Borbón also missed the entire 1997 season. The injury required Tommy John reconstructive elbow surgery and extensive time in rehabilitation. In the offseason Borbón appeared on *Saturday Night Live* with teammates Gerald Williams and Mark Wohlers and a slew of fellow major leaguers in a skit titled "Baseball Dreams" in which a boy's dream of meeting major-league ballplayers quickly turns to a nightmare with their uncouth behavior.

A brief attempt at a comeback was waged in the minors during the 1998 season. During spring training, in his first live game action in 19 months, Borbón was pulled after facing only five batters. He experienced pain in his elbow from torn scar tissue from his surgery.[12] The injury, it turned out, was not serious. His return to the mound, however, was met with mixed results. He pitched without injury for the rest of the season, but had a 5.52 ERA in 39 games (45⅔ innings) with stops along the way at Braves affiliates in Single-A, Double-A, and Triple-A. Collectively, Borbón struggled, walking 23 batters and allowing 54 hits. At the end of the season he was granted free agency and his tenure with the Atlanta Braves organization ended unceremoniously.

In December 1998, at the age of 31, Borbón signed a one-year contract with the Los Angeles Dodgers for $375,000. During the 1999 season he pitched in 50⅔ innings and allowed 39 hits in a then career-high 70 games. He posted a record of 4-3 with a 4.09 ERA and one save. After the season Borbón was traded to the Toronto Blue Jays with outfielder Raul Mondesi for Shawn Green and minor-leaguer Jorge Nunez. After the trade he and the Blue Jays agreed upon an $800,000 salary for the coming season. It was eventually parlayed into a two-year, $3.2 million extension.

After his rebound year with the Dodgers, the move to the American League East proved difficult for Borbón. In 59 games with the Blue Jays, he struggled to a 6.48 ERA and a 1-1 record with only one save. In 41⅔ innings he surrendered 45 hits and issued 38 walks. On average he allowed nearly two baserunners an inning.

The 2001 season in Toronto went much better for Borbón despite a losing record of 2-4. The Blue Jays finished third in the American League East with an 80-82 record, and Borbón dropped his

ERA nearly three runs from the previous season, to 3.71. For the second time in his major-league career, he appeared in at least 70 games. His 71 appearances ranked fifth for relievers in the American League. Borbón allowed 48 hits and walked 12 in a career-high 53⅓ innings. Owing in part to his improved control, his WHIP went from 1.992 in 2000 to 1.125 in 2001.

Continued success for Borbón, however, was fleeting. A difficult start to the 2002 season led to a 4.97 ERA and 1-2 record in 16 games with the Blue Jays. And on May 15 Borbón was traded to his hometown Houston Astros as part of a conditional deal. In response to the trade, Borbón said, "It was a shock. When they called me in, I thought they either released me or traded me. … It will be a great opportunity for me to be with my family all year long."[13] The Blue Jays took on $800,000 of his $1.6 million contract to push the trade through.[14]

The change of scenery to the National League Central Division did not help. A rough start to the 2002 season only got worse. In 56 games with the Astros, Borbón logged 37⅔ innings. Again he struggled to keep runners off the bases. For the season he allowed 41 hits and walked 19. It all resulted in, at the time, a career-high ERA of 5.50 for the season. After the season Borbón was granted free agency by the Astros. In January 2003 he signed a free-agent deal that led to a return to the Dodgers. He was released during spring training.

Hoping to revive his career, Borbón signed with the Long Island Ducks of the independent Atlantic League. Regaining his footing on the mound, he posted a 5-2 record and a 2.08 ERA, and threw two complete games in six starts. His success in independent ball earned Borbón another chance at the major leagues.

He signed with the St. Louis Cardinals on July 28, 2003. At 35, Borbón made seven appearances for the Triple-A Memphis Redbirds before moving to the major-league roster. When he was called up to the Cardinals, they became the fifth major-league team for which he had played. The union did not last long. In seven games he posted a 20.25 ERA with 14 hits allowed in only four innings. He was released on September 9, 2003. It was his final action in the major leagues.

Over the next few seasons Borbón bounced around the minor leagues with several teams. He signed a free-agent contract with the San Diego Padres in December 2003 but was released during spring training. On May 12, 2004, Borbón signed with the Montreal Expos and was sent to the Triple-A Edmonton Trappers, where he struggled. With the Expos organization less than a month, he was released on June 8. In July he pitched one game for the independent Long Island Ducks.

Borbón began the 2005 season with a return to the Long Island Ducks. For the first time in over a decade, he pitched solely in the role of starter. In seven starts, Borbón logged 47 innings on the way to a 3-3 record and a 5.36 ERA. In June he signed a free-agent contract with the Los Angeles Angels, but with short and unsuccessful stints at the Double-A Arkansas Travelers and the Triple-A Salt Lake Stingers, Borbón was released on August 12.

Borbón's last season playing professional baseball came in 2006: four innings pitched in two games with the Bridgeport Bluefish of the Atlantic League. With that, his career as a professional baseball player was over at the age of 38.

As a left-handed reliever, Borbón was afforded ample chances to pitch professionally for 17 years. In total, he spent parts of nine seasons in the majors and parts of 12 seasons in the minors and independent leagues. He suited up for a total of 17 teams. The opportunities as a left-handed reliever also helped typecast him as a gap reliever. First and foremost, he was used to get out the left-handed bat. Early in his career he had wanted "to be a stopper."[15]

On a few rare occasions, Borbón had the opportunity for some in-game at-bats: seven in the major leagues. A lone hit in 1996 left him with a career batting average of .143. The hit was a single to center field off Mark Guthrie of the Los Angeles Dodgers in the top of the ninth inning of a 6-4 Braves victory on August 4. Borbón also recorded the win in the game.

For his major-league career, Borbón finished with a .500 record at 16-16. He pitched in 368 games, compiled a 4.68 ERA, finished 83 games, and earned six saves. He struck out 224 and allowed 259 hits in 271 innings pitched. His penchant for wildness led him to walk 134, nearly one every two innings. It was all good for a WHIP of 1.45.

Borbón briefly served as a pitching coach for the Class-A Cedar Rapids Kernels in 2007. Since retirement he has also worked as a sports agent.

Sources

In addition to the sources cited in the Notes, information was gathered from Borbón's Hall of Fame clippings file, Baseball-Reference.com, BaseballAlmanac.com, Retrosheet.org, and SABR.org, as well as from the *Albany Times* and *USA Today*.

Notes

1. I.J. Rosenberg, "Braves 1995 Recall: Pitcher Pedro Borbon," *Atlanta Journal-Constitution*, August 5, 2015. Retrieved from ajc.com/sports/baseball/braves-1995-recall-pitcher-pedro-borbon/lecAiwJCWkjcfkoNmZQtDJ/.
2. Mark Bradley, "Borbon Jr. the Flip Side to His Father," *Atlanta Journal-Constitution*, June 30, 1996.
3. Bradley.
4. Bradley.
5. Bradley.
6. Claire Smith, "Young Borbon Inherits Post-Season Spotlight," *New York Times*, October 27, 1995.
7. Rosenberg.
8. Bradley.
9. Smith.
10. Smith.
11. Bradley.
12. Associated Press, "Borbon's Career Not on the Rocks," *New York Post*, March 4, 1998.
13. Associated Press, "Jays Trade Borbon," *New York Post*, May 17, 2002.
14. "Jays Trade Borbon."
15. Bradley.

Terry Clark

BY TONY OLIVER

Terry Clark

Like the Cheesecake Factory menu, the 1979 baseball amateur draft had something for everyone. A total of 870 players were selected, including five future managers (Ron Gardenhire, Don Mattingly, Bob Geren, Bud Black, Bob Melvin); one World Series MVP (Orel Hershiser), the record-holder for most consecutive hits in one World Series (Billy Hatcher); one broadcaster (Harold Reynolds); and several All-Stars (Reynolds, Hershiser, Mattingly, Tim Wallach, Jimmy Key, Brett Butler, Glenn Davis, Andy Van Slyke). It even featured two Hall of Famers, although of a different sport: John Elway and Dan Marino would choose the gridiron glory over the baseball diamond and forge historic careers.

Yet a case could be made that the most memorable career was that of the 575th pick. Terry Clark, an 18-year-old right-hander from Los Angeles, was chosen in the 23rd round by St. Louis. He would enjoy several years in the majors and twice as many in the minors, three campaigns in the Caribbean winter leagues, and almost two decades as a minor-league coach. His story is marked by perseverance, a strong will, arduous work, and an indefatigable desire to play baseball. His major-league sojourn was longer than the historical average of 5½ years, yet it featured an interregnum in the minors after nine major-league years and before an additional two seasons bookending his career.[1] It was a Shakespearean five-act play held in a variety of parks, a religious service celebrated both in grand cathedrals and humble chapels.

Terry Lee Clark was born on October 18, 1960, in Los Angeles to a working-class family; his father was a truck driver and his mother stayed at home with the children. Less than a week before his birth, Pittsburgh had defeated the Yankees for the World Series; the Pirates would celebrate the franchise's first title since 1925. The West Coast, long the domain of the Pacific Coast League, had recently welcomed the Dodgers and the Giants, émigrés from the pinstripe-dominated Gotham baseball scene, while the Los Angeles Angels were preparing for their maiden season in 1961.

Having graduated from La Puente High School at age 17, Clark attended Mount San Antonio College in Walnut, California, for a year and caught the eye of scout Angel Figueroa during a "thoroughbred" game. His college coach, Art Mazmanian, was a former All-American from the University of Southern California who played seven years in the minor leagues, mostly in the

Yankees' farm system.[2] Clark had played shortstop and the outfield growing up, but his strong right arm was better suited to getting hitters out at the plate, and the Cardinals sent him to their Appalachian League affiliate in Johnson City along with his fellow draftees.

His manager, fellow Californian Nick Leyva, himself a former minor leaguer, sized up his new pitcher and mentioned that he would be the team's closer. "I didn't even know what that meant," said Clark, noting that Leyva told him he would pitch in the eighth and ninth innings when the team was ahead.[3] This was music to Clark's ears, since he "enjoyed pitching more days in a row." He saw action in 23 games, capturing four wins, two losses, and eight saves, securing a promotion once the new year began.

Leyva was again his skipper and three fellow 1979 draftees (Van Slyke, Mark Salas, and Earl Weaver, no relation to the legendary Orioles manager) also suited up for the South Atlantic League's Gastonia Cardinals. The club finished 1980 second in its division with Clark pitching out of the bullpen; he was involved in 21 decisions (four wins, seven losses, and 10 saves) and 28 other games with a 3.17 ERA, comfortably below the league average of 4.25. While the others moved on, Clark stayed with the team in 1981, improving his numbers to a 4-5 record, 13 saves, and a stellar 2.16 ERA over 53 games, and the Cardinals promoted him to the Florida State League for the 1982 campaign. Once more coupled with Leyva, he turned in a 19-save, 10-win season on the back of a 2.55 ERA for St. Petersburg. Despite not starting a game, he tied Walt Pierce for the team lead in victories while setting the pace for saves.

The 1983 season saw Clark suiting up for the Arkansas Cardinals in the Double-A Texas League. The roster included future Cardinals stalwarts and NL MVPs Willie McGee (1985) and Terry Pendleton (1991). Clark contributed 15 saves, a 6-6 record, and a 3.21 ERA in 52 games. His performance earned him a promotion for 1984 to Triple-A Louisville, which already had two closers, Andy Hassler and Jeff Keener. Clark thus played the role of a set-up man, contributing 34⅓ innings with a 4.72 ERA for the 1984 Jim Fregosi-led team.

The big-league Cardinals lost a heartbreaking 1985 World Series to the Royals, but Double-A Arkansas played sub-.500 ball. McGee and Pendleton had made the jump to the parent club and the fall classic, while Clark made it backward, returning to the Travelers for another season. Jim Riggleman entrusted him with the ball on 42 occasions, but the role was ever-changing; Clark began seven games, closed eight, and appeared in 35 others. The result was a career-worst 4.93 ERA and a release during the National League Championship Series. For the first time in this life, Clark was out of a job.

The mild California winter provided some comfort and the siren call of his hometown club, the California Angels, was soothing on a crisp February 1986 day. He returned to the Texas League, this time wearing the Midland uniform, for a 57-game campaign that again saw him play a relief role. DeWayne Buice was the established closer and finished 42 games (14 saves, 8-6 record), while Clark appeared in 57, ending 32 with four saves. It was enough to merit a one-way ticket to Canada in 1987 to pitch for the Triple-A Edmonton Trappers. Neither Buice nor Clark was the main stopper, as skipper Tom Kotchman employed 12 other men to finish games (six of whom earned saves). Clark contributed a 3.84 ERA in 20 starts and 13 relief appearances, with eight wins, nine losses, and four saves.

Clark sought some additional work during the winter of 1987, signing with the Azucareros (sugar-cane workers) del Este in La Romana, Dominican Republic. The Azucareros finished fifth in the six-team league, missing the playoffs.[4] Playing alongside future big leaguers Chuck Finley, Dante Bichette, Mike Cook, Orestes Destrade, and Hensley Meulens, Clark gave skipper Cookie Rojas a solid rotation arm.[5] He took the mound on 14 occasions, finishing two games en route to four wins and six losses with a 2.32 ERA.[6] It was a successful audition, with Clark playing in front of large crowds against high-caliber competition. He began 1988 once again north of the border and provided the Trappers with 16 solid starts (7-6, 4.91 ERA in 113⅔ innings) before the much-desired call arrived to reach "The Show."

Only a year and a half removed from their surprising 1986 American League West title, the California Angels had taken a considerable step back in 1987, dropping to sixth place in their division. After parting ways with manager Gene Mauch, the team named Rojas to be its skipper. Though Rojas would not finish the season, being dismissed in late September with a 75-79 record, he had seen enough of Clark in the Dominican Winter League when he took the reins of the team. Dan Petry had suffered an injury and Rojas did not hesitate to call up Clark. "I joined the team in Toronto and Cookie told me I'd be starting in Cleveland. It was a great place to debut, since the stadium held 80,000 but only 15,000 showed up. … It took all the pressure off me from facing an away crowd."

On July 7, 1988, Clark took the mound for the Angels against the Indians. His first pitch to Julio Franco was a strike: "Bob Boone was behind the plate and he said, don't shake me off." The rookie took the veteran's advice and it paid off handsomely, as he got past a first-inning run by the Indians to hurl five strong innings (one run, five hits, no walks, 54 pitches, 33 of which were strikes). Rojas lifted him to begin the sixth and Greg Minton recorded his second save of the year by pitching a now-remarkable four innings in relief. Clark's counterpart on the hill was future major-league pitching coach and manager John Farrell, and the second batter for the home team was eventual Cleveland manager Terry Francona. An even smaller crowd than Clark remembered (10,889) witnessed the contest, which took 2 hours and 37 minutes but did not materially impact either club, both of which would end up with losing records. He told the Associated Press, "[T]his was something I've always dreamed about. … After the fifth inning, it was the biggest relief of my life. I told myself, '[Y]ou got here, did the job, and now sit back and enjoy it.'"[7]

Clark won his first three starts, dominating Detroit on July 17 (eight innings, no runs) and the Indians again on July 22 (7⅓ frames, two runs). His July 27 game against the eventual American League champion Athletics was rough, as he lasted five innings while giving up seven runs, with Oakland exploding in the first and fifth innings, but as the calendar turned to August, he boasted a 3-0 record and a 3.55 ERA in 25⅓ innings. The new month began auspiciously, with a complete-game victory against Seattle and six efficient innings vs. the White Sox before three straight difficult outings against Oakland, New York, and Boston. Clark hurled his first shutout against the Yankees on August 27 to improve his mark to 6-2. September proved cruel as he suffered four losses in five games, finishing the year with a 6-6 pitching line in 94 innings.

Of the 141 men who made their big-league debut in 1988, only nine were older than Clark, and only two (Geren and Tony Fossas) were from his 1979 draft class. Still, with 15 starts under his belt, the future seemed bright. But Rojas had been fired with eight games left in the campaign, depriving Clark of a supporter. New manager Doug Rader shuffled the 1989 rotation, adding future Hall of Famer Bert Blyleven as the first starter and wunderkind Jim Abbott as the fifth. Clark returned to Edmonton and showed he had little to prove (11-5, 3.58 ERA in 20 starts) before being recalled once the rosters expanded. He started two games (August 26 at Texas and September 1 in New York) but was hit hard (six total innings, seven runs), earning a demotion to the bullpen. He appeared in two other Angels losses but allowed only one run in five innings. The late turnaround failed to impress the Angels brass, who released him on October 6.

Clark did not have to wait long for his next contract; Houston signed him on January 26,

1990. He began the year with Tucson, then the Astros' Triple-A affiliate. He started 22 games and pitched in seven others, winning 11 and losing four along with one save. The Astros finished 75-87, in a fourth-place tie with the Padres in the National League West, with Clark enjoying only a brief call-up in the summer. Facing Atlanta, he threw four innings and allowed seven runs (six earned) in the second game of a doubleheader. Houston erupted for six runs in the sixth frame to remove him from the decision, but the Braves rallied for a walk-off victory. The game included a personal highlight, as he smacked the first pitch he saw from Braves starter Tony Castillo to center field for a leadoff single. He advanced to second on Eric Yelding's single and scored on a hit by Javier Ortiz. Clark grounded out in his second and last at-bat, this time closing the fourth inning and his Astros career; he was released on October 15, 1991.

A team from Clark's past came calling on January 6, 1992. Cleveland, his initial opponent in the big leagues, signed him to a minor-league deal and assigned him to Triple-A Colorado Springs. The club was led by future major-league skipper Charlie Manuel and featured eventual Hall of Famer Jim Thome. Clark started nine games, posting a 4-4 record with a 3.77 ERA (the league average was 4.40), but for the first time since 1987, he would not reach the upper echelon. The team released him on July 23 after he injured his elbow and underwent Tommy John surgery. After a hard year of rehabilitation, the San Diego Padres offered Clark a contract and he reported to Class-A Rancho Cucamonga to get back into throwing form. His teammates included fellow 1979 draftee Scott Garrelts and former All-Star Bruce Hurst, themselves getting some work on their road back from injuries. He was promoted to Double-A Wichita, where he relieved in 19 games (29⅔ innings, 2.43 ERA) before being granted free agency on October 15.

Having thrown fewer than 50 innings since injuring his elbow, Clark waited for clubs to inquire about his availability. In the pre-Twitter, pre-Facebook, pre-YouTube era, ingenuity and phone calls ruled the day, and Clark told his agent he "wanted to be back in the big leagues." The Braves signed him on November 24, 1993, but networking led him to Phil Regan, helming the perennial winners of the Venezuelan League, Caracas. Regan had managed teams in the Dominican winter league, where he first saw Clark in action.[8] He is well-regarded in Caracas, a team he led for eight campaigns, including a 1989-1990 title.[9]

Clark packed his bags and trekked to South America, providing the Leones with a robust five wins, four saves, and a 1.87 ERA (second lowest in the league) in 1993-1994 as the club finished second.[10] He was sensational in the round-robin semifinals, hurling 9⅔ pristine innings in six games, but saw his luck turn in the finals against Magallanes, allowing four runs in as many frames. Atlanta, winner of three straight division titles, was impressed and invited Clark to spring training. "I pitched 18 innings in the Grapefruit League but ultimately started in Richmond," he said, though he contributed 61 appearances (a career high) and a 3.02 ERA in Triple A. A late-season call-up was possible until the players strike wiped out the last seven weeks of the major-league campaign.

Hungry for more baseball, Clark returned to Caracas for the 1994-1995 season, this time powering the Leones to the league title. Although his ERA swelled to 5.70, he once again started games; feeling overused in relief, he marched into the owner's office and "asked for an opportunity to start." He repaid the trust by pitching four games in the semifinals (3 starts, 1-1, 24⅓ innings, 2.96 ERA) as well as two in the finals (1-1 with a 3.52 ERA) as the Leones roared.[11] The team traveled to San Juan for the Caribbean Series but encountered the formidable Puerto Rican "Dream Team," dropping five of the six contests. Clark could only marvel at what he encountered: "What a team: Edgar Martinez, Roberto Alomar, Juan González, and so many others." The second game for both squads was an extra-innings affair, with Ugueth Urbina walking Carlos Delgado with the bases loaded in the 10th to give Puerto Rico a 4-3 victory.[12]

Clark returned to Florida for spring training and impressed the Braves enough to make the Opening Day roster. He was ecstatic: "Bobby Cox broke the news to me, stating, '[Y]ou should have made the team last year.'" The rotation of Greg Maddux, Tom Glavine, John Smoltz, Steve Avery, and Kent Mercker was the league's best; Clark would pitch in relief. The strike had caused a few weeks' worth of games to be canceled, so the team had an odd schedule to start the season, with a two-game set at home against the Giants before traveling for a three-game series with the Dodgers. Atlanta won the first pair but dropped the third, a 9-1 drubbing in Los Angeles. Avery allowed a double to Delino DeShields to start the game; he stole third and scored on a wild throw by Charlie O'Brien. Two other Dodgers crossed the plate in the bottom of the fourth before Cox pulled his young left-hander. Motioning to the bullpen, he brought in Clark, making his first major-league appearance in almost five years. Having inherited men on second and third, there was little room for error as he walked Carlos Hernández on five pitches. However, pitcher Pedro Astacio meekly tapped the ball back to Clark, who tossed it to O'Brien at the plate before the catcher threw to Ryan Klesko at first to complete an inning-ending double play. Seven pitches later, Clark was back in the dugout, marveling at how a brief time on the big-league mound followed such a prolonged absence from it. Thirsty for runs and with the luxury of early-season rested arms, Cox pinch-hit for Clark in the next half inning with Dwight Smith, who laced a single to left field against Astacio.

Clark next saw action on May 2, when the Braves visited the Marlins. Normally, a Maddux start against a poor team would make relief pitching unlikely, but the abbreviated spring training prompted big-league skippers to be cautious with their players. Maddux tossed 5⅔ strong frames (three hits, one run); Greg McMichael and Mark Wohlers provided 2⅓ innings of unblemished support. Since the Braves had scored seven runs, the game no longer represented a save situation, and Cox called on Clark to close. He walked Jeff Conine on five pitches, retired former minor-league teammate Pendleton on a groundout, and enticed Greg Colbrunn and Charles Johnson to fly out. Eighteen pitches, 10 of which were strikes, and a second appearance without yielding a hit for Clark. The team swept Florida and returned home for a four-game set against Philadelphia.

The Phillies would finish second in the division but their 69-75 record masked the intensity of manager Fregosi, for whom Clark had played in the minor leagues, and veterans Darren Daulton, Lenny Dykstra, and Curt Schilling. The Phillies swept the Braves, with the May 5 contest being Clark's last for Atlanta. Mercker started the game and was shelled early, yielding five runs in two innings; Jason Schmidt allowed two more in three frames. Cox called on Clark to take over in the sixth, but the Phillies, ahead 7-3, were not done. Seven men went to the plate and forced Clark to throw 27 pitches. Kevin Stocker and Dykstra scored, though Gregg Jefferies and Dave Hollins were stranded on base. In a matter of minutes, Clark's ERA ballooned from 0.00 to 6.75. The Braves went in order in the sixth, as Tyler Green employed only 10 pitches to retire Jeff Blauser, Chipper Jones, and Fred McGriff, giving Clark little rest before returning to the field. Veteran Charlie Hayes forced a walk during an eight-pitch battle and Dave Gallagher singled on Clark's first offering. Though he was on the ropes, Clark retired Tony Longmire, Mickey Morandini, and Dykstra to close the top of the seventh. Cox double-switched Javy López and Clark for O'Brien and Pedro Borbón in the eighth, sending Clark to the showers.

The front office wanted to give Clark more time to work on his mechanics. "John Schuerholz said, 'We want to send you back to Richmond to work on some things.' I asked for some time to think about it, and spoke to my former manager

Phil Regan, who was now in Baltimore. He said they could use me, so I asked Atlanta for my release. Schuerholz was surprised and asked me if I was sure." He said he fondly remembered his time in the Braves organization, especially the insight he gained from his fellow hurlers: "Leo Mazzone may get the credit, but Maddux was the true pitching coach of those teams. He spent so much time with the pitchers."

Clark wanted to remain on a big-league roster; he took his wisdom, carefully crafted through winter-, major-, and minor-league campaigns, to the Orioles, inking a deal on June 1. The front office assigned him to Triple-A Rochester, where he appeared in nine games, compiling five saves, one win and two losses. Baltimore called him up in early June and he appeared in a June 8 contest against Seattle, finishing an 8-2 Oriole win by tossing one inning. His next eight appearances yielded no runs; he picked up two holds along the way. (While holds are not an official statistic recognized by Major League Baseball, they are nevertheless commonly captured on box scores.)[13] He lost to the Blue Jays on June 30, tossing two-plus innings but leaving the game with a runner on base that team closer Armando Benítez allowed to score. As the calendar page turned, his return to the American League revealed a formidable 0.87 ERA (one run in 10⅓ innings).

Regan leaned on the veteran right-hander, placing him in 14 games during which he faced 44 batters and allowed only three runs. He garnered a win on July 7 against the White Sox despite facing only two batters. August proved more challenging, as he lost four games, won one, and picked up a save on August 18 against Oakland. The Orioles were in third place behind two solid yet unspectacular clubs; the Red Sox and Yankees would both make the revamped postseason, but the class of the American League resided in the Midwest. The Cleveland Indians romped through the junior circuit en route to a 100-44 record (.694). However, the pinnacle moment of the season occurred on September 6, and Clark had not just a front-row view, but an active role.

Like Clark, Cal Ripken Jr. was born in 1960 but reached the majors in relatively quick fashion. As Clark was compiling a solid 2.55 ERA for the Florida State League Cardinals, Ripken was setting up shop in the left side of the Baltimore infield. On May 30, 1982, his name was penciled into the Orioles lineup, where it would remain uninterrupted until September 19, 1998, for a total of 2,632 consecutive games. The prior record-holder, Lou Gehrig, had seen his own mark end at 2,130 and Ripken stood to pass him on September 6, 1995. Future Hall of Famer Mike Mussina took the mound for the Orioles and handcuffed the now-renamed Anaheim Angels to two runs in 7⅔ innings. The 3-hour 35-minute game was paused in the middle of the fifth to recognize Ripken's feat, and neither his teammates nor the crowd would allow the contest to resume until the stoic shortstop took a literal lap around the ballpark. With the Orioles ahead 4-1, Mussina retired his first two batters in the top of the eighth before yielding a triple to Jim Edmonds. After a standing ovation, the Camden Yards faithful saw Clark allow a double to Tim Salmon, driving in Edmonds, before Regan played the percentages and brought in lefty specialist Jesse Orosco against the dangerous veteran Chili Davis. For the four months with Baltimore, he appeared in 38 contests, forging two victories, five defeats, one save, seven holds, and a 3.46 ERA. Those figures would warrant a return to the Orioles, but the front office dismissed Regan and brought in Davey Johnson. A hard-nosed manager who had led the Mets to the 1986 World Series title, Johnson had also won two championships with the Orioles in 1966 and 1970 as a second baseman. The team decided not to bring back Clark, granting him free agency on December 21, 1995. He fondly recalled the pitching staff of Mussina, Kevin Brown, Ben McDonald, Jamie Moyer, and Scott Erickson.

Kansas City signed Clark in February 1996 and he made the team out of spring training. He appeared on Opening Day, yielding one hit and one walk while retiring two batters in a 4-2 Royals loss to the Orioles. He appeared in 11 other games in April, allowing runs in seven of them. His sole May contest was strong as he yielded one hit in three innings against Oakland. Ironically, this last game would be his best, but Kansas City sent him to Triple-A Omaha.

At Omaha Clark limited opponents to a 2.56 ERA in 45⅔ innings, collecting three wins, two saves, and one loss. The organization placed him on waivers on July 23, with the Astros picking him up for the stretch run. He pitched in five games and allowed 10 runs (eight earned) in 6⅓ innings for Houston and was not offered a new contract at the end of the season.

Cleveland signed Clark for 1997 and sent him to Triple-A Buffalo. Displaying his customary versatility, Clark started 10 games (7-3 record), saved three others, and did not feature in 12 decisions. The Indians recalled him and he started four games, losing three and getting a no-decision. After 26⅓ innings, he was placed on waivers and was claimed by the Rangers on August 4. He appeared in nine games, starting five to end the season with a 1-4 record and a 5.87 ERA. His last appearance was against his first team, the Angels, and he finished the contest by hurling 1⅓ innings, striking out Tony Phillips as his last batter. Although he re-signed with the franchise on December 16, the club assigned Clark to Triple-A Oklahoma for the 1998 campaign. A robust 12-5, 3.38 ERA output in 165⅓ innings followed, but Texas did not give him another opportunity in the majors. He signed with Oakland for a 21st season of professional baseball; the Athletics wished to have veteran leadership and guidance for a trio of prospects, Mark Mulder, Barry Zito, and Tim Hudson. The 1999 Vancouver Canadians, who would move the following year to Sacramento, employed Clark in 14 games before he retired.

Over more than two decades, Clark accumulated 143 wins (major and minor leagues, excluding the Caribbean circuits). He can boast of a perfect pitching line (nine plate appearances without conceding a base) against Hall of Famers Roberto Alomar, Alan Trammell, and George Brett. "It wasn't the big guys who got me," he recalled as he remembered Greg Gagne besting him (2-for-4). Other memorable hitters also enjoyed success at the plate: Jay Buhner (6-for-10), Wade Boggs (6-for-10), Rickey Henderson (5-for-9) and the ageless Julio Franco, whom he faced more than anyone else (13 plate appearances), and who would reach base seven times with four singles and three uncharacteristic walks. On the opposite side of the ledger, Clark boasts a .667 batting mark, surpassing even Ty Cobb. Granted, his three plate appearances are an infinitesimal fraction of the Georgia Peach's 13,099, but baseball has always been a game of averages. Minor-league skipper Bob Skinner gave him a few at-bats in the minor leagues; he always had a keen eye at the plate even if his power was nowhere near Babe Ruth's. He cited Mussina, Brown, and Al Downing among his favorite teammates.

As a testament to Clark's knowledge and reputation, the Cleveland organization wasted no time adding him to its coaching ranks. He rolled up his sleeves in the 2000 New York-Penn League, a summer sandbox for drafted players, leading the Mahoning Valley Scrappers hurlers to a 3.71 ERA and a runner-up finish to the Staten Island Yankees. He ascended to the Eastern League with the Akron Aeros, nurturing young prospects Cliff Lee and Jake Westbrook among others and shaving off almost an entire run from the team's ERA in his second year (2002). He again worked his magic, this time in 2003 and 2004 for the Triple-A Buffalo Bisons, who moved from third to first place during his two seasons, though the team's ERA paradoxically worsened in his second year with the team.

Another of Clark's former clubs, the Texas Rangers, hired him to instruct their young pitchers. The Texas League's Frisco RoughRiders turned around their fortunes, moving from fourth to third place, and eventually to consecutive first-place finishes during his 2005-2008 tenure. His pupils included future big leaguers C.J. Wilson, Edison Volquez, Adam Eaton, Armando Galarraga, and Derek Holland. The organization assigned him to Triple A and he first coached the Oklahoma Redhawks (2009-2010) before the club switched affiliations to the Dodgers. The Round Rock Express, formerly an Astros farm club, became the Rangers' farm team, and Clark instructed the hurlers in 2011-2012.

The Mariners poached Clark and named him the pitching coach for the Jackson Generals, a post he held for one season.[14] He was replaced by Lance Painter but remained with the organization as its minor-league pitching coordinator in 2014, a role that allowed him greater oversight over the team's prospects. The flexibility was quite beneficial as the year gave the Clark family a new milestone. His son Matt Clark had starred at Riverside Community College in California. He was chosen by the Pittsburgh Pirates in the 2007 draft but opted to return to school. A year later, the San Diego Padres selected him in the 12th round after he had transferred to powerhouse Louisiana State University. He progressed through the farm system and earned ample time with Tucson in the Pacific Coast League, where his father coached the Round Rock Express. It was tailor-made for Hollywood; a young prospect hoping to inflict pain on his father's pitching staff. Media loved the story, including a sports-beat reporter named Julia Morales. She covered the event, including Clark the younger's walk-off home run in the series, and later joined the family by marrying Matt.[15] Both the Padres and Mets released him, but Milwaukee saw promise in the first baseman, signing him as a free agent on July 4, 2014. He slugged .605 for the Nashville Sounds before earning a shot at the big leagues in September. His father was "lucky enough to see his first game, first hit, and first home run" during the Brewers' September schedule.

Milwaukee released Matt in the offseason, but Clark the younger has continued his professional baseball dream with the Dominican, Mexican, and Japanese leagues. The Clarks became the 217th pair of fathers and sons to play in the grandest of stages.[16]

The Chicago Cubs approached Clark about their pitching coach opportunity with the Double-A Tennessee Smokies. A Southern League franchise led by Mark Johnson, the team raised prospects Kris Bryant, Javier Báez, and Kyle Hendricks before they became centerpieces of the curse-breaking 2016 Cubs. Clark stepped down at the beginning of 2019.

Though Clark spent parts of six seasons on big-league rosters, he never went the distance (March through September) on the roster or enjoyed a taste of the postseason. As the 25th anniversary of the Braves 1995 World Series title drew near, Clark was nonchalant: "They have invited me to a few celebrations, but my minor-league commitments have kept me from participating."

Acknowledgments

Terry Clark for graciously agreeing to an interview with the author.

Matt Clark for connecting the author with Terry Clark.

Notes

1. University of Colorado at Boulder. "Average Major League Baseball Career 5.6 Years, Says New Study." ScienceDaily, July 11, 2007. sciencedaily.com/releases/2007/07/070709131254.htm.
2. Uyen Mai, "Legendary Coach Maz Passes Away." Mount San Antonio College Newsroom, March 22, 2019. mtsac.edu/newsroom/news/posts/2019-03-22-coach-maz-passes.html.
3. Unless otherwise specified, quotations from Terry Clark stem from the author's interview with him on August 16, 2019.
4. winterballdata.com/TEMPORADAS/1987.htm.
5. history.winterballdata.com/?view_page=team&sok=Ver+Equipo&season_id=34&phase_id=1&team_id=5.
6. history.winterballdata.com/?view_page=player&s_ok=+&season_id=&player_id=828&team_id=.
7. Associated Press, "Angels' Clark Sees Minton Preserve Win Over Indians." Oxnard (California) Press-Courier, July 8, 1988. news.google.com/newspapers?id=icVdAAAAIBAJ&sjid=P14NAAAAIBAJ&dq=terry-clark%20angels&pg=3417%2C1299766.

8 Buster Olney, "Regan Manages to Realize His Goal," *Baltimore Sun*, February 26, 1995. baltimoresun.com/news/bs-xpm-1995-02-26-1995057152-story.html.

9 leones.com/campeonatos.php.

10 pelotabinaria.com.ve/beisbol/mostrar.php?ID=clartero01.

11 pelotabinaria.com.ve/beisbol/mostrar.php?ID=clartero01.

12 "El legendario Dream Team de Puerto Rico en la Serie del Caribe 1995," *El Diario NY*, February 2, 2017. eldiariony.com/2017/02/02/el-legendario-dream-team-de-puerto-rico-en-la-serie-del-caribe-de-1995/.

13 mlb.mlb.com/mlb/official_info/about_mlb/rules_regulations.jsp.

14 Chris Harris, "Generals Announce Coaching Staff for 2013 Season," MiLB.com, December 10, 2012. milb.com/jackson/news/generals-announce-coaching-staff-for-2013-season/c-40594668.

15 Jeff Balke, "Julia Morales Will Do Anything to Keep Fans Engaged." *Houstonia*, September 2018. houstoniamag.com/articles/2018/8/17/julia-morales-astros.

16 baseball-almanac.com/family/fam2a.shtml.

Brad Clontz

BY JESSE ASBURY

Brad Clontz

John Bradley Clontz was born on April 25, 1971, in Stuart, Virginia (population 1,400), five miles north of the state's border with North Carolina. Outside of Clontz, Stuart's best-known native son is Leonard Wood, who formed in 1950 with his four brothers what became a successful auto-racing empire, perhaps what southwestern Virginia is best known for from a sports perspective: Wood Brothers Racing. Clontz attended Patrick County High School in Stuart, where he played on the varsity baseball team. Clontz's mother, Carol Price Clontz, worked for Smithfield Foods, a meat-packing facility in Smithfield, Virginia. She retired in 2008 and died in 2018. His father, Robert Clontz, worked for about a decade as an engineer for Newport News Shipbuilding, then taught himself to paint and became a wildlife artist, permanently leaving his job as an engineer in 1980. He died in 1994.

Clontz attended Virginia Tech University in Blacksburg, Virginia, 58 miles north of his home in Stuart. He spent three seasons as a pitcher on the Hokie baseball team from 1990 to 1992. In his first season, he earned five saves and a 4-1 record in 32 innings as the team's bullpen ace.[1] Most impressively, he allowed earned runs in only three of his 21 appearances and did not give up a home run.[2] In 1991 he moved from the bullpen to the starting rotation. He then spent the summer playing in the Cape Cod League and was named the league's relief pitcher of the year.[3] That year, while pitching for the Wareham Gatemen, he pitched in 24 games and recorded 11 saves and a microscopic 0.91 ERA.[4]

In 1992 Clontz, again in the Hokies' starting rotation, earned second team All-Metro Conference honors.[5] That season, his third and final in college, he set two school records for innings pitched (130) and wins (12) that still stood as of 2019. His 115 strikeouts that season rank second in the Tech history books.[6]

Clontz, whom *Baseball America* listed as the 38th-ranked college pitcher by the end of the 1992 season,[7] was drafted by the Atlanta Braves in the 10th round of that year's amateur draft in June. After signing, he pitched in 21 games split between rookie ball in Pulaski, Virginia, and A ball in Macon, Georgia. Appearing mainly as a reliever, he ended the year with three saves and a 3.45 ERA. The next season, 1993, while playing for the Durham Bulls (High-A Carolina

League), Clontz pitched in 51 games, earned 10 saves, and recorded a 2.75 ERA. In 1994, splitting time between Greenville (Double-A Southern League) and Richmond (Triple-A International League), Clontz pitched in 63 games, recorded 38 saves, and turned in a 1.53 ERA in 70⅔ innings. *Baseball America* named him a first-team Minor League All-Star,[8] and he was named the Southern League's Most Outstanding Pitcher for his work with Greenville.[9] Atlanta designated him the organization's minor leaguer of the year.[10]

In spring training in 1995, Clontz impressed his future Atlanta teammates with his unconventional submarine delivery and his repertoire of sinkers, sliders, and breaking balls. Outfielder David Justice told sportswriters that Clontz might already be the best closer in the majors, despite the fact that he had yet to face a single batter.[11] Pitching coach Leo Mazzone said Clontz was "going to be given the opportunity" to earn his spot on the team, while also adding that "there's no way in hell I'm going to put pressure on the kid."[12] The Braves, who had a revolving door at the closer position throughout the early 1990s, were still looking for someone to permanently fill that role. Greg McMichael, the Braves' primary closer in 1994, ended the year with a league-leading 10 blown saves.[13] Clontz seemed to have as good a chance as anyone to earn a prominent spot in the bullpen once spring training ended. His hard work was rewarded, and he was added to the active roster. New teammate Greg Maddux, fresh off winning his third straight Cy Young Award, helped to make the rookie feel like part of the team by arranging to have a limousine pick up Clontz and fellow rookie pitcher Jason Schmidt and take them to his home in Georgia, where they stayed before getting their own housing situated. Clontz recounted that this was his first time in a limo.[14]

The strike-shortened 1995 season began for the Braves on April 26, one day after Clontz's 24th birthday. He made his major-league debut in this Opening Day game against the San Francisco Giants, pitching a perfect ninth inning to secure a 12-5 win for the Braves. Clontz recorded his first major-league strikeout against the first batter he faced, Giants first baseman J.R. Phillips.

The next day, in another game against the Giants, Clontz earned his first major-league save in a 6-4 Atlanta victory, getting pinch-hitters Jeff Reed and Tom Lampkin to ground out before striking out Robby Thompson to end the game. He recorded three more saves in quick succession, getting his fourth in Atlanta's 13th game of the season, a 3-2 win over the Mets. As the season wore on, however, Clontz saw his save opportunities dwindle as fifth-year veteran Mark Wohlers established himself as manager Bobby Cox's go-to fireman. Clontz was used primarily in middle relief for the remainder of the regular season, appearing in 59 games and recording no more saves after the one against the Mets. He earned his first win as a major leaguer on June 28 against the Montreal Expos, pitching two perfect innings in the eighth and ninth. David Justice hit a walk-off home run in the bottom of the ninth off Mel Rojas to clinch the 4-3 win for Clontz and the Braves. He won seven more games in the regular season, finishing with an 8-1 record and a 3.65 ERA in 69 innings pitched.

The Braves won the NL East championship by 21 games over the Mets. Clontz's work as a reliable setup man during the season earned him a spot on the 25-man playoff roster. In the Braves' run through the 1995 playoffs, he put together the best postseason stretch of his career. Appearing in four games, including Games Three and Five of the World Series against the Cleveland Indians, Clontz recorded a 1.80 ERA, striking out four batters and allowing three hits in five innings pitched. The only run Clontz allowed in the postseason came against the next to last batter he faced, future Hall of Famer Jim Thome, who hit a solo home run off Clontz in the bottom of the eighth inning in Game Five of the World Series at Jacobs Field in Cleveland. The Braves lost three of the four postseason games Clontz pitched in, but defeated the Indians in six games in the World Series, winning the franchise's first title since its move to Atlanta in 1966.

In 1996 Clontz saw a significant increase in his usage. He led the National League's pitchers with 81 appearances and pitched 80⅔ innings. Seeing Clontz's early success against right-handed hitters, who hit just .222 against him during his career, manager Cox began using Clontz frequently to face one or two dangerous right-handed bats in high-leverage situations. He recorded only one save as Wohlers' stranglehold on the closer role continued. Clontz's increased usage may have also led to an increase in his ERA, which ballooned to 5.69 in 1996 after the respectable 3.65 ERA in his rookie year.

The Braves made the postseason again in 1996 and Clontz again pitched in four playoff games, including three World Series contests against the New York Yankees. In 2⅓ innings, Clontz recorded a perfect 0.00 ERA and allowed only one hit, a single by the Yankees' Luis Sojo in Game Three of the World Series. The Braves lost the Series in six games in what was becoming an all-too-common result for the "Team of the '90s."

Originally built to serve as a venue to house some of the events of the 1996 Summer Olympics, Atlanta's new Turner Field became the Braves' home starting with the 1997 season.[15] In their home opener, an April 4 contest against the Chicago Cubs, Clontz became the pitcher of record in the first Braves game in Turner Field. Coming on in the top of the seventh in relief of Terrell Wade, Clontz took on the heart of the Cubs order, pitching 1⅓ scoreless innings and allowing only a walk to Ryne Sandberg.[16] The Braves won, 5-4, after Mike Mordecai scored in the bottom of the eighth on Chipper Jones's single to left field.[17]

Off the field, Clontz became fast friends with third baseman Jones, the future Hall of Famer who, like Clontz, played his first full season with Atlanta in 1995. Both in their mid-20s during their time as teammates, the two were often seen together after games enjoying the bar scene, watching basketball games, and looking for female companionship at home and on the road.[18] Jones, who was married at this time to his first wife, employed "Clontzy" as a middleman of sorts: "Girls knew if they wanted to get in touch with me, they called Brad, and Brad would get the word to me."[19] As Jones's first marriage was ending due to his infidelity, Clontz's position as conduit allowed him access to some surprising information. Clontz, in fact, relayed to Jones that one of the women he had been with had given birth to his child, who was eight months old at the time Jones received the news.[20]

Clontz had a rebound year in 1997. His usage diminished (48 innings in 51 appearances) but his ERA improved (3.75). As in 1996, he recorded only one save, finishing with a 5-1 record and 42 strikeouts. Throughout the decade of the 1990s and into the next, the Braves would win the National League East and clinch another opportunity for October baseball. After a three-game sweep of the Houston Astros in the 1997 NLDS, they fell to the eventual World Series champion Florida Marlins in a hard-fought six-game series. For the first time in his brief career, Clontz failed to pitch in a postseason contest. He never pitched in a playoff game again. With the emergence of Wohlers as a shutdown closer, and with a bullpen featuring a bevy of young arms as well as veteran Alan Embree and the recently signed Kerry Ligtenberg (whom the Braves acquired from a team in an independent league in exchange for a gross of baseballs and four dozen bats),[21] Clontz's role on the team was in jeopardy.

On March 30, 1998, Clontz was released by the Braves. On April 9 he signed with the Los Angeles Dodgers. Clontz pitched in 18 games for his new team, going 2-0 with no saves, a 5.66 ERA and 14 strikeouts in 20⅔ innings. His two wins for the Dodgers came four days apart, a 12-inning, 4-3 win on April 26 against the Cubs and a 14-6 victory over the Pittsburgh Pirates on April 30. On June 4 Clontz and Japanese superstar Hideo Nomo were traded to the New York Mets for Greg McMichael, Clontz's former Braves teammate (whose closer role with the Braves he had claimed in 1995, if only briefly), and Dave Mlicki. The next day Clontz made his debut with the Mets, pitching a scoreless eighth inning against the Boston Red Sox. He pitched in only one more game for the Mets, recording a 9.00 ERA in three innings pitched. At the end of the 1998 season, Clontz was granted free agency and signed with the Boston Red Sox by year's end.

After failing to make the Red Sox' major-league roster during spring training in 1999, Clontz was released and, two days later, signed with the Pirates. In what became the last full season he spent in the major leagues, in 56 games (49⅓ innings, third most on the team), Clontz struck out 40, recorded a pair of saves, and finished with a 2.74 ERA. In December he was traded to the Arizona Diamondbacks for minor-league relief pitcher Roberto Manzueta. Arizona released Clontz before the 2000 season began, and once again he was signed by the Pirates as a free agent. That season Clontz made his final appearance in the majors. On April 30, against Cincinnati, he struggled against the bottom of the Reds' batting order, allowing a home run to Juan Castro and giving up a triple to Pokey Reese. He was pulled after facing Reese, and the Reds went on to win 6-2. Overall, Clontz appeared in only five games that season, pitching seven innings while recording a 5.14 ERA and eight strikeouts. Clontz ended his six-year, four-team major-league career with 272 appearances, 210 strikeouts, 277⅔ innings pitched, eight saves, and a 4.34 ERA.

After being released by the Pirates at the end of the 2000 season, Clontz spent the next six seasons pitching exclusively in the minor leagues for four different organizations. In 2001 he returned to pitch in the Braves' farm system, pitching in nine games for the high-A Myrtle Beach Pelicans after initially appearing in 21 games for the Colorado Rockies' Triple-A affiliate in Colorado Springs. After a season away from baseball in 2002, he returned to Colorado Springs in 2003. In 2004 he pitched for the Oklahoma City Redhawks, then the Texas Rangers' Triple-A affiliate. Finally, in 2005 and 2006, Clontz pitched for the Florida Marlins' Triple-A affiliate in Albuquerque. In what was his final season of professional baseball, he appeared in 57 games for the Isotopes, compiling a 6-5 record, 23 saves, and an ERA of 3.57. Between his two seasons in Albuquerque, Clontz also appeared in 43 games for the Somerset Patriots of the independent Atlantic League, earning nine saves and posting an impressive 1.60 ERA. The Marlins granted him free agency at the end of the 2006 season.

After his baseball career ended, Clontz kept himself busy both in and out of baseball. In 2012 Steve Etheridge of ESPN.com wrote that Clontz had been recording dubstep music, a type of electronic dance music.[22] His Soundcloud site features two hour-long mixes of dance beats that would fit in perfectly in a modern baseball clubhouse but seems odd coming from, as Etheridge put it, "a 41-year-old former disciple of Bobby Cox."[23] Beginning in 2015, he went to work as a player rep for Proformance Baseball, the Richmond-based sports agency that represented Clontz during his playing days.[24] During this time, Clontz also managed a travel baseball team and hosted casino events in Las Vegas.[25] From 2016 to 2018, Clontz also worked as a concierge and marketing executive for MGM Resorts. As of 2019 he was employed by Baha Mar resorts as a director of customer development.[26]

Clontz became a season-ticket holder for Virginia Tech football in 1998.[27] At home games he could often be found outside Lane Stadium, tailgating at Hokie home games. He was known to put his DJ skills on display during his tailgates, entertaining friends and fellow fans all day (or night) long.[28] Clontz also lent his marketing skills and outgoing personality to aid Virginia Tech's baseball program in its fundraising efforts, including attending Baseball Night in Blacksburg, the team's annual fundraiser, alongside fellow former Hokie Franklin Stubbs.[29] In 2011 Clontz was inducted into the Virginia Tech Sports Hall of Fame.[30]

Clontz also became a fixture at gatherings honoring former Braves players, including the annual Alumni Weekends, hosted at the Braves' SunTrust Park.[31] Asked about the Braves' magical 1995 season, when the rookie Clontz joined a team that won Atlanta's first professional sports championship, Clontz said, "You just dream of those things but not coming so early in your career. … I get chills when people talk to me about it."[32] He said he embraced every opportunity to wear his World Series ring at events like the Alumni Weekend and the All-Star Game, stating, "That ring always attracts people."[33]

Sources

In addition to the sources cited in the Notes, the author consulted Baseball-Reference.com and Retrosheet.org.

Notes

1 "Six Named to Tech Hall of Fame," hokiesports.com/news/2011/8/21/20110821aaa_4584.aspx.

2 "Six Named to Tech Hall of Fame."

3 "Six Named to Tech Hall of Fame."

4 "Six Named to Tech Hall of Fame."

5 Virginia Tech Baseball Record Book. Conference History. www2.hokiesports.com/baseball/extras/recordbook.pdf.

6 Virginia Tech Baseball Record Book. Conference History. Clontz was coached at Virginia Tech by Chuck Hartman, who put together a 961-591-8 record in his 28 seasons (1979-2006) as Hokie skipper. Forty of his former players were drafted by major-league teams, including former Dodger Franklin Stubbs, who like Clontz went on to win a World Series during his professional career. Virginia Tech Baseball Record Book.

7 "Six Named to Tech Hall of Fame."

8 thebaseballcube.com/players/profile.asp?ID=9980.

9 thebaseballcube.com/players/profile.asp?ID=9980#Awards.

10 Randall Mell, "Clontz Hopes to Submerge as Closer," *South Florida Sun Sentinel* (Fort Lauderdale, Florida), April 15, 1995 sun-sentinel.com/news/fl-xpm-1995-04-15-9504150015-story.html.

11 Mell.

12 Mell.

13 Mell.

14 Mell.

15 "Turner Field/Atlanta Braves." ballparkdigest.com/201204184748/major-league-baseball/visits/turner-field-atlanta-braves.

16 "Turner Field/Atlanta Braves."

17 "Turner Field/Atlanta Braves."

18 Chipper Jones and Carroll Walton, *Ballplayer* (New York: Dutton, 2017), 197.

19 Jones and Walton, 203.

20 Jones and Walton, 214.

21 Joe Christensen, "Once Acquired for Bats and Balls, Ligtenberg Looks to Fit Like a Glove," *Baltimore Sun*, March 13, 2003.

22 Steve Etheridge, "Ex-Brave Brad Clontz Does Dubstep Music," ESPN Playbook, August 22, 2012. espn.com/blog/music/post/_/id/2710/ex-brave-brad-clontz-makes-dubstep.

23 Etheridge.

24 linkedin.com/in/brad-clontz-1b32023/?trk=people-guest_profile-result-card_result-card_full-click.

25 I.J. Rosenberg, "Braves Recall: Brad Clontz," *Atlanta Journal-Constitution*, July 15, 2015.

26 linkedin.com/in/brad-clontz-1b32023/?trk=people-guest_profile-result-card_result-card_full-click.

27 Carroll Walton, "Former Braves Pitcher Aces VA Tech Tailgating," *Inside Tailgating*, November 22, 2017. insidetailgating.com/blog/2017/11/22/former-braves-pitcher-aces-va-tech-tailgating/

28 Walton.

29 Mike Barber, "Clontz, Stubbs Still Helping Tech Baseball," *Richmond Times-Dispatch*, February 11, 2013.

30 "Six Named to Tech Hall of Fame."

31 "Meet Popular Atlanta Braves Alumni This Weekend," WSB-TV 2 Atlanta, August 20, 2019. wsbtv.com/entertainment/things-2-do/meet-popular-atlanta-braves-alumni-this-weekend/975612074

32 Rosenberg.

33 Rosenberg.

Mike Devereaux

BY GREG KING

Mike Devereaux

"You dream of things like this, but you never think of it happening to you. It's something out of the movies."[1]
—Mike Devereaux, October 15, 1995, after being named NLCS MVP

Mike Devereaux became an instant hero on an Atlanta Braves team filled with future Hall of Famers. Having played with five different teams in a major-league career spanning 12 years, Devereaux's most prestigious career highlight came in October 1995 when he was named the Most Valuable Player of the National League Championship Series. The Braves had acquired the veteran outfielder in late August as an added insurance measure for their pennant drive. Devereaux not only provided the game-winning hit in extra innings in Game One of the NLCS against the Cincinnati Reds, but his three-run homer in Game Four was the capstone that propelled the Braves back to the World Series for the third time in five seasons, one that they won.

Born on April 10, 1963, in Casper, Wyoming, Michael Devereaux was the youngest of four children born to Fred and Mary Devereaux. Fred was an electrical engineer by profession and Mary a part-time schoolteacher. Mike, following after the births of his sister, Phreda, and brothers, Fred Jr. and Ron, took a shine to baseball early. The three Devereaux brothers all played Little League, Babe Ruth, and American Legion baseball, and because they were all born a year apart, for two seasons they played on the same team. When school was in session, however, the Devereaux household focused equally on education. There was no television viewing until all homework was completed, and on school nights, the kids had to adhere to established bedtimes. And weekend nights carried a curfew.

But make no mistake about it. Baseball became something of an obsession for Devereaux. He became an avid fan of the Oakland A's during their run of three consecutive World Series championships in the early 1970s, and especially of their star, Reggie Jackson

Meanwhile, Fred Devereaux, president of the local Little League, was able to coax a number of big-league ballplayers to come to Casper to speak with the kids, among them Gaylord Perry, Johnny Bench, Pete Rose and Reggie Jackson.[2] Devereaux's interest in the game continued to grow, especially in his early teenage years. His father, who would serve as Mike's coach until he was 16, encouraged his youngest son to pursue his passion and take it as far as he could. Devereaux later recalled, "When I was 13, 14, and 15, I was in Babe Ruth and I realized that I loved the game more than anything else. I couldn't wait to go to school and play afterwards."[3]

Devereaux attended Casper's Kelly Walsh High School, but it had no formal baseball program. That proved to be no deterrent. He donned a uniform for the Casper Oilers each summer to play American Legion ball; his first year he played in multiple positions, including shortstop, pitcher, and outfielder, while brothers Fred typically pitched and Ron caught. The brothers helped lead the Oilers to three consecutive American Legion state titles. For three successive years, each one of the Devereaux brothers at age 18 in turn was named MVP in American Legion Baseball for the state for that season. Mike became a standout player on Kelly Walsh's teams in basketball, football, and track and field, and was named All-State, helping his high school win state championships in his senior year. In track and field competition, his athleticism allowed him to establish new state records in the 100-meter, 200-meter, and 400-meter dashes, and the high jump. In fact, it was for these sporting achievements away from the baseball field that he was inducted into the National High School Hall of Fame in 2014, and all his college scholarship offers were for football. But baseball was his favorite sport, and he was determined to play it.[4]

After his high school graduation in June 1981, Devereaux enrolled at Mesa Community College in Arizona, where he joined his brother Ron on the Thunderbirds baseball squad, playing outfield. The team took third in the National Junior College World Series in June 1982.[5] While Mike was at Mesa, a teammate, shortstop Steve Murray, called him Devo, a nickname that stuck. At season's end, Devereaux was selected as the team's MVP and named First Team All-Conference.[6]

The star athlete accepted a scholarship from perennial baseball powerhouse Arizona State University in nearby Tempe for his junior and senior college years, 1984 and 1985. He played right field. In 1984, Devereaux was joined in the outfield by future big leaguers Barry Bonds in center and Oddibe McDowell in left. Has there ever been a better college outfield? Devereaux homered in his first game as a Sun Devil, the team going on to reach the College World Series in 1984. Devereaux launched a go-ahead homer in the seventh inning of the first game of the CWS, and went 3-for-7 in the tournament, though Cal State Fullerton won the national championship. ASU finished the 1984 season with a 55-20 record.[7] The Cleveland Indians selected Devereaux in the 26th round of the June 1984 amateur draft, picking him in a low round likely because he was scheduled to have major reconstructive knee surgery.[8] He elected not to sign, continued pursuit of his degree, and played outfield for ASU a second season, batting .296, including a noteworthy season opener against UC Santa Barbara, in which he collected four doubles, tying a university record.[9]

Several months later, just as he was graduating with his bachelor of science degree in finance, the Los Angeles Dodgers selected Devereaux in the fifth round of the June 1985 draft. He signed his first professional contract with Dodgers scout Dennis Haren. He was assigned to play outfield with their rookie-league team in Great Falls, Montana, in the Pioneer League, managed by Kevin Kennedy, where in 70 games his offensive talents became apparent. Devereaux was named the league's Player of the Year, batting a robust .356 and leading the league in runs (73), hits (103), RBIs (67), total bases (152), and stolen bases (40), helping the team compile an impressive 54-16 (.771) record. The organization then sent him to the Arizona Instructional League, where he played in 28 games.[10]

For the 1986 season, the Dodgers had Devereaux jump over both their low and high Class-A farm teams and placed him with the Double-A San Antonio Dodgers, in the Texas League. In 115 games with San Antonio, the right-hander batted .302 and collected 10 home runs, 53 RBIs, and 31 stolen bases. He returned to the team in 1987 and led the league in a number of categories, including at-bats (562) and games (135), while belting 26 home runs and batting .301. He also demonstrated a flair with the glove, his speed providing for several spectacular running catches. Devereaux led outfielders with 349 total chances in 1987, and he carried a league-best .991 fielding average. He was named to the league All-Star team and was voted San Antonio's Player of the Year.[11]

Devereaux played outfield in three games at the end of the season for the Triple-A Albuquerque Dukes of the Pacific Coast League, and while there received a surprise call from Dodgers manager Tommy Lasorda asking him if he was ready to come up to "The Show." The next day, September 2, 1987, at age 24, he was in the starting lineup to make his major-league debut, playing right field in Dodger Stadium. Devereaux had never even been to a major-league ballpark. "I swung at the very first pitch I saw and got a hit," he said. "So [laughing] I got *that* out of the way."[12] His single off the Philadelphia Phillies' Don Carman was the first of nearly 1,000 hits he would accumulate in his big-league career. In 19 games with the Dodgers in September, Devereaux played all three outfield positions. He went 12-for-54, batting .222, but had two three-hit games and a game-winning RBI. In the fall, just as he had the previous year, he played in the Arizona Instructional League, where he hit near .400. In three consecutive offseasons, from November to January Devereaux continued to hone his skills, playing for Santurce, San Juan, in the Puerto Rican Winter League, which had a professional working agreement with the Dodgers. Jay Bell and Rubén Sierra were among his teammates.[13]

Given his early success in the minors, Devereaux was hopeful of landing a spot on the Dodgers 1988 major-league roster, and thought he enhanced his chances after batting .414 in spring-training exhibition games in the Grapefruit League. But the competition was fierce. In the offseason between 1987 and 1988, the Dodgers had added veteran outfielders Kirk Gibson and Mike Davis, who joined regular starters John Shelby and Mike Marshall. Los Angeles brought Devereaux up in April to play center field to replace an injured Shelby; he started in four games but batted only .115 before being optioned back to Albuquerque, where he continued to excel. Playing in 109 games, Devereaux sported a .340 batting average in 423 plate appearances and finished fourth in the PCL in batting.

For a second consecutive year he was part of the September call-up. At the time, the Dodgers were in a tight race in the Western Division, and he was not expected to see much playing time. Devereaux was in the starting lineup for only one game, with 43 at-bats in 30 games, and could not get enough plate appearances to gain any traction, batting just .116. On September 21 against the San Diego Padres, Devereaux was inserted into a second game of a doubleheader as a pinch-runner, and two innings later, drove in the winning run with a walk-off single to bring the Dodgers one win closer to a division title. A week later, he was linked to a notable game in Dodgers annals. On September 28 Devereaux entered a game against San Diego as part of a double switch for Orel Hershiser after the Dodgers starter had completed the 10th inning to give him the major-league consecutive scoreless inning record. The Dodgers, however, left Devereaux off their postseason roster, a team that went on to defeat the Oakland A's in the 1988 World Series.

In his four minor-league seasons with the Dodgers, Devereaux collectively batted .320 (549 hits in 1,716 at-bats) and averaged 35 steals a year. As the Dodgers looked ahead to the 1989 season, they already had a crowded outfield, and, moreover, their 1985 first-round draft pick, outfielder Chris Gwynn, was waiting in the wings. Trade speculation involving Devereaux began when the Dodgers were negotiating a swap with the Baltimore Orioles that resulted in the acquisition of first baseman Eddie Murray on December 4, 1988, for Brian Holton, Ken Howell, and Juan Bell. Still, the Orioles and Dodgers continued discussions and Devereaux's name was among those mentioned in the swirling rumors. On March 12, 1989, in the midst of both team's spring-training schedules, the Dodgers traded Devereaux to the Orioles for pitcher Mike Morgan.[14] When asked his opinion of the transaction at the time, manager Lasorda remarked, "It's hard to give up a person of the caliber of Mike Devereaux. Sometimes you have to trade guys you think the world of."[15]

What kind of team would Devereaux be joining? Though the Orioles dropped 107 games in 1988, including a record 21 consecutive losses to open a season, he reacted favorably when he learned of the swap. "It takes a big load off my mind," Devereaux told the *Los Angeles Times*. "Now that this is over, I can concentrate on baseball. I'd like to be playing in LA, but I just want to be playing in the major leagues."[16] He explained that he felt no ill will toward the Dodgers and respected their decision for trading him, allowing them to fill their pitching needs while at the same time providing him an opportunity to play on a big-league ballclub.[17]

In 1989, his debut season with Baltimore, Devereaux had a key role as both an outfielder and a designated hitter. Standing an even 6 feet tall and weighing 195 pounds, the right-hander swung a distinctive black bat which, he said, made it difficult for rival outfielders to get a jump on the batted ball based on his own observations peering in from the outfield.[18] He had a good rookie season by all measures, batting .266, stealing 22 bases, and playing in 122 games. There were several highlights in his inaugural year. These include his first big-league home run, on April 21, against the Minnesota Twins' Allan Anderson, and a four-hit game against the Milwaukee Brewers on June 8.

In one memorable game, on July 15, in a jam-packed Memorial Stadium, he became the first Orioles rookie since Cal Ripken Jr. in 1982 to hit a walk-off home run when he launched a pitch from the Angels' Bob McClure that wrapped around the left-field foul pole, producing a thrilling come-from-behind 11-9 win. The Angels vociferously protested that the ball had been foul, but the umpire stood firm. Three weeks later, on August 6, Devereaux hit another walk-off homer, against the Texas Rangers' Jeff Russell, in a 3-2 win. Another signature moment occurred in a late-season game when Nolan Ryan intentionally walked a batter in order to face Devereaux – only to have the rookie blast a three-run home run off the future Hall of Famer.

Surprisingly, given their dismal record in the preceding season, the Orioles, managed by Frank Robinson, played inspired baseball all summer long and the rookie Devereaux played a key role in what became known as the "Why Not?" team's magical run. Baltimore led the American League East Division for most of the summer and fell just shy of making the postseason, finishing second, two games behind the Toronto Blue Jays. "We were right there until the end and it was just heartbreaking to come up short," Devereaux said in 2009.[19] Still later, looking back on that season from the vantage point of three decades, he said, "It was going to be an incredible season either way but it would have just been just icing on the cake to have been able to bring a championship back to Baltimore with all the support we had here." Devereaux added, "We didn't even win it and we got a parade. … Pretty cool"[20]

In 1990 the Orioles regressed as a team, finishing fifth in the AL East. Platooning again, Devereaux saw his season average dip to .240, primarily due to getting off to a poor start in the first six weeks of the season. Things greatly improved afterward; he was named American League Player of the Week in late July, when he batted over .420, with two doubles, a triple, and three home runs, including the first of his three career grand slams, and followed the next night with an eighth-inning homer that broke up a no-hitter being hurled by the Tigers' Jeff Robinson.

In 1991 Devereaux finally got his chance to be the everyday starting center fielder after the Orioles traded Steve Finley to the Houston Astros. In addition to his solid defense, Devereaux hit .260, contributing 19 home runs and driving in 59 runs in 608 at-bats. He became only the second Oriole to get 10 or more doubles, triples, home runs, and stolen bases; Phil Bradley had been the first. Still, the season was not a stellar one in the annals of the franchise; the Orioles finished a distant 24 games behind Toronto. Reflecting back to this period after he had retired, Devereaux remarked that after experiencing firsthand the team's thrilling highs of his rookie year, the 1990 and 1991 campaigns were especially disappointing. But even losing taught both baseball and life lessons, and Devereaux felt thankful that Frank Robinson was in his corner, though he was not one to sugarcoat things. He said that sometimes after he struck out and was heading back to the dugout he would see the clearly disappointed manager just shaking his head.[21]

The team departed venerable Memorial Stadium for Oriole Park at Camden Yards in 1992. Not only did Devereaux permanently etch his name into the record books when he became the first Oriole to hit a home run in the new ballpark when he did so against Cleveland's Jack Armstrong on April 9, but in his new surroundings he experienced the best season of his major-league career. He appeared to benefit from a shift in the batting order, being moved from first to hitting second in the lineup; in addition to clubbing 24 home runs, and speeding to third on 11 triples, Devereaux amassed 107 RBIs, 37 of them either game-tying or go-ahead runs. With the bases loaded, he went 13-for-25, a .520 clip.

Moreover, beyond his clutch hitting, Orioles fans appreciated Devereaux's dramatic center-field play in which he frequently robbed opposing teams of hits, including some that were otherwise destined to go over the fence. One such spectacular play, a ball snatched from the stands that would have resulted in a three-run home run by the Blue Jays' Joe Carter on June 5, 1992, was aptly described by Thomas Boswell in the *Washington Post* the following day: "Devo took his life in his hands. He didn't leap straight up. He didn't have time. He launched himself at what looked like a 45-degree angle, his legs jack-knifed across each other. His right cheek smashed into the very top of the wall just as his arm shot into the second row of seats. How the ball found the glove, no one will ever know."[22]

At season's end Baltimore's baseball beat writers and broadcasters voted Devereaux the winner of the Louis M. Hatter Most Valuable Orioles Award, a year in which the outfielder led the team in 10 offensive categories. He finished seventh in votes for the AL MVP, and was named to *The Sporting News* AL all-star team. "It all came together that year," Devereaux said. "I batted second and with Cal [Ripken] hitting behind me, I got all those good pitches."[23]

While the center fielder batted a steady .250 in 1993, and missed nearly a month of play with a stint on the DL due to a shoulder injury and sore heel, it was the 1994 season in particular he would have liked to have erased. After hitting a home run and triple earlier in a game on May 8, 1994, in front of over 47,000 hometown fans, Devereaux was nailed on the cheek by a rising fastball thrown by the Indians' Chad Ogea on May 8. It was a game featured on ESPN's *Sunday Night Baseball* and later discussed by broadcaster Jon Miller, who was behind the mic for the game, in his book, *Confessions of a Baseball Purist*. Though Devo did not miss much playing time from the errant pitch, he was placed on the DL for two weeks in June with a pulled right hamstring, and he never fully regained his form. When the season was shut down after the players struck in August, Devereaux was hitting barely above .200. His time with Baltimore was drawing to a close, with his contract about to expire and the club making it clear it intended to look in a new direction.[24]

Devereaux filed for free agency in October 1994, and inked a one-year contract with the

Chicago White Sox on April 8, 1995, just as the strike ended. He played exceptionally well for the White Sox as their everyday right fielder. He enjoyed playing on the South Side, and was having a banner year. In 333 at-bats, Devereaux collected 102 hits and was batting .306. Five days before the September 1 trading deadline, Devereaux went to the Atlanta Braves in a straight-up exchange for minor-league outfield prospect Andre King.[25]

Braves outfielder Ryan Klesko was enjoying a good season, but he had just turned 24 that summer. John Schuerholz, Atlanta's general manager, sought to add a veteran right-handed hitter and a solid defensive presence to their roster for their latest pennant drive. Devereaux was pleased with the trade. Though he had fun playing with Chicago, the White Sox were well under .500 and struggling mightily in the standings, and he would now be playing for a team that habitually made it into the postseason, and at the time of the transaction had a double-digit lead over the second-place Phillies for the East Division title. Moreover, just six months earlier, Devereaux had decided to buy property in the Atlanta suburbs to build his dream house. In fact, because he had earlier told teammates of his impending residency shift to Georgia, when informed of the trade, Devereaux initially thought his manager, Terry Bevington, was pulling a prank on him. But his trade to Atlanta resulted in reduced playing time during the remainder of the regular season, with most of his appearances coming in as a defensive replacement in late innings, or stepping up to the plate as a pinch-hitter and staying in the game. Devereaux had just 55 plate appearances, batting .255. His most significant contributions to the Atlanta team, however, were yet to come with his first opportunity to play in the postseason.[26]

In Game One of the 1995 NLCS, on October 10, hosted by the Cincinnati Reds, the Braves and Reds were in a tight pitching duel that had gone into extra innings. With the game knotted 1-1 in the 11th inning, Devereaux's line-drive single drove in Fred McGriff in an important win on the road. Even after getting the clutch game-winning hit, however, few gave much thought to his role going forward in the series. That is, until manager Bobby Cox penciled in Devereaux to start Game Four on October 14 in place of right fielder David Justice, who had been sidelined after being hit by a ball during batting practice before the game. "It was funny how some things work out and being in the right place at the right time," Devereaux said in 2019 about that opportunity to be in the lineup.[27] In the seventh inning, Devereaux delivered the decisive blow, muscling a three-run home run against the Reds bullpen ace, Mike Jackson, as the Braves swept aside the Reds in four games. "It's a feeling I never believed I could have," he said after receiving the NLCS MVP Award for his key hits, batting .308, and driving in five runs. "It's a lot of fun. I'm definitely going to enjoy the moment."[28]

Devereaux appeared in five of the six World Series games against the Indians, in a platooning role. He went up to the plate six times, and got on base three times, with a hit and two walks, batting .250. Devereaux was patrolling the outfield and was on the field to joyously celebrate with his teammates when Marquis Grissom snared the ball for the final out in Game Six to give the Braves their first World Series championship since 1957. The Braves did not figure Devo to be in the club's long-term plans, however, and he was granted free agency after the season.

Always a crowd favorite, Devereaux returned home to Baltimore the following season, signing a one-year contract on January 11, 1996. He was sorry not to have been present the prior year when Cal Ripken broke the consecutive-game streak set by Lou Gehrig (though he watched the historic game on ESPN like much of America). He hoped that with smart defensive play in the Camden Yards outfield with which he was so familiar and by putting up good offensive numbers on the other side of the ledger, he would have a fair chance to be an everyday starting outfielder, which he had been as recently as the preceding year with the White Sox. The new Orioles manager, Davey Johnson, who had just come over from managing the Reds, however, told Devereaux he thought he had always been a player who had come off the bench throughout his career. That had not been the case, of course, since his earliest days in Memorial Stadium, until he got to Atlanta. Which, in essence, ultimately proved to be a trade-off. Devereaux would not have received the NLCS MVP Award or the World Series championship ring had he not suited up with the Braves, but he would end up paying a steep price. His image now had been reshaped to one as a platoon player, a narrative created just in his short six-week stint with the Braves.[29] "It's tough to sit on the bench and then go in and out of the lineup," a frustrated Devereaux told the *Baltimore Sun* near the midway point of the season. "It's something I am not accustomed to."[30]

With reduced playing time, coupled with a nagging shoulder injury, Devereaux's batting average tumbled to .229, though he hit .421 coming off the bench, frequently in key situations. He contributed defensively, including making seven outfield assists. The Orioles had a successful season in 1996, winning a wild-card spot and going on to defeat the heavily favored Indians three games to one in a best-of-five AL Division Series; Devo had an appearance in all the games. Baltimore advanced to face New York in the AL Championship Series, and were defeated four games to one. Devereaux had only a few at-bats in the two combined playoff series, and coming in as a late-inning defensive replacement in the outfield and pinch-runner. He was granted free agency after the season.

Devereaux signed a one-year contract with the Texas Rangers on January 6, 1997, but things did not work out well that season. Though his defensive play in the outfield was flawless, he got off to a slow start offensively, due in part to incurring a strained hamstring in April. He had stepped up to the plate only 80 times over a span of 29 games when he was released in June. He still believed he could play baseball at a big-league level and contribute his skills to help a team win, and to stay active, he signed on to play for a team in Venezuela for three months.

Coming full circle, Devereaux rejoined his original signing team, the Dodgers, agreeing to a contract on January 16, 1998. Devo was well aware he would be competing for one of the team's coveted outfield spots, but he thought it was worth the gamble. The Dodgers had a number of younger outfield prospects they were looking to promote, but he thought they also may have had a desire to add a veteran to the club mix. Devereaux did all that was asked of him, showed hustle in spring training and made the roster as the season opened. In limited plate appearances in April, he was hitting over .300 but was nonetheless released in the first week of May to make room for their highly-touted rookie Paul Konerko, then coming off the DL.

Now 35 years old, Devereaux signed with the San Diego Padres organization a month later. He reported to their Triple-A team in Las Vegas, where he was playing regularly and was in the wings hoping to get called up, but was injured and was placed on the DL in late July. Though he attended several tryouts over ensuing years, he could not catch on and never made it back up to the majors again. He had certainly found success; in his 12 seasons as a major leaguer, he had connected for 105 home runs, and carried a respectable .254 career batting average. He said he loved the game and wished he could have been at it longer. He thought that as an established veteran, having had larger salaries in the past, he was competing with the ballplayers just starting out in their careers who were more economical for organizations and that baseball executives probably perceived he would want more money. But he just wanted to play baseball. It was not about the money.[31]

"That was tough, because, and this is every ballplayer, I'm sure, that thinks … they can still play and I still thought I could," Devereaux said a decade after he had played his last big-league game. "It took probably about five, six years before I really settled into the fact that I'm not going to be playing anymore."[32]

After retiring, Devereaux stepped away from baseball, and concentrated on spending time with his family and growing business interests. He initially got involved in the private sector combining his entrepreneurial marketing and people skills, including working for a business providing outsourcing services, where he managed 35 people, and also for a time serving as a representative for a start-up company working to supply natural foods, including dietary and vitamin supplements, fortified dairy products, and citrus fruits, to major-league clubs, but in the era when baseball was extremely skittish about bringing any products from outside vendors into the clubhouses, it was admittedly a tough sell. He kept his hand in baseball by also starting up in 2003 and running for seven years a baseball academy near Atlanta at which he provided personal hitting instruction for youngsters 6 through 18.[33]

After being out of Organized Baseball for several years, Devereaux decidedly missed it. He had always been interested in sharing his knowledge on hitting and so he returned to the game in 2010, getting involved in player development in the minor leagues. He was offered a job as a field coach for the Orioles' affiliate in the Class-A South Atlantic League, the Delmarva Shorebirds. The following season he shifted to become a field coach with another Orioles Class-A affiliate, the Frederick Keys in the Carolina League. In 2012 Devo was hired by the Colorado Rockies to be the hitting coach for the Asheville Tourists, in the SAL, a job he held for five years. In 2017 Devereaux was assigned to coach the Boise Hawks, the Rockies' affiliate in the short-season Class-A Northwest League. After six years with the Rockies, Devereaux moved into the Cincinnati Reds system. He became the hitting coach of the Pensacola Blue Wahoos in the Double-A Southern League in 2018. They changed their major-league affiliation in 2019, and Devo took on a new assignment as the hitting coach for the Reds' team in the Class-A Midwest League, the Dayton Dragons.[34]

Baseball has changed since Devereaux first broke in, of course. While understanding the importance of using today's analytical data, he said he believed there is an overemphasis on teaching younger players coming up to produce launch angles, leading to uppercut swings, which can be detrimental for long-term player development. By trying to hit the ball over the fence, in part to try to avoid the extreme defensive shifts in today's game, players are instead increasingly rolling over on the ball or striking out, he commented. To neutralize the shift, batters should learn to hit the ball where the ball is pitched and practice hitting it the other way, spraying hard line drives, and using all fields.[35] Reflecting back to his earliest days, he said, "I was blessed to have been coached by former big leaguers in the Dodgers and Orioles system, some of the veterans who themselves were Hall of Famers."[36] This included receiving tips from, among others, Roy Campanella, Tommy Lasorda, Sandy Koufax, Frank Robinson, Brooks Robinson, Jim Palmer, and Eddie Murray, all today enshrined in Cooperstown. Other former players he gave credit to include Boog Powell, Johnny Oates, Tommy McCraw, and Curt Motton.[37]

As a player who worked hard to achieve his own dreams, Devereaux always wanted to repay the opportunity he had to give back to the community. While with the Orioles he was involved with both the Back to School and Athletes Against Drugs programs in the Washington metro area, visiting schools and advising at-risk youth on approaches to help sidestep life's pitfalls. He also founded Mike Devereaux's Orioles, a program supplying baseball equipment and upgrading local ballfields for young people. Nor did he forget his hometown, establishing the Thumbs Up Youth Foundation in Casper, Wyoming, an academic program in area schools promoting the growth and development of students by stressing the importance of good study habits and setting personal goals. He has participated in the Legends for Youth Baseball Clinics sponsored by the Major League Baseball Players Alumni Association. A resident of Ruskin, Florida, outside Tampa, in 2020, Devereaux is married and is the parent to five children, the youngest of whom are a 7-year-old daughter and an 8-year-old son, whom, he said, he enjoyed personally coaching, much as his father did with him and his brothers while growing up in Casper. It's a family tradition being passed down to another generation.[38]

Sources

In addition to the sources cited in the Notes, the author consulted Baseball-Reference.com and the 1986-1989 and 1998 Media Guides of the Los Angeles Dodgers and the 1990-1993 Media Guides of the Baltimore Orioles.

Berney, Louis. *Tales from the Baltimore Orioles Dugout* (New York: Sports Publishing, 1916).

Dempsey, Rick, and Dave Ginsberg. *If These Walls Could Talk: Baltimore Orioles* (Chicago: Triumph Books, 2017), provided context for the Baltimore Orioles during this era.

The author wishes to thank Mike Devereaux for a telephone interview, conducted on November 25, 2019, and providing follow-up information via email.

Notes

1. "Devereaux Delivered as MVP," *Honolulu Advertiser*, October 15, 1995.

2. Mike Devereaux, email communication, December 4, 2019. He was such a fan of Jackson, in fact, that when Reggie became a Yankee in 1977, Devereaux switched his allegiance to New York. He had also idolized Dave Winfield growing up and was thrilled to later play against him. He harkened back to an "incredible" conversation he had with Winfield during an extended rain delay in Cleveland in 1995, the last season of Winfield's Hall of Fame career.

3. Don Marcus, "Devereaux Beats Odds to Become a Star," *Baltimore Sun*, September 20, 1992; SABR, US Baseball Questionnaires, 1945-2005, Box Number: 555698, Michael Devereaux, June 24, 1985; "Devereaux Spends Time Chasing Big League 'Dream,'" *Casper Star-Tribune*, June 11, 1987.

4. Sally Ann Shurmur, "Casper's Fred Devereaux Doing Well on the Mound," *Casper Star-Tribune*, July 9, 1980; Shurmur, "Devereaux Faces New Chapter," *Casper Star-Tribune*, May 27, 1981. Devereaux was inducted into the National Federation of State High School Associations National High School Hall of Fame in 2014. Email communication from Mike Devereaux, November 28, 2019. The American Legion chapter in Casper sponsors the annual Mike Devereaux Invitational, a round-robin baseball tournament to be held for the 13th time in July 2020. legion.org/baseball/tournaments/invitational/159124/mike-devereaux-invitational, accessed November 17, 2019.

5. Technically it was called the National Junior College Athletic Association Tournament.

6. Jay Thorne, "Thunderbirds' Coach Pleased with Tourney," *Arizona Republic* (Phoenix), June 9, 1982; Initially Mike's two older brothers had attended ASU, but Ron had transferred to Mesa Community College for his sophomore year before going on to graduate from Texas A&M and Fred Jr. had transferred from ASU to the University of Houston. Mike's sister, Phreda, went on to graduate from Harvard University, earning straight-A grades. Mike Devereaux, email communications, November 28 and December 4, 2019.

7. "Three-Team Dogfight Expected for Six-Pac Title," *Arizona Republic*, February 26, 1984; Bill Landen, "Sidelights to Be a Part of Tournament," *Casper Star-Tribune*, March 8, 1984.

8. Devereaux had wrecked his knee during basketball practice in his senior year and was told he would not be able to play baseball in college without undergoing major reconstructive surgery. He underwent arthroscopic surgery on his knee and was out for eight months. After some additional treatment, he did not miss any regular-season games with Mesa Community College, though he played wearing a brace. Mike had the recommended reconstructive knee procedure at the end of his freshman year in college; the medical team told him he would be out for an entire year. But when the baseball season came around, through sheer determination and by adhering to a rigorous physical therapy regime, Devereaux was not only back in uniform, but he overcame the surgery to steal 16 bases in 20 attempts in 1984. He had beaten the long odds, which could have conceivably derailed his major-league career even before it began. He gave ample praise to his surgeon. The knee never bothered Devereaux again during his big-league career. William J. Weiss, *1986 Los Angeles Dodgers Organizational Record Book* (St. Petersburg, Florida: Baseball Library, 1987), n.p.; Mike Devereaux, email communication, November 28, 2019.

9. Arizona State University, *Sun Devil Baseball Media Guide*, 2018: 33; 41; 67.

10. Weiss, *1986 Los Angeles Dodgers Organizational Record Book*.

11. Weiss, *1987 Los Angeles Dodgers Organizational Record Book* (St. Petersburg: Baseball Library, 1986), n.p.

12. "Michael Devereaux – Elected to the National High School Hall of Fame – Class of 2014." YouTube.com video uploaded on July 14, 2014, accessed at youtu.be/YGbIszZH5Js.

13. Mike Devereaux, telephone interview, November 25, 2019.

14. Sportswriter Thomas Boswell once related the story of how Orioles general manager Roland Hemond, who had had his eye on Devereaux as he was progressing through the minors, essentially stole him away from the Dodgers. Hemond had nonchalantly inquired about their young prospect in his early

trade discussions with the Dodgers, deliberately mispronouncing his name. Thomas Boswell, "Fans Shouldn't Judge This Week's Trade Just Yet," *Austin American-Statesman*, August 3, 1997.

15 Bob Wolf, "Devereaux Is Traded to Orioles in Exchange for Pitcher Mike Morgan," *Los Angeles Times*, March 12, 1989.

16 Wolf.

17 Mike Devereaux, telephone interview, November 25, 2019.

18 Mike Devereaux, telephone interview, November 25, 2019.

19 Mike Klingaman, "Catching Up with Mike Devereaux: Why Not? A Fair Question," *Baltimore Sun*, August 26, 2009.

20 "Mike Devereaux Reminisces on 1989 'Why Not' Orioles," YouTube.com video uploaded on August 9, 2019, accessed at youtu.be/channel/UCs6xk3YBIP3LMtoc9hDZQiQ.

21 "Mike Devereaux Reminisces on 1989 'Why Not' Orioles"; Mike Devereaux, telephone interview, November 25, 2019.

22 Thomas Boswell, "Devo Steals, Chase Is On," *Washington Post*, June 6, 1992.

23 Klingaman.

24 Tom Keegan, "Devereaux's Cheek Swollen but Unbroken," *Baltimore Sun*, May 9, 1994; Jon Miller, *Confessions of a Baseball Purist* (New York: Simon and Schuster, 1998), 127-128; Ken Rosenthal, "Signing on with White Sox Right Turn for Devereaux," *Baltimore Sun*, April 11, 1995.

25 A Braves second-round draft pick, King never made it beyond Double-A, and he was out of baseball altogether before reaching the age of 24. See King's statistics at baseball-referencecom; accessed October 23, 2019.

26 Andrew Bagnato, "Devereaux's Blast Socks It to Reds," *Chicago Tribune*, October 15, 1995; Steve Dilbeck, "Devereaux Journeys into Hero's Role," *San Bernardino County* (California) *Sun*, October 11, 1995. One of the thrills of going to the Braves for Devereaux was meeting up on a few occasions with one of his boyhood heroes, Hank Aaron. Bob Berhaus, "Inspiring Blast from the Past," *Asheville* (North Carolina) *Citizen-Times*, April 9, 2014.

27 Mike Devereaux, telephone interview, November 25, 2019.

28 Ailene Voison, "Devereaux Latest Hero in Braves Playoff Lore," *Atlanta Constitution*, October 15, 1995; "Devereaux Delivered as MVP."

29 Mike Devereaux, telephone interview, November 25, 2019.

30 Jason LaCanfora, "Devereaux Not Thrilled by Brave New World," *Baltimore Sun*, June 22, 1996.

31 Mike Devereaux, telephone interview, November 25, 2019.

32 Patrick Schmiedt, "Devereaux Makes Peace with Life After Majors," *Casper Star-Tribune*, June 29, 2008.

33 Jack Daly, "Devereaux Still Chasing … This Time It's His Toddler, Not Fly Balls," *Casper Star-Tribune*, May 11, 2003; Mike Devereaux, telephone interview, November 25, 2019.

34 Keith Jarrett, "Three for Three: Tourists Have Led the League in Batting Each Year Under Devereaux," *Asheville Citizen-Times*, July 31, 2014; *Pensacola* (Florida) *News Journal*, January 18, 2018; Marc Pendleton, "Dragons to Bring Back Manager for Third Straight Season," *Dayton* (Ohio) *Journal-News*, January 10, 2019.

35 "Mike Devereaux Reminisces on 1989 'Why Not' Orioles"; "The Ross Grimsley Show," pressboxonline.com/2019/07/25/former-oriole-current-minor-league-coach-mike-devereaux-on-changes-in-player-development, accessed October 7, 2019.

36 Mike Devereaux, telephone interview, November 25, 2019.

37 Mike Devereaux, email communication, December 4, 2019; Ted Leavengood, "Touring the Bases with Mike Devereaux," seamheads.com/2011/06/09/touring-the-bases-with-mike-devereaux, accessed November 17, 2019.

38 Russ Blake, "Devereaux: Starring at Camden Yards"; "Thumbs Up Youth Foundation," *Casper Star-Tribune*, January 28, 1996; "Major League Baseball Players Alumni Association Brings Legends for Youth Baseball Clinic Series to Sarasota, FL," October 6, 2019; news.cision.com accessed November 7, 2019; Mike Devereaux, telephone interview, November 25, 2019.

Ed Giovanola

BY CLAYTON TRUTOR

Ed Giovanola

Ed Giovanola was a utility infielder who played in 218 major-league games over the course of five seasons from 1995 to 1999. He batted left-handed and threw right-handed. Giovanola was a versatile infielder who played second base, third base, and shortstop during a professional baseball career that spanned 10 seasons. In the majors, he played for the Atlanta Braves (1995-1997) and the San Diego Padres (1998-1999). Despite the brevity of his big-league career, Giovanola played on three teams that won the National League pennant, the 1995 and 1996 Braves and the 1998 Padres. He earned a World Series ring as a member of the 1995 Braves. Giovanola made one major-league appearance as a pitcher, throwing 1⅓ scoreless innings for the Padres on August 25, 1999, against the Philadelphia Phillies. This game also proved to be his major-league finale.

Edward Thomas Giovanola was born on March 4, 1969, in Los Gatos, California, in the San Francisco South Bay. His parents, John and Kathleen Giovanola, settled in Santa Clara County not long after John's graduation from Santa Clara University, where he was a standout second baseman on the university's 1962 team that reached the finals of the College World Series, losing to Michigan. John Giovanola went on to a successful career as an executive for a cement company.[1] In high school, Ed Giovanola starred as a middle infielder for the Bellarmine College Prep Bells, one of California's most storied high-school baseball programs. Bellarmine has produced 14 big leaguers, including Joe Albanese, Pat Burrell, and Wayne Belardi.[2] Giovanola capped his high-school career in 1987 by being named to the *San Jose Mercury-News* All-County Baseball team as an infielder.[3] He followed in his father's footsteps and earned a scholarship to play baseball for the Santa Clara University Broncos, one of the powers of the West Coast Conference. In Giovanola's freshman year, the Broncos reached the NCAA tournament. As a sophomore, Giovanola earned first-team All-American honors as a second baseman.[4] He graduated in 1992 with a degree in economics.[5]

Giovanola was selected by the Braves in the seventh round of the 1990 amateur draft. He arguably proved to be the third-best major-league player the Braves selected that year, behind first overall selection Chipper Jones and 10th-round selection Tony Graffanino.[6]

The 21-year-old Giovanola began his professional baseball career with the Idaho Falls Braves of the Rookie-level Pioneer League. He tattooed the baseball in Idaho Falls, compiling an eye-popping .388 batting average and an equally impressive .474 on-base percentage in 25 games. The Braves quickly moved Giovanola up to the Sumter (South Carolina) Braves of the Class-A South Atlantic League, where his hitting cooled to a more modest .244 in 35 games. Giovanola displayed enough promise to earn a promotion in 1991 to the Durham Bulls of the Class-A Carolina League. He spent considerable time at every infield position except first base for the 1991 Bulls, posting just 15 errors over a 101-game season while hitting .254.

The next two summers of Giovanola's career were spent with Greenville (South Carolina) of the Double-A Southern League. Giovanola played on a stacked Greenville Braves club that demonstrated the talent-scouting and acquisition acumen of the John Schuerholz-era (1990-2007) Atlanta organization. This Grady Little-managed team went 100-43, winning the East Division by an astounding 30 games, and defeated the Chattanooga Lookouts in five games to win the Southern League championship. Giovanola's teammates on the 1992 Greenville Braves included Chipper Jones, Javy Lopez, Mike Mordecai, and Tony Tarasco. Giovanola was a part-time performer for the club, posting a .267 batting average in 302 plate appearances.

Giovanola returned to Greenville for the 1993 season, playing primarily third base. His most successful 1992 teammates had advanced in the Braves organization, and the Greenville team returned to earth in 1993, posting a 75-67 mark. The 24-year-old infielder made the most of his opportunities, hitting .281 with a .408 on-base percentage. His performance earned him a promotion in 1994 to the Triple-A Richmond Braves, for whom he batted .282 in 98 games. He was in line for a September call-up to Atlanta, but the strike-shortened season prevented him from making his major-league debut.

In 1995 with Richmond, Giovanola batted .321 in 99 games while playing primarily shortstop. Called up in September, he played in 13 games, seven of them at second base. The 26-year-old made his major-league debut on September 10, 1995, replacing Chipper Jones at third base in the third inning of a 5-4, 11-inning loss to the Florida Marlins. He walked twice in five plate appearances, going 0-for-3 in the game. Overall, he struggled at the plate, getting just one hit and three walks in 17 plate appearances. He had been called up after the deadline for naming postseason rosters, and didn't play as the Braves won the World Series against Cleveland, its first World Series championship since the franchise relocated to Atlanta.

Giovanola bounced between Richmond and Atlanta in 1996. Despite his strong play at the Triple-A level, he had a hard time earning a permanent spot on the Atlanta roster, which had significant depth in the middle infield, including Mark Lemke, Jeff Blauser, and Rafael Belliard. He played in 43 games for the 1996 Braves, hitting .232 in 82 at-bats. He played in 25 games as a shortstop, six as a third baseman, and five as a second baseman.

Giovanola spent most of 1997 in Richmond, batting .291 in 116 games. He played in just 14 big-league games, all in August and September and mostly at third base. Giovanola had 10 plate appearances with the Braves in 1997. The Braves put him on waivers after the season, and on October 13 the San Diego Padres acquired the 28-year-old.

Giovanola played in a career-high 92 games for the 1998 Padres as a utility infielder, filling in primarily at second base for Quilvio Veras and at third for Ken Caminiti.[7] He batted .230 in 139 at-bats. Giovanola hit his only major-league home run on June 27 in a 5-1 win against the Anaheim Angels. In the eighth inning, Giovanola lined a Shigetoshi Hasegawa fastball over the right-field fence at San Diego's Qualcomm Stadium. The Padres won their second NL West title in three years that season, winning a franchise-record 98 games and taking the division by 9½ games over the San Francisco Giants. For the fourth consecutive season, Giovanola played on a team that made baseball's postseason but was not included on any of their playoff rosters.

The 1999 season was Giovanola's final campaign in Organized Baseball. He played in 56 games as the Padres finished fourth in the NL West and in 36 games for the Las Vegas Stars, who finished third in the Pacific-South Division of the Triple-A Pacific Coast League. Giovanola played primarily second, third, and shortstop for San Diego and fell below the Mendoza Line for the first time in his career, hitting just .190.[8]

In his final game as a major leaguer, Giovanola made his professional debut as a pitcher. This was, in fact, his first pitching appearance since Little League.[9] On August 25, 1999, he recorded the final four outs for the Padres in a 15-1 blowout loss to the Philadelphia Phillies. Giovanola, the Padres' sixth pitcher of the afternoon, surrendered one hit and two walks while retiring Alex Arias, Kevin Sefcik, Gary Bennett, and Kevin Jordan, all on fly balls.[10] The Padres released him at season's end and the 30-year-old retired from baseball shortly thereafter. Giovanola settled in San Diego County. He has worked in the wireless phone business as a retail store manager for T-Mobile. As of 2019 he was working as a national sales manager for the realtor Allison James Estates.[11]

Sources

In addition to the sources cited in the Notes, the author relied on Baseball Reference.com.

Notes

1 "John Giovanola '63," *Santa Clara University Athletics* 2019. Accessed July 20, 2019: scu.edu/athletics/broncobench/hall-of-fame/hall-of-fame-inductees/giovanola-john/; Michael Kelly, "Paddy's Boys Still Together," *Santa Clara University Athletics*, June 12, 2001. Accessed July 20, 2019: santaclarabroncos.com/sports/m-basebl/2000-01/releases/061301aaa.html.

2 "High Schools That Have Produced the Most MLB Players," *MaxPreps*, March 31, 2014: maxpreps.com/news/v7K4hqw19oKNxI5snRRHTQ/high-schools-that-have-produced-the-most-mlb-players.htm.

3 Dennis Knight, "All-Mercury News Baseball Teams from the 1980s," *San Jose Mercury-News*, May 7, 2010. Accessed July 20, 2019: blogs.mercurynews.com/hssports/2010/05/07/all-mercury-news-baseball-teams-from-the-1980s/.

4 Dave Mendonca, "South Bay Coach's 'Cup of Coffee' in Major Leagues," *San Jose Mercury News*, August 23, 2017. Accessed July 20, 2019: mercurynews.com/2017/08/23/local-coachs-cup-of-coffee-in-major-leagues/; "SCU Baseball History," *Santa Clara Athletics*, July 6, 2001. Accessed July 20, 2019: santaclarabroncos.com/sports/m-basebl/archive/070601aaa.html#yearly.

5 "Ed Giovanola," LinkedIn. Accessed July 20, 2019: linkedin.com/in/ed-giovanola-42912846.

6 Alan Carpenter, "The Atlanta Braves and the 1990 MLB Draft," *Tomahawk Talk*, December 31, 2017. Accessed July 20, 2019: tomahawktake.com/2017/12/31/atlanta-braves-1990-mlb-draft/.

7 James Clark, "Remembering the 1998 San Diego Padres," *East Village Times*, 2018. Accessed July 20, 2019: eastvillagetimes.com/2018/05/remembering-the-1998-san-diego-padres/12/ 2018

8 According to MLB.com, "The Mendoza Line was a term coined by a teammate of Mario Mendoza on the 1979 Mariners – usually credited to Tom Paciorek or Bruce Bochte – as a joke on the light-hitting shortstop, who typically carried an average around .200 (though he actually finished with a career mark of .215)." m.mlb.com/glossary/idioms/mendoza-line.

9 Jonathan Fraser Light, "Hitters Who Pitched," *The Cultural Encyclopedia of Baseball* (Jefferson, North Carolina: McFarland and Company, 2005), 417.

10 Joe Lanek, "Position Players Who Pitched for the Padres," *Gaslamp Ball*, February 26, 2013. Accessed July 20, 2019: gaslampball.com/2013/2/26/4031628/position-players-who-have-pitched-for-the-padres.

11 "Ed Giovanola," LinkedIn, 2019: Accessed July 20, 2019: linkedin.com/in/ed-giovanola-42912846.

Tom Glavine

BY JOSEPH WANCHO

Tom Glavine

"Yeah we followed his lead, and it doesn't take a rocket scientist to figure out that his kind of poise, his mentality, his way of going about his business, well, that's what won him over 300 games"
—Chipper Jones[1]

The Atlanta Braves were on the cusp of nirvana. The World Series trophy was glistening in the late October sun, waiting to be grasped by the winner of the 1995 fall classic. Atlanta-Fulton County Stadium was rocking on its foundation as the Braves fans serenaded their team with chants of "Whoa, Whoa, Whoooooaaa," while flexing their Tomahawk Chop before and during Game Six. The anticipation of celebrating the team's first World Series championship since relocating from Milwaukee in 1966 was almost unbearable.

In the center of the diamond, the Braves pinned their hopes on left-handed pitcher Tom Glavine. The pitcher with the boyish looks was as lethal a southpaw as any who toed a pitching rubber in history. He made his major-league debut in 1987, and Braves fans had watched him grow into the dominant pitcher they hoped would make their dreams come true.

But a World Series championship had been elusive for Atlanta. After posting a 65-97 record in 1990, the Braves were the talk of baseball when they went from last to first in 1991 with a 94-68 record. Bobby Cox was being hailed as the best manager in baseball with his Lazarus-like miracle of the Braves' rise from the basement to the penthouse of the National League West.

After winning a thrilling League Championship Series against Pittsburgh in 1991 in seven games, the Braves met Minnesota in the World Series. Their dreams were dashed when they dropped a 1-0 10-inning Game Seven to Jack Morris and the Twins. The following season, the Braves again won the West, topped the Pirates in a seven-game LCS, and came up short in the World Series again when Toronto beat them in six games. In 1993 Philadelphia ousted the Braves in the LCS in six games. The postseason was canceled in 1994 after the players strike in August detonated the rest of the season.

Now, in front of a capacity crowd, chanting and willing their team to victory, Glavine held the fans' hopes in his golden left arm.

Thomas Michael Glavine was born on March 25, 1966, in Concord, Massachusetts. He was one of four children (brothers Fred Jr. and Mike and sister Debbie) born to Fred and Millie Glavine.

Fred Sr. worked his whole life in construction, and built the family home in Billerica, Massachusetts. He operated his own company, Fred Glavine Construction. Tom worked for his father's company when he got older, pouring house foundations and building swimming pools. It was tough work, but Tom enjoyed seeing how a house was built from the ground up. But he was smart enough to know that he needed to take precautions against lifting too much weight or putting his treasured left shoulder in peril.

Before Glavine threw a baseball, he was playing hockey at the age of 5. Glavine said hockey, not baseball, was his first love.[2] At Billerica Memorial High School, Glavine was a star in both sports. He played center in hockey and enjoyed the constant action and the perpetual movement required of the position. When he played youth hockey, it was not uncommon for there to be 100 or so games on the schedule. As a senior, Glavine led Eastern Massachusetts, in scoring, totaling 44 goals, and 41 assists. Jack Fletcher, who was the coach of Chelmsford, Billerica's chief rival, appreciated Glavine's talent on the rink. "He's been a nightmare for me for four years," said Fletcher. "He centered their third line his freshman year. I guess Roger (Billerica hickey coach Roger Richard) hid him there. I could see how good he was then. He seems to come through. He stepped in, bingo, he did the job."[3]

Glavine was exposed to hockey, either on the rink or playing in the street with his friends. And while the climate in eastern Massachusetts was ideal for someone to lace up the hockey skates, it was not so for baseball. Billerica Memorial might have played around 20 games in the regular season and then the playoffs. Behind Glavine, who also played some center field, Billerica won the East Mass. Baseball championship. A teammate of his was Gary Disarcina, the future shortstop of the Angels.

Glavine also excelled in the classroom. He signed a letter of intent to attend the University of Lowell. His decision was based in part because the school was located close to home and because he would be able to play both hockey and baseball. Glavine was looking forward to being a student-athlete, and playing the two sports he loved at a higher level.

Glavine had established himself as a superior pitcher in baseball, and a left-handed one at that. Shortly after the NHL draft, the Atlanta Braves selected him in the second round of the amateur draft on June 4, 1984. Five days later, Glavine was selected in the fourth round of the National Hockey League draft by the Los Angeles Kings.

It was baseball that won out when Braves scouting director Paul Snyder offered Glavine $80,000 to sign. Fred Sr., who had handled the negotiations, waited until Snyder made an offer that was deemed acceptable. Glavine said goodbye to college and the NHL and headed to the Gulf Coast League to play for the Bradenton Braves rookie league team.

Two important relationships helped Glavine that first year away from home. The first was infielder Mark Lemke, who was in the minors for the second season. Lemke's road to the big leagues was a bit bumpier than the one Glavine took. But once he got there, they were teammates for several seasons and good friends for life. Initially, Glavine threw the ball hard, trying to show the Braves he was worthy of the $80,000 bonus they gave him. But he began to feel a soreness in his pitching arm. The trainer prescribed rest. Enter Johnny Sain, the roving pitching instructor for the Braves' minor-league affiliates. Sain had been a great pitcher for the Boston Braves and the New York Yankees, as well as a pitching coach for years with the Yankees. He knew a little about his craft. "We're going to throw every day to get your arm strong," said Sain.[4]

As they followed that plan, the pain started to ease and Glavine posted a 2-3 record with a 3.34 ERA. His strikeouts outnumbered his walks, 34 to 13. This trend would follow Glavine through his professional career. Not only could he bring the heat, but he was an excellent control pitcher.

Glavine climbed up the Braves' minor-league chain, having successful years at Sumter of the Class-A South Atlantic League in 1985 and Greenville of the Double-A Southern League in 1986. At Double A, Glavine posted a 9-6 record and a 2.35 ERA. He started to throw a change-up. At Greenville, Glavine went 11-6 with a 3.41 ERA. He earned a promotion to Richmond, the Braves' top farm club, in the Triple-A International League. His first start was on the road at Pawtucket on July 31. With many family and friends in attendance, Glavine was knocked around. He gave up eight runs on four hits, including a grand slam, in 2⅓ innings. Pawtucket won the game, 18-0. The rest of his season at Richmond followed suit, as Glavine went 1-5 with a 5.63 ERA in seven starts. For one of the few times in his professional career, Glavine walked more (27) than he struck out (12).

The Detroit Tigers were making a push for the American League East Division title in 1987. To strengthen their pitching corps down the stretch, the Tigers traded pitching prospect John Smoltz to Atlanta for veteran starter Doyle Alexander. The Braves had a spot open on their pitching staff and called Glavine up from Richmond. Although his won-lost record was 6-12, his ERA was 3.35. It was a clear indication that he was pitching better and that he was losing some tough games.

Glavine made his major-league debut on August 17, 1987, against Houston at the Astrodome. Atlanta (50-67) was out of contention for a playoff spot in the NL West. Houston (58-59) was in third place, three games behind San Francisco and Cincinnati. The Astros hammered Glavine, putting six runs on the board in 3⅔ innings as they whipped the Braves, 11-2. "If I worry about what happened, it won't do me any good," said Glavine. "I have to take what I did positive, and take it out in my next start."[5]

That thinking by Glavine proved beneficial. He won his next start, on August 22, against Pittsburgh, 10-3, his first victory in the majors. In nine starts he finished with a 2-4 record and a 5.54 ERA. It was something to build on.

Over the next three seasons, the Braves occupied the basement of the NL West. Manager Chuck Tanner was relieved early in the 1988 season. He was replaced by Russ Nixon, and eventually by Bobby Cox in 1990. Glavine led the league in losses with 17 in 1988. Not one Atlanta starter reached double digits in wins. The high point for Glavine came on September 7 against San Francisco. He hurled his first complete game, a three-hitter, in a 4-1 win.

The transformation of the Braves began in 1990, although it may have been clouded by their third consecutive finish in last place. Starting pitcher Charlie Leibrandt was traded to Atlanta in the offseason. Together with outfielder Lonnie Smith and third baseman Jim Presley, the Braves had three veteran players who contributed on the diamond and off. Glavine, in addition to Smoltz and the Braves' number-one pick in 1988, Steve Avery, were a rotation in the making. Jeff Blauser, Ron Gant, and Lemke all came up through the Braves farm system. Dave Justice, who was a fourth-round pick by Atlanta in 1985, burst onto the scene and walked away with Rookie of the Year honors from both *The Sporting News* and the Baseball Writers Association of America.

The Braves added two veteran free agents to their roster for the 1991 season to solidify the left side of their infield: Rafael Belliard at shortstop and Terry Pendleton at third base. But it was Glavine (20-11, 2.55 ERA) who tied John Smiley of Pittsburgh for the league lead in wins. Glavine also shared the league lead in complete games (9) with Dennis Martinez of Montreal.

On June 19, 1991, Atlanta toppled the Phillies, 9-2, at Veterans Stadium. Glavine struck out a career-high 12 batters. "We know when we walk on the field with Glavine in there, all we need is two or three runs," said Gant.[6]

Glavine was selected by Cincinnati Reds manager Lou Piniella to start the All-Star Game at Toronto's SkyDome on July 9. He rang up three

AL All-Stars in two innings of work. "It might not have showed, but (nerves) were there," said Glavine. "I was nervous."[7]

The Braves were new to this division race thing. As September came to a close, Los Angeles held a one-game lead over Atlanta. But the Dodgers went 2-3 in October, while Atlanta posted a 4-1 record. Atlanta won its first division title since 1982.

Glavine dropped two games in the League Championship Series, but the Braves topped the Pirates in seven games and won their first pennant since 1958, when they were in Milwaukee. They were matched against Minnesota in the World Series. Glavine broke through with his first postseason win on October 24 in Game Five to even his record at 1-1 in the fall classic. But in a Series that went seven games, it was Jack Morris who stood the tallest, going 10 innings for a 1-0 win in Game Seven.

Glavine received the Cy Young Award that season. "I'm not going to say I'm the best pitcher, but I've always felt I had the ability to be considered one of the better pitchers," he said. "It was just a matter of developing the ability I had. I'm not cocky, but I think I'm a confident person. When I go out there, I'm confident in my ability to win."[8]

The 1992 season was almost a carbon copy of 1991. Glavine won 20 games again, and the Braves won the NL West. Atlanta faced Pittsburgh again in the LCS and were victorious in seven games again. Glavine was not at his best, losing both starts to Pirates knuckleballer Tim Wakefield.

Against Toronto in the World Series, Glavine started Game One. The Blue Jays started Morris, who had signed with Toronto as a free agent. Glavine responded to the challenge by shaking off the hangover from the LCS and pitched the Braves to victory. He went the distance, gave up just four hits, and struck out six in the Braves' 3-1 win. "You sit here the last four days and read about how terrible you are in the postseason," said Glavine. "It seems like this time of year, they throw out everything you did over the course of the year. If I didn't win 20 games, we wouldn't have been here. It's a little aggravating. It shows people's true colors during the heat of battle."[9]

Glavine did have an admirer in the opposing dugout. Toronto manager Cito Gaston knew full well why his team lost the opener. "He kept the ball on the outside of the plate where we couldn't get to it," said Gaston.[10]

The Blue Jays won the Series in six games. The Braves had now made it to the Series two years in a row but lost. To try to rectify that trend, they pulled off perhaps the biggest free-agent signing of the offseason. Greg Maddux, the reigning Cy Young Award winner with the Chicago Cubs in 1992, signed a five-year deal worth $28 million. (Maddux turned down $34.5 million from the New York Yankees.)

Atlanta now sported three top starters, Glavine, Smoltz, and now Maddux. With Avery as the fourth starter, the Braves had the premier starting rotation in the major leagues. The results in 1993 were as anticipated: Glavine (22-6, 3.20 ERA), Maddux (20-10, 2.36), Smoltz (15-11, 3.62), and Avery (18-6, 2.94). Glavine tied John Burkett of San Francisco for the league lead in wins while Maddux was tops in ERA.

Another development came in the way of matrimony for Glavine. He and Carri Ann Dobbins were wed on November 7, 1992. They had one daughter, Amber Nicole.

In spite of Atlanta's stable of outstanding hurlers, they were tied with San Francisco with identical 103-58 records going into the last game of the 1993 season. The Giants closed out the season in Los Angeles, and were drubbed in the last game, 12-1, Atlanta closed at home against Colorado. Glavine defeated the expansion Rockies and the Braves won the division by one game.

The Braves' pennant streak was snapped at two years, as Philadelphia ousted Atlanta in six games in the NLCS.

The 1994 season saw realignment in both leagues. Each broke out into three divisions from two. Now there was a Central Division in addition to East and West Divisions. The Braves were moved into the East along with Montreal, Philadelphia, Florida, and the New York Mets. The extra division also created an extra layer to the playoffs, adding a wild-card team to the three division winners in the postseason.

The players strike ended the season on August 12, 1994. "Everything (baseball team owners have) done has been to set up a confrontation," said union leader Donald Fehr. "All it suggests is it's going to be a long strike."[11] Fehr wasn't kidding: The strike not only canceled the rest of the 1994 season and the postseason, it bled over to 1995, when the first 20 games were also chopped from the schedule. Glavine, who was the Braves' player representative, came under fire for comments he made in the press. Atlanta, not known as a strong union city, took offense at Glavine's talk of freedom. When he considered crossing the picket line to join the replacement players, Phil Niekro said that Glavine was being "greedy."[12] He took shots at owners during negotiations. "They guys (owners) are getting more than they ever thought they were going to get," said Glavine. "So why is it so hard to get a deal? The answer to that question is, they've always wanted more. More to the point where they have total control over players' careers…."[13] But the fans were ready to criticize any player, but specifically those who spoke their mind, like Glavine. "He was vilified as the leader of the union," said Braves President Stan Kasten. "The fans' anger was misplaced. He was just doing his job and exhibiting the same determination and passion that makes us love him on the mound."[14]

In 1995 the Braves got off to a slow start. At the end of June they trailed the Phillies by four games. But the teams reversed their positions in July as the Braves went 20-7 and the Phillies posted a 9-20 record. Atlanta was now in first place, eight games ahead of the Phillies. They did not look back and won the division by 21 games over the Mets and Philadelphia.

On August 10 the Braves edged the Reds, 2-1. Glavine did not get a decision, going eight innings and giving up only an unearned run. However, he did provide Atlanta with its first run when he hit the only home run of his big-league career in the sixth inning. "It was one of the better games I had this year – nothing was easy," said Glavine. "It was a battle, but I found a way to keep us in it."[15]

Atlanta ousted Colorado in the LDS in four games, then swept Cincinnati in the LCS. Glavine made a start in each series, but did not get a decision.

After a three-year hiatus, the Braves returned to the fall classic. Their opponent was the Cleveland Indians, who were making their first postseason appearance in 41 years. Cleveland was the top offensive team in the majors and had the best pitching staff in the AL. The adage that good pitching will always top good hitting was certainly true in this series. The Braves won Game One, 3-2, behind Maddux. Glavine followed suit in Game Two, winning 4-3. The Indians won two of three at Jacobs Field, and the series returned to Atlanta with the Braves leading three games to two.

Glavine started Game Seven, against Dennis Martinez. It was a tightly pitched game, but Glavine was a bit better. He didn't allow a hit until a leadoff single by Tony Peña in the top of the sixth. David Justice's solo home run off relief pitcher Jim Poole in the bottom of the inning gave the Braves a 1-0 lead.

Glavine kept the Indians hitless over the next two innings before turning the matter over to Mark Wohlers, who pitched a 1-2-3 ninth inning to give the Braves their first World Series title since 1957. Glavine was named the Series' Most Valuable Player. "It's just really great how it came down to all of this. It's the best feeling in the world," he commented.[16] Cox might have uttered the understatement of the evening: "He pitched a perfect game."[17]

One might think that the Braves would be the talk of Atlanta. After all, they had won the city's first World Series championship (and as of

2019, their only one). But a once-in-a-lifetime event was taking place in Atlanta. The Summer Olympics were returning to the United States in 1996 and Atlanta was the host city. More than 10,000 athletes would compete in 26 sports at various venues across the city.

Because Fulton County Stadium was a venue that would be used frequently, the Braves were forced to vacate the city and embarked on a 17-game road trip from July 18 through August 4. The Braves went 9-8 on the trip, which saw them begin in Houston and travel to St. Louis, San Francisco, San Diego, and Los Angeles. In the next to last game, on August 3, the Braves edged the Dodgers, 5-3, in an 18-inning affair. Glavine did not pitch in the game, but he pinch-hit for reliever Brad Clontz. He popped out to the catcher in the 12th inning.

The Braves (96-66) won the East again, outdistancing the Expos (88-74) by eight games. Atlanta swept the Dodgers in the LDS. Glavine nailed down the series by winning Game Three, 5-2. (Wohlers earned a save in all three games.) In the LCS, the St. Louis Cardinals took a 3-1 series lead, but the Braves won three straight games to clinch the pennant. Glavine was on the hill for Game Seven. The Braves hammered St. Louis, 15-0. Glavine pitched seven innings, scattering three hits.

The Braves' opponent in the World Series was the New York Yankees. Atlanta won the first two games, but the Yankees won four straight games to take the Series. Having pitched Game Seven of the LCS, Glavine pitched only one game in the World Series. He toed the rubber for Game Three. Although he pitched well (seven innings, four hits, eight strikeouts, one earned run), Glavine left on the short end of a 2-1 score. The Yankees won, 5-2.

Glavine turned author with the release of *None but the Braves: A Pitcher, A Team, A Champion* in 1996 by Harper.

The next two seasons Atlanta was eliminated in the LCS. In 1997 the Florida Marlins bested them and in 1998, it was the San Diego Padres.

For Glavine, the end of the Braves season in 1998 may have left a bitter taste. But his pitching in the regular season (20-6, 2.47 ERA) earned him his second Cy Young Award. "Having won it one time, I've had a burning desire to win it again," said Glavine, "just to prove the first time wasn't a fluke."[18]

In 1997 Tom and Carri Ann divorced. On November 14, 1998, Glavine married Christine St. Onge of Newton Highlands, Massachusetts. They had three children together: Peyton, Mason, and Kienan. Christine had a son, Jonathan, from a previous marriage.

Atlanta won the East again in 1999 and it was beginning to sound like a broken record with their dominance year in, year out. Glavine (14-11, 4.12 ERA) may not have been as sharp as in years past: He led the league in hits allowed (259). But it was the first of four straight seasons that he led the league in games started. At 33, and with a lot of innings pitched so far, it was a testament to how great Glavine kept himself in shape. But through June 4, Glavine was 3-7 with a 5.00 ERA. He did bounce back to have a decent season, but instead of leading the pitching staff, Glavine was third in wins and fourth in ERA.

The Braves breezed through the postseason, disposing of the Astros in four games in the LDS and the Mets in six games in the LCS. In a rematch of the 1996 World Series, they faced the Yankees. The Yankees swept the Braves. Glavine, who came down with the flu, was scratched from starting Game One at home. He recovered to start Game Three at Yankee Stadium. The Braves were leading 5-2 going into the bottom of the seventh inning. But a solo home run by Tino Martinez cut into the lead. Glavine came out for the bottom of the eighth. A single by Joe Girardi and a homer by Chuck Knoblauch tied the score, 5-5, ending Glavine's night. "I know everybody's going to ask why you left him in," said Cox, "but he was throwing great. He didn't want to come out of the game. I asked him if he was tired and he said no."[19]

Glavine led the NL in wins (21-9, 3.40 ERA) in 2000. From July through September, he was 14-4 and was leading the charge to another division title. The Braves had tight competition: The Mets were formidable foes. The Braves were 7-6 against the Mets. The one-game difference was the margin by which they won the division. Then they were swept by the Cardinals in the LDS. Glavine, who started Game Two, was shelled, giving up seven runs in 2⅓ innings.

Over the next two seasons, the Braves continued to dominate the East. But in 2001 they were ousted by Arizona in the LCS and in 2002 by San Francisco in the LDS. In 2002 Glavine tied Kevin Millwood for most wins on the team with 18. At 36 years old, he was still going strong, starting over 30 games a season and pitching well over 200 innings.

But Glavine's time in Atlanta had come to an end. The Braves had signed Smoltz to a three-year, $30 million deal. Glavine, feeling he had proved his worth, wanted the same treatment. But the Braves balked at his asking price. The negotiations became contentious and personal. In the end, Glavine found a willing team to sign him. He signed a three-year, $35 million deal with the Mets that include a vesting option for a fourth year.[20]

Asked what it's like to play in New York, Glavine said: "There's no place better to play when you're going good, and there's no place worse to be when you're not. You just try to stay on the good side as much as you possibly can because when it's not going good, it's a difficult place to play because they let you know."[21]

Based on his answer, it may have been difficult for Glavine in the first two seasons with the Mets. For the first season since 1990, he finished below .500 (9-14, 4.52 ERA) in 2003, with a five-game losing streak from May 24 through June 28. A familiar face joined the Mets in September when they called up Mike Glavine from Triple-A Norfolk. In his debut on September 14, Mike pinch-hit for his older brother and grounded out.

Glavine, who was noticeably distressed at two misplays by outfielder Roger Cedeño, summed up his feelings after the 7-3 loss to Montreal. "If I gave off some kind of indication emotionally about what I thought, my apologies. But as hard as you try to keep your emotions in check, sometimes you get frustrated. It's the nature of the game. In a season like this where so many things have gone wrong for all of us, I think sometimes it's a little harder to hide your emotions than others."[22]

It may not have helped that Atlanta was cruising to another division title, while the Mets were mired in last place, 34½ games behind the Braves.

The 2004 season was not much better for Glavine and the Mets. The Mets inched up to fourth place in the East, but Glavine again finished under .500 (11-14, 3.60 ERA). The highlight of the season came on May 23, when he threw a career-best one-hitter against Colorado at Shea Stadium. Kit Pellow broke up the no-hit bid with a double in the eighth inning

The Mets (97-65) put an end to the Braves' dominance in 2006, finishing in first place in the East. Glavine (15-7, 3.82 ERA) and Steve Trachsel (15-8, 4.97 ERA) were the only two Mets hurlers to post double-digit wins. But they had a premier closer in Billy Wagner, who had 40 saves in 2006. The Mets swept the Dodgers in the LDS, with Glavine getting the win in Game Two. But they lost to St. Louis in seven games in the LCS, Glavine was opposed by the Cardinals' Jeff Weaver, in both starts in the Championship Series and went 1-1. In Game Seven, a two-run home run in the top of the ninth inning by Yadier Molina was the difference as the Cardinals won, 3-1.

For 2007 the 41-year-old Glavine signed a one-year deal with the Mets for $10 million. On August 5 he beat Chicago 8-3 at Wrigley Field for his 300th career win. With a packed house and a national television audience looking on, Glavine pitched 6⅓ innings and gave up two earned runs. As important as a game as it was for Glavine, the Mets stayed ahead of the Braves by 4½ games as the season headed into the stretch. "The feeling right now is probably relief," said Glavine. "Leading up to this, there are a lot of emotions going into it, but now that it's over, there's a sense of relief."[23] He was the 23rd major-league pitcher to achieve the milestone.

On September 23 the Mets led Philadelphia by 2½ games. But they dropped their six of their last seven games and fell into second place as the Phillies won the division.

Glavine returned to Atlanta for the 2008 season, but started only 13 games before calling it quits, making his last start on August 14. His won-lost record for season was 2-4, the same mark as in his first year in 1987. For his career Glavine was 305-203, with a 3.54 ERA. He totaled 2,607 strikeouts against 1,500 walks. Glavine pitched 4,413⅓ innings, and had 56 complete games and 25 shutouts. He had five seasons of 20 or more wins. He was elected to 10 All-Star teams.

In retirement, Glavine has worked as a special assistant in the Braves' front office. In 2010 he became a guest analyst for Braves games on Fox Sports South and Fox Sports Southeast.

On August 6, 2010, the Braves inducted Glavine into their Hall of Fame and retired his number 47. "I hope at the end of the day whether you watched the game here at the stadium or on TV, when you saw number 47 walk to the mound, you knew I was going to give you everything I had," Glavine told the rain-soaked capacity crowd at Turner Field.[24]

Glavine was a first-ballot inductee to the National Baseball Hall of Fame in 2014 when he received 91.1 percent of the vote from the Baseball Writers Association of America. Greg Maddux, Bobby Cox, Frank Thomas, Tony La Russa, and Joe Torre joined Glavine in the HOF Class of 2014.

In 2016 Glavine collaborated on a second book with *Boston Globe* sportswriter Nick Cafardo, *Tom Glavine: Inside Pitch*. The book was essentially a continuation from the one written 20 years earlier

As of 2019 Glavine lived in Alpharetta, Georgia, just outside Atlanta. His son Peyton was selected by the Los Angeles Angels in the 37th round of the 2017 draft, but chose to enroll at Auburn University.

And like dad, he is a lefty.

Notes

1 National Baseball Hall of Fame website, Tom Glavine's page, baseballhall.org/hall-of-famers/glavine-tom Accessed April 11, 2019'

2 Tom Glavine with Nick Cafardo, *Inside Pitch: Playing and Broadcasting the Game I Love* (Chicago: Triumph Books, 2016), 32.

3 Jerry Higgins, "Glavine Billerica's Mr. Clutch," *Boston Globe*, February 21, 1984: 32.

4 Tom Glavine with Nick Cafardo, 52.

5 Gerry Fraley, "Astros Tough on Glavine, Braves 11-2," *Atlanta Constitution*, August 18, 1987: 7-D.

6 I.J. Rosenberg, "Glavine Leads Way as Braves End Skid," *Atlanta Constitution*, June 20, 1991: G9.

7 Joe Strauss, "Glavine Escapes Unscathed," *Atlanta Constitution*, July 10, 1991: G4.

8 Joe Strauss, "Cy Young for a Young Gun," *Atlanta Constitution*, November 13, 1991: F7.

9 Steve Hummer, "Glavine Forgets Postseason Blues while Braves Chase Down a Ghost," *Atlanta Constitution*, October 18, 1992: E3.

10 Ibid.

11 Mike Fish, "Handful of Owners Hold Key," *Atlanta Constitution*, August 13, 1994: D4.

12 Steve Marantz, "The Two Sides of Tom Glavine," *The Sporting News*, May 1, 1995: 44.

13 Marantz, 46.

14 Bob Nightengale, "Glavine Focused on Union, Pitching," *USA Today Baseball Weekly*, August 21-27, 2002: 9.

15 I.J. Rosenberg, "Lopez's Hit in 9th Sends Reds Packing," *Atlanta Constitution*, August 11, 1995: E1.

16 I.J. Rosenberg," Tommy-Hawked! Glavine Helps Deliver First World Series Title to Atlanta," *Atlanta Constitution*, October 29, 1995: E1.

17 Rosenberg, "Tommy-Hawked!"

18 Thomas Stinson. "Glavine Awarded Cy Over Hoffman," *Atlanta Constitution*, November 18, 1996: E1.

19 Murray Chass, "Yanks Come Off the Mat to Foil Braves' Strategy," *New York Times*, October 27, 1999: D1.

20 Jack Curry, "At Long Last, a Good Move," *New York Times*, December 6, 2002: D5.

21 Glavine and Cafardo, *Inside Pitch*, 298.

22 Rafael Hermosa, "Milestones for Glavine, for Better and Worse," *New York Times*, September 15, 2003: D7.

23 Ben Shpigel, "300 Mets' Glavine Reaches Milestone After a Week of Anxious Moments," *New York Times*, August 6, 2007: D1.

24 Carroll Rogers, "Emotional Glavine Gets Fitting Ovation," *Atlanta Journal-Constitution*, August 7, 2010: C3.

Marquis Grissom

BY ALAN MORRIS

Marquis Grissom

On a chilly October night, Marquis Grissom gracefully glided to his right from his position in center field at Atlanta's Fulton County Stadium and gloved the final out of the 1995 World Series. After three tries, the Atlanta Braves were the champions of professional baseball. The man who gloved that final out was the only native Atlantan on the team, having grown up 12 miles south of the Braves home field. Marquis was a team player from the beginning. He had seven brothers and seven sisters and their parents, Marquis and Julia Grissom, expected everyone to pitch in. Marquis remembers stacking firewood on the porch and drawing buckets of water from the well as he did his part.

The story of how Grissom began his baseball career is worthy of an HBO special. He's about 10 years old and playing stickball in the street in front of his house when a big Cadillac makes its way through the Red Oak neighborhood of College Park, Georgia. It is moving slowly and causing a delay of the ballgame as the kids leave the street hollering at the driver to move on so they can play. Several decide to teach the driver a lesson and hurl rocks toward the car as it moves up the hill. Marquis waits until the car turns behind a house and he lets fly. The car stops and turns around as some of the kids scatter. The driver gets out of his car and wants to know who threw that last rock. Everyone points at Marquis. He confesses and the man asks, "Where do you live, son?" Marquis points to the house across the street and the man says, "Follow me." When they get inside, the man introduces himself as T.J. Wilson, an off-duty Atlanta policeman, and says, "Your son just hit my car with a rock but if you will allow him to play on my ball team, I will call it even." Marquis is stunned and then relieved when his mama says, "OK as long as he has time to do his homework and chores, you can have him."[1]

Marquis Grissom worked at the Ford plant in Atlanta. One day he parked a new Mercury Marquis and said to himself, "Doggone, that sounds good – Marquis." It was April 17, 1967, and he put it down on the birth certificate of his 14th child, Marquis Deon Grissom.[2] While his father worked at the Ford plant, his mother tended the family garden, took care of the house, and did her best to instill discipline in a houseful of kids.

"I wanted two boys and two girls," Julia Grissom told a reporter from the *Atlanta Constitution*. "But things just kept happening."[3] Marquis' dad built their house with his own hands with help from some of the older children. "It was a big house. It had seven rooms and three bathrooms, but we could have used more," Marquis said of growing up just south of the Atlanta airport.[4] He played football, baseball, and basketball and ran track at Lakeshore High School. Marquis earned his nickname "Grip" because he always had a ball in his hand and he could easily palm a basketball. He loved sports and knew that participating in sports would keep him off the streets and out of trouble. His mother "never gave me any breathing room." She made sure Marquis did right.[5]

Marquis figured he would end up playing football because it was his favorite sport. "I was a running back and loved the game even though my mother didn't want me to play –afraid I would get hurt."[6] He had offers of college scholarships as a senior but he was drafted by the Cincinnati Reds and offered a $17,000 bonus as a pitcher. "I wanted the money but my mom and dad and high-school coach discussed it and put it to a vote. I voted for the money but everyone else voted for me to go to college. I was outvoted."[7] Marquis went to Florida A&M in Tallahassee on a baseball scholarship.

Grissom batted .448, hit 12 home runs, and led the nation's collegians in triples, and after his sophomore year he was drafted again, this time by the Montreal Expos, who offered him $48,000. He was 21 years old and ready to go, this time without a vote. Everyone knew he was ready for pro ball.

Grissom began his pro career with the Jamestown (New York) Expos. Perhaps because it was his first time north of the Mason-Dixon Line or just the jitters, he got off to a terrible start and was ready to pack his bags and head south. "I called my girlfriend and told her I was taking one more road trip and if I didn't start hitting, I was going back to college."[8] That call must have been the magic because the next day he went 4-for-5 and everything changed. He ran off a string of multi-hit games and finished the season with a .323 average. The next season was with the Double-A Jacksonville (Florida) Expos and the same thing happened. After a slow start he got his average up to .299 with 24 stolen bases and was promoted to Triple-A Indianapolis. He was on the fast track to the major leagues.

After only a year and a half in the minors, Grissom's major-league debut occurred on August 22, 1989, at Stade Olympique in Montreal. Facing the perennial All-Star Fernando Valenzuela, he popped out to the catcher leading off the game against the LA Dodgers. He grounded to third in his next at-bat and then in the bottom of the fifth got his first major-league hit, a sharp single to center scoring a runner. The Expos went on to win the game, 4-2. Grissom finished the season with a .257 BA, and .360 OBP.

During the 1990 season people began to notice the rookie outfielder, who started 68 games for the Expos, at all three outfield positions. He batted .257 with an on-base percentage of .320 and stole 22 bases while being caught stealing only twice. His fielding was superb. He made only two errors and his strong arm (remember, he was drafted as a pitcher) resulted in four assists. The Expos finished in third place with only one regular position player (Tim Wallach) over 30 years old. Grissom placed seventh in Rookie of the Year balloting.

The next season Grissom became the Expos' starting center fielder. He batted .267 with an on-base percentage of .310. He led all major leaguers with 76 stolen bases. The team fell to sixth place but with a nucleus of young talent like Grissom (24), Larry Walker (24), and Delino DeShields (22), along with veterans Tim Wallach (33) and Andres Galarraga (30), it was not surprising that Expos fans were getting excited.

Grissom became a leader of the '92 Expos team. After GM Dan Duquette replaced manager Tom Runnells with Felipe Alou, the Expos challenged the Pirates for the National League East title. Grissom batted .276 with an OBP of .322 and again led all major leaguers with 78 stolen bases. He placed ninth in balloting for the National League MVP. He was a star on the rise.

He was featured in a *Sports Illustrated* story in the fall as the Expos were attempting to overtake the Pirates. Grissom credited new manager Alou with helping change the atmosphere in the clubhouse. "He said if we lost 10 in a row, he might be fired, but none of us would lose our jobs. ... It's much nicer now. You make a mistake, you know it's a mistake. No one has to tell you … that's how Felipe treats us."[9] Grissom also had good things to say about coach Tommy Harper. "He's like a second father to me. We talk about everything, not just baseball. I learn things from him every day about stealing bases."[10]

After his baseball career was over, Grissom said that Harper also taught him how to be a better center fielder. Harper suggested that he play a shallow center field because with his speed he could catch up to balls hit deep and turn shallow fly balls into outs much as Willie Mays did.[11] Grissom also paid tribute to Bobby Cox, whom he called the best manager ever in the major leagues.

It all came together for Grissom in the 1993 and 1994 seasons but it did not begin well. He lost a bitter salary arbitration battle with the Expos in February before the '93 season began. He felt a "lack of respect ... words were said I'll never forget."[12] Before the hearing Grissom had imagined spending his whole career with the Expos. "I love playing with the Expos and I love the fans in Montreal. I was thinking about wanting to play all my baseball there," he said.[13] He loved his teammates and believed they had the talent to win it all. He was happy with manager Felipe Alou and was enjoying his success. He did not let the bitter dispute with management affect his attitude toward the game.

At the All-Star break, Grissom had 93 hits, 53 RBIs, and 19 stolen bases. He was named to the All-Star team for the first time and was the lead-off batter for the National League. The Expos battled the Phillies all year for first place in the East. At the end, they came in second with a record of 94 wins and 68 loses. No small accomplishment for one of the youngest teams in the major leagues with the second lowest payroll. Grissom ended the year with the highest WAR on the team. He won his first Gold Glove award and placed eighth in MVP balloting.

The '94 season began with high hopes for the Expos, still one of the youngest teams but loaded with talent. Manager Felipe Alou had the highest respect from his players and was voted the NL Manager of the Year. Had it not been for the players strike in August, it is likely the Expos would have won the National League East championship and perhaps made it to their first World Series. When the strike began, the Expos had a six-game lead over the second-place Atlanta Braves. Grissom was batting .288 with a .344 on-base percentage, 11 home runs, and 36 stolen bases. He made his second All-Star team and homered off Randy Johnson, helping lead the National League to a win. At the end of the season he received his second Gold Glove award.

The '94 postseason playoffs and World Series were canceled with the Expos having the best record in baseball. But there was trouble in Montreal as the team owners began to express doubts that they could afford to keep the team together. The newspapers called it a "Fire Sale."[14] On April 6, 1995, the Expos traded Grissom to the Atlanta Braves after six years with the club that drafted him and saw him become a multitalented star. The Expos received three players in exchange: outfielders Roberto Kelly and Tony Tarasco, and minor-league pitcher Esteban Yan. One newspaper headline in Atlanta read, "Trade Should Put Braves in World Series."[15] These prophetic words were followed with "[T]his deal will make the Braves infinitely more fun to watch and you can argue he is the most exciting player in the league, the best lead-off hitter, the best defensive center fielder."[16] In addition to being a star, Grissom was an Atlanta native and now a hometown player.

Grissom did not fail to succeed. Along with starters Fred McGriff, David Justice, Chipper Jones, Ryan Klesko, and Javy Lopez, he gave the Braves an intimidating batting order. With these bats and a starting rotation that featured future Hall of Famers Greg Maddux, Tom Glavine, and John Smoltz, the Braves were destined to again make it deep into the postseason. Grissom had a solid year as the leadoff hitter, batting just .258 but scoring 80 runs. He earned his third straight Gold Glove Award. But it was in the postseason that he became a hero. He batted .524 in the Division Series with three home runs, two doubles, four RBIs, and two stolen bases. He was 5-for-5 in the final game as the Braves dispatched the Rockies in four games.

The Braves easily swept the Reds in the Championship Series and Grissom carried a .400 postseason average heading into the World Series. He was a major contributor to the Braves' triumph over Cleveland. He went 9-for-25 (.360), scored three runs, and stole three bases. It was only fitting that the Atlanta native squeezed his mitt on a lazy fly ball to center field for the final out to secure the first championship for the Atlanta Braves.

John Smoltz said after the Braves victory: "He's one of my biggest weapons. ... If you give him any hangtime at all, he'll catch it. He plays shallow, he can run back on the ball, he has a great arm – put that together with his offense, I think he's the best center fielder in the National League."[17]

The Braves were delighted with their 1995 season and the play of their new center fielder/leadoff man. No one was surprised when the Braves offered him a four-year contract worth $19.2 million. Grissom signed the contract and told the *Atlanta Journal-Constitution*, "I'm speechless, we just won the World Series, I'm living at home. It's like: what can happen next?"[18]

What happened next was his best year. Grissom set career highs in home runs (23), triples (10), and batting average (.308). He scored 106 runs and had 207 hits, 74 RBIs, and 328 total bases. He made only one error and had 10 outfield assists. He received his fourth Gold Glove Award and helped the Braves repeat as National League champions. In the World Series they fell to the Yankees in six games. Toward the end of the '96 season a sportswriter said Grissom "brings to the ballpark a belief in work being its own reward and great good sense."[19]

In a move that shocked Braves fans and players, Grissom and David Justice were traded to the Cleveland Indians for Kenny Lofton and Alan Embree before the '97 season. Coming off his best season, Grissom did his best to put on a happy face but he was clearly disappointed, as were many teammates. Chipper Jones summed up the clubhouse sentiment: "Everybody's bummed."[20] Fans questioned why anyone would break up a team that had made it to the World Series for the past two years. Grissom's family could not hold back tears. His wife, Tia, tearfully responded to a reporter's question, "He told me he was traded and I said, 'Come on, quit joking around,' but he said he would never joke around about that. He was upset. He was trying to not be upset, but he was."[21]

The Braves front office made the case that the franchise was confident the trade would not weaken the club. The team had two young outfielders, Andruw Jones and Jermaine Dye, who needed major-league playing time, and still had Ryan Klesko. Lofton was a proven leadoff hitter and Gold Glove center fielder.

Grissom was welcomed to Cleveland and although his '97 regular season was not his best (.262, 22 stolen bases), he shined in the postseason and helped lead the Indians to the World Series, his third Series in a row. Grissom was the MVP of the ALCS, in which he hit a three-run homer in Game Two and stole home in the 12th inning to win Game Three in Cleveland. The Indians lost to the surprising Florida Marlins in the World Series, in which Grissom completed a 15-game Series hitting streak. (The only player to exceed this record was Hank Bauer of the Yankees.)

After one season in Cleveland, the Indians re-signed Kenny Lofton and traded Grissom to the Milwaukee Brewers. He struggled during a three-year stint with the Brewers as his speed and hitting eye declined. He was the regular center fielder but the Brewers were a mediocre team in a strong Central Division.

The Brewers traded Grissom to the Los Angeles Dodgers before the 2001 season. Dodgers general manager Kevin Malone was familiar with Grissom from his days in Montreal. "I've known Marquis since 1988, and this is not only a championship player, he's a championship person," Malone said. "He's a gamer. He wants to win. He's a competitor. What he will bring to this team is a tremendous attitude and tremendous makeup."[22] Grissom spent two years with the Dodgers but in his second season played only 102 games as he tried to overcome hamstring problems.

But good fortune seemed to follow Grissom. The San Francisco Giants hired Felipe Alou as their manager. It was no surprise that the team wanted to get his former center fielder back. Grissom, a free agent, signed with the Giants. He was excited: "At this point in my career, I'm just glad to have the opportunity to come back and be a starter again."[23] He did not disappoint. He batted .300, hit 20 home runs, stole 11 bases, and had 79 RBIs. Near the end of the regular season, the Giants gave Grissom their highest honor, the Willie Mac award. Players, coaches, and training staff vote on the award, which honors the team's most inspirational player. In the words of Willie McCovey, after whom the award is named, "That's something isn't it, he had stretches last year when he got hot, and I could not understand why he was out of the Dodgers lineup."[24]

The Giants entered the postseason with high hopes but were eliminated in the first round by the Florida Marlins, three games to one.

As the starting center fielder in 2004 Grissom's batting average dipped to .279 but he knocked in 90 runs and scored 78. The Giants made a run at the National League West title but lost by two games to the Dodgers. They were in and out of first place all season but failed to make the playoffs.

The Giants put together a veteran lineup for the 2005 season but injuries to key players including Barry Bonds and Grissom contributed to a losing season. Grissom played in only 44 games and batted a career-worst .212 with only one stolen base. He considered hanging up his spikes but felt he had enough left to give it another try. The Chicago Cubs invited him to spring training in 2006. It became obvious that he was not going to make the major-league roster so he called it quits. Just before the season opened, Grissom said, "I came into spring training … to see if I could go out and play baseball again for another year. It didn't work out."[25]

Only 10 major leaguers have retired with 2,000 hits, 200 home runs, and 400 stolen bases: Craig Biggio, Roberto Alomar, Barry Bonds, Rickey Henderson, Paul Molitor, Joe Morgan, Johnny Damon, Bobby Abreu, Jimmy Rollins, and Marquis Grissom. All are in the Hall of Fame except Bonds, Abreu, Damon, Rollins, and Grissom. Bonds would easily be in the Hall if it were not for being tainted with the PED controversy. In 2011, his first year of eligibility, Grissom received four votes and was dropped from the ballot. His legacy is a powerful work ethic and an enduring love for the game.

After retiring as a player, Grissom started the Marquis Grissom Baseball Association. The MGBA is more than a training ground for young ballplayers, it is focused on being a tutorial program, helping Atlanta-area youngsters with math and language skills and preparing them for taking college entrance exams.[26] He said this is his way of paying back for the coaches he had as a young man. "I got so much out of my youth coaches and what they taught me at an early age really made a difference. … I didn't have a ride to practice … equipment, not much at all, but those coaches were there for me … and I wanted to do the same thing. … [I]t was time to give back."[27] As of 2019, 1,600 students had participated in the MGBA program and a high percentage of them have received college scholarships.[28]

In 2009 Grissom was lured back into the major leagues by Stan Kasten, who as president of the Braves was primarily responsible for bringing him to the team. Kasten recalled Grissom's first day with the Braves when he observed him giving teammate Tony Graffanino tips on how to take leads when preparing to steal a base. "I thought, wow, that's really impressive. That's a future coach."[29] It took Kasten two years to persuade him to come work as the first-base coach for the Washington Nationals. One year was enough. Grissom missed working with his baseball association in Atlanta.

One of the first things Grissom did with the money he made as a professional ballplayer was to build his parents a house on land his dad had purchased a few years earlier. He did not stop there. As his salary and stardom increased, he began buying houses for his seven brothers and seven sisters. He talked to them about how to use the money saved on house payments to plan for their children's education. He bought himself a nice 11,000-square-feet house and several luxury cars because that's what ballplayers did. "I look at that stuff now – I didn't overdo it, but even the stuff I got, I don't need it. I look back now, it don't mean nothing," he said.[30]

Sources

In addition to the sources cited in the Notes, the author consulted Baseball-Reference.com, *Baseball Digest* (December 1993), and "The Art of Excellence," an interview with Marquis Grissom with Glenn Zweig on You Tube, at youtube.com/watch?v=oCqELgJ8C_M.

Notes

1. Greg McMichael, "Behind the Braves," podcast, YouTube February 2, 2019. youtube.com/watch?v=wnNd-DHEW45U&t=423s.
2. Dave Kindred, "The Grissom Trail: From a Pasture to Center Field," *Atlanta Constitution*, October 15, 1995: 47.
3. Kindred, "The Grissom Trail."
4. Leigh Montville, "We Are Family," *Sports Illustrated*, September 28, 1992: 38-41.
5. Kindred, "The Grissom Trail."
6. Montville.
7. Montville.
8. Montville.
9. Montville.
10. Montville.
11. McMichael podcast February 2019.
12. Ian McDonald, "Bitter Grissom Planning Post Expos Career," *The Gazette* (Montreal), February 26, 1993: 43.
13. McDonald.
14. Jeff Blair, "Fire Sale II: Grissom to Braves," *The Gazette*, April 7, 1995: 39.
15. Tim Tucker, "Trade Should Put Braves in World Series," *Atlanta Constitution*, April 7, 1995: 44.
16. Tucker.
17. Carroll Rogers, "A Brave New World," *The Gazette*, October 22, 1995: 27.
18. "Baseball Notes," *The Gazette*, November 12, 1995: 22.
19. Dave Kindred, "The Secret of Grissom Plain and Simple: Work," *Atlanta Constitution*, September 22, 1996: 53.
20. Steve Hummer, "In a Cold Deal, Sentimentality Not Thrown In," *Atlanta Constitution*, March 26, 1997: 43.
21. I.J. Rosenberg, "Grissom's Wife 'Very Shocked,'" *Atlanta Constitution*, March 26, 1997: 98.
22. Jason Reid, "Dodgers Send White to Brewers," *Los Angeles Times*, March 26, 2001: 149.
23. Janie McCauley, "Work Makes Grissom Go," *San Francisco Examiner*, March 4, 2003: 24.
24. Brian Murphy, "Giants Notebook: Grissom Wins 'Willie Mac' Award," SFGate.com, September 27, 2003. sfgate.com/sports/article/GIANTS-NOTEBOOK-Grissom-wins-Willie-Mac-Award-2585941.php.
25. Associated Press, "Ex-Braves Grissom Calls it Quits," *Atlanta Constitution*, March 39, 2006: D4.
26. I.J. Rosenberg, "Whatever Happened to Marquis Grissom," *Atlanta Journal-Constitution*, July 2, 2015. ajc.com/sports/baseball/whatever-happened-marquis-grissom/FufBZxFQwvo5yzh5WcYqMP/.
27. Rosenberg.
28. mgba.org.
29. Chico Harlan, "Washington Nationals Coach Marquis Grissom Changes Lives Through his Baseball Association," *Washington Post*, March 18, 2009.
30. Harlan.

Chipper Jones

BY JACOB POMRENKE

Chipper Jones

For generations, many American fathers have raised their sons with dreams of emulating their baseball hero, Mickey Mantle. Chipper Jones's father was no different. From an early age, his son reminded him of The Mick: a small-town country boy with charming good looks, a Southern drawl, and a preternatural ability to hit a baseball from both sides of the plate.

"As a kid, I didn't even know what Mantle looked like," Jones said. "I only heard my dad talk about him. I just thought he had to be the coolest guy ever because he had the coolest name ever."[1]

Mantle's story was already the stuff of legend before Jones ever picked up a bat: his prodigious power and speed, his string of never-ending injuries and — despite an overwhelmingly successful career by any measure — his struggle to live up to fans' folk-hero expectations of him on and off the field.

No baseball player has followed Mickey Mantle's path more closely than the cocky kid from Pierson, Florida. Groomed for superstardom, with a cool nickname to match his father's Hall of Fame idol, Jones exceeded even the lofty goals that had been set for him from the beginning. The Atlanta Braves selected him as the No. 1 pick in the 1990 amateur draft and over the next two decades, he helped lead the franchise to its greatest heights, winning a World Series in his rookie season, earning the National League's Most Valuable Player award, and becoming the face of a baseball dynasty.

"I never wanted to play anywhere else," Jones said. "I'm a Southern kid, and I wanted to play in a Southern town where I felt comfortable. And I felt comfortable from day one in the Braves organization."[2]

After announcing his retirement in 2012, the Braves third baseman was so respected around the major leagues that opposing teams showered him with gifts on a ceremonial farewell tour. He even drew ovations in Mantle's adopted hometown of New York, where he had tormented Mets and Yankees fans for so long with an inordinate supply of game-winning hits. In turn, they enjoyed heckling the brash Atlanta star for his outspoken comments and the revelation of an adulterous affair that tarnished his image early in his career.

Over the years, Jones's off-field troubles receded from the spotlight as he built his credentials for Cooperstown. With 468 home runs and 2,726 hits, Jones stands alongside Mantle as one of the greatest switch-hitters the game has ever seen, ranking near the top of almost every major offensive category for players who batted from both sides. He was elected to the Baseball Hall of Fame in 2018 in his first year of eligibility. In receiving 97.2 percent of votes from the baseball writers, he ranked behind only George Brett among third basemen in the sport's history.

Almost from the moment Larry and Lynne Jones's only son was born on April 24, 1972, in DeLand, Florida, Larry Wayne Jones Jr. looked so much like his father that a relative described him as a "chip off the old block"[3] — and he was called Chipper from then on. The Joneses lived on a 10-acre leatherleaf fern farm in nearby Pierson, a small, blue-collar town known as the "Fern Capital of the World." Larry Sr., who had played baseball at Stetson University, was a math teacher and varsity coach at Taylor High School and Lynne was a professional equestrienne. "Our den was full of her trophies," Chipper said. "She had that little strut about her, that little look in her eye."[4] His father taught him how to play baseball, but he learned to carry an attitude of what his mother called "necessary arrogance" from watching her ride dressage horses in competition.

Larry painted a strike zone on the back of a wooden garage at Lynne's horse farm and pitched tennis balls or Wiffle balls to young Chipper. "We'd get out there and throw the ball just as hard as God let us," Larry said.[5] They would play one-on-one games in the backyard, running through the lineup of the Los Angeles Dodgers, father and son's shared favorite team. When Steve Garvey or Ron Cey came up, Chipper would bat right-handed like the real major leaguers did. When Reggie Smith or Ken Landreaux was up, he would switch to the left side. By the time Chipper was 11 years old, his father could no longer beat him in their backyard games.

Jones's natural right-handed swing led him to step "in the bucket" toward third base, a bad habit he was never able to break. Larry suggested that he add a toe tap before starting his swing to keep his timing and balance intact; that became a signature element of his hitting style, mimicked by young players[6] all over the Atlanta area. "Nobody knew my swing inside and out like [my dad]," Chipper said later. "He built it."[7] Throughout his career, whenever Jones was in a particularly frustrating slump, he called Larry Sr. for help first. The Braves' hitting coaches learned to step aside for the one person who could always find whatever flaw was in Chipper's swing and fix it. "It got to be almost comical how hot I got every time Dad came to town," he said. "The Braves should have put him on the payroll."[8]

One of Jones's first breakout moments came at age 12, when he hit three home runs in a game against a powerhouse team from Altamonte Springs that included future major-leaguer Jason Varitek. Altamonte Springs won and advanced to the Little League World Series, but Jones's performance turned heads.[9] By the time he reached the eighth grade, Jones was good enough to play on the varsity team at Taylor High School. His father quit his job as the school's baseball coach to ward off any complaints about favoritism, but Jones's talent was plain for all to see.

After his freshman year, Jones transferred to a prestigious private academy, The Bolles School, about 100 miles away in Jacksonville. His parents thought his teachers at Taylor were cutting him too much slack because of his athletic prowess. "He was making straight A's and he never cracked a book," Lynne said.[10] As a self-described country boy, Jones didn't fit in well at Bolles. Despite being named starting quarterback[11] on the football team as a sophomore, he quickly grew overwhelmed and homesick. "I went … from a one-stoplight town to a big city, pulling into a parking lot full of better cars than I drove and a lot of rich kids," he said. "It was tough, a big growing-up process."[12]

Jones eventually grew more comfortable, but his move to a private school alienated some of the old friends he had grown up with in Pierson. "I felt like a traitor the first time I went back," he said. "You could see the contempt on people's faces." His Bolles team eliminated Taylor High in the playoffs in three consecutive seasons. Jones never forgot his mixed feelings about leaving home, and he said those memories strongly influenced his decision not to test free agency and stay with the Atlanta Braves during his entire professional career.[13]

During Jones's senior year, dozens of major-league scouts attended his games and even his private batting-practice sessions in the hitting cage. His baseball coach, Don Suriano, tried to shield him from all the attention but it was a futile effort. Jones was named as the Florida state player of the year after hitting .488 as a switch-hitting shortstop; he also went 7-3 with a 1.00 ERA as a pitcher.

The consensus top pick in the amateur draft, and the national high school player of the year, was pitcher Todd Van Poppel from Arlington, Texas. The 6-foot-5 right-hander was armed with a 95-mph fastball and a big curveball; he was already drawing comparisons to fellow Texans Nolan Ryan and Roger Clemens. The Atlanta Braves held the No. 1 selection, but Van Poppel made it clear that he would not sign with the lowly Braves — or anyone else. He planned to attend the University of Texas, Clemens's alma mater. The Braves had finished last in the NL West in three of the last four years and were on their way to 97 losses and another last-place finish in 1990.

"We all heard that Todd Van Poppel didn't want to play here," said Braves pitcher and future Hall of Famer Tom Glavine, who was in his fourth big-league season then. "I think we all took it personally. I think we were all like 'Okay, screw you. We don't want you to play here.'"[14]

Jones and Van Poppel had met each other once before, when they both visited the University of Miami at the same time. Neither could have imagined they would be linked together in baseball history. "If Todd Van Poppel didn't want to be an Atlanta Brave," Jones said later, "I was more than happy to take his place."[15]

Braves scouts Tony DeMacio and Dean Jongewaard met with the Jones family the day after his high school graduation to begin salary talks. But Chipper had no interest in starting off on the wrong foot with the Braves. "The Braves want to get their number one player signed, sealed, and delivered," he said. "I'm not out to hold up any ball club."[16] He settled for a $275,000 signing bonus — nearly a million dollars less than Van Poppel got from the Oakland A's as the No. 14 pick in the same draft.

Jones joined the Braves' rookie-league camp in Bradenton, Florida, about a three-hour drive from his hometown of Pierson. But a hand injury suffered during a fight with a high school teammate hampered his swing and he hit just .229 in 44 games. In a desperate attempt to improve his batting average and his confidence, he received permission from manager Jim Procopio to hit right-handed for a few games. That decision angered the Braves' brass and cost Procopio his job. They didn't care about the 18-year-old phenom's stats, only his development.

Jones spent the fall of 1990 in an instructional league at West Palm Beach, where he met Hall of Famer Willie Stargell and former Washington Senators slugger Frank Howard, who were both working for the Braves as hitting instructors. Stargell recommended that he use a bigger, heavier bat, advising him that his body would catch up soon, which it did as he filled out to 6-foot-4 and 210 pounds. "We'll have you hitting 30 homers in no time, son," Stargell said. Jones called his dad to ask for a second opinion. "When Willie Stargell tells you something," Larry said, "you respect him enough to heed that advice."[17]

Jones's hitting quickly came around — in his second pro season, with Single-A Macon, he hit .326 with 15 homers, 24 doubles, 11 triples, and 40 stolen bases — but his fielding at shortstop left a lot to be desired. He made a whopping 71 errors in 135 games and worked hard every day with infield coach Carlos Rios to get his defense up to a major-league level. Still, his bat was already strong enough that *Baseball America* named him as the minor leagues' No. 4 prospect entering the 1992 season.[18]

After starting the year in High-A with the Durham Bulls, Jones was promoted to the Braves' Double-A affiliate in Greenville, South Carolina. Managed by future Boston Red Sox skipper Grady Little, the G-Braves were loaded, with future major leaguers Javy Lopez (the league MVP), Tony Tarasco, and Pedro Borbon on the roster. The Braves finished 100-43, won the Southern League championship, and were recognized by Minor League Baseball as one of the greatest teams of all-time.[19] The 20-year-old Jones did his part, hitting .346 with a league-best 11 triples in 67 games.

Jones missed a playoff game that fall for a reason he later regretted — to get married. His bride, Karin Fulford, was a Wesleyan College student that he had met in Macon the year before. They wed on September 12, 1992, as his teammates were playing the Chattanooga Lookouts in the championship series. Neither the Braves nor Jones's parents were happy with his decision, and the bad timing foreshadowed an unhappy marriage.

The following year, Jones was back in the playoffs with Triple-A Richmond on the day he learned the Braves were bringing him up to the big leagues. He made his debut on September 11, 1993, as a ninth-inning defensive replacement at shortstop in a blowout win at San Diego. The Braves were in the middle of one of the most dramatic pennant races in National League history, needing every one of their 104 victories to overtake the San Francisco Giants and win the West Division by a single game.

The rookie Jones soaked up the atmosphere — "I had the best seat in the house," he said[20] — but didn't see much playing time. He recorded his first hit on September 14 at home in Atlanta, a pinch-hit single batting right-handed against Cincinnati Reds lefty Kevin Wickander. But he only had two other at-bats in the season's final three weeks. Manager Bobby Cox left him off the playoff roster, but invited him to travel with the team to Philadelphia for the NL Championship Series. The Braves, gassed from the tension of a tight pennant race, lost to the Phillies in six games.

Jones entered spring training in 1994 preparing to back up the veteran Terry Pendleton at third base and split time at shortstop. Then left fielder Ron Gant broke his leg in a preseason motorcycle accident, opening a position in the Braves' starting lineup. Jones began working out in the outfield, a position he had only played sparingly as a teenager, learning the ropes from Deion Sanders and Otis Nixon. He was having a strong spring, hitting .375 with three home runs, when he was seriously injured two weeks before Opening Day.

On March 18, in an exhibition game against the New York Yankees, Jones attempted to avoid a tag while running to first base when he heard his left knee pop. The diagnosis was grim: a full tear of the nterior cruciate ligament, ending his promising season before it had even begun. The 1994 season ended prematurely for everyone in August when major-league players went on strike and the World Series was cancelled because of the ongoing labor dispute. Jones had to wait through an excruciatingly long offseason before he could get back on the field.

On April 26, 1995, Jones finally saw his name in the Braves' starting lineup, playing third base and batting third in the order — wearing his favored No. 10 jersey for the first time, the same number his dad had always worn. Only two-thirds of the seats were filled at Atlanta-Fulton County Stadium as fans reluctantly welcomed back the striking major-league players, but "I wasn't going to let anything ruin my first Opening Day," Jones said.[21]

Jones's excitement was so overwhelming that he ran over his starting pitcher, Greg Maddux, on an infield popup by the Giants' Barry Bonds in the first inning. The reigning Cy Young Award winner verbally berated him on the field and in the dugout for the next few innings: "Settle the [expletive] down, you [expletive] rookie!"[22] Jones redeemed himself a few minutes later by driving in the Braves' first run of the season with an RBI single. He added another RBI single and scored three runs in the season opener. Thirteen months after a devastating knee injury, his hard work was about to pay off in a big way.

There was no more fitting place for Jones to hit his first home run than at Shea Stadium. With the Braves' move to the NL East division following baseball's realignment in '94, their growing rivalry with the New York Mets turned into one of the sport's most heated matchups for the rest of the decade. Jones, who often seemed to save his best performances for games against the Mets, would later find himself at the center of New York fans' ire both on and off the field.

His first of many game-winning hits against the Mets came on May 9. Batting left-handed against Josias Manzanillo, Jones broke a 2-2 tie in the ninth inning by lining a fastball into the upper deck in right field. "I don't think my feet hit the ground the whole time I was rounding the bases," he said.[23] That first home run opened the floodgates: he went deep four more times in the next seven games. Less than a week later, he hit a walk-off home run against the Florida Marlins' intimidating closer, Robb Nen. That stretch, he said, helped him turn a corner: "I went from questioning if I belonged to knowing I did."[24]

Jones couldn't sustain that kind of hot streak all season, but he finished with a solid .265 average, 23 home runs, and 86 RBIs as the Braves ran away with the NL East by 21 games. In a controversial Rookie of the Year vote, Jones finished runner-up to Japanese sensation Hideo Nomo of the Los Angeles Dodgers. The 26-year-old Nomo had pitched for five years in Japan's top-flight league before coming over to MLB as a free agent and leading the National League in strikeouts in his first season.

Jones may have missed out on the individual honor, but he and the Braves had greater heights to climb in the postseason. Major League Baseball had added a new wild-card team and an extra round of playoffs, and Jones's debut in the NL Division Series against the Colorado Rockies was one to remember. In Game One at a sold-out Coors Field in Denver, he hit a home run in the third inning and made a diving stop of Andres Galarraga's line drive in the eighth to help preserve a 4-4 tie. Then in the top of the ninth, he drilled a hanging slider by Curt Leskanic over the wall in right-center field to give the Braves a crucial 5-4 win to open the best-of-five series.

Atlanta downed the Rockies in four games and Jones again made an impact in Game One of the NLCS against the Cincinnati Reds. With the Braves down 1-0, the rookie third baseman led off the ninth inning with a single off Reds lefty Pete Schourek and scored the tying run two batters later on a groundout. The Braves won the series opener in 11 innings and went on to sweep the Reds to clinch the National League pennant, their third in the past five years. Jones recorded a base hit in each of his first eight playoff games, and batted .308 in that postseason. "I've been through a lot of pressure games in my life," he said. "Some guys live for crunch time. I'm one of them."[25]

Jones played solidly in the World Series against the Cleveland Indians, reaching base three times in the 1-0 victory in Game Six that secured the Braves' first championship since moving to Atlanta in 1966. After Marquis Grissom caught the final out in center field, Jones was the first player to reach the mound and join the celebration with closer Mark Wohlers and catcher Javy Lopez. He ended up at the bottom of the dogpile; it was "the best pain you'll ever experience in your life," he recalled.[26]

The Braves secured Jones's services for four more years by signing him to an $8.25 million extension during the offseason.[27] His salary jumped from $114,000, near the league minimum in '95, to $825,000 a year later, and his financial woes during the dark days of the strike — when he and wife Karin had to borrow money from her family to pay the bills[28] — were long gone.

That security off the field led Jones to more greatness on the field in 1996, when he hit 30 home runs and began an eight-year streak of 100 or more RBIs as the Braves won their second consecutive NL pennant. Jones was selected by Bobby Cox to his first All-Star team that summer, along with five of his teammates, and he started at third base in place of the injured Matt Williams. Jones finished fourth in the MVP voting behind San Diego's Ken Caminiti.

The Braves quickly disposed of the Los Angeles Dodgers in the NL Division Series, then fell behind the St. Louis Cardinals three games to one in the league championship series. Dennis Eckersley's fist-pumping histrionics in closing out Game Four fired up the Braves' offense and the defending champions pummeled the Cardinals in the next three games, outscoring St. Louis 32-1 to win the NLCS. Jones hit .440 during the series.

After sweeping the New York Yankees on the road in the first two games of the World Series, the Braves looked well positioned to win back-to-back titles and stake their claim as one of baseball's great dynasties. "We were the hottest team on the planet," Jones said. "Then all of a sudden, we weren't."[29] The Yankees won all three games in Atlanta, rallying from a 6-0 deficit in Game Four on Jim Leyritz's game-tying home run, and closed out the Braves in Game Six at Yankee Stadium. Jones was left standing on deck with the tying and go-ahead runs on base as Mark Lemke popped out to end the Series.

The Braves began the 1997 season with a new home stadium, Turner Field, and a new roster, having traded away team leaders David Justice and Marquis Grissom to the Cleveland Indians in a blockbuster deal before spring training. The outspoken Justice, who had hit the World Series-clinching home run for the Braves in 1995, had been Jones's mentor, his "big brother" in the clubhouse. After the trade, Justice said, "The team is Chipper's now."[30]

When the Braves moved into Turner Field, they also began a new game-day tradition, allowing players to select their own "walk-up" music before their at-bats. The song Jones chose, Ozzy Osbourne's "Crazy Train," became associated with him for the rest of his career. In his autobiography, Jones gleefully reminisced about digging in against the rival Mets and hearing catcher Mike Piazza express his disgust under his breath when the iconic opening guitar riff blasted throughout the stadium. "He didn't hate the song," Jones recalled. "He hated the spectacle of what might happen when I got into the box."[31]

Jones's exploits against the Mets soon became the stuff of legend. As the Braves-Mets rivalry heated up, New York fans increasingly focused their wrath on Jones, who gave them plenty of ammunition when his troubled personal life went public during the 1998-99 offseason.

With his marriage to Karin crumbling, Jones decided to come clean by giving an interview in which he admitted to having multiple affairs and fathering a child with a waitress from a Hooter's restaurant whom he met during spring training. "I've messed up royally," he said. "I wish you were allowed one mulligan in life. To be able to rewind two years and play it all over again, I'd do it in a heartbeat."[32] The revelation shattered his all-American image and it took years for his reputation to recover. Visiting fans heckled him mercilessly and he sometimes wore cotton in his ears to muffle the boos.

Nowhere were the boos louder than at Shea Stadium in New York. Mets fans took to chanting Jones's given name — "Lar-ry! Lar-ry!" — after pitcher Orel Hershiser mentioned in an interview that the Braves' star hated being called by that name.[33] Piazza added to the furor when he told a reporter he couldn't "call a grown man Chipper."[34]

Jones shrugged off the fans' enmity and his own personal issues to deliver a career-defining MVP season in 1999. A tip from the Braves' new hitting coach, Don Baylor, helped transform his game. Despite being a natural right-hander, Jones had only hit 12 of his 108 home runs thus far against lefty pitchers, and NL managers learned to take advantage of his weakness by turning him around to bat righty in crucial situations. Baylor pushed him to develop the same confident attitude — the "necessary arrogance" his mom had long ago instilled in him — from either side of the plate.

The new mind-set paid dividends immediately, as Jones hit his first home run of the 1999 season off the Arizona Diamondbacks' left-handed ace, Randy Johnson. He went on to hit .352 with a career-high 15 homers from the right side that year, setting an NL record for most home runs (45) by a switch-hitter. But he saved his most damaging blows for the Braves' bitter rivals from New York.

In late September, the Mets came to Atlanta just one game back in the NL East standings with 12 to play. Six of those games were against the Braves, and Jones made the most of his first real pennant race. In a memorable three-game sweep at Turner Field, Jones hit four home runs — two from each side of the plate, every one of them giving the Braves a lead. A week later, he reached base five times in three games as the Braves took the return series at Shea Stadium and cruised to the division title.

Jones's dominance against the Mets propelled him to NL MVP honors at the end of the season; he received 29 of 32 first-place votes from the baseball writers after batting .319 with 116 runs scored, 110 RBIs, and setting career highs in home runs (45), walks (126), and stolen bases (25).

But he wasn't quite finished with the Mets, and New York fans weren't done with "Larry." The Mets regrouped to take the National League's wild-card playoff berth, then they upset the 100-win Arizona Diamondbacks in the division series to set up an intense rematch with the Braves in the NLCS.

The Mets' brash manager, Bobby Valentine, had spent the final weeks of the regular season accusing the Braves of underhanded tactics, including tipping pitches to their hitters, and there was no love lost between the two teams. Jones added fuel to an already blazing fire when, after enduring hours of hostile taunting from the Shea Stadium faithful, he snapped back to a reporter, "Now all those Mets fans can go home and put their Yankees stuff on."[35]

In the NLCS, with boos and "Lar-ry" chants raining down on him every time he stepped into the batter's box at Shea Stadium, Chipper reached base in 15 of his 29 plate appearances (four of his nine walks were intentional), but only recorded one RBI. The Braves won a tense series, clinching the pennant on Andruw Jones's bases-loaded walk in the 11th inning of Game Six.

The World Series against New York's more illustrious American League team was billed as the battle for the "Team of the '90s" title, but it proved to be an anticlimactic end to the season. The Yankees swept the Braves to capture their third World Series in four seasons. Jones managed just three hits in the four games, including a home run off Orlando "El Duque" Hernandez in Game One.

After his MVP season, the Braves offered their star third baseman a six-year, $90 million contract extension, which briefly made him the highest-paid position player in baseball. Jones's agent, Steve Hammond, took his time accepting and Chipper replaced him with his childhood friend, B.B. Abbott, and soon signed the deal. With his new contract in hand, he bought a 4,000-acre ranch in south Texas that he renamed the Double Dime, after the uniform number 10 that he and his father both wore.

Jones's messy marriage with Karin ended that same offseason. By the time the 2000 season began, he had remarried to Sharon Logonov, a Florida native, in his parents' front yard in Pierson. Their first son, Larry III, who they called Trey, was born in June. Their second son, Shea, born in 2004, was named in part after the Mets' home stadium, where Chipper always had such great success. His relationship with New York fans had once been hostile, but it evolved into something more like mutual respect after the tragic events of September 11, 2001, took an edge off the Braves-Mets rivalry. "I didn't mean [my son's name] to be a slap in the face to the fans of New York," Jones said. "I enjoyed playing on that stage. Other than Atlanta, there's nowhere else I wanted to play more than New York."[36]

Following the 2001 season, GM John Schuerholz and team president Stan Kasten approached Jones about moving to left field so they could sign former All-Star third baseman Vinny Castilla. Jones was reluctant to switch positions, but he had played in the outfield before and agreed to move for the good of the team. Jones enjoyed a chance to get away from the pressure of the infield. "I used to spend so much mental preparation on defense, either working on it or worrying about it," he said. "I'm sure it took away from my offense."[37]

Castilla provided a solid option at third base but he re-signed with the Colorado Rockies as a free agent after just two seasons in Atlanta, turning over the position to Mark DeRosa. In 2003, the Braves signed Gary Sheffield to play right field. With perennial Gold Glove winner Andruw Jones in center field and Chipper Jones in left, they made for one of the most formidable outfields in baseball. With the two right-handed sluggers between him, Chipper was moved to the cleanup position instead of his customary No. 3 spot in the lineup. No matter where he played, he continued to produce at the plate, averaging 26 homers and 103 RBIs in his two full-time seasons as a left fielder.

With the Jones boys anchoring the lineup, and a rotating cast of starting pitchers — with Russ Ortiz, Mike Hampton, and Tim Hudson replacing the Big Three of Glavine, Maddux, and John Smoltz, now the closer — the Braves continued to dominate the NL East in the early 2000s. But they only made it out of the first round once, in 2001, and Atlanta players quickly grew tired of answering questions about October.

"People say we haven't lived up to expectations because we've won only one World Series — but that's one more than a lot of other teams have won," Jones said. "We're of the mind-set that if we keep giving ourselves opportunities in the postseason, one of these days it'll bounce our way again."[38]

In 2004, the Braves struggled out of the gate and it appeared as if their postseason streak might be in jeopardy. Jones strained his right hamstring chasing down a ball in left field in April and was out for three weeks. When he returned, his batting average spiraled down and he was hitting .214 at the All-Star break. With DeRosa struggling at third base and Jones still hobbled by nagging injuries, manager Bobby Cox decided to move his star back to his old position.

The switch might have saved the Braves' season; they played .680 ball in the second half and finished with a 96-66 record. Jones batted a career-low .248, but belted 11 of his 30 home runs in August as the Braves overtook the Philadelphia Phillies for yet another NL East title. However, they bowed out again in the NLDS, this time to the Houston Astros.

Atlanta again got off to a slow start in 2005 and fell behind the Washington Nationals by the Fourth of July. But an infusion of young talent that included rookies Brian McCann and Jeff Francoeur — coined the "Baby Braves" — spurred a second-half run to the team's 14th consecutive division title, a major-league record that may never be equaled. At age 33, Jones was the team's elder statesman, contributing 21 home runs. But he missed more than 50 games after tearing a ligament in his left foot.

The Braves finally failed to reach the postseason for the first time in Jones's career in 2006. Following the inaugural World Baseball Classic, in which he hit two home runs for the United States team, he batted .324 for the Braves, including a career-long 20-game hitting streak and his only three-homer game. But he was sidelined for another 52 games with nagging injuries, which would plague him for the rest of his career. He averaged just 122 games played during his final nine seasons. By the time he retired, he'd had six knee operations and survived the baseball grind "on a daily dose … of Percocet and a Red Bull."[39]

After another solid season in 2007 — in which he hit .337, led the National League in OPS, and finished sixth in the MVP voting — Jones surprised everyone, including himself, with a white-hot start in 2008. He recorded hits in 18 of his first 19 games and kept his average over .400 for more than two months. When he hit his 400th career home run on June 5 against Florida Marlins right-hander Ricky Nolasco, his batting average stood at an astounding .418, inspiring talk that the 36-year-old could become the first player since Ted Williams in 1941 to surpass the .400 mark. Jones tried to downplay his chances and called the talk premature. "I don't think anybody can do it," he said.[40]

Two weeks later, his average fell below the .400 mark on June 19 in Texas, on the final game of a 10-day, four-city road trip. Still, he was hitting .376 with 18 home runs at the All-Star break. A shoulder injury sapped his power and he was limited to four home runs in the season's last two months. Jones was reduced to a pinch-hitting role during the last two weeks and finished with a .364 average. He held off a late-season charge from St. Louis Cardinals slugger Albert Pujols to lead the NL in hitting for the first and only time.

"I don't know if I would have won the batting title if I hadn't had a sore shoulder," he said. "If I'd been out there getting four, five at-bats a day, grinding on that shoulder, the numbers probably would have suffered."[41]

Before the 2009 season, Jones signed a four-year, $61 million extension that would keep him in a Braves uniform for the rest of his career. "I've been good to the Braves, but they've been better to me," he said. "They never even let me get to a free-agency year. The money I've made in the game is ridiculous, but I'd like to think it hasn't changed me."[42]

Jones played sparingly in the second World Baseball Classic that spring before leaving the United States team early with an oblique injury. His batting average dropped down to earth by 100 points to .264 and he grew so frustrated with his poor play that he met with Braves officials early in 2010 to discuss possible retirement plans. Bobby Cox, the only big-league manager he had ever played for, had already decided it would be his final season. With the Braves leading the NL East for most of the year and a postseason berth in sight, it felt like a fitting time to say goodbye after one last October run together.

Another devastating injury put an end to Jones's thoughts of calling it a career. On August 10 at Houston, he charged in on a ground ball by the Astros' Hunter Pence and blew out his left knee — shredding the same knee ligament he had torn 16 years earlier as a rookie in 1994. "In that instant, I knew retirement was out the window," he said. "No way did I want to go out like that. I couldn't retire limping off the field … for Bobby's swan song."[43]

Jones was forced to watch from the sidelines as the Braves lost a tight NL Division Series to the San Francisco Giants, ending Cox's Hall of Fame managerial career. With his hand-picked successor, Fredi Gonzalez, taking the reins in the Braves' dugout, Jones made it back on the field by Opening Day in 2011. That year, he passed Mickey Mantle with his 1,510th career RBI, placing him second only to Eddie Murray among all switch-hitters in baseball history. But Atlanta's season ended on a sour note again when they blew an 8½-game lead in the wild-card standings in September and finished out of the postseason on the final day.

During spring training in 2012, the 40-year-old Jones decided to announce this would be his final season. His farewell tour got off to an ominous start: Hours before his emotional retirement press conference, he injured his knee again during a team stretching session and underwent surgery for a torn meniscus that forced him to miss Opening

Day.[44] But he hit a home run in his first game back, the first indelible moment in a year full of them.

In every city Jones visited, opposing teams showered him with gifts: a Stetson cowboy hat from the Houston Astros; a customized surfboard from the San Diego Padres; a signed third-base bag from the Washington Nationals; and an original piece of art commemorating his career by his archrivals, the New York Mets, against whom he batted .309 with 49 home runs and 159 RBIs during his career.

His 468th and final home run was a memorable one: a three-run, walk-off blast against Phillies closer Jonathan Papelbon on September 2 at Turner Field, helping the Braves qualify for the postseason one last time, as a participant in the first NL Wild Card Game against the St. Louis Cardinals. In his final major-league appearance on October 5, Jones made a crucial error to start the Cardinals' go-ahead rally in the fourth inning and went 1-for-5 in an elimination game that was marred by a controversial infield-fly ruling which cost the Braves an opportunity to tie the score.

In retirement, Jones has stayed away from baseball for the most part. He has hosted a series of hunting shows on television from his Texas ranch and he returns to Atlanta occasionally when the Braves ask him to offer hitting tips to the team's young players and minor-league prospects. He also keeps busy raising his young family and coaching his sons' sports teams. After three kids with Sharon, their marriage ended in 2012 and he remarried to model Taylor Higgins in 2015.

An all-around hitter who batted over .300 from both sides of the plate — the only switch-hitter in major-league history with more than 1,000 plate appearances to do so — Jones's career was honored when he was elected to the Hall of Fame on the first ballot in 2018. He became the sixth member of the Braves' dynasty to make it to Cooperstown, along with teammates Greg Maddux, Tom Glavine, and John Smoltz, manager Bobby Cox, and GM John Schuerholz.

"For us to have that little fraternity in a little piece of heaven up there in Cooperstown, New York, it's something that we can and should be very proud of, because we did an awful lot of winning," Jones said.[45]

Notes

1. Chipper Jones and Carroll Rogers Walton, *Ballplayer* (New York: Dutton, 2017), 6. All page numbers are locations from the Kindle version of this book.

2. Jerry Crasnick, "One and Done for Chipper Jones," ESPN.com, March 22, 2012. Accessed online at http://www.espn.com/mlb/spring2012/story/_/id/7723234/chipper-jones-retire-2012-season on April 12, 2018.

3. *Ballplayer*, 6.

4. *Ballplayer*, 13-14.

5. Jack Wilkinson, "Chipper: The Natural," *Atlanta Journal-Constitution*, March 23, 1997: F6.

6. Including this author, who grew up near Atlanta and closely followed Jones's career from beginning to end.

7. *Ballplayer*, 296-97.

8. *Ballplayer*, 296-97.

9. Wilkinson.

10. Wilkinson.

11. Jones switched to wide receiver at Bolles and led the state in receptions during his senior year, drawing attention from coaches Steve Spurrier at the University of Florida and Bobby Bowden at Florida State University. But he told them his future was in baseball.

12. Wilkinson.13

13. *Ballplayer*, 32-34.

14. Cory McCartney, "Chipper Jones or Todd Van Poppel? Inside decision that led to Braves picking franchise icon," Fox Sports, January 24, 2018. Accessed online at https://www.foxsports.com/south/story/chipper-jones-todd-van-poppel-012418 on February 10, 2018.

15. *Ballplayer*, 61.

16. Russ White, "Braves Choose Chipper," *Orlando Sentinel*, June 5, 1990.

17. *Ballplayer*, 70-71, 89-90. Jones eventually settled on a 35-inch, 34-ounce Rawlings MS20 bat that he borrowed from Ron Gant; he used that model for his entire major-league career.

18. John Manuel, "Top 100 Prospects: Year by Year," *Baseball America*, February 19, 2014, accessed online at https://www.baseballamerica.com/majors/top-100-prospects-year-by-year on February 10, 2018.

19 Bill Weiss and Marshall Wright, "Top 100 Teams," MiLB.com, accessed online at http://www.milb.com/milb/history/top100.jsp?idx=23 on February 10, 2018.

20 *Ballplayer*, 105.

21 *Ballplayer*, 125.

22 *Ballplayer*, 126.

23 *Ballplayer*, 128.

24 *Ballplayer*, 130.

25 Tim Kurkjian, "Pressure-Treated," *Sports Illustrated*, October 16, 1995. Accessed online at https://www.si.com/vault/1995/10/16/207235/pressure-treated on April 12, 2018.

26 *Ballplayer*, 147.

27 I.J. Rosenberg, "Jones Gets 4-Year Deal from Braves," *Atlanta Journal-Constitution*, February 17, 1996: F1.

28 *Ballplayer*, 149-50.

29 *Ballplayer*, 160.

30 Terence Moore, "Like It or Not, Chipper Must Lead Team Now," *Atlanta-Journal Constitution*, April 9, 1997: B1.

31 *Ballplayer*, 324.

32 Bill Zack, "Chipper Jones Admits to Fathering Illegitimate Child," *Savannah Morning News*, October 22, 1998, accessed online at http://savannahnow.com/stories/102298/SPTchipper.html on February 19, 2018.

33 John Romano, "Braves-Mets: War of the Words," *Tampa Bay Times*, October 12, 1999: 10C.

34 *Tampa Tribune*, October 23, 1999, 4.

35 Carroll Rogers, "Braves Dim Mets' Playoff Chances," *Atlanta Journal-Constitution*, October 1, 1999: D1.

36 *Ballplayer*, 248-49.

37 Guy Curtright, "Switch to Left All Right," *Atlanta Journal-Constitution*, March 31, 2002: P5.

38 "Chipper Jones," *Sports Illustrated*, October 3, 2005. Accessed online at https://www.si.com/vault/2005/10/03/8357601/chipper-jones on April 12, 2018.

39 *Ballplayer*, 315.

40 Associated Press, "Chipper: .400 and holding," June 8, 2008.

41 *Ballplayer*, 307.

42 Chipper Jones, "Bottom of the 19th: The Walk-off," *Sports Illustrated*, September 17, 2012. Accessed online at https://www.si.com/vault/2012/09/17/106233934/bottom-of-the-19th-the-walkoff on April 12, 2018.

43 *Ballplayer*, 310-11.

44 Jayson Stark, "Chipper Jones to Have Knee Surgery," ESPN.com, March 24, 2012. Accessed online at http://www.espn.com/mlb/spring2012/story/_/id/7731316/2012-spring-training-chipper-jones-arthroscopic-surgery-torn-knee-meniscus on April 16, 2018.

45 Mark Bowman, "Head of the Class: Chipper Elected to Hall," MLB.com, January 24, 2018. Accessed online at https://www.mlb.com/news/chipper-jones-elected-to-baseball-hall-of-fame/c-265267272 on April 16, 2018.

David Justice

BY SEAN TETERS

David Justice

Every major leaguer dreams of making the postseason and hoisting the World Series trophy. A few will get to not only hoist the trophy, but be the hero of the World Series. Not many players can say that they hit a home run to win the deciding game of the World Series, or that they hit a go-ahead three-run homer to clinch a World Series berth, or that they went to the postseason in 11 straight seasons and won two World Series trophies. David Justice, one of the most prolific postseason heroes of the 1990s, can say all of those things.

Justice, a Braves right fielder from his 16-game debut in 1989 until the end of the 1996 season, was a part of five major-league organizations and played in the majors for four of them: the Braves (1989-1996), Cleveland Indians (1997-2000), New York Yankees (2000-2001), New York Mets (offseason 2001) and the Moneyball Oakland Athletics (2002, his final season). In his 14 major-league seasons, Justice compiled a slash line of .266/.376/.410, with 305 home runs, 1,571 hits, and 1,017 RBIs.

David Christopher Justice was born on April 14, 1966, in Cincinnati to Robert and Nettie Justice. His father, a security guard, left the family when Justice was a child, and Nettie took care of him as a housekeeper and caterer.[1] He attended a Catholic high school, Covington Latin High School, in Covington, Kentucky, across the Ohio River from Cincinnati. The school is known for its academic excellence, and Justice excelled while there; He skipped both seventh and eighth grades and graduated at the age of 16. While in high school he was a star basketball player, holding the school's all-time scoring record and averaging nearly 26 points a game during his senior season. Covington Latin did not have a baseball team; Justice played American Legion baseball over the summers during his high-school years. Justice attended Thomas More College in nearby Crestview Hills, Kentucky, on a basketball scholarship, and once said, "I didn't love baseball back then."[2] Scouts from the Braves had seen the potential in the multisport star and the Braves drafted him in the fourth round of the June 1985 amateur draft.

The Braves sent Justice to the Pulaski Braves of the rookie-level Appalachian League. He batted just .245, but after hitting 10 home runs in 66 games and posting an OPS of .793 he was promoted to the low Class-A Sumter Braves in 1986. There Justice had his best minor-league season, slashing .300/.425/.509 with 10 home runs and 61 RBIs in 61 games. Justice led the team in most offensive categories. (His future Atlanta teammate Mark Lemke led the team in most of the others.)

Justice was promoted to the Durham Bulls (Class A-advanced) in midseason and finished the season with a combined .290/.419/.497 line with 22 home runs and 105 RBIs. His performance, particularly his power bat, earned him a move up to Double-A Greenville for 1987.

Justice struggled to adjust to Double-A ball as a 21-year-old (.227, 6 home runs), and was again at Greenville to start the 1988 season. Justice showed progress that season (.278, 9 home runs in 58 games) and was promoted to Triple-A Richmond, where he batted only .203 in 70 games. But in 1989 Justice put together a solid season: .261/.360/.430, a team-high 12 home runs, and a .789 OPS, second highest on the team. After the season *Baseball America* ranked him the number-nine prospect in the International League.

Justice was called up by the Braves for a week in late May. He made his major-league debut on May 24, starting in right field in a home game against the Pittsburgh Pirates. In his first at-bat, against righty Bob Walk, Justice grounded out to shortstop. The game went into extra innings, and in the 12th Justice got his first major-league hit, a line-drive single to right off Randy Kramer. Justice had only the one hit in 20 at-bats before being sent back to Richmond on the 31st. He was called back up in September and on the 19th hit his first major-league home run, off Houston ace Mike Scott. Justice started the 1990 season with Richmond but was brought up after batting .356 in 12 games. Justice hit 28 home runs playing either right field or first base in 127 games and was voted the National League Rookie of the Year.

From 1990 to 1996 Justice was a staple in the Braves lineup. In 801 games over that period he posted a .276/.375/.501 slash line with an .877 OPS. Justice was one of 25 players who hit over 150 homers and had more than 500 RBIs during the seven-year period, despite being hurt for most of the '96 season.

Dale Murphy's trade to the Philadelphia Phillies in early August 1990 paved the way for Justice to be moved permanently to right field. Francisco Cabrera replaced Justice at first base for the remainder of the season. Justice opened the 1991 season as the Braves' regular right fielder. That season he missed more than 50 games with injuries but returned with plenty of time to help the Braves World Series push. In 109 games he drove in 87 runs. During the NLCS vs. Pittsburgh, Justice hit his first postseason home run, off Pirates pitcher Bob Walk (the same pitcher he faced for his first major-league at-bat in 1989). In the World Series Atlanta faced the Minnesota Twins in what became known as the "Worst to First" Series. In 1990 both the Twins and the Braves had finished in last place in their divisions.

The Series went seven games; five were decided by a single run, and three games went into extra innings. The Series was headlined by the Game Seven pitching matchup of veteran Jack Morris and 24-year-old John Smoltz. The two dueled for nearly eight innings, with Smoltz leaving in the eighth inning with one out and giving up no runs. The Twins won the game and the Series in the 10th on Gene Larkin's RBI single. Morris went all the way for the shutout. Justice hit two homers and drove in six runs in the Series.

On face value some of Justice's numbers didn't look so good for the 1992 season but it was in part due to a slow start at the plate. Through May he hit just .190 with 4 homers and 11 RBIs in 35 games. For the remaining 109 games, Justice hit .279 with 17 homers and 61 RBIs. He posted one of his highest WAR totals for his career during the season, with a bWAR of 4.9 and an fWAR of 5.1. The Braves once again won the NL West in 1992 with a record of 98-64, and faced the Pittsburgh Pirates again in the NL Championship Series. During the NLCS, Justice hit .280 with two homers, but perhaps his biggest at-bat was in the ninth inning of Game Seven, when with the Braves losing 2-0 he hit a groundball off Doug Drabek that was booted by Pirates second baseman José Lind, which allowed Terry Pendleton to move to third base and Justice to reach first. Pendleton scored on a fly ball, which set the stage later in the inning for pinch-hitter Francisco Cabrera. On Cabrera's two-out single, Justice scored the tying run from third base and watched as Sid Bream rumbled home to send Atlanta into hysterics with a walk-off win. Justice had a disappointing World Series, going 3-for-19 as the Braves dropped their second straight Series, to Toronto in six games. That offseason, Justice married actress Halle Berry shortly after midnight on January 1, 1993 (though the wedding began on December 31, 1992) in a ceremony at their Atlanta-area home.[3]

In 1993 Justice arguably had his best season in the majors: a .270/.357/.515 slash line with 40 homers and 120 RBIs. He batted .288 and slugged .518 with runners in scoring position. He made his first All-Star team as the National League's starting right fielder and had one hit in the game. The Braves, and Justice, had a disappointing postseason as they fell to the Philadelphia Phillies in six games of the NLCS. Justice batted .143 with no homers and four RBIs. He placed third in the MVP voting behind Barry Bonds and Lenny Dykstra, and won his first Silver Slugger award.

The major leagues saw some reshuffling in 1994, with the Central Division being added to both leagues after the expansion in '93. In the strike-shortened season of 1994 Justice was batting .313 when the season came to a sudden halt. He made his second straight All-Star team, starting in right field again. Atlanta was down six games to Montreal in the NL East when the strike ended the season in August, maintaining their streak of division titles since the season hadn't been completed.

The strike settled, the 1995 season began with great expectations for the Braves, who were seemingly a staple in the NL postseason, having won their division the previous three seasons (excluding the 1994 season). The expansion to three divisions required the creation of a division series and a wild-card team. Justice had a down year at the plate (.253, 24 home runs, 78 RBIs in 120 games) but made headlines for very different reasons during the Braves' 1995 World Series year.

The Braves defeated Colorado in the NLDS and Cincinnati in the NLCS. They faced Cleveland in the World Series. Indians shortstop Omar Vizquel said of the Braves: "They know they can't win a World Series. … They already lost twice. When you have that on your mind, it's tough to get out."[4] It was no secret that the two teams were in for a difficult Series, with Cleveland having one of the more elite offenses and the Braves having the three-headed monster of Glavine-Maddux-Smoltz on the mound. Before Game Six, Justice criticized Braves fans in the media, saying, "If we get down 1-0 tonight the fans probably will boo us out of the stadium. … You have to do something great to get them out of their seats. Shoot, up in Cleveland, they were down three runs in the ninth inning and were still on their feet."[5] Justice was voicing his concern, as he felt that the fans weren't as excited and into the games as they were back when the Braves' great run began in 1991. Justice was booed by the Atlanta fans in the introductions before Game, Six, which Justice afterward admitted that he deserved, and that he had learned his lesson.[6]

Game Six of the World Series was possibly the biggest game of Justice's life. The Braves were leading the Series, three games to two. After his comments, which the *Atlanta Journal Constitution* ran under the headline "Justice Takes a Rip at Braves Fans," he was not the Atlanta crowd's favorite player. After he drew a seven-pitch walk in the bottom of the second inning, there was a mixture of boos and cheers from the crowd. In the bottom of the fourth, Justice crashed a two-out double into the left-center gap and off the wall, but was stranded at third with the bases loaded to end the inning. (The double was Justice's first extra-base hit of the 1995 postseason.) In the bottom of the sixth, Justice, leading off against Indians lefty reliever Jim Poole, unloaded on a 1-and-1 inside fastball and drove it over the right-field fence, giving the Braves a 1-0 lead. On the national broadcast Bob Costas said, "Dave Justice, all is forgiven in Atlanta." The lead held, as Tom Glavine threw eight shutout innings, turning it over to Mark Wohlers, who locked up the victory for Atlanta and clinched the city's first World Series triumph. Justice was Atlanta's hero.

After playing in only 40 games in 1996 season because of a shoulder injury, Justice was traded on March 25, 1997, to the Indians along with Marquis Grissom for outfielder Kenny Lofton and reliever Alan Embree. Braves GM John Schuerholz said in 2016 that it was the most difficult trade he's ever had to make, but cited a need to clear some payroll and acquire pitching as the motives behind the deal.[7]

After spending 12 years with the Braves organization, Justice moved to Cleveland, where he became the starting left fielder and had a career year. He made his third All-Star team and won his second Silver Slugger Award. He had a slash of .329/.418/.596 with a career-high 1.013 OPS. The Indians ran through the first two rounds of the playoffs, with Justice batting .300 average with two RBIs in the first two rounds. He batted only .185 in the World Series against the Florida Marlins, but had four RBIs as the Indians dropped the Series in seven games. After the season he was named the AL Comeback Player of the Year. He and Halle Berry divorced in June.[8]

Justice hit career home run 200 on May 3, 1998, off Jason Johnson of the Tampa Bay Devil Rays. But in that season and the next, his home-run production fell off to 21 each season, but with 88 RBIs each season. In 2000 he played relatively well for the first three months, hitting .262 with 21 homers and 58 RBIs through June. The New York Yankees were in the market for a power outfield bat, and obtained Justice for three players on June 29. For the Yankees, Justice split time between left field, right field, and DH, and went on a tear. He slashed .321/.402/.614 for the second half of the season, with 19 home runs and 57 RBIs. Justice finished the season with a .961 OPS.

The Yankees made the postseason and took on Oakland in the ALDS. Justice had a rather unspectacular ALDS (4-for-21) but stole the show in the ALCS against Seattle. In Game Six the Yankees (leading the Series three games to two) were down 4-3 in the bottom of the seventh. After Jose Vizcaino and Derek Jeter reached base, Justice, facing Arthur Rhodes, launched a 3-and-1 fastball off the upper-deck façade of Yankee Stadium, giving the Yankees a 6-4 lead that they held for a 9-6 victory and the pennant. Justice was named the ALCS MVP after mashing two homers and two doubles and driving in eight runs. He won his second career World Series as the Yankees defeated the Mets in five games. Justice didn't play his best in the Series but did collect three RBIs despite batting just .158 and going homerless.

Before the 2001 season, Justice married Rebecca Villalobos in February.[9] In 2001, at age 35, Justice played in only 111 games and his offense fell off sharply (.241, 51 RBIs). The Yankees traded him to the Mets after the season for Robin Ventura. After only seven days in the Mets organization, he was traded to Oakland for Mark Guthrie and Tyler Yates. Justice played in 118 games, mostly in left field or as the DH, and hit 11 homers with 49 RBIs. On July 28 he hit his 300th major-league home run, and went on to hit just five more. He was 37 years old in 2002 and retired as a player after the Athletics dropped Game Five of the ALDS to the Minnesota Twins.

Justice worked as a broadcaster for ESPN for two seasons. He also was an analyst for the Yankees' YES network for a few years, before leaving the network in 2008 after the 2007 California wildfires destroyed his family's home in San Diego County.[10] Justice was mentioned in the Mitchell Report in December 2007 that tied numerous players from the '90s and early 2000's to steroid and HGH use. Justice denied the claims on numerous occasions and said he hoped that other players in the report would do the same if the reports were untrue.[11] On August 17, 2007, Justice became the first player from the Braves run of 14 straight division titles to be inducted into the Braves Hall of Fame.[12] He also became eligible for the Baseball Hall of Fame in 2008, but received only one vote, which removed him from the ballot.

Justice and his wife, Rebecca, have three children: David Jr., Dionisio, and Raquel.[13] In the 2011 film *Moneyball,* Justice was portrayed by actor Steven Bishop in the story of the 2002 Oakland A's. (He said none of his scenes in the film actually happened in real life.)

Justice finished his 14-year major-league career with 305 home runs, 1,017 RBIs, and 1,571 hits. He is third in postseason RBIs with 63, fourth in postseason games played (112), and ninth in postseason hits (89). He finished with two top-five MVP finishes, a three-time All-Star, Rookie of the Year award, two-time Silver Slugger, an ALCS MVP, and two World Series championships. As of 2020 he resided in San Diego with his family.

Sources

In addition to the sources cited in the Notes, the author relied on Baseball-Reference.com and Fangraphs.com.

Notes

1. "Justice, David 1966," Encyclopedia.com, encyclopedia.com/education/news-wires-white-papers-and-books/justice-david-1966. Accessed December 11, 2019.
2. I.J. Rosenberg, "Whatever Happened to … David Justice," *Atlanta Journal Constitution,* September 17, 2015.
3. Don O'Briant, "Ringing in '93 – with Wedding Bells," *Atlanta Journal Constitution,* January 10, 1993.
4. Buster Olney, "Justice Asks Braves Fans to Prove Comments Wrong/Outfielder Says Support Isn't What It Was in '91," *Baltimore Sun,* October 29, 1995.
5. Jerome Holtzman, "In 1 Swing, Justice's Jeers Turn to Cheers," *Chicago Tribune,* October 29, 1995.
6. Holtzman..
7. I.J. Rosenberg, "Schuerholz: David Justice Trade Was Hardest to Make," *Atlanta Journal Constitution,* March 31, 2016.
8. "Divorce Between Halle Berry, David Justice Final," *Albany* (Georgia) *Herald,* June 25, 1997.
9. Michael Miller, "David Justice Opens Up about His Divorce from Halle Berry," *People,* November 9, 2015.
10. Andrea Naversen, "At Home with David & Rebecca Justice," *Ranch & Coast,* March 5, 2012.
11. "Justice Denies Claims Against Him in Mitchell Report," ESPN, December 14, 2007.
12. I.J. Rosenberg, "Whatever Happened to … David Justice."
13. Naversen.

Mike Kelly

BY JOEL RIPPEL

Mike Kelly

As a high-school baseball player in talent-rich Southern California, Mike Kelly was a late bloomer and didn't get a lot of attention from the Division I college baseball programs in the area.

"I had a good senior year," Kelly said, "but none of the local schools, the USCs, the UCLAs or the Cal State Fullertons, had any interest in me. I got no offers from any of those schools."[1]

Kelly would go on to put together one of the most memorable college baseball careers.

Michael Raymond Kelly was born to Ben and Betty Kelly in Los Angeles on June 2, 1970, and grew up in the Orange County suburb of Los Alamitos.

"Some of my earliest memories are of playing Wiffle Ball with my dad in the back yard," Kelly said. "I don't even know how old I was. My parents have been there since Day One. They were at every game in Little League. Every game in high school. They would drive out to see me play at (college). They've always been there."[2]

Kelly's high-school season got the attention of at least one major college program.

The Los Alamitos Griffins went 12-14 in Kelly's junior year (1987). In 1988 the Griffins and Kelly blossomed. He hit .486 as the Griffins improved to 21-7. Kelly was named first-team All-Orange County by the *Orange County Register* and third-team All-CIF (California Interscholastic Federation) Southern Section 5-A Division.

"(Arizona State coach) Jim Brock came out to see me play," said Kelly. "I think it was an all-star game. I hit a home run that game. He congratulated me on the home run and all that. I ended up getting a scholarship to ASU."[3]

After the season, Kelly was selected in the 24th round of the amateur draft by the New York Mets. That would cause Brock some concern.

Kelly had until the first day of fall classes at Arizona State to accept the Mets' reported offer of $70,000. On August 24 he attended the first day of classes, meaning he could not sign with the Mets. That was a relief to Brock; five members of Kelly's recruiting class had already signed professional contracts.

Kelly and fellow Orange County products Tommy Adams, who turned down a reported $90,000 offer from the Atlanta Braves, and Jim Austin, who had been drafted by the Kansas City Royals, showed for the first day of the fall semester at Arizona State.

"You look at their athletic ability and project it two or three years down the road and it's pretty exciting," said Brock.[4]

From the start of his freshman season, Kelly stood out. In nine games during the Sun Devils' fall practice schedule, Kelly hit .361, second-best on the team.

The Sun Devils, ranked fifth in the 1989 preseason poll by *Baseball America*, opened their 1989 season in early January by playing seven games in Taiwan. Kelly hit .400 with two home runs and seven RBIs as the Sun Devils went 5-2 to earn the championship of the International Baseball Invitational in Taichung City.

Kelly's potential was on display from the start. On March 28, in the Sun Devils' 7-6 loss to Washington State in the Riverside (California) Invitational, Kelly hit a home run that traveled an estimated 475 feet. The home run, his ninth of the season, cleared a 40-foot screen above the left-field fence.

In ASU's 3-2 victory over California in Tempe on April 23, Kelly hit a "drive to center (that) was still rising when it hit about one foot from the top of the 30-foot-high batter's eye in center field, 400 feet from home plate."[5]

For the season, Kelly batted .300 with 10 home runs and 56 RBIs in 58 games and was named a second-team All-American as the Sun Devils went 42-19.

His sophomore season was better. He hit .376 with 21 home runs and 82 RBIs in 68 games – the Sun Devils were 52-16 – to earn Pac-10 Player of the Year honors, and he was a consensus National Player of the Year.

Besides his offense, Kelly's sophomore season was highlighted by two memorable catches.

On May 12, with the Sun Devils leading Arizona 4-2 in the sixth inning in Tucson, Arizona's Jack Johnson hit a long drive to center with two runners on and two outs. Kelly raced to the fence at the 400-foot mark and leaped and caught the ball above the fence to preserve the Sun Devils' lead in an eventual 6-4 victory.

Asked if Kelly's catch was the best he had seen in his 19 seasons as ASU coach, Brock said, "College, pro, any form of baseball – it was the best. We've had guys reach over the fence before, but never with such an impact on a game. And he made one earlier in the game that can stand on its own merits. It was just about as good as you'll see."[6]

Kelly had made a sparkling catch earlier in the season. In a 9-5 loss to Texas in Austin on February 11, with the bases loaded in the bottom of the eighth, Kelly ran down a line drive near the warning track in right-center.

As a junior in 1991, Kelly hit .373 with 15 home runs and 56 RBIs to repeat as an All-American. Later in the year he was named the 1991 Golden Spikes Award winner as the top amateur baseball player in the nation.

In three seasons for the Sun Devils, Kelly hit .350 with 46 home runs (third-best in ASU history behind Bob Horner's 56 and Jeff Larish's 51) and 194 RBIs (sixth-best). He stole 59 bases in 68 attempts.

On June 3, 1991, the day after his 21st birthday, Kelly didn't have to wait long to hear his name announced. Seven minutes after the draft began – with the New York Yankees selecting high-school pitcher Brien Taylor with the first pick – the Atlanta Braves chose Kelly.

In the previous three drafts, the Braves had selected high-school players as their top pick – Chipper Jones in 1990, Tyler Houston in 1989, and Steve Avery in 1988.

"It's true we've always leaned to high-school kids," Braves director of player development and scouting Chuck LaMar said. "However, this is a unique individual. Mike is still improving. Usually in college, what you see is what you get. But in Mike Kelly's case, he's a collegiate player who has not reached his potential. We had 14 different people, over 30 games, look at him. We wanted to see him on the road, at home, under the lights and in the daytime."[7]

Talks between Kelly and the Braves took seven weeks before Kelly agreed to a reported package of $625,000 on July 22.

"It's taken a while for us to get this thing worked out," Kelly said, "but it has come together just fine. Both sides are happy about how it turned out. I'm thrilled about the opportunity to make this goal of mine to play professional baseball come true. This has been one of if not the most exciting times in my life. As soon as I meet the players and the coaches, I'm sure things will begin to settle down."[8]

The Braves were pleased with Kelly's signing. "Obviously we feel he has an outstanding future because of the way he approaches the game both physically and mentally," said LaMar. "He's a combination of speed and power that we want to build our major-league club around."[9]

Kelly joined the Braves in Pittsburgh for two days of workouts before being assigned to Durham of the Class-A Carolina League. After a slow start (1-for-10, 5 K's), he hit .250 with 6 home runs and 17 RBIs in 35 games.

Kelly was invited to Atlanta spring training as a nonroster player in 1992. But in the first week of camp, during a routine physical examination, a growth was found in his groin area. The growth – a benign tumor – was removed surgically and Kelly was sidelined until March 24.

He was assigned to Greenville of the Double-A Southern League. In 133 games, he batted .229 with 25 home runs and 71 RBIs. Greenville, whose roster included Chipper Jones and Javy Lopez, was 100-43.

Kelly was invited to spring training again in 1993. He played sparingly, batting .200 with one RBI in five games before being sent to the Braves' minor-league camp. Kelly spent the 1993 season with Richmond of the Triple-A International League. In 123 games, he batted .243 with 19 home runs and 58 RBIs.

Kelly went into spring training in 1994 battling Jarvis Brown for the final spot on the Braves' 25-man Opening Day roster. The Braves were looking for an outfielder to fill the roster spot that opened after Ron Gant suffered a broken leg, which sidelined him all season.

Kelly had a good spring, hitting .400 with two home runs and seven RBIs, and sealed his spot on the roster in the Braves' 7-5 exhibition victory over the Baltimore on April 1 in Atlanta. Kelly went 2-for-4 and in the third inning banged into the wall in left-center while making a catch of a drive hit by the Orioles' Chris Hoiles.

"It felt great. I was pumped," said Kelly. "I didn't expect to be with this club out of spring training. But when Chipper (Jones) got hurt. I got a chance. They told me in West Palm I'd made the club. I couldn't make myself believe it until I got to the stadium and saw my uni hanging there. And when I stepped out on the field this morning, I finally felt like a big leaguer."[10]

"Mike did a good job, but I'm not surprised," Braves manager Bobby Cox said. "He had a great spring – hit the ball well and played good defense."[11]

In the Braves' final exhibition game, Kelly scored the winning run in a 4-3 victory over the Chicago White Sox in Atlanta. The victory gave the Braves a 20-7 spring-training record, their best since moving to Atlanta.

The Braves opened the season with a seven-game road trip to the West Coast and won all seven. Kelly played a key role in three of the victories.

On April 5, the second game of the season, Kelly made his major-league debut. He entered the game in the bottom of the sixth inning as a defensive replacement for left fielder Ryan Klesko. In his first major-league at-bat, in the eighth inning against Padres reliever A.J. Sager, he popped out to second base.

On April 7 Kelly ran for Klesko in the ninth inning and scored the tying run. In the 11th inning, facing Sager again, he doubled to left for his first major-league hit. Kelly scored the go-ahead run on David Justice's single in the Braves' 10-8 victory over the Padres.

On April 9 Kelly again entered a game as a pinch-runner, scoring the winning run on a single by Jeff Blauser in the Braves' 2-1 victory over the Dodgers in Los Angeles.

Kelly got his first three major-league RBIs when he delivered a bases-loaded double in the eighth inning to break a 6-6 tie in the Braves' 9-6 victory over the Marlins on April 26 in Miami. The double – his fourth of the season – lifted his batting average to .250 in 20 at-bats.

Over the next week, Kelly, who was platooning with Klesko in left field, went 0-for-7. On May 4, the Braves sent him to Richmond. "I would love to keep playing him up here, but I can't justify playing him once every seven or days," said Cox.[12]

Kelly said, "It is probably the best thing for me to go down and get some at-bats."[13] He was recalled on July 8.

On July 18, Kelly's first major-league home run lifted the Braves to a 3-2 victory over the Pirates in Pittsburgh. Kelly, who was 3-for-4 for his first multiple-hit game in the majors, led off the seventh inning with a home run to left-center off Steve Cooke to break a 2-2 tie.

Kelly's final major-league games of the season were memorable. He went 6-for-14 in a three-game series (August 9-11) in Colorado. In the Braves' 13-0 victory on August 11, he went 4-for-6 with a double and two RBIs. It was the final day of the season, as the Major League Baseball Players Association went on strike.

But Kelly's season wasn't over. On August 12, he was optioned to Richmond.

"He didn't have to (accept the assignment), but we always expected that he would take it," general manager John Schuerholz said. "This is an opportunity for him to keep playing."[14]

Kelly finished the season in Richmond. For the season, he hit .262 with 15 home runs and 45 RBIs in 82 games with Richmond. In 30 games with Atlanta, Kelly batted .273 with 2 home runs, and 9 RBIs. With 13 of his 21 hits for extra bases, he had a slugging percentage of .506.

Spring training was delayed in 1995 before the players and owners reached a settlement on April 2. Kelly had a quiet spring, hitting one home run in the Braves' 11 exhibition games. When the regular season opened on April 26, he was on the Braves' roster.

On Opening Day in Atlanta, Kelly was the Braves' starting left fielder against San Francisco Giants left-hander Terry Mulholland. He platooned with Klesko in left field, then was sent to Richmond on August 11 after the Braves acquired outfielder Luis Polonia from the New York Yankees. Kelly was hitting .194 with 46 strikeouts in 129 at-bats.

"Mike needs the at-bats, it's as simple as that," said Cox.[15]

Kelly got off to a slow start in Richmond, but over the final three weeks of the International League regular season, he went 11-for-30 to finish with a .289 average in 15 games for Richmond.

After Richmond's playoff series was over, Kelly joined the Braves on September 10 in Miami and doubled as a pinch-hitter in the Braves' 5-4 loss in 11 innings to the Marlins. It was his only hit in the final three weeks of the regular season; he played in 12 games as a pinch-hitter or defensive replacement and went 1-for-8 with one RBI. Overall, in 97 games with the Braves, he hit .190 with 3 home runs and 17 RBIs.

In the final week of the regular season, the Braves asked Kelly to play winter ball, and he went to Venezuela. In late November, after hitting just .217 in 19 games, Kelly abruptly ended his season and returned to the United States.

On January 9, 1996, the Braves traded Kelly to the Cincinnati Reds for minor-league pitcher Chad Fox and a player to be named.

According to the *Atlanta Journal Constitution*, "Kelly … had fallen out of favor with the club over the last season, especially last month when he abruptly left his winter league team in Venezuela. He will have a chance to play regularly for the Reds – the club lost left fielder Ron Gant and backup Jerome Walton to free agency."[16]

"I left Venezuela because I was sick the whole time and losing weight and it was hurting my performance," said Kelly. "I wanted to be traded. Atlanta has a lot of great players and breaking into that lineup was no easy task."[17]

"He has not had much of an opportunity with the structure of our club," said Schuerholz. "It was disappointing that he left (winter ball). I wish he would have stayed and worked at it hard."[18]

Kelly made a quick impression in the Reds training camp, hitting three home runs in his first 10 spring-training at-bats, and late in spring training was given a vote of confidence by Reds manager Ray Knight.

Said Kelly: "He just came over and said, 'Mike, you know you're going to be my center fielder. I'm going to just let you go out there and play and probably give you 500 at-bats. Just go out there and have fun and relax.'"[19]

Kelly was 0-for-11 in the Reds' first four games, then went 8-for-23 between April 6 and April 15 and 0-for-7 in three games between April 16 and April 19, which dropped his batting average to .195. He was optioned to Triple-A Indianapolis.

"I saw a guy in spring training who was much more aggressive at the plate, defensively and on the bases – and playing happy," Knight said. "I think his lack of success at the plate caused him to struggle a bit in every aspect of the game. I told him he hadn't let me down. He needs to work on the mental part of the game. He needs to be aggressive in the outfield and not be tentative. … I don't want him to fear failure. It seemed like he was always worried."[20]

Kelly was recalled in the first week of July, then was returned to Indianapolis on July 12.

Kelly spent the rest of the season in Indianapolis. Overall, he hit .209 with 8 home runs and 30 RBIs in 88 games. On September 1, when the Reds recalled five players from Indianapolis, Kelly remained with Indianapolis for its two American Association playoff series.

Despite a solid spring training with the Reds in 1997 – 13-for-41 (.317) with three home runs and six RBIs – Kelly was outrighted to Chattanooga on March 27 after clearing waivers. After hearing the news, Kelly said he thought about retiring.

"I'd be lying if I said I didn't think about going home," Kelly said. "(His father Ben Kelly) said I was too young to quit. Basically, it was 'keep the faith.'"[21]

Kelly got off to a good start in Chattanooga. In 15 games, he hit .350 with 3 home runs and 12 RBIs to earn a promotion to Indianapolis. In 27 games with Indianapolis, he hit .348 with 7 home runs and 18 RBIs. On May 24 he was recalled by the Reds.

"I'm happy for him," Knight said. "I think it's a testament to his intestinal fortitude. … he was demoted to Double A and it had no negative effect on him. He tore up that league, and was tearing up Triple A, too."[22]

Kelly spent the rest of the season with the Reds, hitting a career-high .293 with 6 home runs and 19 RBIs in 73 games.

On November 11 the Reds traded Kelly to the expansion Tampa Bay Devil Rays after they agreed to take Dmitri Young in the expansion draft and send him to the Reds. Acquired a week before the expansion draft, Kelly became the first player on the Devil Rays roster.

"I'm pretty excited and pretty surprised at the same time," Kelly said. "I always figured there'd be a chance I wouldn't be protected and might be taken, but it never entered my mind I'd be traded to the Devil Rays."[23]

Kelly enjoyed a good training camp with the Devil Rays, hitting .390. On Opening Day he went 0-for-5 and suffered a groin strain. The injury sidelined Kelly the next six games, and on April 9 he was placed on the 15-day disabled list retroactive to April 1.

On April 15, Kelly was sent to Triple-A Durham on a rehabilitation assignment. After four games with Durham, he was activated on April 22.

He returned to the lineup on April 23, going 3-for-5 with two home runs – his first multihome-run game in the majors – in a 12-5 victory at Texas. He spent the rest of the season with Devil Rays, hitting .240 with 10 home runs and 33 RBIs in 106 games.

With about a week to go in spring training in 1999, the Devil Rays released Kelly.

"It wasn't an easy decision," said manager Larry Rothschild. "I think Mike Kelly will be in the major leagues somewhere this season. Mike is a class person who I have lot of respect for, and he is a talented baseball player. We beat our heads in trying to figure out how we could get that talent to show up."[24]

For general manager Chuck LaMar, who was with the Braves when Kelly was drafted, the decision was difficult. "We would not have won as many games as we did last year (63) without the contribution of Mike Kelly," LaMar said. "Today was a tough day because we appreciate what Mike did last year for us, and he's always been a class act on and off the field."[25]

Two days after being released by the Devil Rays, Kelly signed a minor-league contract with the Colorado Rockies. When the Rockies placed Larry Walker on the disabled list in the first week of the regular season, Kelly was recalled. He made his Rockies' debut on April 9 when he doubled in a run as a pinch-hitter in a game against the Dodgers in Los Angeles. Two days later he went 0-for-1 in the Rockies' 8-5 loss to San Diego in Denver. It was his last major-league at-bat.

After Walker was reactivated on April 14, Kelly was returned to Colorado Springs. He spent the rest of the season there, batting .277 with 9 and 50 RBIs in 114 games.

Kelly was granted free agency on October 4 and signed a minor-league contract with the New York Mets. He was in spring training with the Mets but was reassigned to their minor-league camp on March 19, 2000, then released on the 30th.

Kelly did not play in 2000, 2001 or 2002. In January of 2003, he signed a minor-league contract with the Kansas City Royals. He spent the 2003 season with Triple-A Omaha. He hit a career-high .296 with 14 home runs and 65 RBI in 100 games and played in the Triple-A All-Star Game in July.

After the season Kelly again became a free agent. In February of 2004, he signed a minor-league contract with the New York Yankees. He spent the season with Triple-A Columbus, hitting .253 with 15 home runs and 50 RBIs in 84 games. After the season, he retired at the age of 34.

In the spring of 2014, Arizona State honored Kelly by placing his jersey number on the Sun Devils' Wall of Fame. In June of 2015, Kelly was inducted into the College Baseball Hall of Fame.

Sources

In addition to the sources cited in the Notes, the author consulted collegebaseballhall.org, Baseball-Reference.com, Newspapers.com, Retrosheet.org and thesundevils.com.

Notes

1. Mike Kelly Hall of Fame Induction, July 2, 2015, collegebaseballhall.org.
2. Mike Kelly Hall of Fame Induction.
3. Mike Kelly Hall of Fame Induction.
4. Bob Eger, "Baseball Recruits Are Set," *Arizona Republic* (Phoenix), August 25, 1988: E8.
5. Eger, "ASU Catches Break on Dropped Fly, Sweeps Cal," *Arizona Republic*, April 24, 1989: D4.
6. Eger, "Kelly Snatches Victory from Jaws of Defeat for ASU," *Arizona Republic*, May 13, 1990: D1.
7. Eger, "Braves Tap ASU's Kelly," *Arizona Republic*, June 4, 1991: D1.
8. "Braves Sign Ex-Los Alamitos, ASU Standout Kelly," *Orange County Register* (Anaheim, California), July 23, 1991: E4.
9. "Braves Sign Ex-Los Alamitos, ASU Standout Kelly."
10. Tom McCollister, "Kelly Shines in 7-5 Victory over Orioles," *Atlanta Journal Constitution*, April 2, 1994: D1.
11. McCollister.
12. I.J. Rosenberg, "Kelly Sent to Richmond; Brown Recalled," *Atlanta Journal Constitution*, May 5, 1994: G6.
13. Rosenberg, "Kelly Sent to Richmond."
14. Rosenberg, "Mike Kelly to Play at Richmond During Strike," *Atlanta Journal Constitution*, August 13, 1994. D4.

15 Rosenberg, "Yanks' Polonia Acquired for Bench Help," *Atlanta Journal-Constitution*, August 12, 1995: D5.

16 Rosenberg, "Braves Trade Kelly to Reds," *Atlanta Journal Constitution*, January 10, 1996: C5.

17 Rosenberg, "Braves Trade Kelly to Reds."

18 Rosenberg, "Braves Trade Kelly to Reds."

19 Associated Press, "Kelly Gets Chance as Reds Starter," *Orange County Register*, March 31, 1996: C2.

20 Chris Haft, "Howard Back; Kelly Demoted," *Cincinnati Enquirer*, April 21, 1996: C6.

21 John Fay, "Kelly Owes Promotion to Demotion," *Cincinnati Enquirer*, May 25, 1997: C5.

22 Fay.

23 John Erardi, "Are Reds Deals with New Clubs the Only Deals?" *Cincinnati Enquirer*, November 12, 1997: D1.

24 Joe Henderson, "Kelly, First Roster Ray, Is Cut," *Tampa Tribune*, April 1, 1999: 76.

25 Henderson.

Ryan Klesko

BY JOEL RIPPEL

Ryan Klesko

Ryan Klesko caught the attention of scouts early in his high-school baseball career. Scouts clamored for the prime spots behind home plate to watch Klesko, a freshman on the Westminster (California) High School varsity.

Klesko hit 278 home runs and batted .279 in a 16-year major-league career. But the scouts weren't there to watch him hit. They were there to watch him pitch.

"I went to Ron LeFebvre's pitching school eight years," Klesko said. "At first I was going for fun. But after a certain point I was good enough that I knew I would do something in baseball after high school. I thought it would be pitching."[1]

Klesko, a hard-throwing left-hander, struck out 138 in 96⅔ innings as a sophomore and junior and compiled a 13-6 won-lost record in his first three seasons on the Westminster varsity. After his junior season (in 1988) he was a member of the US Junior Olympic Team. But an elbow injury limited him to playing first base as a high-school senior.

"I was always a pretty good hitter, too," Klesko said. "When I was a freshman and sophomore at Ron's school, I started batting against college pitchers and I did fine. I knew I could make it as a hitter, too."[2]

Klesko credited his mother, Lorene, with helping him reach the major leagues. Klesko's parents, Howard and Lorene, divorced while he was in high school. Before the divorce, Howard Klesko was frequently gone for work in Southern California oil fields, so Lorene, who worked packing aerospace parts, took on a second job cleaning houses on weekends to pay for Ryan's pitching lessons, built a pitching mound in the backyard of their home and took on the role of catcher for him (something she also did for his two sisters, who were good softball players).

"When I was a kid, my mom would watch baseball on TV and say to me, 'See those guys? You're going to be one of them someday,'" said Klesko. "I never thought it was possible, but she always believed in me."[3]

During his senior year, Klesko hit .347 with 5 home runs and 18 RBIs and earned All-Sunset League honors for the fourth consecutive season. In early May of 1989, he signed a letter of intent to play baseball for Arizona State. In early June, Klesko was selected in the fifth round of the amateur draft. Eleven days after the draft, the Braves opened a three-game series at Dodger Stadium and invited Klesko to take batting practice.

"A lot of teams came to see me when I was in high school," said Klesko. "They thought only of me as a pitcher. It had everything to do with how hard I threw. That is what they wanted. I was a good hitter in high school but they weren't focused on anything else and I played in an awful big park so it was hard to hit it out. It all worked out after hitting with the Braves at Dodger Stadium. I think they really realized then just how good I could hit and the power I had."[4]

Several days later, the Braves signed Klesko and assigned him to their farm team in the rookie Gulf Coast League. Florida was an adjustment for Klesko.

"I remember getting to Bradenton and it was hot as crap and hot and rainy at the same time," he said. "There were also these big mosquitoes. I went in and told the coach I hated it, was depressed and wanted to go home. I said how do I get out of here? He said hit! So I did, and I was gone very quickly."[5]

Klesko responded by hitting .404 with one home run and 16 RBIs in 17 games with the GCL Braves and was promoted to Sumter (South Carolina) of the Class-A South Atlantic League. In 25 games with Sumter, he hit .289 with one home run and 12 RBIs.

Klesko returned to Sumter in 1990 and hit .368 with 10 home runs and 38 RBIs in 63 games. He was named a South Atlantic League All-Star and was named the league's top prospect. At midseason he was promoted to Durham of the high Class-A Carolina League and hit .274 with 7 home runs and 47 RBIs in 77 games.

He got off to a slow start in 1991 with Greenville of the Double-A Southern League. As the youngest everyday player in the Southern League (he turned 20 in June), he hit just .190 in April. But he regrouped to hit .347 with 9 home runs and 38 RBIs in May and June. For the season, he hit .291 with 14 home runs and 67 RBIs in 126 games. He walked 75 times and had a .404 on-base percentage as he earned the league's MVP honor and was named the number-2 prospect (behind Royce Clayton) in minor-league baseball by Howe Sportsdata.[6]

In his fourth professional season, Klesko made his Triple-A and major-league debuts. In 123 games with Richmond of the International League, he batted .251 with 17 home runs and 59 RBIs. He was called up by the Braves on September 11 and made his big-league debut the next day in Houston. Facing veteran reliever Doug Jones as a pinch-hitter in the ninth inning, he struck out in the Braves' 9-3 victory. Over the next three weeks, Klesko saw pinch-hitting duty and made one start at first base. On October 1, against San Francisco in Atlanta, he went 0-for-4 with his first major-league RBI (on an infield grounder) in the Braves' 6-5 victory in 10 innings. In 13 games, he was hitless in 14 at-bats.

Klesko opened the 1993 season in Richmond but was recalled by the Braves on April 19. Three days later, in Miami, he got his first major-league hit – a pinch-single in the ninth inning off the Marlins' Bryan Harvey. On April 27, in Atlanta, he hit his first major-league home run – a pinch-hit, two-run home run in the ninth inning off Pittsburgh's Tim Wakefield. The home run tied the game and forced extra innings before the Pirates won 6-2 in 11 innings. Klesko hit .273 in 14 games but was returned to Richmond on May 18.

Back at Richmond, Klesko batted .274 with 22 home runs and 74 RBIs in 98 games. A highlight came when he was named the most valuable player representing the International League in the Triple-A All-Star Game after going 4-for-4 with two home runs and three RBIs in the National League's 14-3 victory over the AL.[7]

On September 10 Klesko rejoined the Braves. On September 15 in Atlanta, he hit a two-run home run as a pinch-hitter to start the Braves' five-run rally in the bottom of the ninth in a 7-6 victory over Cincinnati. In his two stints with the Braves, Klesko was 6-for-17 with two home runs and five RBIs in 22 games.

Klesko made Atlanta's Opening Day roster in 1994. Other than brief minor-league rehab stints in 1995 and 2006, he spent the rest of his 19-year professional career in the major leagues. His opportunity to make the Opening Day roster involved a move from first base to the outfield. Ron Gant, a mainstay in Atlanta's outfield the previous four seasons, suffered a broken leg in a dirt-bike accident just before the start of spring training. The injury forced Gant to miss the entire season and Braves manager Bobby Cox used a platoon of Klesko and Dave Gallagher in left field. Klesko batted .278 with 17 homers in 245 at-bats and 92 games before the season ended when the players strike began on August 12. Klesko finished third (behind the Dodgers' Raul Mondesi and Houston's John Hudek) in the National League Rookie of the Year voting.

In the abbreviated spring training of 1995, Klesko had the best batting average (.370) of Braves regulars, but he again opened the season in a platoon with Mike Kelly. In the Braves' sixth game of the season (May 2 at Florida), Klesko suffered a thumb injury and he was placed on the 15-day disabled list. He returned to the lineup on May 18.

Klesko struggled at the plate in his return (with no home runs in his first 57 at-bats of the season), but in early June he started hitting. He broke out on June 6 with his first two home runs of the season (including the first grand slam of his career) and a career-high six RBIs in Atlanta's 17-3 victory over the visiting Chicago Cubs. One other noteworthy home run came on July 24, when he homered off Pirates reliever Dan Plesac in Pittsburgh. It was the first home run of his career off a left-hander.

For the season, Klesko hit .310 with 23 home runs and 70 RBIs in 107 games and 329 at-bats. The Braves made the 1995 postseason, and in the Division Series against Colorado, he went 7-for-15 with an RBI. Klesko went hitless in the Braves' four-game sweep of Cincinnati in the Championship Series, but he took center stage in the World Series.

After the Braves defeated Cleveland in the first two games in Atlanta, Klesko hit home runs in all three games at Jacobs Field in Cleveland to become the first player to homer in three consecutive World Series road games. His home run in the sixth inning of the Braves' 5-2 victory in Game Four landed near where his mother, Lorene, was sitting in the bleachers.

"It missed her by about 10 feet," said Klesko. "She went down and got it, but she had to bribe them for it. It cost her a baseball bat, two balls autographed by our whole team and a couple of pictures. But it was worth it."[8]

For the Series, won by the Braves in six games, Klesko was 5-for-16 with three home runs and four RBIs.

Klesko got off to a good start in 1996. He hit 10 home runs – a club record for April – with 20 RBIs and a .337 batting average. In early June he had at least one RBI in seven consecutive games (June 2-9). Healthy all season, he played in 153 games and batted .282 with a career-high 34 home runs and then career-high 93 RBIs. Klesko batted just .176 with two home runs and five RBIs in 14 postseason games as the Braves reached the World Series again (losing to the Yankees).

Klesko's production declined a little in 1997 as he hit 24 home runs and had 84 RBIs in 143 games, but he finished the regular season strong. From August 28 to September 17, he hit six home runs in 13 games. One of those home runs helped Klesko reach a milestone. On September 17 he slugged his fifth career grand slam in the Braves' 10-2 victory over the New York Mets. The grand slam – the 100th home run of Klesko's career – was Atlanta's 12th of the season, which broke the major-league record of 11 (set in 1996 by Baltimore and Seattle). In the opening game of the NLDS, his solo home run in the second inning gave the Braves a 2-0 lead in their 2-1 victory over Houston. He homered in each of the first two games (against Florida) in the NLCS.

Klesko's 1998 season was interrupted when he had an appendectomy on June 29. He missed the

Braves' six games before the All-Star break and their first three games after the break before returning to action on July 12. For the season, he batted .274 with 18 home runs and 70 RBIs. But after striking out 129 times in 1996 and 130 times in 1997, he struck out only 66 times.

The 1999 season, which saw Klesko split his time between first base and left field, was his last in Atlanta. In 133 games, he hit .297 with 21 home runs and 80 RBIs. In 12 playoff games, Klesko hit .219 and one home run as the Braves made their third World Series appearance in five seasons.

On December 22 the Braves traded Klesko, second baseman Bret Boone, and pitching prospect Jason Shiell to the San Diego Padres for first baseman Wally Joyner, outfielder Reggie Sanders, and second baseman Quilvio Veras.

"I was upset at first because the Braves were so good. But (Padres manager) Bruce (Bochy) brought me in and said I was going to be an everyday player," Klesko said. "I remember when (Braves general manager) John (Schuerholz) told me about the trade. He said, 'Ryan, I think you are going to be happy.' I knew then that I was going to San Diego, Anaheim, or Los Angeles. It was fun going back home and I had good seasons there. I cut down on my swing and stride and things worked out."[9]

Klesko's first season in Southern California was one of his best overall. As the Padres' first baseman, he batted .283 with 26 home runs and 92 RBIs in 145 games. He set career highs in walks (91) and stolen bases (23).

His second season with the Padres saw him record another 20-home run, 20-stolen base season – joining Dave Winfield as the only Padre (at that point) to have accomplished that more than once – and was highlighted by his only All-Star Game appearance. In 84 games before the All-Star break, he hit 17 home runs and had 75 RBIs (a team record for RBIs prior to the All-Star break). On July 10 in Seattle, he drove in the NL's only run with a sacrifice fly in the AL's 4-1 victory. In 146 games, Klesko batted .286 with 30 home runs and career highs in RBIs (113) and runs scored (105).

In 2002, Klesko's regular-season debut was delayed as he sat out the first four games (April 1-5) for his involvement in a bench-clearing brawl between the Padres and the Anaheim Angels in an exhibition game in Tempe, Arizona, on March 9. In the first inning of that game, Klesko had charged the mound after being hit in the lower back by a pitch from Aaron Sele.

After the four-game penalty, Klesko was in the lineup almost every day as he batted .300 – his highest average since he hit .310 for Atlanta in 1995 – with 29 home runs and 95 RBIs in 146 games. The season was highlighted by a career-high 16-game hitting streak (April 9-28) and reaching base safely in 56 consecutive games from April 9 to June 14 (the longest streak in the major leagues that season). After the season, he was named the Padres' MVP by the San Diego Chapter of the Baseball Writers' Association of America.

After playing in 145, 146, and 146 games, respectively, in the previous seasons, Klesko was limited to 121 games in 2003 and missed the final month of the season after shoulder surgery. For the season, he hit a then career-low .252 with 21 home runs and 67 RBIs.

His 2004 season got off to a slow start and included a stint on the 15-day disabled list (May 28-June 16) because of a right oblique strain. But he batted .310 after the All-Star break to finish with a .291 average in 127 games. He hit 32 doubles but only nine home runs to go with 66 RBIs. He reached a milestone when he hit his 250th career home run in the Padres' 14-5 victory over the Reds in Cincinnati on August 13.

The 2005 season saw Klesko lead the Padres in home runs (18) for the third time and the Padres' return to the postseason for the first time since 1998. Klesko was 2-for-10 in the Cardinals' three-game sweep of the Padres in the NLDS.

Klesko missed all but the final two weeks of the 2006 season. Bothered by soreness in his throwing shoulder in spring training, he started the season on the disabled list. After receiving two cortisone shots, he considered trying to play through the pain. But after having an MRI, Klesko underwent surgery on April 10.

"It's probably best to go ahead and do it instead of having a roller-coaster all year," said Klesko. "The MRI did not show very good news."[10]

Klesko hoped he would be able to return around the All-Star break but wasn't activated until late September after an eight-game rehab assignment with Lake Elsinore (California League). Over the final two weeks of the season with the Padres, he was 3-for-4 with two walks and two RBIs as a pinch-hitter. He was on the Padres' postseason roster and went 2-for-3 as a pinch-hitter in their loss to the St. Louis Cardinals in the NLDS. After the season the Padres declined the option of Klesko's 2007 contract.

On December 19, 2006, Klesko agreed to a one-year, $1.75 million contract with the San Francisco Giants, where he was reunited with Bruce Bochy, who left the Padres after the 2006 season to become the Giants manager. In 116 games in 2007, he batted .260 with six home runs and 44 RBIs in 362 at-bats. After the season Klesko filed for free agency. In April of 2008, he announced his retirement. For his 16-season major-league career, he batted .279 with 278 home runs and 987 RBIs in 1,736 regular-season games. In 62 postseason games – in seven seasons – he batted .236 with 10 home runs and 22 RBIs.

Klesko was asked about spending the early portion of his big-league career being platooned by Braves manager Bobby Cox.

"Bobby and I were always good," said Klesko, "but I wanted to play every game. I think he would want any player to want to be out there every day. What it came down to is, I played for two of the best managers in the game in Bobby Cox and Bruce Bochy. I did get to hit a lot more against lefties under Bruce but the Braves gave me my chance and we won big there."[11]

After retiring, Klesko made his home near Macon, Georgia, with his wife and son. He has invested in real estate (more than 7,000 acres in several states) and he owns 17 rental homes. He has hosted an outdoor television program called *Campfire Stories* on the Pursuit channel on Direct TV.

Sources

In addition to the sources cited in the Notes, the author also consulted Baseball-Reference.com, mlb.com, newspapers.com, and retrosheet.com.

Notes

1. Mike Eisenbath, "Minor League Report: Making His Big Pitch at the Plate," *The Sporting News*, September 2, 1991: 33.
2. Ibid.
3. Gerry Callahan, "Baseball. Sultan of Swat," *Sports Illustrated*, April 8, 1996: 66.
4. I.J. Rosenberg, "Whatever Happened to Ryan Klesko," myajc.com, August 6, 2015.
5. Ibid.
6. Jim Keller, "Top 10 for the Future," *The Sporting News*, September 2, 1991: 33.
7. The Triple-A All-Star Game featured players from each of the three Triple-A leagues (American Association, International League, and Pacific Coast League). An MVP from each league was designated after the game.
8. I.J. Rosenberg, "Klesko Will Start in Left Despite Pain in Thumb," *Atlanta Journal/Constitution*, October 28, 1995: D5.
9. I.J. Rosenberg, "Whatever Happened to Ryan Klesko," myajc.com, August 6, 2015.
10. "Around The Majors: Padres' Klesko Out Two to Four Months," *Los Angeles Times*, April 9, 2006: D10.
11. I.J. Rosenberg, "Whatever Happened to Ryan Klesko," myajc.com, August 6, 2015.

Brian Kowitz

BY JACK ZERBY

Brian Kowitz

Brian Kowitz, a speedy, defensively-gifted outfielder, worked his way from college stardom through five-plus minor-league seasons to a call-up with the Atlanta Braves that, brief as it was, earned him a World Series championship ring.

The compact (5-foot-10, 180 pounds) Kowitz was a schoolboy phenom in Baltimore, then an Atlantic Coast Conference Player of the Year before the Braves made him a ninth-round pick in the June 1990 draft and he embarked on his professional career. Although he advanced steadily through the minors and was having a solid International League season at Triple-A Richmond when promoted to the majors in June 1995, Kowitz was returned to Richmond when David Justice came off the disabled list. By the next season Kowitz cut his ties with Atlanta and bounced around other International League outposts affiliated with American League teams. At age 26, he left Organized Baseball, finished his bachelor's degree, then returned to play a few games of professional independent baseball in 2000. After baseball he concentrated on a career in finance and insurance and became active in community affairs in suburban Baltimore.

Brian Mark Kowitz ("Co-wits") was born in Baltimore on August 7, 1969, to Jack and Patricia A. Kowitz. Jack, a retired lawyer, and Patricia now live in Southwest Florida. Brian has a younger brother, David, a Baltimore attorney.

Jack's parents – Brian's paternal grandparents – Ben and Shirley Schneiderman Kowitz, met in the Budzyn concentration camp in Poland during World War II; Holocaust survivors, they reunited and were married in 1945. They emigrated to Baltimore in 1949. Initially working as a night-shift upholsterer, Ben saved enough money to open a grocery store, and at the time of his death in 2002, owned a chain of 13 grocery stores in West and Southwest Baltimore, managed by his sons Joseph and Ervin.[1] Like Jack, a fourth Kowitz son, Ronald, is also a retired lawyer.

Left-handed all the way, Brian excelled at baseball, basketball, and football at Boys' Latin School of Maryland, a Baltimore prep school better known for its lacrosse program. As a senior in the 1986-87 academic year, he passed for more than 900 yards as the Lakers' quarterback, led the basketball team with just shy of 17 points per game,[2] and was named honorable mention as an outfielder on the All-Metro-Baltimore baseball team.[3] In the summer of 1987 he was a member of the Randallstown-Baltimore County Liberty Road

League senior all-star team in National Amateur Baseball Federation competition; Kowitz's bases-loaded double in the top of the eighth inning paced his team to the Federation World Series title in Youngstown, Ohio, as Liberty Road defeated the Long Island Tigers, 7-6.[4]

Kowitz moved on to a solid baseball career at Clemson University, although he had been predicted to have the lowest ceiling of the three scholarship players the South Carolina baseball powerhouse recruited from the Baltimore area in 1987.[5] He manned all three outfield spots for the Tigers for three seasons with only a single error committed near the end of his junior-year campaign in 1990 marring his defensive work, and authored a 37-game hitting streak that same season, lifting him to a .403 batting average.[6] He explained, "I'm more mature at the plate. I'm taking every pitch one at a time. Plus, I'm hitting the left-handed curveball, and I've never done that in the past."[7] He also gave credit to the academic preparation he received at Boys' Latin: "I'm dyslexic, and I got the attention I needed at BL."[8]

Kowitz's fine season was rewarded with his selection as 1990 Atlantic Coast Conference Player of the Year. His 1989 Clemson coach, Bill Wilhelm, said, "I think it's very appropriate that Brian got this award because I know how hard he's worked to make himself a better player."[9] Kowitz was a Clemson honor-roll student with a three-year grade-point average over 3.0,[10] but Wilhelm predicted that he could have a decision to make that spring: continue school or opt for a professional baseball contract.

The Braves fulfilled that prediction, selecting Kowitz in the ninth round of the June 1990 draft. He signed, putting school and his solid academics on a back burner for the time being. Atlanta started him at the short-season Rookie League level, with Pulaski (Virginia) in the Appalachian League. Kowitz got off to an excellent start, hitting .324 with some speed (13-for-20 in stolen bases) and surprising power (of his 59 hits, 13 were doubles, one a triple, and eight were home runs); he slugged Appalachian League pitching at a .538 rate, the highest in his professional career. He was named to the Appalachian League All-Star team[11] and was promoted three rungs to Double-A Greenville (South Carolina) in the Southern League for 20 games as the 1990 season wound down.

To open the 1991 season, Kowitz, seen by the Braves as a leadoff hitting possibility, was assigned one level lower than Greenville, to the venerable Durham Bulls in the high-A Carolina League. He hit .254 in 354 plate appearances there and again earned promotion to Greenville, this time for 35 games. Kowitz played with the same teams but in a different progression in 1992. He opened the season at Greenville and hit .286 in 21 games, but on May 10 was assigned back to Durham. There, as Kowitz became more familiar with professional pitching and was spotted lower in the batting order, he upped his average to .301 and drove in an impressive 64 runs.

Atlanta kept Kowitz at Greenville for most of the 1993 season. He solved Southern Association pitching for a .278 average in 514 plate appearances – working 60 walks against 56 strikeouts; this time his late-season move was to the Triple-A Richmond Braves in the International League. Kowitz got 54 plate appearances there in 12 games and closed out the year at .277 between Greenville and Richmond.

With all of baseball, Kowitz went through tumult when a Players Association strike ended major-league play after August 11, 1994, wiped out the postseason, and extended into February 1995.

That season, 1994, Kowitz had been initially assigned to the Braves' minor-league spring-training camp. He was called up to the big club near the end of camp and responded with game-winning hits on March 27 and April 2.[12] Atlanta manager Bobby Cox had high praise for Kowitz after these heroics: "I like Brian Kowitz. He's a college kid and he never makes an error. And he's always hit. I've always thought that he was going to hit with us."[13] But with an outfield of Justice, Ryan Klesko, and Roberto Kelly, and with Deion Sanders and Tony Tarasco in reserve, Kowitz, now 25, was ticketed for further Triple-A seasoning at Richmond in 1994. He excelled there, hitting an even .300 in 519 plate appearances as an everyday outfielder, driving home 57 runs, and stealing 22 bases in 30 tries. He even got a pitching win on May 12, when he was called in from left field as Richmond's fifth pitcher in the 15th inning of a scoreless tie against Scranton/Wilkes-Barre at Richmond. Kowitz navigated two scoreless innings but gave up the first run of the game in the top of the 17th. Leading off the home half, however, he singled, then scored the tying run and was the winning pitcher as Richmond scored again later in the inning and won, 2-1, in 5 hours and 7 minutes.[14]

That September, as major-league play had been stilled by the strike but the minors continued, Kowitz was a crucial element in Richmond's Governor's Cup three-game sweep over Syracuse to the 1994 International League championship, with a pair of home runs in the Braves' 11-7 win in the second game.

But despite his accomplishments in late spring training, Cox's accolades, his fine season in Triple A, and his contributions in the league championship series, Kowitz wasn't on Atlanta's 40-man roster when the Rule 5 draft rolled around in December 1994. Uncertainty about whether the strike would wipe out the 1995 season could have been a factor, but for whatever reason, the Braves left Kowitz exposed. The Minnesota Twins selected him and placed him on their 40-man roster; Kowitz, hoping to make the majors with Minnesota, worked on conditioning back at home in Owings Mills, the Baltimore suburb where he grew up, as the strike continued and baseball ownership used replacement players in an ersatz and embarrassing "spring training."[15] Minor leaguers – those not holding coveted 40-man roster spots as Kowitz did – were faced with deciding whether to endanger their potential major-league careers by participating in games with the replacements. Few did; Kowitz was spared the decision.

The strike was ultimately settled[16] on March 31 – but only by a court injunction issued by future Supreme Court Justice Sonia Sotomayor in the US District Court in Manhattan – the replacements scattered, and the Players Association players, including Kowitz, reported for their delayed spring training on April 5.[17]

Kowitz had to have been buoyed by an item in the April 10 *Sporting News* putting him in the mix for Minnesota's left-field job.[18] And his camp play was impressive enough to warrant a Twins contract reported on April 15,[19] but as the belated spring training drew to an end, he suffered a hamstring injury[20] serious enough for Minnesota to place him on waivers and then, when he cleared, return him to the Atlanta organization under the terms of Rule 5. By April 24 the Twin was once again a Brave.[21]

When the hamstring healed it was back to Richmond once again for Kowitz, who had come so frustratingly close to opening the season with Minnesota. He aptly called it "an emotional roller coaster," adding, "I did a lot in Richmond the year before and I had to go back and do it again. I was so mentally prepared to be in Minnesota. It kind of took a little piece out of me."[22]

Kowitz had been keeping track of the numbers in the Atlanta outfield and knew that the Braves had traded two outfielders (Tarasco and Kelly) for one (Marquis Grissom) going into 1995. "'I thought I'd be the next guy who came up,'" Kowitz said. He was right. In early June a nagging shoulder injury put David Justice on the disabled list, leaving the Braves in need of a left-handed-hitting outfielder with some seasoning. They summoned Kowitz, who said: "You have to be in the right place at the right time."[23]

He arrived in Atlanta from Richmond on Friday, June 2, 1995. The Braves were hosting the Houston Astros for a weekend series at Atlanta-Fulton County Stadium. On Friday and Saturday, Kowitz took in the major-league atmosphere from the dugout, but on Sunday, June 4, he got Cox's call as a fifth-inning pinch-hitter for starter Tom

Glavine, who was on the wrong end of a 5-0 score. Kowitz wasted no time, ramming the first pitch he saw from Shane Reynolds down the left-field line for a double that scored Charlie O'Brien from third base with Atlanta's first run of the game.

Obviously liking what he had seen and perhaps recalling Kowitz's late 1994 spring training, Cox installed Kowitz in right field, hitting leadoff, for the next four homestand games, against the Cubs, then the Cardinals. On June 5 the rookie kept his on-base percentage perfect with a hit-batsman to lead off the Atlanta first inning, then scored on Chipper Jones's double; in the sixth he executed a perfect bunt that scored O'Brien from third, and "Bobby Cox loved it."[24] Kowitz singled in wins over Chicago on June 6 and 7 and again on June 10 against St. Louis. But that was it for him as a starter. Cox put Mike Kelly in right field and the leadoff spot on June 11; Kowitz got into that game only as a pinch-hitter for pitcher Steve Bedrosian in the third inning. He drew a walk.

Through Kowitz's five starts the Braves went 4-1. He fielded six of six chances perfectly playing all three outfield positions over 53 innings, but after his perfect start at the plate, he had cooled and hit only .167 in 28 plate appearances in 10 games.

Justice was reactivated from the disabled list on June 18. Kowitz was optioned back to Richmond, where he finished out the season with a respectable .280/.360/.365 offensive line in a combined 100 games with the call-up sandwiched in. But although Richmond failed to make the 1995 International League playoffs and he was available, he didn't get a September recall as the Braves won the NL East title. Having appeared on Atlanta's major-league roster during the season, Kowitz was honored with a World Series Championship ring after the Braves defeated the Cleveland Indians in six games to win the 1995 World Series. Glavine, for whom Kowitz had pinch-hit back on June 4 in his debut, won Games Two and Six and was named Series MVP.

During the 1995-96 offseason Kowitz married his fiancée, Amy Schwartz, of Pikesville, Maryland. As Kowitz was making his major-league debut that summer, Amy was finishing her master's degree in special education at Johns Hopkins University in Baltimore.[25]

Kowitz had a Series ring but the disappointment of being characterized by a Gannett News Service sportswriter as "going nowhere in the Braves system,"[26] as he contemplated his seventh year with the Atlanta organization. Dropped from Atlanta's 40-man roster, Kowitz declared free agency[27] and went to 1996 spring training as a nonroster invitee with the Detroit Tigers. By March 16, however, he was assigned to minor-league camp and started the season back in Triple A with the Toledo Mud Hens. After hitting a disappointing .191 in 24 games with Toledo, he was released and caught on in May with the Blue Jays' Syracuse Chiefs, the club he had helped defeat for the International League title two years earlier.[28] He hit marginally better (.241) with Syracuse over 34 games, but he had become a career minor-leaguer, was limited by an ankle injury,[29] and seemed to see baseball's handwriting on the wall for him.

So instead of trying to catch on with yet another major-league organization in 1997, Kowitz went back to Baltimore County, enrolled at Towson University and finished his bachelor's degree in sports management and business administration. With his education complete, and getting started with his life's work, he took a 13-game foray back into professional baseball in 2000, playing 13 late-season games with the independent Aberdeen (Maryland) Arsenal of the Atlantic League. Now 30, he hit a refreshing .432, playing mainly as a first baseman.

After Towson, with the brief detour in Aberdeen, Kowitz concentrated on the financial-services industry. He operated his own planning firm for seven years through 2011, then became a principal in Heller Kowitz Insurance Advisors in Lutherville, Maryland. He continued there as of 2019, focusing his practice on insurance products for professional athletes, sports executives, doctors, lawyers, and businessmen. He joined the advisory board and was an instructor with The Baseball Warehouse, a Baltimore-area entity that "educates players, coaches, and parents regarding the many aspects of [baseball], with the goal of promoting and bettering the game of baseball at all levels."[30]

Kowitz, a member of both the Boys' Latin School and Clemson University athletic halls of fame, is active with charities and other community groups in and around his and Amy's home in Owings Mills, coaches youth baseball, basketball, and football teams, and supports Jemicy School, an Owings Mills lower-through-upper-and-preparatory school focused on educating students with dyslexia and related language-based learning challenges. Two of the Kowitzes' three children attend the Jemicy School.[31]

Sources and acknowledgments

In addition to the sources cited in the Notes, the author used the Baseball-Reference and Retrosheet.org websites for player and team pages, box scores, and game logs. Except for the citation from *The Sporting News*, accessed through the Paper of Record.com website, all newspaper citations were accessed through Newspapers.com.

I appreciate the time Brian Kowitz took from his busy family life and business commitments to review a draft of this biography and provide input. Brian Bark, Brian's friend since prep school and collegiate baseball days, fellow Atlanta farmhand, neighbor, and himself a former major leaguer with the 1995 Boston Red Sox, was a helpful contact.

Notes

1. Ben Kowitz obituary, *Baltimore Sun*, February 20, 2002: B8.
2. *Evening Sun* (Baltimore), February 12, 1987: 74
3. *Evening Sun*, June 4, 1987: 26.
4. *Baltimore Sun*, August 11, 1987: 37. Kowitz continued to play summer amateur baseball for Johnny's Auto Sales in a Baltimore league through his college career. He had a 33-game hitting streak for Johnny's in 1989. See: McMullin, Note 5.
5. Paul McMullen, "Kowitz Is Surprise Bumper Crop of Latest Baltimore Harvest," *Evening Sun* (Baltimore), May 11, 1990: 30.
6. Ibid.; "Boys' Latin Grad Kowitz Named Top Player in the ACC," *Baltimore Sun*, May 20, 1990: 91; Batting average from 1990 Clemson University entry, Baseball Cube.com, accessed March 2, 2019.
7. McMullen; "Boys' Latin Grad." Kowitz hit .274, then .270, in his first two Clemson seasons.
8. McMullin.
9. "Boys' Latin Grad."
10. McMullin.
11. "Kowitz Named," *Greenville* (South Carolina) *News*, September 5, 1990: 15.
12. "The Name Is Kowitz," *Greenville News*, April 3, 1994: 25.
13. Ibid.
14. And that was just the first game of a doubleheader. Richmond won the second game as well. *Times-Leader* (Wilkes-Barre, Pennsylvania), May 13, 1994: 25.
15. See Tom Verducci, "The Sham Spring," *Sports Illustrated*, February 23, 2015, accessed at si.com/vault, March 1, 2019.
16. Gershon Rabinowitz, "Revisiting Replacement Players," blog at Baseball Essential.com, posted March 15, 2015, accessed February 25, 2019.
17. Due to the late start of spring training, the 1995 Atlanta Braves didn't open their regular season until April 26. Both major leagues played shortened schedules of 154 games rather than 162 in 1995, hearkening back to the last pre-expansion seasons, 1960 for the American League and 1961 for the National League.
18. Scott Miller, "Minnesota Twins," *The Sporting News*, April 10, 1995: 39.
19. (Minneapolis) *Star Tribune*, April 15, 1995: 22.
20. Lem Satterfield, "Rave Brave Reviews Could Earn Kowitz Encore," *Baltimore Sun*, July 5, 1995: 37.
21. (Minneapolis) *Star Tribune*, April 25, 1995: 26.
22. Tim Luke, "Braves Notes," *Greenville News*, June 4, 1995.
23. Mark Bradley, "Kowitz Finally Finds Right Place at the Right Time," *Atlanta Constitution*, June 5, 1995: 37.
24. Bill Tanton, "Boys' Latin Hits Big Time with Kowitz," Baltimore Sun.com, posted June 15, 1995, accessed February 25, 2019.
25. Satterfield.
26. Tom Gage, Gannett, "Lots of New Faces in Detroit Camp," *Battle Creek* (Michigan) *Enquirer*, February 13, 1996: 11, 13.
27. I.J. Rosenberg, "Braves Open Roster Spot with Kowitz a Free Agent," *Atlanta Constitution*, November 28, 1995: 76.
28. *Tampa Tribune*, May 23, 1996: 89.
29. *Baltimore Sun*, September 4, 2000: 40.
30. Brian Kowitz entry, LinkedIn.com, accessed February 25, 2019.
31. Ibid.

Mark Lemke

BY PAUL HOFMANN

Mark Lemke

Referred to as "the original dirt player" by Atlanta Braves manager Bobby Cox, Mark Lemke was a throwback second baseman who rarely left the field with a clean uniform.[1] Standing at 5-feet-10-inches and weighing between 165 and 170 pounds, the undersized second baseman contributed in ways that didn't always show up in a box score. Affectionately called the Lemmer by teammates, Lemke was a clutch player who will always be remembered for his performance in the 1991 World Series.

Jimy Williams, who managed Lemke with the Boston Red Sox and coached him with the Braves, described Lemke's workmanlike approach to the game as follows: "I've just seen him make so many plays and be in the middle of so many rallies at key times, in big games. … He brings his own little sack lunch to the table, while all the other guys are eating filet."[2]

Mark Alan Lemke was born on August 13, 1965, in Utica, New York, 40 miles northwest of Cooperstown, and grew up in Whitesboro, a suburb of Utica. He was the youngest of four children of Roger and Patricia Lemke.[3] Roger, a graduate of the University of Notre Dame, worked as a federal government contract administrator in Rome, New York. Patricia was employed as an employment counselor.

Mark Lemke may not be the most famous member of the Lemke clan. His family tree includes a presidential candidate. Lemke is the second cousin twice removed of William Lemke, an eight-term Republican member of the US House of Representatives from North Dakota and the 1936 Union Party presidential candidate.[4] When asked about his distant relationship to the one-time presidential candidate, Lemke responded, "I have been asked about that a lot and haven't disputed it because it sounds pretty good."[5]

Mark attended Sacred Heart Elementary School and Notre Dame High School in Utica. At Notre Dame he played both baseball and basketball. According to Lemke, he actually took basketball more seriously.[6] However, the diminutive guard attracted little interest from college basketball coaches.

Lemke did attract interest on the baseball diamond. He received a scholarship offer to play baseball at Purdue University and drew the attention of a scout working the upstate New York area. Cy Williams, who worked for the Major League Scouting Bureau and recommended Lemke as a high-school prospect, compared the undersized infielder to one of the grittiest players of all time, Pete Rose. "His style of play does sort of remind you of Pete Rose," Williams said in June 1983. "That is not to say he is the next Pete Rose, but I think he has the ability and desire to become a professional baseball player. He seems to be the type of kid who uses every ounce of his ability."[7]

Indeed, Lemke was the type of player who got the most out of his ability. When asked how he made it to the majors despite his size, Lemke said, "It's kind of hard to explain. I look at guys going into the Hall of Fame and think about the fact that I played for many years with them … pretty amazing. I guess the best way to describe why I made it is I just grinded it. I was very determined."[8] Lemke also credited his family for the development of his grittiness and ability to grind on the baseball field. "I have a sister and brother who are pharmacists and another sister who is a doctor. I was the youngest so I had a lot to look up to. I also had parents who taught me the right things."[9]

On the third day of the 1983 June amateur draft, Lemke was selected in the 27th round by the Atlanta Braves. Until then Lemke had his mind set on attending Purdue. After being drafted by the Braves, he was brought to Atlanta with the rest of the team's draft picks, including future major leaguers Ron Gant and Jay Buhner. It was at that point that he started to ask himself, "What do you want to do – go to school or play ball?"[10] Lemke remembered his father advising him, "You don't want to go to school … if all you're going to think about is baseball. … You can always go to school."[11] Lemke followed his heart and signed with the Braves.

The 17-year-old Lemke was assigned to the team's Gulf Coast League affiliate in Bradenton, Florida, where he had his first eye-opening experience in professional baseball: "You think they are drafting you as the second baseman of the future and you go to rookie ball and all of a sudden, there are 15 other second basemen."[12] In 53 games Lemke hit .263 with 19 RBIs as the rookie-league Braves finished in second place in the Gulf Coast League's North Division.

Lemke returned to Bradenton to start the 1984 season. His roommate that year was Tom Glavine, a left-handed pitcher the Braves had taken in the second round of the 1984 draft. Glavine, who along with Lemke traveled his way up through the Braves' minor-league system, was embarking on a Hall of Fame career.[13] Lemke hit .276 with 3 home runs and 32 RBIs before being promoted to the Anderson (South Carolina) Braves of the Class-A South Atlantic League. At Anderson, Lemke struggled to make the adjustment to higher caliber pitching. He hit an anemic .149 with 5 RBIs in 42 games.

Now 19 years old, Lemke began the 1985 season with the Sumter (South Carolina) Braves.[14] Splitting second-base duties with future Braves outfielder Gant, Lemke appeared in 90 games and showed only modest improvement at the plate. He finished the year with a .216 average, no home runs, and 20 RBIs. At this stage of his career, Lemke was not highly thought of as a prospect in the Braves organization. However, the same fire and determination that characterized his major-league career allowed him to move on from his early offensive struggles.

Lemke returned to Sumter for the 1986 season and split time between third base (77 games) and second base (50 games). The switch-hitting infielder hit .272 and began to demonstrate an ability to hit for power. His 18 home runs and 66 RBIs helped him earn a spot on the Sally League all-star team as a utility infielder and a promotion to the Durham Bulls of the High-A Carolina League for the 1987 season.[15]

Settling in at second base, Lemke hit .292 with 20 home runs and 68 RBIs at Durham and earned a berth on the league all-star team.[16] His success with the Bulls helped him emerge as a bona-fide second-base prospect for the Braves. At the end of the season, he was called up to the Greenville Braves of the Double-A Southern League and joined future Braves Jeff Blauser, David Justice,

Tommy Greene, Pete Smith, and Gant, playing in six games.

Lemke returned to Greenville to start the 1988 season. It was about this time that he thought he had the ability to make it to the parent club. Reflecting back on that year, Lemke said, "I knew then I had the talent and it now was going to become the mental side of the game if I was going to make it."[17] That year he hit .270 with 16 home runs and 80 RBIs. He also stole 18 bases in 20 attempts. When the Double-A season ended, Lemke earned a September call-up to Atlanta.

Lemke made his major-league debut in Atlanta on September 17, 1988. Starting at second base in both games of a doubleheader against the San Diego Padres, he went 0-for-3 (with a walk and a run scored) as the Braves dropped a 9-4 decision in the opener to right-hander Eric Show. The next day he collected his first major-league hit, a second-inning groundball single to right field off Padres right-hander Andy Hawkins. During the late-season call-up, Lemke appeared in 16 games and finished with a .224 average.

Lemke failed to make the Braves roster coming out of spring training in 1989. After the Braves acquired left-handed-hitting Jeff Treadway during spring training, they had the luxury of farming Lemke out for another year of seasoning to the Richmond Braves of the Triple-A International League. Lemke was Richmond's everyday second baseman and enjoyed a productive season at the plate. In 146 games he hit .276 with 5 home runs and a team-leading 61 RBIs, and was named to the circuit's all-star team.

In a foreshadowing of what was to come to Atlanta the Triple-A Braves won the International League's Western Division title with a record of 81-65 and went on to capture the International League championship with a three-games-to-one victory over the Syracuse Chiefs. The Braves were swept in four games by the American Association's Indianapolis Indians in the Triple-A Classic.

After the playoffs Lemke earned his second call-up to Atlanta. He batted only .182 in 14 games, but hit his first major-league home run on September 14 in San Diego. With runners on second and third and two down in the top of the seventh, Lemke pinch-hit for Treadway. He deposited a 2-and-0 Eric Nolte fastball into the seats in left field. The three-run shot put the Braves up 12-3 as they rolled to a 13-4 drubbing of the Padres.

Lemke made the Braves roster as a utility infielder in 1990. After working his way through the Braves' minor-league system without a sterling pedigree, he welcomed the news that he had finally made the big-league roster. "It's a relief. I wasn't sitting around trying to figure out what was going on because of what happened last year." Lemke said, referring to his being one of the last cuts in 1990. "I was hoping to work on some skills and get the most out of my three weeks here [in spring training]."[18]

Lemke started the season slowly. He was hitting only .171 with 6 RBIs when he twisted his left ankle when he fell in the passage from the clubhouse to the dugout during a rain delay.[19] The injury landed him on the disabled list and kept him out of the lineup for six weeks. In 102 games that year, Lemke hit .226 with 21 RBIs.

During the 1990 season, the Braves started the initial stages of transitioning from perennial doormat to consistent winners. The team got off to a 25-40 start before general manager Bobby Cox relieved manager Russ Nixon of his duties and replaced him with himself. Cox fared only slightly better during the remainder of the season, guiding the Braves to a record of 40-57, as the team (65-97) once again finished the season in last place. Unbeknownst to the casual fan, Cox had begun molding the young Braves into a cohesive unit that competed on a daily basis. Years later, Lemke commented on what he thought Cox brought to the team, "I think to a man, we would all say he was the best. He gave us confidence that we could compete and win at that level and that is a hard thing with young kids," recalled Lemke.[20]

This new winning attitude ushered in a new era of baseball in Atlanta in 1991, one of the longest sustained periods of success in major-league history (14 consecutive division titles), that culminated with a World Series title in 1995.

Cox returned to the dugout in 1991 and Lemke and Treadway platooned for most of the season, allowing the Braves to take advantage of Treadway's ability to hit right-handers and Lemke's defense.[21] As the season progressed it was apparent the Braves were moving more toward Lemke as the regular second baseman, and by the end of the season he was getting most of the playing time there. He finished the season with a .234 average, 2 home runs, and 23 RBIs as the Braves completed a worst-to-first turnaround with a record of 94-68.

Twenty years later, Lemke reflected on the Braves' reversal of fortune. "We knew we were going to be better that year, but how much better, I don't think any knew," he said."[22] In a separate interview he reminisced on the atmosphere during the Braves' stretch-run battle with the Los Angeles Dodgers. "It was the most incredible ride any of us could imagine. … That September with the Dodgers was like a playoff scenario every night."[23]

Lemke started six games, and appeared in all seven, in the 1991 National League Championship Series against the Pittsburgh Pirates. In Game Two he went 2-for-4 and drove in David Justice with the game's only run with a sixth-inning double off Zane Smith. For the series, Lemke went 4-for-20 (.200) as the Braves rallied from a three-games-to-two deficit, winning the last two games on the road, to reach the franchise's first World Series since 1958.

The Braves second baseman caught fire in the World Series against the American League champion Minnesota Twins. Lemke played in six games and batted .417 with 10 hits in 24 at-bats, including a double, three triples and four RBIs. He was the first player to collect three triples in the World Series since Yankees third baseman Billy Johnson accomplished the feat in 1947. Lemke, who was not known for his speed, recalled that he nearly had a fourth. "A triple for a guy like myself is hard and there was one other hit I had in the Series that I thought could have been a triple but I stopped at second."[24]

Had it not been for a walk-off home run by Kirby Puckett in the 11th inning of Game Six and a 10-inning Game Seven masterpiece pitched by Jack Morris, Atlanta might have won the Series and Lemke might have been named World Series MVP.[25]

Although the Braves failed to win the World Series, more than 750,000 fans turned out for the team's near-victory parade. "The parade was the highlight," Lemke said. "It was all a good experience. I don't know if I'd want to go through it every offseason. But I enjoyed it while I was there."[26]

Coming off the success of the previous fall, Lemke won the full-time job at second base in the spring of 1992. That season he appeared in a career-high 55 games. Lemke's reliable defensive play at second base more than compensated for his modest offensive contributions (.227 batting average, 6 home runs, 26 RBIs) as the Braves went 98-64 and repeated as NL West champions.

The 1992 NLCS was a rematch of the previous year's. Lemke went 7-for-21 with two RBIs as the Braves once again beat the Pirates in seven games to advance to the World Series. Lemke went 4-for-19 in the World Series and collected the game-winning RBI in Game Two and another RBI in Game Four as the Braves fell to the Toronto Blue Jays in six games.

After the season the Braves released Treadway, solidifying Lemke's position as the team's starting second baseman. He responded with an improved season at the plate. In 151 games, all but one at second base, Lemke hit .252 with a career-high 7 home runs and 49 RBIs as the Braves won their third consecutive NL West title. Despite outhitting and outscoring Philadelphia in the NLCS, the Braves dropped the series in six games. Lemke went 5-for-24 and drove in five runs, four of which came in Game Three when he hit a three-run double.

Lemke enjoyed his best all-around season in 1994. In 104 games he hit a career-high .294 with 3 home runs and 31 RBIs. He had a career-high .994 fielding percentage at second base.[27] When play was suspended on August 12 because of the players strike, the Braves were 68-46, six games behind the NL East-leading Montreal Expos.

The strike lingered into the 1995 season, canceling the first 18 games of the season. Lemke lost another four weeks when he landed on the disabled list with a partially torn left hamstring in late June. The injury was so severe that Lemke reportedly had difficulty "just standing."[28] Limited to 116 games during the regular season, Lemke hit .253 with 5 home runs and 38 RBIs as the Braves captured the NL East title, their fourth division title in five years.

Lemke hit .211 in the Braves' four-game victory over the Colorado Rockies in the Division Series. He followed that with a .167 average in the Braves' four-game sweep of the Cincinnati Reds in the NLCS. Advancing to the World Series for the first time since 1992, Lemke and the Braves met the American League champion Cleveland Indians. Lemke started all six games at second and hit .273 as the Braves won the franchise's first World Series title since 1957, when they were still in Milwaukee.

Lemke's gritty play continued to take its toll when he landed on the disabled list with a jammed thumb in late May 1996. The injury forced Lemke to miss 18 games. Limited to 135 games, he hit .255 with 5 home runs and 37 RBIs as the Braves again captured the NL East title.

The defending World Series champion Braves opened the playoffs with a three-game sweep of the Los Angeles Dodgers in the NLDS. Although he went only 2-for-12 in the series, Lemke was once again clutch as he drove in two runs in the clinching game with a fourth-inning double off Japanese sensation Hideo Nomo.

The 1996 NLCS was a hard-fought seven-game battle between the Braves and the Central Division champion St. Louis Cardinals. After falling behind three games to one, the Braves rallied to win the series. Lemke hit safely in all seven games, batting .444 (12-for-27) with two doubles, a home run, and five RBIs to help the Braves capture their second consecutive pennant.

In Game One of the NLCS, Lemke erased a 1-0 deficit and drove home two runs with a fifth-inning single to right-center. The Braves went on to win, 4-2. In Game Four, he led off the sixth inning with his only postseason home run, a shot to deep right off right-hander Andy Benes. In Game Five, a 14-0 Braves blowout victory, Lemke went 4-for-5 with an RBI single. In Game Six he added a 2-for-4 performance and another RBI single. In the seventh and final game, an anticlimactic 15-0 Braves win, Lemke went 2-for-4.

The Braves and Lemke got off to a fast start in the 1996 World Series. In a 12-1 Game One victory over the Yankees, Lemke went 2-for-4, including a sixth-inning RBI single. In Game Two he hit a first-inning ground-rule double and scored the game's first run when Fred McGriff drove him home with a single to left field. Lemke added a second hit, a single to center, and scored a second run in the top of the fifth to help the Braves to a 4-0 victory and two-games-to-none lead in the Series. With the Series headed back to Atlanta, the Braves were well positioned to repeat as champions.

After going 4-for-8 in the Series' first two games, Lemke managed only two more hits (an RBI single in Game Three and a harmless single in Game Four) in 18 trips to the plate during the Series' last four games. He made the last out in the Series, when he hit a pop foul that Yankees third baseman Charlie Hayes squeezed to end the Braves' one-year reign as World Series champions.

Lemke recalled the final out of the series. "I had [John Wetteland] right where I wanted him. … I give a lot of credit to Wetteland. I really remember that at-bat. If he had thrown a curve, I'd probably strike out. He kept throwing the fastball on the outside corner and I'd fight off the pitch. If he throws high with a fastball, I walk. He throws it over the plate and I tear it up. The only thing better I could have done was flick it a little farther (into the stands)."[29]

The 1996 World Series was Lemke's last appearance in the postseason. In 62 postseason games over five seasons, he hit .272 with 10 doubles, 3 triples, a home run, and 25 RBIs. True to his career statistics, the numbers do not accurately reflect Lemke's contributions or impact on the Braves' playoff successes. His clutch playoff performances, be it exploding offensively as he did in the 1991 World Series or quickly turning a double play at second, often set the tone for the entire team.

For the third consecutive season, Lemke missed a considerable amount of time in 1997 due to injury. In early June he missed a week with a vision problem that helped drop his batting average to .232. On August 20, with the team headed toward another NL East division title, he sustained a season-ending sprained ankle. The injury occurred when Houston Astros left fielder Derek Bell took Lemke out with a "football-style, roll block" at second base.[30] At the time he was hitting .245 with 2 home runs and 26 RBIs. Unable to recover prior to the playoffs, he was kept off the Braves' playoff roster.

After the season Lemke, 32, filed for free agency. Hampered by injuries over the past few seasons, he found a soft market for his services. The Red Sox originally offered him only $250,000 per year, an 87.5 percent cut from the $2 million he had earned the previous year with the Braves. Lemke rejected the Red Sox twice before finally coming to terms on a one-year, $1 million contract at the end of spring training.[31] The deal reunited Lemke with Jimy Williams, who was the bench coach when Lemke was in Atlanta, and former teammate Steve Avery.

Lemke, who missed nearly all of spring training before coming to terms with the Red Sox, got off to a slow start. At the end of April he was hitting a microscopic .108. He began to turn things around in May and hit .255 between May 1 and 19, raising his average to .193. However, on May 19 his baseball career effectively came to an end. In the top of the sixth inning of a game at Fenway Park, Lemke was involved in a collision at second base with Chicago White Sox catcher Chad Kreuter and suffered a concussion. The gritty Lemke returned to the lineup on May 25 against the Toronto Blue Jays and went 0-for-3. He was pinch-hit for by Lou Merloni in the top of the ninth inning. This was Lemke's final major-league appearance.

For weeks Lemke was unable to play and suffered from concussion symptoms: fatigue, dizziness, headaches, and difficulty concentrating.[32] On July 15 the Red Sox moved him to the 60-day disabled list, signaling an end to his season and Red Sox career.

As the season wound down, the Red Sox acquired second baseman Chris Snopek from the White Sox to fortify their playoff push. At the time of the move, Williams reminded everyone of Lemke's contributions to the team. "Mark Lemke hit .187 and helped us win a lot of games," Williams said. "Don't always look at stats. Look at what the player does, maybe moving runners, making plays, taking an extra base. There's a lot more important things than those stats."[33]

While Williams's comments were designed to point out Lemke's contributions to the Red Sox that year, they also served as a commentary to his entire career. Lemke's contributions to the Braves teams of the 1990s are not accurately measured by his career .246 average, 32 home runs, and 270 RBIs.

Surprisingly, given his tenacious style of play, Lemke is the holder of an obscure major-league record. Lemke has the record for most career plate appearances (3,664) without being hit by a pitch. One would expect a player with Lemke's desire to do anything possible to win to have been hit by a pitch at least once in his career.

After Boston, Lemke retired but came back as a knuckleball pitcher and coach with the New Jersey Jackals of the independent Northern League East for two seasons (1999-2000). In his first year with the Jackals, who had former major leaguer Pete Rose Jr. on the roster, he made 11 appearances on the mound, five as a starter. Despite an inflated ERA of 6.68, he finished the season with a record of 5-1. The Jackals finished the year with a record of 45-40 and in second place in the NEAS's South Division. He made only one appearance in 2000. In 2⅔ innings he walked seven, gave up nine hits and yielded 12 earned runs. The Jackals finished in last place with a record of 31-53.

Following his foray into independent-league baseball, Lemke moved to Alpharetta, Georgia, and began dabbling in real estate. In December 2003 he was reunited with former Braves teammate John Rocker as a victim in a real-estate scam. A real-estate investor allegedly bilked Rocker and Lemke out of more than $500,000. Lemke alone reportedly lost $408,000.[34]

In 2006 Lemke began working on the Braves' pregame radio show and as a fill-in for radio analyst Don Sutton. "I love it, though it is something I didn't anticipate doing," he said. "I do quite a bit of prep work but I will tell you Twitter really helps me get ready for games."[35]

Lemke, who is not married, currently resides in Sandy Springs, a suburb on the northern tier of the metropolitan Atlanta area.

Sources

In addition to the sources cited in the Notes, the author relied on baseball-reference.com and Retrosheet.org.

Notes

1. I.J. Rosenberg, "Whatever Happened to … Mark Lemke," *Atlanta Journal-Constitution*, January 9, 2015. Retrieved from ajc.com/sports/baseball/whatever-happened-mark-lemke/VmSeJBHyLoEgUnUc3cnQFK/.
2. Rosenberg, "Whatever Happened to … Mark Lemke."
3. Patricia Lemke, personal correspondence, November 11, 2019.
4. In 1936 William Lemke accepted the nomination of the Union Party, a short-lived third party, for president. He received 892,378 votes, just under 2 percent, and no electoral votes. Lemke did outpoll Republican Alf Landon in five North Dakota counties and was the last third-party presidential candidate to outpoll a major-party nominee in any non-Southern county until George Wallace outpolled Hubert Humphrey in Kane County, Utah, in 1968.
5. I.J. Rosenberg, "Whatever Happened to … Mark Lemke."
6. I.J. Rosenberg, "Whatever Happened to … Mark Lemke."
7. Ronald Blum, "Lemke Does It Again for Atlanta," *Sumter (South Carolina) Item*, October 23, 1991: 3D.
8. I.J. Rosenberg, "Whatever Happened to … Mark Lemke."
9. I.J. Rosenberg, "Whatever Happened to … Mark Lemke."
10. Fran Perritano, "Tuesday Conversation with Mark Lemke," *Utica (New York) Observer-Dispatch*, April 6, 2010. Retrieved from uticaod.com/article/20100406/News/304069930.
11. Perritano.
12. I.J. Rosenberg, "Whatever Happened to … Mark Lemke."
13. John Feinstein, *Living on the Black* (New York: Little Brown and Company, 2008), 12.
14. The Sumter Braves replaced the Anderson Braves as Atlanta's Class-A affiliate in the Sally League.
15. "Sports Notebook: Braves Patient in Pursuit of Dawson," *Atlanta Constitution*, August 29, 1986: 67.
16. Gerry Fraley, "Garcia Working Out Again, May Get September Try at Third Base," *Atlanta Constitution*, August 30, 1987: 59.
17. I.J. Rosenberg. "Whatever Happened to … Mark Lemke."
18. Joe Strauss, "Nixon Leaves No Doubt on Plans for Lemke: 'He's Got to be Here,'" *Atlanta Constitution*, March 25, 1990: 53.
19. "Injury Update," *Atlanta Constitution*, May 30, 1990: 70.
20. "Injury Update."
21. Treadway had a .325 average against right-handed pitchers, but hit only .250 against left-handers. Lemke hit .254 against left-handers and only .219 against right-handers. Lemke was the stronger defensive second baseman.
22. Tim Tucker, "Special Year Had Set Championship Stage," *Atlanta Constitution*, August 12, 2011: C9.
23. I.J. Rosenberg, "Whatever Happened to … Mark Lemke."
24. I.J. Rosenberg, "Whatever Happened to … Mark Lemke."
25. Perritano.
26. Craig Davis, "Lemke Never Walked on This Street Before," *South Florida Sun-Sentinel* (Fort Lauderdale, Florida), February 27, 1992: 41.
27. Lemke had a perfect 1.000 fielding percentage at second base for the Red Sox in 1998. However, that came in only 31 games.

28 I.J. Rosenberg, "Braves Notebook: Alou Eyes Maddux as All-Star Starter," *Atlanta Constitution*, June 27, 1995: 58.

29 Perritano.

30 Jack Wilkinson, "Ankle Sprain Puts Lemke on DL," *Atlanta Constitution*, August 23, 1997: 138.

31 I.J. Rosenberg, "Lemke, Red Sox Reach Deal," *Atlanta Constitution*, March 27, 1998: 60.

32 Gordon Edes and Dan Shaughnessy, "To Lemke It's Not Personal: He Has Nothing Against Kreuter," *Boston Globe*, June 10, 1998: 82.

33 Shira Springer and Gordon Edes, "Surprised Package Arrives," *Boston Globe*, September 2, 1998: 38.

34 Ernie Suggs, "Unhappy Reunion for ex-Braves," *Atlanta Constitution*, December 10, 2003: B4.

35 I.J. Rosenberg, "Whatever happened to … Mark Lemke."

Javy Lopez

BY KYLE EATON

Javy Lopez

Javier Torres "Javy" Lopez was born on November 5, 1970, in the city of Ponce, Puerto Rico. Lopez was a right-handed-hitting catcher who played for the Atlanta Braves, Baltimore Orioles, and Boston Red Sox over his 15-year major-league career, though he is primarily known for his time with the Braves. Lopez was a three-time All-Star and one-time Silver Slugger recipient, and in 1995 was a World Series champion, all with the Atlanta Braves. Lopez is listed at 6-feet-3 and 185 pounds,[1] but by his own admission, his weight climbed to at least 248 pounds during his career.[2]

Javy was the second youngest of five children (two boys, Juan Eduardo and Javy, and three girls, Sandra, Betsy, and Elaine) in his household, and learned from an early age the value of hard work from his parents and his lower-middle-class upbringing. Lopez's mother, Evelia Torres, held many jobs ranging from bank teller to teacher, but she eventually left the work force to better provide supervision and care for her children. This left Jacinto Lopez, Javy's father, an auto-parts dealer, former employee of a credit union, and occasional car salesman, as the primary source of income for the family. The modest, four-bedroom house in which Javy grew up lies in close proximity to the other homes on his block, and lent itself perfectly to providing close familial and neighborly ties. The values growing up in this modest family created a bond that Lopez has reflected upon.[3]

Javy's first swings came when he took an old bat and a bucket of rocks to the roof of his house and hit the rocks into the vacant lot across the street. Jacinto Lopez recalled the stamina Javy displayed while doing this: "I'd be on the couch and he would be up there swinging at stones. I would say to myself, gosh, this kid never gets tired."[4] At 7 years old Lopez began playing baseball at a neighborhood church on a concrete field with a rubber ball.[5] Whenever a bat or tape to make a ball could not be found, Javy and his friends improvised with broomsticks and soda-bottle caps. Any materials that could be feasibly used as a bat or ball were used.[6]

Lopez did not know the idiosyncrasies of baseball but he did enjoy playing the game and began to develop a knack for it as well. His father took him to a recreational league when he saw his son's potential. Once the duo started playing catch, coaches took notice of Javy's potential and put him on a team. Javy demonstrated a strong arm, but lacked the touch or control to pitch, the agility to play shortstop, or the swiftness to patrol the outfield. But he hit well, so the coaches kept plugging him in at different positions until one worked for him. Lopez benefited from baseball being a year-round sport in Puerto Rico. As soon as one season ended, Lopez went to another team to play. The repetition and extra coaching were invaluable in developing his defensive skills, and it was by the time he made his third team that Lopez began to find his way and started to feel comfortable on the diamond.[7] Baseball even taught Lopez an early life lesson. His uncle bought him his first baseball glove and Javy left it on the patio one day. Someone stole the glove and Javy learned how to properly keep track of his belongings.[8]

By age 13 Lopez still did not have a true position, but one of his managers, Johnny Rodriquez, tried him at catcher. Lopez was not great at blocking balls or catching bad pitches, but his arm was strong enough to compensate for his rawness behind the plate; he threw out a plethora of runners on his first day as a catcher, and thus his position was found.

Lopez's hard work was rewarded when he was signed as an amateur free agent by the Atlanta Braves in 1987.[9] He turned down offers from the New York Yankees, San Diego Padres, and Montreal Expos to sign with the Braves, who offered $45,000 while the Padres and Expos were offering $75,000. Jacinto Lopez explained: "TBS used to be the only station that showed games here, so we were Braves fans."[10] After Lopez signed with the Braves, even more teams began to pursue him, but he honored his contract. Lopez said, "You know what? Forget it! I'm going to be in Atlanta, on TBS!"[11]

For what it is worth, Lopez might not have been the best athlete, or even the best baseball player in his family, at least for a time. His sister Elaine was at one point regarded as one of the best beach volleyball players in Puerto Rico, if not the best. Elaine also was married to former American League MVP Juan Gonzalez for a time, causing a fun debate on which member of the extended Lopez family was the best baseball player.[12]

Lopez started with the Braves' team in the Gulf Coast League (rookie) as a 17-year-old in 1988. Each subsequent year he advanced a level, and in September 1992 he made the jump from Double-A Greenville (Southern League) to the Braves. No stop was without trials and tribulations, but Lopez continued to show promise. For example, Lopez had 31 passed balls playing for Burlington, Iowa (Midwest League). Lopez blamed his fear of the ball, the cold weather, and the pitchers lacking the ability to properly grip the ball in that climate.[13]

During his rise through the minors, Lopez paused in 1991, while playing for Durham (Carolina League) to marry his childhood sweetheart, Analy Hernandez.[14]

Called up from Greenville, Lopez made his major-league debut on September 18, 1992, at Atlanta-Fulton County Stadium, hitting a pinch-hit double off Houston's Rob Murphy in his first at-bat. He was 6-for-16 in a nine-game audition, then opened the 1993 season playing for the Triple-A Richmond Braves. Called up in August, he played in only eight games but hit his first major-league home run on August 21 at Wrigley Field against Chicago Cubs reliever Shawn Boskie.

By Opening Day of the 1994 season, the 23-year-old Lopez had become the Braves' starting catcher, replacing Damon Berryhill. He performed well enough to earn a top-10 spot in the National League Rookie of the Year balloting, and learned quite a bit about handling a major-league pitching staff – one with three future Hall of Famers, Greg Maddux, John Smoltz, and Tom Glavine.

It was, however, a starter from the back end of the rotation, Kent Mercker, who provided Lopez his most memorable game in 1994. On April 8 the Braves were visiting the Los Angeles Dodgers for their fifth game of the season. Kent Mercker was on the mound for the Braves and Lopez was behind the plate. Despite some first-inning trouble (two walks), Lopez was able to guide Mercker out of the inning unscathed. Mercker finished the game with 10 strikeouts, four walks, and zero hits allowed. As of 2019 the game was the last no-hitter pitched by a member of the Braves.

After the strike-shortened season of 1994, and the late start to the 1995 season as the strike wound down, Lopez solidified his spot in the starting lineup for the perennial playoff contender Braves. He improved in every major statistical category, and by the end of the season there was no doubt who the backstop of the future was for the Braves. In the postseason Lopez helped the Braves slug their way past the Colorado Rockies and Cincinnati Reds, and provided one of the greatest plays of the World Series, against the Cleveland Indians.

In the bottom of the sixth inning Lopez hit a line-drive, two-run home run off Dennis Martinez that gave the Braves a 4-2 lead, which they did not relinquish.

In the top of the eighth, the Indians' Manny Ramirez was on first and slugger Jim Thome was at bat. Lopez had observed Ramirez's penchant for a large lead off the bag and decided to take a chance at stealing an out. Lopez recalled, "McGriff looked at me, and I signaled to him by touching the ground and picking up the dirt. He signaled back by tugging on his pants."[15] On a 2-and-2 count, Alejandro Peña threw a pitch up and in, which Thome did not offer at. Lopez flung the ball to Fred McGriff at first, catching Ramirez by surprise for the second out of the inning. Thome walked on the next pitch, and without Lopez's pickoff throw, the eighth inning might have unfolded differently. "It was the best feeling in the world," Lopez recalled.[16]

The Braves won the World Series in six games. Just nine days after Lopez jumped into Mark Wohlers' arms as a World Series champion,[17] Javy and Analy welcomed the couple's first son, Javier Alexander, to the world. It was certainly about as good a two-week stretch anyone can hope to have.[18]

The 1996 regular season was a respectable one for Lopez. He eclipsed the 20-home-run mark for the first time. But Lopez again saved his best performances for the postseason. In the NLCS he helped guide the Braves back from a three-games-to-one deficit against the St. Louis Cardinals by going 13-for-24 with two home runs, five doubles, and three walks. Lopez did not maintain this torrid pace in the World Series, which the Braves lost in six games after taking a 2-games-to-none lead over the New York Yankees. Lopez was 4-for-25.

Lopez was selected for the National League All-Star team in 1997 and 1998. He showed solid power, called a respectable game behind the plate. Lopez finished the 1998 season with 34 home runs, two shy of Joe Torre's franchise record of 36 home runs by a catcher.[19] In both seasons the Braves were defeated in the NLCS.

In 1999 Lopez suffered the first major setback in his career. Lopez was having another strong year statistically, but in late July Lopez suffered a torn ACL, and his season was finished.[20] Also that year Lopez's mother died after having a stroke, and his father had quadruple bypass surgery. As Jacinto Lopez recovered in the Lopez family home, Javy decided to buy the house next door and moved in Jacinto's twin sister, Lourdes, where she helped take care of Jacinto and kept him company. Lopez also decided to provide everything his father needed financially so he did not have to return to his high-stress job as a newspaper distributor. Professionally, Lopez watched the Braves make another World Series run, but were swept by the Yankees. Lopez wondered how much he could have helped the Braves in the Series. Lopez was also coming to terms with his failing marriage, a brother addicted to drugs, and his sister Elaine's pending divorce from Juan Gonzalez. He acknowledged that the combination of all of these issues left Lopez in quite a negative state of mind.[21] During this tumultuous time, Lopez's second son, Kelvin Gabriel, was born.[22]

Lopez returned with a solid 2000 season, but the decline in his game was starting to become evident. His batting and power numbers slipped in 2001 and 2002, and rumors that the Braves would move on from Lopez became more and more audible. A team built around a pitching staff cannot afford to have a liability at catcher, especially a catcher paid as an All-Star-caliber player but who no longer performed as one, and this was on a team with growing budgetary concerns. One of the issues that plagued Lopez throughout the 2002 season was a contentious divorce and the fear that Lopez might become estranged from his two sons. The mental toll of the divorce and custody battle was tremendous, and were probably a strong factor in some of Lopez's shortcomings on the field.[23]

Then … The 2003 season was undoubtedly Lopez's best, statistically speaking. He was at a crucial juncture in his career. Lopez was 32 years old and played a position in which players do not typically age gracefully. He had come off a dismal 2002 season, and faced the realization that the Braves had recently acquired their supposed catcher of the future in Johnny Estrada. Long gone were the All-Star campaigns of 1997 and 1998, and the postseason heroics of the mid-1990s. The reality was that Lopez was a hit-first catcher with some pop who no longer could hit – or at least that was what the baseball world believed. Lopez heard the critics, and in many regards he agreed with their assessment of the state of his game.

Lopez entered the 2003 season with a new mental approach and a revamped conditioning program. No longer the flabby 248-pound catcher eating everything in sight, he was a lean 210-pounder who lifted weights multiple times per week instead of once or twice a month, the regimen he followed in previous seasons.[24] Whether these improvements were the result of hard work and determination or chemical enhancements, as was the theme of baseball of the period, could be debated for years to come. Lopez even created some doubt on his new physique with interviews in which he was a little too coy about the subject. In an interview in 2010 he reflected upon 2003: "Well, everybody seen players getting big, hitting the ball harder, home runs and stuff. All of a sudden – boom – they got the big contract and everybody's like, 'You know what, did that, it worked for him, why not do it?'… I mean, how can I explain this? It's like if you're going to race cars, if you're going to race a car and some people are using nitro in the fuel [Lopez laughed], and you see them winning all the time, and you're using regular gas – you know what? If they're using nitro and they've been winning, well, I'd be stupid enough not to use nitro, too."[25]

But the fact remains that Lopez showed tremendous results from his lifestyle changes, regardless of how they were obtained, and slugged his way to an incredible 2003 season. Even the noticeable focus on his diet and conditioning did not create immediate benefits. Lopez had to stop fighting his psyche in the batter's box – taking every out as an indictment of his abilities –and had to have faith in his natural abilities. Also, Lopez opened his stance a bit, and began to reap the benefits. He made consistent and hard contact.[26] His new approach, conveniently in a contract season, created Lopez's finest season in the big leagues with career highs in home runs (43), RBIs (109), batting average (.328), on-base percentage (.378), and slugging percentage (.687). Lopez established the major-league record for home runs by a catcher, 42 (one of his home runs came via a pinch-hit against the Mets in July). He played in his third and final All-Star Game (he was the starting catcher for the National League) and was poised to cash in on his success in the coming free-agency period. But all of this success still did not mean that Lopez would be catching one of the best pitchers of his generation, Greg Maddux.

One of the most discussed aspects of Lopez's career was his professional relationship with Maddux. Attempting to explain why the most talented catcher on the roster was not catching Maddux, arguably the best pitcher in the league, article after article was published suggesting that, at least at some level, there was a rift between the two.

Both players downplayed the drama, but every time Maddux toed the rubber and Lopez was not behind the plate, there would be a comment or question about it. In fact, between September 8, 1998, and September 28, 2003, if Lopez caught a pitch from Maddux, it was because Lopez entered the game late as a pinch-hitter, and manager Bobby Cox did not want to remove his ace pitcher from the game just yet.[27] Fueling the controversy was the fact that in 1994, when Maddux led the league with a 1.56 ERA, Lopez caught 22 of his 25 starts. So, on paper at least, it seemed as if the two players could coexist in the same game.

Eddie Perez was a longtime backup catcher with the Braves and personal favorite of Maddux; he also downplayed the rift. Perez said a player knowing when he would get to play or have a day off was important for staying mentally sharp throughout the grind of the long season, and Maddux was able to provide this for two players, Lopez and his backup, each season.[28] Even in the playoffs, Bobby Cox adhered to his distaste for pairing Maddux and Lopez in the battery despite endless objections and questions from the media. It just seemed to be regarded as certain that Lopez was not going to be catching Maddux, regardless of the magnitude of the situation.[29] After his career was over, Lopez did admit that it bothered him that he did not catch Maddux in some of the biggest situations for the Braves. He wondered if the Braves could have won even more if he had caught Maddux, and he wondered how much more gaudy his own 2003 season would have been with the added at-bats from catching Maddux on a consistent basis.[30]

After his dominant 2003, Lopez did test the free-agency waters and landed in Baltimore, which was attempting to revamp its offense. Lopez played in a career-high 150 games, and batted .316. It was easily his second best season in the majors. Despite his impressive stats, Lopez was on a losing team for the first time in his career and watched the postseason from home, but at least he was not watching alone.[31] The move to Baltimore coincided with another major happening in his life. On June 23, 2004, he married his second wife, Gina.[32]

The 2004 season was Lopez's high-water mark with the Orioles, and in August of 2006 he was jettisoned to the Boston Red Sox for a journeyman player, Adam Stern. He played in 18 uneventful games before being released in September. Lopez was re-entering the free-agency pool with much less luster than in his previous free-agency campaigns. Lopez signed with the Colorado Rockies but was released before the 2007 season began. He tried a comeback with the Braves in spring training in 2008, but decided to retire when it became evident that he just could not hit the ball the way he once did and he was reassigned to the minor-league camp.[33]

Lopez retired with a career batting average of .287, 260 home runs, a World Series ring, an NLCS MVP award, three All-Star team selections, one Silver Slugger Award, over $61 million in earnings, and an incredible pickoff throw in the 1995 World Series. He had played on 11 division winners, and had that magical 2003 season when he set the season record for home runs by a catcher.

Lopez founded Bones Bats, a company that made hardwood bats, so that he would still have some connection to baseball.[34] He chose to use the word Bones instead of his name because he knew no player would buy a bat to use in the major leagues with another player's name on it. Appealing to major-league players with the bat did not work, and most of the sales were to the amateur ranks and dealers. Bones Bats did not prosper as Lopez had hoped, but he felt strongly about his product and said he would continue to produce bats as long as he felt this way.[35]

Lopez occasionally traveled to Florida to help coach the Braves young players during spring training. He was inducted into the Atlanta Braves Hall of Fame during the 2015 season.[36]

Lopez and Gina settled in Suwanee, Georgia, in the Atlanta metropolitan area. They had two sons, Brody, born in 2014, and Gavin, born in 2010. He began to play in charity golf tournaments.[37] Lopez also enrolled in Leadership Gwinnett to learn more about his community and its government, and to network with people outside of baseball.[38] He also spent more time at his longtime hobby of remote-control airplane flying.[39] Lopez also strove to make at least two trips a year to his native Puerto Rico, especially for New Year's Eve, which was a time for rejoicing and celebration with his family and friends at his sister's home.[40]

Notes

1. Both baseball-reference.com and retrosheet.org list Lopez at that height and weight.
2. Associated Press, "Javy Lopez: What a Difference a Year Makes," *Augusta Chronicle*, June 28, 2003.
3. Javy Lopez and Gary Caruso, *Behind the Plate: A Catcher's View of the Braves Dynasty* (Chicago: Triumph Books, 2012), 15-16.
4. "Braves: Javy Lopez Returns to His Roots. Puerto Rico Welcomes Native Son Home," *Savannah Morning News*, April 15, 2003.
5. Lopez and Caruso, 20.
6. "Braves: Javy Lopez Returns to his Roots."
7. Lopez and Caruso, 20-22.
8. "Braves: Javy Lopez Returns to his Roots."
9. Lopez and Caruso, 22-29.
10. "Braves: Javy Lopez Returns to his Roots."
11. Lopez and Caruso, 28.
12. I.J. Rosenberg, "Whatever Happened To: Ex-Brave Javy Lopez," *Atlanta Journal-Constitution*, October 1, 2015.
13. Lopez and Caruso, 32.
14. Lopez and Caruso, 109.
15. I.J. Rosenberg, "Javy Lopez Remembers Picking Off Manny Ramirez," *Atlanta Journal-Constitution*, October 1, 2015.
16. Gene Sapakoff, "Javy Lopez Recalls 'Goofy' Maddux, Respect for Former Braves Coach Cox," *Charleston* (South Carolina) *Post and Courier*, January 28, 2014.
17. Lopez and Caruso, 111.
18. Sapakoff.
19. Mike Berardino, "Lopez Finally Grabbing Headlines," *South Florida Sun Sentinel* (Fort Lauderdale), September 13, 1998.
20. "Braves Lose Lopez For Season," cbsnews.com/news/braves-lose-lopez-for-season/, accessed February 1, 2017.
21. Lopez and Caruso, 103-104.
22. Lopez and Caruso, 111.
23. Roch Kubatko, "Clearing His Mind, Though Not His Plate," *Baltimore Sun*, February 23, 2004.
24. Associated Press, "Javy Lopez: What a Difference a Year Makes," *Augusta Chronicle*, June 28, 2003.
25. Craig Calcaterra, "Javy Lopez on Steroids: 'I'd be Stupid Not to Use Nitro Too," Hardball Talk, http://mlb.nbcsports.com/2010/02/05/javy-lopez-on-steroids-i/, accessed December 14, 2016.
26. Associated Press, "Javy Lopez: What a Difference a Year Makes."
27. Rafael Hermoso, "Baseball: If Maddux Is Pitching, Lopez Isn't Catching," *New York Times*, October 5, 2002.
28. Mark Bowman, "For Perez, a Front-Row Squat at Maddux's Greatness," MLB.com, m.mlb.com/news/article/66355592/former-braves-catcher-eddie-perez-reflects-on-greg-madduxs-greatness/, accessed January 15, 2017.
29. Rafael Hermoso, "Baseball: If Maddux Is Pitching, Lopez Isn't Catching."
30. Fox Sports South, "Javy Lopez Q&A, Yardbarker.com, yardbarker.com/mlb/articles/javy_lopez_q_a/s1_10297_10268746?, accessed February 1, 2017.
31. Roch Kubatko, "Orioles, J. Lopez Agree to Contract," *Baltimore Sun*, December 22, 2003.
32. Lopez and Caruso, 116.
33. Associated Press, "Catcher Javy Lopez Retires After Getting Cut by the Braves," *USA Today*, March 23, 2008.
34. Fox Sports South, "Javy Lopez Q&A.
35. Lopez and Caruso, 175-176.
36. "Javy Lopez to the Braves HOF," NotintheHallofFame.com, notinhalloffame.com/home/news/4514-javy-lopez-to-the-braves-hof, accessed December 14, 2016.
37. I.J. Rosenberg, "Whatever Happened To: Ex-Brave Javy Lopez."
38. Lopez and Caruso, 177-178.
39. Bill Zach, "Lopez Finds Escape Through His Planes," Online Athens, onlineathens.com/stories/111900/spo_1119000073.

shtml#.WI-x97YrLR0, accessed January 31, 2017; Matt Hennie, "Javy Lopez and His Multi-Million-Dollar Home," projectq.us/atlanta/javy_lopez_and_his_multi-million_dollar_home, accessed January 31, 2017.

40   Lopez and Caruso, 16.

Greg Maddux

BY STEW THORNLEY

Greg Maddux

On August 26, 1995, Greg Maddux was at Wrigley Field in Chicago, formerly his home stadium. Now a member of the Atlanta Braves, Maddux was on the verge of tying a major-league record with his 16th consecutive road victory. With two out in the top of the third, Maddux singled to left, starting a five-run rally. He took the mound in the bottom of the inning with a 5-0 lead. In the press box, a writer muttered, "This is like giving a 15-0 lead to a regular human being."[1]

The comment reflected the dominance Maddux had established in the 1990s and the awe and wonder in which he was held as he reached the peak of his career. Maddux got his win in this game – and another five before the season closed. He became the first pitcher to win four consecutive Cy Young Awards. In 1994 and 1995, Maddux posted an earned run average (ERA) that was minuscule in any circumstances, historic in relation to the league ERA each year.

Gregory Alan Maddux was born April 14, 1966, in San Angelo, Texas, where his dad was stationed at the time. Dave Maddux had graduated from high school in Decatur County, Indiana, in 1957 and joined the U. S. Air Force, where he was involved in accounting and finance for 22 years. When his girlfriend, Linda, graduated a year later, the couple was married.[2] A daughter, Terri Lynn, was born in 1959 while Dave was stationed at Elmendorf Air Force Base in Anchorage.

The family was at Wright-Patterson Air Force Base in Dayton, Ohio, when son Mike was born in 1961. After two years in Taiwan, the Madduxes were stateside again when Greg was born. Soon after, with the Vietnam War going on, Dave had a one-year tour in Thailand. Linda took the kids back to Decatur County, where a number of family members lived.[3]

When Dave returned from Thailand, the transfers continued – to Minot, North Dakota, for a year; Riverside, California, for three years; and Spain for another three years. It was in Spain that the Maddux children were most active in sports. Terri was on the track team in high school and continued her love of running, including marathons, through her life. The boys participated in football. All three played basketball.

On the diamond, Terri, like most girls, was shunted away from baseball and into softball. Mike and Greg played in a sanctioned Little League. "Kids would come home from practice in the hot sun, and the first thing they would do is head outside into the yard to play more baseball in the hot sun," Linda said. "Finally, I came to the realization that they were doing what they wanted to do. And they all survived."

Dave Maddux got his final transfer in August 1976, to Nellis Air Force Base in Las Vegas. He eventually received orders to move back to Elmendorf Air Force Base. Linda recalled that once they would have embraced this assignment. "When we were kids we had decided we would want to go to Elmendorf to retire," she said. "By this time, we had two kids in college, and we wouldn't consider leaving them behind."[4] Instead, Dave retired from the military and became a poker dealer at various casinos in Las Vegas.

Terri was starting her junior year at the University of Nevada, Las Vegas (UNLV), at this time, and Mike was entering his first year at the University of Texas, El Paso. As for Greg, he found himself in a different school district from where his siblings had been, at Rancho High School, which had served those living at the military base. With Dave a civilian, the Madduxes moved to the southeast side of Las Vegas, and Greg attended Valley High School.

Greg played junior-varsity basketball, as Mike had done, but both brothers were discouraged from the sport by coaches, who wanted them to focus on their pitching potential in baseball. During Maddux's junior year, Valley High School won the state baseball championship under coach Rodger Fairless.

Beyond what he learned from Fairless, Maddux had a tutor in Ralph Medar, a former scout, who oversaw workouts and organized pickup games on Sunday mornings in Las Vegas. "Ralph was the first pitching coach I ever had," Maddux told John McMurray for an article in *Baseball Digest*. "He worked with me when I was 15 years old, and he taught me that movement was more important than velocity. He helped me make the ball move and sink as opposed to seeing how hard I could throw it. I think I was fortunate to learn that lesson at such a young age."[5]

Maddux didn't turn heads with out-of-this-world stuff, a blazing fastball or a 12-to-6 curve ball. Never having had the luxury of such gifts, Maddux instead learned to pitch. Throughout his career, he was known for his control, late movement on his pitches, and knowing what he was doing. From an early age, Maddux established his reputation for being a cerebral pitcher, studying hitters and getting them out on pitches that hardly seemed imposing on their way to the plate – at least the first half of the way.

Maddux planned on attending the University of Arizona in Tucson and playing for Jerry Kindall, who had won two national championships as a coach and was on his way to a third. Linda remembers how impressed she was when meeting Kindall. "We had heard that Jerry took good care of his pitchers," she said, adding that Kindall was known for being "not so intent on winning that he would burn out his pitchers."[6]

However, Maddux was drafted in the second round by the Chicago Cubs in June 1984, and the bonus offered was enough that two weeks later he decided to skip college and sign a pro contract. He put the bonus money aside, in case baseball didn't work out and he wanted to go back to college, and lived off his minor-league salary in addition to money he had saved during summer jobs he worked at Sears and Wendy's in Las Vegas.

Maddux progressed through the minors with the steady rhythm that defined his work on the mound: Rookie League in 1984, Class A in 1985, and a three-level rise the following season, from Double-A to Triple-A to the majors as a September call-up.

Maddux made his major-league debut as a pinch-runner for the Cubs in the 17th inning of a game against Houston September 3, a game that had started the day before and was suspended by darkness. He stayed in the game and pitched the 18th inning, giving up a run and taking the loss. Four days later, he was the starter against Cincinnati and went the distance in an 11-3 win, which stopped a seven-game Chicago losing streak.

Maddux made five starts for the Cubs in 1986, the last one at Philadelphia. The opposing starter was his brother Mike, who had also reached the majors that season. Greg prevailed in this game, winning 8-3.

Opponents in 1986, Greg and Mike became teammates for the first time after the 1987 season, playing winter ball in Maracaibo, Venezuela. The pitching coach was Dick Pole, who had worked with Greg in the minors and would again with the Cubs. Pole is often credited with teaching Maddux the value of a ground out. "Dick always told me. 'You don't have to strike him out, you just got to get him out,'" Maddux said.[7]

Pole was also discovering in Maddux a fearlessness on the mound, one that allowed him to throw any pitch in any situation. Pole said that when he was a pitching coach for other teams, he warned that Maddux would throw a change up on a full count in the ninth. Invariably, however, batters would still get caught looking in these situations.[8]

Maddux had one more brief stint in the minors, in 1987, and then was up for good. He had a great start in 1988, earning a berth on the All-Star team, before cooling off. After a slow start in 1989, he picked it up. Combined, he had 37 wins and an ERA of 3.07 for the two years.

In 1992, Maddux had 10 wins by early July and was picked for the All-Star Game, in which he relieved starter Tom Glavine of Atlanta, who had a 13-3 record and seemed on his way to a second consecutive Cy Young Award. However, Maddux was outstanding over the remainder of the year, finishing the season with a 2.18 ERA, third in the majors, and leading major-league pitchers with 268 innings pitched. Although Wins above Replacement (WAR) was not yet in wide use, later analyses showed that Maddux led all players in 1992 with a WAR of 9.4 (9.2 as a pitcher).[9] Maddux got the Cy Young Award, and Glavine finished second.

Maddux was a free agent after the 1992 season and was the top player on the market. His agent, Scott Boras, was negotiating with Cubs general manager Larry Himes and, characteristically, was expecting top dollar. The Cubs were offering a five-year contract for $27.5 million (guaranteed with another $1.5 million in incentives). When Maddux didn't sign right away, the Cubs signed free-agent Jose Guzman and appeared to back off on their offer to Maddux. The New York Yankees topped all offers to Maddux at $34 million (reportedly increased to $37.5 million[10]), and Maddux seemed ready to go to the Bronx. A late entry by Atlanta at $28 million caught his attention, and Maddux signed with the Braves.

Maddux had a few reasons for signing for less money than what he could have gotten from the Yankees, including that he thought Atlanta would be a better place to raise a family than New York. Maddux had married Kathy Ronnow, whom he had known since high school, in 1988. By the end of 1993, they had a daughter, Amanda Paige (who goes by Paige). In 1997 they had a son, Chase.

A player departing a team as a free agent often leaves hard feelings with fans, and Maddux was back at Wrigley Field for the season opener in 1993. He wasn't fazed by the booing he received as the Braves won the game, 1-0, with Maddux outdueling the Cubs' Mike Morgan (who was also a graduate of Valley High School in Las Vegas).

Although he understood the fans' reaction, Maddux was hurt by comments made by former teammates, such as Ryne Sandberg, about his signing with the Braves. The charges included that he had planned to sign with the Braves all along and used the Cubs (and then the Yankees) to get a larger offer. Maddux said he made repeated calls to the Cubs during the final stage of negotiations and if the team would have put its original offer back on the table, he would have considered it "heavily."[11] (Unbeknownst to Maddux at the time of his final call, the Cubs had just signed free-agent Randy Myers. The Cubs had also signed another pitcher, Dan Plesac. According to Himes,

"We went over the numbers on those," meaning there wasn't money left for Maddux.)[12]

What didn't work out for the Cubs became a boon to the Braves. Maddux was eventually called by Houston general manager Gerry Hunsicker, "The greatest free-agent signing in baseball history."

Atlanta pitching coach Leo Mazzone said, "When we signed Maddux, I didn't realize at the time it was going to be the greatest free-agent signing in the history of the game. But I knew I was going to get a lot smarter, real quick."[13]

Maddux was joining a team that had won the last two National League pennants with a rotation that had Glavine, a former and future Cy Young recipient; John Smoltz, a future Cy Young recipient; and another top young pitcher, lefthander Steve Avery. Not surprisingly, the Braves staff allowed the fewest runs in the National League in 1993. With a strong lineup – including shortstop Jeff Blauser and outfielders David Justice and Ron Gant – the Braves were near the top in runs scored, as well. The one team in their division to rival them in both categories, the San Francisco Giants, battled the Braves to the end. Maddux was the winning pitcher in the Braves' penultimate game, and the next day Glavine was the winner while the Giants were losing. Atlanta, with 104 wins, beat out the Giants by a game for the title in the National League West.

Steve Avery started the first game of the playoffs, which the Braves lost to the Philadelphia Phillies in 10 innings. Maddux, fully rested for Game 2, pitched seven strong innings as the Braves tied the series. The Phillies won two of the next three, and the Braves faced elimination in Game 6, with Maddux back on the mound. This time he didn't make it through the sixth, giving up six runs (five earned), and the Phillies won to advance to the World Series.

During the regular season, Maddux led the league with 267 innings and an ERA of 2.36 and received the Cy Young Award again. What was coming, however, was even better.

The 1994 and 1995 seasons were truncated by a players' strike, and Maddux pitched barely over 200 innings, although it was enough to lead the majors both years. His earned run average in 1994 was 1.56. Two years before, when Maddux received his first Cy Young Award, National League teams averaged 3.9 runs per game, and the league ERA was 3.50. In 1994, the averages were 4.6 and 4.21, respectively.

Maddux's 1994 ERA was only 37.1 percent of the league average, even better than what Bob Gibson had achieved with his 1.12 ERA in 1968, the Year of the Pitcher. Maddux in 1995 had a 1.63 ERA, 39 percent of the league average.

Writers, analysts, and others were touting Maddux as the best right-handed pitcher since Walter Johnson. A number of outstanding southpaws pitched in the period between Johnson and Maddux – Lefty Grove, Warren Spahn, and Sandy Koufax, and pundits generally conceded that Maddux was not on the same level as Koufax.

Pitchers can be compared in many ways, and the difference in innings pitched then and later is relevant to any discussion about the greatest. In terms of ERA relative to the league average, Maddux has few rivals, including Koufax. In addition, the ballpark factors show Dodger Stadium – Koufax's home park in his prime – to be pitcher friendlier than Maddux's home parks with the Braves, Atlanta-Fulton County Stadium and Turner Field.[14]

Maddux finished this four-year run of greatness by pitching in his first World Series. With seven days' rest, he started the first game of the 1995 World Series and was outstanding. The first batter he faced, Cleveland's Kenny Lofton, reached base on an error and came around to score. The only other baserunners off Maddux were Jim Thome, with a fifth-inning single, and Lofton, who singled in the ninth and came around to score on an error. Atlanta won the game, 3-2. Maddux had the chance to finish off the Series five days later but wasn't as sharp. He gave up two runs in the last of the first. After the Braves tied the game, he gave up two more runs and took the loss. The Braves still won the series, taking the next game 1-0 on a David Justice home run and a one-hitter by Glavine and Mark Wohlers.

Maddux pitched in two more World Series. In Game 2 of the 1996 Series he pitched eight scoreless innings, allowing six hits and no walks, as the Braves beat the New York Yankees, 4-0. He was the losing pitcher in the final game as the Yankees won the World Series, 4 games to 2. In 1999 the Yankees beat the Braves again, this one a sweep. Maddux pitched the opening game and carried a 1-0 lead into the eighth inning before giving up four runs. His performance in five World Series games was good – he had a 2.09 ERA in those games. Between 1989 and 2008 Maddux appeared in 35 postseason games and had a 3.27 ERA in 198 innings.

As for the regular season, Maddux continued in top form although he didn't receive any more Cy Young Awards. Between 1996 and 2000, he was in the top 5 in the balloting four times. His 1997 season was of the caliber that it would have been the best in the league in a lot of years. However, this year Pedro Martinez of Montreal was beginning a string of Maddux-like seasons.

Martinez, with the Expos and Boston Red Sox, received the Cy Young Award three times in four years, with a second-place finish the other year. In 2000 Martinez had a 1.74 ERA when the league average was 4.91, a performance even better than what Maddux had produced in 1994.

Martinez's fantastic seasons served to highlight the dominance of Maddux around the same period. The pair had produced three of the top five performances in terms of ERA+ (the pitcher's ERA compared to the league ERA with adjustments made for the pitcher's home ballpark). The others in the top five had occurred in the Deadball Era (Dutch Leonard in 1914) and the 19th century (Tim Keefe in 1880).

Although Martinez was gone as a Cy Young rival after 1997, the National League continued to have strong contenders for the award. Maddux's teammates received it in 1996 (Smoltz) and 1998 (Glavine); Randy Johnson of Arizona then started a string of four Cy Young Awards.

Maddux continued as a top pitcher into the 21st century, even if he was no longer a perennial contender for the Cy Young Award. He pitched with the Braves through 2003 before signing as a free agent with the Cubs before the 2004 season. Over the next few years he pitched for the Los Angeles Dodgers and San Diego Padres. Maddux's last game was in relief for the Dodgers in the final game of the 2008 National League Championship Series. He pitched two innings and gave up two unearned runs as Philadelphia beat Los Angeles for the pennant. A free agent at the end of the season, Maddux called it a career, announcing his retirement in December.

Between traditional statistics, such as wins, and ones more recently embraced, such as ERA+, Maddux was outstanding both in peak and career value. Much is made of him winning at least 15 games a year between 1988 and 2004. He finished with 355 career wins, the most of any pitcher other than Warren Spahn who had pitched after 1930.

Maddux struck out 3,371 batters in 5,008.1 innings, an average of about 6 per 9 innings. Although this may not raise eyebrows, a key to his success was his control – he walked just 999 batters, an average of 1.8 per 9 innings. In 2001 Maddux set a National League record with 72.1 straight innings without a walk, a streak that was broken with an intentional walk. During his Cy Young Award seasons, Maddux led the National League in Fielding Independent Pitching (FIP) all four years.[15]

Bob Nightengale of *USA Today* pointed out how Maddux had dominated the game for years without being a power pitcher: "Maddux, whose fastball is routinely clocked at only 88 mph, remarkably throws more fastballs than any established pitcher in the game. The difference is control and movement. He can throw the fastball with nearly pinpoint control, while the ball darts and spins as if he's controlling it like a yo-yo."[16]

"He can throw you a strike and still not give you anything good to hit," said Braves pitching coach Leo Mazzone. "He's a master at that. It's the greatest command I've ever seen on a consistent basis."[17]

Mazzone and others have told of Maddux's penchant for telling his pitching coach, manager, and teammates about how he will get out of an inning, such as saying that he'll get the batter to foul out to the third baseman on the second pitch to him.[18]

Jeff Torborg, who caught flamethrowers Sandy Koufax and Nolan Ryan, later observed and marveled at Maddux carving up batters in a completely different manner. Torborg commented on how Maddux could throw a pitch so that it appeared it would be a ball but then break over the plate after the batter had decided not to swing. Torborg said Maddux stood out because, unlike most pitchers, he could start the ball out on either side of the plate and have it break back for a strike.[19]

Maddux summed up his style in an interview with Bob Nightengale in 2001:

"The best pitch in baseball is a located fastball. That will always be the best pitch. You can set up everything you want off that.

"[Hall of Fame pitcher] Don Sutton used to always say to make sure all your pitches look the same when they're 5 feet out of your hand. Then find ways to make the ball end up in different places and at different speeds. The more ways you can put it in more places at more speeds, the better.

"That's pitching."[20]

However the stats are sliced, Maddux stands out as one of the best pitchers ever, and he was easily elected to the Hall of Fame in 2014. He was inducted with his teammate, Tom Glavine, and his manager while with the Braves, Bobby Cox. His number 31 was retired by both the Braves and the Cubs (with the latter, the retirement of 31 is for both Maddux and Ferguson Jenkins).

The Madduxes made Las Vegas their permanent home, even as Greg moved around the majors as a pitcher and later in assorted duties with teams. He worked with the Cubs as an assistant to the general manager, focusing on working with pitchers from 2010 to 2012. He then worked with the Texas Rangers, where brother Mike was the pitching coach, and later as a special assistant with the Los Angeles Dodgers. In between he was the pitching coach for the United States in the 2013 World Baseball Classic.

His son, Chase, made it as a right-handed pitcher on the UNLV baseball team, and in 2016 Greg joined the Rebels as a volunteer assistant coach.[21]

In 1995, when Maddux was at his peak, Tom Verducci wrote in *Sports Illustrated*, "His career is a masterpiece, available for all to see every fifth day or so as he works atop the pitching mounds of National League ballparks.

"The rest of us, should we recognize our good fortune, could be eyewitnesses to genius. Did you see van Gogh paint? No, you could respond, but I saw Greg Maddux pitch."[22]

Notes

1. Overheard by the author of this article, who was in the press box that Saturday afternoon.
2. The information on the Madduxes and the details of their children growing up came from a telephone interview between the author and Linda Maddux, May 16, 1995.
3. Dave was one of 10 children, three of them boys. Linda was one of three girls.
4. Telephone interview with Linda Maddux, May 16, 1995.
5. John McMurray, "Greg Maddux: Consistency, Hard Work, and Pitching Smarts Made Him a Winner," *Baseball Digest*, September 2007: 40.
6. Telephone interview with Linda Maddux, May 16, 1995.
7. Carroll Rogers Walton, "More to Maddux Than Meets the Eye," *Atlanta Journal-Constitution*, July 17, 2009, accessed February 23, 2018 from https://www.ajc.com/sports/baseball/more-maddux-than-meets-the-eye/BnbkvNMtw20N4vErpjatCI/.
8. Carrie Muskat, "Like Clockwork: In-out, Up-down," *USA Today Baseball Weekly*, November 21-25, 1995: 20.
9. baseball-reference.com is the source for WAR. Maddux probably received a little bump in his WAR for his fielding; he received the Gold Glove for the third time in 1992, and he got the award 18 times in his career.

10 Joey Reaves, "Maddux and Dawson Sign Off," *Chicago Tribune,* December 10, 1992: 3, Section 4.

11 Alan Solomon, "Hurt, Maddux Answers Critics," *Chicago Tribune,* December 13, 1992: 16, Section 3.

12 Alan Solomon, "Maddux Agent Tried Cubs Again," *Chicago Tribune,* December 10, 1992: 3, Section 4.

13 Bob Nightengale, "Inside the Mind of Maddux," *USA Today Baseball Weekly,* August 15-21, 2001: 14.

14 baseball-reference.com has Maddux with an ERA+ (the pitcher's ERA relative to the league ERA, is adjusted to the pitcher's home park) of 271 in 1994 and 260 in 1995. Koufax, Spahn, and Grove never approached those figures.

15 FIP focuses on elements of pitching – walks, hit batters, home runs, and strikeouts – that are independent of fielding.

16 Bob Nightengale, "Inside the Mind of Maddux," *USA Today Baseball Weekly,* August 15-21, 2001: 14.

17 Carrie Muskat, "Like Clockwork: In-out, Up-down," *USA Today Baseball Weekly,* November 21-25, 1995: 22.

18 These stories emerged during a player panel – moderated by Pete Van Wieren with panelists Phil Niekro, Mark Lemke, Bobby Cox, and Ron Gant - at the SABR convention in Atlanta, August 6, 2010.

19 Murray Chass, "Koufax and Maddux: Unequaled Mastery," *The New York Times,* August 17, 1997: 24.

20 Bob Nightengale, "Inside the Mind of Maddux," *USA Today Baseball Weekly,* August 15-21, 2001: 14.

21 "Baseball Hall of Famer Joins Rebel Staff," UNLV Rebels press release, July 6, 2016, http://www.unlvrebels.com/sports/m-basebl/spec-rel/070616aaa.html.

22 Tom Verducci, "Once in a Lifetime," *Sports Illustrated,* August 14, 1995: 24.

Darrell May

BY DARIN WATSON

Darrell May

Courtesy Atlanta National League Baseball Club LLC.

Even though any player who reaches the major leagues is supremely talented, perseverance is a key factor for many of them. The ability to keep trying often separates major and minor leaguers. For Darrell May, perseverance included transitions between several organizations and a stint in Japan, before finding himself as the leader of the pitching staff on a surprising team, and then narrowly avoiding the stigma of a 20-loss season.

Darrell Kevin May was born on June 13, 1972, in San Bernardino, California. The son of Robert and Judy May, he joined a family that already included older brother Jeff, 10½ years Darrell's senior. Robert May grew up in West Virginia, one of 12 children in his family. After working in the coal mines, he joined the Air Force and served as a mechanic. Out of the service, he went to work as a cable splicer for many phone companies. Judy also came from a good-sized family: She was one of six children in hers. She was a stay-at-home mom, a full-time job by itself.

Before Darrell was born, Judy had been told by doctors that she couldn't get pregnant again, so his arrival was a pleasant surprise. The Mays moved to Oregon nine months after Darrell was born, settling in Rogue River next door to his maternal grandparents and his mother's sister. His father had fallen in love with the area, which reminded him of his home state West Virginia; and being near family was a plus.

The family lived on 10 acres of land in the natural beauty of southern Oregon, with plenty of room for baseball. Jeff was a very good basketball player, and Darrell wanted to follow in his footsteps. But Darrell suffered from asthma, and in his first day of practice in seventh grade, his asthma was so bad he couldn't run up and down the court one time without needing his inhaler. After a few days of that, it was apparent that Darrell would need to find another sport. Wrestling took over his fall and winter sports schedule, with baseball remaining his spring and summer sport.

In Oregon the May family became acquainted with another Southern California import, John "Buzzy" Black ("I remember hearing one time that he could never sit still, so he got the nickname Buzzy," May said.[1])

Black had coached Little League baseball for decades in Southern California, and when he saw 10-year-old Darrell's potential, he decided it was time to get back into coaching. Black would guide May throughout high school, and even when May was in the majors, Black would analyze video of his pupil and send him suggestions.

After graduating from Rogue River High School, May headed back to California for his college education. He attended Sacramento City College, excited at the chance to play for coach Jerry Weinstein, who was in the middle of a career that would see him win 830 games and a national title at the school.[2] At first, Sacramento City College was not in May's plans, but some Rogue River High School alumni who were friends with Black pushed for May to go there. On his way to a recruiting visit to Taft Community College in California, May stopped and threw a bullpen session for Weinstein, whose interest was piqued.

"After talking with him and the coaches and looking at all his memorabilia in his office and the guys who have been through that program, I didn't look anywhere else. I knew that's where I was going," May said.

The Oakland Athletics, with Dave Wilder scouting him, selected May after his freshman year, in the 14th round of the June 1991 draft. Despite his high-school success, May had not been scouted, so the lure of professional baseball was strong. But May decided to continue his education for one more year at least. Under the rules at the time, the Athletics retained his draft rights until the 1992 draft. As that draft neared, May was committed to the University of Tennessee. When Oakland contacted him again in a last-ditch effort to sign him, Wilder had moved on to Atlanta. May's new contact with Oakland insisted that the team's offer was a lower number than May remembered. May called Wilder on the second day of the 1992 draft, mainly out of curiosity over which offer was correct. Once Wilder realized May was available, he persuaded the Braves to draft him, with a better offer than Oakland had presented despite the lower draft position.

Atlanta was becoming famous for its ability to develop pitchers as an organization, with names like Tom Glavine, Steve Avery, Kent Mercker, Mike Stanton, and Mark Wohlers leading the Braves' renaissance in the early 1990s. That was an enticement to sign with the Braves, as was the team's offer to pay for May to continue his college education.

"To this day, if anybody asks, 'what was your favorite organization?'... Braves, definitely," May said. "I saw how consistent it was at every level. Every coach teaches differently, but what they taught and how they taught, from Single A to Double A to Triple A, it was going to be the same."

May's first day of professional baseball was his 20th birthday. Despite his low draft position (or perhaps unburdened by not being highly drafted), May progressed steadily through the Braves system. All along the way, he showed an ability to throw strikes, with 2.22 walks per nine innings for his minor-league stops from 1992 to 1995.

All of that got him to the doorstep of the major leagues. By the time rosters expanded in September 1995, the Braves had a healthy lead in the NL East and were looking to the postseason. When Mercker tweaked his back, Atlanta summoned May to the majors, with Richmond manager Grady Little delivering the news to him after May had pitched 4⅔ no-hit innings in a game that was eventually rained out in Richmond's last series of the year.

"He asked me at the end of the game if I was riding the bus back or driving (from Norfolk to Richmond). I said I was riding the bus. He said, 'Well, don't be late.' I remember I was pissed off because I prided myself on being early. I did not ever want to be late, I didn't want to be the guy other guys were waiting on, so I was like, 'Why did he say that, did he see me late or something?' Well, the reason he didn't want me to be late was because he had to tell me I was getting called up to the big leagues. So we got back to Richmond, he calls me into his office. I thought, 'Oh no, what's going on?' He goes, 'I hate to inform this to you, but Kent Mercker hurt his back. You're going up.' I was like, 'What?!?' I kind of thought I had hit my plateau in this organization because of the studs we had at the big-league level," May said.

May made his major-league debut on September 10. With a 17-game lead in the division and 19 games left to play, the Braves were already setting up their playoff rotation. So Maddux started but pitched only one inning. He was followed by Jason Schmidt for three innings. May entered the game to pitch the bottom of the fifth with Atlanta ahead, 4-2. He allowed a single to Greg Colbrunn, then got a fly out and two grounders to end the inning. His second inning of work was a little rougher, as Quilvio Veras led off with a bunt single, then stole second and third. He scored on a sacrifice fly, but May recovered nicely to work through the heart of the Florida order, giving up a single to Jeff Conine but getting fly balls from Gary Sheffield and Terry Pendleton. Ultimately, the Marlins scored an unearned run in the ninth and then got the winning run in the 11th for a 5-4 win, but it was still a successful debut for May.

May pitched in one more game in 1995, two nights later in Colorado. This outing was uglier, as the Rockies scored four runs on five hits in his second inning of work en route to a 12-2 win. However, he did notch his first strikeout in the big leagues, getting Vinny Castilla on a swing and miss to end the inning.

For a young pitcher, joining the 1995 Braves was intimidating. But it was also educational, with the chance to study three eventual Hall of Famers (Glavine, John Smoltz, and Greg Maddux) up close.

"They were very welcoming. They would ride you, they would be hard on you. They were intimidating in their card games, playing hearts in the locker room with those guys. You get on one of the guys or give them a bunch of points and he'll ride you a little bit, but on the slope everybody was very professional, take care of business, let you take care of your business, do your own thing. Well, those guys did their own thing. I did what (pitching coach) Leo Mazzone told me."

As a rookie and a quiet personality, May mostly tried to absorb lessons from that trio by watching, but would occasionally ask questions. As a left-hander without overpowering stuff, Glavine in particular was a role model.

Those two games in 1995 would be May's only appearances in a Braves uniform. In 1996, at the end of spring training, Atlanta tried to sneak him through waivers, as he was out of options. Pittsburgh claimed him on waivers. He posted a 7-6 mark for their Triple-A team in Calgary, and appeared in five games at the major-league level before being waived by the Pirates. The California Angels claimed him in September, and he broke camp with the major-league team in 1997. He had pitched sparingly when he was demoted to Triple-A Vancouver in mid-May, but came back up in mid-July and pitched well in a long-relief role: a 3.86 ERA in 23⅓ innings before a rough September. Still, he seemed to be in the Angels' plans for 1998.

Until the end of spring training, anyway. Despite assurances that he would be the fifth starter, despite working with Angels pitching coach Marcel Lachemann over the winter, and despite a good spring training, May once again fell victim to a numbers game.

"I was told, whether it was true or not, they had signed a couple guys to guaranteed contracts. They weren't doing well at all, but they were guaranteed contracts. They were going to keep them," May said.

The Angels kept May on the roster until the end of spring training, hoping to sneak him through waivers. In the meantime, the Hanshin Tigers of the Japan Central League were interested. They had actually been scouting May for a while but the Angels had been unwilling to sell May to them.

"As a kid, I didn't grow up wanting to play baseball in Japan. I didn't want to meet with them. My agent had to talk me into meeting with them, just to hear them out. We met with them. … I was blown away with how much money they were willing to pay a guy that had, I think, maybe one year of big-league experience under my belt," May said.

The money was persuasive, as May figured he could help his family and still come back to the United States and try his luck with a minor-league team. Despite some trepidation, May signed a two-year deal with Hanshin.

"I didn't want a two-year contract, because if I didn't like it, I didn't want to have to come back for a second year. They convinced me they don't sign any foreigners to less than two-year deals," May said.

But May discovered that of six foreign players in the organization, he was one of only two signed for more than one year. He stuck with it, though. May seemed to do particularly well against the Yomiuri Giants, who have a fierce rivalry with Hanshin. So when May's two years with Hanshin were done, the Giants must have taken some delight in signing him as a free agent. After a successful 2000 season that included May finishing third in the league in strikeouts, he signed with Yomiuri for one more season.

Looking back, May said he enjoyed his time in Japan much more than he expected he would when he signed with Hanshin. Japanese teams pay for players' apartments, so while he was making more money than he had in major-league baseball, he was also able to save more. The cultural differences were eventually overcome, as well.

"You think baseball is baseball, but it's completely different over there. Once the game starts, there's a lot of similarities. Most people wouldn't notice the differences but being there and playing it, you definitely see the difference. Once I learned some of the language and adjusted to their style of baseball, I had a lot more fun with it and I really enjoyed playing in Tokyo," May said.

During that 2001 season, Allard Baird, then general manager of the Kansas City Royals, began scouting some Japanese players and noticed May. Baird was impressed with May's poise and command.

"The thing was not only what we saw on the field but the Giants over there are like the New York Yankees and are playing before about 45,000 people every night. So here's a guy who came over from the States, is playing for their big-market team and that's added pressure," Baird said.[3]

Meanwhile, May credited his time in Japan with preparing him to be in a major-league rotation.

"I needed to develop my breaking ball and, in Japan, they're good breaking-ball hitters. I talked to a lot of coaches who said you've got an average fastball and you've got to hit your spots," he said.[4]

May's 2002 got off to a rocky start, as he started the season on the disabled list with a torn groin. In his first game back, he re-injured it. It wasn't until June 6 that he picked up his first big league win in five years, pitching five innings in Kansas City's 4-3 win over the Chicago White Sox.

The 2002 Royals were in turmoil. Contraction rumors swirled early in the season before word came that the Royals were not a candidate. Manager Tony Muser was fired in late April, followed by pitching coach Al Nipper in June. The team became the first 100-game loser in franchise history.

All of which made 2003 that much sweeter for May and the Royals. The team jumped out to a 16-3 start, which stunned everybody outside the locker room. They reached the All-Star break with a seven-game lead in the American League Central Division. But Minnesota caught fire in the second half and captured the division title. Kansas City still ended up with an 83-79 record, the franchise's first winning mark since the strike-interrupted 1994 season.

Those facts obscure the almost comical lengths (such as signing Jose Lima, without scouting him first, out of an independent league and sticking him in the rotation) Baird had to go to in order to round out the pitching staff. Nearly every pitcher on the Opening Day roster was hurt at some point, as the Royals used a whopping 29 pitchers, 15 of whom made at least one start. May took the ball a team-high 32 times. (Chris George and Jeremy Affeldt tied for second with 18 games started.) And he would have taken it more often.

"I was trying to talk them into giving me the ball every four days, coming from the Braves organization where we threw two bullpens between starts. There were times where they put me in the bullpen between starts because they knew I was used to it," May said.

Of all those pitchers, May was the only one to reach double digits in wins. He also led the team in innings pitched, ERA, and strikeouts. As the veteran of the season-starting rotation (the only one older than 24), May did everything they could ask of him and was given the team's pitcher-of-the-year award at season's end.

Expectations were high for the 2004 Royals. But after a walk-off win over the White Sox on Opening Day, things fell apart quickly. May stayed dependable, making a team-high 31 starts. But while 2003 was a storybook season, this was a nightmare. Despite pitching for a team on its way to 104 losses, May's record was 9-12 in mid-August. Then he took six losses in a row; the Royals were shut out in the last three. With three turns left in the rotation, May had a chance to lose 20 games. Detroit's Mike Maroth had been saddled with 20 losses the previous season, but Brian Kingman of the Oakland A's was the last pitcher before him to do so, in 1980. A stigma had grown around the number.

A frustrated May said, "You try to keep in perspective. I can't put the blame on anybody else. But, realistically, I know there are a lot of games that easily could have gone the other way. Let's put it this way: There are a lot of games where I felt like I did my job that ended up as losses."[5]

As it was, May ended up with a league-leading 19 losses. The Royals were looking ahead to next season and had switched to a six-man rotation, so May's start on September 28, a 5-1 loss to Cleveland in game 157, was his last of the year. It was also his last appearance in a Royals uniform. On November 8, 2004, he was traded to San Diego with relief pitcher Ryan Bukvich for outfielder Terrence Long, pitcher Dennis Tankersley, and cash.

May's time in San Diego was brief. After just 22 appearances, he was traded to the New York Yankees with pitcher Tim Redding and cash for relief pitcher Paul Quantrill. May appeared in just two games for the Yankees, making his final appearance on July 15. He finished the season at Triple-A Columbus, then latched on with the Minnesota Twins as a free agent.

May's role in Minnesota was to serve as a fifth starter until prospect Francisco Liriano was ready to step in. During spring training, it became apparent the youngster was ready.

"He went into spring training and just dealt. It was fun to watch. He had the nastiest slider I think I've ever seen from a lefty other than Randy Johnson. So I understood why they took him," May said.

May caught on with Cincinnati, pitching at Triple-A Louisville. But with a wife and two young daughters growing up quickly, he was already contemplating retirement. When his younger daughter, who had not seen him in a month and a half, didn't recognize him, he knew it was time.

In retirement, May was coaching some high-school and small-college baseball in the Austin, Texas, area. He was also giving lessons. One student showed some promise, and May told his parents they would need to think about agents someday soon. May called his former agent, Paul Cohen, and that led to an offer for May to work with Cohen's agency. From his home base in Austin, he was put in charge of recruiting players in Texas for the agency. As opposed to coaching or scouting, the job allowed him to spend more time at home with wife Heather (the pair were married in 2000) and daughters Grace and Brynley.

Sources

The author is extremely grateful to Darrell May for agreeing to a phone interview, conducted on August 2, 2019.

In addition to the sources cited in the Notes, the author accessed the *Kansas City Star*, Baseball-reference.com, and Sccpanthers.com.

THE 1995 WORLD CHAMPION ATLANTA BRAVES

Notes

1. Telephone interview with Darrell May, August 2, 2019. Unless otherwise indicated, all quotations from May are from this interview.
2. All-Time Win/Loss Record, sccpanthers.com/sports/bsb/all_time_win_loss, accessed August 17, 2019.
3. Dick Kaegel, "May Took Indirect Route to KC," *Kansas City Star*, February 20, 2002.
4. Dick Kaegel, "May Day Finally Arrives for First Time Since 1997," *Kansas City Star*, June 7, 2002.
5. Bob Dutton, "Dreaded 20 Would Put May at a Loss," *Kansas City Star*, September 12, 2004.

Fred McGriff

BY PETER M. GORDON

Fred McGriff

"I was blessed," said Fred McGriff, reflecting on his career in baseball.[1]

McGriff signed his first pro contract when he was 17. During his 19-year major-league career, McGriff was a five-time All-Star, won the Silver Slugger award three times, and hit 30 or more home runs 10 times. In 1995 he led the Braves to their first world championship in Atlanta, and in 1998 brought professionalism and credibility to one of the worst teams ever, the expansion Tampa Bay Devil Rays.

In 1992, McGriff became the first player to lead both the American and National Leagues in home runs since the nineteenth century. He was also the first player to hit 30 or more home runs for five different teams. ESPN's Chris Berman gave Fred McGriff one of the most memorable baseball nicknames of the 1990s: "Crime Dog," after the cartoon public service announcement dog McGruff.

McGriff was born in Tampa, Florida, on October 31, 1963, the youngest son of Eliza and Earl McGriff. He had two sisters, Sandra and Terri, and two brothers, Michael and Dexter. Earl McGriff told *Sports Illustrated*, "We let our children produce at their own speed. We didn't push them. We didn't hold them back."[1]

Fred McGriff grew up four blocks from Al Lopez Field, the longtime spring training home of the Cincinnati Reds, which gave him a lot of exposure to major-league baseball at an early age. "I can't remember going to my first game," he once said. "I mean, I was always at a baseball game. I lived at ballgames. I always loved the game."[2]

McGriff started playing organized ball in the West Tampa Little League. At Jefferson High School he played for coach Emeterio "Pop" Cuesta. In his long career, Cuesta also coached major leaguers Luis Gonzalez and Tino Martinez. Cuesta cut McGriff from the team during his sophomore year. Being cut from the team must have hurt McGriff, but perhaps it also motivated him, since he got back on the high school team and went on to a successful major-league career.

In June 2011 at a ceremony honoring Cuesta's 40th anniversary of coaching baseball, McGriff asked him why. Cuesta responded to the audience, "First of all, this is not the Fred McGriff here as a sophomore. The Fred McGriff that was here was about 5-foot-6, 5-foot-7 with glasses. I told him to hit the ball, I mean, he hit it, but it wouldn't go very far."[3]

McGriff grew very quickly into a solid prospect during his junior year of high school. In 1981, after his senior year, the New York Yankees selected him in the ninth round of the amateur draft. McGriff had been offered several college scholarships, but decided to sign with the Yankees.

In a brief stint in the Gulf Coast League in 1981, McGriff hit just .148, but next season raised his average to .272 in 62 games. He led the league with 9 home runs and 41 RBIs in 62 games. After the season the Yankees traded McGriff, outfielder Dave Collins, pitcher Mike Morgan, and cash to Toronto for pitcher Dale Murray and infielder Tom Dodd (Rob Neyer included this trade in his book, *Rob Neyer's Big Book of Baseball Blunders*, as one of the worst trades the Yankees ever made.).[4]

While McGriff was in the minors he visited a coach and swing doctor in Orlando, Tom Emanski. McGriff found Emanski's coaching helpful, and the relationship he developed with Emanski would also become very lucrative for McGriff.

The Blue Jays sent their new acquisition to Kinston in the Carolina League. In 1984 McGriff was named the number-two prospect in the Blue Jays' system by *Baseball America*. After moving up through Toronto's minor-league system, McGriff was called to the big club from Syracuse in mid-May of 1986. He made his major-league debut, at the age of 22, on May 17, 1986, against the Cleveland Indians as a defensive replacement for Willie Upshaw. The next day McGriff started his first game, as the designated hitter and lined the first pitch he saw into left field for a single. He got into one more game before the Jays returned him to Syracuse for the rest of the season, where he hit .259 with 19 home runs and 74 RBIs.

The next season McGriff made the Blue Jays roster as a DH/first baseman, platooning sometimes with Cecil Fielder. McGriff hit .247 with 20 home runs in 107 games. He hit his first major-league home run on April 17 against the Boston Red Sox' Bob Stanley in Toronto – a three-run shot with two out in the bottom of the fifth that gave the Blue Jays a 7-5 lead in a game they won 10-5

Tom Emanski called McGriff during the season to ask a favor. As McGriff told the *New York Times*, "I'm in the big leagues and we're playing in Chicago. After the game he picks me up right outside the stadium and we go to a Little League park. He just gives me this shirt and this hat and says put them on. He had his own little video camera so he shoots the video. At the time I was just like, OK give me one percent. I didn't know it was going to turn into anything."[5]

The video, *Tom Emanski's Defensive Drills*, became one of the best-selling baseball instructional videos of the 1990s, thanks to an ad campaign on ESPN featuring McGriff's endorsement. McGriff said he was kidded in every locker room whenever that commercial aired on ESPN. "I'm sure he made millions," McGriff added, "but the thing is, he did a great job and he did help me get to the big leagues. He helped me make a great living also."[6] McGriff's percentage added up to a great deal of money over the years.

In 1988 the Blue Jays made McGriff their regular first baseman. He played 154 games and hit .282 with 34 home runs (second in the AL to Jose Canseco) and 82 RBIs, beginning a streak of seven straight years hitting 30 or more homers.

In 1989 the Blue Jays moved to the Skydome, and McGriff blossomed into one of the most dangerous sluggers in the majors. On June 5 he celebrated the first game in the new park with a home run. McGriff batted .269, led the AL with 36 home runs, and won his first Silver Slugger award. Teammate Lloyd Moseby said of McGriff, "You know that highlight reel that shows the Willie Mays catch and then switches to the fan who grabs his head with his hands in amazement? Fred McGriff does that to you when he hits a home run."[7] The Blue Jays won the AL East, but lost in the ALCS to the Oakland A's. McGriff hit a disappointing 3-for-21 in the series.

McGriff suffered through a slump early in 1990, but managed to finish strongly, batting .300

with 35 home runs and 88 RBIs. Then, after the season, the Blue Jays made a blockbuster trade with the San Diego Padres, sending the 26-year-old McGriff and shortstop Tony Fernandez, to the San Diego Padres for catcher Roberto Alomar and outfielder Joe Carter. The trade worked out well for the Blue Jays, who won the AL East in 1991 and back-to-back World Series in 1992 and 1993. In 1991, McGriff hit .278 with 31 home runs and 106 RBIs as the Padres finished third in the NL West.

McGriff started 1992 on fire, hitting homers in four of his first five games, including a grand slam. In July he homered in four consecutive games, was voted onto the NL All-Star team, and went 2-for-3 in the game. He finished the season with a .286 batting average, led the league with 35 home runs and drove in 104 runs. That earned him a second Silver Slugger award, and he finished sixth in MVP voting, his best showing so far. McGriff became the first player to lead two different major leagues in home runs since Harry Stovey (National League and American Association) in the 19th century.

McGriff earned just over $4 million in 1992 and signed a 1993 contract for $4.2 million. He got off to a terrible start, batting just .190 in April. Although he improved to .275 by July, the Padres were going nowhere, and the front office was ordered to cut payroll. The Atlanta Braves needed a hard-hitting first baseman, and on July 18 relieved the Padres of McGriff's services and salary for three prospects: Vince Moore, Donnie Elliot, and Melvin Nieves.

When McGriff came to Atlanta the Braves were in second place in the NL West, nine games behind the San Francisco Giants. McGriff joined the Braves in Atlanta for a game against the Cardinals on July 20. Before the game, a fire broke out in the press box. No one was hurt, the fire was put out, and the game started. Coincidentally or not, McGriff's presence appeared to ignite the Braves. They were behind 5-0 entering the bottom of the sixth. Jeff Blauser hit a three-run homer and Ron Gant singled. McGriff then launched a two-run homer that tied the game. The Braves went on to win 8-5.

Years later, McGriff told a reporter how he felt about the trade and his first game with Atlanta. He said, "The Padres were having a fire sale, so it didn't surprise me … my ribs were really bothering me when I was traded, and the Braves let me go home to Tampa for a day or two to rest them. Then my plan was to come up for the first game in the St. Louis series, but I intentionally left my house in Tampa at noon because I knew I would get up to the game right before it started and would get another night off to rest my ribs. But then came the fire, I was in the lineup and the game started after 9. I spent most of my time before the game in the training room with the trainer working on my ribs. Then I went out and hit that homer. It was crazy."[9]

In the 68 games McGriff played from July 20 to the end of the season, the Braves went 51-17. McGriff hit 19 homers, drove in 55 runs, and had a 1.004 OPS. In his book *The Time of Bobby Cox*, author Lang Whitaker wrote, "With McGriff on the team, the Braves were definitely combustible. Fred McGriff got the Braves red hot."[10]

The Braves passed the Giants and won the West Division championship by one game with a record of 104-58. For the season, McGriff finished with a .291 batting average, 37 home runs, and 101 RBIs. Although the Braves lost the NLCS to the Philadelphia Phillies in six games, McGriff stayed hot, batting .435 for the series with one home run and four RBIs. He won another Silver Slugger award and finished fourth in the MVP voting – his career high.

Teammate Ron Gant gave McGriff a great deal of credit for the Braves' surge, telling a sportswriter, "He just makes everyone else a better hitter. I hit in front of him. It wasn't that the pitchers were throwing me different pitches. They were throwing me the same pitches, but I was just more of an aggressive hitter with him hitting behind me. He just makes everyone else better."[11]

McGriff appeared to be on his way to a career year in 1994, batting .310 with 23 home runs and 63 RBIs at the All-Star break. In the All-Star Game his two-run pinch-hit homer in the ninth inning off Lee Smith tied the score, and he was named the game's MVP after the National League won in the 10th. Of the home run, he said, "It was a fastball away. He blew the second pitch by me. I was thinking, let it go, be aggressive, take your whacks. If you don't get him, get ready for Thursday and play the Marlins."[12]

A month after the All Star-Game the season ended for everyone. Players responded to the owners' efforts to unilaterally enforce new policies that would lead to a salary cap by striking on August 12, 1994. The strike led to the first World Series cancellation in 90 years and delayed the start of the 1995 season. McGriff finished 1994 with a full season's work: 34 homers, 94 RBIs, and a .318 batting average in only 113 games. Since McGriff finished his career with 493 home runs, it's tempting to think that had the season continued, McGriff could have hit at least eight more homers. Perhaps getting over the 500-home run mark would have made a difference in McGriff's Hall of Fame support.

When the 1995 season opened on April 26, McGriff showed his long hiatus hadn't cooled down his bat, as he went 4-for-5 with two home runs against the San Francisco Giants. The Braves had high expectations for success in 1995. McGriff said, "It was win or bust that year."[13] McGriff played every game that season, made his third All-Star Game, and helped the Braves win the NL East crown with a .280 batting average, 27 home runs, and 93 RBIs.

The Braves beat the Colorado Rockies in the NLDS four games to one and swept the Cincinnati Reds in the NLCS to face the Cleveland Indians in the World Series. McGriff batted a sizzling .438 in the NLCS to spark the team. In Game One of the World Series, he homered off Orel Hershiser in his first World Series at-bat. McGriff batted .261 for the Series. He hit another home run in Game Three. He also had two doubles and a .609 slugging average as the Braves defeated Cleveland in six games for their first Series victory, and the only Series win for a Bobby Cox-managed team.

McGriff had another solid year in 1996 to lead the Braves to another division championship. On May 19, he reached the 300-lifetime homer mark. He finished the season with a .295 batting average, 28 homers, and 107 RBIs. The Braves won the pennant but lost to the Yankees in the World Series.

The Braves reached the postseason again in 1997, even though McGriff's home runs declined to 22, but with 97 RBIs. He didn't make the All-Star team, and the Braves lost to the Florida Marlins in the NLCS. Two new teams, the Tampa Bay Devil Rays and the Arizona Diamondbacks, were admitted to the major leagues for 1998. On the day of the expansion draft, the Braves sold McGriff to the Devil Rays, sending the Crime Dog back to his home town. Ever the gracious professional, McGriff simply said about moving from one of the best teams in baseball to an expansion team, "Going back and getting to play in front of my parents in our hometown was really special."[14]

On April 1, 1998, McGriff drove in four runs to spark the Devil Rays to the franchise's first win, over the Tigers. He had a poor year for the Rays by his standards, hitting .284 with just 19 home runs and 81 RBIs. (He did lead the team in those categories.) McGriff rebounded in 1999, hitting 32 homers, driving in 104 runs, and batting .310.

In 2000 the Devil Rays signed some high-profile free agents, including Vinny Castilla and Greg Vaughn, to join McGriff and Jose Canseco. They dubbed their new lineup 'The Hit Show," and raised expectations high for the 2000 season. But only McGriff and Vaughn had decent seasons. On June 2 McGriff hit a home run off the New York Mets' Glendon Rusch that made him the 31st major leaguer to reach 400 homers. McGriff also represented the Devil Rays in the All-Star game.

He finished the season with 27 home runs, 106 RBIs, and a batting average of .277. On September 23 McGriff became the second player (along with Frank Robinson) to hit 200 home runs in both leagues when he homered off Roy Halladay of the Blue Jays.

McGriff started slowly in 2001 but soon heated up and was hitting over .300 for the Devil Rays when the team traded him to the Cubs. McGriff, 37, was being paid $6.5 million. When the deal was originally made on July 8, McGriff invoked his no-trade clause. Later in the month he accepted the deal and went to Chicago.

The Cubs wanted a strong left-handed bat to hit behind Sammy Sosa, on his way to 64 home runs. In 49 games with the Cubs, McGriff hit 12 homers. For the full season he hit 31, with 102 RBIs and a .306 batting average.

The Cubs picked up their option on McGriff for 2002. Taking advantage of the hitter-friendly Wrigley Field, McGriff hit 30 homers drove in 103 runs with a .273 batting average. This was McGriff's 10th 30-homer season, and he became the first player to hit 30 or more homers with five different teams. Despite McGriff's hitting, the Cubs finished fifth in the NL Central Division, and the team opted not to re-sign the 39-year-old, making him a free agent for the first time in his career.

The Los Angeles Dodgers signed McGriff for the 2003 season for $3.75 million, about half his Cubs salary. They hoped McGriff could give them the same steady power in the middle of the order and perhaps attract some fans who wanted to see him break the 500-home-run barrier.

For the first time in his career, McGriff's body broke down. He missed extended periods with knee, hip, and groin injuries. When he was playing, the injuries hurt his game. He played in 86 games and ended up with 13 homers and 41 RBIs. Worse, he batted only .249. Still, McGriff ended the season only nine home runs away from 500, and with an offseason to rehab many thought he would make it.

The Dodgers did not re-sign McGriff for 2004. In March the 40-year-old signed with the Devil Rays and started the season with the Triple-A Durham Bulls. On May 28 he joined the Devil Rays, who were noted for bringing in older players close to achieving milestones to improve attendance. McGriff hit a home run on May 31 to spark a 7-5 win over the Minnesota Twins. That started a small hot streak, and by June 17 he was batting .269. He hit his second home run that day. That was the high point – McGriff slumped to a .181 average by July 15, and didn't hit another home run.

That July 15 game was McGriff's last. The Devil Rays released him on July 28. He officially retired during spring training 2005, seven home runs shy of 500. His 493 home runs tied him with Lou Gehrig. He also ended his career with 2,490 hits, 1,550 RBIs and 1,349 runs scored. He batted .284 with a .377 on-base percentage, and an .886 OPS (on-base percentage plus slugging average). McGriff hit even better in postseason play. In 50 games he batted .303 with 10 home runs and 37 RBIs, with a .917 OPS. He hit four home runs in 12 World Series Games.

McGriff became eligible for election to the Hall of Fame in 2010 and received 21.5 percent of the vote. Many writers thought McGriff would eventually be voted in, but he never came close to receiving the required 75% of votes. In 2019, his last year of eligibility on the baseball writers' ballot, McGriff received 39.8% of the vote – good for 10th place, but not for the Hall of Fame. Some suggested McGriff's chances were hurt by playing for five different teams in his career, some say it was because he didn't hit 500 home runs. Hall of Famer Chipper Jones, his teammate on the Braves, thought McGriff should get elected. "There was nobody I enjoyed hitting in front of more than Fred McGriff."[15]

Baseball made McGriff a wealthy man. He earned over $65 million in salary during his playing career, which was supplemented by his royalty percentage from the Tom Emanski video. After his playing career was over, McGriff consulted and coached for some of his former teams, including the Blue Jays. He spent 2007 through 2010 as a consultant for the Rays (formerly the Devil Rays), as the team moved from the AL East depths to a World Series appearance and regular contention for the division title. He also hosted a sports radio talk show in Tampa. In 2015, the 20th anniversary of the Braves' World Series victory, the Braves signed McGriff to serve as a spring-training instructor and scout. As of 2019, McGriff still worked for the Braves, and sold his house in Tampa.

Sources

In addition to the sources cited in the Notes, the author also consulted Baseballamerica.com, baseballhall.org, Baseball-reference.com, draysbay.com, MLB.com, *Orlando Sentinel*, Retrosheet.org, *Sports Illustrated*, and SABR.org.

Notes

1. David O'Brien, "McGriff Q & A Part 2," *Atlanta Journal Constitution*, March 9, 2018. https://www.ajc.com/sports/baseball/mcgriff-part-hall-fame-snub-and-advice-for-prospects/kWtUEZUP9eGY6wD3bxnv3J
2. Ralph Wiley, "Give Us a Smile, Hit It a Mile – Fred McGriff," *Sports Illustrated*, May 8, 1989. https://www.si.com/vault/1989/05/08/119855/give-us-a-smile-hit-it-a-mile-fred-mcgriff-of-the-toronto-blue-jays-is-mr-nice-guy----until-he-punishes-opposing-pitchers-with-his-tape-measure-home-runs
2. Wiley.
3. Eddie Daniels, "Jefferson's Pop Cuesta Honored for 40 Years of Coaching," *Tampa Tribune*, June 4, 2011. http://ttt-tbdev.newscyclecloud.com/sports/preps/jefferson-dragons/baseball-jeffersons-pop-cuesta-honored-for--years-of-coaching-235095
4. Rob Neyer, *Rob Neyer's Big Book of Baseball Blunders* (New York: Simon & Schuster, 2006), 209-210.
5. Tyler Kepner, "Deciphering Hall Ballot Without Superstar," *New York Times*, January 5, 2010: B15.
6. Kepner.
7. Wiley.
9. O'Brien.
10. Lang Whitaker, *In the Time of Bobby Cox* (New York: Scribner, 2011), 111-112
11. Claire Smith, "McGriff and Turnaround are Same Word to the Braves," *New York Times*, October 5, 1993: B16
12. Smith.
13. Wiley.
14. O'Brien.
15. Marc Topkin, "Know Who Thinks Fred McGriff Deserves to Be in the Hall of Fame? New Member Chipper Jones," *Tampa Bay Times*, January 25, 2019. https://www.tampabay.com/blogs/rays/2018/01/25/know-who-thinks-fred-mcgriff-deserves-to-be-in-the-hall-of-fame-new-member-chipper-jones/

Greg McMichael

BY SCOTT BRIMER

Greg McMichael

Gregory Winston McMichael was born on December 1, 1966, in Knoxville Tennessee. He was the youngest of three children and a multisport athlete growing up. He always hanging around ballfields with his older brothers while they played. He enjoyed sports and competition and developed his skills as a ballplayer. McMichael's father, Allen owned an insurance company and his mother, Sylvia ran a hair salon.

Tricia Foley, a sports content producer and blogger wrote, "The McMichaels were an all-American family, until he reached the fifth grade and his parents decided to end their marriage. Less than three years later he had developed a rare congenital cartilage disease, osteochondritis dissecan. The doctors told him that the cartilage in his knees had died and it would need to be removed. His world came crashing down when they advised him he could no longer participate in sports that would be strenuous on his knees.

"For someone to tell you that basically your career is over with and [you're] only 13 years old, I felt like I lost my identity and who I was," McMichael said.[1]

Over the next few years McMichael had a tough time and hung out with the wrong kind of people. He turned to sports to help cope. He gave up all other sports and focused on baseball, which was the least damaging to his knees. Meanwhile his parents were eventually able to overcome their differences and remarry.

McMichael attended the Webb School, a private high school in Knoxville and led them to a state championship in 1985, the year he graduated. While in high school he developed into a fine right-handed pitcher and was offered a scholarship at the University of Tennessee, where he pitched from 1986 to 1988. "In college there was a time when I didn't think I was good enough," McMichael said. "If it were up to me, I would've quit, because it got too hard or too difficult. And there was always something I call gut checks in your life that was one of them."[2]

His freshman year at Tennessee he had a difficult time adjusting to college baseball but he stuck with it. During his junior year at Tennessee, Mark Connor arrived to become the head coach from the New York Yankees and took over the baseball program, which turned out to be good for McMichael. Connor encouraged him and was able to fine-tune his skills as a pitcher. McMichael also played ball with Athletes in Action and in the Alaskan League for two years, honing his skills as a pitcher.³ Connor taught him well and he was ready for the next step.

In 1988 McMichael was drafted in the seventh round of the June 1988 major-league amateur draft by the Cleveland Indians after he had been scouted by Roy Clark. He progressed through the Cleveland system and advanced to Triple A but injured his knee once again. Dom Chiti, an evaluator with Cleveland, recommended that he retire from baseball but McMichael disagreed, saying, "God will tell me when it's time." He parted ways with Cleveland with positive feelings about his time there. McMichael said he believed he may have been a victim both of new talent coming into the system and the fact that the Indians had to make a tough call regarding his knee surgeries. The team let him go. He reconnected with Roy Clark, then with the Braves. Clark came to see him pitch and felt that Greg still had what it would take to be a productive pitcher and the Braves signed him in 1991.

McMichael reported to the High Class-A Durham Bulls in 1991 and started his career with the Braves. He was trying hard to fit in and was having a hard time. He wasn't pitching very well, his knees were hurting, and he was newly married. McMichael was at a crossroads and considering retirement from baseball. He planned to see manager Grady Little and tell him about his decision. As he walked in to see the manager at the Durham Bulls ballpark, Roy Clark showed up and they discussed his plans. Clark advised him to not retire and urged him to reconsider.⁴ McMichael was struck by the confidence Clark showed and decided to not see Little but to go home and think about it and pray with his wife, Jennifer, for guidance.

He had developed tendinitis because he was overcompensating for his knee pain and was placed on the disabled list at the All-Star break. Greg and Jennifer decided that they needed to be more patient. He came off the DL and was slotted as a reliever. A fellow pitcher told him that a scout in the stands one night thought that if he had a changeup he would be in the major leagues.⁵ McMichael started working on his changeup and was told by Nate Minchey, a fellow pitcher, it was a good pitch that he could control and to use it more. Catcher Javy Lopez encouraged him to keep throwing the changeup and his pitching coaches agreed. Lopez said that it was the slowest changeup he had ever caught.⁶ McMichael threw predominantly changeups for the next six weeks of the 1991 season and did very well increasing his strikeout rate.

At this point McMichael was 25 and battling for a roster spot. Chuck LaMar, Director of Player Development and Scouting, was down for the beginning of spring training in 1992 to evaluate pitchers. McMichael later learned that at the start of spring training he was on everyone's release list … except for Bill Slack who was his pitching coach. The day he was evaluated he increased his speed from 84 to 88 mph and made the Double-A Greenville roster as the closer. After a month in Greenville striking out two batters per inning and exclusively using his changeup, he was promoted to Triple-A Richmond. During this time his knee pain had diminished. McMichael likes to say "that God took the pain away, but He gave me a changeup."⁷

After the 1992 season the Braves sent McMichael to Puerto Rico to pitch in winter ball. He improved while there, led the league in strikeouts, and made the All-Star team. He believed his stint in Puerto Rico helped because he was able to gain confidence pitching against established major-league players like Sandy Alomar Jr. and Juan Gonzalez.

In 1993 McMichael went to Braves spring training as a non-roster invitee. When he reported to West Palm Beach he was in awe when he walked in the locker room. In his first spring training game he struck out two out of the three batters he faced. When he came off the mound Bobby Cox nonchalantly let him know he had done a good job. There were a lot of opportunities during spring training and but McMichael only gave up his first run in his final spring season game. He made the most of his chance, made the team, and went to Atlanta.

McMichael was the only rookie on the team that year. Because of his experience in baseball to this point, he never wanted to get to excited – but this was it, he made it. There were five pitchers vying for three slots; McMichael, Steve Bedrosian, Mark Davis, Mark Wohlers, and Jay Howell. Cox called Bedrosian, Howell, and McMichael into his office and let them know they had made the team. The 1993 team was loaded with outstanding pitchers and McMichael was amazed and happy that he was selected to be on the team.[8]

It was three weeks before McMichael made his debut as a reliever, against the Chicago Cubs on April 12. He walked the first batter he faced and struck out the second. A fly out and another strikeout ended the inning. By the end of June he was the closer. McMichael recalled a game when he was facing Larry Walker of the Montreal Expos and had to step off the mound to gather himself. He coached himself and prayed, knowing that he could only do his best and not be something he wasn't. His mantra was to "keep it simple." He then threw three changeups in a row and got him out.[9] This was a pivotal moment in McMichael's career in baseball. He appeared in 74 games, closing 40 of them. He got stronger as the year went on and racked up 15 saves in August and September. McMichael finished the year with 19 saves and a 2.06 earned-run average in 91⅔ innings of work.

McMichael was runner-up to Mike Piazza for the Rookie of the Year honors at the close of his breakout year.[10]

In the strike-shortened 1994 season, McMichael pitched in 51 games and racked up 21 saves. The team was in second place in the National League East Division when the season came to an end, leaving everyone to wonder if the Braves could have caught the Montreal Expos. In 1994 to acknowledge his accomplishments he was inducted to the Tennessee Sports Hall of Fame.

The 1995 Braves season was the 125th season in the history of the franchise and its 30th season in Atlanta. The team started slowly, but came on strong after the All-Star break. McMichael pitched in 67 games and posted seven wins, two losses, and two saves.

In the 1995 World Series McMichael pitched in three games and had a 2.70 ERA. According to McMichael, "I don't remember the first appearances (in Atlanta), but remember the second one in Cleveland. We had just been to the Rock & Roll Hall of Fame and their park in Cleveland was one of the newer ones in baseball then, and it was loud and jamming and a happening place. I remember being on the mound and I think the biggest impression to me was the atmosphere in the stadium. It was also pretty cool coming back and pitching against the team that drafted you."[11] He earned his World Series ring against the team that released him, but he was not bitter about it. He felt that being released by Cleveland was one of the best things that happened for him in baseball.[12] In his five years with the Braves. McMichael had an ERA of 2.96, 44 saves, a WHIP of 1.213, and a WAR of 5.7.

In November of 1996 McMichael was traded to the New York Mets for Paul Byrd. In 1997 he got his only two major-league hits. McMichael's time playing in the Big Apple was enjoyable and he felt it was a great experience.[13] In June of 1998 he was traded to the LA Dodgers with Dave Mlicki for Hideo Nomo and Brad Clontz, and then was quickly traded back on July 10 for Brian Bohanon. He continued to pitch for the Mets until July 1999, when he was traded to Oakland with Jason Isringhausen for Billy Taylor.

On November 3, 1999, McMichael was declared a free agent and was signed by the Cubs on February 8, 2000. The Cubs released him on March 23. Three days later, he signed as a free agent with the Braves, coming back home to Atlanta, where he pitched in 15 games without a decision.

McMichael retired after the season because of a rotator cuff injury and his baseball career ended. He finished with a 6.7 WAR, 31 wins and 29 losses, an ERA of 3.25, 53 saves, 459 strikeouts, and a WHIP of 1.292.

McMichael opened Hardball Warehouse, a baseball academy, to teach baseball to youngsters. At the time he said, "I've thought about doing something like this for a long time. It would keep me up at nights sometimes. That's good and bad. But it definitely keeps you focused on your ideas."14 In 2010 McMichael took on a new challenge, as the Braves senior adviser for alumni relations. In this position he was responsible for the Braves fantasy camps, setting up Braves Alumni weekends, and keeping former Braves in touch with the team. He became the co-host of the Braves Podcast, and spoke to youth groups.

Looking back on his career in baseball McMichael said what he missed most of all was the competition and the adrenaline rush he got from competing at such a high level.15 McMichael and his family live in the Atlanta area.

Sources

In preparing this biography, the writer relied on Baseball-Reference.com, the ultimatemets database, email correspondence with Greg McMichael, articles from the *Atlanta Journal* and several Behind the Braves Podcasts.

Notes

1. Tricia Foley, "Dreams, Faith and Baseball: A Chat with Greg McMichael," trichefoley.com, April 10, 2015. trichefoley.com/2015/04/10/dreams-faith-and-baseball-a-chat-with-greg-mcmichael/.
2. Tricia Foley.
3. "Behind the Braves Podcast," MLB.com, June 25, 2019. mlb.mlb.com/fan_forum/podcasts/index.jsp?c_id=mlb&podcast=behind_the_braves. Unless otherwise attributed, most of McMichael's thoughts about his development come from this same podcast.
4. "Behind the Braves Podcast," June 25, 2019.
5. The names of the pitcher and scout are not known.
6. "Behind the Braves Podcast," December 11, 2019. mlb.mlb.com/fan_forum/podcasts/index.jsp?c_id=mlb&podcast=behind_the_braves.
7. "Behind the Braves Podcast," June 25, 2019.
8. Martin Gandy, "Interview with Former Braves Reliever Greg McMichael," TalkingChop.com, December 20, 2010. talkingchop.com/2010/12/20/1887074/interview-with-former-braves-reliever-greg-mcmichael.
9. "Behind the Braves Podcast," June 25, 2019.
10. "Behind the Braves Podcast," June 25, 2019.
11. I.J. Rosenberg, "Whatever Happened to Greg McMichael," AJC.com, November 4, 2016.ajc.com/sports/baseball/whatever-happened-greg-mcmichael/qeIaOCTyQ9oP6KAvfvYkqN/.
12. "Behind the Braves Podcast," June 25, 2019.
13. Mark Bowman, "Where Have You Gone, Greg McMichael," MLB.com, February 6, 2003. mlb.mlb.com/content/printer_friendly/atl/y2003/m02/d06/c198005.jsp.
14. Mark Bowman.
15. Martin Gandy.

Kent Mercker

BY CLAYTON TRUTOR

Kent Mercker

A journeyman in the best sense of the word, Kent Mercker made his name over the course of an 18-season career as a young, hard-throwing left-hander in the Atlanta Braves' bullpen before moving to the back end of the Braves' dream rotation in the mid-1990s that featured future Hall of Famers Greg Maddux, Tom Glavine, and John Smoltz as well as Steve Avery. Mercker's tenure with the Braves was highlighted by both team and individual accomplishments. He was a member of the Braves' 1991 and 1992 pennant-winning teams as well as the 1995 world championship team.

On September 11, 1991, Mercker pitched six hitless innings and got the win in a combined 1-0 no-hitter against the San Diego Padres with Mark Wohlers and Alejandro Pena. On April 8, 1994, Mercker pitched a no-hitter against the Los Angeles Dodgers.[1] His career was in turmoil through the late 1990s, as he bounced from club to club, unable to sustain the promise of his early career. Around the turn of the century, Mercker transitioned back to the bullpen, reinventing himself into a crafty set-up man who relied on his control, changeups, and breaking pitches to get hitters out instead of his heat. A steady presence in unsteady "steroid-era" bullpens, Mercker enjoyed some of his greatest success when he was well into his 30s.[2]

In the midst of his transition to the bullpen, Mercker suffered a life-threatening cerebral hemorrhage while on the mound for the Angels. On May 11, 2000, he was pitching at home against the Texas Rangers in a rare appearance as a starter. In the second inning Mercker began to feel dizzy on the mound before dropping to one knee. Angels medical staffers took him to the University of California-Irvine Hospital, where tests revealed that he had suffered a cerebral hemorrhage. Mercker spent days in the intensive-care unit. Hospital staff members prevented the bleeding on his brain from developing into an aneurysm, which likely would have killed him. Mercker spent three months back home in Athens, Ohio, recovering before returning to the Angels bullpen in mid-August.[3]

For his courage and determination in a life-threatening situation, the Boston Chapter of the Baseball Writers Association of America named Mercker a co-recipient of the 2000 Tony Conigliaro Award, along with Tampa Bay's Tony Saunders, who recovered from a career-threatening broken arm the same season. Mercker and Saunders shared the award, which is given annually to the player who "best overcomes an obstacle and adversity through the attributes of spirit, determination, and courage that were the trademarks of Conigliaro."[4]

Kent Franklin Mercker was born on February 1, 1968, in Indianapolis. The son of Franklin and Norma Mercker, he moved with his family several times during his childhood due to his father's job as a salesman. The family settled in Dublin, Ohio in 1980. Mercker was one of Ohio's finest high-school baseball players of the 1980s. Over four seasons he posted a 32-3 record pitching for the Dublin-Coffman High School Shamrocks. As a senior, the left-handed Mercker was clocked pitching as fast as 93 miles per hour. In 1983 he led the nearby Worthington American Legion baseball team to a third-place finish in the American Legion World Series.[5]

The Atlanta Braves selected the 6-foot-1, 175-pound pitcher Mercker in the first round of the June 1986 amateur draft. He proceeded quickly through the Braves organization, reaching Triple-A Richmond soon after his 21st birthday. The youngest player on the Richmond roster, Mercker went 9-12 for the 1989 International League champions, posting a 3.20 ERA in 27 starts. He received a September call-up with the sad-sack, 63-win 1989 Atlanta Braves. Mercker pitched in two games for the Braves that September. He was shelled in both outings, one of them a start, surrendering six earned runs and eight hits in 4⅓ innings.

Mercker began the 1990 season in Richmond and in late June was promoted to Atlanta. Aside from rehab assignments, he never again pitched in the minor leagues. He became a fixture in the Braves bullpen in the second half of the 1990 season, picking up seven saves in 36 appearances for yet another cellar-dwelling Braves team.

Mercker went 5-3 with a 2.58 ERA in the Braves' 1991 dream season, working primarily as a middle reliever and occasionally as a closer (six saves). He made four starts, including one on September 11 when he pitched the first six innings of a combined no-hitter against San Diego. Mercker made three appearances for the Braves in the postseason. He took the loss at home in Game Four of the NLCS, which tied the series with Pittsburgh at two games apiece. Mercker surrendered a 10th-inning walk to the Pirates' Andy Van Slyke, who wound up scoring the winning run when Mike Lavalliere singled him home off Mercker's replacement, Mark Wohlers. He made two brief appearances in the seven-game 1991 World Series, holding the Minnesota Twins scoreless both times.

Mercker remained a steady presence in his 53 appearances out of the Braves bullpen in 1992. He pitched well in the NLCS, a rematch between the Braves and Pirates. Mercker held the Pirates scoreless in three innings over two outings, one of which was a blowout victory for Pittsburgh (Game Five) and the other a decisive victory for Atlanta (Game Six). He suffered a rib injury during the Braves' victory celebration after Game Seven, and was not on the World Series roster.[6]

Mercker returned to top form in 1993, posting a 3-1 record and 2.86 ERA in 43 appearances. He started six games from late July through September, pitching effectively but never lasting more than six innings. Mercker made a career-high five postseason appearances in 1993, all in the Braves' defeat by the Philadelphia Phillies in six-games in the NLCS. In five innings of work, Mercker gave up just one run. He did not figure in any decisions.

In 1994 Braves manager Bobby Cox decided to make Mercker his fifth starter. The decision paid immediate dividends, as the 26-year-old lefty pitched a no-hitter and struck out 10 Los Angeles Dodgers on April 8, his first start of the season. In his first season as a regular starter, Mercker won nine of his 13 decisions and posted a 3.45 ERA during the strike-shortened season.[7] His record was second best among Braves starters, next to Greg Maddux, who posted a 16-6 record with a 1.56 ERA for the second-place Braves.

After the promise of 1994, Mercker's 1995 season proved disappointing. Though his performance was competitive with that of most fifth starters, Mercker did not develop into an ace. He went 7-8 with a 4.15 ERA. Mercker made two postseason appearances during the Braves' run to the 1995 World Series. In Game Three of the NLDS, he got Colorado Rockies catcher Joe Girardi to fly out to end the 10th inning in a 7-5 defeat. In Game Three of the World Series, he surrendered an earned run in two innings of relief work against the Cleveland Indians in a 7-6 defeat at Jacobs Field that narrowed the Braves' Series lead to two games to one.

In December 1995 the Braves traded Mercker to the Baltimore Orioles for right-handed reliever Joe Borowski and minor-league pitcher Chaad Stewart. Mercker struggled in Baltimore to a 3-6 record with a 7.76 ERA in 14 appearances, 12 of which were starts. In late July the Orioles sent Mercker to Cleveland for 39-year-old future Hall of Fame first baseman and designated hitter Eddie Murray. Mercker returned to a familiar role in Cleveland, posting a 3.09 ERA in 10 relief appearances, but the Indians left him off their playoff roster. (The Indians ended up losing the ALDS in four games to the wild-card Orioles. Eddie Murray, the man for whom Mercker was traded, batted .400 in the series and reached based in 9 of 18 plate appearances.)

On December 10, 1996, Mercker signed a one-year free-agent contract with the Cincinnati Reds. He was a hard-luck 8-11 as a starter for the 1997 Reds. His 3.92 ERA was well under the league-wide ERA of 4.24. His performance in Cincinnati impressed the St. Louis Cardinals enough for them to sign him to a two-year deal that ended up being worth $3.8 million. Mercker worked a career-high 161⅔ innings and won a career-high 11 games against 11 losses in 1998. His ERA ballooned to 5.07, but that mirrored a league-wide uptick in ERA to 4.31. Mercker's teammate Mark McGwire contributed significantly to the National League's skyrocketing ERAs with his record-breaking 70 home runs. Mercker posted a 6-5 record for the Cardinals in 1999, but his ERA remained over 5.00.

On August 24, 1999, the Cardinals dealt Mercker to the Red Sox for left-handed pitcher Mike Matthews and minor-league catcher Dave Benham. Mercker returned to form during his brief stint in Boston, going 2-0 in five starts with a 3.51 ERA for the wild-card-bound Red Sox. He made three postseason appearances for the Red Sox, who defeated the Indians in five games in the Division Series before losing to the Yankees in five games in the ALCS. Mercker started Game Four of the ALDS, lasting 1⅔ innings and surrendering two earned runs before being replaced by Rich Garces. Garces ended up with the win in Boston's wild 23-7 victory. Mercker started Game One of the ALCS and received a no-decision in a 4-3 loss at Yankee Stadium. He lasted four innings and gave up two earned runs. Mercker took the loss in Game Five of the ALCS, the victory that clinched the pennant for the Yankees. He surrendered two runs in 3⅔ innings in the 6-1 defeat.

In January 2000 the free-agent Mercker signed a one-year, $850,000 deal with Anaheim. In a season shortened by his life-threatening cerebral hemorrhage, he made 21 appearances, 14 as a reliever and 7 as a starter. The Angels declined to offer him a new contract after the season. His 6.52 ERA and 1-3 record in 2000, as well as his medical problems, tightened the market for his services. Mercker signed a free-agent deal with the Red Sox in January 2001, but Boston released him near the end of spring training.

Mercker signed a one-year, $500,000 deal with the Colorado Rockies on February 7, 2002. Playing his first full season since 1999, he went 3-1 with a 6.14 ERA for the Rockies in 58 appearances. Mercker signed with the Reds in January 2003 and turned his career around, becoming the set-up man he had been evolving into over the previous few seasons. In 49 appearances, Mercker posted a 2.35 ERA. The Braves re-acquired Mercker down the stretch of their 2003 playoff run, and Mercker shined, surrendering just two earned runs in 17 innings of work for a 1.06 ERA. Mercker made one playoff appearance for the 2003 Braves, who lost in the Division Series to the Chicago Cubs. He pitched a scoreless eighth inning in the Braves' 4-2 home loss in Game One.

Mercker joined the Cubs in the offseason. At age 36, he made 71 relief appearances in 2004. After the season he signed a two-year, $2.75 million deal with the Reds. The seemingly ageless Mercker made a career-high 78 appearances for the 2005 Reds. Before season-ending elbow surgery in mid-August, he pitched in 37 games in 2006 and was released after the season. Mercker sat out the 2007 season to allow his elbow to heal. In 2008 Mercker, now 40, signed a one-year free-agent contract with the Reds. Forty-year-old Kent Mercker went 1-0 in 15 appearances, missing significant action with back trouble. He pitched his last game of the season on May 31, and he got a walk-off victory over his original team, the Braves. After the season, the Reds released him and he retired.

Mercker retired with a 74-67 career mark and a 4.16 ERA, strong considering that he spent much of his 18-year career pitching in one of the most explosive offensive eras in major-league history. The left-handed hitting Mercker had a career .113 batting average with 18 RBIs. Four of them came on Mercker's only home run, a fourth-inning grand-slam off the Florida Marlins' Jesus Sanchez on September 2, 1998.

As of 2015, Mercker resided in his hometown of Dublin with his wife, Julia, and three daughters. In 2009 he became an occasional broadcaster on Reds radio and television broadcasts. He also worked as a professional development adviser for athletes with Excel Sports Management, based in New York City.[8]

Sources

In addition to the sources cited in the Notes, the author also consulted Baseball-Reference.com and Baseball-Almanac.com

Notes

1. Bob Nightengale, "A No-Hitter By Decision," *Los Angeles Times*, September 12, 1991. Accessed online on March 1, 2016: articles.latimes.com/1991-09-12/sports/sp-3120_1_kent_mercker; Maryann Hudson, "Dodgers No Hit; Mercker Big Hit," *Los Angeles Times*, April 9, 1994. Accessed online on March 1, 2016: articles.latimes.com/1994-04-09/sports/sp-43980_1_kent_mercker.

2. "Mercker Enjoying Home Life During Rehab," *Dublin Villager*, July 23, 2008. Accessed online on March 1, 2016: thisweeknews.com/content/stories/dublin/news/2008/07/23/0724dumerckerstory.html.

3. Ibid.; Chris Foster, "Angels' Mercker Recovers From Cerebral Hemorrhage to Pitch Again," *Los Angeles Times*, August 12, 2000. Accessed on March 1, 2016: articles.latimes.com/2000/aug/12/sports/sp-3268.

4. United Press International, "Red Sox Sign Mercker," January 5, 2001. Accessed online on March 1, 2016: upi.com/Archives/2001/01/05/Red-Sox-sign-Kent-Mercker/5888978670800/.

5. Dejan Kovacevic, "Braves' Mercker Traces Pitching Career to Claridge," *Pittsburgh Post-Gazette*, August 1, 1991: E9.

6. Milton Kent, "World Series Notebook," *Baltimore Sun*, October 18, 1992. Accessed online on March 1, 2016: articles.baltimoresun.com/1992-10-18/sports/1992292143_1_blue-jays-league-championship-series-rotation.

7. "Dodgers No Hit; Mercker Big Hit"; "No. 35, Kent Mercker," *Braves Journal*, October 19, 2006. Accessed online on March 1, 2016: bravesjournal.us/?p=2750.

8. "Linked-in Profile: Kent Mercker," Linkedin.com. Accessed online on March 1, 2016: linkedin.com/in/kent-mercker-95386b84; Tommy Poe, "Random Ex-Brave: Kent Mercker," *Walk Off Walk*. Accessed online on March 1, 2016: blog.walkoffwalk.net/2015/07/random-ex-brave-kent-mercker.html.

Mike Mordecai

BY MARK S. STERNMAN

Mike Mordecai

A longtime utility infielder who played a dozen years for three National League teams, Mike Mordecai made more appearances for the Montreal Expos than for any other club, but had his most memorable moments with key postseason hits that helped the Atlanta Braves and the Florida Marlins win World Series titles.

An Alabama native who attended high school and college in his birth state, "Mordecai was a three-sport star at Hewitt-Trussville, but stuck with baseball for college. At the University of South Alabama, he was a two-time All-American and named to the All-Sun Belt Conference team each year. In 1987, he helped the Jaguars to the conference title."[1]

After languishing in the minors for six years, Mordecai played four games in the strike-shortened 1994 campaign. On May 10, facing Philadelphia's closer Doug Jones, Mordecai got his first career hit and his only one of the season by pulling a three-run homer to left on a 1-and-2 pitch in the bottom of the ninth.[2] The blast helped Atlanta rally from an 8-1 ninth-inning deficit in a game the Braves won 9-8 in 15 innings in a most unlikely fashion: a walk-off bunt single by relief pitcher Mike Stanton.

Mordecai made the 1995 Braves after hitting .412 in spring training[3] and became a father with the birth of daughter Taylor Mae on April 27. He had his best offensive season as a 27-year-old rookie with career highs in on-base percentage (.353) and slugging (.480).

Atlanta faced Colorado in a tightly contested Division Series. The Braves won the opening game, 5-4, but trailed 4-3 going into the ninth inning of Game Two. A double by Chipper Jones and a single by Fred McGriff quickly tied the score. Three batters later, Mordecai batted for reliever Alejandro Peña with two on, two outs, and the game still tied. Darren Holmes, the third pitcher the Rockies used in the frame, fell behind Mordecai. "With a 3-and-0 count, I was looking for a fastball," Mordecai said. "I had to get it if he gave it to me, and he gave it to me. You look at the playoffs as a chance to prove something."[4] Mordecai's hard RBI groundball single between the second-base bag and the shortstop[5] gave Atlanta a 5-4 lead in a game the Braves would win 7-4.

Mordecai had the right mentality for a long-term reserve. "Usually it's the seventh, eighth, or ninth innings when you have to deliver," he said.

"You are in the game to help secure the 'W' already set up by the name guys. You're in there to finish the deal, and that is what it's all about. It doesn't matter whether people know your name or not at that point. It's all about winning."[6]

In Game Three, Atlanta trailed 5-3 in the seventh when Mordecai had another key RBI pinch-hit, a double this time that plated Ryan Klesko. Mordecai remained in the game and came up for a second time with one out in the bottom of the ninth. The Rockies clung to a 5-4 lead as Mordecai and Holmes again went head-to-head with runners on the corners this time. Mordecai's fly to left failed to score the tying run, but Luis Polonia did by singling with two outs. Colorado won the game in extra innings, but Atlanta captured the fourth game, the NLCS, and the World Series.

Beginning in 1996, Mordecai went into a three-year batting slump with OPS figures of .639, .449, and .602. A series of injuries started his slide. Mordecai had surgery on his elbow after the World Series[7] and "a hairline fracture in his right wrist"[8] that landed him on the disabled list during the first month of the 1996 season.

Mordecai hit his nadir in 1997 by batting just .173 with only three extra-base hits in 89 plate appearances. The Braves allowed him to sign as a free agent with division rival Montreal. While the move allowed Mordecai to go north geographically, he now played on a team well south of Atlanta in the standings.

A resurgence of sorts north of the border began in 1999 when Mordecai broke the 100-game mark for the only time in his career and also set a career high in homers with five and walks with 20. Stephanie Myles, who covered the Expos for the *Montreal Gazette* and was a correspondent for *The Sporting News,* damned Mordecai with faint praise, writing of him in 1999 that he "struggled less this year than last. He has had problems hitting breaking pitches, but that largely has been the result of not playing enough. Mordecai has hit well when he has made several consecutive starts, and his defense has been exemplary."[9]

Mordecai married Jennifer Meredith (his second wife) on February 5, 2000. She gave birth to their first son, Jackson, on August 2. Sons Jacob and John followed.

In 2001 Mordecai attained highs in hits (71), doubles (17), and RBIs (32). On Opening Day, Myles wrote, he "made his major league debut as the emergency catcher after backup Sandy Martinez blew out his elbow … in Chicago. Mordecai … played every position in the infield this year, and … is the type of player who figures to be a manager someday."[10]

Commissioner Bud Selig sought to execute the Expos (and Twins) via contraction, but he could not immediately eliminate the once-proud Montreal franchise. Selig nevertheless provided Expos owner Jeffrey Loria with a golden parachute that safely and softly landed him with the Florida Marlins franchise, while the suits at the Manhattan offices of Major League Baseball tightened the Montreal purse strings, essentially sealing their Canadian doom. Who would root for a team owned by absentee owners in another country that declined to invest in the ballpark or the roster? Opting to focus on baseball rather these machinations, Mordecai opined optimistically during 2002 spring training: "I look at the season as one long audition. … The eyes of baseball will be on us."[11]

The eyes of baseball rarely focused on Mordecai, but Loria's new team ironically rescued him. On July 11, 2002, Florida and Montreal made a trade that eventually involved seven players. The Expos included Mordecai as a throw-in with the bold-faced names of Carl Pavano and Graeme Lloyd going to the Marlins and Cliff Floyd and Wilton Guerrero returning to Canada.

Florida won its second World Series in 2003. Mordecai played in neither the NLDS nor the World Series, and had only one hit in six NLCS plate appearances, but his second and last postseason double put an exclamation point on one of the most notorious innings in baseball history.

The Marlins battled the Cubs in the NLCS. The teams split the first two games. In Game Three Florida trailed 4-3 in the bottom of the eighth. Miguel Cabrera led off with a single. Mordecai pinch-hit and sacrificed Cabrera to second. With two outs, Todd Hollandsworth singled in the tying run. Mordecai stayed in the game and had a chance to win the game. Facing Joe Borowski with two outs and the bases loaded, Mordecai flied to center. Chicago won 5-4 in 11 innings.

The Cubs won Game Four before the Marlins took Game Five. Chicago needed but one win in two Wrigley Field contests to return to the World Series for the first time since 1945. As part of a double switch, Mordecai entered Game Six in the bottom of the seventh inning with Florida down 2-0. The Cubs soon extended their lead to 3-0. When Chicago's Mark Prior retired Mordecai to start the eighth, the Marlins had a win expectancy of only 5 percent.

Juan Pierre doubled before Luis Castillo hit a foul fly. Moises Alou, the left fielder for the Cubs, seemingly had a play as the ball descended into the front rows of the Wrigley stands, but Chicago fan Steve Bartman ended up with the ball, Castillo ended up walking, and a nightmare scenario for the cursed Cubs had commenced.

Mordecai would bat again in the same frame. After Castillo, Florida batters singled, reached on an error, doubled, walked (intentionally), hit a sacrifice fly, and walked (again intentionally). Kyle Farnsworth faced Mordecai with two outs and the bases loaded. The Marlins led 4-3. Doing color commentary on Fox, Al Leiter, a still-active left-handed pitcher with the Mets, presciently commented before the 2-and-1 pitch that Mordecai "has always been a very good fastball hitter."

In the 20th and final plate appearance of his postseason career, Mordecai cleared the sacks with a screaming double off the bottom of the ivy-covered wall in left-center. Leiter continued, saying Mordecai "waited for the fastball and jumped all over it."[12] Thanks to the two-bagger, Florida now enjoyed a commanding 7-3 advantage. Pierre drove Mordecai in with a single, and the Marlins maintained the 8-3 score to even the NLCS.

"When I faced Farnsworth … the adrenaline was flowing because we were back in the game," Mordecai recalled. "I knew he threw hard and the ball ran a little bit. I was thinking, 'Just one more run and we have a two-run lead. I'll take that.' I felt like if I could fake a bunt on that first pitch and draw the infield in a little bit, I might hit a blooper off the end of the bat and that might be the difference.

"I missed a really good pitch when I led the inning off against Prior. Didn't put a good swing on it. I worked the count in my favor and put a better swing on a 2-and-1 pitch and hit a ball to the left-center field gap off the wall. That was an exciting time."[13]

Although still playing in Florida, Mordecai became a footnote in Montreal baseball history on September 29, 2004. The Marlins led the Expos 9-1 with two outs in the bottom of the ninth at Stade Olympique. Terrmel Sledge popped to third. Mordecai made the putout that finished the game and ended the run that the Expos had begun in Montreal in 1969. (The franchise ended the season at Shea Stadium.)

"I'm probably the last guy who should have caught that ball, but it happened the way it happened," said Mordecai. "It was weird walking off the field, because I'm thinking, 'Man, I really grew up here as a big-league ballplayer and now that's it, they're moving.'"[14]

Mordecai retired after the 2004 season but stayed with the Florida organization. In 2005 he managed the short-season Jamestown Jammers to a 31-44 record. "We started good and finished bad," Mordecai said. "I enjoyed it a lot."[15]

Just short of enough service time to qualify for a 10-year pension, Mordecai returned to the Marlins after the rosters expanded in September with Florida in the mix for the wild card. The specter of Mordecai magic lurked. After rejoining the team, he humble-bragged, "Obviously, some of the younger [players] have never been in a race like this. I've done it a couple of times. ... Does that mean I'm any more capable of helping out than they are? You never know. We'll just have to wait and see how that pans out."[16]

Mordecai went hitless in two at-bats, and the Marlins missed the playoffs.

Mordecai has bounced around baseball ever since. He coached at Houston Academy in Dothan, Alabama, before joining Toronto as a minor-league infield coordinator. In that role, "he earned rave reviews for his defensive work with then prospect Brett Lawrie."[17]

In 2019 Mordecai returned to minor-league managing with Toronto's Double-A New Hampshire Fisher Cats. "I would like an opportunity to manage at the major league level," Mordecai told a newsman. "To get to that position there are many different routes. ... I'm here to help players. I want to do what's best for the organization. ... I'm relaxed, but there are expectations."[18]

Mordecai seemingly gave up on or postponed these plans when partway through the season he announced he would leave the Toronto organization and return to coaching at Northside Methodist Academy in Dothan. "Getting back close to the family and spending some time at home with my wife and kids and still be a part of baseball and teaching young people, not only sports, but the game of life is what has drawn me (back to Dothan)," Mordecai said. ... "I feel like I kind of fulfilled everything I wanted to do (in the big leagues). ... I would love to be a big-league manager someday, but there are way too much hoops of fire to jump through for that to happen."[19]

Notes

1. Michael Seale, "Who Is the Most Famous Former Husky?" [Trussville, Alabama] *Patch*, June 27, 2018. "Mordecai is one of the all-time greats to play at South Alabama. In his three years, he led USA to one Sun Belt title and two NCAA Tournament appearances, including the regional championship in 1987. ... Owns four school records including career marks for runs scored (235) and hits (277). ... He holds single-season records for at-bats (262) and runs scored (94). ... Ranks third in career batting average (.373) and RBI (174). ... Played in 195 career games, fourth best in USA history. ... Ranks sixth in career homers with 26." usajaguars.com/hof.aspx?hof=24 (accessed August 5, 2019).

2. Jones threw a changeup or a hanging offspeed pitch that stayed in the middle of the plate. See youtube.com/watch?time_continue=2124&v=zE2MBAAwa_Q (accessed August 2, 2019).

3. Todd Thompson, "Mordecai Recalls Games in Sheffield," *Florence* (Alabama) *Times Daily,* December 23, 1995: 3D.

4. Jay Privman, "Braves Pull Away From Rockies for 2-0 Lead," *New York Times*, October 5, 1995.

5. youtube.com/watch?v=fSkMRUFGLKY (accessed August 5, 2019).

6. Craig Barnes, "Handy Man to Have Around," *South Florida Sun-Sentinel* (Fort Lauderdale), March 16, 2003.

7. Tim Luke, "Atlanta Braves," *The Sporting News*, February 5, 1996: 45.

8. Bill Zack, "Atlanta Braves," *The Sporting News*, April 29, 1996: 28.

9. Stephanie Myles, "Montreal," *The Sporting News*, October 4, 1999: 59.

10. Stephanie Myles, "Montreal Expos," *The Sporting News*, September 10, 2001: 48. Mordecai allegedly had a gift for discerning pitches. "In Mordecai's estimation, if he sees three pitchers per game a week he can pinpoint how 10 or 12 are tipping. He has been looking for tendencies since his A-ball days in 1989. Juan C. Rodriguez, "Private Eye Mordecai Is Marlins' Top Dugout Spy," *South Florida Sun-Sentinel*, March 21, 2004.

11. Michael Farber, "Last Swing in Montreal," *Sports Illustrated*, March 18, 2002. The Expos hung on in Montreal for three more years, and the mastermind of their move unjustly sailed on to Cooperstown (adding delayed insult to previous injury, Selig went to the Hall of Fame in the same class as Montreal stalwart Tim Raines), a stupefying outcome for those who see a commissioner's job as growing rather than contracting a sport.

12. youtube.com/watch?v=nOyQEmAs6u8 (accessed August 5, 2019).

13. Roger Brown, "New Fisher Cats Manager Helped Ruin Some Childhoods," *New Hampshire Union Leader* (Manchester), January 14, 2019.

14. Shi Davidi, "Former Expo Mike Mordecai Flooded with Memories in Return to Montreal," Sportsnet, March 26, 2018. Actually, Mordecai aptly made the catch given his appreciation for international players. Fifteen years later, he observed, "If Lou Gehrig or Babe Ruth or Jackie Robinson came back today and saw the game, they might not recognize it. They would say, 'What the hell?' to the defensive shifts or the relievers starting games. But you know what? If you told them that there's a

right fielder from Germany or a pitcher from Lithuania or a catcher who's from Italy, they might actually like that. They would see that the national pastime has gone global." Steve Wulf, "Twins' Max Kepler Leading Baseball's Charge Into Europe," ESPN, June 27, 2019.

15 Associated Press, "The Marlins' Mordecai: Player-Manager-Player," *New York Times*, September 25, 2005.

16 Kevin Baxter, "Vet Is 'Ready to Help,'" *Miami Herald*, September 14, 2005.

17 baseballcoachesclinic.com/site/mike-mordecai/ (accessed August 2, 2019).

18 Roger Brown, "Fishers Make Former Major Leaguer Mordecai New Manager," *New Hampshire Union Leader*, January 10, 2019.

19 David Mundee, "Mordecai Returning to Coach Baseball at Northside Methodist," *Dothan* (Alabama) *Eagle*, July 31, 2019.

Matt Murray

BY BILL NOWLIN

Matt Murray

Matt Murray spent seven seasons working his way up through the minor leagues, finally making it to the majors in 1995 – when he pitched briefly for two first-place teams, the Atlanta Braves and the Boston Red Sox. The Red Sox were swept in the Division Series by the Cleveland Indians, who went on to face the Braves in the 1995 World Series. The Braves won that year's Series, four games to two. Murray watched the games on TV.

A native of the City of Boston, Matthew Michael Murray was born there, in the Dorchester section, on September 26, 1970. In a 2019 interview, Murray said, "We lived in Mattapan my first couple of years and then we moved to the North Shore. Swampscott. My mother was a property site manager in Salem Heights and my father was in sales. Mostly machine parts, but when he was 40 he went back to college and became a licensed therapist. It was a big change. I had just one brother, Chris. He played football at Colgate in his freshman year but then realized it was a full-time job and decided, 'I'm just going to be a student.'"[1]

Matt was actually drafted before completing high school, which is typically not permitted. He was a second-round draft selection of the Atlanta Braves in the June 1988 amateur draft, but he had only completed his junior year at Loomis Chaffee School in Windsor, Connecticut, a large prep school. Garry Brown of the *Springfield* (Massachusetts) *Union-News* explained: "He actually has another year of prep school to go, but because his original high school class in his native Swampscott graduates this month, he is draft-eligible. Murray may be the only draftee who will have to go back to secondary school to get his diploma after he turns pro."[2]

Brown wrote that Murray could be "one of the real sleepers in the draft." Murray threw right-handed, though he batted left. He was already 6-feet-6 when he was drafted and was listed at 200 pounds. Braves scout Paul Ricciarini is credited with recommending Murray.[3]

Seventeen years old at the time, Murray was assigned to the Pulaski Braves in the rookie-level Appalachian League. He appeared in 13 games (with eight starts), striking out 76 batters in the 54 innings he worked. His record was 2-4 with a 4.17 ERA.

The 1989 season saw Murray work in Sumter, South Carolina, for the Single-A South Atlantic (Sally) League. He started 12 games and was 3-5 with a 4.33 ERA (the team was 60-81). He also pitched in two Rookie League games that year and was 1-0.

His third year in pro ball was 1990 – he was still only 19 years old – and he played Single-A ball again, this time in the Midwest League for the Burlington

(Iowa) Braves. He had a very good season, 11-7 (3.26) with 134 strikeouts in 163 innings. He started 26 games and completed six of them.

In 1991 Murray appeared in only two games (1-0), for the Durham Bulls of the Class-A+ Carolina League. He didn't pitch again until 1993. Murray recalled: "1991 opening game, I pitched seven innings and felt a little twinge in my elbow. The next day, I could barely move my arm. It was not torn. Based on the MRI, they thought it was frayed and that I could rehab it. So I rehabbed that entire year and then went to spring training in '92 and felt it pop. I had the surgery in April of '92. It was quite an ordeal. Lots of rehab. Lots of downtime." He had won that opening game, though.

The Braves franchise in the Sally League in 1993 was the Macon Braves. Murray joined them in July on a rehab assignment and stuck; he started 15 games and recorded a superb 1.83 earned-run average. His record was 7-3, and again he struck out almost as many batters (77) as innings he pitched (83⅔).

In 1994, on his second successive one-year contract, he pitched for two teams – Class A+ Durham, where he was 6-7 with a 3.79 ERA in 15 starts and the Double-A Southern League's Greenville (South Carolina) Braves. At the higher level, he struggled more; he was 3-4 (5.08) in 12 starts. After the season, Murray was designated for assignment.[4] He was sent to Richmond, and could have been claimed by another team in the December Rule 5 draft, but was not.

In 1995 Murray made the major leagues. In fact, he played for four teams before the season was done. First up were five starts with Greenville; he was 4-0 (with a 1.53 ERA). He was promoted to the Richmond Braves in the Triple-A International League. There, Murray was 10-3 with a 2.78 ERA. Even as the season was just getting underway, and he had won his first two games with Richmond, Braves manager Bobby Cox suggested that Murray might be in line for a September call-up. "All that waiting has paid off," Cox said. "We've been waiting on him for three or four years."[5]

On August 11 pitcher Steve Bedrosian announced his retirement.[6] The Braves brought up Murray to take Bedrosian's place on the roster. He was excited about the opportunity. He admitted that he had considered quitting baseball when faced with the elbow surgery. "I really thought about it," he said, "but my family wouldn't let me." He said, "It's been a long road. It's the pinnacle of something I started out to do a long time ago. It's really a matter of saying, 'I deserve to be here and believing it.'"[7]

Matt recalled when he had nearly packed it in. That was '94. "I played in Low-A ball in '93, rehabbing, and had some success. In '94 I went back to Durham, where I had been three years prior to that, and I gave up 20 home runs in the first half! What do I do? I was at a crossroads. I'm 24 and I can't get anybody out in A ball. I spoke to my manager, Matt West, and my pitching coach, Bill Slack. They gave me some great advice – to concentrate on the progress I was making. I was trying to be perfect. A lot of my former teammates were in the major leagues – Mark Wohlers, Javy Lopez, and all those guys. They taught me that the ink was dry on the last pitch and to look forward. I asked my wife, "Should I come home, and go to work?" She said, 'No, this is your dream. You've got to keep going.' I had a good support system from my coaches and my family."

Murray debuted in the major leagues the night after his recall, August 12, coming into a home game. The Rockies led the Braves, 5-2, after five innings. Murray retired the first three batters he faced, retiring the side in the sixth. But in the seventh, he walked the first batter, gave up a single, and then surrendered a three-run homer to Larry Walker. He got the next three batters, but was replaced by a pinch-hitter in the bottom of the seventh.

The Marlins came to Atlanta and just two days later, Murray got a start. He pitched 4⅔ innings, but with two outs and two baserunners in the top of the fifth, he was replaced by reliever Brad Clontz, who gave up back-to-back singles, allowing both inherited runners to score and thus adding two earned runs to Murray's line.

On the 19th in St. Louis, he worked two innings, giving up a solo home run to Scott Hemond.

On August 29, back in Atlanta, the Astros and Braves were tied, 9-9, after 11 innings. Murray pitched a scoreless top of the 12th, but in the 13th gave up a solo home run to Houston's Tony Eusebio. A double and a stolen base, with a suicide-squeeze sacrifice bunt, scored another run. It was his fourth and final outing for the Atlanta Braves.

As the Braves began to consider their postseason roster, they had added Mike Devereaux near the end of August and there was some thought that they might keep the veteran Rod Nichols, sending Murray back to Triple A.[8] As it happens, they sent Murray to the American League instead.

"I had been in the Braves organization my whole career," Murray recalled. "John Schuerholz brought me in the office and said, 'I've got good news and bad news. What do you want first?' I said, 'Give me the bad news.' 'The bad news is you're no longer a Brave.' Oh, man. 'What's the good news?' 'The good news is you're going home.' Just for a split-second, I thought, 'Are they releasing me? That's good news?' He could tell I was confused, and he said, 'We traded you to the Boston Red Sox.'"

Matt's family still lived in Swampscott. He'd been a Red Sox fan growing up, 16 when the Red Sox and Mets squared off in the 1986 World Series. Little did he know he would later become a teammate of Roger Clemens.

"It was bittersweet," he said. He'd been with the Braves organization for a long time. "And we were having a pretty good year! But I got traded to the Red Sox and it was just a whirlwind. My family. Friends. Tickets. They [Red Sox] had their roster pretty much set. Once they clinched, they had their playoff roster to set up, so I only pitched twice. Once in relief in Yankee Stadium, and then I got to start in Fenway Park. If I could pick two places where I would want to pitch. …"

On August 31 Murray was the player to be named later, sent to the Red Sox to complete a trade made at the July 31 trading deadline, when the Sox also acquired Mike Stanton. Braves GM Schuerholz then acquired veteran pitcher Alejandro Peña, optioning Terrell Wade to Richmond and outrighting Rod Nichols. Murray was out of options, so rather than release him, they dealt him to Boston. The Red Sox sent two minor-league prospects to the Braves as well, RHP Michael Jacobs and outfielder Marc Lewis.

Murray left one first-place team for another; the Red Sox held a 14-game lead over the second-place New York Yankees in the American League East. The Braves had a 14½-game lead over the second-place Phillies.

GM Dan Duquette of the Red Sox had begun to make some moves, too, designating Juan Bell for assignment and bringing outfielder Matt Stairs back up. Lee Tinsley was put on the 15-day DL. Pitcher Vaughn Eshelman was complaining of some left-shoulder stiffness, according to manager Kevin Kennedy. Early in September, Boston had six players on the 15-day disabled list.

Murray appeared in only two games for the Red Sox. On September 8, at Yankee Stadium, the Yankees scored five runs off starter Tim Wakefield in the first two innings. Wakefield settled down and didn't allow a hit for the next four innings, but with New York holding a 5-0 lead after 6½ innings, Kennedy gave the ball to Murray. He faced only four batters and they all reached base. Randy Velarde walked. Wade Boggs doubled Velarde in. Bernie Williams singled, Boggs taking third, and then Paul O'Neill doubled to right field, scoring Boggs and Williams. Brian Bark took over for Murray.

On September 25 the Detroit Tigers were visiting Fenway Park and Bostonians got their chance to see the Boston-born Murray, who was given the starting assignment, a last-minute replacement for Erik Hanson. He set down the side in the first inning. He gave up a couple of hits, but no runs, in the top of the second, then saw the Red

Sox put up a run on the board in the bottom of the inning. In the top of the third, he walked the first batter on five pitches, but then saw the next two batters reach base on errors by right fielder Stairs and shortstop John Valentin. The bases were loaded, with nobody out. Chris Gomez singled, tying the game at 1-1. But then Travis Fryman swung at the first pitch and hit a grand slam down the left-field line. Another base on balls and a single put two more runners on base, but a double-play ball hit back to Murray himself finally secured the first (and second) outs of the inning. A sixth run scored, though, when Phil Nevin singled weakly to third base. There was a third error behind Murray but it did not affect the scoring.

The Red Sox scored once in the bottom of the third. Kennedy stuck with Murray, but a double, groundout, and another RBI single by Gomez made it 7-2, Tigers, and Ken Ryan was brought in to relieve.

That was the last Murray pitched in the majors. He had been 0-2 (6.75 ERA) for the Braves in 10⅔ innings and 0-1 (18.90) in 3⅓ innings for the Red Sox.

The Red Sox signed Murray for 1996, but outrighted him to Pawtucket on March 22. "I think I pitched twice in spring training for the Red Sox," he said. The Philadelphia Phillies picked him up off waivers and assigned him to Triple-A Scranton/Wilkes-Barre (International League). He fared poorly there, with a record of 1-8 (7.67) in 13 starts. The Phillies let him go, and the Braves noticed – they reacquired him on August 9, sending him to Richmond. In 12 innings (two starts, three relief stints), Murray was 1-2 (6.00).

"I had shoulder surgery at the end of 1996. I hurt my shoulder in spring training that year rushing to get ready to get back to the major leagues with the Phillies. They were pitching-depleted. I battled through that whole year with shoulder issues but then had surgery at the end of the year. It was terrible. I had pitched two innings in all of spring training, but I pitched six innings my first time with the Phillies. I felt OK. The next one, I think I threw seven innings and then we broke camp. My first game was in Syracuse and it was like 26 degrees. I threw seven innings and started having inflammation. It was just a bad year."

For the next three seasons, Murray played independent league baseball.

In 1997 he pitched for the Catskill Cougars in the Northeast League. He was 0-3 in six games. The next two years were in the Atlantic League, with the Newburgh Black Diamonds (5-7, 3.21 in 18 starts) in 1998 and then – his final year in baseball – with the Lehigh Valley Black Diamonds in 1999. (The franchise had moved.) Murray was 3-1 (3.75) in six starts.

"After the surgery, I just was rehabbing. Trying to get my feet back under me. Get my arm in shape.

"Catskill. 1997. That was through my agent. I think he had a connection there. My manager was Wally Backman. It was great. He was the best. That was just me trying to get my arm back in shape. The next year, a former teammate of mine was playing in the independent league so I went and joined him. A guy named Earl Steinmetz. 1998. I think that was the first year of the Atlantic League. They were building a stadium but it wasn't done. They had no home stadium. You talk about going back to minor-league days; we bused *every* day!

"I went to Taiwan, too. That was '99. Six months. My arm wasn't coming back. I was 28 at the time. My daughter was born. Every game in Taiwan was televised and I was watching the replay, watching myself pitch. I pitched okay, seven or eight innings, but I was just watching myself pitch and I said, 'It's time to call it quits.' Terrible. I called my agent that night and said, 'Just get me home. I want to play one more time back in the States.' So he called the Black Diamonds and they had a spot open. I went back there. Got to play in Nashua, New Hampshire, so my family got to see me pitch for the last time. And that was it."

The Murrays divorced and Matt has not remarried. They had two children, Jackson and

Madeline. As of 2019 both Matt and Nikki lived in Calhoun, Georgia, where she was from. "She remarried and lives about a tenth of a mile from me," Matt said. "We have a good relationship. Our kids are older now – one's going to be a senior in high school and the other a senior in college. We had such a roller-coaster marriage. We got married in '95. I started in Double A. Got promoted to Triple A. Promoted to the big leagues. Then traded to Boston. Just a whirlwind in the first couple of years of marriage, but we hung in there. Once real life settled in, we found we had different goals. We get along well. Her husband and I get along. I said, "From now on, we're business partners and our job is to raise our two kids as best we can.""

After baseball, "I left and I started working for Mohawk Industries, a flooring manufacturer. I lived in Calhoun, Georgia. That's where Mohawk's corporate headquarters is. My next-door neighbor – her sister was there. I was still unsure if I really wanted to quit and I was having a conversation with my neighbor. Her sister asked, 'Are you still playing baseball?' I said, 'I'm not sure.' She said, 'Well, I need a salesperson. Today. I had a salesperson quit yesterday.' I said, 'I don't know anything about carpet.' She said, 'Don't worry about it. We'll train you.' The rest is history.

"I started in sales, and then I moved into the Mohawk Home Division. When I got divorced, I didn't want to have to travel. I had my children every other week. So I moved into product development. Now I'm the product director for the floor-mat division of Mohawk."

What was it like, he was asked, to have played for both the 1995 Atlanta Braves and the 1995 Boston Red Sox, both teams that went into the postseason that year?

"With the Red Sox, we finished the season in Milwaukee. I wasn't on the playoff roster so I went home. I was in Georgia watching it on TV. It was just one of those surreal things. I thought, 'Wow, imagine if it was the Red Sox playing the Braves in the World Series.'

"After the season, Linda Miller – I think it's her name – called me and said, 'Hey, it's Linda with the Atlanta Braves. I've got a question for you.' I said, 'OK.' Because I'd been traded, I didn't know if it was about insurance or travel or whatever it was. 'I need your ring size.' I said, '*What*? Don't joke with me.' She said, 'I'm serious. Ted [Turner] wants everyone who was on the team, anyone involved, to have a World Series ring.'

"I was in Triple A the next year with the Phillies and when we came to Richmond, where the Triple-A affiliate of the Braves was, the GM – who I knew really well – gave me my World Series ring."

Does it come up sometime when he's in the business world, that he had played baseball? Does it help him in some way?

"It really doesn't. It's not something that I boast about. I hardly ever wear my World Series ring. I've worked with people for six years, and they'll ask, 'Why didn't you tell me?' 'It was a former part of my life.' 'You don't like talking about it?' 'I love talking about it, but …'"

The memories are good. Murray had particularly nice words for 1995 Braves manager Bobby Cox: "He treated everybody the same, whether you're a superstar or a guy like me. He was actually the general manager when I got drafted in '88. He was just one of the true … truly one of the finest people – not just managers, but one of the finest people I've ever met."

Notes

1. Matt Murray interview with author on May 10, 2019. Unless otherwise indicated, all quotations directly attributed to Murray come from this interview.
2. Garry Brown, "John McNamara Falling into Red Sox Managerial Pattern?" *Springfield* (Massachusetts) *Union-News*, June 4, 1988: 21.
3. Garry Brown, "Fenton Reports to L.A. Kings Camp Without a Contract," *Springfield Union-News*, September 10, 1988: 6. This article presents Murray's weight as 200. Murray later added another 40 pounds and is so listed in current databases.
4. "Transactions," *Fort Worth Star-Telegram*, November 19, 1994: 48.

5   Bill Zack, "Wohlers Says Mattingly Helped 'Mental Approach,'" *Marietta* (Georgia) *Journal*, May 10, 1995: 18.

6   They also acquired Luis Polonia on the same day, for minor-league outfielder Troy Hughes.

7   Bill Zack, "Schuerholz Seeks Right-Hand Hitter," *Augusta* (Georgia) *Chronicle*. August 13, 1995: 22.

8   Bill Zack, "New Brave Devereaux Excited About Being with New Ballclub," *Marietta Journal*, August 27, 1995: 24.

Rod Nichols

BY MATTHEW L. BLOSS

Rod Nichols

Rodney Lea Nichols was born on December 29, 1964, in Burlington, Iowa. His family relocated to Albuquerque, New Mexico when Rod was about three years old, but he has always remained an Iowan at heart. Nichols early on adopted Iowa as one of his favorite college teams. "Back in the day, if you got the Hawkeyes on TV, you watched them," says Rod. Growing up in New Mexico, if there was a chance to see a game, I did."[1]

Nichols grew up in Albuquerque, where he managed to snag a job as batboy for the Albuquerque Dukes, the Triple-A farm team of the Los Angeles Dodgers, after his freshman and sophomore years in high school (1978 and 1979). According to Rod, "That's when I decided I wanted a career in professional baseball."[2]

Nichols started attracting attention early, as a standout right-handed pitcher on the Highland High School team, before moving on to three years at the University of New Mexico, 1983-85.

Nichols led the Lobos in wins (6) and ERA (3.93) in 1984, and in 1985 he was selected in the fifth round of the amateur draft by the Cleveland Indians.[3] He was the only one of five teammates drafted that year to play in the major leagues, and one of the 14 former Lobos to make the major leagues overall. Including Nichols, seven players drafted in the fifth round that year made the majors. Some other players of note selected in the 1985 draft were B.J. Surhoff, Will Clark, Bobby Witt, Barry Bonds, and Rafael Palmeiro.

After being drafted, Nichols spent three seasons as a starting pitcher in the minors with stops in Class-A Batavia, Waterloo, and Williamsport prior to being called up to the major leagues. His progress was slowed by a shoulder injury that required surgery in 1986.[4] Nichols, possessing a slow curve and a Luis Tiant-esque twisting windup, became known within the Cleveland organization when, after a rough inning with Batavia, he flushed his glove down the clubhouse toilet.[5] He was called up in 1989 to replace pitcher Bud Black, who had been placed on the disabled list with an arm injury.[6] The decision to promote Nichols may have been helped by the five scoreless innings he pitched during the only Colorado Springs Sky Sox game Cleveland Indians President Hank Peters attended that season.[7]

After starting the season in Triple A with the Pacific Coast League's Colorado Springs Sky Sox, and despite a 2-6 record with a 5.68 earned-run average, Nichols made his debut for the Indians in Cleveland on July 30, 1988, against the Minnesota

Twins, pitching seven innings and allowing three earned runs on five hits and striking out five, taking the loss in a seven-inning game shortened by weather. He found himself in an early hole after giving up a three-run home run to the Twins' Gary Gaetti in the first inning, but he settled down and after the game said, "I was nervous when I walked the first batter of the game, but I was all right after the home run. It was like a big burden had been lifted. It was a weird feeling."[8] Manager Doc Edwards said, "He pitched well. He hit a few 88s and his fastball stayed between 85-87 miles per hour most of the time."[9]

Nichols pitched in 10 more games in his rookie year, which he split with stints with Colorado Springs and Kinston of the Class-A Carolina League. With the Indians he made nine more starts and finished with a record of 1-7 and a 5.06 ERA in 69⅓ innings pitched.

Nichols earned his first major-league win against the New York Yankees pitching in Yankee Stadium on September 7 and going 6⅓ innings, allowing four earned runs and striking out four. After pitching and getting the win in Yankee Stadium, Nichols said, "This is everybody's dream come true as a kid."[10] In another rookie-year highlight, Nichols lost 1-0 to the Toronto Blue Jays in Cleveland on September 24, pitching a complete game. In his last three starts in 1988, the Indians were shut out in all three games. After the season Nichols pitched winter ball in the Dominican Republic.[11]

In the 1989 season, also split with Colorado Springs, Nichols pitched in 15 games for the Indians, making 11 starts and finishing with a 4-6 record and a 4.40 ERA in 71⅔ innings. The season was highlighted by a three-start winning streak; he won on July 28 at home against the Boston Red Sox, on August 3 against the Red Sox at Fenway Park, and on August 9 against the Yankees at Yankee Stadium. In a victory over the Detroit Tigers on September 14 in Cleveland, Nichols went eight innings and struck out a season-high 10 batters.

Nichols' 1990 season was also split between Colorado Springs and the Indians. With the Indians he was 0-3 in four appearances, two of them starts, with a 7.88 ERA in 16 innings. He was 12-9 (5.13) with the Sky Sox.

Nichols spent the entire 1991 season as a starter and reliever with Cleveland. He went 2-11 but had a solid 3.54 ERA in 137 innings. Nichols picked up his only career save in a scoreless four-inning relief appearance on June 19 against the Chicago White Sox. His two victories were a 2-1 complete-game win against the Oakland Athletics in Oakland on July 17 and a 3-0 shutout of the Chicago White Sox on August 25 in Cleveland.

In 1992 Nichols again split time between the Indians and Colorado Springs, starting nine games and relieving in 21 others. His record was 4-3 with a 4.53 ERA in 105⅓ innings.

Nichols became a free agent on December 19, 1992, and signed with the Los Angeles Dodgers for the 1993 season. He pitched in only four games for the Dodgers (0-1, 5.68); he spent most of the season in the Pacific Coast League with the Albuquerque Dukes, where he won eight games and lost five.

Released after the season, Nichols signed with the Kansas City Royals but spent the entire 1994 season in Triple A with the American Association's Omaha Royals, compiling a 5-10 record and a 5.64 earned-run average. In 1995 Nichols admitted that he was "bad" n 1994 and "didn't deserve a chance" to return to the majors.[12]

Again a free agent, Nichols signed with the Braves for the 1995 season. He spent all but two weeks with the Triple-A Richmond Braves. He was called up in August after the team traded Mike Stanton to the Red Sox and needed a reliever.[13] He made five pitching appearances for the Braves, giving up 14 hits in 6⅔ innings. Before being called up, Nichols was leading the International League with 24 saves and ended up making the International League All-Star team as a reliever.[14] He was returned to Richmond on August 29. Despite his success that season in

Triple-A – when he was called up general manager John Scheurholz decribed him as "a machine" – Nichols was unable to duplicate it at the major-league level. After learning he was being demoted, a disappointed but appreciative Nichols said, "Like I told Bobby (Cox), I appreciate the opportunity. I've got no complaints. I'm just sorry things didn't work out. I'm bummed. I wanted to stay around."[15]

After spending the entire 1996 season in Triple A with Richmond, Nichols signed with the Fukuoka Daiei Hawks of the Japanese Pacific League, where he made just three appearances in 1997, for a total of three innings, ending his playing career.

After a few years off, Nichols joined the Philadelphia Phillies as a minor-league pitching coach in 2000, spending the next 13 seasons with the Piedmont Boll Weevils, Lakewood BlueClaws, Reading Phillies, Scranton-Wilkes Barre Red Barons, Ottawa Lynx, and the Lehigh Valley IronPigs, before getting back to the major leagues as the Phillies' bullpen coach, 2013-15. Rod then joined the Chicago Cubs organization and spent the 2016-19 seasons as the pitching coach of their Triple-A team – back "home" in Iowa.[16]

Rod currently lives with his wife, Sharon, and family in Helena, Montana. Their son, Chris, was drafted by the Phillies in 2012, and pitched in their farm system for two seasons.[17]

Sources

In addition to the sources cited in the Notes, the author consulted Baseball-Reference.com and Baseball-Almanac.

Notes

1 Tommy Birch, "I-Cubs' Nichols Glad to Be Back in Iowa," *Des Moines Register*, May 28, 2016. desmoinesregister.com/story/sports/baseball/2016/05/28/sunday-stretch-rod-nichols-iowa-cubs-baseball-notebook/85083456/.

2 "Sports Briefs," *Albuquerque Journal*, April 14, 1979: C-2.

3 "New Mexico Baseball History and Records," golobos.com/documents/2019/2/6/Baseball_History_and_Records_Through_2018__.pdf.

4 Sheldon Ocker, "Nichols Is Impressive Despite Tribe's Defeat," *Akron Beacon Journal*, July 31, 1988: E1. infoweb.newsbank.com/apps/news/document-view?p=AWNB&docref=news/0EB6291F44107433.

5 Ocker, "Nichols Is Impressive Despite Tribe's Defeat."

6 "Horner's Shoulder Injury Could Threaten Career," *St. Petersburg Times*, July 30, 1988: 5C. infoweb.newsbank.com/apps/news/document-view?p=AWNB&docref=news/0EB528D4D3FD14CF.

7 Mike Klis, "Stadium Seems to Take a Toll; Nichols Gets Call from Cleveland," *Gazette Telegraph* (Colorado Springs), July 29, 1988: 4. infoweb.newsbank.com/apps/news/document-view?p=AWNB&docref=news/0F34BCE2A939F95E.

8 Ocker, "Nichols Is Impressive Despite Tribe's Defeat."

9 Ocker, "Nichols Is Impressive Despite Tribe's Defeat."

10 Ocker, "Medina Displays His Power in Indians' Win," *Akron Beacon Journal*, September 8, 1988: E1. infoweb.newsbank.com/apps/news/document-view?p=AWNB&docref=news/0EB6293DDF322B1.

11 Mike Klis, 'Eddie Williams Unsure Where He'll Play, Colorado Springs Faces Murderous Slate; Denver Series Off," *Gazette Telegraph*, December 11, 1988: 10. infoweb.newsbank.com/apps/news/document-view?p=AWNB&docref=news/0F-34CFB53331BEA.

12 Bill Zack, "Deal for Duncan Didn't Come Through," *Augusta* (Georgia) *Chronicle*, August 2, 1995: C02. infoweb.newsbank.com/apps/news/document-view?p=AWNB&docref=news/1036CDBE184B8F6A.

13 I.J. Rosenberg, "Promotion Unlikely for Replacement Lefty Despite Braves' Need for a Left-Handed Reliever/ Dale Polley Figures He's Stuck at AAA Richmond," *Atlanta Journal and Constitution*, August 15, 1995: D5. infoweb.newsbank.com/apps/news/document-view?p=AWNB&docref=news/0EADA1EE63F3BDF9.

14 Steve Wiseman, "A Knight-mare Season Ends," *Charlotte Observer*, September 3, 1995: 5G. infoweb.newsbank.com/apps/news/document-view?p=AWNB&docref=news/0EB6CE5913637DAE.

15 Bill Zack, "Schuerholz Acquires Pena in Marlins Deal," *Augusta Chronicle*, September 2, 1995: C02. infoweb.newsbank.com/apps/news/document-view?p=AWNB&docref=news/1036CC867A333FB6.

16 Tommy Birch.

17 Stephanie Pendrys, "Back on Campus: Chris Nichols," MILB.com, December 7, 2012. milb.com/milb/news/back-on-campus-chris-nichols/c-40569560.

Charlie O'Brien

BY STEVE WEST

Charlie O'Brien

A baseball writer once compared Charlie O'Brien to Barry Bonds. Using the game of Monopoly to describe the range of players in fantasy baseball, he wrote, "Barry Bonds is Boardwalk. He costs the most money. Charlie O'Brien is like Mediterranean. He goes the cheapest."[1] Okay, it wasn't the most flattering comparison, but Charlie would take it. He didn't really care what people said about him. He had a 15-year career and a World Series ring, all because he was one of the best play-callers in the game.

Charles Hugh O'Brien was born on May 1, 1960, in Tulsa, Oklahoma. His father, Charles Raymond O'Brien, was a partner in the family business, O'Brien Meat Company. His mother, Ann Kelley, was a homemaker in charge of their nine children. The family had a sporting background, with Charles having played football and baseball at the University of Tulsa. During his major-league career Charlie wore several uniform numbers, but mostly his preference was for the number 22, to match his father's football number.

Charlie played baseball and hockey from a young age, and first put on catcher's gear at age 5. He admired Reds catcher Johnny Bench as a youth. "I tried to catch like Bench," he said. "I tried to hit like him, too. But that went away pretty quick."[2]

O'Brien's younger brother John played a few seasons in the Cardinals system in the early 1990s, not advancing past Class-A ball, then spent several years in independent leagues.

O'Brien starred at Bishop Kelley High School in Tulsa, winning two state championships. He was picked in the 14th round of the 1978 amateur draft by Texas, but chose to go to college. He attended Wichita State in Kansas, where he played alongside seven future major leaguers on a highly successful team. Among his teammates was pitcher Erik Sonberg, who achieved lasting fame by being drafted one spot ahead of Roger Clemens in the 1983 draft. Sonberg reached Triple A but never pitched in the majors. He later became a member of the O'Brien family when he married Charlie's sister.

In 1982, under legendary college coach Gene Stephenson, Wichita State set an NCAA record that still stood in 2020 by winning 73 games, but lost to Miami in the College World Series championship game. O'Brien paired with Russ Morman and Phil Stephenson to become the first trio of NCAA teammates to each have 100 RBIs in a season. O'Brien was named an All-American that year, and Gene Stephenson was impressed.

"Charlie is the best catcher in the college ranks right now, I believe," he said.[3]

O'Brien had been drafted as a junior by Seattle in 1981 (21st round), but signed with Oakland after going in the fifth round of the 1982 draft. He received a bonus reported as $12,500.[4]

O'Brien split his first minor-league season at two Single-A stops, and found himself up against Oakland's other top catching prospect, Mickey Tettleton. The competition between them continued for years, but in the early days O'Brien proved better and was promoted to Double A for 1983. He had an excellent season there, hitting .291 with 14 home runs, but missed the last month with a back injury. He was promoted to Triple-A Tacoma in 1984, but leg and back injuries once more curtailed his season.

With a traffic jam at catcher in the A's system, O'Brien was sent to Double-A Huntsville at the beginning of 1985. Teammate Luis Polonia later claimed that he and O'Brien got into a fight one day, with Polonia saying, "I broke the bus window with his head."[5] Polonia went on to say that O'Brien promised payback, which he got during an on-field fight in 1989. O'Brien denied they had ever fought.

O'Brien was surprisingly called up to the parent club in late May as rumors swirled that Oakland was going to trade starting catcher Mike Heath. His major-league debut on June 2 was inauspicious, as he caught the eighth inning of a 10-1 loss in Baltimore. He spent his time on the bench behind Heath (who was not traded) and Tettleton. O'Brien spent a month with the A's but got in just one more appearance – also as a one-inning defensive replacement – before being optioned to Class-A Modesto. The reason for the three-level drop was that the higher-level teams already had starting catchers.[6] After a couple of weeks in Modesto, though, he was promoted to Tacoma.

O'Brien returned to Oakland in mid-August when Tettleton went on the disabled list. This time he got into four games, with one start, before being sent back down on Tettleton's return. He was called back up when rosters expanded. He got into several games defensively, and made his second start of the season in the last game of the season, where he also got his first career RBI.

The A's surprised O'Brien by trading him to Milwaukee at the end of spring training in 1986. The Brewers sent him to Triple A, which was discouraging, but he ran into Steve Carlton as he was leaving. "'You'll be back,' he said. 'You're too good a catcher. I like the way you catch.' Hearing that from a Hall of Fame guy like Carlton was great. He didn't have to take the time to say that. Gives you confidence."[7]

After a few weeks at Vancouver, where he got little playing time behind B.J. Surhoff, O'Brien was sent down to Double-A El Paso. He reignited his status as a top prospect by hitting .324 with 15 home runs. A chipped thumb from a foul tip slowed him at the start of 1987, and he was sent to Triple-A Denver. He spent the year there, except for a few weeks in May when he was called up to the Brewers because Surhoff's father died and backup catcher Bill Schroeder had a sore elbow. O'Brien got into 10 games, all of them starts, and while he hit just .200, he impressed by throwing out 9 of 14 attempted basestealers. Oddly enough, on a team that finished the season 91-71, and was 20-4 when he was called up, Milwaukee lost all 10 games that O'Brien played in.

He started 1988 back in Denver, but was called up again in mid-June. O'Brien played well enough that he mostly took over the backup catcher role from Schroeder, playing in 40 games in the second half of the season. Despite a .220 batting average, he did manage to hit his first career home run in July, off Kansas City's Floyd Bannister.

The 1989 season began with Surhoff as the primary catcher, but as the year went by and Surhoff struggled at the plate, O'Brien got more playing time based on his defense. By the end of the season, pitcher Chris Bosio requested that O'Brien be his personal catcher, the first of a number of pitchers who made that request in O'Brien's career.

Around this time O'Brien began standing out by wearing brightly-colored catcher's gear. In Milwaukee he wore a bright yellow chest protector, and with the Mets he switched to orange. "This way, if my mom and dad are watching the highlights on TV and there's a play at the plate, they'll be able to tell right away if I'm catching," he said.[8]

O'Brien struggled with the bat during 1990, hitting just .186 with the Brewers. His defense was still strong, but the Mets traded for him just before the deadline, needing a catcher for the pennant run. With starter Mackey Sasser hurt, O'Brien was called upon to start 25 of the last 33 games for the Mets, including twice catching both ends of a doubleheader. He could not help, though, as the Mets slowly fell away by the end of the season.

At the start of 1991 the Mets named O'Brien as the starter, but poor hitting – he was as low as .146 in July – meant that he slipped down the pecking order. He had spent the winter working on his hitting, coming off a career-low .178 between the Brewers and Mets, but nothing seemed to help.

In fact, to get more playing time in the second half, O'Brien relied on an old trick – becoming someone's personal catcher. This time it was Dwight Gooden. Caught by all three catchers, Gooden had struggled to a 4.39 ERA through the end of June, but O'Brien caught him exclusively from then on and his ERA fell to 2.28. "There's something about it. I know what he wants to do and that makes him feel comfortable," O'Brien said.[9] Perhaps it was something else, though, an ability to not back down from the star pitcher. "Charlie wouldn't be as nice as other catchers when he approached you. ... He was very direct. He would get right in your face, basically nose-to-nose, if he felt like you weren't giving one hundred percent out there or that you weren't giving it your all every pitch," Gooden said.[10]

The bad news for O'Brien was the arrival of a young catcher at the end of the season. Todd Hundley had shown good catching skills in the minors, and just as importantly a good bat. This gave him a leg up over O'Brien. Hundley came up in September 1991 and caught almost every day. O'Brien did catch the last game of the season, when his pitcher, David Cone, tied the National League record with 19 strikeouts.

The 1992 season opened with manager Jeff Torborg calling Hundley his starter. O'Brien remained as Gooden's personal catcher, which accounted for almost half of the games he caught in 1992. Late in September, O'Brien broke his wrist when a foul ball hit it, ending his season with a week left. He took the opportunity to have surgery on both knees, cleaning up some ongoing issues.

O'Brien went into 1993 once more as backup to Hundley, but switched away from being Gooden's personal catcher to sharing the workload more evenly. He also hit .255, his highest average for a full season to that point, which was well-timed as he entered free agency for the first time.

O'Brien later said that he didn't like playing for the Mets. His feeling was that the players had too much fun away from the team to care about winning. They didn't have a tough manager to take care of that, and there was no player who was enough of a leader that he would be willing to call out others.

O'Brien signed a two-year, $1.1 million deal with the Atlanta Braves. The goal was for him to be the veteran backup behind rookie phenom Javy Lopez, and help Lopez improve on the defensive and game-calling side. Being the backup didn't bother him. "It's not a label I cherish, but I've made a living doing it," he said.[11] Braves manager Bobby Cox said that O'Brien would get playing time. "To me he's the best catch and throw guy in the league."[12]

O'Brien ended up catching more than a third of the games in the strike-shortened season. He got more playing time each month as Lopez did not perform as expected. O'Brien also became the personal catcher for John Smoltz, catching every one of his games as the Braves preferred the veteran catcher for the sometimes-wild pitcher. He made headlines in May for a different reason: After Smoltz hit the Mets' John Cangelosi to start a brawl, O'Brien ended up on the cover of *Sports Illustrated*, shown punching Cangelosi to the ground. "Hopefully, my kids won't see it," he said.[13] He received a $1,000 fine for the fight.

The following season Smoltz switched to being caught exclusively by Lopez, and O'Brien caught almost all of Greg Maddux's starts. The pitchers talked about the differences between the two catchers, but Lopez chafed at not being able to get into a groove by catching every day. Maddux had confidence in O'Brien. "We work well together. I very seldom shake him off. I watch all the catchers on TV closely and to me, Charlie is easily the best in baseball," Maddux said.[14]

It worked, as the Braves lapped the field in their division, then cruised through the playoffs to win the 1995 World Series. O'Brien started every one of Maddux's starts in the playoffs, but was regularly replaced by Lopez in the middle innings when the Braves were looking for a bigger bat. His one offensive highlight was a three-run home run off Cincinnati's David Wells to give the Braves a lead they did not relinquish in Game Three of the NLCS. "Close your eyes and swing," he said. "Sometimes it works."[15]

The Braves let O'Brien go to free agency, and he left Atlanta as a world champion. Still, he was irked at the way they treated him, even down to getting his World Series ring. "I got my ring from a UPS deliveryman. Out of sight, out of mind."[16]

O'Brien signed a two-year deal with Toronto for $1.125 million. For the first time he was the starting catcher, and he set career highs in almost all counting stats, including 13 home runs in his 109 games. The home runs were a surprise for O'Brien. "I never go up expecting to hit them out. I'm just a hacker. If it goes, it goes. I don't think about it," he said.[17]

In 1997 Toronto splashed $6.5 million on free agent catcher Benito Santiago. Santiago's 1997 ended up worse than O'Brien's 1996 in most categories, and by midseason O'Brien was getting more playing time. When Roger Clemens chose O'Brien as his personal catcher, Santiago was so irritated that he threatened to demand a trade. He instead reasserted himself and hit 100 points higher in the second half of the season, pushing O'Brien back to the backup spot. A rare batting highlight for O'Brien came on May 14 in Detroit, when his career-high six-RBI day was led by his first grand slam.

Around this time O'Brien became frustrated with his mask, and the headaches that came from being hit by foul tips. Watching hockey, he realized that goalies were hit with much harder force by a puck but were much better protected by their helmets. He began working with a Canadian company to adapt a hockey-style mask for baseball. The helmet he came up with provided better protection and visibility.[18] It took months for Major League Baseball to approve it for game use, which annoyed O'Brien. "These things are safe enough for hockey goalies, so why is it taking so long?"[19] He finally used his mask in a game for the first time against the Yankees. Yankees catcher Jim Leyritz immediately ordered one for himself.

The mask quickly spread around the league, with a number of players wearing it the next season. Within a few years the helmet-style mask became widely used at all levels of the game.

O'Brien became a free agent at the end of 1997, and had a few parting shots as he left Toronto. In particular he ripped into Santiago, unhappy at the feud that had developed between them. He said that Santiago was overpaid for the production he had brought. "I don't know what I did wrong there, but if they want to pay a guy (Santiago) $3 million who hits just 13 home runs, well, they got him."[20]

O'Brien signed another two-year deal, this time with the White Sox for $1.4 million. They signed O'Brien and Chad Kreuter on the same day, apparently figuring to let the two veteran catchers battle to see which would be the starter. They split time until O'Brien suffered a chip fracture of his right thumb in July and went on the disabled list for the first time in his career. While on the DL, he was sent to Anaheim for two minor-league pitchers at the trade deadline.

Anaheim was leading the AL West and looking to pick up the veteran catcher for the stretch. When O'Brien arrived, his thumb was examined by doctors, who determined it was not healing and he would miss another month. The Angels activated him in early September, but he played in just five games before being hit by a pitch and breaking another finger, which ended his season. Oddly enough, the Angels then acquired Kreuter to finish out the season while O'Brien went back on the DL. Neither of them provided any help as the Angels fell out of contention.

O'Brien didn't fare any better in 1999, when a torn ligament in his foot put him on the DL in early June. He returned after six weeks out, but just a week later was released, having hit .097 for the season.

O'Brien wasn't quite ready to give it up. He signed a minor-league deal with Montreal for the 2000 season. After another foot injury cost him most of spring training and the first month of the season, he was sent to Double-A Harrisburg to start the season. He was called up to the Expos after a couple of weeks. He spent a month with Montreal before being released, with the final straw apparently coming when he allowed five stolen bases in a game against the Yankees. Montreal offered him a job as the bullpen catcher, but he decided it was time to go home.

O'Brien had married Traci Rodriguez, and they had four children – two girls and two boys. While they grew up in Tulsa, Oklahoma, the family had regularly spent summers wherever their father was playing, and had recollections of interactions with players on a personal level.

O'Brien bought a ranch in northeast Oklahoma, and named it the Catch-22 Ranch, for his uniform number. O'Brien was an avid hunter, and during his career he went hunting with several other players, among them Chipper Jones and Will Clark. He appeared on hunting shows on ESPN and other channels. As of 2020, on his ranch he hosted tour groups on hunting trips. He created a company, Charlie O' Products, which creates and sells items for hunters. He has also hosted a show for hunters, *Deer Thugs*, which aired on cable TV.

O'Brien's two boys, Chris and Cameron, played college and then minor-league baseball. Charlie coached their high-school teams, but stopped coaching when they went to college. He and Traci regularly traveled to see their sons play in college and the minor leagues, although he wasn't necessarily a good watcher. "The game moves so much quicker on the field than it does from the stands. After seeing it from the angle that I saw it from for all those years, it's kind of boring to be up in the stands."[21]

Chris followed his father's footsteps to Wichita State, and was taken by the Dodgers in the 18th round of the 2011 draft. Playing mostly catcher, he reached Triple A in the Orioles system before retiring after the 2017 season. Cameron attended several colleges, was undrafted, and spent two seasons in Low-A ball for Toronto. Both brothers received 50-game suspensions for taking amphetamines, which effectively ended their playing careers.

O'Brien gained notoriety in 2012 when he appeared as a defense witness in the perjury trial of his former teammate, Roger Clemens. In his testimony, he was emphatic in his belief that Clemens never took steroids, although he struggled to remember things about other teammates. However his testimony appeared, it was not too damaging; Clemens was acquitted.

O'Brien wrote a book about his career, called *The Cy Young Catcher*. In it he claimed to have caught a record 13 pitchers who won the Cy Young Award, and detailed each of their careers and his interactions with them. Although the claim is technically true, O'Brien caught just four of them during their Cy Young-winning years (Maddux twice, Pat Hentgen, and Clemens). Of the rest, some were very late in their careers (he caught Pete Vuckovich only in spring training) and others very early. (Chris Carpenter won his Cy Young several years after O'Brien had retired.)

Many pitchers had good things to say about O'Brien's ability as a defensive catcher and the way he called a game. If selecting him as a personal catcher wasn't enough, to a man they praised how he called a game, and how he was able to get in sync with his pitcher. "From the first time I met him, he seemed like a guy who was born to be a catcher," said Don Sutton. "He received the ball with almost pillow-like hands. He knew how to throw. But I think he had that innate sense of what a pitcher was trying to do, and how can we use that to get the hitter."[22]

Sources

In preparing this biography, the author relied primarily on Charlie O'Brien's book, *The Cy Young Catcher*, and on baseball-reference.com.

Notes

1. Stephen Nover, "Leagues Can Keep Games Interesting Even for Most Jaded," *Las Vegas Review-Journal*, December 12, 1993: 2E.
2. Marty Noble, "O'Brien Hit One for All Journeymen," *Augusta* (Georgia) *Chronicle*, October 15, 1995: 10B.
3. "Oelkers Hurls WSU to 11th Win in Row," *Wichita* (Kansas) *Eagle*, March 22, 1982: 5B.
4. Randy Brown, "Unsuccessful in Series Bid, WSU Looks at 1983," *Wichita* (Kansas) *Eagle*, June 14, 1982: 1B.
5. Claire Smith, "Yankees," *Stamford* (Connecticut) *Advocate*, September 22, 1989: B5.
6. "The A's," *San Francisco Chronicle*, July 2, 1985: 46.
7. Charlie O'Brien and Doug Wedge, *The Cy Young Catcher* (College Station, Texas: Texas A&M University Press, 2015), 13.
8. "Seventh-Inning Stretch," *Cleveland Plain Dealer*, August 5, 1990: 11C.
9. Nat Gottlieb, "O'Brien Delighted with Doctor's Duty," *Trenton* (New Jersey) *Evening Times*, July 23, 1991: B2.
10. O'Brien, *The Cy Young Catcher*, 45.
11. Bill Zack, "O'Brien Relishes Tutor's Role as Backup to Braves' Lopez," *Augusta* (Georgia) *Chronicle*, March 21, 1994: 1B.
12. Tom Saladino, "O'Brien Insurance for Braves," *Brunswick* (Georgia) *News*, March 19, 1994: 3B.
13. Bill Zack, "Braves Notes," *Augusta* (Georgia) *Chronicle*, May 20, 1994: 2C.
14. "Sizzling Maddux Rolls On," *Columbia* (South Carolina) *State*, September 1, 1995: C4.
15. Marty Noble, "O'Brien Hit One for All Journeymen," *Augusta* (Georgia) *Chronicle*, October 15, 1995: 10B.
16. O'Brien, *The Cy Young Catcher*, 179.
17. "Extra Bases," *Fort Worth Star-Telegram*, May 3, 1996: C4.
18. Cliff Gromer, "Blue Plate Special," *Popular Mechanics*, April 1997: 59.
19. Simon Gonzalez, "Baseball Report," *Fort Worth Star-Telegram*, August 18, 1996: C8.
20. "Catcher O'Brien Rips Santiago, Blue Jays," *Las Vegas Review-Journal*, November 24, 1997: 14C.
21. O'Brien, *The Cy Young Catcher*, 2.
22. O'Brien, *The Cy Young Catcher*, 177.

José Oliva

BY NICK WADDELL

José Oliva

José Galvez Oliva was born on March 3, 1971, in San Pedro de Macoris, Dominican Republic. He was signed as a shortstop by the Texas Rangers on November 12, 1987 and was assigned to the Gulf Coast League Rangers where he spent the 1988 season. He appeared in 27 games and hit .214. He was promoted to the Pioneer League for 1989, and again played mostly shortstop for the Butte Copper Kings. Oliva's stats showed a player trying to adjust to baseball in America: He was second on the team with 15 errors and had the second-worst batting average on the team (.211). Oliva was in the bottom half of the team for almost every stat, but the Rangers still wanted to see what he could do at the next level.

Oliva spent 1990 with Gastonia of the low-A South Atlantic League. He led Gastonia with 38 errors as the starting shortstop and played a bit of third base too. Oliva's bat showed a bit of power with 10 home runs, and 52 RBIs, but he led the team in strikeouts.

Moved up again in 1991, Oliva played for Port Charlotte of the High-A Florida State League. He switched positions and became the starting third baseman. Oliva began to show some of the power that would be his calling card in his major-league career when he led the league with 14 home runs.

Oliva was promoted to Double A for 1992 and played for the Tulsa Drillers. He showcased a more mature game, hitting .270 with 16 home runs, and was voted the best defensive third baseman in the Texas League, despite 28 errors and a .915 fielding percentage. The solid minor-league track record, along with his age, forced the Rangers to protect Oliva before the 1992 expansion draft that brought the Colorado Rockies and Florida Marlins to the major leagues; however, he was traded less than a month later. The Rangers sent the 21-year-old Oliva to the Braves for left-handed pitcher Charlie Leibrandt and minor-league pitcher Pat Gomez. The Braves needed to move Leibrandt's salary in order to sign reigning Cy Young Award winner Greg Maddux.

Oliva spent 1993 with the Triple-A Richmond Braves, and was being groomed to take over in Atlanta for third baseman Terry Pendleton after Pendleton's contract expired in 1994.[1] This was due in large part to Oliva's defensive showing in 1992, but also because Richmond had a shortstop in young Chipper Jones. Oliva showed power by hitting 21 home runs and drove in 65 runs, but his average struggled to top .200 all season. He was hitting .204 through early July, but was able to raise his average to .235 by the end of the season.

Oliva entered the 1994 season with uncertainty. He was still viewed as a top prospect in the Braves' system, but his position was not firmly set. Atlanta's top prospect, Chipper Jones, was going to play at least some third base because he was blocked at the major-league level by shortstop Jeff Blauser.[2] Jones tore his ACL during spring training and missed all of the 1994 season. Oliva responded to the opportunity to have third base to himself by showing why he was considered to be a top prospect. In his first 40 games in 1994 he batted .286. By late June Oliva's average had dropped to .260, but he still showed power with 17 home runs. This was enough for the Braves to call him up when Terry Pendleton was forced to the disabled list with a strained back.[3]

Oliva's first start came on July 6, 1994, against the Pittsburgh Pirates. In his second at-bat he led off the bottom of the fifth with a single to center for his first major-league hit. He collected two more hits in his second start, on July 9, against the St Louis Cardinals. The next day Oliva started again. In the bottom of the second, on a 2-and-2 count, Oliva went deep against Allen Watson for his first major-league home run. In his first eight major-league games, Oliva hit .455 with four home runs, including two against the Florida Marlins on July 16. By the time he was sent back to Richmond at the end of the month, his average had dropped to .288. But Oliva had made a strong impression on the Braves. "He had a much wilder swing when I saw him before. He'd lift his front foot way up and missed a ton of pitches. Now he's got a softer foot and great coverage. He's a different hitter," manager Bobby Cox said.[4] Oliva was sent down due to the Braves' need for a right-handed leadoff batter against left-handed pitchers. Mike Kelly, who had been sent down at the end of July, fit the bill, and took Oliva's spot on the roster. Oliva helped Richmond win the International League championship with a 3-0 sweep of the Syracuse Chiefs.

Despite the strong performance, Oliva again faced uncertainty entering the 1995 season. The Braves had to make tough decisions. The team released Terry Pendleton, which opened up a starting position. If the Braves brought back shortstop Jeff Blauser, then Chipper Jones would most likely move to third base. If Blauser moved on in free agency, Jones would most likely play shortstop and Oliva could play third base. The players strike and lockout further complicated the situation, since teams could not sign players until an agreement was reached.

Oliva had a scary health issue to start 1995. He was hospitalized for two weeks for a liver infection. Oliva had complained of stomach and back pain while on a promotional tour. Doctors in the Dominican Republic diagnosed him with food poisoning and gave him treatment. The pain persisted into winter ball, when Oliva had trouble swinging the bat. Braves team doctor David Watson ran tests that showed the liver infection. Oliva was immediately hospitalized.[5] He recovered, and had a strong spring to make the club as a backup infielder; Chipper Jones was named the starting third baseman. During the shortened spring training, Oliva saw time at first base as well. But he was not happy with the demotion to bench player, and his attitude was reflected in his play. During one spring training game, catcher Javy Lopez threw to Oliva after a strikeout; Oliva was not paying attention and was struck by the ball. During another game, he failed to run out a ground ball. Oliva had told media prior to the game that he was unhappy with the decision to play Jones at third over him.[6]

Oliva got his chance at third, however, when a thumb injury to Ryan Klesko forced Chipper Jones to left field. In his first eight at-bats, Oliva hit two home runs. His confidence in himself was evident. "If I play every day this year, I guarantee I win rookie of the year," Oliva said.[7] He also explained his rocky spring: "This year in spring training, they didn't give me the job. I was real down in spring training, felt real bad. But you wait for your time."[8]

Oliva failed to make the most of his time. He hit for power during the short stretch (four home runs, three doubles), but failed to hit for average (.189). His defense was also weak; he had six errors in nine games. Oliva attributed his numbers to the lack of consistent playing time. "If I play consistently, I'll put up good numbers," he said. "I was struggling defensively, six errors in nine games, but that's not me. It wouldn't be that way all year if I played. It's a concentration problem, worrying about going to the bench. I try to be so perfect, I mess up."[9] Oliva stayed with Atlanta largely because he was out of minor-league options. The Braves would have had to put Oliva on waivers if they wanted to send him down. Eventually, the Braves solved the issue by trading Oliva to the Cardinals for minor-league outfielder Anton French. The Cardinals were desperate for some power and, as Bobby Cox later said, Oliva had "more than big-league power. He's got major-league power."[10]

Cardinals manager Mike Jorgensen did not know where to play Oliva. "I don't know if he can play first base or the outfield or not, but we'll find out," Jorgensen said.[11]

Oliva failed to make a good first impression on his new team. He was given three days to join the Cardinals in order to give the club time to make a roster move, but still arrived late to the Cardinals' series opener in Cincinnati and was removed from the lineup.[12] The woes would continue onto the field as well. Oliva hit only .122 with two home runs for the Cardinals.

Despite the poor numbers in a limited sample, the Cardinals re-signed Oliva to a one-year deal before the 1996 season. But Oliva never received the chance to make his mark on the club. Early in spring training, he dove for a ball while playing first base and tore ligaments in his thumb. He sat out a few weeks but could not put up good enough numbers to make the team. He was sent to Triple-A Louisville, where he hit 31 home runs and drove in 86 runs. Although he was not the starting third baseman, Oliva put up strong defensive numbers as well; he made only four errors at third and two at first base.

The Cardinals decided to not resign Oliva after the season, but the Mets offered a minor-league deal, which Oliva accepted. He was excited by the prospect of playing for the Mets. "My dream since I was a little kid was to play in New York. Maybe my dream will come true," Oliva said.[13] Just as in seasons past, Oliva did not show enough to warrant a big-league spot, and he was optioned to Triple-A Norfolk during spring training. Oliva caught the eye of scouts from the Chinese Professional Baseball League and signed with the Brothers Elephants of Taipei.

Oliva verbally agreed to a minor-league deal with the Seattle Mariners on December 19, 1997, and was expected to officially sign the contract on December 22.[14] In the early morning of December 22, Oliva and a female passenger were involved in a car accident near Santo Domingo. The convertible he was driving hit an object in the road, and Oliva was thrown from the vehicle. His uninjured passenger waited an hour for help to arrive while Oliva's condition worsened. He suffered multiple severe wounds to his head, throat, and lungs. The injuries were too much to overcome, and Oliva died shortly after arrival at a hospital.[15] He was 26 years old.

Sources

In addition to the sources cited in the Notes, the author consulted baseballalmanac.com and Baseball-Reference.com.

Notes

1. Terence Moore, "Future as Bright as Present for Braves," *Atlanta Constitution*, April 4, 1993.
2. I.J. Rosenberg, "The Future," *Atlanta Constitution*, February 27, 1994.
3. I.J. Rosenberg, "Pendleton Goes on DL; Oliva Called Up," *Atlanta Constitution*, June 30, 1994.
4. Joe Strauss, "Despite Hot Start, Oliva Faces Demotion," *Atlanta Constitution*, July 31, 1994.

5. "Braves' Third Baseman Oliva Leaves Hospital After Infection," *Atlanta Constitution*, February 4, 1995.
6. I.J. Rosenberg, "Braves Notebook," *Atlanta Constitution*, April 20, 1995.
7. Jack Wilkinson and Thomas Stinson, "Oliva: I'm Rookie of Year if Regular at Third," *Atlanta Constitution*, May 6, 1995.
8. Wilkinson and Stinson.
9. Tim Tucker, "Return to Bench Peeves, Saddens Oliva," *Atlanta Constitution*, May 18, 1995.
10. Rick Hummel, "Braves Were Reluctant in Sending Oliva to Cards," *St. Louis Post-Dispatch*, September 5, 1995.
11. Rick Hummel, "Cardinals Get Oliva in Trade with Atlanta," *St. Louis Post-Dispatch*, August 26, 1995.
12. Rick Hummel, "Newest Cardinal's Tardiness Gives Cooper Surprise Start," *St. Louis Post-Dispatch*, August 29, 1995.
13. Thomas Hill, "Camping Out," *New York Daily News*, February 22, 1997.
14. "Former Brave Oliva Killed in Car Accident," *Atlanta Constitution*, December 23, 1997.
15. "Former Brave Oliva Killed in Car Accident."

Alejandro Peña

BY ALAN COHEN

Alejandro Peña

"In a year that has been so improbable, the impossible has happened!"

—Vin Scully, October 15, 1988[1]

Alejandro Peña appeared in three World Series during his 15-season major-league career, but his first appearance was the kind of thing that you can only dream about. He was called in from the Los Angeles Dodgers bullpen in Game One of the 1988 World Series. His team was trailing the Oakland A's 4-3 at the Dodgers' ballpark. He pitched two scoreless innings, striking out three and allowing one hit, a harmless infield single with two outs in the ninth inning by Stan Javier. Peña was due up fourth in the ninth inning and it was determined that he would be removed for a pinch-hitter. With two outs, A's reliever Dennis Eckersley walked pinch-hitter Mike Davis as Dave Anderson, the apparent pinch-hitter for Peña, looked on from the on-deck circle.[2] But as Davis headed to first base, Kirk Gibson grabbed a bat and Anderson returned to the dugout. "Gibson, half man, half beast, whose arrival as a free agent in February had so dramatically transformed the Dodgers, now limped toward the plate to face Eckersley," an eyewitness wrote.[3] Peña was in the clubhouse when Gibson's iconic two-run pinch-hit homer on a 3-and-2 slider gave the Dodgers the lead in the World Series and Alejandro Peña had his first and only World Series win.

Alejandro Peña Vasquez was born on June 25, 1959, in the peasant village of Cambioso, Puerto Plata, Dominican Republic. As a boy, he worked with his father, also Alejandro, building dirt ovens near their home. It was hard work, and on Sunday, when they paused from work, young Alejandro would play baseball. One of seven children (five boys and two girls), he played third base as a youngster, and it wasn't until he was 15 that he played in any semblance of an organized league.

The timeline is unclear as to how Peña evolved from a scrawny third baseman to a hard-throwing pitcher, but Antonio Taveras, Alex Taveras, and Ralph Avila were involved in changing the direction of Peña's life. The first time he showed up for a Dodgers tryout on the island, he showed a strong arm and Avila told him that "his only chance, in my opinion, to sign a contract was to become a pitcher."[4] Alex Taveras, a Dodgers infielder who lived in the Dominican Republic, concurred that Peña would not make it as a third baseman.

Five months later, Peña had established himself as a pitcher and was playing semipro ball on Hispaniola, the island that the Dominican Republic shares with Haiti. Antonio Taveras, Alex's father, was a scout for the Dodgers, and he advised Avila that it was time to take another look at Peña. Avila picks up the story at this point: "The next night the son of a gun struck out 15 batters, strictly with fastballs. I knew if I didn't sign him, someone else would do it."[5] Peña signed with Avila as a free agent in 1978 for $4,000 and a $500 monthly stipend.

Peña was with Clinton in the Midwest League in 1979, going 3-3 with a 4.18 ERA. In 1980 he went 10-3 for Vero Beach in the Florida State League. He was promoted to Triple A during the 1981 season. At the time he was called up, he had a league-leading 22 saves with a 1.61 ERA for Albuquerque. His presence had positioned them to win the Pacific Coast League championship at the end of the season. They won the Southern Division by 25 games and defeated Tacoma in the postseason series for the league championship.

Peña was called up by the Dodgers on August 12, 1981, shortly after the end of the players strike. The 6-foot-1, 205-pound right-hander traveled to Atlanta and made his major-league debut the following evening, pitching a scoreless ninth inning against the Braves in a game the Dodgers lost 9-1. The following day, he picked up his first major-league save, pitching the final four innings against the Braves in a 5-0 Dodgers win. It was his longest outing of the 1981 season to date. (His longest outing with Albuquerque had been 2⅓ innings.)[6] At Pittsburgh on August 25, Peña entered the game after the Pirates had tied the score in the bottom of the ninth inning. There were two outs and the winning run was on second base. He induced Tony Peña to hit a comebacker for the inning's third out and the game went into extra innings. There was no scoring in the 10th inning as Peña retired the side in order. He picked up his first career win when the Dodgers broke through for two 11th-inning runs and Tom Niedenfuer came on for the save, pitching the bottom of the 11th inning.

Peña appeared in 14 games in 1981, had a 1-1 record, and was credited with two saves. His ERA was 2.84. The Dodgers advanced to the World Series, defeating the Expos in the League Championship Series. Peña appeared twice during the five games against Montreal, pitching 2⅓ scoreless innings. He did not play in the World Series win over the Yankees after being diagnosed early in the Series with a bleeding ulcer. He had collapsed after the second game and was admitted to a Los Angeles area hospital for observation.

Tellie (short for Telesila) Ceballos was a telephone operator in Los Angeles in 1981. She had been born on August 13, 1958 and came to the United States when she was 12 years old. She met Peña shortly after the World Series, and the two went out on a dinner date. They married in 1983. They have two children, Alejandro Jr. (born June 16, 1984) and Arianna Cristina (born October 19, 1989). As of 2015 their son was a doctor in Phoenix and their daughter, lived in Georgia and was an aspiring musician.[7]

Even with love in his life, Peña was the quiet man in the clubhouse because he had trouble leaning English. Although there were several Spanish-speaking players on the team. Peña, coming from a peasant village, had far less sophistication than his Latin comrades.

In 1982 Peña was off to a good start with the Dodgers, with a 1.29 ERA in his first 13 appearances, but then ran into some difficulties. By July 15 he was 0-2, and his ERA had soared to 4.54. He was sent back to Albuquerque, where he did not fare much better, for the balance of the season.

In the offseason between 1982 and 1983, Peña pitched for Licey in the Dominican Winter League, and was managed by Dodgers coach Manny Mota. Peña sought the opportunity to pitch as a starter and Mota gave him the chance. Peña recorded four shutouts and found his way into the Dodgers rotation in 1983.

Peña spent two years in the rotation. In 1983 he pitched in 34 games, 26 as a starter. Most of his eight relief appearances came early in the season. Through June 12, despite missing two weeks with migraine headaches, he had relieved on eight occasions and started five times. At the time, he sported a 5-1 record and a 2.32 ERA. Three of those first five wins had been as a starter, including his first shutout, on May 24 at Philadelphia. That shutout came on the heels of shutouts by Bob Welch and Fernando Valenzuela, and represented the first time that the Dodger staff had pitched three consecutive shutouts since 1966 when Claude Osteen, Don Drysdale (with relief help from Phil Regan), and Sandy Koufax pitched successive shutouts from September 9 through September 11 while leading the Dodgers to the pennant. For the season, Peña went 12-9 with a 2.75 ERA. The Dodgers won the NL West and Peña pitched once in the League Championship Series against the Phillies, an ineffective relief stint in which he allowed two runs in 2⅔ innings. The Dodgers lost the best-of-five series in four games.

In 1984 Peña had his best season and narrowly missed being selected for the All-Star team, as teammate Fernando Valenzuela was chosen by manager Paul Owens. At the break, he was 10-4 with a 2.40 ERA and three shutouts. But the impact of a career-high 199⅓ innings took a toll and in early August he began to experience pain in his throwing shoulder. The pain subsided and on August 12 he defeated the Giants, 5-4, in 10 innings. However, the pain returned, and he pitched only three times the rest of the season. His season ended with a 12-6 record and a league-leading 2.48 ERA. He had hurled eight complete games and led the league with four shutouts.

The situation was made worse by Peña's language issues. In interviews with the media, he had to use the services of interpreter Jaime Jarrin. He was unable to properly communicate his condition to the Dodgers' medical personnel, and surgery was delayed. Peña would be essentially on the shelf for two seasons. It was hoped that rest during the offseason would help with the shoulder pain, but surgery proved necessary. Dr. Frank Jobe performed shoulder surgery (an arthroscopy) the following February.[8] Peña was on the DL for virtually the entire 1985 season, making only two late-season relief appearances.

Peña was restricted to bullpen activity early in 1986, making nine unproductive appearances. In July he returned to the starting rotation. He picked up his first victory since 1984 on July 7, when he allowed two hits in five innings as the Dodgers defeated the Cardinals, 1-0. It was his only win of the season. He pitched in 24 games in 1986 (10 as a starter) and went 1-2 with one save and a 4.89 ERA.

The man who started each of his 28 appearances in 1984 would evolve into a relief pitcher over the next three seasons and would be relieving exclusively starting in 1988, when he appeared in a career-high 60 games. Speaking of his new role, he said, "I like this role. I like the pressure and the close situations of this game. It looks like this motivates me more than starting did. I believe I've become a good short man. I hope other people believe it too."[9] Although his won-lost record was only 6-7, he had 12 saves and struck out 83 batters in 94⅓ innings. The Dodgers won the NL West and Peña returned to the postseason for his third appearance. He had a win and a save against the Mets in the NLCS.

In Game Two, the Mets rallied in the ninth inning, had reduced the deficit to three runs and had two runners on base with one out when Peña was summoned. He secured the victory by getting Gary Carter on a fly ball to right field. In Game Three he was part of an eighth-inning bullpen implosion, yielding a double to Wally Backman as New York scored five runs against four Dodgers relievers and took a 2-1 lead in the best-of-seven series. In Game Four at New York, Peña entered the game in the ninth inning with the score tied 4-4. He pitched three scoreless innings, not allowing a hit, before being removed for a pinch-hitter.

He wound up getting the win when Kirk Gibson homered in the top of the 12th inning.

After Kirk Gibson launched his game-winning homer in Game One of the World Series, the Dodgers defeated the A's in five games.

Peña was in peak form and his fastball was being clocked in the mid-90s. However, the speed of his fastball was in stark contrast to his pace of play. He was slow, methodical, patient, and deliberate on the mound for his entire career and was not about to change. "I've been that way my whole career. Why change it now?" he said. "I've been successful, so why would I want to make a change? If I can get a hitter out with this style, why would I want to pitch fast?"[10]

The Dodgers failed to repeat in 1989. Peña was 4-3 with a 2.13 ERA in 53 games, but only five saves as the Dodgers handed the closer role to Jay Howell. Los Angeles finished in fourth place with a 77-83 record and there were changes to be made. At the end of the season, Peña was traded to the Mets along with outfielder/first baseman Mike Marshall for infielder Juan Samuel. In his nine years with the Dodgers, Peña had gone 38-38 with 32 saves and a 2.92 ERA.

He arrived in New York as the Mets were beginning to look less like the championship squad they had been when they won the World Series in 1986 and a divisional championship in 1988 before falling to the Dodgers in the NLCS.

During the 1990 season, Peña went 3-3 with five saves and a 3.20 ERA. The Mets were treading water in the early part of the season. Bud Harrelson had replaced Davey Johnson as manager on May 29, and on June 4, after they lost five of six, the Mets' record stood at 21-26. Then they turned their season around. Between June 5 and August 3, they won 40 of 55 games to take over the division lead. During that stretch Peña was credited with a win, a save, and four holds. But after Labor Day, the Mets could not maintain their momentum and finished in second place, four games behind the Pirates.

Peña started the 1991 season with the Mets but was dealt to the Atlanta Braves on August 28. By then the Mets had fallen from contention and were in fourth place, 13½ games behind the division leaders. Peña had an excellent season with the Mets, going 6-1 with four saves and a 2.71 ERA. However, they realized that their chances at re-signing Peña, who was to become a free agent at season's end, were nominal and they obtained Joe Roa and Tony Castillo from Atlanta. The Braves, meanwhile, needed bullpen assistance, as their ace reliever, Juan Berenguer, had been injured. As Atlanta sportswriter Mark Bradley noted, Peña went from a capsized ship to a luxury liner.[11] He had a phenomenal five-week stretch run with the Braves, going 2-0 and saving 11 games in 15 appearances. From September 3 through October 4, he appeared in 14 games, all of which were won by Atlanta.

One of those saves was against the Padres on September 11. In that game, he came on in the ninth inning with the Braves leading 1-0. The Padres had gone hitless in eight innings against Kent Mercker and Mark Wohlers. Peña quickly got the first two batters, but Darrin Jackson hit a Baltimore chop to the left side of the infield that third baseman Terry Pendleton lost in the lights. The ball bounded off shortstop Rafael Belliard's glove and Jackson reached safely. The official scorer Mark Frederickson ruled the play an error by Pendleton. The no-hitter remained intact, and when the next batter, Tony Gwynn, skied to left fielder Otis Nixon, Peña had completed the combined no-hitter.[12]

The Braves, who had finished in last place the prior season, went 21-8 during Peña's hot streak and won the NL West by one game. On October 5, the day after Peña's last save of the season (and third in as many days), his services weren't needed as John Smoltz pitched a complete-game win over Houston, clinching the division title for the Braves. In the League Championship Series, they defeated the Pittsburgh Pirates in seven games. Peña recorded saves in three of the wins. He appeared in four games, was not scored upon, didn't allow any inherited runners to score, and yielded only one hit in 4⅓ innings. In Game Three, he entered the game in the bottom of the eighth inning. The Braves led 7-3, but the Bucs had loaded the bases with one out off Mike Stanton and Wohlers. Orlando Merced fouled out on a 3-and-1 fastball and got Jay Bell struck out looking. Peña had a 1-2-3 ninth for the save and Atlanta moved ahead in the series, two games to one.

In Game Six, with the Braves down 3-2 in the series, Peña came on to pitch the ninth inning at Pittsburgh with Atlanta leading 1-0. The Bucs' Gary Varsho opened the bottom of the ninth with a single to center field. He was bunted to second. With two out and Andy Van Slyke at the plate, Peña hurled a wild pitch and the potential tying run was at third base. The count went to 1-and-2 on Van Slyke and a classic pitcher-batter duel followed. The Pirates center fielder fouled off four consecutive pitches, the last three of which were hard-hit balls. During the first seven pitches of the at-bat, Peña had thrown a variety of pitches. Van Slyke said, "He threw a slider, a fastball, a forkball."[13] Braves catcher Greg Olson, who had driven in the only run of the game with a double in the top of the ninth, thought it was time for something different and called for a changeup. Van Slyke was frozen at the plate and looked at strike three. After the game, Van Slyke said, "I didn't even know he had that pitch."[14] The changeup had been in Peña's arsenal since early in 1984 when he had learned the pitch from coach Silvano Quesada while pitching for Licey in the Dominican Winter League, and perfected the pitch under the tutelage of Dodgers pitching coach Ron Perranoski.[15]

The Braves lost the World Series to the Twins in seven games. In Game Seven at the noisy Metrodome, Peña entered the scoreless battle in the bottom of the ninth inning. The first two batters in the inning had singled off Mike Stanton. Peña came in and put out the fire. The game advanced to extra innings. In the bottom of the 10th, the Twins loaded the bases on a double, a sacrifice, and two intentional walks. As reported by *Sports Illustrated*'s Steve Rushin, pinch-hitter Gene Larkin "slapped the first pitch he got from Alejandro Peña to left center, over the head of Brian Hunter, who, like the rest of the Atlanta outfield, was playing only 30 yards in back of the infield in an effort to prevent Minnesota's Dan Gladden from doing precisely what he did: bound home from third base in the bottom of the 10th, through a cross-current of crazed, dazed teammates, who were leaping from the third base dugout and onto the field."[16]

Peña re-signed with the Braves after the season for $2.65 million, a substantial increase over the $1 million he was paid in 1991. Although Cleveland had made a two-year offer, Peña chose to sign a one-year deal with the Braves "because it's the most fun he ever had," according to his agent, Tom Reich.[17]

But the promise of the last five weeks of 1991 did not extend into 1992. Not right away, anyway. Although Peña had three saves in April, his May performance was horrific. In seven appearances that month, his 0-3 record included a blown save, and his ERA was 9.72. On May 16, after a poor performance, the crowd turned angry as Peña left the mound, and when he returned to the parking lot, he found that his car had been vandalized by someone using a key to scratch off some of the paint. He was no longer his team's closer. He was placed on the DL (eventually it was determined that his problems were in part due to bronchitis, strep throat, and a sinus infection). Once Peña returned from the DL, pitching coach Leo Mazzone detected a flaw in his delivery having to do with the release point.[18] And slowly Peña turned things around.

Healthy and delivering the ball like the Peña of old, Alexandro returned to form, and on July 8, with the Braves in danger of losing their fourth consecutive game, was given the ball in the ninth inning against the Mets in Atlanta. The "forgotten closer" entered the game with the bases loaded and none out. The Braves were leading 2-1. Peña got Howard Johnson on a popup and induced Willie Randolph to hit into a double play.[19] The save was his fourth of the season and first since April 28. From June 18, when he returned from the DL, through the end of the season, Peña saved 12 games and had a 2.30 ERA. From July 8 success through July 25, the Braves went on a tear. They won 13 games in a row to surge from six games behind the division lead to two games in front of the pack. Peña's only win of the season and eight of his saves came during the first 12 games of the streak, and he was credited with a hold in the Braves' 13th consecutive win.

The Braves once again finished first and faced the Pirates in the NLCS. But Peña's season was over. Experiencing elbow pain (tendinitis), he had spent time in late August and early September on the DL. The pain reached its threshold, surprisingly enough, after one of his best efforts. At Pittsburgh on August 17, he pitched the bottom of the 10th inning to save a 5-4 win. The last batter was Barry Bonds. As manager Bobby Cox recalled, "First pitch: fastball, whoosh! Second pitch: another fastball – and it was harder than the first. Third pitch: fastball again, and I swear it had more velocity than either of the first two. I'm just gaping at Peña. As for Bonds (who took the pitch for strike three), his eyes were bulging out; they were bigger than billiard balls. So, we all run out to the mound to shake Alejandro's hand, and just as I'm reaching for him, he says, 'Don't do it. My arm is killing me.'"[20] Peña was placed on the DL, and his September work had been limited to three nonsave appearances.

Toward the end of the season, Peña's wife, Tellie, organized an auction event where the wives of the Braves players raised money for victims of Hurricane Andrew by auctioning off broken bats, autographed jerseys and other items.[21] For Peña, the season would end on a sour note. On September 30, with the division championship already clinched, the Braves asked Peña to pitch the eighth inning against the Giants with the Braves trailing 1-0. Although he completed the inning, retiring three of the four batters he faced, he was in pain.[22] Peña was not used in the NLCS and was left off the roster when the Braves lost to the Blue Jays in the World Series.

A free agent once again, Peña signed with the Pirates during the offseason, but did not play in 1993. On March 26 he underwent surgery to rebuild a ligament in his pitching elbow. The procedure involved removing a ligament from his right wrist and reattaching it in his elbow. His contract with the Pirates was restructured into a two-year deal, and he returned to the mound in 1994. When his contract was restructured, Peña showed great class. He could have just made his salary, more than $1 million, for 1993 and moved on. He chose to return his signing bonus of $500,000 and signed a two-year deal calling for $175,000 in 1993 and $1.35 million in 1994. In describing the contract, he said, "I could live with myself better. I didn't feel right taking the money and not doing anything for the team. I didn't want to take the money and then go play for somebody else."[23]

Sidelined by bleeding ulcers at the beginning of the 1994 season, Peña started the season on the DL. He returned to the mound in May and was named the Pirates closer in June, after a great four-inning stint on May 26 when he came on the 10th inning and allowed no hits as the Pirates won in 13 innings. He had a brilliant month with seven saves, but his season ended on June 28. He was in immense pain after throwing the final pitch in his seventh save of the season, and an examination indicated that he had ligament damage in his elbow. He was finished for the season and the Pirates released him on June 30.[24]

Peña pitched for three major-league teams in 1995. He started the season with the Red Sox and was pitching well in his first 10 appearances with a save, a hold, and a 2.70 ERA. But then he hit a bad spell. He was scored on in six of his last seven appearances with Boston and his ERA ballooned to 7.40. The Red Sox released him on June 13. Two weeks later, he signed with the Charlotte Knights, the Triple-A affiliate of the Florida Marlins and pitched in nine games, saving five and posting a 0.96 ERA. The Marlins called him up on July 29.

With the help of a sinker developed under the tutelage of Marlins pitching coach Larry Rothschild during August was credited with six holds and two wins in 13 games. His ERA was 1.50 and he struck out 21 batters in 18 innings. At month's end he was traded back to the Braves for Chris Seelbach.

The Braves were a virtual cinch for a playoff berth, leading the NL East by 14½ games when Peña arrived. He was given the number 26 that he had worn in 1991 and became the set-up man for closer Mark Wohlers. He shored up the pitching-rich Braves, getting into 14 games. He was credited with three holds and struck out 18 batters in 13 innings.

In the best-of-five Division Series against Colorado, Peña was credited with wins in the first two games. In each instance, he gave up a run-scoring double after entering the game, only to see his teammates rally to win after he became the pitcher of record. In Game Four, he took over for Greg Maddux in the eighth inning with the Braves leading by six runs. Dante Bichette greeted him with a single and then Peña retired the next six batters and was mobbed at the mound after he struck out John Vander Wal for the final out of the game and series. In the NLCS against Cincinnati, Peña pitched in three of the four games as the Braves swept the Reds. He pitched the eighth inning in Games One, Two, and Four and was not scored upon.

"Oh yeah, I thought I'd be here again. I never give up on myself. I thought I had a couple of good years left even after Boston let me go this year."

– Alejandro Peña, October 22, 1995 on the eve of Game Seven of the 1995 World Series.[25]

In the World Series against Cleveland, Peña entered Game Two in the seventh inning. The Braves led 4-3 and there were runners at the corners with two outs. Albert Belle came to the plate. Eddie Murray lurked in the on-deck circle. Peña remarked about facing Belle. "Early this season, when I was with Boston, he hit a homer off me (on a fastball). This was revenge. I started him with a slider and then got him with three straight fastballs."[26] He got Belle out on a popup that catcher Javy Lopez caught behind home plate.

In the eighth inning Peña got two outs before walking Jim Thome, and Bobby Cox brought in Mark Wohlers, who got credit for the save. Peña was credited with a hold, and the Braves led the series, 2 games to none. The third game of the Series went into extra innings, and Peña came in to pitch the 11th. After successes in each of his first seven postseason appearances in 1995, Peña had a bad outing, yielding a leadoff double to Carlos Baerga and a game-winning single to Eddie Murray. He wasn't expecting to pitch that night as he had strained his lower back in pre-game warmups. After the game, he admitted, "I couldn't follow through, but I had to pitch." (The Braves had already gone through four relievers)."[27] It was Peña's last appearance in the Series. The Braves won in six games, and Peña had gone 2-1 with a 1.29 ERA in eight 1995 postseason outings.

Peña was once again a free agent after the 1995 season. After signing a minor-league contract with the Marlins in December 1995, he had an excellent spring training and made the major-league roster. But after pitching in four April games, he was placed on the disabled list on the 17th with a strained rotator cuff. Dr. James Andrews performed surgery on June 18, but Peña never pitched again professionally.

For his 15-year major-league career, Peña was 56-52 with a 3.11 ERA. As a starter he had seven shutouts, and as a reliever he had 74 saves.

After he retired from baseball Peña paid serious attention to his golf game at his home in Georgia and stayed out of the game for more than 10 years. He was the pitching coach for the Dominican Summer League Dodgers from 2010 through 2013.

THE 1995 WORLD CHAMPION ATLANTA BRAVES

Sources

In addition to the sources cited in the Notes, the author used Baseball-Reference.com. and Peña's file at the National Baseball Hall of Fame and Museum.

Notes

1 Orel Hershiser (with Jerry B. Jenkins), *Out of the Blue* (Brentwood, Tennessee: Wolgemuth and Hyatt Publishers, 1989), 188.

2 Larry Schwartz, "Hollywood Ending for L.A., Gibson's HR Wins in Ninth," *Bergen Record* (Hackensack, New Jersey), October 16, 1988: S01.

3 Peter Gammons, "The Home Run," *Sports Illustrated*, October 24, 1988.

4 Gordon Edes, "Alejandro's Pain Is Real," *Los Angeles Times*, March 5, 1986: Sports-1.

5 Ibid.

6 Gordon Verrell, "Dodgers: Kiddies in Pen," *The Sporting News*, September 5, 1981: 47.

7 I.J. Rosenberg, "Whatever Happened to Alejandro Peña?" *Atlanta Journal Constitution*, May 2, 2015.

8 Verrell, "Fastball No Longer in Peña's Arsenal," *The Sporting News*, March 11, 1985: 32.

9 Terry Johnson, "No Stopping Him: To Dodgers' Relief, Peña Back in Form," *Daily Breeze* (Torrance, California), April 25, 1989: D3.

10 Ibid.

11 Mark Bradley, "Peña Feels Lucky to Be a Brave," *Atlanta Journal*, August 30, 1991: H2.

12 Bob Nightingale, "A No-Hitter by Decision in Baseball: Mercker, Wohlers, Peña get Help from Scorer's Controversial Ruling as the Braves Beat the Padres, 1-0," *Los Angeles Times*, September 12, 1991: 1.

13 Joe Sexton, "Baseball: Peña Strikes a Big Blow," *New York Times*, October 17, 1991: B15.

14 Murray Chass, "Baseball: No Runs, No Pennant: Braves Force Game Seven," *New York Times*, October 17, 1991: B13.

15 Terry Johnson, "Peña Gets Results with New Pitch," *Daily Breeze* (Torrance, California), April 30, 1984: D1.

16 Steve Rushin, "A Series to Savor," *Sports Illustrated*, November 4, 1991.

17 Associated Press, "Atlanta Keeps Peña," *Augusta* (Georgia) *Chronicle*, December 20, 1991: 1B.

18 I.J. Rosenberg, "The Fire Burns Again: To Braves' Relief, Alejandro Peña has Regained His Health and Fastball to Fuel 11-Game Win Streak," *Atlanta Constitution*, July 24, 1992: E1.

19 Rosenberg, "Mets Fall 2-1, as Peña Saves Glavine's 13th," *Atlanta Constitution*, July 9, 1992: D1.

20 Dave Nightingale, "Hurtin' and Uncertain," *The Sporting News*, October 5, 1992: 10.

21 Susannah Vesey, "What Am I Bid?" *Atlanta Constitution*, September 25, 1992: G2.

22 Aileen Voisin, "Baseball: The Braves 1992 NL West Division Champions: Peña Feels Pain in His Elbow While Pitching Scoreless 8th," *Atlanta Constitution*, October 1, 1992: E8.

23 John Mehno, "Giving Something Back," *The Sporting News*, March 21, 1994: 16.

24 Ron Cook, "Peña's Release a Sad Farewell," *Pittsburgh Post-Gazette*, July 1, 1994: C1.

25 Lyle Spencer, "Peña Still has Shades of '88 Series in Him," *Riverside* (California) *Press-Enterprise*, October 23, 1995: D01.

26 Scott Tolley, "Indians Get Home Cooking," *Palm Beach* (Florida) *Post*, October 23, 1955: 3C.

27 Mike Berardino, "Hired Guns' Shine at Just the Right Time in Braves Title Run," *Augusta* (Georgia) *Chronicle*, October 30, 1995: 4C.

Eddie Pérez

BY TONY OLIVER

Eddie Pérez

Catchers, like musicians, use both hands for their craft: the gloved one captures the ball while the other acts as a conductor's baton to guide the action. Johnny Bench, arguably the best player to don the tools of ignorance, stated, "The catcher is in the middle of everything. He sees it best."[1] The statement is both literal and figurative; not only is he the sole defensive player with a frontal view of the mound, but it is his guidance that traditionally starts every micro-battle between hitter and pitcher. Braves fans – both the ones in the South and those who were raised on "America's Team" during their TBS heyday – were privy to a clinic in the late 1990s thanks to Eddie Pérez.

Born on May 4, 1968, Eddie was blessed with a comfortable upbringing in then-prosperous Venezuela. For most of the second half of the twentieth century, the country's vast oil reserves afforded a standard of living envied by its Latin American neighbors. Growing up in Ciudad Ojeda in the state of Zulia, he and his siblings enjoyed the allure of baseball without the sport representing a one-way ticket out of poverty: "My family loved baseball. … All my brothers and my dad played. I don't recall specifically when I started."[2] His father worked in the oil industry as a shore captain and his mother stayed at home with the children. (Both parents now reside in Atlanta.)

Although the Águilas of Zulia played in Maracaibo, only 90 minutes across the namesake lake, Eddie rooted for the Tigres of Aragua, who played more than seven hours away, near the capital city of Caracas: "My dad took me to see two games. Zulia played against Aragua and I preferred the latter, even though people rooted for the Águilas." Later he lived out two dreams, playing 10 winter-league seasons with his favorite club before winding down his active career at home: "Aragua traded me to Zulia, which hurt me a lot; it was a transition, but I liked playing at home, seeing my family and friends on the stands."

Perez was mesmerized by the exploits of Davey Concepción, the National League's premier shortstop during the 1970s and a vital member of the fearsome Big Red Machine. In the days before cable broadcasts, a "game of the week" was the main drug to fuel the country's baseball addiction, and appearances by Cincinnati were appointment television. Concepción was the heir to "Little Louie" Aparicio, whose Spanish nicknames focus on his stature on the diamond: "El Grande" and "El Rey David." Much like Puerto Rican players wearing number 21 in honor of Roberto Clemente despite being born after his tragic death, Aparicio's contribution to the fertile grounds of Venezuelan baseball has bloomed for generations after his retirement. As Aparicio's number 11 and Concepción's 13 were popular, Eddie opted to split the difference and choose number 12.

Prior to Cal Ripken and Alex Rodriguez, shortstops were hardly tall, and Eddie had grown to 6-feet-1 by his teens. Eddie did not have to look far to determine a position to play: His father was a celebrated amateur catcher. In the major leagues, Baudillo "Bo" Díaz had replaced Bench behind the plate in Cincinnati, giving Venezuelans another established big-league hero. Though Eddie and Bo never met, they share a connection via Carlos Hernández, Eddie's contemporary behind the plate in the big leagues. Díaz played with Hernández in Venezuela and the latter, in turn, shared some of those tips with Pérez.

At the tender age of 7, Eddie was turning enough heads to play his first children's Campeonato Nacional. Blessed with the twin graces of natural ability and a patient father who taught him the fine art of catching, he progressed through the youth levels to star in the 1986 Big League World Series tournament in Fort Lauderdale, Florida. Venezuela lost its first game against Taiwan but then reeled off eight consecutive victories to win the tournament. Eddie earned Most Valuable Player (MVP) honors with seven home runs and 16 runs batted in.[3] The event, held from 1968 through 2016, picked up where the Little League World Series ended, affording 15- to 18-year-old youth the opportunity to showcase their talents in front of scouts. It was Venezuela's first and only title, prompting joy in the state capital of Maracaibo and a massive opportunity for Eddie, but his decision was far from easy.

In the days before cell phones and email, messages were relayed via landline telephones and intermediaries; his performance in Fort Lauderdale garnered Eddie some scout interest and the chance to further impress the scouts. "The Aguada Tigres gave me a tryout; about 50 or 60 kids showed up, 10 of whom were from Zulia, like me. I was the only one signed. Since I was underage, my dad said: 'Here's the deal, $15,000 is more than I've ever earned in a year. That means nothing, though: It's your decision.'"

Having finished high school, Pérez was planning to enroll in college like his older siblings and weighed the pros and cons of leaving Venezuela to prove his mettle in the United States. "My dad asked if I was sure if I wanted to sign the contract. My brothers criticized me – 'Are you crazy?' they would say." He remembers his father cautioning him how life would change: While he would indeed be playing baseball, he'd have to cook for himself, launder his clothes, and handle a host of other domestic duties typically glossed over by scouts spinning tales of stardom and riches. Pedro González, himself a former major leaguer with the Yankees and Indians, gave Pérez an honest opinion of the opportunity: While the $15,000 offered by Atlanta was a sizable sum, Eddie also had an offer with his favorite club, the Tigres de Aragua, for 200,000 bolívares, (about $10,700, 18.7 bolívares being worth $1 in early 1986).[4] "It was both luck and a blessing to follow my dad's footsteps (playing catcher). Eight years in the minors, always as a backup, followed by 11 years in the big leagues and another 10 as a coach. Every career has obstacles and I never gave up. Moreover, the franchise taught me not just to be a good ballplayer but also a good person, off the field and with the community. I've been with them more than 30 years."[5]

Ultimately Pérez decided to follow his dreams. After signing with Atlanta on September 27, 1986, he packed his bags for the Gulf Coast League, where he started the 1987 campaign. Playing with future big leaguers Derek Lilliquist, Keith Mitchell, and Ben Rivera, Pérez appeared in 31 games and fielded at a .980 clip while hitting .202. The team finished last with a 20-43 record but gave the 19-year-old his first exposure to life outside of Venezuela.

It was a slow climb for Pérez. He amassed 721 games in the minors across the Gulf, Class A, Double A, and Triple A affiliates of the Braves franchise. The 1988 season saw him at Burlington of the Midwest League, with another last-place finish; 1989 at Sumter of the South Atlantic League, with a club 1½ games out of the cellar; 1990 split between Sumter and Durham (Carolina League), where both clubs posted winning records; 1991 between Durham and Greenville (Southern League). The 1992 and 1993 seasons were spent at Greenville and 1994/1995 at Richmond (International League) before Pérez got the much-desired call from Atlanta. From 1987 through 1995, he played in 698 games in the minors, garnering 2,456 plate appearances and producing a .246 batting average. (After establishing himself in the majors, Pérez played 23 minor-league games in 2001 and 2006 during rehabilitation assignments.)

On September 10, 1995, he debuted in the major leagues in Miami, pinch-hitting in the getaway game of a series against the Marlins. Although the Braves were six weeks away from winning the World Series, they lost that contest 5-4 in extra innings. Greg Maddux started but pitched only one inning, as Atlanta manager Bobby Cox gave work to six other hurlers in preparation for the extended postseason (this was the first campaign with the Division Series, since the 1994 strike canceled the playoffs). With the score tied, 4-4, Mark Wohlers' spot was up in the 10th inning and Pérez was summoned to bat against Terry Matthews. He recalled the game fondly, stating, "I was happy in the big leagues after so many years in the minors. In the last game of the series, I was asked by Bobby Cox to bat and I struck out." He caught Pedro Borbón Jr. for two innings and witnessed former Brave Terry Pendleton cross the plate for the Marlins win.

Of the 120 major-league baseball players whose first career at-bat produced a home run, two have been Venezuelans: Gerardo Parra (2009) and Alex Cabrera (2000).[6] Pérez narrowly missed being the first, leaving the yard for his first hit during his first start (and second plate appearance) on September 15, 1995. While Atlanta had already clinched the NL East (and ended up winning by a comfortable 21-game margin), the game was far from meaningless. Pérez recalls not just the game but the circumstances with flawless details: "Pat Corrales called me and said: 'I have good news and bad news: You're starting but you're catching John Smoltz, who had been struggling.' Javy López told me 'good luck.'… Charlie O'Brien said good luck too, but stay calm, call your game. Smoltz shook me off twice: Barry Larkin hit a home run and Hal Morris doubled. He struck out 11 batters in eight innings pitched and (Greg) McMichael closed."

Starting behind the plate for the first time, Pérez hit seventh in the batting order and recorded 12 putouts, one assist, and one double play. Pérez connected off veteran left-hander Mike Jackson in the seventh inning to drive home David Justice. The home run provided the difference as the Braves beat the Reds 3-1 in front of 31,882 fans for Smoltz's 11th victory of the season and McMichael's second save. The first of Pérez's 40 career round-trippers was particularly memorable: His boyhood idol Concepción was on hand during one of his appearances at Riverfront Stadium. They met and shook hands after the game. During Pérez's phone call to his parents' home, it was hard to figure out which accomplishment pleased him more: "The game ended, and I was so happy, calling my family from a pay phone and when I left the stadium I ran into Davey who was there signing autographs. He came over. … I couldn't believe it, this was my dream, my first hit, and meeting Davey. I still have the ball."

For the season, Pérez appeared in seven games and had four hits in 13 at-bats; he struck out twice, did not walk, and collected a double in addition to the earlier home run. He pinch-hit, started another game at catcher supporting Steve Avery, pinch-ran, and played first base for half a game. As the backstop, he tallied 25 innings with no errors, two assists, and two double plays; the starters yielded only two runs in 18 innings over the two games he started, demonstrating a facility to call the game. The Braves opted not to include him in the postseason roster, choosing the regular-season tandem of O'Brien and López for all three rounds. The Braves, however, liked what they saw from Pérez and declined to offer O'Brien an extension after the World Series, making Pérez the heir to the second catcher spot on the roster.

The 1996 and 1997 seasons brought plentiful action for Pérez. As the backup catcher, he played in 141 total games, collecting 373 at-bats and 81 hits, 25 of which were for extra bases. He tasted the postseason in both years, playing in 10 games but reaching base only twice, on a hit against the Dodgers in the NLDS and a walk against the Cardinals in the National League Championship Series, both in 1996. The Braves, so-called team of the 1990s, played good baseball against the Marlins and the Yankees but could not best their foes in the fall.

In 1996 Pérez saw action in 68 games, 39 as a starter. The Braves were 26-13 with his name in the starting lineup. He had a six-game hitting streak and at one point reached based in eight consecutive games. The back-of-the-baseball-card statistics did not tell the whole tale; as the Braves knew, his game-calling abilities provided value beyond his offensive output. Braves pitchers compiled a 3.02 ERA when he was their backstop, more than half a run better than starting catcher López. The next year, his batting average dipped by 41 points (from .256 to .215) while his OPS dropped by more than 100 points (from .697 to .594). His handling of the staff continued to be exemplary, with a catcher's ERA of 3.24 as the Braves led the league with a 3.18 mark.

The 1998 campaign yielded batting highs for Pérez. Appearing in 73 games and garnering 206 plate appearances, he hit .336 with a .404 OBP and a .537 slugging percentage. Pérez attributed his success to a sound mindset: "I want to remain here, and I need to hit. If I don't, I won't stay. Great hitting catchers like Javy and (Mike) Piazza were there … so I focused on hitting." While his lumber was white-hot, his focus on the mound did not waver; Braves pitchers allowed a scant 2.60 runs per nine innings when he was on the lineup. Atlanta's starters combined for 88 victories with Glavine picking up 20, Maddux earning 18, Kevin Millwood and Smoltz tying at 17 and Denny Neagle winning 16 as the team's fifth starter. The juggernaut finished the campaign at 106-56, establishing a franchise record.

Pérez also found an unlikely source of hitting prowess: Maddux. "Few people know this, but Maddux knows more about hitting than pitching. He wouldn't talk more unless asked. … In LA, I said if I don't hit, I am not sure I won't catch you again. He said try to hit to third base. That day I had three hits. I asked him why he hadn't told me before; he said, 'You never asked.'" Beyond Maddux, Pérez sought hitting tips from Chipper Jones, former teammate Fred McGriff, and fellow Venezuelan Fred Manrique. He was consistent throughout the year, overcoming a 1-for-8 start with three multihit games in April to reach .385 by month's end. His average dipped below .300 for only a fraction of July. Although Atlanta swept the Cubs in the NLDS, the Braves fell to the San Diego Padres in the NLCS in six games. Pérez collected three hits against the Friars and one against the Cubs, establishing personal postseason marks he would shatter the next year. The sole hit against Chicago was decisive, an eighth-inning grand slam off Rod Beck to give the Braves and Maddux the win.

The 1999 season saw Atlanta seek an elusive second World Series title en route to its seventh consecutive division championship. (The Braves accomplished the task during 14 consecutive seasons, a major-league record, although one aided by the cancellation of the 1994 postseason since they trailed the Montréal Expos.) Pérez appeared in a career-high 104 games due to his former minor-league roommate Lopez's season-ending injury in late July. Though he hit a pedestrian .249, his on-base average and slugging both improved by 21 and 39 points after his playing time increased in August and September. Despite the extra games and the sweltering Georgia summer, Pérez logged a 3.55 catcher's ERA on 3,182 opponents' plate appearances, the second-best mark in the majors for backstops with such workload. He powered the Braves to a World Series appearance by hitting .500 while slugging .900 against the Mets in the NLCS. Pérez was voted the series MVP, echoing his 1987 amateur accolades. Had fans been told before the series began that a catcher would win the award, most would have guessed future Hall of Famer Piazza, who donned the mask for the Mets. However, Piazza was not in a groove, going 4-for-24 during the six-game affair.

While expectations were high for the World Series (a rematch of the 1996 fall classic), Atlanta could not answer the Yankees, who swept the Braves en route to their third title in four years.

With López back to full health in 2000, Pérez returned to full-time backup duty. He suffered through right-shoulder injuries in consecutive seasons, suiting up for only 32 combined games in 2000 and 2001.[7] The Braves nevertheless won the NL East but failed to advance to the World Series, dropping three straight contests to the Cardinals in the 2000 NLDS and a tough five-game series against eventual champion Arizona in the 2001 NLCS. Pérez watched the postseason from home while nursing his injuries.

The 2002 season saw Pérez switch leagues for the first time, after the Braves traded him to Cleveland for a player to be named later (Jason Fitzgerald) on March 28. Eight days earlier, Atlanta had shipped Paul Bako and José Cabrera to Milwaukee for Henry Blanco. A fellow Venezuelan, Blanco was two years younger than Pérez and had averaged close to 100 games for the Brewers in the prior two seasons. He played until age 41 in the majors, appearing in 971 games (914 as the catcher), a representative of the strong Venezuelan catching corps that followed Pérez. Steve Torrealba, a second-generation Venezuelan major leaguer, played a handful of games for the Braves as well in 2002, having debuted in the big leagues the prior October against the Marlins by replacing Pérez in the ninth inning and singling in his first at-bat. Though Pérez was leaving the Braves, his mark on the franchise was well-felt and his countrymen had set up a club behind the plate.

With the 74-88 Indians, Pérez appeared in 42 games in 2002. While the team was 18-24 in games he played, they were 16-18 in his starts, proving his ability to manage the pitching staff, as attested by his 4.37 catcher's ERA, three-quarters of a run better than starting backstop Einar Díaz's 5.18. The Indians were in transition, fielding a team with veterans like future Hall of Famer Jim Thome, Omar Vizquel, Ellis Burks, Bartolo Colón, and Chuck Finley, alongside youngsters CC Sabathia and Milton Bradley. Pérez backed up Díaz but also provided tutelage to a young Víctor Martínez, who was beginning his career in the majors. Pérez knew his stay with the Indians would be short-lived, given the promise of Martínez and the presence of a younger option, Josh Bard, on the roster.

The 2003 season brought him back to the National League with the Brewers, who were in the 11th of a brutal stretch of 12 consecutive losing seasons. Pérez was the main catcher for Milwaukee, appearing in 107 games and slashing .271/.304/.420 while playing his customary solid defense. The Brewers improved their 2002 mark by 12 games, though their pitching worsened by almost a third of a run. Pérez hit his second (and last) career regular-season grand slam in San Diego, victimizing Carlton Loewer on May 28 in the first inning of an 8-6 loss, and his only career walk-off round-tripper, against Cincinnati's Scott Williamson on May 17. His batting average reached .316 in the summer, but he fell into a slump to finish the year.

The Brewers did not offer Pérez a contract for 2004, granting him an opportunity to reunite with the Braves. Although only Chipper Jones and

John Smoltz remained from the 1990s core, Pérez welcomed the opportunity to show the ropes to young prospect Brian McCann, who would enjoy seven All-Star seasons with the Braves. Pérez played in 74 games, collecting 39 hits (15 of which were for extra bases) as the Braves reached the NLDS in 2004. Atlanta lost a hard-fought series to the Astros in five games, three of which Pérez entered as part of a double switch. He was hitless in three at-bats.

Baseball is at its core a game of matchups. Every manager seeks an advantage, no matter how small, against his opponent. Often the pendulum swings in unexpected ways, as was the case of Randy Johnson and Pérez. By the time both met on May 18, 2004, Pérez boasted of a 6-for-13 batting line against the Hall of Fame-bound lefty. In their last matchup, he was tasked with a seemingly impossible feat: pinch-hit against the Big Unit as Johnson attempted to pitch a perfect game. "I think I hit .400 or .500 vs. RJ. I was surprised that day that I wasn't in the starting lineup since Bobby liked to play the hitters with strong history. I was watching the game and Pat said, you're going up, and I grabbed the bat. Everything was working for Randy; I could see how he was dominating all our hitters. One of my most memorable at-bats … perfect games are so hard to do." Facing a 98-mph fastball, Pérez struck out to end the game.

The 2005 season proved to be a tough one for Pérez. After appearing in 15 games through May 18, he did not see action until the end of the year due to tendinitis in his right shoulder. Brian McCann established himself as the regular during his absence, wrapping up the season with a .745 OPS as a 21-year-old and helping the staff finish sixth in NL ERA. Pérez's curtain call came on September 27, 2005, during a 12-3 blowout against the Rockies. He pinch-hit for Danny Kolb and grounded out on a 2-and-1 pitch from Randy Williams. He had made his final on-the-field appearance on May 14, starting behind the plate and guiding Mike Hampton to two innings of work and Adam Bernero to three frames before yielding to Johnny Estrada.

The Braves signed Pérez to a minor-league deal on January 6, 2006, and he did not return to the majors. He appeared in 13 games for the Southern League's Mississippi Braves and provided a veteran presence for prospect Jarrod Saltalamacchia. He played an unofficial role assisting his former teammate Jeff Blauser, who managed the team. The franchise was transitioning; it would experience its first losing season since 1990, failing to make the postseason. During Pérez's years with the Braves, the team played deep into every October, but the next playoff trip would not come until 2010.

To watch Pérez catch Maddux was akin to seeing a world-class ballet performance between favorite partners. Baseball players in general are creatures of habit but pitchers are more inclined to seek the comforts of routines. The sabermetrics explosion has given us statistics like pitch framing and catcher's ERA to better measure the defensive contributions of catchers. Savvy pitchers, though, have long trusted their feelings, recollections, and overall easiness by "feel." Like a nervous animal prognosticating an earthquake, *they just knew*. During their tenure with the Braves, Maddux and Pérez teamed up for 832⅓ innings, dozens of wins, and hundreds of moments that could serve as clinics for players and fans alike.[8]

On June 17, 1996, Pérez found himself in the starting lineup for Maddux's start. He tripled and supported Maddux's eight innings with zero walks and only four hits allowed. The relationship clicked to such a degree that the rest of the campaign saw a marked difference in the pitcher's effectiveness: His 1.89 ERA in Pérez's 114 innings caught was about half of regular López's 3.44 ERA in 131 innings. While the proper calculation and recording of catcher's ERA was not yet en vogue, the organization took notice and made Pérez the starter for Maddux's starts the rest of the year despite the more potent bat of López.

Maddux's exploits are legendary, and readers wishing the stories were apocryphal may be surprised. While the tandem had played together during 1994 and 1995 spring training, the decision to pair them was made by Cox, who noticed the ace's level of comfort with the team's backup catcher. Unlike other positions, where starters are expected to play 95 percent of the games, a starting catcher may average 120 to 130 starts to account for the wear and tear on the body and the "always-on" concentration before, during, and after the game. While a position player must account for the opposing pitcher's "stuff," a catcher must prepare for every single one of the other team's players.

Pérez himself was eager to praise Maddux. From the way he caught the ball to the way he held it in the right hand, Maddux was always providing signals on his preferred methods. Seemingly insignificant gestures like the way he touched his cap — typically a signal between hitters and third-base coaches — gave Pérez clues on what Maddux was thinking. The pitcher's 1994-1995 partner in crime, O'Brien, had departed for Toronto during the 1995 offseason. The organization knew, from the small sample of 1994/1995 spring training games and a batch of September contests, that Pérez was ready to fulfill two roles: overall backup and Maddux's catcher. Although the baseball fan saw their connection only on the field, they also spent time in the dugout, going over hitters and observing the intricacies of the opponents' lineups. Pérez took the opportunity to ask Maddux questions about each situation for future reference: "Umpires would often ask me how come Maddux never pitched a no-hitter. I would say he didn't want to. … He purposely wanted batters to have some hits off him so he could dominate them the next time."

Pérez never took the opportunity for granted, but he worked hard to ensure that the Braves star was comfortable on the mound. "I never heard that Maddux demanded me as his catcher," Pérez said. "It was Bobby's decision. It started in the 1994 spring training, he seemed at ease with me. In 1995 spring training I caught a lot of his games too and Bobby noticed. I think it also had to do with ensuring Javy had a day off and I had a day to play that was scheduled. Communication between Maddux and me was important; he wanted us to sit together and talk about the game and a lot of people didn't see that. Perhaps Maddux told Bobby, I don't know. Maddux was different, I learned quickly, and Charlie O'Brien helped me tremendously. When we first started, he'd tell me what to throw — a lot of people didn't know it. I had to learn fast; in a month I picked up and wanted to call the game. He shook me off three times, and I asked him how we did. He jokingly said it was three times too many. I learned a lot from him that has helped me not only as a player but also as a coach."

Pérez's favorite anecdote about Maddux: "In 1998 we were discussing the opposite team, going over batter by batter, how to pitch to each in individual situations. Against Jeff Bagwell, nothing inside, everything outside. In the seventh or eighth, we were ahead 8-0, Bagwell came up with the bases empty. Maddux said inside and I was annoyed; I always wanted to be on the same page as Maddux. He shook me off three times and said inside. I thought he was crazy. … Bagwell hit a massive foul shot and Maddux still asked for it inside. Next pitch, home run, a long shot. I was mad and asked him why, he said we'll talk later. Maddux pitches eight innings and then Wohlers picked up the save in the ninth. In the dugout I was mad at him and he said, 'In two months, Bagwell will come up and seek that pitch.' Two months later, in Houston, Bagwell came up with two men on base, we were up 3-1 in the seventh inning, Bagwell sought the inside ball, but Maddux pitched three outside changeups to strike him out. I was happy celebrating and thought he'd be mad as he didn't like such emotions during the game. … So he pulled me aside and said, 'Remember two months ago? The pitch we threw him?' I didn't recall at the time, but thought about it, and then remembered the prior pitch."

Has the anecdote been embellished? Perhaps, but much like a myth, it has plenty of historical origins. Rob Neyer tried to verify it and found one instance of its possible occurrence.[9] He concluded that the story wasn't as "good" as originally called, but one might beg to differ. Maddux "allowed" the round-tripper to Bagwell while staked with a four-run lead early in the game, rather than in the later innings. This attests to the pitcher's confidence in his stuff, his catcher, and his team's offensive prowess. The comeuppance did not occur late in a playoff game, but rather early in one (first inning). But the result was the same: Bagwell chased a pitch Maddux knew he'd be seeking.

Like many Latin American players, Pérez could not resist the siren song of winter baseball. He returned to Venezuela for 12 straight campaigns (1987-1988 through 1998-1999), playing in 420 regular-season games and another 72 in the postseason. He won two Golden Gloves (1993-1994 and 1994-1995) and was selected as the league's MVP (known as the Vitico Davalillo Award) in 1994-1995. Aragua won 34 games and lost 26, placing second in team ERA (2.78) and third in team batting (.262). The magic did not carry over to the round-robin: Aragua finished last with a 3-9 mark as their bats and arms grew cold.[10] (Winter Leagues in the Caribbean typically begin in November and go through January, so they are titled after both years.)

After the 1996-1997 season, Pérez was traded to Zulia, where he would finish his playing career. His lifetime numbers (.254 average in 1,564 at-bats) are eerily similar to his major-league tally of .253 in 1,525 at-bats.[11] While his playing career in the winter leagues did not result in a league title, Pérez was able to play with many major leaguers, including Concepción for the latter's final three campaigns in the Venezuelan circuit.[12] However, Pérez's voyage into the Venezuelan record books did not stop with his retirement.

Bitten by the coaching bug with Atlanta, Pérez was tapped to lead the Zulia team in 2008-2009 and 2009-2010, posting a 61-66 regular-season record and a 9-18 mark in the postseason. He returned in 2014-2015, compiling a 35-28 line good for third place. More than 20 major leaguers played for the team, including fellow Venezuelan catcher Sandy León, who established himself as a "pitcher's catcher" for the Boston Red Sox.

In 2015-2016 Pérez moved to the Aragua franchise. Though the Tigres had won the title in 2003-2004, 2004-2005, 2006-2007, 2007-2008, 2008-2009, and 2011-2012, they'd been led by a foreign-born manager. Pérez managed the club to the Venezuelan Winter League title, and became the first *criollo*, or Venezuelan, to achieve the goal for the franchise.[13] The team became the runner-up in the Caribbean Series, losing a tough final game to México's Venados of Mazatlán.

"Specialist" is sometimes a backhanded compliment in baseball. Stone-gloved hitters are often derided as "DH's in waiting." Lefty-One-Out-Guys (LOOGYs) are lambasted for lengthening the game and slowing its pace. Charlie Finley even employed a "designated pinch-runner," the much-derided Herb Washington who would not enjoy a single plate appearance but appeared in 105 major-league games and scored 33 runs.

Historically, shortstops and catchers have seen their defensive value weighed above their offensive contributions. Paradoxically, the pendulum is swinging away from shortstops and toward catchers as more complex and definite metrics to value fielding contributions gain popularity among fans and front offices. General managers have, perhaps belatedly, recognized catchers' contributions beyond passed balls and caught-stealing percentage to include pitcher effectiveness, once thought to be the sole responsibility of hurlers. Yet while Joe Tinker and Ozzie Smith have gained Cooperstown immortality thanks to their leather exploits, catchers with similar careers (Bob Boone, Jim Sundberg, Jason Kendall) have been all but ignored by voters.

Catchers are like teaching assistants, their entire livelihoods providing an apprenticeship not enjoyed by the other positions. Yet this trait is often missed by even hard-core fans. The Milwaukee Brewers' classic logo combined a "B" for Brewers and a "M" for Milwaukee into a silhouette of a catcher's mitt that many missed, much like the contribution of the masked men.

Catchers are the second least represented position in Cooperstown, with only 18 immortalized with a Hall of Fame plaque. (The fewest are the 17 third basemen.) Only two backstops have made it in their first year of eligibility, Bench and Iván Rodríguez. Not Yogi Berra (second year). Not Roy Campanella (seventh year). Not Bill Dickey (11th year). Not Piazza (fourth year). Catchers are unlikely to spend 20 years in the majors as their wear and tear is evident even if they switch positions in their older years (as Bench and Berra did), so their opportunity to amass counting statistics like hits and runs is limited, making their offensive numbers less impressive than those of their teammates.

Their job is never done; every game has a post-mortem to discuss what worked, what did not, and what should change. While other positions receive such scouting updates, they do not generate the due diligence expected of the catcher, whose view includes not just the pitcher and his mechanics but also the placement of the fielders. Given that only 70 percent of plate appearances yield a play on the field, their position plays an outsized role in the outcome of a game.[14]

Like a Sherpa, the catcher guides the pitcher through the game, but his responsibility changes as the game progresses. The average 2018 major-league game saw 4.5 hurlers take the mound; yielding new personnel, new conversations, new signs, and new strategy.[15] These tasks were added to the time squatting behind the plate, catching 100-mph balls, handling wild pitches and foul tips, focusing on the baserunners, and ensuring that the pitcher's confidence is strong regardless of the scoreboard. A baseball card, often focused only on hitting prowess, cannot adequately capture the catcher's performance, which is much more correlated to the team's winning percentage than to any other measure.

After the 2006 season, the Braves offered Pérez the role of bullpen coach, understanding that his wealth of knowledge would be integral to the young roster. The Braves had finished 2006 with a 79-83 record, the first losing campaign since 1990. Pérez kept the role for a decade (until 2016), seeing the team both rise and fall again in the NL East. He was shifted to the first-base job on May 17, 2016, and kept the position until the end of 2017, bringing a total of 11 full seasons as a member of the Braves' major-league coaching staff.[16]

Pérez's son Andrés was drafted by Atlanta in the 36th round of the 2016 amateur draft.[17] Buoyed by the robust support network of American collegiate sports and academics, the 6-foot-7 Andrés received a scholarship to the University of North Georgia.[18] Pérez the elder recognized the opportunity but was quick to highlight the reality: "It is different than in Venezuela. There I would have gone to study and forgotten about baseball. My son can play and study. Had he been in Venezuela, I would suggest he take the $5,000 or $20,000 given the reality of the country."

Pérez enthused about the new wave of his countrymen reaching the major leagues, although as a proud Venezuelan, he is heartbroken about the main catalyst. As of the conclusion of the 2018 season, 392 Venezuelans had played in the major leagues, with almost two-thirds of them reaching the "Big Show" after Pérez's debut. While Vizquel, Andrés "The Big Cat" Galarraga, Díaz, Aparicio, and Chico Carrasquel reached the baseball pinnacle before Pérez, younger stars like José Altuve and Miguel Cabrera have followed in his footsteps. In the spring of 2017, Pérez beckoned the call of the motherland by serving as the bench coach for the Venezuelan team in the World Baseball Classic.

"There'll be lots more (Venezuelan players) due to the (political) situation. Before, one could be doing OK with a college education especially in the oil industry. Fandom has always been there, people love baseball. It was easier for us to make a living, especially in the West, all of life's necessities." As Pérez and the author spoke on the phone in early 2019, the United States and dozens of other countries had recognized Juan Guaidó as the legitimate president of Venezuela, triggering a showdown with Nicolás Maduro.

Pérez's catching exploits emboldened Victor Martínez and Salvador Pérez, perennial All-Stars at the position. At the end of the 2018 season, Pérez's career placed him 11th among Venezuelan catchers in games played. Ever humble, he downplayed his role in fomenting the boom of his countrymen in the major leagues. Of the 10 players above him, only one – Díaz – debuted before Pérez. While playing for the Indians in 2002, Pérez mentored Martínez, a decade younger and still unpolished behind the plate. Pérez recalled telling Indians skipper Charlie Manuel, "V-Mart will be your top catcher" and Martínez himself, "I am not a fraction of the player you will be." But above all, he credited Díaz, who "opened the doors with the great job he did, may he rest in peace."

As Venezuela's economy has collapsed, the possibility of a middle-class life has all but disappeared. Inflation reached one million percent in 2018, rendering the bolívar almost worthless and forcing those with means to subsist by turning to the black market for their needs.[19] Players who fail to reach the majors may not have a good education as a backup plan. Though Pérez wished the younger generation the best of luck, he said he was deeply concerned about the underlying conditions: "Some schools have 12- to 14-year-olds with poor education. Education has worsened for the younger generation; the baseball schools don't cover education."

Pérez garnered another milestone in 2014 as he became an American citizen, cementing his ties to the Atlanta area and the franchise that has employed him for almost three decades.[20] Prior to the 2019 season, Pérez was named a special adviser for player development, granting him oversight of the next generation Braves while they make their way through the system.[21]

From his new perch, Pérez hoped to counsel not just the Braves' farmhands but also the system within the major leagues. "Working with the Braves, I am focused on ensuring they don't just play well but also learn English. … We'll soon pass the Dominicans (in percentage of major-league players). Venezuelan players seek that better future, just like Dominicans did. There will be lots of great players, representing Latin America and Venezuela, but it saddens me to see the younger players struggle to read. (The major leagues) must do a better job."

Acknowledgments

- Eddie Pérez for graciously discussing his career via a phone interview.
- Greg McMichael, Atlanta Braves director of alumni relations, for connecting the author to Eddie Pérez.
- JJ Montilla, Venezuelan sportswriter, for sharing the Venezuelan Baseball reference site Pelota Binaria, which includes winter league statistics.
- Pete Palmer and Jim Wheeler for detailed disabled-list records.

Sources

In addition to the sources cited in the Notes, the author relied extensively on Baseball-Reference.com.

Notes

1 brainyquote.com/authors/johnny_bench.

2 Eddie Pérez, telephone interview, January 29, 2019. Unless otherwise indicated, all quotations directly attributed to Pérez come from this interview.

3 Robert Lohrer, "Broward Loses Big League Title," *South Florida Sentinel* (Fort Lauderdale), August 17, 1986. sun-sentinel.com/news/fl-xpm-1986-08-17-8602180967-story.html.

4 govinfo.gov/content/pkg/GOVPUB-T63_100-dd1437db9d97161a1d6cd2945151dd6c/pdf/GOVPUB-T63_100-dd1437db9d97161a1d6cd2945151dd6c.pdf.

5 govinfo.gov/content/pkg/GOVPUB-T63_100-dd1437db9d97161a1d6cd2945151dd6c/pdf/GOVPUB-T63_100-dd1437db9d97161a1d6cd2945151dd6c.pdf.

6 As of the conclusion of the 2018 season: baseball-almanac.com/feats/feats5.shtml.

7. Associated Press, " Braves' Perez May Miss Season," *New York Times*, March 22, 2001. nytimes.com/2001/03/22/sports/plus-baseball-braves-perez-may-miss-season.html.

8. Tom Ley, "Here's an Awesome Story About Greg Maddux," Deadspin.com, January 8, 2014. deadspin.com/heres-an-awesome-story-about-greg-maddux-1497441759.

9. Rob Neyer, *Rob Neyer's Big Book of Baseball Legends: The Truth, the Lies, and Everything Else* (New York: Touchstone, 2008), 14-16.

10. pelotabinaria.com.ve/beisbol/temporadas.php?TE=1994-95.

11. pelotabinaria.com.ve/beisbol/mostrar.php?ID=pereedu002.

12. pelotabinaria.com.ve/beisbol/mostrar.php?ID=concdav001.

13. Mark Bowman, "Perez Eyeing Venezuelan Winter League Title," MLB.com, January 21, 2016. mlb.com/braves/news/braves-eddie-perez-eyeing-winter-league-title/c-162485118.

14. Mike Axisa, "MLB's Biggest Problem Is Not Pace of Play and It's Only Getting Worse in 2018," CBSSports.com, April 15, 2018. cbssports.com/mlb/news/mlbs-biggest-problem-is-not-pace-of-play-and-its-only-getting-worse-in-2018/.

15. Jim Albert, "Historical Look at Pitcher Usage," January 28, 2019. baseballwithr.wordpress.com/2019/01/28/historical-look-at-pitcher-usage/.

16. atlanta.braves.mlb.com/team/coach_staff_bio.jsp?c_id=atl&coachorstaffid=120407.

17. David O'Brien, "Eddie Perez's Son Drafted by Braves in 36th Round," *Atlanta Journal-Constitution*, June 11, 2016. ajc.com/sports/baseball/eddie-perez-son-drafted-braves-36th-round/PaN3SAsQzLVtLzgKdpMTYL/.

18. ungathletics.com/roster.aspx?rp_id=3060.

19. Reuters, "IMF Projects Venezuela Inflation Will Hit 1,000,000 Percent in 2018," Reuters.com, July 23, 2018. reuters.com/article/us-venezuela-economy/imf-projects-venezuela-inflation-will-hit-1000000-percent-in-2018-idUSKBN1KD2L9.

20. Michael Cunningham, "Braves Coach Perez Becomes American Citizen" *Atlanta Journal-Constitution*, August 14, 2014. ajc.com/sports/braves-coach-perez-becomes-american-citizen/YvxtkUA6bXj9L4A9MaO6LJ/.

21. mlb.com/braves/team/front-office.

Luis Polonia

BY JOHN STRUTH

Luis Polonia

Luis Polonia had a nomadic career, playing for six teams in his 12 major-league seasons. He was a .293 career hitter, and played for four World Series teams, including the champion 1995 Atlanta Braves and 2000 New York Yankees.[1] He made a name for himself in Latin America, eventually being elected to the Caribbean Baseball Hall of Fame. His career was not without controversy both on and off the field. A visceral man, he could be happy one moment and testy or bitter the next. One thing he did not lack, however, was confidence.

Polonia was born on December 10, 1963, in Santiago, Dominican Republic. His father, Luciano, was a physician. Before Luciano went into medicine, he played "alongside Juan Marichal, Julian Javier and the Alou brothers. But Luciano Polonia is 5'4", and never got a chance to leave the Dominican Republic."[2] Luis had at least three siblings – Umberto, Francisco, and Jose.[3] In January 1984 Luis was signed as an amateur free agent by Juan Marichal, who was then scouting for the Oakland Athletics. He was discovered playing in the Dominican League, where he had distinguished himself at an early age.

Polonia began his professional career in 1984, playing with the Madison Muskies of the Class-A Midwest League. He batted .307, stole 55 bases, set the team mark with 10 triples, and scored 103 runs in 135 games played. He was a fan favorite in Madison, and was named the team's most valuable player by both the club and the fans.[4]

Polonia moved up to Huntsville, the A's Double-A affiliate, in 1985, and in 1986 played for Tacoma, their Triple-A team. He hit .289 for Huntsville and .301 for Tacoma. Beginning the 1987 season in Tacoma, Polonia was batting .321 after 14 games, with 18 runs scored, when he had sufficiently impressed the A's to be called up to Oakland after an on-field collision between Mike Davis and Dwayne Murphy sidelined Murphy.

Shortly after his call-up, Polonia hit his first major-league home run and first triple in a game against the Boston Red Sox on April 28. He was very excited about his first major-league home run. As for the triple, he said, "I was going for the triple, I hate doubles."[5]

Polonia continued to impress his teammates and manager Tony LaRussa into early June. Mike Davis said, "Some kind of way we have to keep Luis in this lineup. To me he's the igniter of our ball club right now."[6]

In August Polonia ended a prolonged slump with a double, triple, sacrifice fly, and three RBIs against the Seattle Mariners. Perhaps what ignited his turnaround was that before the game he got into a scuffle with teammate Jose Canseco. What began as a shouting match soon turned to a shoving match. Reggie Jackson and hitting coach Bob Watson stepped in between the two before the fight escalated. Polonia said, "Sometimes when you joke around with somebody, you take the joke. But if you don't feel good, you don't take it. ... I'm not afraid of nobody. I'm not going to hurt Jose, but I could find a lot of ways to do it. I'm not afraid."[7] Polonia ultimately acquitted himself well in his rookie campaign. He hit a solid .287, stole 27 bases, and scored 78 runs in 125 games played. The A's finished the season at .500 but had a nucleus of young players and veteran leadership that promised good things to come.

The 1988 campaign began with Polonia anticipating a full season with the A's. They had other plans and he was assigned to Tacoma. For a 24-year-old, with one partial year of big-league experience under his belt, he made waves by asking for a trade. "Right now, that's my wish. I'm tired of coming down to the minors every year and waiting for someone to get hurt," he said. "What should I expect? They signed three guys. Who got the worst part? Luis Polonia. I always get the worst part."[8]

He did eventually get a call-up and spent the second half of the season with the A's. What was apparent throughout the season was that Polonia did not fit into the A's plans as more than a fourth outfielder. And he was an outfielder with a liability: a poor fielder. In fact, after he cost the A's a game in the World Series with two misplays, the *Los Angeles Times* wrote of him: "The misadventures of Oakland's Luis Polonia in the outfield Tuesday night recalled this line from the Times staffer Mike Penner: 'He was best described last season by a teammate who provided a scouting report in the form of a Jeopardy question. A. Catch-22. Q. What do you get when you hit 100 fly balls to Luis Polonia?'"[9] Despite that sentiment, in 84 games and 288 at-bats, Polonia hit .292 scored 51 runs, and stole 24 bases. But between his complaining about going down to the minors and poor fielding, his stay with the A's was on shaky ground.

Polonia began the 1989 season with Oakland but was traded to the New York Yankees on June 21. He began his season slowly and by late April was hitting .214. By the time the trade was consummated, Polonia's average had risen to .286 in 59 games. He was traded, along with Eric Plunk and Greg Cadaret, for Rickey Henderson. Polonia was excited to be a Yankee, in part because of the large Dominican presence in the city. For the Yankees he batted .313 in 66 games.

One event in Milwaukee changed Polonia's fortunes with the team. On August 17 he was arrested and charged with sexually assaulted an underage girl. The next day Polonia pleaded no contest, avoiding a felony charge. He was freed and ordered to return for sentencing after the season. On October 2 Polonia was sentenced to 60 days and fined $1,500. He was also ordered "to make a $10,000 contribution to Sinai Samaritan Medical Center's sexual assault treatment center in Milwaukee."[10]

Polonia began 1990 as a Yankee. But he was on tenuous footing due largely to the Milwaukee incident. After only 11 games played he was traded on April 29 to the California Angels. "On the surface, it was merely an exchange of a hit man for a guy [Claudell Washington] with pop, a case of both the Yankees and Angels filling vital needs," a New York sportswriter wrote. "That's the obvious reason for the trade. The underlying implications are more intriguing. Polonia became persona non grata after he pleaded guilty to having sex with a minor. ... Polonia, on the other hand, never fit in. He was a lead off hitter, but the Yankees already had a good one in Steve Sax. And he was a defensive liability. Then the Milwaukee incident made him vulnerable."[11]

For Polonia the trade to the Angels was a boon: Through 1993 he was an everyday player. It probably helped that he and manager Doug Rader seemed to hit off. What he could not shake was the backlash that persisted from his sexual-assault conviction.

Two separate incidents, the first during the 1990 season and the second in 1991, illustrate Polonia's difficulties with fans. In July the *Los Angeles Times* reported, "The Alameda County district attorney will decide today whether claims by an 18-year-old spectator that he was struck by Angel outfielder Luis Polonia Thursday at the Oakland Coliseum warrant the filing of charges. … Polonia allegedly slapped or pushed a fan after batting practice Thursday, when he heard the youngster shout insults. … Polonia allegedly reached over the railing and made contact with the boy."[12]

In May the *Arkansas Gazette* (Little Rock) reported, "This season Polonia, a California Angels outfielder and Angel Manager Doug Rader got into a screaming match with [Jim] Northrup because Northrup called Polonia, 'Luis Lockup.' … Polonia told Rader he was threatened and Rader attempted, unsuccessfully to have Northrup ejected. … 'Luis Polonia was in a rage because I called him "Luis Lockup." Okay, now he was guilty. What kind of example is that?'" Northrup said.[13]

Not all was bad for Polonia, however. He quickly found a home with his new team, and on August 29 got a break that turned him from a platoon player to an everyday player. Against the Texas Rangers, with the score tied in the seventh inning. Jack Howell had reached second base and Texas manager Bobby Valentine had Dick Schofield intentionally walked. Rangers southpaw John Barfield was on the mound.

"Luis Polonia looked to his left, but no one stirred," wrote the *Los Angeles Times*. "… Polonia looked to his right. Still no one moved. He looked to his manager, Doug Rader, and Polonia heard the words he never thought he would hear."

Polonia reported that Rader told him, "Get ready to hit against the left-hander…Go out there," adding, "that was the best thing he could do for me."[14] Polonia singled in Howell. That opened the floodgates, and before the inning was over the Angels scored seven times.

Two weeks earlier Polonia had exacted some revenge on the Yankees, when he struck an inside-the-park grand slam against them on August 14. Reflecting on the game, he said, "I got my heart broken by the Yankees and A's. I get on fire every time I face them. I feel like I want to do so much. My heart is burning. … It was the Yankees who got burned Tuesday night."[15]

Polonia finished the season batting .336 with the Angels. He played in 109 games. He also worked his way into everyday status moving into the new season. Polonia averaged 150 games played over the next three seasons. He averaged about 50 stolen bases a season and 80 runs scored. However, his batting averages dropped each season from .296 to .286 to .271. Entering free agency, Polonia signed with Yankees.

Polonia had always maintained that he wanted to return to New York. But by 1995 his role had changed and he found playing time diminished. Polonia and Yankees manager Buck Showalter did not see eye to eye.

Polonia batted a solid .311 in 95 games in 1994. He was a positive contributor to the Yankees' season. His teammates appreciated him and didn't mind poking fun at him either: "The Yankees hung a bat wrapped in tinfoil in their clubhouse yesterday to commemorate Luis Polonia's home run Tuesday night. They called it the Silver Slugger Award. It was Polonia's first home run in 650 at-bats."[16] The Yankees were in first place when the players strike ended the season in August. As he cleaned out his locker, Polonia said, "A weird day. … I'm going to stay five, six days. Something might happen."[17] As the article added: "It didn't."

Right from the start of the 1995 season, Polonia and Showalter were at odds. This had carried over from the previous year when Polonia was benched four consecutive games against left-handed starters in July. Showalter was upfront with Polonia, telling him he would see limited playing time against southpaws. But Polonia didn't take that well. "I'm not happy. I know he's experimenting, but I don't like the idea. I don't like playing ball, hitting eighth or ninth. I think I did excellent last year. ... I was having fun. ... Imagine me hitting only against right-handers and hitting eighth."[18]

Polonia poked the wrong bear. With less playing time, he became more anxious. Not a recipe for success! In June he said, "I don't want to be traded but if it comes to the point where I'm the one who will be sitting, they should be reasonable and let me go somewhere where I can play."[19]

Reasonable the Yankees were, shipping Polonia off to Atlanta on August 11. The Braves acquired him to help the team in their stretch drive. Polonia played sparingly, getting in 28 games. In the playoffs and World Series, he contributed to the Braves championship run. In Game One of the Division Series between the Braves and Colorado Rockies, Polonia drove in David Justice on a slow roller that tied a tight ballgame in the sixth inning. A sacrifice by Polonia in Game One of the National League Championship Series with Cincinnati set up the winning run in the 11th inning. In the World Series against the Cleveland Indians, Polonia played the field in Games Three through Five, and was 4-for-14 with a home run and 4 RBIs.

With free agency looming, Polonia signed a nonguaranteed contract with the Seattle Mariners over the winter. He was released during spring training. On April 19 he signed with the Baltimore Orioles and was assigned to their Triple-A affiliate in Rochester. After 13 games he was called up to Baltimore.

Polonia's play did not impress the Orioles. On June 19 he made a baserunning blunder that seemed to seal his ultimate fate. Wrote the *Baltimore Sun*: "... (T)he biggest offender in this game of Stupid Oriole Tricks was Luis Polonia, who got picked off second while dustin' and adjustin' his uniform pants. ... 'He wasn't even looking at the pitcher or shortstop,' [manager] Davey Johnson said, "He was looking at the ground. Then the guy turned around. We're just not paying attention. That was just a vapor lock."[20]

The Orioles designated Polonia for assignment on August 2. In 58 games played, he had hit .240. On his way out the door, an obviously bitter Polonia took a parting shot. Buster Olney reported, "Polonia sharply criticized the way the Orioles play, saying that while they have the talent to win, they won't unless they approach the game more unselfishly." Olney went on, quoting Polonia, "People on the Orioles are always worrying about what other people do, criticizing, instead of just going out and playing the game right."[21]

"Players are critical? 'Players and coaches,' he said."[22]

Two weeks later, on August 17, Polonia again signed with the Braves. Perhaps they were hoping that he would repeat his previous success. During the remainder of the season he was used sparingly. In 31 at-bats he hit .419. He also didn't see much playing time in the postseason, going hitless in 10 at-bats and drawing a walk. But he was asked to contribute to the Braves in a unique way. "Polonia is the only Brave who has played for the Yankees, who has a feel for the dynamics of Yankee Stadium, who has some idea what it is like to play before the most rabid and volatile fans around. ... Polonia said the biggest topic of conversation would be the dimensions of the playing field."[23]

Perhaps it helped Atlanta. They won the first two games of the World Series, played in New York, before succumbing to the Yankees, four games to two.

When the season ended, Polonia had no contract. In March 1997 he signed with the Tampa Bay Devil Rays. They assigned him to the Mexico City Tigres. He hit .377 in 110 games, scored 105 runs, and stole 48 bases. That led to an invitation to spring training. However, Tampa Bay did not sign Polonia and he returned to Mexico City for the 1998 campaign. He had another stellar season, hitting .381.

On December 18, 1998, Polonia signed a minor-league contract with the Detroit Tigers. He was assigned to Toledo, their Triple-A affiliate, to start the season. After 42 games, he was called up. By mid-June Tigers manager Larry Parrish had said that Polonia had won the leadoff job. For Polonia, Detroit represented a triumph of perseverance. He said, "When you hang in there, God always gives you a chance. He gave me two bad years, maybe to see how I could take it. I always kept my faith."[24]

Used almost exclusively as a designated hitter, Polonia played in 87 games. He hit .324, and added some pop, hitting 21 doubles, 8 triples, and 10 home runs. His .526 slugging percentage was 100 points over any other season in his career. This earned him a return for the 2000 season.

Opening Day. Comerica Park. Luis Polonia, leading off for the Tigers, tripled. He then was singled in, scoring the first run in the ballpark's history. It could be argued that it was the highlight of his Detroit season in 2000. Though he continued to hit well, the Tigers were interested in seeing some of their younger prospects at the major-league level. As the trade deadline approached, they had another incentive to move on from Polonia. With just 52 more at-bats, he would be guaranteed a contract for 2001. Unable to trade him by the deadline, they released Polonia on July 31. In 80 games, he had hit .273.

Polonia didn't have to wait long before the Yankees came calling. He signed on for a third stint with them on August 3. Joe Torre said of the signing, "We're at a point now where we have to look at the little things that help you win a game here, there. … I've always liked him as a hitter. He's got some speed. That makes up for problems he has defensively. And he works hard."[25]

In 37 games Polonia hit .286. His primary role was to spell David Justice in the field, allowing Justice to DH as the season wore along. Seeing limited play in the postseason, he did have one notable appearance in the World Series. In Game One his single helped the Yankees overcome a one-run deficit in the ninth inning. The Yankees went on to win the game in extra innings. They also went on to win the World Series, defeating the New York Mets. This was Polonia's swan song. After the Series he was made a free agent and never returned to the major leagues.

Polonia was not finished with baseball. He returned to play with the Mexico City Tigres for the 2001 and 2002 seasons. He also continued playing winter ball with the Dominican Republic. That led to continued appearances in the Caribbean Series, which the Dominican team won with regularity. In total Polonia made 14 appearances in that series. He also represented the Dominican Republic in the World Baseball Classic. In 2006, at age 42, he replaced an injured Vladimir Guerrero in the WBC.

Polonia also opened a baseball academy in the Dominican Republic. In 2016 he was named to the Caribbean Baseball Hall of Fame He finished his playing career in 2010.

Polonia had three children. One son, Rodney, was signed by the Pirates organization. His two other children went into careers as entertainers: Albert is a rap artist, Bianca an entertainer and singer. Luis also acted in the 2018 film *Jugando a' Bailar*. Surprisingly, he plays a baseball player.

Polonia ultimately had a long and fruitful career. He played in 1,379 games and batted .293. He played an important role on two pennant-winning teams, the 1988 A's and 1994 Yankees, who didn't play postseason baseball because of a labor dispute. He played in four World Series with the: A's, Braves (twice), and Yankees.

Perhaps he overvalued his own contributions. Certainly he felt he was an everyday player. With the exception of the California Angels, not one team he played for felt the same way. His strengths were that he could hit, he had speed, and from accounts, he was a good teammate.

His weaknesses were that he was a one-dimensional singles hitter. He was a poor baserunner, and while he stole 321 bases in the major leagues, he was thrown out 145 times, leading the league in that category three times. He was also a poor fielder. His career wins above replacement score (WAR) stands at 9.0.

But Polonia really stands out for his tenacity. He never stopped believing in himself. It would have been easy to give up his dream after spending two years in Mexico City, but he picked himself up and refused to let his dream die away. Twice, in mid- and late career, he signed minor-league contracts, and then earned a spot on a major-league roster. So it can be said of him, he had a good career.

Sources

In addition to the sources cited in the Notes, the author also consulted:

baseball-reference.com/bullpen/Caribbean_Baseball_Hall_of_Fame#2011.

baseball-reference.com/players/p/polonlu01.shtml.

Notes

1 Polonia also played in the 1988 World Series with the Oakland Athletics and in the 1996 Series with the Braves.

2 Robyn Norwood, "Polonia Aims to Give Angels a Quick Start," *Los Angeles Times*, March 3, 1992: 222.

3 Mark Kriegel, "Bronx Beams as Luis Makes Turn for Home," *New York Daily News*, April 4, 1994: 52.

4 "Polonia's First Season a Most Valuable One," *Wisconsin State Journal* (Madison), September 12, 1984: 23.

5 Frank Blackman, "Polonia Just Having Fun," *San Francisco Examiner*, April 29, 1987: 58.

6 Frank Blackman, "Polonia Has Made His Mark: A's Must Find Him a Spot," *San Francisco Examiner*, June 2, 1987: 53.

7 Frank Blackman, "Pugnacious Polonia Beats Up Mariners," *San Francisco Examiner*, August 11, 1987: 51, 55.

8 Frank Blackman, "Majors: Polonia Wants Trade," *San Francisco Examiner*, April 11, 1988: 56.

9 "Boston Masterpieces Hang in the Garden," *Los Angeles Times*, October 20, 1988: 183.

10 Michael Kay, "Luis Gets Sixty Days," *New York Daily News*, October 3, 1989: 68.

11 Phil Pepe, "Luis Swapped for Claudell," *New York Daily News*, April 30, 1990: 43.

12 Helene Elliott, "Bay Area District Attorney Mulls Charges Against Angels' Polonia," *Los Angeles Times*, July 27, 1990: 50.

13 Ken Boatmen, "Players See, Know Their Enemies," *Arkansas Gazette* (Little Rock), May 29, 1991: 42.

14 Helene Elliott, "Angels Let Polonia Hit, and Hit He Does," *Los Angeles Times*, August 30, 1990: 54.

15 Helene Elliott, "An Inside Job for Polonia," *Los Angeles Times*, August 15, 1990: 114, 118.

16 Jeff Bradley, "Flashes," *New York Daily News*, June 30, 1994: 78.

17 Jeff Bradley, "Short Year," *New York Daily News*, August 12, 1994: 23.

18 Jeff Bradley, "Buck Tinkering Peeves Polonia," *New York Daily News*, April 18, 1995: 44.

19 Tom Pedulla, "Ripken, Orioles Pound Yankees," *Journal News* (White Plains, New York), June 20, 1995: 25.

20 Ken Rosenthal, "It Might Be Difficult to Seek Shelter, When You're Not in the Storm," *Baltimore Sun*, June 20, 1996: 173.

21 Buster Olney, "Polonia, Heading Toward Exit, Takes a Shot," *Baltimore Sun*, August 3, 1996: 31.

22 Olney.

23 Curtis Bunn, "Polonia Spreading The News About Playing in New York," *Atlanta Constitution*, October 19, 1996: C11.

24 John Lowe, "Polonia's Arrival a Top Surprise," *Detroit Free Press*, June 10, 1999: 49.

25 Ronald Blum, "Yanks Re-Sign Luis Polonia," *Ithaca Journal*, August 4, 2000: 17.

Jason Schmidt

BY COSME VIVANCO

Jason Schmidt

Midway through the 2001 major-league baseball season, the Pittsburgh Pirates traded right-hander Jason Schmidt to the San Francisco Giants. Schmidt, who compiled a 49-53 record throughout the first six years of his career, would blossom into one of the elite pitchers in the National League during the mid-2000s.

Jason David Schmidt was born on January 29, 1973 in Lewiston, Idaho. When Schmidt was 5, his parents divorced, and his mother Vicki married Ray Schmidt, a machinist at a paper mill. Jason and his sister formed a bond with their stepfather through baseball. His stepdad bought him his first glove and stressed him on the importance of the fundamentals. "I told him to make me play catch whether I felt like it or not," Schmidt said. "We'd go to the street, and he'd sit on a bucket we used to wash the car. He'd have me throw to him, and if I didn't hit the glove, he wouldn't budge. The ball would roll down the street and I had to go get it. My control got better fast."[1]

While living in Washington State, he attended Kelso High School where played football and basketball in addition to baseball. In his senior year he tossed a no-hitter where he struck out 20 out of 23 batters he faced. Schmidt had a perfect game through five innings of work before he walked two batters in the sixth frame. "It was like everything was flowing together that game," Schmidt said. But he admitted that the absence of professional scouts lend him the luxury of feeling comfortable on the mound. "I say they (the scouts) don't bother me, but sometimes you feel like you can't do certain things if they're there," Schmidt said. "Sometimes I throw a roundhouse curve and they don't like to see that."[2]

He was honored with Washington's Gatorade State Player of the year award and All-State MVP in baseball. Schmidt was offered a scholarship from the University of Arizona, but chose to sign with the Atlanta Braves, who selected him in the eighth round of the 1991 amateur draft. Jason Schmidt made his debut with the Braves organization in 1991 as a member of the Gulf Coast Braves. He made 11 starts and finished the year with a 3-4 mark and a 2.38 ERA. He toiled through the farm system from 1992 to 1995. While working his up to through the minors, Schmidt made the habit of calling his mother on the way from the ballpark.

"It was my stress relief after a game," he said. "Call my mom."[3]

Schmidt made his major-league debut in a relief appearance against the Los Angeles Dodgers on April 28, 1995. On September 3, 1995, he made his big-league debut as a starter, replacing the injured Kent Mercker. Schmidt pitched eight scoreless innings, giving up six hits and striking out seven as the Braves topped the Cubs 2-0. "I thought I was dreaming out there," he said. "It was the seventh inning and I had a shutout, and I'm thinking no way this could be happening."[4] Schmidt finished the year with a 2-2 record and a 5.76 ERA. He didn't make a postseason appearance that year.

The following year, the promising Braves prospect was shipped to the Pittsburgh Pirates in a midseason trade that brought Denny Neagle to Atlanta. On September 23, 1996, Schmidt pitched his best game to date when he went the distance in a 4-3 loss to the Chicago Cubs, striking out 11 and walking none. "He has an outstanding arm, one of the better arms in the league," manager Jim Leyland said. "I don't think you'd want to do that [have him throw 137 pitches] on a consistent basis, but he was throwing 94 [miles per hour] in the ninth inning. He has a chance to be a good one."[5]

And while Leyland lamented the notion of pushing a pitcher of Schmidt's caliber to the limit, being the rotation's workhorse would be a blessing and a curse throughout Schmidt's major-league career.

Prior to the 1997 season, Jason Schmidt received news that almost put a dent to his big-league dreams. While spending time at his winter home, he began to experience lightheadedness. Medical tests revealed an irregular heartbeat. Schmidt was diagnosed with hypervagotonia, a condition that affects young, well-conditioned athletes. "I was obviously worried about this," Schmidt said. "I mean I'm only 24 years old and you don't think something like this can happen to you. All I kept thinking about was that I was getting married Nov. 1 and how my baseball career might be flashing in front of my eyes. It was a little scary (Tuesday) when one of the doctors asked me if one of the other doctors had mentioned a pacemaker to me. Then the doctor just said, "Forget I ever said that. ' Still, it made me think and it certainly makes me feel fortunate that I'm OK and everything is fine."[6]

Nevertheless, he made his season debut on April 6, 1997 against the Los Angeles Dodgers. He pitched six innings, striking out three and walking three as the Pirates lost to the home team, 6-3. Schmidt pitched his best game on July 2 against the Chicago White Sox. He went the distance, striking out 10 and walking one in a 3-1 complete-game victory. Schmidt ended the year with a 10-9 record and a 4.60 ERA as the Pittsburgh Pirates finished second in the NL central division with a 79-83. The following season, he went 11-14 with a 4.07 ERA, losing five of his last six decisions to cap off a disappointing year.

In 1999, Schmidt ended the year with a 13-11 record and a 4.19 ERA. His most notable performance was on April 21 when he pitched eight innings and struck out 11 in a 2-0 loss to the San Diego Padres. The following year he missed two weeks in April due to shoulder inflammation, which flared up again in June. During his second stint on the DL, the then 27-year old Schmidt was examined by the world-renowned Dr. James Andrews in Birmingham, Alabama. "I want to get a total checkup from him," Schmidt said Monday. "He's the best in the business. I want him to look at it and see what he thinks. I want to find out what is wrong once and for all." He eventually found himself under the knife to repair a partial fraying of the rotator cuff.[7]

Schmidt returned to the mound on May 11, 2001, securing a 3-0 victory against the Milwaukee Brewers. He went 6-6 with a 4.61 ERA with the Pittsburgh Pirates when he was traded to the San Francisco Giants with John Vander Wal for Armando Rios and Ryan Vogelsong. The benefit to Schmidt was the opportunity to play for a team that had World Series aspirations. "That's the No. 1 thing, a chance to be in the pennant race and the playoffs. That's what you play for," Schmidt said.[8]

In his first outing as a member of the San Francisco Giants, Jason Schmidt went up against the club that he had called home for the last six seasons, the Pittsburgh Pirates. He pitched seven strong innings, striking out eight and giving up one hit and one earned run as the Giants defeated the Pirates, 3-1. He finished 2001 strong with the Giants, compiling a 7-1 record with a 3.39 ERA. On December 18, he re-signed with the club as a free agent for a deal worth five years and $41 million. In his 2002 debut against the Chicago Cubs, Schmidt gave up four earned runs on seven hits in a 10-4 loss. But throughout the season, Schmidt displayed the dazzling potential befitting a number one starter. On June 8 in Yankee Stadium he struck out a career-high 13 in eight innings as the Giants, behind Barry Bonds' first home run in the "house that Ruth built," topped the Yankees 4-3. Eleven days later, he pitched a complete game shutout against the Tampa Bay Devil Rays, striking out 11 and walking one as the Giants cruised to an 8-0 win. On July 28, he handcuffed the rival Los Angeles Dodgers for a 3-1 win behind 10 strikeouts. On August 20, Schmidt tied his career high in strikeouts as the Giants squeaked pass the New York Mets for a 1-0 win.

The San Francisco Giants finished the year with 95-66 record in the NL West – good enough to secure the wild card for the 2002 postseason run. In his first-ever playoff game, against the Atlanta Braves, Schmidt started strong but began to tire in the sixth when he walked three Braves in a row after striking out Julio Franco. He gave up four earned runs as the Braves cruised to a 10-2 win in game three of the NLDS. "They had their big heart of the lineup coming up there, so I just tried to be a little bit more careful to a couple of the guys," said Schmidt who threw 104 pitches in 5 1/3 innings. "Looking back, I could have been a little more aggressive."[9]

In his next postseason appearance, Jason Schmidt found better success as he stymied the St. Louis Cardinals in seven innings of work, striking out eight and giving up one earned run as the Giants dispatched St. Louis 4-1 in Game Two of the 2002 NLCS. "He was excellent," Cardinal manager Tony La Russa said. "His control was excellent. His stuff was excellent. The couple times he got behind the count, the 2-0 or 3-1 pitch he made wasn't backing off his good stuff and throwing the ball down the middle. He really, really pitched well."[10]

The San Francisco Giants went on to capture their first NL flag since 1962. On October 19, 2002, Schmidt took the mound as the Giants starter in the first game of the 2002 World Series. He picked up the win, going five innings as the Giants beat the Anaheim Angels, 4-3. Five days later, Schmidt struck out eight in 4 ½ innings in a no-decision as the Giants thrashed the Angels 16-4 to put them one game away from winning their first World Series since 1951. However, the dreams of Giants fans were shattered as the club blew a 5-0 lead in Game Six and lost the decisive game 7, 4-1 as the Angels celebrated their first World Series title in franchise history.

Schmidt had finished the 2002 regular season with a 13-8 record and a 3.45 ERA. He struck out 196 and walked 76 batters. His WHIP of 1.192 was the lowest in his career up to that point.

His 2003 season was his break-out year.

In his 2003 debut, Schmidt picked up the win with a strong 7 ½ inning outing against the San Diego Padres for a 8-1 victory. At the end of April, he stifled the Cubs for a 5-0 shutout victory that included 12 strikeouts. On May 16, he tied his career high of 13 strikeouts in a 7-5 win over the New York Mets. On June 19, Schmidt pitched a gem against the rival Dodgers for a 2-0 win. On July 15, 2003, Schmidt started in his first All-Star Game going up against former teammate Esteban Loaiza of the Chicago White Sox. He pitched back-to-back gems against the Milwaukee Brewers and the San Diego Padres towards the end of September. The San Francisco Giants finished 2003 with a 100-61 and a NL West division title. In Game One of the 2003 NLDS against the Florida Marlins, Jason Schmidt hindered the Marlins with a 2-0 shutout win to give the Giants a 1-0 advantage in the series.

It was the last win of 2003, as the Marlins won three straight to send the Giants home early for the winter.

Schmidt finished the 2003 regular season with a 17-5 record and a NL-leading 2.34 ERA. He struck out 208 and walked 46. He led the majors in WHIP with a 0.953 and tied for the major-league lead in shutouts with three. He finished second in the Cy Young Award voting behind Dodgers closer Eric Gagne.

When he was not mowing down hitters, he was often making teammates laugh with practical jokes. Behind his locker would be a highly sophisticated flatulence machine that would be used on rookies or callups to the big leagues. "I'll hide it somewhere in his locker and wait for the reporters to ask, 'How do you feel?" and then hit it," Schmidt says. "You keep hitting it after the questions, make sure they can't say a word."[11] He'll squirt mustard into a jelly doughnut and set them in the pregame spread. He would stack paper cups on the batboy's protective helmet.

But more importantly he became the Giants' workhorse in the rotation. Averaging about 115 pitches per start, it's a safe bet that without Schmidt's arm, the Giants would have fallen out of contention in the NL west.

On May 18, 2004, Jason Schmidt stepped onto the mound at the famed Wrigley Field and dazzled the night crowd with an incredible performance. Hurling 144 pitches in nine innings, Schmidt held the Cubs to one hit, outdueling Cubs right-hander Matt Clement in the process. The only run that scored was on a Pedro Feliz single that scored Barry Bonds. Schmidt also tied his career high in strikeouts with 13 on the night that Randy Johnson pitched a perfect game against Schmidt's former club, the Atlanta Braves.

"When he's on, he's as tough as anyone in this league," Cubs manager Dusty Baker said.[12]

"I'll take the shutout and the win any say. I can't argue with that," Schmidt said. "No-hitters, there's a lot of luck involved. If I never get one, so be it. I'm not going to lose sleep over that."[13]

A month later he tossed another one-hitter, this time against the Boston Red Sox. Striking out nine on a 133 pitches as the Giants beat the Red Sox, 4-0.

"I like this one better," Schmidt said, comparing it to his 1-0 win against the Cubs on May 18. "I can say I actually felt good. I felt sharp. All my pitches were working. It felt smooth today."[14]

Schmidt ended 2004 with an 18-7 record with a 3.20 ERA. He struck out a career high 251. He tied for the league lead in shutouts with three. He made his second All-Star appearance and finished fourth in the Cy Young voting. However, the Giants missed the postseason.

On April 5, 2005, Jason Schmidt earned an opening day victory over the Los Angeles Dodgers. Going seven innings and striking out nine as the Giants beat their rival 4-2. In May, he went on the 15-day DL with a right shoulder strain. Schmidt returned to the club on May 24, earning a 5-3 win over the Dodgers in SBC Park. On June 22, he pitched his best game of the year against the Arizona Diamondbacks, striking out 10 in eight innings to hand Arizona a 4-0 loss. In September he suffered a right groin strain that listed him day-to-day. He finished 2005 with a 12-7 record and 3.20 ERA. The San Francisco Giants finished in third place in the NL West with a 75-87 mark.

On June 6, 2006, Jason Schmidt had the performance of his career against the Florida Marlins. He struck out 16 in a complete-game win on 124 pitches to give the Giants a 2-1 win. It was not only a career high, but he also tied the franchise's all-time single game strikeouts record held by Christy Mathewson. A ninth-inning wild pitch moved runners to second and third with no outs. Schmidt struck out the final three batters to preserve the victory. It was Schmidt's 20th career complete game and his third of the season.

The scene after the historic contest was fitting of a postseason celebration. His five-year old daughter Makynlee was waiting for her dad as he came up the steps. His teammates cheered, offered hugs and handshakes and clapped for Schmidt as he walked into the clubhouse.

"That's a highlight of my career, coming in here and getting that reception from the guys," Schmidt said. "That surprised me. I guess because I was so locked into the game."[15]

Schmidt ended 2006 with an 11-9 record 3.59 ERA.

On December 6, 2006, Jason Schmidt signed a free contract with the Los Angeles Dodgers. The deal was worth three years and $47 million. His addition looked to bolster a solid rotation that included Derek Lowe, Brad Penny, and left-hander Randy Wolf.

"Jason is a top of the rotation starter who can dominate a game as well as any pitcher in the major leagues," Dodgers general manager Ned Colletti said. "He's a proven winner and that's something that's very hard to find."[16]

Dodgers brass hoped that signing of Schmidt would give their World Series aspirations another boost, but Schmidt's tenure with the Dodgers was marred with frequent trips to the disabled list.

In his first start as a Dodger, Schmidt earned a 5-4 win over the Milwaukee Brewers. In his Dodger Stadium debut, he left the game in the fifth with tightness in his right hamstring. In his next start against the San Diego Padres, he was rocked for five earned runs and seven hits in two-plus innings. Retiring only six of the 16 batters he faced. He eventually made a trip to the 15-day disabled list with bursitis in his throwing shoulder. Schmidt returned from the DL on June 5 against the San Diego Padres. He pitched six innings, but came up without the decision as the Dodgers lost to the Padres, 1-0. On June 20, 2007, Schmidt had surgery to repair a torn labrum in his right shoulder. The Dodgers organization was optimistic that he could make a return to All-Star form. "I think the odds are with him as opposed to against him," said Stan Conte, the Dodgers director of medical services.[17] He missed the entire 2008 season.

During spring training 2009, Schmidt pitched in an intrasquad game, throwing 11 pitches, nine of them for strikes. He notice a remarkable difference in the way he pitched as opposed to the previous season when he tried to stepped back onto the mound, only to being relegated to the disabled list for an entire year.

"Coming in tomorrow, being able to play catch, that's the bigger hurdle than anything," Schmidt said. "Last year I kind of knew when the game was over how I was going to fell. I feel really good about it right now."[18]

In a spring training game against the Texas Rangers, Schmidt only pitched two innings. He gave up a three-run home run but he gave Dodgers manager Joe Torre a glimmer of hope that he could return to the rotation as the club's fifth starter.

Schmidt dispatched the Rangers on 12 pitches in the first inning. He struck out Andruw Jones and Travis Metcalf with a slider but gave up the three-run blast to Taylor Teagarden.

In his first trip to the mound in two years, Jason Schmidt earned a tough 7-5 win over the Cincinnati Reds. The Reds tagged him for three earned runs in the first inning, but he shook it off and finished strong to come up with his first win in two years. "I had hoped to just go out there and make it respectable but I'm happy with the result," Schmidt said.[19] His fastball never registered above 87 mph on the radar gun, but the most remarkable feat was for the former All-Star to make it back onto the field after an arduous journey that included shoulder surgery and numerous rehab assignments.

For a day, he returned to form against his old team, the Atlanta Braves. On July 31, he pitched six solid innings. Schmidt walked five, but gave up only one hit as the Dodgers beat the Braves 5-0. "Just to be out there is kind of a miracle in itself, "the 36-year-old said. "I wasn't sure if they wanted me to," Schmidt said of the Dodgers. "I wasn't sure if I wanted to. It ended up going a lot better than I expected."[20] It would be the last taste of success in Schmidt's major-league career.

On August 5, the veteran right-hander surrendered four earned runs and five hits in 3 2/3 innings against the Milwaukee Brewers. It was his second consecutive start where he failed to make it out of the fourth inning. The Dodgers lost the game, 4-1. In his four starts since returning from a two-year layoff from shoulder surgery, the former All-Star posted a 2-2 record with a 5.60 ERA. Two days later the Dodgers moved Schmidt to the 15-day DL for what the club deemed a "shoulder injury." In his comeback after two years being on the shelf, Schmidt looked strong, but in his final two starts, looked subpar. The possibility that his career could come to a crashing halt loomed large.

He filed for free agency in November 2009, but eventually retired from the sport.

For his major-league career, Jason Schmidt recorded a 130-96 mark with a 3.96 ERA. His most successful run was with the San Francisco Giants, where he finished with a 78-37 to go along with a 3.36 ERA. Being the workhorse of the rotation brought him and the team success, but it paved a way for an injury bug to his shoulder that led to close of his major-league career.

He made his debut on the Hall of Fame ballot in 2015, but ended up with no votes for enshrinement.

Jason Schmidt briefly made his mark as one of baseball's most dominating pitchers. And while his career was plagued with injuries, he will be remembered for having an explosive pitching arsenal that left opposing batters perplexed. The success in San Francisco opened new opportunities for Jason Schmidt. It made him an All-Star, it gave him the chance to play on baseball's grandest stage, and made him wealthier than he could imagine, but he never allowed it to define who he was.

"I try not to let baseball define me as a person," Schmidt said. "I'm not the kind who will drop my name at a restaurant to get a table right away. I'd rather wait an hour. I don't like to be noticed.

"When the time comes to walk away, I won't have a hard time shedding the title of ballplayer."[21]

Sources

In addition to the sources cited in the Notes, the author consulted baseball-reference.com and retrosheet.org.

Notes

1. Steve Henson, "Schmidt Keeps the Wolves at Bay," *Los Angeles Times*, April 9, 2007, https://www.latimes.com/archives/la-xpm-2007-apr-09-sp-schmidt9-story.html

2. Al Wasser, "Despite His Slow Start, Kelso Ace Has Numbers That Add Up to a Bright Future," *Longview Daily News*, April 20, 1991: B3.

3. Steve Henson.

4. I.J. Rosenberg, "Schmidt Opens A Few Eyes in 2-0 Blanking of Cubs," *Atlanta Constitution*, September 4, 1995: D1.

5. Paul Meyer, "Pirates' 11-game Streak Snapped in 4-3 Loss to Cubs," *Pittsburgh Post-Gazette*, September 24, 1996: C1.

6. "Jason Schmidt Gets OK to Resume Activities," *Longview Daily News*, March 14, 1997: D1.

7. Alan Robinson, "Pirates' Schmidt Goes on DL," *Tyrone Daily Herald*, June 13, 2000: 4.

8. Robert Dvorchak, "Giant Step" *Pittsburgh Post-Gazette*, July 31, 2001: D-3.

9. Jason Reid, "Baker Feels Heat for Loss," *Los Angeles Times*, October 6, 2002: D17.

10. Joe Strauss, "Cards Hit the Road with 2-0 Deficit; Giants Can Clinch Series at Home," *St. Louis Post-Dispatch*, Oct 11, 2002: D4.

11. Daniel G. Habib, "Jason Schmidt Has Got To Be Kidding Every Fifth Day, The Giants' Ace And CY Young Front-Runner Mows Down Batters. The Rest Of The Time He's The League Leader In Practical Jokes," *Sports Illustrated*, July 26, 2004, https://www.si.com/vault/2004/07/26/377606/jason-schmidt-has-got-to-be-kidding-every-fifth-day-the-giants-ace-and-cy-young-front-runner-mows-down-batters-the-rest-of-the-time-hes-the-league-leader-in-practical-jokes

12. Paul Sullivan, "About Schmidt: 1-hit Masterwork," *Chicago Tribune*, May 19, 2004: 1.

13. Nancy Armour, "Schmidt Throws One-Hitter," *Napa Valley Register*, May 19, 2004: D2.

14. "Schmidt One-Hits Red Sox," *Kenosha News*, June 21, 2004: B5.

15. Janie McCauley, "Schmidt Mows Down Marlins," *Santa Maria Times*, June 7, 2006: D3.

16 ESPN News Services, "Dodgers Ink Schmidt to Three-Year, $47M Contract," December 6, 2006. https://www.espn.com/mlb/news/story?id=2688596

17 Ben Bolch, "Schmidt Gets Good Odds on Recovery," *Los Angeles Times*, June 22, 2007: D6.

18 Dylan Hernandez, "Schmidt Feeling Good after Session," *Los Angeles Times*, February 24, 2009: D3.

19 Dylan Hernandez, "Schmidt's Win Not Totally Off the Wall," *Los Angeles Times*, July 21, 2009: C1.

20 Charles Odum, "Schmidt Pitches Gem for Win," *Desert Sun*, August 1, 2009: C5.

21 Steve Henson, "Schmidt Keeps the Wolves at Bay," *Los Angeles Times*, April 9, 2007, https://www.latimes.com/archives/la-xpm-2007-apr-09-sp-schmidt9-story.html

Mike Sharperson

BY SAM GAZDZIAK

Mike Sharperson

Mike Sharperson was a super-utility man, a valuable role-player who could play any infield position or come off the bench to pinch-hit. While supersubs rarely get the credit they deserve, his skills were such that he made the National League All-Star team. Sharperson spent parts of eight seasons in the major leagues, winning a World Series with the 1988 Los Angeles Dodgers and also logging time with the Toronto Blue Jays and Atlanta Braves. Tragically, he was killed in a car accident while driving to his next major-league opportunity.

Michael Tyrone Sharperson was born on October 4, 1961, in Orangeburg, South Carolina. His parents were Ethel and Mike Sr., and he had two siblings, sister Leslie and brother Vincent. Mike Sr. held a variety of jobs, including slaughtering pigs, fixing sinks, and pushing brooms. Mike Jr. recalled years later a time when he and his brother visited the slaughterhouse where their father worked.

"It was blood everywhere, and my brother and I couldn't believe it. We asked my dad, 'Why do you put up with this?' He said it was because he made good money and could take care of us. I'll never forget that."[1]

Things did not come easy for the Sharperson family. His great-grandmother, who lived to be 106, spoke about the days of slavery. His grandfather talked about the cotton gin. Though Mike Jr. grew up poor, he was proud and principled. He was not invited to the parties held by the rich students in high school. He showed up anyway, with his friends in tow.

"We were the have-nots, but when we showed up, nobody would tell us that we weren't invited," recalled John Butler, a childhood friend. "That's the way Juice [Sharperson's nickname] is. Real quiet, but real proud."[2]

Sharperson was a 1979 graduate of Orangeburg-Wilkinson High School and played baseball for four years, three as a starter at shortstop and the outfield. One of his teammates was future big leaguer Herm Winningham. Sharperson was also a starting wide receiver on the football team and an honor-roll student.[3] He and Winningham also played on the Post 4 American Legion team that won the South Carolina state championship in 1978. Sharperson was drafted by the Pittsburgh Pirates in the 41st round of the 1979 June amateur draft, but he elected to attend DeKalb Junior College (now named Georgia Perimeter College).

Sharperson kept getting drafted at every opportunity. The Expos selected him in the second round of the 1980 January Draft-Secondary Phase, and the Tigers took him in the fourth round of the 1981 January Draft-Secondary Phase. He spurned those offers, not because of money, but because he told his parents he would attend college for two years.[4]

In his second season playing ball at DeKalb, Sharperson hit .392 with 50 RBIs and was a third-team Junior College All-American pick. The Blue Jays picked him in the first round of the 1981 June Draft-Secondary Phase. Though he had accepted a scholarship offer from the University of South Carolina, he decided to begin his professional baseball career with the Jays.[5] Sharperson was the 11th overall pick, and his 5.5 career WAR is higher than that of anyone else taken in that round.

The Florence Blue Jays of the South Atlantic League – located less than 100 miles from his hometown of Orangeburg – were Sharperson's first stop in a five-year journey to the major leagues. In 111 games, the 20-year-old slashed .255/.376/.337. He drew 59 walks and had an equal number of strikeouts, and he stole 28 bases in 35 attempts. Fielding was his weakness. Sharperson played 102 games at shortstop and made 32 errors for a .925 fielding percentage. Overall, the team was high on him as a future Blue Jay.

"Most of the scouts and members of the organization are feeling like I have a good shot of making the big leagues in two or three years with a lot of work," Sharperson said in January 1983.[6]

Sharperson moved up to the Kinston Blue Jays of the high Class-A Carolina League in 1983. He raised his fielding percentage at shortstop to .952, and he also demonstrated his versatility in the field. He played four games at second base, 11 games at third, and even a game as catcher. He batted .266 with 20 stolen bases and five home runs, a career high that he matched in two other minor-league seasons.

"What impresses me about Mike is his range both to his left and to his right," said Kinston statistician Dan Lovallo. "He makes a lot of spectacular plays look routine. When he gets hits, he always does in key situations."[7]

The Blue Jays advanced Sharperson to Double-A Knoxville in 1984, and he responded with a team-best .304 batting average, ahead of future major-league stars Fred McGriff and Cecil Fielder. A switch to second base didn't hurt him defensively, as he had a .973 fielding average and was a part of 103 double plays.

Sharperson's next stop was the Syracuse Chiefs of the Triple-A International League. He played there in 1985 and 1986, turning in two very similar seasons. He batted .289 and scored 86 runs each year. He had 155 hits and 59 RBIs in 1985 and 150 hits and 45 RBIs in 1986. Each season, he was named the Toronto minor-league player of the year. His stolen bases declined significantly, to a total of 31 in those two seasons while being thrown out 28 times. On the plus side, he fielded second base admirably, with .977 and .974 fielding averages.

Sharperson hit just four home runs for Syracuse in 1986, but that didn't mean he was completely powerless. Years after the fact, he talked about the time he beat both McGriff and Fielder in a home-run-hitting contest that summer.

"I hit four homers in five swings," he said. "And every time I see one of those guys, I bring it up."[8]

Sharperson had been invited to the Blue Jays spring-training camps, but Damaso Garcia was established firmly at second base. He said that Garcia's presence basically ruined spring training for him, because he knew there was no room for him on the big-league club.[9] But during the 1986 offseason, Garcia was traded to the Braves, creating an opportunity for Sharperson to win the job in 1987.

"There were times when I thought, 'Hey, why even work? It's not going to get you everywhere,'" Sharperson said of his past springs. "I could have just taken it easy at Syracuse. But I kept a good attitude, kept working, and now I'm glad I did."[10]

Sharperson said that when he heard about Garcia's trade to Atlanta, he and his wife, Diane, wanted to throw a party, but they decided to hold off until he officially won the job.[11]

In the spring, Sharperson held off Manuel Lee and was named the Blue Jays' Opening Day second baseman. The 25-year-old made his major-league debut in Toronto on April 6, 1987, against the Cleveland Indians. Batting ninth, he flied out to left and struck out against Tom Candiotti. In the bottom of the sixth inning, he stepped up to face Doug Jones with runners on first and second. He doubled to left field, scoring Ernie Whitt, and he came around to score a couple of batters later on Lloyd Moseby's single. Along with a 1-for-4 day, he also handled four chances at second base flawlessly.

Sharperson hit safety in each of his first four games and then went hitless in three. His batting average seesawed back and forth, getting as high as .265 on April 22. After that, he slumped badly. He was demoted after a game in Seattle on May 23. He was hitting just .208 at the time. Sharperson was given the news of his demotion in the middle of his cross-country flight back to Toronto.

Sharperson started 75 games at third base and nine at second base in Syracuse. He batted .299 with 21 doubles and 5 home runs in 88 games, while playing well in the field at both positions. On September 22 Toronto traded him to the Dodgers for right-handed pitcher Juan Guzman.

"By adding Mike to our club, we have strengthened ourselves in the middle infield," said Dodgers executive vice president Fred Claire.[12]

At the time of the trade, Guzman had a 20-16 record and 4.03 ERA after three seasons in the low minors with the Dodgers. He would become an All-Star pitcher with the Blue Jays and looked like a pitching ace until injuries curtailed his effectiveness. Still, Guzman's first three major-league seasons were sensational enough that the trade was looked upon poorly by Dodgers fans, particularly when Sharperson failed to solidify the infield as promised.

After the trade, Sharperson was added to the Dodgers' big-league roster. He didn't start immediately, as he had been sitting at home for three weeks without picking up a bat. The Blue Jays had failed to recall him to the majors after Syracuse's season ended. Sharperson did get into the lineup and started 10 games – seven at third base and three at second. He recorded nine hits in 33 at-bats for a .273 average, including two doubles. The Dodgers envisioned him challenging Steve Sax at second base in 1988. Sharperson, for his part, was just happy to be out of the Blue Jays organization, as he felt he had never been given a real chance in the majors.

"I don't think 98 at-bats is a fair shot," he said of his brief time with the Jays at the start of the season. "The numbers I had in Syracuse the last two years deserved a whole year in Toronto. Also, it was my first time in the big leagues and it takes time to adjust."[13]

Sharperson did not make it past the first significant round of cuts in 1988 spring training with the Dodgers and began the season with the Triple-A Albuquerque Dukes. He hit .319 in 56 games with 19 stolen bases before he was needed by the Dodgers after shortstop Alfredo Griffin broke his hand. Sharperson was brought back to the majors on May 22. He appeared in 46 games, but only four of those appearances were starts. The bulk of his work came as a late-inning defensive replacement in the infield, primarily at second base. He was also used as a pinch-hitter, though he struggled in that role (3-for-22).

While his chances to step up to the plate were few and far between, Sharperson made the most of his opportunities. He had three hits in four at-bats in May and then hit .308 in June. He was batting .343 on July 25 when he was sent back to Albuquerque after Griffin returned from the disabled list. Sharperson returned to the Dodgers in late August. While he slumped in September, batting .200 in 20 at-bats, Sharperson ended the year with a .271 batting average.

Still, Sharperson made the postseason roster only because utility infielder Dave Anderson aggravated a back injury two days before the end of the season.[14] He appeared in two games of the seven-game NL Championship Series against the New York Mets. In Game Three, he pinch-hit for Danny Heep (who was pinch-hitting for starting pitcher Orel Hershiser) and drew a bases-loaded walk from Mets reliever Randy Myers in the eighth inning. He had walked only once in 64 regular-season plate appearances. That walk broke a 3-3 tie, but the Dodgers bullpen imploded in the bottom of the inning, resulting in an 8-4 Mets win. Sharperson played shortstop for that final inning. He bunted into a force play as a pinch-hitter in the 11th inning of Game Four and took over third base for the rest of the game, which the Dodgers won 5-4 in 12 innings. Sharperson was on the 25-man roster for the World Series, but he did not play as Los Angeles defeated the Oakland A's in five games.

The Dodgers slipped to fourth place in 1989, with a 77-83 record. Sharperson bounced back and forth between Los Angeles and Albuquerque. Griffin was once again healthy enough to play shortstop, and free agent Willie Randolph took over the starting second-base spot. When Sharperson didn't make the 25-man roster out of spring training, he flew home to Stone Mountain, Georgia, instead of Albuquerque. He threatened to quit baseball entirely and even made plans to work in a nearby carpet factory. Diane persuaded her husband to report to Triple A for the start of the season.[15]

Sharperson started the season in Albuquerque, saw limited action with the Dodgers in May when Kirk Gibson was sent to the disabled list, and returned again to the big leagues at the start of August. He hit .309 for the Dukes and helped them finish first in the Pacific Coast League South Division. He played in 27 games for Los Angeles and had a .250 average, with seven hits and five RBIs. He did find ways to lead the Dodgers to victories, though. He hit a tie-breaking sacrifice fly against the Giants on August 13 for a 3-2 win and drew a bases-loaded walk against the Braves' Mike Stanton in the bottom of the ninth inning for a 1-0 win on September 16.

Sharperson was poised to spend 1990 as a Dodgers utility infielder once again; then third baseman Jeff Hamilton went down early with an injury. This time, Sharperson was given the chance to fill in as the starter. He still kept the role of a supersub, starting games at all four infield positions and pinch-hitting in 25 games. He played in more than 100 major-league games for the first time in his career and finished 1990 with a slash line of .297/.376/.373. He had an OPS+ of 110 and even hit his first major-league home run – his first three home runs, in fact. The first, off the Mets' Ron Darling on August 16, came four years and 446 at-bats after he made his major-league debut. It ended his status as a "Zero Hero" – a player who'd gone the longest without a homer. The distinction, as noted by *Philadelphia Inquirer* sportswriter Jayson Stark, had been held previously by Felix Fermin, Lance Johnson, and Alvaro Espinoza before it went to Sharperson. He passed the mantle of Zero Hero on to Junior Noboa.[16]

To his Dodgers teammates and manager, Sharperson was far from a zero. Tommy Lasorda called him a manager's delight.

"He's unselfish, he gets along with everybody on the club and plays hard," Lasorda said. "That's my idea of a team player. I need a few more like him."[17]

Sharperson, in turn, enjoyed his expanded role, even if he wasn't playing every inning of every game. He knew his role.

"Sure it would be nice if they elected a utility man to the All-Star team. But I don't think that will happen anytime soon," he said. "I'll just take my playing time and be happy with that."[18]

He would be proved wrong about utility players getting All-Star nods, but it would be a couple of years away.

Sharperson, a slow starter, spent the first portion of the 1991 season hitting under .200. He then racked up five hits in two games against the Cubs and Pirates on June 19 and 20, including his first home run of the year, to raise his batting average nearly 100 points to .234. He hit .290 the rest of the season to end with a .278 average in 105 games, with 20 RBIs and two home runs. It wasn't enough to help the Dodgers finish first, as the 93-win team finished a game behind the Braves.

The Dodgers fell from second place all the way into the cellar in 1992, with a 63-99 record. Sharperson, however, had his best all-around season; he slashed .300/.387/.394, with a 124 OPS+. In 128 games, he hit 21 doubles and 3 home runs while driving in 36 runs and drawing 47 walks. All those numbers were career highs. An injury to second baseman Juan Samuel gave him the opportunity to start regularly, and by the All-Star break, he was hitting .328. He would have ranked third in the National League in batting average, but he didn't have enough at-bats to qualify for the batting title. Still, on a team that featured stars like Darryl Strawberry, Brett Butler, Eric Davis, Orel Hershiser, and Eric Karros, Sharperson – and only Sharperson – was selected to the NL All-Star team to represent the Dodgers. His selection was prompted by the rule that every major-league team be represented at the All-Star Game. It was an unconventional pick, but given his production, a logical one.

Sharperson's mother, Ethel, flew to San Diego to see her son. Mike Sr., though, did not like flying and couldn't make it. Mike Jr. did what he could to give his father the All-Star experience by taking videos and talking to him on the phone. While the Home Run Derby was taking place, Sharperson was in the American League dugout collecting autographs.[19] He struck out against the A's Dennis Eckersley in his only All-Star at-bat, but he enjoyed the experience to the fullest.

"If nothing else, I hope that because I made the All-Star team, kids today who don't think they have a chance will decide to keep trying," he said.[20]

Sharperson never had the chance to repeat his success. The Dodgers revamped their roster in 1993, adding second baseman Jody Reed and third baseman Tim Wallach, and Sharperson was moved back to the role of pinch-hitter and utility infielder. Once again he struggled at the start of the season, with a sub-.200 average into July. Though he eventually raised his average to a respectable .256, only 12 of his 73 appearances were in the starting lineup. The bulk of his appearances – 53 – came as a pinch-hitter. He hit .255 in that role, but it seemed clear that the Dodgers just did not envision him as a starter.

The Dodgers let Sharperson go as a free agent at the end of the 1993 season but signed him to a minor-league deal in February 1994. He was released in April, when manager Lasorda decided to keep an extra pitcher on the roster. Sharperson had no hard feelings over the decision.

"The Dodgers were fair to me," he said. "They took care of me and my family. I had some great years with them. They provided me a chance to make an All-Star team, and I had a chance to win a world championship. I also made some money there."[21]

Sharperson signed a minor-league contract with the Boston Red Sox and performed well for Triple-A Pawtucket, hitting .298 in 37 games. However, he didn't fit into the Red Sox youth movement plans and was released. He then caught on with the Iowa Cubs; Ron Clark, Sharperson's manager in Kinston, was the Cubs' coordinator of minor-league instruction. He thought Sharperson had a career ahead of him as a coach when his playing days were over. Sharperson wasn't ready to retire yet and signed with the Cubs to try to get back to the majors.[22] He hit .278 with Iowa, but any hopes of joining the Cubs were dashed when the players strike brought the 1994 season to an early end.

As he once more entered the offseason as a free agent, Sharperson was left in a tough position because of the strike. He wanted to land a job with a major-league team, but he was unwilling to cross the picket line to do it. He ultimately signed with the Braves in February and reported to the team's minor-league training camp, but he would not play in any spring-training games with the replacement players whom the Braves (and every other team) had brought to spring training. He did say that he would be willing to report to Triple-A Richmond should the strike carry over to the start of the season.

Sharperson stood out from the other minor leaguers at camp, not only for his experience but for his Dodgers World Series ring. "I'm starting to wear it a little more now, because I've got a feeling that Atlanta is going to win another one, and hopefully I'll be a part of that," he said, prophetically. "I'm going to bring it out and let some of the guys see it … just to loosen everybody up and just to give them a reminder of what one does look like."[23]

The strike came to an end, and Sharperson's position during the strike didn't cause any problems with his teammates once they showed up to camp. His chances to contribute to the Braves' World Series run were extremely limited, however. He made the Opening Day roster because Ryan Klesko started the season on the disabled list. Used exclusively as a pinch-hitter, he went hitless in his first four games before he entered the May 16 game to replace Jose Oliva in the top of the seventh. In the bottom of the eighth, he lined a two-run double to left field to help the Braves to an easy 15-3 win over the Rockies.

Sharperson was sent back to Richmond when Klesko was activated from the DL but returned when Mark Lemke was hurt. He went hitless in two at-bats and was returned to Triple A. All told, he went 1-for-7 with the Braves, who did indeed win the World Series as Sharperson predicted. He batted .319 for Richmond and left the Braves as a free agent after the season.

Sharperson was one of a group of 14 nonroster players invited to spring training by the San Diego Padres in 1996. He spent most of spring training playing the corner infield positions and was one of the last roster cuts. The Padres opted to keep outfielder Chris Gwynn on the roster, and Sharperson was assigned to Las Vegas Stars of the Pacific Coast League.[24]

Sharperson proceeded to demonstrate that he had plenty of baseball left in him. He had four hits and two RBIs in a game against Tucson on April 30, broke a scoreless tie against Calgary with a two-run homer on May 11 and drove in two more runs the next day. In 32 games with the Stars, Sharperson had a .304 batting average and 21 RBIs as the everyday third baseman.

His work impressed Stars manager Jerry Royster. "I wasn't sure what he had left. He came here and he proved what he had," Royster said. "He was the best player on our team, if not in the league."[25]

Sharperson's play was also noticed by the Padres, who were dealing with injuries at the big-league level. Third baseman Ken Caminiti had groin and shoulder injuries and was expected to be put on the disabled list. The Padres juggled their 40-man roster by putting prospect Homer Bush on the 60-day DL to free up a spot for Sharperson.[26]

The first reports that the Padres were planning a roster move came on May 21. San Diego, though, was hesitant about putting Caminiti on the DL and losing the eventual National League MVP for 15 days. Manager Bruce Bochy said he preferred to get by until Caminiti was healthy, so the Padres held steady.[27]

Caminiti continued to miss games and, according to Padres spokesman Roger Riley, Sharperson was told on Saturday, May 25, to fly to Montreal and meet the team there. There was no guarantee that he would be promoted to the big-league roster, but the team wanted him there in case Caminiti wasn't ready for the series against the Expos.[28]

At about 2:45 A.M. on May 26, Sharperson was driving out of Las Vegas on I-15 South and missed his exit. He attempted to swerve onto the exit anyway, but he lost control of his vehicle in the rain and crashed. Sharperson was not wearing his seat belt and was ejected from the vehicle through the sun roof.[29] He died about two hours later, on the operating table at University Medical Center. Highway Patrol trooper Steve Harney said that wearing a seat belt might have made a difference.[30] Sharperson was 34 years old.

Stars manager Royster was in tears as he talked about the loss of his player. "This really, really hurts. The guys are trying to sort this thing out. Baseball has lost a real friend. Baseball will definitely mourn the death of Mike Sharperson."[31]

Tommy Lasorda, Sharperson's former Dodgers manager, said he was "sick all day" over the news.

"I loved Mike Sharperson. I loved him and his family very dearly. He was a great guy to have on the team."[32]

In parts of eight major-league seasons, Sharperson had a slash line of .280/355/.364. He had 337 hits that included 61 doubles, 5 triples, and 10 home runs. He played 256 games at third base, 156 at second base, 41 at shortstop, and 19 at first base. He also played an inning in right field in 1993.

Sharperson is buried at Belleville Memorial Gardens in Orangeburg, South Carolina.

Sources

In addition to the sources cited in the Notes, the author consulted Baseball-Reference.com.

Notes

1. Bill Plaschke, "Bringing Game Home," *Los Angeles Times*, July 14, 1992.
2. Plaschke.
3. "Post 4 Profile, Mike Sharperson," *Times and Democrat* (Orangeburg, South Carolina), July 6, 1979.
4. Plaschke.
5. "Sharperson, Wilson Sign Baseball Pacts with Carolina," *Times and Democrat*, July 10, 1981.
6. Gage Bleakley, "Two Baseball Pros Were Among the Best from Area," *Times and Democrat*, January 18, 1983.
7. Gage Bleakley, "Local Stars Hope for Chance to Make the Big Leagues," *Times and Democrat*, May 29, 1983.
8. Tim Sullivan, "Sharperson More Like Commonperson," *Cincinnati Enquirer*, July 15, 1992.
9. Robbie Andreu, "Jays Rookie Sharperson Enjoying Spring Camp A.D. – after Damaso," *South Florida Sun Sentinel* (Fort Lauderdale), March 18, 1987.
10. Andreu.
11. Andreu.
12. "Baseball Notes: Dodgers Trade Guzman," *Greenville* (South Carolina) *News*, September 22, 1987.
13. Sam McMannis, "Newest Dodger: Is He Just a Face in the Crowd, or a Challenger to Sax?," *Los Angeles Times*, September 23, 1987.
14. Ken Rosenthal, "Jogging GMs Hammered Out A's-L.A. Deal," *Baltimore Evening Sun*, October 14, 1988.
15. Plaschke.
16. Jayson Stark, "A Quiz for Those Who Know Their No-Hitters," *Philadelphia Inquirer*, August 21, 1990.
17. "Sharperson Has All Bases Covered with the Dodgers," *Atlanta Constitution*, July 5, 1990.
18. "Sharperson Has All Bases Covered."
19. Plaschke.
20. Plaschke.
21. Randy Peterson, "Wanted: Return to Majors," *Des Moines Register*, July 31, 1994.
22. Peterson.
23. Tim Luke, "Playing a Waiting Game…," *Greenville* (North Carolina) *News*, February 23, 1995.
24. "Around the Majors," *Los Angeles Times*, March 30, 1996.
25. "Sharperson Dies after Car Accident," *Daily News* (New York), May 27, 1996.
26. "NL Report," *Philadelphia Daily News*, May 21, 1996.
27. "Padres Will Forgo Placing Caminiti on the DL," *Arizona Daily Star* (Tucson), May 23, 1996.
28. "Sharperson Dies after Car Accident."
29. Mike Downey, "'Sharpie' Is Remembered Fondly by Padres and Dodgers," *Los Angeles Times*, May 29, 1996.
30. "Sharperson Dies after Car Accident."
31. "Sharperson Dies after Car Accident."
32. "Sharperson Dies after Car Accident."

Dwight Smith

BY SAM GAZDZIAK

Dwight Smith

Dwight Smith entered the major leagues with a bang, thanks to a dynamic rookie season that included clutch hits, a playoff appearance, Rookie of the Year votes, and even a chance to sing the National Anthem. He never matched the success of that first season, but Smith still had a respectable eight-year career in the major leagues that included a World Series championship. Smith played for the Chicago Cubs (1989-93), California Angels (1994), Baltimore Orioles (1994), and Atlanta Braves (1995-96).

John Dwight Smith was born in Tallahassee, Florida, on November 8, 1963. His baseball skills became evident at a pretty early age, but his other natural talent was evident as well – singing. As early as five years old, Smith was singing in a church choir in Varnville, South Carolina, where he grew up. His three older brothers didn't play sports, but they all loved music. Smith followed in their path.

"I probably sing more than I play baseball," he said in his rookie season of 1989 "I play baseball maybe seven or eight months a year, but I sing every day. In the car, in the shower, in my room, I'm always singing, trying new things."[1]

Smith's parents were Wallace Smith and Anne Mary "Annie Mae" Grant. They attended Samaritan Baptist Church in Varnville, and Smith's religious beliefs helped keep him balanced during the ups and downs of a professional baseball career.[2] Annie Mary was widowed when Dwight was 7 years old and had to be the sole supporter for four young boys. Smith later said that she was always positive and cheerful and supported him in all his endeavors. When she died in 1985, her last words to him were, "Make the big leagues, Dwight, and cut your album."[3]

Smith attended Wade Hampton High School in Varnville. He was a baseball and football player there, but he decided that pursuing baseball would be the best way to get a college scholarship and prepare for a professional career.[4] In his senior year, the lefty-hitting outfielder hit .457 with 5 home runs, 16 RBIs, and 25 stolen bases. He signed a baseball grant-in-aid with Spartanburg Methodist College in July 1982.[5]

Spartanburg College was a good fit for Smith for several reasons. It had the same small-town feel that the easygoing Smith liked. It also had a good music program, allowing him to pursue a major in music. The school's baseball team made it to the Junior College World Series in his freshman year of 1983.

Smith was one of eight SMC players named to the all-Western Region 10 baseball team in 1984. That summer he was drafted by the Cubs in the third round of the 1984 June Draft-Secondary Phase. Previously, the Blue Jays had picked Smith in the third round of the 1984 Draft-Regular Phase, held in January. He didn't sign with the Jays, but he did agree to terms with Chicago and reported to Pikeville, Kentucky, to begin his professional baseball career.

Smith hit .236 for the Pikeville Cubs in 1984, with 39 stolen bases in 61 games. He moved up through the ranks of the Cubs minor leagues in orderly fashion, from Rookie-ball Pikeville in 1984 to low-A Geneva in 1985, to A-ball Peoria in 1986 and Double-A Pittsfield in 1987. At every step along the way, his numbers got better and better. The 1986 season with the Peoria Chiefs was the one that made Smith a true prospect; he batted .310 with 22 doubles, 11 triples, and 11 home runs. He stole 53 bases and was rated as a fastest baserunner and best defensive outfielder in the Midwest League, according to a *Baseball America* poll of team managers.[6]

During the offseason, Smith would return to South Carolina and sang in talent shows and nightclubs. When asked if he wanted to pursue a music career after baseball, he replied, "I'd like to sing professionally while I'm *in* baseball."[7]

Smith began the 1987 season in Pittsfield by hitting well over .400 through late May. He cooled off but still ended the year with a .337 batting average, 18 home runs, 72 RBIs, and 60 stolen bases. He had a classic Dwight Smith game on June 21. Before the game he sang the National Anthem. Though he had the day off, he came to bat as a pinch-hitter in the bottom of the eighth inning. He walked, advanced to second base, stole third, and scored as Pittsfield tied the game. He won the game in the bottom of the ninth with a long sacrifice fly.[8]

Smith was the MVP of the 1987 Eastern League All-Star Game, banging out an RBI double in the third inning and stealing a base in the seventh inning. He scored two runs in the 6-0 win. "This is most definitely the highlight of my career," he said after the game. "But I hope next year at this time I'll be in Wrigley."[9]

He was close. Smith spent 1988 in Triple-A Des Moines and wowing the organization.

"I don't know that any player does it better," said Iowa manager Pete Mackanin.

"He surprised me the first time. He's awesome," said teammate Mark Grace.

Of course, they were referring to Smith's singing ability, but Cubs instructor and Hall of Famer Billy Williams was referring to Smith's baseball skills when he said, "He's one of those can't-miss people. Dwight Smith will be in the big leagues someday."[10]

After a strong year at Iowa in 1988, Smith entered the Cubs spring-training camp in 1989 with a legitimate chance to emerge as the starting left fielder. Instead, he was one of the first cuts. Not only did he hit poorly, but his fielding was bad enough that Cubs manager Don Zimmer had an easy time sending him to Triple-A Iowa.

"I put a lot of pressure on myself. I read too many papers about Dwight Smith going to have a shot," said Smith, who frequently referred to himself in the third person during his career. "I learned something from that. I learned that you can't get the best out of whatever you do if you're going to press. You've got to relax and let it happen."[11]

"I saw a Dwight Smith in spring training that I didn't want to see no more," Zimmer said. Smith handled his demotion like a seasoned veteran, surprising the skipper. "He said, 'You put me in the lineup. I've got no complaints. You're not seeing the real Dwight Smith.'"[12]

The real Dwight Smith made an appearance in the major leagues soon enough. He was batting .325 in Iowa when the Cubs were bitten by the injury bug. The entire starting outfield of Mitch Webster, Jerome Walton, and Andre Dawson all went on the disabled list, and Smith was part of a group of rookies brought up to help fill out the outfield. He made his debut on May 1 in San Francisco. He went 0-for-3 and was thrown out trying to steal a base. He picked up two hits in each of the next two games and was off and running in the majors.

In his first 25 games, Smith hit .365 with 7 doubles, 2 triples and 2 home runs. Even his fielding showed significant improvement. Originally starting in right field to spell an injured Dawson, Smith eventually locked down left field for the rest of the season. Even if he wasn't a Gold Glove candidate, he was no longer an embarrassment. It could have been part of Smith's growth development. It also could have been the fact that Dawson gave the rookie one of his Gold Gloves in spring training.

"It meant a lot to me as far as my confidence to think someone like Andre Dawson would do that for little Dwight Smith," said the rookie.[13]

Smith's first career home run came during a 15-3 demolition of the Mets on June 5. He sent a 1-and-0 pitch from starter David Cone into the left-field bleachers for a three-run homer in the first inning. He added a double, single, and walk before the game's end. Zimmer decided to test the rookie the next day by letting him start against lefty Bob Ojeda. Smith responded with another homer, giving the Cubs a lead in an eventual 8-4 win.

Smith, ever the entertainer, even got a chance to show off his singing skills by performing the National Anthem in a game at Wrigley Field on July 21. Like so much of his rookie season, it was a note-perfect performance. He finished his rookie campaign with a .324 batting average, 9 home runs, and 52 RBIs. The Cubs, led by Walton and Smith at the top of the lineup, surprised baseball by winning 93 games and finishing first in the NL East. They lost to the Giants in the NL Championship Series in five games; Smith hit .200 in four games.

Walton was named the NL Rookie of the Year, with 22 of 24 first-place votes. Smith received the remaining two votes and was the runner-up. Realistically, he had the better offensive season than Walton – compare his slash line of .324/.382/.493 and 141 OPS+ to Walton's .293/.335/.385 and 100 OPS+ -- but Walton had a 30-game hitting streak that raised his profile considerably. Walton was quick to credit his teammate for his own success in the majors.

"It helped me a lot once Dwight got here. I had someone on my level to chat with. Dwight is a comedian," Walton said.[14]

Both rookies regressed in 1990. Smith's average dropped to .262, and by the end of the year, the slumping outfielder was moved to a part-time role. He was the subject of trade rumors, and once the Cubs signed left fielder George Bell in the offseason, he indicated that he would be open to leaving.

"For personal reasons, I don't want to leave Chicago. For career reasons, I probably need to," he said, adding that he would be the same gregarious, fun-loving kid if he remained a Cub.[15]

The presence of Bell in left field did cut into Smith's playing time. He appeared in 90 games and hit an abysmal .228. He barely saw left field at all and was used instead as a pinch-hitter and reserve right fielder, giving Dawson extra days off to rest his bad knees. He still had opportunities for heroics, but they were few and far between. He gave Dawson a day off on June 30 when the Cubs battled the Cardinals. With the Cubs down 4-1, Smith launched a game-tying home run off Jose DeLeon to help spur an eventual 7-4 win.

The 1992 Cubs were a much different team, with a new general manager (Larry Himes) and new manager (Jim Lefebvre). Bell had been traded to the crosstown White Sox over the offseason. Despite the new look, Smith was stuck in the same role as pinch-hitter and reserve outfielder. He was even sent back to Triple-A Iowa at the end of April when he was hitting .216, though the demotion lasted only three games. He raised his batting average to .276 by the end of the season in his limited playing time, and his 14 pinch hits from that season are one of the best in Cubs history.[16] Still, he couldn't help but feel that the Cubs had given up on him.

"All throughout my career, I've proven I can play day in and day out if I'm given a chance. You see good numbers when I'm playing every day. But Dwight Smith doesn't burn any bridges. Dwight Smith still has a smile on his face," he said.[17]

Smith's fortunes changed in 1993. While he still wasn't playing every day, he became a regular center fielder against right-handed pitching and responded with the best season since his rookie campaign. He slammed a career-high 11 home runs and slashed .300/.355/.494 in 111 games. His 343 plate appearances were his most since 1989. After the season, though, his Cubs career abruptly came to an end when the team declined to offer him a contract. Smith, who made $680,000 in 1993 and was arbitration-eligible, was caught in a payroll crunch; the Cubs opted to keep Glenallen Hill over Smith as their reserve outfielder.

Smith was given the news around Christmastime and was understandably hurt at leaving the only professional organization he'd ever known. "It was almost like home – and almost like your parents put you out," he told the *Chicago Tribune*. "I guess I was a Cub and now I'm a bear. So I've got to find my own food."[18]

Smith spent the offseason recording a demo R&B album called *R U Down*. From a baseball perspective, he signed with the California Angels on February 1, 1994. If there were any questions about how his Cubs teammates felt about Smith, they were answered the first time the Angels and Cubs faced off in a spring-training game. The Cubs had fastened a sign on the left-field fence that read "Dwight Smith Field," and his friends gave him a hero's welcome on the field. Angels manager Buck Rodgers was caught unprepared for the love-in.

"Amazing. Wasn't he the fourth outfielder on this club?" he said.[19]

In 45 games as an Angels left fielder and occasional designated hitter, Smith hit .262 with 5 home runs and 18 RBIs, platooning in left field with Bo Jackson. Smith lost his spot in the lineup when the Angels brought Jim Edmonds to the major leagues. He was traded to the Baltimore Orioles on June 14 for a player to be named later. The Orioles needed a left-handed bat off the bench as they competed for a postseason berth, and Smith made the best of his time there. He hit .311 in 28 games with three homers, as the Orioles finished with 63 wins, 6½ games behind the Yankees in the strike-shortened season. He became a free agent after the rest of the season was canceled. The strike carried over into 1995, delaying the start of the season. Smith signed with the Atlanta Braves on April 12, 1995. The move to the Braves was close to home for him, as he lived in nearby Fairburn in the offseason. It also gave him the opportunity to focus on something he's missed in his career to date.

"After six seasons, you are looking for rings, not rebuilding. The Braves are where it's at," he said.[20]

With an outfield of Ryan Klesko, Marquis Grissom, and David Justice, there weren't many opportunities for him to start. He did have plenty of chances to pinch-hit – 82 of his 103 games came off the bench. He didn't shine as a pinch-hitter, with 16 hits in the role for a .232 average. Thanks to some timely hitting in his spot starts, Smith hit .252 with the Braves overall. One of those starts came against the Cubs on August 27. He went 2-for-3 with a run scored in his return to Wrigley Field.

Smith once again had the chance to sing the National Anthem at Atlanta-Fulton County Stadium. This time, his performance was noticed by Atlanta resident and Braves fan Elton John. The singing legend was so impressed that he went to the ballpark days later and requested to speak with Smith during batting practice. He also gave him a business card and asked Smith to send him his demo tape.

Smith appeared in all four games of the 1995 NL Division Series against the Colorado Rockies (and sang the National Anthem once). He had two hits in three at-bats, including an RBI pinch hit in Game One that momentarily gave the Braves a 4-3 lead. Atlanta would lose that lead but win the game, 5-4. Smith was 0-for-2 in the NL Championship Series against Cincinnati and had a hit and a walk in three plate appearances against Cleveland in the World Series. His one World Series base hit came off Dennis Martinez in a 4-3 win over the Indians in Game Two.

Smith returned to the Braves in 1996, and he was reunited with his former Cubs teammate Jerome Walton. United on the baseball field at least. The two friends lived around the corner from each other in Fairburn. But they enjoyed being teammates again.

"To be able to come home and play with him is just a blessing," Walton said. "He really keeps you on your toes, makes the game fun. That's the main thing I miss about Smitty."[21]

Smith struggled through the season, getting just 16 pinch-hits in 69 at-bats and batting .203 overall. The Braves once again finished in first place in their division and made it to the World Series, losing to the Yankees. Smith was kept off the postseason roster.

Smith, now 33 years old, was granted free agency after the season, and for the first time in his career, he found no major-league teams interested in his services. He signed with the Tampa Bay Devil Rays in early 1997, with the idea that he would spend the summer playing with the Mexico City Tigers for a chance to join the Rays in their inaugural 1998 season.[22] Instead, he suffered a sciatic nerve injury and never made it to Mexico. He ended up playing for the St. Paul Saints of the independent Northern League instead, hitting .352 in 74 games there. He returned to the Devil Rays in spring training in 1998, but he was released – on a day that he was scheduled to sing the National Anthem.[23] He played in 20 games for the Rochester Red Wings, the Triple-A affiliate of the Orioles, in 1998, to conclude his professional playing career.

In eight major-league seasons, Smith slashed .275/.333/.422, with 497 hits that included 88 doubles, 20 triples, and 46 home runs. He drove in 226 runs and scored 244 times. He hit .273 in 13 postseason games with the Cubs and Braves and was a career .269 as a pinch-hitter, with 87 hits and eight pinch-hit homers. Smith was also considered an all-time great teammate.

"He was the best pinch-hitter in Cub history, and he was the greatest guy I ever saw in a clubhouse," said Mark Grace. "He has a great sense of humor, kept everybody loose. And he can sing and dance and does great imitations. He's hilarious. He probably could be a stand-up comic."[24]

Smith had some legal problems after his retirement. On September 8, 2006, Smith, 42, was charged with cocaine possession and two traffic violations after being pulled over by Peachtree City police. He was charged with driving on a suspended license and for having no insurance. He was released on $8,000 bond. The *Atlanta Constitution* reported that he previously was arrested on November 22, 2003, in Tyrone, Georgia, and accused of driving under the influence and possession of marijuana.[25] The results of those charges are not known.

By 2020 Smith was mostly known as being the father of Dwight Smith Jr., an outfielder for the Baltimore Orioles. He also has two daughters, Taylor and Shannyn, and he called his wife, Cheryl, the backbone of the family.

"She has worked hard to keep us all intact," he said in 2011.[26]

Dwight Jr. took his first steps by his dad's locker in the Cubs clubhouse in Wrigley Field, and he has mentioned that they talk daily during the season.[27] Even while Smith was working out in the offseason during his playing career, he was spending time with Dwight Jr. A 1997 profile on the elder Smith mentioned that as he worked on his swing, he put a bat in his four-year-old son's hands and let him take his swings from a nearby cage.

"I want to be there for Dwight Jr.," said Smith. "When he hits a home run he can look back over at my face and see how happy I look. He can see Dad out there saying, 'That's my son.'"[28]

Sources

In addition to the sources cited in the Notes, the author consulted Baseball-Reference.com.

Notes

1. "A Song in Their Hearts," *St. Louis Post-Dispatch*, September 8, 1989.
2. Kathleen Myers, "Blue Jays Draft Son of Varnville Baseball Star," *Augusta* (Georgia) *Chronicle*, June 16, 2011.
3. Jerome Holtzman, "No Time Is Down Time for Cubs' Resilient Dwight Smith," *Chicago Tribune*, June 4, 1993.
4. Bill Everhart, "Dwight Right on Time," *Berkshire Eagle* (Northampton, Massachusetts), June 29, 1987.
5. "UNC Arena Construction Set to Begin by August," *Greenville* (South Carolina) *News*, July 16, 1982.
6. Fred Mitchell, "Future Is Green for Cubs," *Chicago Tribune*, August 5, 1986.
7. Bill Everhart, "Dwight Right on Time."
8. Bill Everhart, "Dwight Right on Time."
9. Bill Everhart, "Dwight Smith MVP in 6-0 National win," *Berkshire Eagle*, June 30, 1987.
10. Randy Peterson, "I-Cubs' Smith Hits Right Chord in Both His Jobs," *Des Moines Register*, April 26, 1988.
11. Alan Solomon, "Rookie Leads Cubs' Assault," *Chicago Tribune*, June 6, 1989.
12. Bill Moor, "Smith's Demotion Sparked His Return," *South Bend Tribune*, June 7, 1989.
13. Roman Modrowski, "Cub Rookie Earning His Gold Glove," *Times* (Munster, Indiana), June 27, 1989.
14. "A Song in Their Hearts," *St. Louis Post-Dispatch*, September 8, 1989.
15. Alan Solomon, "Dwight Smith Wants Out – Or Maybe Not," *Dispatch* (Moline, Illinois), December 30, 1990.
16. Chris Kamka, "Cubs Stat Mailbag: The Best Pinch-Hitting Seasons in Team History," NBCSports.com, December 13, 2018. nbcsports.com/chicago/cubs/cubs-stat-mailbag-best-pinch-hitting-seasons-team-history.
17. Randy Peterson. "Cubs' Smith Just Asks for a Chance," *Des Moines Register*, May 20, 1992.
18. Alan Solomon, "Smith Feels Devastated, Says Release by Cubs 'Hurt Me,'" *Chicago Tribune*, December 28, 1993.
19. Jerome Holtzman, "Dwight Smith Still Special to His Ex-Cub Mates," *Chicago Tribune*, March 8, 1994.
20. I.J. Rosenberg, "Smith Delighted to Be with a Contender, Even After 74 Percent Pay Cut," *Atlanta Constitution*, April 14, 1995.
21. Kevin Langbaum, "Buddies Back Up," *Palm Beach Post*, February 20, 1996.
22. Charean Williams, "Devil Rays' Smith Isn't in the Mood to Sing," *Orlando Sentinel*, March 24, 1997.
23. Kevin Wells, "Devil Rays Daily," *Tampa Tribune*, March 26, 1998.
24. Holtzman, "Dwight Smith Still Special to His Ex-Cub Mates."
25. Kathy Jefcoats, "Ex-Braves player Charged with Cocaine Possession," *Atlanta Constitution*, September 12, 2006.
26. Michael Carvell, "Family Prospect," *Atlanta Journal-Constitution*, June 5, 2011.
27. Steve Ewin, "Tracing His Dad's Footsteps to The Show," *The Province* (Vancouver, B.C.), August 16, 2002.
28. Delbert Ellerton, "Player Shares Knowledge with Son, Aspiring Stars," *Atlanta Constitution*, February 20, 1997.

John Smoltz

BY WARREN CORBETT

John Smoltz

The Atlanta Braves' three aces may be the greatest pitching combination in history: the artist Greg Maddux, the stylist Tom Glavine, and the electric John Smoltz. In seven seasons, from 1993 through 1999, the Braves won almost two-thirds of the games started by their Big Three.

Maddux claimed four straight Cy Young Awards, Glavine two Cys, and Smoltz one. Atlanta pitching coach Leo Mazzone said Smoltz "had the best stuff of all of them. Greatest slider I've ever seen from a right-handed pitcher. Powerful fastball. A nasty split-finger. A changeup. And a curveball."[1] Smoltz owed his 22-year career to a live arm, determination, and medical science.

When the Braves won an unequaled 14 consecutive division championships from 1991 through 2005, Smoltz was the only player to celebrate every one.[2] His election to the National Baseball Hall of Fame in 2015 came one year after Maddux and Glavine were inducted along with manager Bobby Cox.

Smoltz is the only pitcher to record more than 200 victories and more than 150 saves, but that is a junk statistic; Dennis Eckersley totaled 197 victories to go with 390 saves. Smoltz's unique achievement was his excellence as a starter, then a closer, then a starter again. He led the National League in wins at age 29, in saves at 35, and in wins at 39.

Before all that, Johnny Smoltz was a good boy.

John Andrew Smoltz was born on May 15, 1967, in Detroit but grew up in Lansing, Michigan, the eldest of three children of John Adam Smoltz and the former Mary Tersigni. His father, a salesman and a joker, embarrassed the children when he decorated his car to look like the calculators he was selling. Both parents moonlighted as accordion teachers. Johnny joined the family business when he was 4, playing at polka parties and winning prizes for musicianship. By age 7 he set a new goal. He told his mother he would be a professional baseball player. Fine, she said, but you should have a backup plan, just in case. Okay, the boy replied, I'll be a gas-station attendant.

In the Smoltz home, the rule was "God first, family second, schoolwork third, athletics fourth."[3] Baseball became Johnny's obsession. He spent hours bouncing a rubber ball off the side of the house, pitching the seventh game of the World Series while providing his own play-by-play broadcast, imitating the voice he heard on the radio, Ernie Harwell. As a teenager he didn't go to parties and generally avoided trouble, channeling his energy to the diamond and the basketball court. He described his younger self as "a people pleaser."[4]

Johnny's grandfather John Frank Smoltz worked for the Detroit Tigers for three decades as an usher and groundskeeper. (His father also worked briefly as an usher.) When Johnny was a junior at Waverly High, the granddad persuaded a Tigers executive to send a scout to see the boy pitch. Scout Ken Madeja was not happy to be chasing yet another tip on somebody's son or nephew or grandson, but he reported back, "This time we got a good tip. This kid is pretty good."[5]

Other teams were taking notice, and several scouts told Johnny he would likely be drafted in the first three rounds. His hometown school, Michigan State, had offered a baseball scholarship, so word got around that he might be difficult to sign. He fell to the 22nd round, when the Tigers claimed him with the 574th pick of the 1985 draft. At the time of his election, Smoltz was the lowest draft choice to make the Hall of Fame.

The Tigers' interest picked up after Smoltz was chosen for the junior Team USA that summer and pitched, and lost, the Junior Olympics championship game to Cuba. He was invited to Tiger Stadium for a workout. While the club negotiated with his father, Johnny was lining up his freshman class schedule and dorm room. He signed the night before classes started. Joining the favorite team of his childhood was "almost too good to be true."[6]

Smoltz was not an immediate success in pro ball. Although he was promoted to Double A in his second season, his ERA for the Eastern League's Glens Falls Tigers was 5.68 in August 1987, with a 4-10 record, when lightning struck. An infamous (in Detroit) trade with Atlanta brought the Tigers a veteran right-hander, Doyle Alexander, who went 9-0 as a two-month rental to help the club win the American League East championship.

In return for Alexander, Detroit gave Atlanta a choice between two young pitchers, left-hander Steve Searcy and Smoltz. Years later the Tigers' then-GM, Bill Lajoie, said, "Smoltz had not done anything out of the ordinary to indicate that he would become the pitcher he has become."[7] But the Braves scouts saw a 6-foot-3 stringbean, just 20 years old, who might be special. The *Atlanta Journal-Constitution* said the Braves' new acquisition was "known for throwing hard but not always accurately."[8]

Smoltz was distraught, feeling rejected by his hometown team and dispatched to the depths of hell, or at least the National League. "As far as I was concerned, the Braves were the worst team in all of baseball."[9] He wasn't far wrong; the club was bad and getting worse.

The Braves did have something the Tigers did not: minor-league pitching coaches. Smoltz said the roving coaches in the Detroit system had given him little instruction, and the advice he had received was often contradictory. Joining Atlanta's Triple-A club in Richmond, he began a 19-year collaboration with Leo Mazzone. Mazzone didn't tamper with Smoltz's mechanics, "one of the most beautiful deliveries I'd ever seen."[10] Instead, he concentrated on improving the youngster's curve and slider.

Improvement came quickly. Smoltz posted a 2.79 ERA at Richmond before Atlanta called him up in July 1988. The frightened 21-year-old made his debut for the last-place Braves against the first-place Mets. Shea Stadium was packed for Tom Seaver Day. Smoltz allowed only one run and four hits in eight innings before Bruce Sutter closed out the rookie's first victory. He won just once more and finished with a 5.48 ERA, but the next year he made the All-Star team in his first full season.

The Braves lost 300 games in Smoltz's first three seasons, finishing last in the NL West every year. While losing, the club was assembling a core of pitchers who were promoted as the "Young Guns." Tom Glavine had been called up after the Alexander-Smoltz trade, and Smoltz never let him forget how he got to the majors. Pete Smith,

Tommy Greene, and Derek Lilliquist showed early promise. Steve Avery and Kent Mercker, a pair of first-round draft choices, joined the staff in 1990. Smoltz thought they benefited from being rushed to the majors with a lousy team, under no pressure to win: "We weren't very good so we had to get our brains beat out and learned from it."[11]

General manager Bobby Cox moved into the manager's chair in midseason 1990 and John Schuerholz took over as GM. They added veteran third baseman Terry Pendleton and first baseman Sid Bream to a young nucleus of hitters including David Justice and Ron Gant. Clearly the Braves were getting better, but no one anticipated the magic of 1991.

Smoltz almost didn't make it for Atlanta's worst-to-first surge. By the All-Star break he stood at 2-11 with a 5.16 ERA. His confidence had collapsed. "Anytime things started to get a little hairy, I would begin to unravel; … it became a foregone conclusion in my mind that once runners were on, they were going to score."[12] In desperation, Schuerholz suggested he see a psychologist, Jack Llewellyn.

Llewellyn calls himself a mental-development coach.[13] After a few sessions with his new patient, Llewellyn gave him a video showing some of his best performances and told him to watch it before every start. "Remembering my little highlight reel helped me break out of it and banish the negative thoughts from my head," Smoltz said.[14] He went 12-2, 2.63 in the second half, then shut out Pittsburgh in the seventh game of the League Championship Series to send Atlanta to the World Series.

That shutout established Smoltz's reputation as a big-game pitcher. He went on to set postseason records with 15 victories (since surpassed by Andy Pettitte) and 199 strikeouts. But the biggest Game Seven of his life is known as the Jack Morris game, not the John Smoltz game. In the deciding contest of the 1991 World Series, Smoltz shut out the Minnesota Twins until he was relieved in the eighth. Morris, refusing to come out, pitched 10 scoreless innings for the victory that sealed the championship.

That was the start of Atlanta's run of 14 straight division titles and the first of many postseason letdowns. The club made it to the World Series five times but won just one championship. After another disappointment in the 1992 Series, Atlanta signed free agent right-hander Greg Maddux, that year's Cy Young Award winner with the Cubs. He joined the 1991 Cy Young winner, Glavine, and Smoltz at the top of the rotation. The three maintained an intense, though unspoken, competition; nobody wanted to be left behind. Smoltz knew where he stood. "My sense is that I was the guy riding in the backseat most of the time," he acknowledged. "As good as Greg was, Tom was right up there with him."[15] With the Big Three and a changing cast of supporting pitchers, Atlanta allowed the fewest runs in the National League for 11 straight seasons, 1992-2002.

The trio bonded over their mutual love of practical jokes, trash talk, and golf. All were dedicated golfers, but Smoltz was the most fanatical – and the best. He also served as the concierge who arranged tee times and rental cars. Of course, he insisted there was more to it than play. "Golf is the closest thing to the anticipation of getting ready to pitch a game," he said. "There are all kinds of things that can go wrong, and it's about how you handle them and what your process is like. When you pitch, you make 115 pitches and decisions, and golf is the same."[16]

Even as he topped the league in strikeouts and starts in 1992, Smoltz began suffering elbow pain. Atlanta's orthopedic surgeon had told him he had, in layman's terms, extraordinarily loose joints. Smoltz thought his flexibility made him a better pitcher, but it also made him a pitching time bomb. By 1994 he had to shut down in July and underwent elbow surgery to remove a bone spur and chips shortly before the season was canceled because of the players' strike.

He rejoined the rotation as the Braves won their only World Series in 1995, over Cleveland.

The next year he moved into the front seat, leading the league in wins with 24 and in strikeouts with almost 10 per nine innings. He won 14 straight decisions. The spectacular season earned him the Cy Young Award (Maddux had won the previous four). In 1996, pitching coach Mazzone said, "John Smoltz was as awesome and dominant a pitcher as I've ever seen."[17]

Smoltz capped the season with one of his best World Series performances. After beating the Yankees in Game One, he came back in the fifth game to strike out 10, allowing just four hits in eight innings. Only two Yankees reached third base, one of them after center fielder Marquis Grissom muffed a fly ball. That man scored an unearned run and Andy Pettitte shut out the Braves for a 1-0 victory. Smoltz said it was the best game of his life, but added, "My arm, for the last seven innings, I ain't lying, my arm was tired, hurting."[18] The Yankees won the Series to begin their own dominant run, claiming four championships in five years.

Smoltz signed a four-year contract at an average $7.75 million per year, making him briefly the highest-paid pitcher in the game. In 1997 he led the league in innings pitched for the second straight year while dealing with more elbow pain. After the season he needed a second arthroscopic surgery. Although he posted a 17-3 record in 1998, around two trips to the disabled list, the pain didn't go away. There were days when he couldn't stand to throw a slider. "I am absolutely serious when I say that I pitched some of my greatest games in some of my worst conditions," he said.[19]

The team doctor told him Tommy John surgery was inevitable, but he resisted. By August 1999, he told a reporter, "I'm at the point right now where I just don't know how long it's going to last. It's pitch to pitch, start to start now."[20] To relieve the pain, he gave up throwing overhand and dropped to a low three-quarters, almost side-arm, delivery. "I basically taught myself how to pitch a whole new way," he said. "Nobody knew how hard it was. I was trying to fake it."[21]

The elbow gave out during spring training in 2000. Smoltz made the dreaded visit to the pitcher's best friend, surgeon James Andrews, for an elbow ligament replacement that cost him the entire season. Returning in 2001, he managed just five starts before heading back to the DL.

Along with Cox and Mazzone, Smoltz concluded that his elbow couldn't stand up to pitching a full game every fifth day. The club sent him to the bullpen and by the end of the season he had taken over as the closer. He recorded 10 saves in 11 chances, then finished all three games of the Division Series as the Braves swept Houston. It was the last postseason series the Braves won during his career; they lost the league championship to Arizona.

Smoltz called the fall of 2001 the Offseason from Hell. With his contract expiring, the Braves told him they wanted him back, but only as a reliever. He balked. He had organized his life around a starting pitcher's schedule, waking up early on his days off to take his children to school and play golf. When he tested free agency, at least half a dozen teams offered him a starting job. The Yankees put a reported $52 million on the table for four years. After agonizing and praying, Smoltz accepted a $30 million, three-year deal, with an option for a fourth year, to close for Atlanta. "I looked at the total picture," he said. "Family, lifestyle, my charity and community work, financial, friends and family. And baseball."[22] He, his wife, Dyan, and their four children were settled in the community and he was leading a fundraising drive to build a new Christian school.

Smoltz had won 159 games as a starter; now he was a reluctant reliever. His personality didn't seem to fit the role. He was hyperactive and something of a control freak. Fellow reliever Mike Remlinger said, "If he's awake, he's full tilt. He's like a 10-year-old."[23] He had to come to the ballpark every day and sit around for six hours waiting to learn whether he would pitch. Smoltz asserted control over his new environment by renovating Turner Field's bullpen, paying to install air-conditioning and bringing a favorite recliner from home.

In his second outing of 2002, Smoltz entered a tie game against the Mets in the ninth and was rocked for eight runs. For the rest of the season he was nearly automatic. He set a National League record with 55 saves (matched by Eric Gagne the next year) while blowing only four opportunities. In 2003 he was even more dominant, with his fastball clocked at 99 mph. He allowed just eight walks and eight earned runs in 64⅓ innings for a 1.12 ERA, with 45 saves in 49 opportunities. He saved 44 more in 2004. In 3½ years, Smoltz racked up a 91 percent success rate closing games. But he had to visit Dr. Andrews again after the 2004 season to clean out more chips in his battered elbow.

Smoltz had accepted the bullpen assignment to preserve his elbow, but he eventually concluded that closing was more dangerous than starting because he was throwing all-out all the time. With Smoltz owning the ninth inning, the Braves had won four more division titles but never advanced past the first round of the playoffs. The Ted Turner era in Atlanta had ended and the new owner, Time Warner, squeezed the club's budget. Glavine and Maddux had left as free agents because the team couldn't afford them. Smoltz believed he could contribute more as a starter. Now he had to convince GM John Schuerholz.

Smoltz made his pitch over dinner at McCormick and Schmick's in December 2004. Schuerholz was skeptical that his arm could hold up for 200 innings; Smoltz hadn't reached that level since 1997. Smoltz told him, "Take my baseball card and turn it over." Schuerholz agreed to bet on his track record as a starter.[24]

It was a gamble at long odds on a pitcher who was nearly 38 years old with an elbow that belonged in a medical textbook. On Opening Day in 2005 Smoltz made his first start in almost four years. The Florida Marlins knocked him out in the second inning after he gave up seven runs. Schuerholz's bet looked like a loser.

Five days later Smoltz struck out 15 Mets, matching his career high, and held them scoreless for 7⅓ innings before he served up a two-run homer. Pedro Martinez pitched a two-hitter to beat him. Smoltz took his place at the top of the Braves rotation, leading the team with 33 starts, 229⅔ innings, and a 1.145 WHIP. He finished 14-7, 3.06. The elbow held up, but he developed pain in his shoulder. He won Game Two of the Division Series against Houston on "pure grit," Schuerholz said.[25] It was the Braves' only postseason victory as their run of division championships finally ended.

Smoltz tied for the NL lead with 16 wins in 2006, followed by 14 the next year. On May 24, 2007, he recorded his 200th career victory when he defeated the Mets. Losing pitcher: Tom Glavine. But shoulder pain sent Smoltz to the disabled list two months later. He opened the 2008 season taking a shot of Novocaine before every start. When he could no longer pitch through the pain, he underwent arthroscopic surgery in June.

Smoltz was determined to keep pitching, but the ball club was no longer willing to gamble on a 42-year-old. Schuerholz offered a contract for 2009 loaded with incentives tied to health and performance. Smoltz's 22 years as a Brave ended with him and Schuerholz barking at each other through the media. For many, his departure turned out the lights on the brightest era in the club's history. "I lost a brother," teammate Chipper Jones said. "If he's retiring, that's one thing. But for him to be playing somewhere else is unacceptable."[26]

Unacceptable or not, it was a fact. Smoltz signed with the Boston Red Sox, even though he wouldn't be able to pitch until June. He interrupted his minor-league rehab stint to get married. He and his first wife had divorced in 2007. His new bride, Kathryn Darden, was a divorcee with two children.

Smoltz joined the Red Sox rotation on June 25. He labored through eight starts, most of them ugly, before Boston released him and his 8.33 ERA. He still refused to quit. The St. Louis Cardinals were willing to give him a shot. In his first start for St. Louis he struck out seven in a row and shut out San Diego for five innings. That was his only victory for the Cardinals, but he pitched well enough to earn a spot on the postseason roster. Relieving in Game Three of the Division Series, he struck out five straight Dodgers in two innings.

The Cardinals did not invite Smoltz back for 2010. He began a new career as a broadcaster with TBS, the television home of the Braves. Later he joined MLB Network and became the lead analyst for Fox Network. He appeared at ease in front of cameras and brought an endless supply of corny jokes. (San Francisco's Candlestick Park was so cold because "there was a Giant fan in every seat.")[27]

One of Smoltz's TV assignments took him to Cooperstown, New York, to cover the induction of Maddux, Glavine, and Cox into baseball's Hall of Fame in 2014. Smoltz followed them into the Hall in 2015, the first year he was eligible. Among the many tributes was this from Bobby Cox: "When John was on the mound, you always thought you were going to win a ballgame."[28]

Sources

Glavine, Tom, with Nick Cafardo. *None but the Braves* (New York: HarperCollins, 1996).

Lopez, Javy, with Gary Caruso. *Behind the Plate: A Catcher's View of the Braves Dynasty* (Chicago: Triumph Books, 2012).

Wilkinson, Jack, with Carroll Rogers. *Game of My Life: Memorable Stories of Braves Baseball* (Champaign, Illinois: Sports Publishing, 2013)

Notes

1. Leo Mazzone and Scott Freeman, *Leo Mazzone's Tales from the Mound* (Champaign, Illinois: Sports Publishing, 2006), 40.
2. The Braves finished second behind Montreal in the strike-shortened 1994 season, when no division champion was crowned.
3. John Smoltz, speech at West Georgia Technical School, Newnan, Georgia. youtube.com/watch?v=UfhuG-uKtJo, accessed February 28, 2015.
4. Ibid.
5. Mark Bowman, "Scouts thrilled they followed tip on Smoltz," mlb.com, January 6, 2015. m.braves.mlb.com/news/article/105722168/scouts-thrilled-they-followed-tip-on-john-smoltz, accessed June 11, 2015.
6. John Smoltz with Don Yeager, *Starting and Closing: Perseverance, Faith, and One More Year* (New York: William Morrow, 2012), 47.
7. Bill Shanks, *Scout's Honor: The Bravest Way to Build a Winning Team* (New York: Sterling & Ross, 2005), 130.
8. Gerry Fraley, "Braves' Alexander Traded to Detroit for Minor Leaguer," *Atlanta Journal-Constitution*, August 13, 1987: C-1.
9. Shanks, 129.
10. Mazzone, 14.
11. Shanks, 137.
12. Smoltz, *Starting and Closing*, 235.
13. centerforwinning.com/.
14. Smoltz, *Starting and Closing*, 237-238.
15. John Feinstein, *Living on the Black* (New York: Little, Brown, 2008), 68.
16. Lindsay Berra, "Off the Diamond, Onto the Fairway," Sports on Earth, May 10, 2015. sportsonearth.com/article/123152242/mlb-players-golf-us-open-john-smoltz-livan-hernandez-chris-sabo-garry-templeton.
17. Mazzone, 55.
18. Charlie Vincent, "'I went through the worst times and now the best times'" *Detroit Free Press*, March 30, 1997: 4-E.
19. Smoltz, *Starting and Closing*, 70.
20. Michael Knisley, "The Unnatural," *The Sporting News*, August 30, 1999: 13.
21. Smoltz press conference, Atlanta, January 6, 2015. accessatlanta.com/videos/news/raw-video-john-smoltz-speaks-on-hall-of-fame/vC9CWn/, accessed June 11, 2015.
22. Smoltz press conference.
23. Tom Verducci, "Atlanta's Endgame Anchored by the Reluctant Closer, John Smoltz," *Sports Illustrated*, August 19, 2001, online archive.
24. Hal Bodley, "Smoltz's unique resume paved way to HOF," mlb.com, January 7, 2015. m.braves.mlb.com/news/article/105863000/hal-bodley-john-smoltzs-unique-resume-paved-way-to-hall-of-fame accessed June 11, 2015.
25. John Schuerholz with Larry Guest, *Built to Win* (New York: Warner Books, 2006), 188.
26. Jeff Schultz, "Smoltz Leaves Braves," *Atlanta Journal-Constitution*, January 9, 2009: D-1.
27. *MLB Central*, MLB Network, June 12, 2015.
28. Bodley, "Smoltz's unique resume."

Mike Stanton

BY NICK WADDELL

Mike Stanton

William Michael Stanton was born on June 2, 1967, in Houston, Texas. His sports path was trending toward football until a blindside block tore his knee cartilage at Midland High School. Stanton was committed to the University of Arkansas, but the school withdrew after the injury. Stanton switched to baseball and was a Texas All-State center fielder. During a tryout for NAIA Southwestern University, Stanton told coaches he could pitch – despite never pitching during high school. The school offered him a scholarship. He eventually transferred to Alvin Junior College (now Alvin Community College) where he was pitching – obviously very successfully – when the Atlanta Braves drafted him in the 13th round in 1987.

The Braves assigned Stanton to the Pulaski Braves of the Rookie-level Appalachian League. Pitching in 15 games, starting 13, he was 4-8 with a 3.24 ERA, but his numbers fail to show Stanton's weak start and strong finish. He began the season 0-5.[1]

Stanton spent most of the 1988 season with the Burlington Braves of the Class-A Midwest League. He was again mostly a starter, starting 23 games in 30 appearances. His stats warranted a promotion to start 1989 at Greenville of the Double-A Southern League, along with a new role. The Braves shifted Stanton to strictly a relief role. He had a 1.58 ERA and 19 saves when he was called up to Triple-A Richmond on July 29. Stanton enjoyed the opportunity to pitch relief. "I like it because I get in more games," he said. "My arm has a quick recovery time. I can throw every day."[2] Stanton made the most of his opportunity in Richmond as well, with eight saves in 13 appearances, and a 0.00 ERA. The Braves took notice and called Stanton up to replace the traded Paul Assenmacher.

The young reliever pitched a scoreless ninth in a 4-1 loss to the Cardinals in his August 24, 1989, major-league debut. Manager Russ Nixon used Stanton in two high-leverage situations against the Cubs. On August 25 Stanton came in to a 3-2 lead with one out in the eighth inning and forced Mark Grace into a foul pop to third. On August 27 he faced two batters in the bottom of the eighth with the Braves leading 2-1. Stanton walked Jerome Walton but got Grace to strike out swinging. Stanton picked up his first save on August 28 by pitching two scoreless innings in a 5-2 win over the Pittsburgh Pirates. The left-hander finished the season with seven saves in eight chances over 20 appearances.

Expectations were high for Stanton heading into the 1990 season. Nixon put his confidence behind Stanton: "Stanton is our number one guy. … I feel confident about Mike Stanton. I don't feel bad about him."[3] The Braves were so high on Stanton that they refused to include him when discussing a trade in late 1989 for Seattle's Jim Presley.[4] The Braves eventually made a deal for Presley, but without including Stanton. Stanton entered the season as the left-handed closer, and with confidence in his fastball/slider combination. "There's no pressure. I just plan to do the same thing I did last year – make them hit the ball and get people out," he said.[5]

Stanton dealt with tendinitis during 1990 spring training, which affected his velocity. He attributed the tendinitis to the shortened spring training caused by the 32-day lockout. Stanton posted an ugly 18.00 ERA through April, and did not appear in the majors again that year. He was first diagnosed with an inflamed rotator cuff and sent to the disabled list in late April.[6] Stanton was kept out of action until June, when he made rehabilitation appearances with Greenville. After feeling discomfort in an appearance, Stanton was held out of action until another rehab appearance in late August. That appearance was Stanton's last; the team shut him down for the season to rest and rehabilitate.

Stanton got off to a hot start in 1991 and did not give up an earned run until May 10. He pitched in a variety of situations and finished the year 5-5 with seven saves and a 2.88 ERA. The solid season continued into the postseason. He made three appearances against the Pittsburgh Pirates in the National League Championship Series, and five appearances against the Minnesota Twins in the World Series. He was the winning pitcher of Game Four in Atlanta, but he saw firsthand the brilliant 10-inning performance by Twins starter Jack Morris in Game Seven. Stanton relieved John Smoltz in the bottom of the eighth. After an intentional walk to Chuck Knoblauch, Stanton got Kent Hrbek to line into an unassisted double play. Stanton gave up two singles to start the bottom of the ninth, but Alejandro Peña was able to prevent those runners from scoring.

Stanton had a difficult 1992. His ERA in May and June was over 8, and he finished with an ERA of 4.10. Manager Bobby Cox used Stanton in a variety of roles throughout the season, and Stanton did not have a defined role. In the postseason he showed his value. In nine game appearances, Stanton did not allow an earned run to the Pirates or the Blue Jays. The Braves fell short of their World Series goal, though, for the second season in a row.

Stanton faced competition entering 1993 from one of Atlanta's top prospects, Mark Wohlers. Wohlers was viewed as a pitcher who got batters from both sides of the plate out, while Stanton was developing a reputation as more of a left-handed specialist. The criticism did not faze Stanton, however. "If I'm on my game, I don't think it matters if a guy's right-handed or left-handed," he said. "If I make my pitches, I'll get guys out."[7] Stanton made his pitches and got guys out. He led the league in saves through May and looked like the pitcher the Braves believed he was in 1990. Stanton believed in himself, too. "[I]t means a lot to me to be leading the league in saves. That is the job people thought I was going to do in 1990, and now things are working out," he said.[8]

The hot start did not last. Stanton lost his closing role to Greg McMichael after failing to show consistency. Stanton understood the move: "It's the penthouse or the outhouse. You either do the job or you give it up. It's as simple as that."[9] He attributed the decline to a mechanical issue. "It's my wrist. It's a matter of a fraction of an inch."[10] Pitching coach Leo Mazzone agreed. "[H]e is going out around the ball instead of getting behind it. … The ball is breaking in to right-handed hitters instead of moving away."[11] The adjustments did not have an immediate impact; Stanton gave up two earned runs in his next outing after those comments and was solidly booed during each home appearance throughout August.

Stanton finished the season strong, however. He broke his thumb in the middle of September but continued to pitch and finished with an ERA of 2.35 for the month. Stanton made only one appearance in the National League Championship Series against the eventual winners, the Philadelphia Phillies. He walked one and gave up a hit, but prevented the Phillies from scoring. The Braves lost the series, but Stanton again showed he could pitch effectively in the postseason.

Before the 1994 season the Braves signed former Baltimore Oriole Gregg Olson to close out games for the Braves. Stanton still viewed himself as a closer, though. He added a changeup in spring training to complement his fastball. He attributed his struggles in late 1993 to one specific game: July 22 against the Pittsburgh Pirates. "It was one of those losses I had a hard time getting rid of. ... 95 percent of relief pitching is having confidence in yourself. If you don't let the shaky times go, bad things are going to happen to you, and I just wouldn't let this one go."[12] Greg McMichael took over the closer role instead of Olson, and Stanton was a trusted setup man. His 3.55 ERA was second best in the Braves bullpen, and he even helped the Braves with his bat. The May 10 game against the Philadelphia Phillies started as a blowout, with the Phillies leading 8-1, until the Braves scored seven in the bottom of the ninth to tie the game. Stanton was called upon to pitch four innings. He was the pitcher of record when, in the bottom of the 15th, he bunted home the winning run with two outs. Although his bat was not called upon to win a game again that season, his pitching helped the Braves stay in the wild-card lead until the lockout halted the season on August 12. The lockout canceled the playoffs and the World Series.

Stanton's contract situation for 1995 was a victim of the lockout. He was nontendered after the 1994 season because of the possibility of a hard salary cap. Once the hard salary cap plan was withdrawn, the Braves tendered him a contract.[13] Stanton reportedly had interest from the Cincinnati Reds and the Baltimore Orioles before Atlanta offered him a deal.

Stanton struggled through the first half of 1995. He figured he was pushing too hard. "I'm not getting away with my mistakes like I have at times before. ... I've made mistakes in pitch selection and pitch location," he said. "And I think at times at home when things go bad, I've been pressing. I just have to sit back and look at things."[14] Things got so bad for Stanton that he was benched for over three weeks without appearing in a game. The Boston Red Sox' failed pursuit of Bret Saberhagen became Stanton's gain. After the Colorado Rockies acquired Saberhagen, the Red Sox turned their attention to their bullpen in an effort to move Rheal Cormier to the rotation.[15] Stanton was acquired by the Red Sox on July 31. He was asked about his struggles through the season, and his response dealt with the fact that Atlanta had a strong rotation and little need for relievers. "I'm a better pitcher than what I've shown but I need to get innings to be an effective reliever. I know they were saying my velocity was down but to me that's just a result of my mechanics being off because of a lack of work."[16] Stanton pitched in 22 games with the Red Sox as a late-innings option in a few high-leverage situations. In those games, Stanton had four holds, one blown save, and one win.

The Red Sox faced the Cleveland Indians in the American League Division Series, which Cleveland swept, 3-0. Stanton appeared only in Game One, but pitched 2⅓ innings of one-hit ball with four strikeouts. Boston wanted to keep the left-handed pitcher in their bullpen, but at a reduced price. Boston offered him a contract worth $750,000, half of his 1995 salary, but Stanton won a contract worth $1.75 million in arbitration.

Stanton began 1996 with the Red Sox, but with the team below .500 and out of playoff contention, it looked to bolster the squad for the next season. The Texas Rangers were making a push for the playoffs, and at the July 31 trade deadline acquired Stanton and a player to be named later (Dwayne Hosey), for right-hander Mark Brandenburg and prospect Kerry Lacy. Stanton was a solid addition to the Rangers bullpen. He pitched 22⅓ innings, mostly as a set-up pitcher. The Rangers won the American League West, but lost to the New York Yankees in the American League Division Series, three games to one. Stanton appeared in three games and pitched well, but he took the loss in Game Two thanks to a wild throw by Rangers third baseman Dean Palmer. After the season the team offered Stanton arbitration, but he declined. Instead, he signed a three-year, $5.45 million deal with the Yankees.

Stanton entered 1997 with a desire to be a closer again. "I want to be the closer. That's where the fame and glory is," he said. "I know I can do the job but it's a matter of an opportunity. … Whatever Joe (Torre) decides, I'll do, but it's my job to make Joe's job as tough as possible."17 The Yankees had let All-Star closer John Wetteland sign with Texas, but Stanton's competition was young Mariano Rivera, who had been a relief pitcher the season before. Stanton pitched well in spring training, but Rivera was named closer and began his journey to the Hall of Fame.

Stanton's Yankees tenure got off to a hot start, except for a rough outing in a loss to the Chicago White Sox on April 20. He left the team in late April to deal with undisclosed family issues, which played a role in the rough outing. Stanton refused to completely blame the family issues, though. "I'm not going to make excuses for anything, but that's not to say it wasn't on my mind the last time out," Stanton told a local newspaper.18 Stanton shook off the effects of the personal issues and pitched to a 2.57 ERA over the season. Because of his effectiveness, Stanton was called upon three times in the Yankees' three-games-to-two Division Series loss to the Cleveland Indians.

Stanton pulled a muscle in his back during spring training in 1998, but he quickly shook off the injury to have an effective start to the season. He picked up a win and four saves in the first month. He was one of the better relievers in May, pitching to a 2.45 ERA with two more wins and five holds. June, however, began three rough months for Stanton. He was suspended in June for hitting Baltimore's Eric Davis. Stanton claimed the ball slid out of his hands, and the situation dictated that Stanton had no reason to hit Davis, but the league saw the incident differently. His original suspension was upheld. Stanton pitched well in September, after the Yankees had acquired veteran Jim Bruske from the San Diego Padres as bullpen insurance.

He was called in against the Cleveland Indians three times in the American League Championship Series. He shut out the Indians in each appearance. His third career trip to the World Series was less than memorable. Stanton made his only appearance against the San Diego Padres in Game Two. The Yankees were leading 9-1 at the time, but Stanton allowed an RBI double to Ruben Rivera, and was charged with another run when Jeff Nelson gave up an RBI single to Mark Sweeney. The Yankees closed out the game and took the World Series by sweeping the Padres.

The 1999 season began disastrously for Stanton with an ERA of 13.50 through the end of April, but he pitched well enough after that to bring it down to 4.33 by the end of the season. The season was marked by Stanton's one and only start in the major leagues. On May 9 vs. the Seattle Mariners, Stanton was called upon to start the game. He provided the Yankees with four innings of two-hit ball. The Yankees went on to win 6-1.

Stanton appeared in three games of the American League Championship Series against his former team, the Red Sox. He faced three batters over three games; he gave up a double, forced a groundout, and walked the third. He was used even more sparingly in the World Series victory over the Atlanta Braves. He struck out the only batter he faced, pinch-hitter Jose Hernandez.

After the season, Stanton re-signed with the Yankees for another three years. The 2001 campaign was the best season of Stanton's career. He was 9-4 with a 2.58 ERA out of the bullpen, and was named to his only All-Star Game. Stanton's hot start to the season carried him through, although the left-hander had an ERA of 4.76 for August and September. He attributed the decline in his performance to arm fatigue.[19] The season was not without controversy, however. Stanton got himself into hot water with the media and the public after the tragic events of September 11. The Mets were providing aid and support to the grieving community, to which Stanton opined that the Mets were engaged in a "PR ploy."[20] His comments were criticized throughout the country.

Stanton did continue his postseason brilliance, despite a rough American League Championship Series against the Seattle Mariners. He pitched three perfect outings against the Oakland A's in the Division Series, including a Game Five win, and was strong in five appearances against the eventual World Series champion Arizona Diamondbacks.

Stanton made his last postseason appearance in 2002, ending his 11-year run (minus the 1994 cancelation of the playoffs). Stanton was roughed up in the Division Series by the eventual World Series champion Anaheim Angels. He gave up three runs in 2⅔ innings of work. Even with the rough postseason, Stanton finished his postseason career with a 5-2 record and a 2.10 ERA.

Stanton signed a two-year deal with the New York Mets after the season, largely due to the Yankees' negotiating tactics. Reports state that the Yankees gave Stanton, Florida Marlins pitcher Chris Hammond, and Mets pitcher Mark Guthrie the same offer (two years, $4.46 million) and 15 minutes to respond. The pitcher who responded first would receive the contract, while the other two would be left out.[21] The 2003 and 2004 seasons were opposite: Stanton pitched in just 50 games for the Mets in 2003, largely due to missing a month because of a sore knee. He bounced back with a career-high 83 appearances in 2004, and a 3.16 ERA.

Stanton returned to the Yankees for the 2005 season, but the reunion ended when the Yankees designated him for assignment in late June. Stanton was ineffective and had an ERA over 7 when he was cut loose. The Washington Nationals signed him as some bullpen insurance. His tenure with the club got off to a rocky start. In the bottom of the 10th inning of a tied game against the Milwaukee Brewers, Stanton relieved Luis Ayala, who left the game with runners at the corners. Before throwing an official pitch, Stanton was called for a balk, forcing in the winning run. The rest of his 2005 tenure with the club was positive, and he finished his time in the capital with an ERA of 3.58. In a rare late-September move, the Red Sox acquired Stanton for the last series of the season, against the Yankees. The Red Sox were one game back of the Yankees in the division and tied for the wild card with the Cleveland Indians. Stanton pitched in only one game, an 8-4 loss to the Yankees. The Red Sox reached the postseason, but since he was traded after the eligibility deadline, he could not be part of their playoff run.

Stanton re-signed with the Washington Nationals before the 2006 season. He pitched well for the Nationals except for a few bad outings against Florida, Colorado, and Cincinnati. The Giants were impressed enough to swing a trade to make a push toward a wild-card berth. Stanton pitched to a 3.09 ERA with the Giants, but it was not enough for the club to make the postseason.

The Cincinnati Reds signed Stanton before 2007 to improve their bullpen. His season started with eight straight appearances without giving up a run. A bad outing against Philadelphia late in April previewed a difficult May, when opponents hit .365 off him. Stanton did get his ERA down to just under 4.00 in mid-July, but the roller-coaster outings wreaked havoc on his stats. Stanton ended 2007 with an ERA of 5.93. His troubles were compounded when he was named in the December 2007 Mitchell Report as having bought Human

Growth Hormones (HGH). Stanton vehemently denied the allegations.

The left-hander sat out 2008 but was invited to spring training with the Chicago Cubs in 2009. A rocky spring (6.48 ERA in 8⅓ innings) made him an easy cut. Stanton retired as a player shortly after being cut.

The left-hander spent 2010 as the varsity baseball coach for Don Bosco Preparatory High School in Ramsey, New Jersey. After the season, Stanton stepped down. He began making appearances on SiriusXM's *MLB Radio Network* as a postseason analyst in 2011. These appearances led Comcast SportsNet Houston to contact him in 2013 regarding an in-studio analyst position. Stanton accepted, and as of 2020 has been an in-studio analyst for the team ever since.

Sources

In addition to the sources cited in the Notes, the author relied on Baseball-Reference.com and Baseball-Almanac.com.

Notes

1 "Pulaski Blanks O's," *Kingsport* (Tennessee) *Times-News*, July 30, 1987.

2 Tom Whitfield, "Stanton Earns Promotion with Record-Breaking AA Relief Work," *Atlanta Constitution*, July 30, 1989.

3 Joe Strauss, "Giants Obtain Reliever Alvarez in Winter Draft," *Atlanta Constitution*, December 5, 1989.

4 Joe Strauss, "Braves Obtain Jim Presley for Eave, Pennington," *Atlanta Constitution*, January 25, 1990.

5 "Nothing Fazes Braves' New Rookie Reliever," Associated Press, April 4, 1990.

6 Joe Strauss, "Stanton on DL with Inflamed Rotator Cuff," *Atlanta Constitution*, April 29, 1990.

7 Mark Bradley, "Stanton Merits Shot," *Atlanta Constitution*, February 28, 1993.

8 I.J. Rosenberg, "Closing the Door," *Atlanta Constitution*, April 23, 1993.

9 I.J. Rosenberg, "Stanton Sits, Watches McMichael's 2nd Save," *Atlanta Constitution*, July 31, 1993.

10 I.J. Rosenberg, "Stanton Finds Fastball Flaw While Watching Videotape," *Atlanta Constitution*, August 5, 1993.

11 I.J. Rosenberg, "Stanton Finds Fastball Flaw."

12 Terence Moore, "After Horrors of '93, Stanton Working on Mental Rehabilitation," *Atlanta Constitution*, March 24, 1994.

13 I.J. Rosenberg, "With Cap Off, Stanton Gets New Offer," *Atlanta Constitution*, March 7, 1995.

14 I.J. Rosenberg, "Stanton's Slumps Are Annual Occurrence," *Atlanta Constitution*, June 25, 1995.

15 Nick Cafardo, "Stanton Deal Should Spin Cormier into the Rotation," *Boston Globe*, August 2, 1995.

16 Cafardo.

17 John Giannone, "Camping Out," *New York Daily News*, February 16, 1997.

18 John Giannone, "Flashes," *New York Daily News*, May 8, 1997.

19 Anthony McCarron, "August's End Will Be Relief for Stanton," *New York Daily News*, August 28, 2001.

20 Roger Rubin, "Stanton Says 9/11 Flap Is History," *New York Daily News*, December 19, 2002.

21 Bill Madden and Anthony McCarron, "Stanton Left Out as Brave Looms," *New York Daily News*, December 7, 2002.

Tom Thobe

BY J. SCOTT SHAFFER

Tom Thobe

Mild temperatures and the consistent sunshine of Southern California have helped young baseball players gain an advantage over prospects from other areas of the country. Yet, the accommodating weather comes with a cost as baseball competes with many other outdoor activities that attract young prospects. For 18-year-old Tom Thobe of Huntington Beach, surfing and skateboarding challenged his passion for baseball.[1] Thus, when Thobe was drafted in June of 1987, he needed to choose between the Pacific waves or moving to Wytheville, Virginia, for his baseball career. After a year, Thobe quit baseball and moved back to California.

As stated by sportswriter John Weyler, "Pitchers who quit the rookie leagues and don't touch a baseball for three years aren't exactly what the scouts are looking for."[2] After three years of full-time employment, skateboarding, surfing, and partying, Tom Thobe began to think about his future.[3] How would he support a family? What was his role in life? Each time he came back to the same conclusion: baseball. Through hard work and a strong support network, Thobe beat the odds and made his major-league debut in 1995 at the age of 25. While his major-league career lasted only a cumulative seven games across two seasons, his baseball experience emphasized the value of resiliency.

Thobe was born in Covington, Kentucky, on September 3, 1969, to Blanche (Lynch) and Jack Thobe. After moving to the West Coast to Huntington Beach, he played high-school baseball for Edison High School, a sports-centric school that has produced multiple professional baseball players including Dale Thayer, Donnie Hill, and Jeff Kent.[4] In 1988 Thobe pitched for the Golden West College Rustlers, 115 innings in 17 games, with a 10-3 record and a 4.30 ERA under coach Fred Hoover.[5] Having been drafted by the Chicago Cubs in the 38th round of the 1987 amateur draft, Thobe decided to leave college ball in May of 1988 by signing the $30,000 bonus and headed for the club's rookie league team.[6]

At age 18, Thobe made his minor-league debut with the Wytheville Cubs. By midseason, he was struggling. He failed to generate strikes from his curveball, leading to an ERA of 8.95, and walked 30 batters while giving up 10 home runs in 57⅓ innings.[7] While competition can be challenging for new players, Thobe's biggest challenge came from himself. As he stated, "I really missed the beach and the whole beach lifestyle. I was young and rebellious and when they told me to stop skateboarding, I just sort of told them where to stick it and kept doing it. Everything was catching up with me and I was ready to get a full-time job and chuck it."[8] His mother blamed his age, saying he was too young and "intimidated by the older players and pro ball."[9] Thobe finished the first season and returned the following spring for minor-league training camp. However, after seeing his workload diminish and receiving his assignment back to Wytheville, Thobe decided to quit, fearing that he could "be buried in the system."[10] He also offered, "Looking back, I didn't really want to be there and everyone knew it, so there was a lot of friction all around. And the main thing was, I just wanted to surf."[11]

Thobe returned home to California, where he was able to pursue his passion for surfing and skateboarding recalling, "when I first came home, I surfed all day and worked at night, making sandwiches."[12] He was finally doing what he dreamed about during his time in Virginia. After a few years of surfing, partying, and working monotonous jobs, the lure of the ocean began to run out. He began by experimenting with drugs and was later arrested for shoplifting.[13] His perspective on life began to change after he met Jennifer Herrmann and began to question how he would support a family.[14] As a 23-year-old without a college education or significant work training, Thobe reverted to what he excelled in during his youth: baseball.

Thobe knew the path back to professional baseball would not be easy. Having learned from his previous minor-league experience, he knew he would have to train physically and mentally to succeed.[15] For his physical workouts, he enlisted the help of his brother J.J. Thobe, a right-handed pitcher who had just been drafted by the Cleveland Indians in 1992.[16] His workouts consisted of running and pitching during pickup baseball games in the area.[17] Mentally, he began reading Anthony Robbins.[18] Robbins, a motivational speaker and philanthropist, emphasized the important pillars in life to include physical health, relationships, emotions, and finances and has been a mentor for influential leaders ranging from President Bill Clinton to Los Angeles Dodgers owner Peter Guber.[19]

Thobe learned about his first opportunity to pitch when his mother mentioned that pro scouts were hosting a tryout at Orange Coast College.[20] He participated in the tryout, but his 86-mph fastball and breaking curveball failed to impress scouts.[21] However, the event did reunite him with his former Golden West College coach, Fred Hoover. Hoover, an inductee into the Community College Baseball Hall of Fame, was one of the most winning coaches in Golden West College history, posting 12 conference championships before becoming the coach of the University of California Irvine.[22] Hoover felt that Thobe should have turned down the Cubs' offer in 1987, saying, "Tom was always a pain in the ass that way. … I think signing was a mistake, but then isn't it for almost all of them? This kid going from Huntington Beach to live in Virginia at 18 years old? C'mon."[23] However, Thobe's performance during the tryout made an impression on Hoover, leading his former coach to take a more active role in his career reboot. Hoover invited Thobe to pitch in the Golden West alumni game and later set up a one-on-one tryout for him.[24] During the tryout, Thobe capitalized on the opportunity, throwing an 88-mph fastball and breaking curveball.[25] Steve Youngward, the local area scout for the Atlanta Braves, liked what he was seeing from the 6-foot-6 lefty and within a week he was off to Braves spring training, receiving his assignment to Class-A ball with the Macon Braves in 1993.[26]

Being given a second chance in the minors thanks to the efforts of his old coach, Thobe continued to leverage mentors. Jim Acker, a 10-year veteran with stints in Toronto, Atlanta, and Seattle, had just been sent to the Macon Braves. Thobe roomed with Acker and began to learn as much as he could from the veteran. As Thobe said, "Before, I just threw it. Jim taught me more than I could've learned in five years of pitching. We talked nonstop about pitching."[27] Specifically, Acker taught Thobe how to throw a slider, as well as strategies for mixing pitches.[28] Acker's mentorship proved valuable to Thobe's success in Macon. Thobe moved up to Double A in 1994 and Triple A in 1995, planting himself as a reliable reliever. By the time he received his first call-up, in mid-September, Thobe was 7-0 with a 1.84 ERA.[29]

In his first major-league appearance, on September 12, Thobe faced the Colorado Rockies in the bottom of the third inning. After forcing a fly out to end the inning, Thobe returned in the next inning with sluggers Dante Bichette and Andres Galarraga due to bat. After allowing a single to Bichette, Thobe got three straight outs to exit the inning unscathed. His next game came seven days later in front of the home crowd. With the Braves trailing the Mets 4-0, Thobe came into the game in the top of the sixth, facing Rico Brogna. After generating a fly ball from Brogna and a groundout from Todd Hundley, Thobe allowed a single to Butch Huskey before getting the last out of the inning on a lineout by Alex Ochoa. Thobe continued into the seventh inning, but allowed two singles to Dave Mlicki and Damon Buford before being turning the game over to Brad Clontz as the Mets scored four runs in the inning. Thobe's final game of the season came against the Mets in Shea Stadium. He replaced Pedro Borbon to start the bottom of the eighth inning with Atlanta trailing the Mets, 6-4. Facing his first three batters, Thobe allowed two runs to score, on a single by Joe Orsulak, a double by Chris Jones, and a two-run single by Jose Vizcaino. Though he had faced only 17 batters in 3⅓ innings with the Braves (with a 10.80 ERA), Thobe had impressed the team and earned praise from Macon Braves manager Randy Ingle, who said, "You'd think that after all that time away from the game he would be very rusty, but he's been incredibly sharp. Every time I've called on him, he's done an outstanding job."[30]

Tom's brother, J.J., made it to the majors in September 1995 and appeared in four games with the Montreal Expos. On September 22 he pitched the bottom of the eighth against the Braves in Atlanta, retiring the side in the order in a game the Braves won, 5-1. Tom watched from the bullpen but the two never appeared in the same game. J.J. pitched for the Columbus Red Stixx (South Atlantic League) in 1996, his final season in Organized Baseball.

Tom Thobe started the 1996 season with Triple-A Richmond. However, by early April, he was back on a major-league mound and off to a good start against the Los Angeles Dodgers. Entering the game in the bottom of the seventh, Thobe got three quick outs from two fly outs and a groundout. Three days later he faced the San Diego Padres. After retiring the side in the bottom of the seventh, Thobe returned in the eighth inning and allowed a Brad Ausmus single before forcing Jody Reed to hit into a double play. In his third appearance, against the Padres at home on the 21st, Thobe entered the game in the top of the 14th and faced four batters, allowing only a single. In the top of the 15th, after giving up a leadoff single to Rickey Henderson, he induced both of the next two batters to ground back to him and both times made an error. Henderson scored on a sacrifice fly and San Diego took a 2-1 lead. They were the only two fielding chances of his career; Thobe thus sports a career fielding percentage of .000. That is also his career batting average.

In an interview with *Orange County Register*, Thobe recounted his one plate appearance, stepping up to bat in the bottom of the 15th with a runner in scoring position and two outs. With no other batters left to substitute, manager Bobby Cox signaled to Thobe to take pitches and possibly draw a walk. However, Thobe missed the signs amid the noise and pressure, took a swing and grounded out to second, ending the Braves' chance to come back.[31] His last appearance on the mound in the big leagues came four days later, on April 25 at San Francisco. Steve Scarsone hit a home run off Thobe in the Giants' 8-0 victory.

Returned to Triple-A Richmond, Thobe struggled to generate strikeouts and saw his ERA and WHIP increase to 6.13 and 1.750 respectively. Furthermore, he was aging. The next season, 1997, he turned 27 years old, did not receive any call-ups to the majors, and was let go by the Braves organization. Thobe played for the Cincinnati Reds' Double-A affiliate in Chattanooga in 1998 before spending his last two seasons in baseball playing for independent-league teams including the Allentown Ambassadors and the Sonoma County Crushers.

After hanging up the spikes, Thobe returned to Orange County, California, where he worked in the hotel industry for 12 years before joining Ben's Asphalt of Santa Ana as a project manager.[32] The company leveraged Thobe's baseball experience with success when it negotiated a contract with the Angels to resurface the stadium parking lot.[33] Thobe continued to support the baseball community by participating in the MLB Players Alumni Association Legends for Youth baseball clinics in Southern California.[34]

Thobe's career illustrates the level of effort, commitment, and support required to advance in professional baseball. He worked hard, both mentally and physically, and was fortunate to have support from his old coach, Fred Hoover, and seasoned veterans like Jim Acker. Thobe recalled the feeling of entering a major-league locker room for his first game. "I walked into the locker room the first time, and my jersey was hanging between [Steve] Avery's and [Greg] Maddux's. That was amazing."[35] The *Orange County Register* noted that his appearances were "seven more than if he'd never tried," and more importantly, Thobe learned the value of "never giving up."[36]

Sources

In addition to the sources cited in the Notes, the author also consulted Baseball-Reference.com.

Notes

1. John Weyler, "Thobe Makes Most of Second Chance: Former Edison High and Golden West Pitcher is Back in the Minor Leagues with a Different Attitude," *Los Angeles Times*, May, 13, 1993, retrieved from latimes.com/archives/la-xpm-1993-05-13-sp-34950-story.html.
2. Weyler.
3. Weyler.
4. "Edison High School," Baseball Cube. Retrieved from thebaseballcube.com/hs/profile.asp?ID=1632#Alumni.
5. "Golden West College 1988 Baseball Statistics." Retrieved from gwcathletics.com/sports/bsb/archive_files/stats/1988_Baseball_Team_Results.pdf.
6. Weyler.
7. Weyler.
8. Weyler.
9. Weyler.
10. Weyler.
11. Weyler.
12. Weyler.
13. Weyler.
14. Weyler.
15. Frank Mickadeit, "Tom Thobe: Big League Mound to Big A Lot," *Orange County Register* (Anaheim, California), March 22, 2012, retrieved from ocregister.com/2012/03/22/tom-thobe-big-league-mound-to-big-a-lot/.
16. Weyler.
17. Mickadeit.
18. Mickadeit.
19. Mickadeit.
20. Mickadeit.
21. Mickadeit.
22. "Legendary GWC Baseball Coach Fred Hoover Dies at Age 81," *Rustler Athletics*, June, 25, 2012, retrieved from gwcathletics.com/sports/bsb/2011-12/releases/20120625s008vf.
23. Weyler.
24. Weyler.
25. Mickadeit.
26. Mickadeit.
27. Weyler.
28. Weyler.
29. Mickadeit.
30. Weyler

31 Mickadeit.

32 Mickadeit.

33 Mickadeit.

34 "Major League Players Alumni Association Brings Legends for Youth Baseball Clinic Series to San Diego," *Cision News*, September, 24, 2015, retrieved from news.cision.com/major-league-baseball-players-alumni-association/r/major-league-baseball-players-alumni-association-brings-legends-for-youth-baseball-clinic-series-to-,c9835503.

35 Mickadeit.

36 Mickadeit.

Terrell Wade

BY BILL JOHNSON

Terrell Wade

The 1991 Atlanta Braves were a team on the rise. Despite, or perhaps as a result of, their moribund performance in the late 1980s, when the team won no more than 72 games in a season and finished no higher than fifth place in the National League West Division, owner Ted Turner overhauled the club's leadership. Notably, he brought in a new general manager, John Schuerholz, who in turn invigorated the organization's scouting enterprise. One of his ascendant scouts, Roy Clark, was empowered to conduct regional tryout camps in hopes of unearthing a few promising nuggets of talent. In one of these camps, Clark discovered an 18-year-old left-handed pitcher with only two years of high school baseball experience, Terrell Wade.

In a plot line seemingly plucked from Clint Eastwood's film *Trouble with the Curve*, in which a lucky scout finds a talented gem in the backwoods of North Carolina, Wade went on to star in the Braves' minor-league system. After several years climbing the minor-league ziggurat, he reached the major leagues in 1995, when he made three appearances for the eventual World Series champions. Wade pitched in the major leagues for three more injury-plagued seasons, and in the minors until 2006, but it was his brief cup of coffee with the 1995 team that netted him a championship ring and a small niche in Atlanta Braves history.

Hawatha Terrell Wade was born on January 25, 1973, in tiny Rembert, South Carolina, the second child of Horace and Francis Mae Wade.[1] Wade's father owned a store near Rembert for a while, but generally earned his living by doing odd jobs throughout the region. Terrell had an older brother, Sherman, and younger siblings, brother Travis and sister Shemikia.[2] Always an athlete, Wade grew up loving basketball and swimming,[3] as well as baseball, the sport at which he truly excelled.

Rembert is a small community near the city of Sumter, and not far from the South Carolina state capital, Columbia, but did not have its own school district. Wade attended Hillcrest High School, but played baseball only in his senior season. According to Hillcrest teammate Brian Benenhaley, "He was a really good athlete. (He) only played baseball in high school one year. His fastball sat around 82-83."[4] According to Benenhaley, the team was not very talented, but Wade "made the team competitive when he pitched."[5] Despite pitching a two-hitter against the much larger Sumter High school, Rell, as he was called by his classmates, was not scouted by any professional team. After graduation, in May 1991, though, the left-hander decided to take his shot.

"I had taken two courses in masonry, and that's what I was going to do," Wade said in discussing why he decided to attend a Braves tryout camp in Sumter.[6] He had played American Legion ball in 1991, in addition to high school, and his coach "told me that I should go out there because I had everything to gain."[7] Wade, by then a 6-foot-3 a lefty with a fastball that had accelerated to the 92-93 MPH range, immediately snared the eye of Roy Clark. Chuck LaMar, then the Braves' director of scouting and player personnel, said in 1994, "I think our scout Roy called me from a pay phone. He said, 'I have a young man we need to sign immediately.'"[8] LaMar further reflected: "Roy Clark covers the Carolinas for us and covers it as good as any scout in baseball and yet he missed him (at first). So we're not patting ourselves on the back. These (tryout-camp discovery) stories are getting fewer and fewer. But they still happen, and it shows what an inexact science judging talent can be."[9]

Unmarried when he signed, Wade did have a four-month-old daughter, Tyresse Chantal. So the $5,000 signing bonus was an immediate paycheck. The pitcher did not disappoint his new team, going 2-0 and striking out 22 with the Braves' Rookie Gulf Coast League squad in Bradenton, Florida. He spent the next year, 1992, in Idaho Falls of the Rookie Pioneer League, where he managed an ERA of only 6.44, but still whiffed 54 batters in 50⅓ innings. That potential earned him a promotion to Macon in the low Class-A South Atlantic League, for 1993. There, Wade emerged as an elite prospect.

He posted an 8-2 mark with Macon, with a 1.73 ERA and 121 strikeouts in 83⅓ innings. He was the league's Pitcher of the Week in June (14-20) and Macon Pitcher of the Month in May, and was named the SAL's top prospect by *Baseball America*.[10] After a midsummer promotion to high Class-A Durham, he was named Carolina League Pitcher of the Week for July 4-10. Wade tossed only 33 innings for the Bulls before being promoted again, this time to Greenville of the Southern League, where he earned his first Double-A victory by throwing a four-hit shutout against Chattanooga on August 12. After the season, Wade received the Phil Niekro Award as the top pitcher in the team's minor-league system, and – despite having departed in July – was named Macon's Player of the Year.

Wade married fiancée Frances Regina during the offseason, but the marriage did not last. On the diamond, though, life was easier. Entering the 1994 season, *Baseball America* made Wade the 29th-ranked prospect in all of baseball, and the fifth-best prospect in the Southern League. With Greenville, he was named the team's Pitcher of the Month in May, after he posted a 3-1 record with a 3.35 ERA, and was named to the Southern League All-Star game. Wade was promoted to Triple-A Richmond on August 13, and won his International League debut, 6-2, over the Toledo Mud Hens. He was 2-2 in four starts for Richmond. Of note, he had held hitters to a .130 batting average (3-for-23) with runners in scoring position.[11] He was invited to major-league spring training in 1995.

On May 1, 1995, Wade reported back to Richmond as *Baseball America*'s number-54 overall prospect. He was named International League Player of the Week May 28-June 3. On August 31, the Braves summoned him to Atlanta, but he was optioned back to Richmond after one game. He was called up on September 10, and he debuted on the 12th, in a two-inning relief appearance against the Colorado Rockies in Denver. He entered in the fifth inning with the Braves trailing 7-1. The first batter Wade faced, slugger Vinny Castilla, homered, but the rookie then got Walt Weiss to ground out, struck out Lance Painter, and got Eric Young to ground to third to end the frame. He followed that with a clean sixth inning, erasing Joe Girardi, Dante Bichette, and Trent Hubbard on a total of six pitches.[12] Wade pitched only two more innings that month. On the last day of the season he was the losing pitcher as the Braves lost to the Mets in 11 innings.

In the afterglow of the 1995 World Series, the Braves invited Wade to big-league camp again, and this time, the phenom was ready. "I feel that it's my year," he said. "In spring training, I need to prove to them that I'm ready. I got the stuff that can get me there."[13] With his occasional wildness controlled, Wade battled a young Jason Schmidt for the fifth spot in the starting rotation. After a spot start on July 24 in which Wade dominated the Cardinals in a 4-1 win, the team made the appointment official, noting that he would be still be "used out of the bullpen until a fifth starter is needed during the first three weeks of August."[14] In the win over the Cardinals, Wade was called on to fill in for an injured Steve Avery, and followed John Smoltz's outing the previous evening in which the future Hall of Famer allowed only five hits in eight innings. "I had some big shoes to fill," Wade said after the game.[15] Wade went only five innings, but mixed a 95-MPH fastball with a slider and a changeup while allowing only one unearned run and two hits, and struck out eight. His team was impressed. Catcher Javy Lopez observed, "We heard a lot about Terrell in the minor leagues. Once he came up, he made us a believer because he's been a really good relief pitcher. Now, he showed us he could be a starter."[16]

The 1996 campaign was the best of Wade's professional pitching career. In 44 games, including eight starts, over 69⅔ innings, he logged a 5-0 record with a 2.97 ERA and 79 strikeouts. The Braves repeated as National League champions, but fell to the Yankees in six games in the World Series. Wade pitched in relief in two of the games, logging two-thirds of an inning and giving up a walk.

In 1997 Wade began to fade. Weighing upward of 235 pounds,[17] he was being considered by manager Bobby Cox as his fifth starter.[18] "He's as thin as he'll be his whole life. He's just a big kid," said Cox. (Last year) he had one or two games where he got a little wild. Other than that, without him, I don't think we win the division."[19] By early June, though, Cox was frustrated with Wade's inconsistency. "I know he can do better. He pitched good last year. This year? In spots, he's looked good, but he's not consistent right now."[20] On June 9, the reason for Wade's problems emerged, when he was diagnosed with a torn flexor in his left elbow. After almost two months of rest, he was sent to Double-A Greenville to pitch 15 innings before returning to Atlanta.[21] His Southern League trip was not successful; a 4.97 ERA in 12⅔ innings. Wade was exposed in the expansion draft after the season, and was selected by Tampa Bay. It was probably no coincidence that Chuck LaMar was the Devil Rays' first general manager.[22]

Wade spent most of the 1998 season in the minors, with St. Petersburg and Durham, and did not appear in a game for Tampa Bay until September 21, when he started against the Boston Red Sox, threw five innings, struck out six, and allowed three earned runs while earning the victory. He final major-league appearance came September 26, in New York against the Yankees, where he took the loss after giving up three runs on nine hits in 5⅔ innings. Overall he pitched in 61 major league games and 126⅓ innings. He struck out 125, won eight games, lost five, and earned a single save. He also had a World Series ring to commemorate his experience.

The Devil Rays sent Wade to Durham in 1999. It would be difficult to imagine a worse season for the pitcher. He gave up 21 home runs and 104 earned runs in 98⅔ innings, which earned him his outright release. The Cincinnati Reds signed him and sent him to Double-A Chattanooga, along with a brief stop at Triple-A Louisville, but Wade's time in Organized Baseball was through. In 2003 he was 3-3 for the Macon Peaches of the independent Southeastern League. In 2004 he went 3-2 with the Pennsylvania Road Warriors and the Atlantic City Surf of the independent Atlantic League, and in 2006 he was 1-1 with the Nashua Pride of the independent Canadian-American League.

After that 2006 season, though, Wade retired from professional baseball. Now married to Nicky (Stokes), in 2019 he lived in the Atlanta area and owned a plumbing and electrical supply business. He has occasionally surfaced at autograph signings.[23]

Notes

1. Howe Sports Data International questionnaire, submitted by Terrell Wade and dated August 30, 1991. Howe Sports Data International, Inc., Boston.
2. Interview with Travis Wade, May 1, 2019, Rembert, South Carolina.
3. Howe questionnaire.
4. Interview with Brian Benenhaley, April 26, 2019.
5. Benenhaley interview.
6. I.J. Rosenberg, "The Find: Got Wade in a Tryout," *Atlanta Constitution*, February 23, 1994: 19.
7. "The Find."
8. "The Find."
9. I.J. Rosenberg, "Braves Find Million Dollar Arm for $5,000," *Atlanta Constitution*, February 23, 1994: 17.
10. *Atlanta Braves Media Guide*, 1996, 345. Baseball America rankings corroborated by Baseball Reference, online at: baseball-reference.com/register/player.fcgi?id=wade--001haw (accessed May 15, 2019).
11. *Atlanta Braves Media Guide*, 1996, 345.
12. Game account from Baseball Reference: baseball-reference.com/boxes/COL/COL199509120.shtml, accessed May 2, 2019.
13. Thomas Stinson, "Wade Seeks Combination to Break In," *Atlanta Constitution*, February 25, 1996: 81.
14. Thomas Stinson, "Wade Tagged," *The Sporting News*, August 5, 1996: 12.
15. Mike Eisenbath, "Braves Rookie Pitcher Wade Slips Into Big Shoes, Finds Them Snug," *St. Louis Post-Dispatch*, July 25, 1996: D-3.
16. Eisenbath.
17. Thomas Stinson, "Wade Mustn't Fade," *Atlanta Constitution*, February 26, 1997: 20.
18. "Taking the Fifth," *The Sporting News*, March 17, 1997: 33.
19. Stinson, "Wade Mustn't Fade."
20. Jack Wilkinson, "Wade's Inconsistency Frustrating Cox," *Atlanta Constitution*, June 8, 1997: E-9.
21. Jack Wilkinson, "Terrell Goes," *Atlanta Constitution*, July 21, 1997: 21.
22. Jack Wilkinson, "Devil Rays," *The Sporting News*, January 5, 1998: 67.
23. Interview with Travis Wade, May 1, 2019.

Mark Wohlers

BY TOM HUFFORD

Mark Wohlers

Most high-school or college pitchers with dreams of a major-league career think about pitching in the World Series, an All-Star Game, hurling a no-hitter, or getting a strikeout to end a big game. Besides these, Mark Wohlers had something else on his mind while growing up – throwing a pitch 100 miles an hour in a big-league game!

Mark Edward Wohlers was born in Holyoke, Massachusetts, on January 23, 1970, the second child of Frederick G. and Irene Kobylanski Wohlers. Fred, a welder, and Irene, a factory worker, divorced when Mark was 9 years old, and he and his sister, Cindy, were raised primarily by their mother. At age 14, Mark began working the 4-to-midnight shift as a dishwasher at Mel's Restaurant, where 16-year-old Cindy was the cashier. He later moved up to busboy, before working his way through high school as a sandwich maker at the local Subway shop.

Mark fashioned a standout career with the Holyoke High School Purple Knights baseball team, highlighted by a no-hitter his junior year, and when not on the mound as a senior, he hit .420 while holding down first base. He was named to the All-Western (Massachusetts) Conference team in 1987 and 1988.

After graduation, Wohlers was selected by the Atlanta Braves in the eighth round of the June 1988 amateur draft. Although he had already agreed to attend the University of Maine to pitch for the Black Bears, he changed his mind when the Braves came calling. He quickly signed, and was sent to the Braves' Appalachian (Rookie) League club in Pulaski, Virginia. Wohlers appeared in 13 games with Pulaski, nine as a starter, posting a 5-3 record with a 3.32 ERA. In 59⅔ innings, Wohlers struck out 49 batters, but walked 50. His best outing was a 3-2 complete-game three-hitter against the Martinsville Phillies, in the second game of a July 11 doubleheader. The effort may have been overlooked by many fans, however; in the first game, Braves first-round draft pick Steve Avery pitched five innings of a 5-0 shutout in his professional debut.[1]

Wohlers moved up to the Braves' Sumter team in the low Class-A South Atlantic League for 1989, but the wildness that plagued him the previous season followed him to South Carolina. In 14 starts for Sumter, the best he could do was to fashion a 2-7 record and a 6.49 ERA, with 51 strikeouts in 68 innings, while allowing 74 hits and 59 walks. When the Appalachian League began play in mid-June, Wohlers was sent back to Pulaski, specifically to work with pitching coach Matt West, who had just completed an eight-year minor-league career, mostly in the Braves system. In eight starts and six relief appearances, Wohlers still struggled, giving up 48 hits in 46 innings, but his control was much better, with only 28 walks to go with 50 strikeouts.

For the beginning of the 1990 season, Wohlers moved back to Sumter, where his Pulaski pitching coach West had joined manager Ned Yost's staff. Based on Wohlers' turnaround work the final half of the previous season, especially his averaging more than one strikeout per inning, Yost and West moved him to the bullpen. Something clicked, and suddenly Wohlers dominated the South Atlantic League, with 85 strikeouts in 52⅔ innings while surrendering only 27 hits and 20 walks. That was enough to earn a late-season promotion to Atlanta's Double-A team in Greenville, South Carolina, where he picked up where he had left off, with another 20 K's in 15⅔ innings. His overall season's work totaled 105 strikeouts against only 34 walks in 68⅓ innings, with a 2.37 ERA.

Wohlers was chosen to receive the 1990 Phil Niekro Award, given annually by the Braves to the outstanding minor-league pitcher in their organization. Before the award was presented at the annual awards banquet of the Braves 400 Club (the team's booster club) in January, he was asked if there was anything special that he would look forward to once he reached the major leagues, and he replied, "It would be a dream come true to throw a pitch 100 miles per hour in a major-league game!"[2]

The 1990 season had been a pivotal one for the Braves at the major-league level. Coming off two consecutive last-place finishes, the club wasn't expected to do much, and it didn't. John Smoltz, with 14 victories, and Tom Glavine, with 10, were the only pitchers to post double-digit wins. The outfield was decent, with Lonnie Smith, Ron Gant, and longtime franchise favorite Dale Murphy. The team's only representative on the National League All-Star team was catcher Greg Olson, who started the season with the Richmond Braves, and whose entire major-league career had consisted of two at-bats with the Minnesota Twins the previous year. Bobby Cox had come down from the front office to take over the managerial reins from Russ Nixon in mid-June and began making some changes with an eye to the future. Lefty Steve Avery was called up from the minors to join Smoltz, Glavine, and Charlie Leibrandt in the starting rotation, and Murphy was traded to Philadelphia to allow Dave Justice, in the midst of a Rookie-of-the-Year season, to move from first base to right field. The team finished the season in last place once again, and clearly there was still need for improvement.

Opportunities would abound in 1991. John Schuerholz had come over from Kansas City to take the position of general manager of the Braves, and was impressed with the young pitching in the team's minor-league system. But he knew that for the team to be successful, the defense had to be improved, so he imported first baseman Sid Bream, third baseman Terry Pendleton, shortstop Rafael Belliard, and outfielders Otis Nixon and Deion Sanders. The only pitchers he added during the offseason, however, were relievers Randy St. Claire and Juan Berenguer. Additional help on the mound would have to come from within the Braves system, and Mark Wohlers had every intention of taking advantage of his opportunity.

Wohlers started the season with a bang at Greenville, managed by former Braves first baseman Chris Chambliss, and was nearly unhittable. Put into the closer's role, he showed that he was making progress on the control problems that had been plaguing him. In 28 games, covering 31⅓ innings, he allowed only nine hits and 13 walks, with 44 strikeouts. He tallied 21 saves out of the bullpen, and his 0.57 ERA was the lowest on the staff among those with at least five innings pitched. That was good enough to earn him a promotion up I-85 to the Braves' Richmond, Virginia, Triple-A team.

"Braves Win! Braves Win! Braves Win!"

The promotion to Triple A didn't faze Wohlers in the least, as he picked up 11 saves in 23 games to go with a 1.03 ERA in 26⅓ innings. In Atlanta, the Braves had suddenly found themselves in dire need of relief help. Juan Berenguer, who had been counted on to be the team's closer, had done a fine job, but broke his arm while wrestling with his children at home on an offday. He last pitched on August 12, and would miss the rest of the season. Wohlers' 1991 season took a dramatic change on August 16, when the Braves announced that they had traded pitcher Dan Petry to the Boston Red Sox and that Wohlers would be called up from Richmond, to join the team the next day in San Diego. He was thrust into the middle of a pennant race, with the revitalized Braves playing their best baseball in nearly a decade. Going into that night's game, the Braves found themselves in second place, only 1½ games behind the Los Angeles Dodgers. Braves Fever had swept the city of Atlanta, and the team had the attention of the whole baseball world. It was just the opportunity Wohlers had been hoping for, and he was thrilled to be a part of it.

Braves manager Bobby Cox had a habit of trying to get a fresh rookie just up to the majors into a game as soon as possible, to help get the "major league jitters" out of the way. In Wohlers' first night on the Braves roster, Cox chose the perfect time to test his new recruit – bottom of the ninth inning, Braves ahead 2-1, two outs and Tony Gwynn on third base, representing the tying run. Bobby called on Mark to replace Mike Stanton, and Wohlers struck out Tim Teufel swinging on a 3-and-2 pitch to pick up his first major-league save and preserve the win for Charlie Leibrandt.

Wohlers was used in five of the first 10 games he was with the big-league club, picking up two saves to go along with his first win – a 14-9 victory over the Montreal Expos, in which he contributed two innings of one-hit ball. He had done his job, allowing no runs and only three hits in his first five games.

On August 27, the day after Wohlers' first major-league win, the Braves beat Montreal 3-2 to move into a first-place tie with the Los Angeles Dodgers. The next day, seeing that winning their division now was a real possibility, Braves GM John Schuerholz went looking for additional pitching help and landed reliever Alejandro Peña from the New York Mets. Pena, in his 11th big-league season, would bring a veteran presence to the bullpen, and proved to be a godsend to the team, going on to win two games and record 11 saves in his 15 appearances. His presence on the team let Wohlers generally be used in the seventh or eighth inning, gaining experience away from the pressure of ninth-inning situations.

At the end of August, the Braves had first place all to themselves – but by only one game over the Dodgers. In the game of Sunday, September 1, at Philadelphia, Wohlers was brought in to start the bottom of the ninth inning of a 4-4 tie game and got through unscathed. Atlanta failed to score in the top of the 10th, but in the bottom of the inning, leadoff batter John Morris hit a long home run to deep center field to give the Phillies a 5-4 walk-off win. It was Morris's only home run of the year, and handed Wohlers his first loss.

Things didn't go any better for Wohlers in his next outing, September 4 in Montreal, when he was brought in to relieve Steve Avery in the top of the sixth inning with the Braves leading 2-1. Avery had allowed two singles leading off the inning, and after Wohlers retired Marquis Grissom on a groundout, he gave up two doubles and a single to surrender the lead.

Wohlers didn't see any action in any of the Braves' next five games, leading into a two-game homestand against the San Diego Padres, starting on September 11. Kent Mercker, in only his second start of the season for the Braves, faced off against the Padres' Greg Harris. Terry Pendleton's fifth-inning home run staked the Braves to a 1-0 lead, and Mercker left the game after the sixth inning. In what was his longest outing of the season, Mercker hadn't allowed a hit when he was replaced by Mark Wohlers. Wohlers responded with two perfect innings before turning things over to Alejandro Peña for the ninth. Peña retired the first two batters before Darrin Jackson reached first on Pendleton's fielding error. He then retired Tony Gwynn to preserve the shutout and what turned out to be the first combined no-hitter (more than one pitcher) in National League history.

From this point on, the Braves won 15 and lost eight, including winning eight of their last nine games. They moved into first place for good on October 2 and held on to finish a game in front of the Dodgers, to claim the NL West Division title.

The Braves opened the National League Championship Series on the road against the East Division champion Pittsburgh Pirates. Tom Glavine started Game One, but left the game after the sixth inning, behind 4-0. Wohlers came in to pitch a scoreless seventh, but the Bucs added another run off Mike Stanton in the eighth and held on for a 5-1 victory. Wohlers pitched again back home in Atlanta in Game Three, giving up a hit and a walk and recording a strikeout in the eighth inning of an eventual 10-3 Braves victory. In Game Four, Wohlers relieved Kent Mercker in the 10th inning of a 2-2 tie, and the first batter he faced, Mike LaValliere, stroked an 0-and-2 pitch into center field to drive in what would prove to be the winning run for the Pirates. The Braves eventually won the Series four games to three, though, sending the team to its first World Series since it relocated from Milwaukee in 1966.

When the Braves headed to Minnesota to take on the Twins in the World Series, Wohlers made his first appearance in Game One, when he followed Charlie Leibrandt and Jim Clancy with the Braves already trailing, 5-1. He held the Twins in check with a scoreless seventh inning, but a Braves rally failed, with a 5-2 final score. Returning home to Atlanta-Fulton County Stadium, Wohlers was used only sparingly, with one-third-inning appearances in Games Three and Four, both Braves victories. Many consider the 1991 World Series the best ever, with six of the seven games being decided by one run and the Twins taking the deciding Game Seven by a 1-0 score in 10 innings. Regardless of the outcome, Braves fans will never forget that magical "Worst to First" season!

As if Wohlers' 1991 year hadn't been eventful enough, at season's end he was named Southern League Pitcher of the Year by *Baseball America*, and received the Minor League Player of the Year Award from *USA Today*.

Wohlers bounced between Richmond and the big-league club for the next two seasons, while learning to harness his control and take command of his fastball. The closer duties in Atlanta were being handled by Pena, Stanton, and Greg McMichael, while Wohlers worked primarily as a set-up man. In 1992 he became an important cog in the bullpen after his second call-up from Richmond in late August, going 14 straight games without allowing an earned run. In the postseason, he worked three scoreless innings in the NLCS against the Pirates, and two shutout stints in the World Series versus Toronto.

In 1993 Wohlers spent the first two months of the season in Richmond, where he fashioned a 1.84 ERA in 29⅓ innings and regained his control, with 39 strikeouts against only 11 walks. After being recalled on June 4, he spent the rest of the season in Atlanta, appearing in 46 games and compiling a 6-2 won-lost record. He made four appearances in the NLCS against Philadelphia, and was charged with the loss in Game Five after giving up Lenny Dykstra's tiebreaking home run in the 10th inning.

It isn't totally correct to say that 1994 was Wohlers's first complete major-league season — because the season itself wasn't complete, due to the players strike on August 12. The stoppage wiped out the rest of the season, and put an end to a successful season for Wohlers. He had surrendered only one home run in 51 innings, and had begun the season with five consecutive wins, the best start by a reliever in Atlanta franchise history. He ended the season by striking out 40 batters in his last 36 innings. During the season, Wohlers was also busy with community activities, by helping the Braves 400 Club raise funds to construct a baseball field at the Devereux Center campus in nearby Kennesaw, Georgia. The Devereux Center is designed to help support the needs of youth with emotional and behavioral challenges. At the field dedication, the Devereux students divided into two teams, with Wohlers pitching for each side. The students fared better than their major-league counterparts, as every single participant registered at least one hit off Wohlers before the game ended.

Wohlers also gathered a great deal of attention during the player strike when he took a job at an Atlanta area auto body shop at a salary of $10 per hour. His job was to arrive at 7 A.M. and have the coffee waiting when co-workers showed up, then to sweep the shop and buff car bodies in preparation for new paint jobs. "I think when I first started working there, the other guys there thought I was going to be some hot shot, not really pulling my load," said Wohlers. "Maybe the first time they saw me standing in a dumpster, trying to cram the trash down to make more room they realized I would be OK."[3] "I worked there 10 hours a day, five days a week," he said. "The way I was brought up, what my family and I went through, I have a pretty good grip on things. I never took anything for granted. I never thought because I played baseball I was better than anyone else."[4]

Nobody has documented exactly when Wohlers first threw a pitch over 100 mph in a major-league game, but there seems no doubt that he did it. There are numerous reports that he hit 103 on the radar gun during a spring-training game against the Marlins in 1995, and it was possible that this was the fastest pitch until Joel Zumaya of the Tigers threw a 104.8 mph fastball against Frank Thomas of the White Sox in a 2006 game.[5] But no one knows for sure.

Spring training started late in 1995, and so did Opening Day, due to the player strike not being settled until April 2. An abbreviated 144-game schedule was started on April 26. No one really stood out and staked a claim to the Braves' closer job right away, indeed through the first 37 games of the season (June 4) only seven saves were credited to the staff – four by Brad Clontz, two by Pedro Borbon Jr., and one by Greg McMichael.[6] On June 5, in his 18th appearance of the season, Wohlers registered his first save, and pretty much claimed the closer's job for the rest of the year. From that point on, he finished the year with 25 saves, while McMichael and Stanton each added one. Wohlers had taken control of his fastball and recorded 90 strikeouts and only 24 walks in 64⅔ innings.

The Braves finished the season with a 90-54 record, the best in the league, and beat the Colorado Rockies three games to one in the NLDS, then swept the Cincinnati Reds four straight in the NLCS to advance to the World Series against the Cleveland Indians. Wohlers was a workhorse during the postseason, working in three of the four NLDS games and all four contests in the NLCS.

Wohlers had worked in World Series Games Two, Three, and Four with mixed results. He picked up a save in Game Two, was charged with a blown save in an eventual 7-6 loss in Game Three, and gave up a home run and a double to the only two batters he faced in a 5-2 victory in Game Four. In Game Six Tom Glavine pitched a one-hit masterpiece, and led 1-0 thanks to David Justice's home run in the sixth inning. Returning to the dugout after the eighth inning, Glavine told manager Bobby Cox, "I'm done."

Manager Cox summoned Wohlers from the bullpen to start the ninth with a simple instruction: "Shut this thing down!" It wasn't like there was no tomorrow for the Braves. This was Game Six, and if they lost there was always tomorrow. But nobody (except for the Indians) wanted to go to a Game Seven. The leadoff batter, Kenny Lofton, lifted a pop foul down the third-base line which somehow shortstop Rafael Belliard got to for the first out. Then Paul Sorrento pinch-hit for Omar Vizquel, and flied out to center fielder Marquis Grissom for out number two. The last hope for the Indians was second baseman Carlos Baerga, who lined Wohlers' first pitch to Grissom in left-center field. With that, the Atlanta Braves brought home their first world championship!

There was every reason to think that the Braves' magic would continue. They were a young, talented team, who had just won a World Series after first-place finishes in 1991-92-93. And they didn't disappoint in 1996. The team took sole possession of first place on May 19 and stayed there the rest of the season, compiling a 96-66 record, taking three straight from the Dodgers in the NLDS and beating the Cardinals in a seven-game NLCS, en route to a World Series date with the New York Yankees. Wohlers was a workhorse once again, with 39 saves and 100 strikeouts in 77⅓ innings, and was named to the National League All-Star team in July, making a ninth-inning appearance in the 6-0 NL win.

After taking the first two Series games from the Yankees in New York, the Braves were excited to be coming back home. Even after dropping Game Three, they felt confident after taking a 6-0 lead in Game Four. The Braves ran into trouble in the sixth, when the Yankees tallied three runs on a walk and three singles against starter Denny Neagle, cutting the Braves' lead in half. After Terrell Wade and Mike Bielecki held the Yankees in check the rest of that inning and through the seventh, Wohlers took over in the top of the eighth. Wohlers set his sights on a two-inning stint to close out the game for the Braves, but things went downhill from the first pitch. Charlie Hayes was way out in front on Wohlers' first offering, sending a slow dribbler that hugged the third-base line before coming to a dead stop in fair territory just before the bag. Darryl Strawberry followed with a single to left, bring up Mariano Duncan with runners on first and second. Duncan lined sharply to shortstop Rafael Belliard who bobbled the ball, and had to settle for a force out at second rather than an almost sure double play. That brought up catcher Jim Leyritz, who had taken over for Joe Girardi the previous inning.

Leyritz remembered asking coach Don Zimmer what Wohlers threw, and Zimmer's response was, "Guy throws 100 miles an hour, just be ready!" He recalled that the feeling in the dugout was "at least we didn't get shut out, we'll get them tomorrow."[7] When he stood in at the plate, he saw Wohlers' fastball as well as his slider, and expected to get a fast one on the 2-and-2 count. Wohlers came in with a slider on the outside edge of the plate – Leyritz guessed wrong, swung anyway, and launched the pitch over the left-field fence to tie the game, 6-6. Mike Aldrete and Tim Raines were then retired on groundouts, but it was too late – the damage had been done.

Wohlers came back out for the ninth inning and held the Yankees scoreless before giving way to Steve Avery for the 10th. Avery allowed the go-ahead run on a single and three walks before giving way to Brad Clontz, who saw another run score on an error. The Yankees took the game by an 8-6 score, evening the Series at two games apiece.

Obviously discouraged at having been within two innings of going up three games to one, with another game at home, the Braves fell 1-0 to Andy Pettitte the next night, and then 3-2 to Jimmy Key in Game Six, seeing their chance at a repeat championship disappear.

Many observers feel that Wohlers was never the same after that Game Six disappointment, although he did have a relatively successful 1997 season, leading the team with 33 saves. In 1998, however, he seemed to lose all control on the mound, and he spent a portion of the season with Triple-A Richmond. It's not that he was just missing with his pitches; he was wild. In 20⅓ innings with the Braves, he walked 33 batters, and ended the season with a 10.18 ERA. His work with Richmond was even worse, with 36 free passes in only 12⅓ innings.

Wohlers' problems were quickly diagnosed – at least in the media and by fans – as a case of "Steve Blass disease," a condition in which a player becomes unable to throw with any semblance of control. The cure for that disease has never been found, but most observers feel that the problem is more psychological than physical. Whatever the trouble was, there was no quick remedy.

Few fans knew that in addition to his problems on the field, Wohlers had off-the-field difficulties at home, as well. In early July, his wife, Nancy, filed for divorce, after a marriage of almost six years. Two weeks later, his mother suffered a heart attack. In the last two weeks of July, he tossed 3⅔ innings in six games, giving up five hits and a whopping 14 walks. Almost unbelievably, he did not record a single strikeout during that stretch, while his ERA for the season ballooned from 5.62 to 10.53. August started out in much the same fashion, and after two games, he was shut down. In exasperation, the Braves placed Wohlers on the 15-day disabled list on August 21, and listed the reason as "inability to pitch."

Through his problems, though, Wohlers did not make excuses. "I try to realize this is only a game, just a small section of my life. … But somebody making 4 million dollars or 5 million dollars, I don't care if you're a baseball player or a doctor, that person has a lot of pressure on him. I've apologized to Bobby Cox. I've apologized to John Schuerholz for the investment they made in me and they're not getting any return. I feel guilty about that."[8]

In the offseason Wohlers worked with Braves' minor-league pitching instructors Guy Hansen and John Ramey, as well as pitching coach Leo Mazzone. Sports psychologist Jack Llewellyn, who had famously worked with starter John Smoltz early in his career, focusing on Smoltz's concentration and mental approach to the game, also worked with Wohlers during the winter and in spring training. The need for him to return to his old self intensified because of an elbow injury to Kerry Ligtenberg, who had stepped up to serve as the Braves' closer the previous year. And by the end of the training season, it appeared that Wohlers' rehab had succeeded.

"We didn't have any right – nor did we anticipate – that Mark would start the year with us and be able to contribute in any measurable fashion to our club's success," said GM Schuerholz in late March. "But he has put himself in a situation where he will be very much able to help us, someone we can rely on."[9]

Wohlers' early work in the 1999 season, however, followed the same pattern as the previous year. He appeared in two of the Braves' first four games, walking six batters without a strikeout and retiring only two of the 10 batters he faced.

On April 16, thinking a change of scenery might help, the Braves traded Wohlers to the Cincinnati Reds for pitcher John Hudek. Almost immediately the Reds put him on the disabled list with an anxiety disorder, before he made short stops with the Reds' Indianapolis, Chattanooga, and Rockford minor-league teams. His season ended when he underwent Tommy John surgery on his elbow on July 6.

Wohlers opened the 2000 season in the Reds' minor-league system, with stints in Louisville and Dayton, before finally reaching the big-league club on July 20, 15 months after his trade from the Braves. He appeared in 20 games, primarily in middle relief, and ended the year with optimism that his control and health problems were behind him.

Indeed, that did seem to be the case, as Wohlers opened the 2001 season with the Reds, and worked in 30 of the team's first 77 games. He exhibited his best control since 1996, walking only seven batters, against 21 strikeouts, in 32 innings. On July 1, the New York Yankees came calling. Locked in a head-to-head battle with the Boston Red Sox for the American League East lead, the Bronx Bombers were looking for some bullpen help, and sent minor-league pitcher Ricardo Aramboles to the Reds for Wohlers. He pitched in 31 games for the Yankees down the stretch, contributing to the eventual elimination of the Red Sox in the AL East. For Wohlers, it was a return to postseason play for the first time since 1997 with the Braves, and he did appear in one game of the ALCS, won by the Yankees over Seattle, four games to one.

At the end of the season, Wohlers was granted free agency, and was signed by the Cleveland Indians to a two-year contract in early January 2002. In his first year with the Tribe, he led the staff with 64 appearances, his highest total since 1997. In late July, Indians closer Bob Wickman went down with an elbow strain, and Wohlers took over the role, recording seven saves over the remaining two months of the season. As far as he was concerned, his career was finally back on track.

In spring training 2003, however, Wohlers experienced pain in his right elbow, and he had bone chips removed from his right elbow just before the season started, putting him on the sidelines until mid-June. In the second game of his rehab assignment at Akron, however, he ruptured the tendon graft he had in his elbow in 1999. On August 1 he underwent his second Tommy John surgery.

On October 17 the Indians declined the 2004 option on Wohlers, making him a free agent. On November 3 the team re-signed Wohlers to a minor-league contract, and invited him to spring training. However, when spring came, he declined to report and in mid-March announced that he would sit out the season for personal reasons. Subsequently, he was released by the Indians, marking the end of his career.

Over his 12-year major-league career, Wohlers posted a 39-29 won-lost record, a 3.97 ERA, and 119 saves. His 112 saves as of the end of the 2019 season stood at fourth place on the all-time Atlanta Braves list, and when he retired he was second only to Gene Garber's 141. He remains the only Braves pitcher to experience the joy of being on the mound for a World Series championship celebration since the team moved to Atlanta in 1966.

During the night of March 1, 2011, Wohlers' house in Milton, Georgia, suffered a major fire, and was destroyed in less than an hour. He credited his wife Kimberly, whom he married in 2000, for getting him and their three children, Jake, Mia, and Charlie, safely out of the home in time.

As of 2020 the family lived in Woodstock, Georgia, where he and Kimberly were in the real estate business. Austyn Wohlers, a daughter from Mark's first marriage, graduated from Emory University in Atlanta in May 2019.

Sources

In addition to the sources cited in the Notes, the author accessed Baseball-Reference.com, Retrosheet.org, and the online archives via Newspaper.com, NewspaperARCHIVE.com, and Ancestry.com.

Notes

1. "Braves Take Twinbill, Avery Pitches Shutout," *Southwest Times* (Pulaski, Virginia), July 12, 1988: 6.

2. Conversation with the author, (president of the Braves 400 Club 1991-92), on January 19, 1991.

3. Buster Olney, "When Strike Came, Wohlers Went to Work- Braves Relief Pitcher Not Afraid of Dirty Hands," *Baltimore Sun*, October 13, 1995. baltimoresun.com/news/bs-xpm-1995-10-13-1995286113-story.html.

4. Gordon Edes, "Braves Believe It – The Pen Is Mightier," *South Florida Sun-Sentinel* (Fort Lauderdale), October 12, 1995. sun-sentinel.com/news/fl-xpm-1995-10-12-9510120051-story.html.

5. Andrew Maggio, "The Top 15 Pitchers with the Hardest Fastballs of All-Time," *The Sportster* (St. Laurent, Quebec), May 14, 2015. thesportster.com/baseball/top-15-pitchers-with-the-hardest-fastballs-of-all-time/.

6. Greg McMichael is credited with a save in the game of May 4, but that game was suspended by rain after eight innings. McMichael did not actually pitch in the contest until September 7, when the game was resumed and completed. McMichael pitched the bottom of the ninth inning for the save.

7. Paul Daugherty, "Doc: Tragedy Has Made Leyritz Stronger," Cincinnati.com, October 31, 2016. cincinnati.com/story/sports/columnists/paul-daugherty/2016/10/31/doc-tragedy-has-made-jim-leyritz-stronger/93089454/.

8. Bruce Webber, "Wildly Out of Control: Is It Pitcher's Motion or Emotion?" *New York Times*, August 23, 1998: Sec. 1, 1.

9. George Dias, "Mind Over Matters" *Orlando Sentinel*, March 21, 1999.

Brad Woodall

BY CLAYTON TRUTOR

Brad Woodall

Brad Woodall was a left-handed pitcher who pitched in five major-league seasons. He played for the Atlanta Braves (1994-1996), the Milwaukee Brewers (1998), and the Chicago Cubs (1999). Woodall made 55 career appearances, 27 as a starter and 28 as a reliever. For his career, Woodall posted a 10-14 record with a 5.31 ERA. He was a switch-hitter. He was 6-feet tall and was listed at 175 pounds. Woodall was a member of the World Series champion 1995 Atlanta Braves and the 1996 National League champion Braves. He made most of his big-league appearances (31 games) for the 1998 Brewers.

Woodall was born in Atlanta on June 25, 1969, the son of James and Janet Woodall, who at some point settled the family in Blythewood, South Carolina, a suburb of Columbia. James Woodall was a small businessman and also worked for IBM.[1] Attending Spring Valley High School in Columbia, Brad starred on the baseball team, which has historically been one of the state's top programs. (Spring Valley has produced several other big-league ballplayers including Bill Landrum and Taylor Guerrieri.[2])

Woodall earned a baseball scholarship to the University of North Carolina, where he became one of the top stars in the Atlantic Coast Conference. Excelling as a pitcher, first baseman, and outfielder, Woodall earned first team All-ACC honors in 1990 and 1991. He was a part of the 1989 team that reached the College World Series, its first since 1978. Woodall earned an economics degree from UNC in 1993. Twelve years later, he earned a graduate degree in entrepreneurial management from the University of Wisconsin.[3]

On June 10, 1991, the Braves signed Woodall as an undrafted free agent. Assigned to Idaho Falls in the Rookie-level Pioneer League, Woodall dominated as a reliever, posting a 1.37 ERA in 28 games and earning 11 saves. He finished the season with the Durham Bulls of the high Class-A Carolina League, making four appearances. Woodall split 1992 between Durham and Double-A Greenville of the Southern League, impressing in both locations. He posted a 2.13 ERA in 24 appearances for Durham and a 3.20 mark for Greenville in 21 appearances. The Grady Little-managed 1992 Greenville Braves were one of the best teams in Southern League history, posting a 100-43 record and winning the league championship with the likes of Chipper Jones, Javy Lopez, and Mike Mordecai on its roster.[4]

Woodall bounced around the Braves' minor-league system in 1993, serving stints in Durham and Greenville and finishing the season in Triple-A Richmond, playing on another stacked team, filled with the fruits of the John Schuerholz-era Braves minor-league system. He worked primarily as a starter, achieving a 10-8 overall mark with a 3.64 ERA in 24 appearances (10 of which were for Richmond). In 1994 Woodall broke out as a star in the International League, posting a 15-6 record and a 2.42 ERA for Richmond, which he helped lead to the International League championship.

In the strike-shortened 1994 major-league season, Woodall also made his big-league debut. On July 22 he started for the Braves against the St. Louis Cardinals at Busch Stadium. Woodall pitched six innings, surrendering three earned runs and five hits in a 3-2 defeat, giving the 25-year-old the loss. Woodall went 1-for-2 at the plate, getting a hit off former Cy Young Award winner Rick Sutcliffe in his first major-league at-bat.

Woodall returned to Richmond for most of the 1995 season but made nine appearances for Atlanta, pitching a total of 10⅓ innings and posting a 1-1 record with an ERA of 6.10. He pitched exclusively out of the bullpen for the Braves, having trouble cracking a staff that included future Hall of Famers Greg Maddux, Tom Glavine, and John Smoltz. The unprecedented depth of Atlanta's pitching staff in the mid-1990s proved to be a detriment to Woodall's career, preventing him from gaining big-league experience as a pitcher in his mid- to late 20s.

In 1996 Woodall again spent most of the season in Richmond, posting a 9-7 record in 21 starts with a 3.38 ERA. He made three starts for Atlanta and a total of eight appearances. He went 2-2 and had an ERA of 7.32. Woodall spent his final year in the Braves organization in 1997, stuck in Richmond. On December 19, 1997, Woodall signed as a free agent with the Milwaukee Brewers, seeking an opportunity to kickstart his career with the Brewers, who had not had a winning season since 1992.

Woodall earned a spot in the Milwaukee rotation in 1998 and he had a 7-9 record in his only full season as a big leaguer, making 20 starts out of a total of 31 appearances. He worked 138 innings for the Brewers and posted an ERA of 4.96. Considering his ERA, Woodall's WHIP of 1.391 was quite solid. Woodall tied for third on the Brewers' staff in wins with Jeff Juden. The Brewers were much different than the teams Woodall grew used to in Atlanta. They won just 74 games in 1998. Woodall's performance in 1998 proved insufficient to earn him a spot on the Brewers' 1999 roster.

At the end of spring training in 1999, the Brewers put Woodall on waivers and the Chicago Cubs claimed him. In April and May of what proved to be his final major-league season, Woodall pitched in six games for the Cubs, starting three and posting an 0-1 mark for the season. He had an ERA of 5.63 in 16 innings pitched. Woodall spent most of the season with the Triple-A Iowa Cubs of the Pacific Coast League. Chicago granted Woodall his free agency soon after the season and he spent the 2000 season out of baseball.

Woodall made a comeback in professional baseball in 2001, spending the season with the Long Island Ducks of the independent Atlantic League. Working primarily as a reliever, he had a strong season, posting a 2.11 ERA with a 3-1 record in 34 appearances. He retired shortly thereafter.

In the major leagues Woodall had 60 plate appearances and recorded a .271 batting average with a .364 on-base percentage. He hit one home run – a solo homer off the Colorado Rockies' John Thomson on September 3, 1998. He pinch-hit in his last game with the Brewers, on September 26, 1998, hitting a single between short and third and driving in a run. It was his third (and final) major-league run batted in.

In 43 fielding chances, Woodall made two errors, for a fielding percentage of .953.

After leaving baseball, Woodall settled in Middleton, Wisconsin, a suburb of Madison. His wife, Kari, became an assistant swim coach at the University of Wisconsin-Madison. He worked as a pitching coach in the Tampa Bay Rays organization and as an assistant baseball coach at the Madison (Wisconsin) Area Technical College, where he worked primarily with pitchers. As of 2020 he owned Woodall Baseball Academy, which trains young baseball and softball players in the Madison area. Besides offering training year-round, Woodall Baseball Academy runs fall baseball instructional leagues: a wood bat league for high-school players and a fall baseball league for elementary- and middle-school students.[5]

Sources

In addition to the sources cited in the Notes, the author relied on Baseball Reference.com.

Notes

1. Fatter Than Joey, "Weekend Dad Mug: Interview with Brad Woodall," *Brew Crew Ball* January 30, 2010. Accessed on July 20, 2019: brewcrewball.com/2010/1/30/1285018/weekend-dad-mug-brad-woodall; "Jim Woodall," *LinkedIn*. Accessed on July 20, 2019: linkedin.com/in/jim-woodall-0b42645b.

2. "Vikings in the MLB/College," *Spring Valley Vikings Baseball* 2018. Accessed on July 20, 2019: hometeamsonline.com/teams/default.asp?u=SPRINGVALLEYBASEBALL&s=baseball&p=custom&pagename=Vikings+in+College%2FMLB.

3. "Brad Woodall," *Woodall Baseball Academy* 2019. Accessed on July 20, 2019: woodallbaseball.com/about/.

4. Robert Castello, "92 G-Braves Enter Hall of Fame," GreenvilleOnline.com, July 24, 2014. Accessed on July 20, 2019: greenvilleonline.com/story/sports/baseball/2014/07/24/g-braves-enter-hall-fame/13135833/.

5. Dennis Punzel, "Know Your Madisonian: Ex-Major Leaguer Brad Woodall Still Pitching Baseball at His Academy," Madison.com, March 28, 2013. Accessed on July 20, 2019: madison.com/wsj/news/local/know-your-madisonian-ex-major-leaguer-brad-woodall-still-pitching/article_ef37cc9e-9706-11e2-9e35-0019bb2963f4.html; "Brad Woodall: Assistant Baseball Coach," Madison College Athletics 2019. Accessed on July 20, 2019: madisoncollegeathletics.com/coaches.aspx?path=&rc=164.

MANAGER & COACHES

Bobby Cox

BY TIM DEALE

Bobby Cox

Fourteen consecutive years in first place. Bobby Cox's teams hold a unique distinction in major-league baseball. Prior to The Streak, the team finished last three years in a row.

Robert Joe Cox was born in Tulsa, Oklahoma, on May 21, 1941. He recalled his younger days: "We moved from Oklahoma when I was about three years old. My childhood was great. The San Joaquin Valley is noted for grapes and fruit. It was a farming community. So anytime you live in a farming community you have a great upbringing. As kids, we worked in the fields with all of the other kids and parents. I grew up in Selma, California, which is a very small town [near Fresno]. It was a climate that you could play a Friday night football game and take batting practice Saturday morning. It was year-round athletics, actually. Which was great!"[1]

The Cardinals had a Class-C farm team in Fresno. "I became a huge Cardinals fan and I can remember as a little kid cutting out the newspaper Stan Musial pictures. My idol growing up was Stan Musial."[2]

Cox graduated from Selma High School and then attended Reedley (California) Junior College, where he was active in sports. "I played them all – football, basketball, and baseball. That's what we did. Actually, one of my ambitions was to be a major-league player and then a high-school football coach. That is what I kind of had in mind."[3]

In 1959 Cox signed with the Los Angeles Dodgers for $40,000 as an amateur free agent.[4]

In 1960 the 5-foot-11, 180-pound, right-handed Cox, started his professional baseball career with the Reno Silver Sox in Reno, Nevada, of the Class-C California League at the age of 19. He played second base and batted .255 with a .389 on-base percentage, a .411 slugging percentage, and .801 on-base plus slugging percentage (OPS). All figures but his batting average were above league average (and there he was just one point below the .256 league average) and he ranked first in range factor, assists, and double plays. Reno won the league championship.

On October 1, 1961, Cox married Mary E. Xavier in Fresno County, California. They had five children, Bobby Jr., Connie, Debbie, Shelly, and Randy.[5] They divorced in 1977.[6] Mary had a nephew named Joseph Xavier, who was drafted by the Oakland Athletics and played in the minors from 1985 to 1990. His last season was with the Greenville (South Carolina) Braves of the Double-A Southern League.

From 1960 to 1964 Cox was in the Dodgers system. The Chicago Cubs drafted him before the 1965 season, when the Dodgers didn't protect him in the minor-league draft. The Cubs traded Cox to the Atlanta Braves on April 28, 1966, and the Braves traded him to the New York Yankees in December 1967.

Cox spent nine seasons in the minors as a player and one as a player-manager. He mostly played third base (522 games) and second (499). He ranked first and second numerous times in defensive categories. His slash line for 10 seasons in the minors was .275/.359/.451/.810. He was among the league leaders a number of times in various categories and he was a member of a second championship team in 1967, the Triple-A Richmond Braves (International League).

Cox played for the Cardenales de Lara in the Venezuelan Winter League for three seasons, 1967-1970.

His major-league debut came for the Yankees and manager Ralph Houk on April 14, 1968. It was a one-run game, the Twins leading, 4-3. With one out in the bottom of the ninth and runners on first and second, Cox pinch-hit against Al Worthington and struck out.

Cox made his first major-league start at third base on April 27, against the Detroit Tigers at Yankee Stadium. He went 0-for-3. There were better games, such as June 21 in Minnesota, when Cox was 3-for-4 with a home run and four RBIs.

Mickey Mantle was in the last year of his big-league career and Cox was able to play alongside him for one season. "1968, that was Mickey Mantle's last year. I couldn't wait to meet him. First year in the big leagues, get to play alongside Mickey – that was a big thrill. Mantle was from Oklahoma, and I was born in Oklahoma. So he tried to help me as much as he could. … Even then, he was still the fastest guy on the team." Asked what his most memorable moment with Mantle was, Cox said, "We turned a triple play, the last triple play the Yankees had. Mickey was playing first."[7]

Cox finished the season with a slash line of .229/.300/.316/.616 in 135 games. The numbers might seem low but the team batting average was .214 and the league slash line was .230/.297/.339/.637.

Cox had a .957 fielding percentage, placing him above league average. He ranked fourth in range factor, fifth in assists, and fifth in double plays in the American League. All of the hard work in the minors paid off as he was named to the Topps All-Star Rookie Team.

When the 1969 season started, Cox was used for pinch-hitting duties and did not start until May. He played in 85 games that year and was a starter in 56. In the final at-bat of the final game of his career, Cox hit a sacrifice fly for an RBI against Luis Tiant, winning the game against the Cleveland Indians.

The slash line for Cox during his major-league baseball career was .225/.310/.309/.619. His fielding percentage was .950 compared with the league average of .952 and a range factor of 3.06 compared with 3.08.

The Yankees sent Cox to the Triple-A Syracuse Chiefs (International League) for 1970. After the season he was released.

Cox's playing career ended at the age of 29 due to a series of "injuries and illness." "Cox battled knee injuries during his time in the majors and never got a chance to be an everyday player beyond 1968."[8]

But there was good news for 1971. "I really didn't have the courage to ask to stay in the game, because I was quitting after the 1970 season. … Then Lee MacPhail, who was the director of player personnel, flew down to Richmond, where Syracuse was finishing the season. He met with me and suggested that I stay in the game. The Yankees had a managerial opening in Fort Lauderdale and he thought that I would be good for that. So, I accepted."[9]

Cox managed the Fort Lauderdale Yankees, a Class-A affiliate in 1971. He was promoted to the Double-A West Haven Yankees for 1972 and won the Eastern League American Division championship. Cox moved up to Triple-A Syracuse in

1973 and guided the team as it improved from a 64-80 record the previous season to 76-70. He stayed with the team from 1973 to 1976, each year improving and winning the International League championship in 1976.

During the years Cox managed the Chiefs, he also managed the Cardenales de Lara in the Venezuelan Winter League from 1974 to 1977.

A promotion in 1977 put Cox in a New York Yankees uniform as the first-base coach and the team won the World Series with Billy Martin at the helm.

Of that season, Cox later said, "I had already managed six years in the minors and managed winter ball in Venezuela. That year was just special because I did get to coach with Billy and we did win a world championship. I have fond memories of that season. Ralph Houk was a big influence when he managed me with the Yankees. Certainly, Billy was. Dick Howser was a coach on Billy's staff. So was Yogi Berra and Elston Howard. So I got to know those guys really well. Pick their brains here and there. But basically when you go into managing, you are what you are. You don't want to change much."[10]

In 1977 the Braves had the worst record in the National League. Club owner Ted Turner hired Cox to manage the team, replacing Dave Bristol. Cox immediately set the tone in the clubhouse upon his arrival. Every spring training he would hand down six rules:

1. No beards.
2. No uniform pants covering the shoe tops.
3. Dress code.
4. Mind the curfew.
5. Be on time.
6. Play hard at all times.

Andruw Jones learned a lesson about not playing hard when he didn't run all-out at a ball hit to center field. Cox pulled him off the field in the middle of the game. Eddie Perez, who played for Cox years later, said, "He taught me to not only be dressed good (at the ballpark), but dress good outside. … He said, 'We've got to dress nice. There's people around. We have to look like a professional player.'" Over the years Cox would bend on the beard rule and allow the pants to go a little bit lower.[11]

In addition to landing his first major-league managerial job, 1978 was also a good one for Bobby in other ways. Cox and Pam Boswell of Rome, Georgia, married. They have a 48-acre farm in Adairsville, Georgia, and a home in Marietta, near Atlanta.[12] They had three children, Keisha, Kami, and Skyla.[13]

Statistically, the 1978 and '79 Braves were last or near last in numerous defensive, pitching, and hitting categories, and finished last in the National League West Division. They ranked last in the league in attendance with less than one million.

Among the numerous young players in 1978 were third baseman Bob Horner, a 20-year-old rookie, straight out of college, who had not played in the minor leagues; and Dale Murphy, 22, who was in his first full year and playing first base. The Braves were the youngest team in the NL with an average age of 25.5.

The Braves finished fourth in 1980. Cox's success at developing players in the minors and putting them in the best position to succeed was working with the young team. For example, he moved Murphy to center field, where he won five Gold Gloves, was an All-Star seven times, and was the league MVP two years in a row.

Cox made an interesting move for the 1981 season when he hired 74-year-old Luke Appling to be one of his coaches. One writer said, "He teaches hitting and provides an earthy link between the game's beer-and-pickled-egg past and today's double-knit conglomerates."[14]

Having the best coaches he could find was something Cox believed in. "At one point people thought Bobby was digging his own grave by having three former managers (Jimy Williams, Don Baylor, and Pat Corrales) on the bench," wrote a Braves historian. "He wanted the best people around him to try and make the team as successful as he could."[15]

The good news was that by 1981 the Braves had improved to sixth in defensive efficiency and the team ERA was fifth, but the runs per game were eighth in the NL. The Braves finished fifth in the West Division, but the attendance improved to ninth in the league. The bad news was that Ted Turner fired Cox.

"I hated to leave because I knew the team was getting ready to do something after all of those years," Cox said in 2009. "It was a struggle there. But we had a lot of young kids coming up and it didn't take much more for us to get over the hump."[16]

Fortunately for Cox, he was hired to manage the 1982 Toronto Blue Jays. Either Cox was attracted to managing young teams that finished in last place or the general managers with young teams wanted him. The Blue Jays were the youngest team in the American League East. They had finished in last place five consecutive seasons. No one knew what was going to happen since Cox's track record with the Braves the previous four seasons was 266 wins and 323 losses. But the Blue Jays' GM, Pat Gillick, had confidence in Cox and believed he could develop the young team.

The Blue Jays tied with the Cleveland Indians for last place in 1982 with some young players playing in their first full seasons. But under Cox's tutelage, they improved to 89-73 in 1983, finishing fourth with the youngest team in the AL East. In 1984 they finished second and in 1985 they were the division champions with the best record in the league. In the postseason the Kansas City Royals beat the Blue Jays in seven games in the League Championship Series. Cox was voted the AL Manager of the Year. The Blue Jays were 10th in attendance in 1982. They were second in 1985.

Ted Turner admitted near-instant regret for his decision in 1981, but he was able to hire Cox back for the 1986 season, as general manager.[17] Chuck Tanner was the manager and Paul Snyder was the scouting director.

Of going back to Atlanta, Cox said, "When Ted offered me the job, number one was family and number two was baseball and family comes over baseball. My family was in Atlanta and we still had kids in school."[18]

As the new GM, Cox had to find a way to reverse what had been happening with the team. They finished last three consecutive seasons. His priority was pitching and defense. "In order to have great pitching, you've got to have great defense. We just didn't. … our defense was horrendous, not good at all."[19] The core of the team that won 14 consecutive division titles was players accumulated by Cox while he was the GM. "Those teams were built on being strong up the middle, having good defense helps the pitching and having good pitching helps the defense. And pitchers had to field their position and cover first base."[20]

Cox said, "We had a four- or five-year plan. Most of it was on drafting, farm system, developing. We spent all of our money drafting players. We didn't want to lose anybody. If a scout wanted somebody, we signed them. That really got the foundation going and all that had to do with Paul Snyder, our scouting director."[21]

The Braves finished last in the six-team NL West in 1986 with a 72-89 record. Meanwhile, Cox was busy restructuring the team and the farm system and the development process as well as drafting and trading players. With pitching his priority, Cox was nurturing and trading for future Hall of Famers Tom Glavine and John Smoltz respectively.[22]

The 1987 team finished 69-92 but moved up to fifth place. Their 1988 record was 54-106, the worst record in the NL. In 1989 the team improved to 63-97 but still had the lowest winning percentage in the league.

Cox had the ability to spot talent. Once he and Snyder went to Jacksonville, Florida, to watch a high-school game. The Braves had been scouting a player in the area who attended The Bolles School, a private school in Jacksonville. When they arrived Cox told Snyder, "Don't show me which one he is. I wanted to try to pick him out."[23] That player was Chipper Jones. He was the number-one draft pick in 1990. After a 19-year career, all with the Braves, Jones was a first-ballot inductee into the Hall of Fame.[24]

Cox talked about hiring himself to be the Braves manager with 97 games remaining in the 1990 season. "I liked being a manager much more than a GM actually," he said. "It's more fun to be around the players on a day-to-day basis. The game itself presents a great challenge each and every day. That's the fun part of baseball."[25]

Russ Nixon was managing the Braves to start the 1990 season but after a 25-40 start, Cox took over and they finished in last place again. The team had an average age of 27.6, second youngest in the majors.

The restructured minor-league system and development process were starting to produce stars. Ron Gant was promoted to the Braves as a second baseman but Cox converted him to the outfield and he received MVP votes in the 1990 season as well as other seasons.

Another of the young stars from the Braves minors was David Justice, who won the Rookie of the Year Award for 1990. Cox said, "He's got as sweet a swing as I've ever seen. … This is as true a swing as I've ever seen."[26]

The pitchers Cox had been developing in the farm system, along with those picked up in trades, were now the bulk of the pitching staff: Tom Glavine, John Smoltz, and Steve Avery, among others.

When John Schuerholz was hired as the GM of the Braves in 1991, he was asked about keeping Cox as the manager and he said, "I don't think I could consider this job without Bobby Cox in the dugout. That's how highly I regarded the man. Some of my friends thought I was crazy to come to Atlanta. … But I knew Bobby and Paul Snyder had put together a robust minor-league system and brought some good young arms to the Braves. I also noticed that when those young pitchers would make a good pitch, balls would go through legs, balls were thrown into the stands, and there were a lot more bad hops than good hops."[27]

Cox and Schuerholz had known each other and made some trades while Schuerholz was the GM of the Kansas City Royals. Schuerholz said, "I can't say enough about Bobby. He had such admiration for the people who put on the uniform and were able to perform at the major-league level. He treated people with honor and respect and had high expectations of individuals and teams. That was very clear to the people involved with him and people played up to those standards."[28]

According to Terry McGuirk, who later became the team's chief executive officer, "Bobby might have showed his best talent as GM. He took an absolutely bankrupt situation and put together the talent, the coaches, the scouts, and the support system. But I don't think he was ever really comfortable in the role."[29]

After becoming GM, Schuerholz, went to work to improve defense. He traded for and signed as free agents Terry Pendleton at third base (who won the 1991 batting title and was the National League MVP); Rafael Belliard at shortstop; Otis Nixon in center field; Lonnie Smith in left field; Deion Sanders as a fourth outfielder; and Sid Bream at first base. They now had a good mix of young players and veterans.

Cox made sure that in the clubhouse everybody was treated equally. There were no areas for certain groups or levels of players, and there would be no music because Cox wanted to create a businesslike atmosphere, with his players concentrating on baseball.[30]

Cox was handed a new deck of cards every spring. But he always managed to make the most of what he had. On the rare occasion when he found a joker in the deck, Cox cut ties quickly. Players like Deion Sanders, Kenny Lofton, John Rocker, and Bret Boone did not fit his formula of a businesslike clubhouse devoid of such distractions as the raucous rock music that permeates and often divides other locker rooms.[31]

Cox had a full season with a team that was solid on defense and had good starting pitching. He led the team to the West Division championship in 1991 with a 94-68 record, one game ahead of the Los Angeles Dodgers. One of the reasons for the turnaround was Smoltz. "I was suffering from a complete collapse of confidence … but my manager, Bobby Cox, never stopped believing in me the entire time," Smoltz said. "It's hard to describe this, I guess, but Bobby just had this ability to believe in people and he had this gentleness about him. Bobby never lost confidence in me. … He believed in something that other people didn't seem to see: my potential."

"It was really right here, at this specific point, that my manager changed the course of my career. No, that's not accurate. He *saved* my career. I mean, you can imagine the kind of flak he was taking for continuing to hand me the ball every five days. The critics were clamoring for the hook, for anything. The sentiment became 'Send him down. Or send him to the bullpen. Do *something*, Bobby! The kid has obviously lost it.' Who knows what would have happened to either of us had I not eventually turned things around; I could have easily cost us both a job. If I have said it once, I have said it a thousand times: I will always be grateful for Bobby Cox."[32] Smoltz had a record of 2-11 during his 1991 struggles and 12-2 after he and Cox turned things around. In 2016 Cox said, "I love sticking with people and I've stuck with a lot of people that really succeeded when people didn't think they would."[33]

The Braves won the National League pennant by defeating the Pittsburgh Pirates in seven games in the NLCS. Six of the games were low-scoring affairs and three of the games were 1-0 with the Braves winning two of them, including the final game when Smoltz pitched a shutout.

The World Series, against the Minnesota Twins, was a fierce battle with five of the seven games decided by one run and three of the games going into extra innings, including the final game when the Twins won 1-0 in the bottom of the 10th inning. This was the first time both teams had gone to the World Series after finishing in last place the year before.[34] Another rarity occurred was that each team won all its home games. That has only happened three times. The Braves had their chances to win Game Seven. They had runners in scoring position numerous times but never had the clutch hit to score a run.

Asked what the key was to not only recognizing talent but also putting players in the right situation to succeed, Cox said, "I think it's your gut instinct, really. I've done a lot of scouting in my life. I used to scout when I was a minor-league manager. During spring training I would go out with the scouts and watch high-school games. Then when I became a GM, I became even more familiar with scouting. Credit Paul Snyder. He's the best that ever lived. If you watch baseball long enough, I think your instincts will tell you what to do."[35]

The 1992 Braves had a couple of changes for Cox. One of the minor-league players he nurtured, Mark Lemke, became the full-time second baseman and there were some pitching changes. The Braves improved to 98-64, winning the NL West again and the pennant.

Then they faced the team Cox had been building a few years before, the Blue Jays, and they lost the World Series in six games. The Braves' closer, Alejandro Peña, wasn't available for the postseason. Cox was forced to use other pitchers to finish games. Four of the games were decided by one run and Toronto won all four. The Braves had opportunities with runners in scoring position to tie or win those games but it didn't happen. The final game went 11 innings and the Braves had the tying run on third base in the bottom of the 11th, but lost.

A couple more pieces were added in 1993. "After debating whether to sign (Greg) Maddux or Barry Bonds, who both hit free agency after the 1992 season, the pitcher won out."[36] The Braves almost signed Barry Bonds, but one wonders how he would have fit into the "everyone is equal clubhouse" of the Braves.

On July 22 the Braves were 55-42, 10 games out of first place. They had just traded for Fred McGriff and he ignited them as they went 8-1 the rest of July. They stayed hot and on September 11 they took over first place and stayed there for the rest of the season. From July 23 to the end of the season the Braves were 49-16 (.754). They went from 13 games over .500 to 46 games over .500 in a matter of 65 games, finishing at 104-58.

Cox said he wanted great pitching and great fielding and he got it. The pitching staff was first in the league by a wide margin in ERA and ERA+. On defense they were tied with the Giants for best in the league in a statistic called Defensive Efficiency.[37]

"He's got half the club on his shoulders and is carrying them. Fact is I don't know if I've ever seen anyone do that. That's Mister Clutch." Cox was talking about Ron Gant after he had 18 runs batted in during an eight-game span in September 1993 to keep the Braves ahead of the Giants late in the season. Author Tom Verducci argued that the amazing stretch wasn't Gant's greatest achievement; "it may have been that he moved Bobby Cox, his phlegmatic manager, to positively gush."[38]

In the NLCS, Atlanta faced the Philadelphia Phillies and lost in six games. The Phillies won three games by one run. In two of those games the Braves had numerous chances to score with runners in scoring position, including the final inning in each game.

During the offseason Cox had knee replacement surgery on both knees.[39]

There were some new players in the 1994 starting lineup. Javy Lopez was signed as an amateur free agent from Puerto Rico when Cox was the GM. Ryan Klesko, drafted by GM Cox, was now a rookie in left field. Klesko and Lopez finished 3rd and 10th respectively in the Rookie of the Year voting. Cox moved other players to new positions during the season and gave another of his draftees a chance to play; Kent Mercker became a starting pitcher.

On August 11, 1994, the remainder of the season was canceled after the players union struck.

Cox did what he always did in 1995 and adapted with the changes in the roster. Chipper Jones came in second in Rookie of the Year voting. Cox, showing again that he was not afraid to change a player's position, moved Jones from shortstop to third base.

The Cox philosophy of great pitching and great fielding continued, with the Braves having the best team ERA and ERA+ and the fielders ranking fourth in the league. The team finished first in the newly-realigned East Division. (The actual change in divisions occurred in 1994.)

The Braves won over the wild-card (established in 1994 and first used in 1995) Colorado Rockies in the Division Series.

In the NLCS, the Braves won four straight over Cincinnati to claim the pennant.

The 1995 World Series could be called a rematch of the 1948 series when the Cleveland Indians defeated the Boston Braves in six games.

The sixth game in 1995 was a 1-0 nail-biter. The Braves led in the Series, three games to two. Glavine was pitching a one-hit shutout after eight innings and 109 pitches. Cox had to decide whether to continue with Glavine or go with his closer.

An Atlanta team had never won a championship in baseball, football, or basketball. Cox's decision would be for one game, but that one game had a tremendous amount of excitement or disappointment riding on it. Cox went to the bullpen for the ninth inning and brought in the closer, Mark Wohlers, who had pitched in three of the previous four games. Wohlers recorded outs one and two in short order. It all came down to one more out. Carlos Baerga, the number-three hitter in the lineup for the Indians, came to bat. On the first pitch, Baerga sent a fly ball to deep left-center field. Center fielder Marquis Grissom gave chase and hauled it in, and the Braves were World Series champions.

The World Series championship was the third in the history of the Braves franchise. They won in 1914 as the Boston Braves and in 1957 as the Milwaukee Braves. Their victory in 1995 made them the only team to win a World Series in three different cities.

The 1996 Braves finished first and beat the Dodgers in the NLDS, three games to one. They overcame the St. Louis Cardinals in seven games in the NLCS to clinch another pennant. They faced the Yankees in the World Series and lost in six games. The Yankees won Games Five and Six by one run, 1-0 and 3-2.

Ted Turner owned the Braves from 1976 to 1996. After the 1996 season his Turner Broadcasting merged with Time Warner. His role with the Braves was diminished. The purse strings got tighter after Turner left.40 The Braves were used to Turner spending money on what they needed. Now things were changing.

In 1997 and 1998 the Braves won in the NLDS but lost in the NLCS. In 1999 they were back to the World Series but were swept by the Yankees.

John Smoltz missed the entire 2000 season after having Tommy John surgery. In 2001, while Smoltz was working his way back to the starting rotation, Cox began using him as a reliever. Then Smoltz became the closer and was extremely good at it for the next three seasons. When the team ran low on starting pitchers, Cox moved him back into the starting rotation for 2005.

Between injuries, free agency and salary restrictions, it was becoming more difficult to continue winning, but Cox was working his magic and the Braves continued their streak of first-place finishes. From 2000 to 2004 they won their division but lost in the Division Series four of the five seasons. In 2001 they won the Division Series but lost to Arizona in the Championship Series.

In 2005 the Braves (90-72) finished first for the 14th season in a row but lost to Houston in the Division Series. Asked in 2009 if 2005 was his finest season of managing because of coping with injuries and 18 rookies during the season and still finishing first, he replied, "I never expect guys to struggle. So when they come up here, I expect them to compete with the team on the other side and not be awed by them or anything else. They're treated just like the veterans. ... There's only one reason why you're up here and that's because you have talent. I do have patience and if somebody gets off slow, I am going to stay with them, because they have talent."41

The first-place streak ended in 2006. For Cox personally, counting the 1985 Blue Jays, Cox had 15 consecutive seasons of first-place finishes when he managed a team for a full season.

During their 14-season streak, the Braves played in 25 postseason series and won 12 of them. Some may point out that the Braves won only one World Series during that time, but John Smoltz had an interesting approach to the question: "Superior pitching wins baseball games, but power pitching is a bonus in the postseason. And starting pitching is great, but timely hitting is better. We went to the World Series five times. Over those five Series we played a total of twenty-nine games. More than half of those games – seventeen to be exact – were decided by one run and we lost twelve of those."42

"The fact that John Schuerholz and Bobby Cox gave us a *chance* to win it all every year –remember, to win it all, you HAVE to make the playoffs first – was amazing. We won when the team was rebuilding, while most teams don't go to the playoffs when they are in transition. We won because our manager could take a variety of different teams with certain weaknesses and win, teams that had a lot of injuries, and still make it."43

Broadcaster Jim Kaat, a three time All-Star and longtime pitcher in the big leagues, said, "That Atlanta team had everything except a quality closer. If you could put somebody like Mariano Rivera on that club, they would be unbeatable."44 Baseball analyst Tim Kurkjian said the same thing: "They didn't have a top-quality 'closer.'"45

"We had so many different types of teams during our streak," said Cox. "We had slugging teams, speed teams, and really young teams but always had pitching. It was fun managing teams stacked with base-stealers. ... I liked to turn the runners loose. ... I'm not only proud of every team I ever managed but proud of the fans and the organization. No manager can win without the right people around him. That starts in the front office, with the general manager and player-development people, but also the coaches."[46]

The closest team in major league baseball to the Braves are the Yankees with nine straight division championships, from 1998 to 2006. The longest streak in other major professional sports is held by the New England Patriots with 11.

Former Mets GM Omar Minaya observed, "If they were to give a Pulitzer Prize in baseball, Bobby Cox and John Schuerholz and their whole organization deserve it. What they've done is more than impressive. ... The 14-year run was possible because Bobby was so adaptable. Playing the hand Schuerholz gave him, he won with different types of teams: some dominated by pitching, some loaded with sluggers, others with speed merchants, and still others with veterans. One year, the Braves even used 18 rookies but still managed to win."[47]

In 2006 the team record was 79-83, for a third-place division finish. Gone were the days of Maddux and Glavine in the rotation although they still had Smoltz, who was now 39. The only remaining position players from the heydays were Chipper Jones and Andruw Jones. From 2007 to 2009 the Braves finished third, fourth, and third respectively.

Tom Glavine came back for the 2008 season to finish his career with Cox and the Braves. Smoltz was in his last year with the Braves. (He was the only player who was with Cox from the beginning of the 14-season streak to the end of it.)

On June 8, 2009, Cox posted win number 2,000 with the Braves, making him just the fourth major-league manager to win 2,000 with one team, joining Connie Mack, John McGraw, and Walter Alston.[48] Cox finished with 2,504 total wins: 2,149 with the Braves and 355 with the Blue Jays.

Before the 2010 season, Cox announced that he would step down at the end of the campaign. The Braves finished in second place in the division with a 91-71 record, making them the wild-card team, in the postseason one last time for Cox. They lost to the Giants three games to one in the Division Series. All four decisions were by one run. Chipper Jones had season-ending knee surgery in August, and in the second game of the series the Braves closer, Billy Wagner, suffered an oblique-muscle injury and did not play afterward. The Braves made seven errors, which were factors in two of their three losses. After Game Two, manager Bruce Bochy led his players to a standing ovation for Cox while the fans (in San Francisco) stood and cheered, "Bobby, Bobby, Bobby!" and the umpires congratulated Cox.[49]

Asked about the errors costing the Series, Cox, a player's manager right to the end, expressed disappointment but remained supportive of his players. Cox congratulated Bochy and the Giants and wished them good luck. He said he was touched by the Giants and fans ovation.[50]

The respect for Cox throughout baseball was shown when the Braves played in different cities in 2010. "Being able to understand and see everybody in baseball, every team, every player just appreciating what he brought to the game of baseball and to see how everybody was just sending him off was something special to see from the same dugout with him, (Tim) Hudson said, it was awesome."[51] City after city meant gifts and ceremonies, a celebration of his impact. While in Washington to play the Nationals, Cox was invited to a reception on Capitol Hill, hosted by U.S. senators.[52]

Another important contribution from Cox to the Braves was the team's rising attendance. When he became the manager they were last in the majors with less than one million per season. During Cox's time they were first, second, and third for numerous seasons, topping three million multiple times.

In September 2014 the Braves brought Cox back to help them choose their next general manager and director of player development after GM Frank Wren was gone.

Tom Glavine spotlighted Cox's qualities when he told the author of a team history, "What made him a great manager was that he was so good at handling his players. He was so good at getting the best and most out of his guys. He treated everybody with the utmost respect and made everybody understand that whether you were a superstar or the 25th man coming out of spring training, you were going to be an important piece of the puzzle. He made guys not only understand that but believe it."[53]

Marquis Grissom summed up for the author why the players played so hard for Cox. (Grissom had played for three managers before he arrived in Atlanta in 1995.) "He's the best, from all the managers that I had. Every day he would ask me, 'How you doing? How's your family doing?' (He was) able to push all of us in the right direction and get the best out of all of us, and I think that says the world about Bobby Cox – and if you can't play for him, you can't play for nobody."[54] Tim Hudson said, "He was a manager who felt like a teammate, a friend and a father figure. I'm proud that I played for one of the best managers a player could ever ask for." Said John Smoltz, "A small part of Bobby Cox changes you as a baseball player. Twenty years with the man changes your life."[55]

Cox's philosophy of having great pitching and great defense produced the most wins during the 1990s. The Braves' record from 1990 through 1999 was 925-629 (.595). The second most wins during the '90s belonged to the Yankees, at 851-702. (.548).

Hall of Fame manager Sparky Anderson said, "I always gave Bobby the name 'The Greatest,' and I believe that. I believe Bobby Cox can out manage every living soul you want to see."[56]

Cox was never one to take credit for anything. That honor was reserved for his players. Cox defined the term 'player's manager.' In fact, he cared so much that he was known to send some of his former players money if they were ever in need.[57]

Hall of Fame GM John Schuerholz said, "It is sad that the story of the Atlanta Braves ends with the word 'but.' People talk about the great run we had. All my cohorts in the business say, 'What a remarkable accomplishment. No one will ever do that.' The media examines what we have done as productive, but the end of the sentence is, 'But only one championship.' Is that what we have become, a society that wants to look at greatness in an effort to find a failing instead of celebrate success?"[58]

The Braves had just one manager, Cox, during a 15-year stretch in which the 29 other teams employed 149 managers. Over the course of winning 14 division titles, the Braves had 272 players wear their uniform. John Smoltz was the only member of the organization in all 14 championship seasons, although he was on the disabled list for the 2000 season. There were 144 pitchers to appear for the Braves, and only five started as many as 160 games: Tom Glavine (400), Greg Maddux (363), Smoltz (319), Steve Avery (181), and Kevin Millwood (160). They used 20 catchers, 35 first basemen, 24 second basemen, 28 third basemen, 20 shortstops, 57 left fielders, 30 center fielders, and 56 right fielders.[59]

Cox and Joe McCarthy are the only major-league managers to have six seasons of 100 or more wins.

Of his relationship with GM Schuerholz, Cox said, "It's as good a relationship as there could possibly be in sports, I think. We get along great. John runs everything by me. I'm involved in everything that John wants to do. Some GMs don't operate that way anymore. I respect him a great deal. I think he respects my knowledge of what we should do: what trades, free agents, and my reasons for and against some of those."[60]

Through the 2019 season, there have been 711 major-league managers.[61] Cox ranks number four in wins. The top five are Connie Mack with 3,731 victories in 53 years; John McGraw with 2,763 in 33 years; Tony La Russa with 2,728 in 33 years, Bobby Cox with 2,504 in 29 years, and Joe Torre with 2,326 in 29 years. McGraw has the best winning percentage of the five managers, .586, Cox is second at .556, followed by Torre, .538; La Russa, .536; and Mack, .486.

Cox ranks first among the five managers in the statistic "Actual Wins Minus Expected Wins." It is a measure of the extent to which a team outperformed or underperformed its talent. His rating is 34.8. He is followed by La Russa, 20.4; Mack, 13.9; Torre, -5.5, and McGraw -11.9.[62]

Bill James, in a series of articles on Hall of Fame managers, ranks them according to points they score in numerous categories he devised. His top six: McGraw, 250 points; McCarthy, 237; Cox, 206; Mack, 197, La Russa, 196; and Torre, 177.[63]

The Baseball Writers' Association of America named Cox the Manager of the Year a record four times, tying him with La Russa. Three managers have won in three different decades, Cox, La Russa, and Buck Showalter. Cox is the only manager to win the award in consecutive years. *The Sporting News* named Cox the Manager of the Year eight times. The closest is Jim Leyland with four.[64]

On August 12, 2011, Cox was inducted into the Atlanta Braves Hall of Fame and his number-6 jersey was retired.[65] In 2014 he was inducted into the Baseball Hall of Fame, along with La Russa and Torre, the same year as Tom Glavine, Greg Maddux, and Frank Thomas.

Before the HOF ceremony started, Tom Seaver was giving instructions on things to remember during the speeches. He said, "All right boys, don't forget your wife's name. Seriously, practice it right now." Talking to Cox, he said, "Now, what's your wife's name?" "Pam," Cox replied. "Don't forget it." Seaver said. Cox didn't. While waiting offstage before the ceremony, Leo Mazzone, the Braves longtime pitching coach and Cox's right-hand man, noticed that Cox was nervous, and as he had done for Atlanta pitchers so many times, played psychologist. "I told (one of Cox's daughters) to text him a message that said, 'We've been in a lot tougher jams than this one,'" Mazzone said. Cox later admitted that his hands shook as he started his speech. Cox started with a joke, "A few years ago I was sitting with Steve Stone, the broadcaster for the Chicago White Sox, at an Arizona Fall League game, and this guy comes up and says, 'Steve, can I have your autograph?' He says, 'Sure.' He signs it, and he says, 'Hey, you don't want Bobby's autograph?' That guy just stared at me and he says, 'Yeah, I know you. You're that guy from Atlanta who gets thrown out all the time, right?' I said, 'Yeah, that's me, but (Tommy) Lasorda, if he didn't quit so early in his career, he would've had the record that I've got now.'"[66]

Cox was ejected 165 times by major-league umpires.[67] About arguing with umpires, he said, "I generally don't go onto the field that much … but 90 percent of the time it's because my player is upset. And I've got to get in there right away and keep him in the game or at least stick up for him. My relationships with umpires, in my mind, is great. I like them, every single one of them. Being a major-league umpire is the single toughest job in sports. It's hard. Those guys are good. But again, I have to stick up for my players. I can get really upset and other times I'm not and I will talk softly and not be as irate."[68] He was ejected from three postseason games and as of 2019 was the only manager to be ejected from two World Series games.

On April 2, 2019, Cox suffered a possible stroke one day after he attended the Braves' home opener at SunTrust Park.[69] Taken to a hospital, he was seeing visitors the next day. He was taken to a rehabilitation facility a few weeks later and was walking.[70]

The International League inducted Cox into its Hall of Fame in April 2020.[71] He was inducted into the Fresno County Athletic Hall of Fame in 1981.[72]

"I've been more busy after I retired than when I was working," Cox said in 2012. He was named chairman of the board of the Atlanta area Northside Bank. He was also a partner in the Lake Point Sporting Community and Town Center project. He and his wife became involved in a number of charity projects, particularly the Homeless Pets Foundation.[73]

Former Brave Greg McMichael summed up Cox's career: "Bobby Cox's contribution to baseball was, building an organization to sustain winning, going from a manager to a general manager and how to lay the foundation for a team to restructure their farm system, develop players, draft and trade for players, and then go back to managing that core group of players and do something no other team has ever done. When he was managing, he always had the player's back, never through anyone under the bus, didn't blame individuals, and didn't say things to the press about his players. He did what was best for the team."[74]

Sources

In addition to the sources cited in the Notes, the author consulted

Bradbury, J.C. *The Baseball Economist* (New York: Penguin Group [USA] Inc., 2007).

James, Bill. *The Bill James Baseball Abstract 1984* (New York: Ballantine Books, 1984).

Whitaker, Lang. *In the Time of Bobby Cox* (New York: Scribner, 2011).

A huge thank-you to the Aiken County (South Carolina) Public Library, Amanda, Carolyn, and Janet.

All baseball facts and statistics for players and managers are from baseball-reference.com.

Notes

1. Kevin Newell, "What About Bob?" *Coach & A.D.*, October 2, 2009. coachad.com/articles/what-about-bob/.= October 2, 2009.
2. youtube.com/watch?v=SCGQ4kAqzHU.
3. Newell.
4. Robert E. Luckett, "Bobby Cox, b. 1941," *New Georgia Encyclopedia*, November 18, 2002. georgiaencyclopedia.org/articles/sports-outdoor-recreation/bobby-cox-b-1941.
5. answers.com/Q/Does_Bobby_Cox_have_children;mlb.mlm.com/team/coach_staff_bio.jsp?c_id=atl&coachorstaffid=87101162759.
6. State of California Marriage Index.
7. Charles Bethea, "Q&A with Bobby Cox," *Atlanta Magazine*, May 1, 2010.
8. sportscollectorsdaily.com/bobby-cox-baseball-cards/;coachad.com/articles/what-about-bob/.
9. Newell.
10. Doug Walker, Cox Settling into Life after Baseball," *Rome (Georgia) News Tribune,* August 5, 2012.
11. northwestgeorgianews.com/rome/cox-settling-into-life-after-baseball/article_28bc93ac-ecb8-5475-abdf-b55b012819ff.html.
12. Newell.
13. Cory McCartney, *Tales from the Atlanta Braves Dugout* (New York: Sports Publishing, 2016), 164.
14. Steve Weller, "His Tales Are Tall, but Braves Listen," *South Florida Sun-Sentinel* (Fort Lauderdale), March 2, 1985.
15. Dan Schlossberg, *When the Braves Ruled the Diamond* (New York: Sports Publishing, 2016), 31.
16. Newell.
17. Romo, "Walk Off: The Bobby Cox Story," romoball.blogspot.com, October 18, 2010.
18. youtube.com/watch?v=1l_3jUFcKg.
19. Schlossberg, xv.
20. Phone interview with Greg McMichael, February 12, 2020.
21. youtube.com/watch?v=1l_3jUFcKg.
22. Schlossberg, 29.
23. Chipper Jones with Carroll Rogers Walton, *Chipper Jones Ballplayer* (New York: Dutton, 2018), ix.
24. McCartney, 84-90.
25. Newell.
26. Bill James, *The New Bill James Historical Baseball Abstract* (New York: The Free Press, 2001), 829.
27. Schlossberg, 6.
28. Schlossberg, 13.
29. Schlossberg, 30.
30. Schlossberg, 27-28.
31. Schlossberg, 33.
32. John Smoltz with Don Yaeger, *Starting and Closing* (New York: William Morrow, 2012), 236.
33. McCartney, 116.
34. John Thorn, Pete Palmer, and Michael Gershman, with Matthew Silverman, Sean Lahman, and Greg Spira, *Total*

Baseball: The Official Encyclopedia of Major League Baseball, 7thEdition (New York: Total Sports Publishing, 2001), 2487.

35 Newell.
36 Schlossberg, 9
37 Baseball-reference.com, league statistics for teams in 1993.
38 Tom Verducci, *Sports Illustrated,* September27, 1993, 43-44.
39 nytimes.com/1993/10/22/sports/braves-manager-has-knee-surgery.html.
40 Schlossberg, 17, 23.
41 Newell.
42 Smoltz, 220-225.
43 Smoltz, 219.
44 Schlossberg. 54.
45 youtube.com/watch?v=nQheZpZ0bTw.
46 Schlossberg, xviii.
47 Schlossberg, 14.
48 baseballhall.org/hall-of-famers/cox-bobby.
49 youtube.com/watch?v=HrJlb636e0U.
50 youtube.com/watch?v=vnU8SisHill.
51 McCartney, 174
52 McCartney, 175.
53 Schlossberg, 31.
54 McCartney, 157
55 Schlossberg, 265.
56 Youtube.com/watch?v=nQheZpZObTw.
57 Adam Ferguson, "Goodbye Bobby Cox: The End of an Era for the Atlanta Braves," Bleacherreport.com, Bleacherreport.com/articles/488856-goodbye-bobby-cox-the –end-of-an-era-for-the-atlanta-braves.
58 mlb.com/news/braves-14-straight-titles-should-be-cheered-c237410912.
59 mlb.com/news/braves-14-straight-titles-should-be-cheered-c237410912.
60 Newell.
61 https://www.baseball-reference.com/managers/
62 *Total Baseball,* 2414.
63 billjamesonline.com, February 18,19, and 20, 2013.
64 https://www.baseball-reference.com/bullpen/Manager_of_the_Year_Award
65 talkingchop.com/2011/3/22/2066442/braves-to-retire-bobby-coxs-number.
66 McCartney, ix-xii.
67 retrosheet.org/boxesetc/C/Pcox-b103.htm.
68 Newell.
69 Tim Darnell, patch.com/georgia/atlanta/braves-hall-fame-manager-bobby-cox-suffers-possible-stroke.
70 wsbtv.com/sports/legendary-braves-manager-bobby-cox-released-from-hospital-following-stroke/943515081/.
71 Dave Lezotte, "Bobby Cox to Be Inducted into International League Hall of Fame," January 20, 2019. milb.com/gwinnett/news/bobby-cox-to-be-inducted-into-international-league-hall-of-fame-303280110.
72 fresnoahof.org.
73 Walker.
74 Greg McMichael interview.

Jim Beauchamp

BY C. PAUL ROGERS III

Jim Beauchamp

In high school in Grove, Oklahoma, Jim Beauchamp was a standout athlete in all sports. But in baseball, he really stood out and with his speed and power drew comparisons to another Oklahoma native son, Mickey Mantle.[1] But injuries and bad luck deprived him of stardom and relegated him to a 10-year major-league career as a journeyman outfielder and pinch-hitter. After his playing career, he became a baseball lifer as a successful minor-league manager and major-league coach for the Atlanta Braves, spending a total of 50 years in the game. While doing so he became the only player to wear an Atlanta uniform in three Atlanta ballparks: Ponce de Leon Park (as a member of the Atlanta Crackers), Atlanta Fulton-County Stadium, and Turner Field.[2]

James Edward Beauchamp was born on August 21, 1939, in Vinita, Oklahoma, the youngest of three children to Dennis and Beulah Beatrice Hurst Beauchamp. His father was a lawyer who practiced law with his father, E.H. Beauchamp. Young Jim's uncle gave him his first baseball glove, a Frankie Crosetti model, and his father early on taught him how to hit and field.[3] The family moved to nearby Grove, where Jim starred in football, basketball, track, and baseball at Grove High School. In basketball the 6-foot-2 Beauchamp averaged 25.2 points a game as a senior. and was named to the All-State second team. He also finished second in the 100-yard dash in the state high-school track meet. In baseball his high-school team played few games, although he played enough to draw the Mantle comparisons.[4] After graduating from high school, he attended Oklahoma State University for a semester in the fall of 1957, but the following spring signed a professional contract with the St. Louis Cardinals for a reported $50,000 bonus.[5] Freddie Hawn, the scout who signed him, had also discovered Lindy McDaniel, Von McDaniel, and Kerry Don McDaniel, the three pitching brothers from Hollis, Oklahoma.[6]

The Cardinals organization thought enough of Beauchamp's potential to send the 18-year-old to the York (Pennsylvania) White Roses in the Class-A Eastern League. Although one of the youngest players in the league, he hit .259 in 114 games in his debut year. That performance earned him a promotion to the Tulsa Oilers of the Double-A Texas League for the 1959 season. He improved slightly in the faster competition to .268 in 119 games and doubled his home-run total to 10 from the previous year's five round-trippers. His biggest night by far was on August 29, when he hit for the cycle, went 5-for-5 and drove in five runs in a 15-3 Oilers win over the Victoria Rosebuds.[7]

After the season Beauchamp suffered the first of several serious injuries while playing in the Winter Instructional League in Florida. In a game in St. Petersburg he crashed head-first into a concrete wall while chasing a foul ball. Even though he had a helmet liner inside of his cap, he knocked himself out and ended up spending eight days in the hospital with a severe concussion.[8]

Perhaps in part due to the severity of that injury, Beauchamp returned in 1960 to Tulsa, where he batted .258 in 527 plate appearances with 12 home runs and 55 runs batted in. He also led the Texas League in stolen bases with 29, his second stolen-base title in a row.[9] In July he smacked a home run in an exhibition game against the parent Cardinals before a record crowd of over 10,000 in Tulsa.[10]

Because of his power and speed, the Cardinals considered the 21-year-old Beauchamp a top prospect and invited him to 1961 spring training, where he duly impressed manager Solly Hemus.[11] He didn't stick with St. Louis, however, and split time between the San Juan/Charleston Marlins of the Triple-A International League and Tulsa. He struggled in Triple A, batting .227 in 73 games and 305 plate appearances, before ending up back with the Oilers. There he found his stroke, hitting .455 in 11 games before severely dislocating his shoulder while diving back into a base.[12]

The injury to Beauchamp's shoulder eventually required surgery and did permanent damage to his throwing ability. He missed most of the 1962 season as a result, appearing in only 53 games for the Atlanta Crackers in the International League. In 180 plate appearances, Beauchamp hit .254 with five home runs.

He was back with Tulsa in 1963 and, still only 23 years old, he resurrected his career. In 137 games he hit .337 with 31 home runs and 105 runs batted in and led the Oilers to the playoff title, all of which led to his being named the Most Valuable Player in the Texas League.[13] On May 30 Beauchamp drove in six runs with a home run, double, and two singles in the longest game in Texas League history, an 18-inning 9-8 Tulsa victory against the Albuquerque Dukes in a game that lasted 5 hours and 47 minutes.[14] But his top performance during the season occurred on July 18, when he hit for the cycle with a single, double, triple, and two home runs to drive in seven runs in a 14-4 win over the El Paso Sun Kings.[15] The Texas League All-Stars played the major-league Houston Colt .45s that year in their version of an All-Star game and Beauchamp won it for the minor leaguers, 7-3, with a walk-off two-out grand slam off Dick Drott in the bottom of the ninth.[16]

Beauchamp had by then become a fan favorite in Tulsa; from 1961 until 1980 the large sign outside Oiler Park announcing the next Oiler home game was modeled after him in his hitting stance.[17]

Beauchamp's 1963 performance in Tulsa earned him a late season call-up to the Cardinals, which was even more of a thrill because 1963 was Stan Musial's last year and Musial had been Beauchamp's boyhood idol.[18] He struck out in his first at-bat, on September 22 against Joe Nuxhall of the Cincinnati Reds in Crosley Field, pinch-hitting for Lew Burdette in the eighth inning of a 5-2 Cardinals loss. He also failed to record a hit in two more late-season pinch-hitting appearances, making him 0-for-3 in his brief big-league debut.

Beauchamp's Texas League All-Star grand slam in 1963 had also attracted the attention of the Colt .45s, who traded outfielder Carl Warwick for him and pitcher Chuck Taylor in February 1964, just before the start of spring training.[19] Beauchamp made the big-league team, in its third year of existence, out of spring training and was in the starting lineup for the second game of the season, against the Milwaukee Braves in Houston. After flying out to center field in his first at-bat, he stroked a double off Braves starter

Denny Lemaster in his second trip to the plate for his first major-league hit, in a 6-5 Houston loss.

Although given a chance to play almost every day in left field, Beauchamp struggled at the plate and was hitting .185 on May 4 when he was sent down to Oklahoma City in the Pacific Coast League. Ironically, he smashed his first major-league home run the day before, against Fred Norman of the Chicago Cubs in a 5-3 Houston win.

Beauchamp quickly regained his batting stroke with the 89ers and slammed 34 homers in 128 games while hitting .285, earning a September call-up with the Colt .45s. One of his homers in Oklahoma was a towering blast that traveled so far out of All-Sports Stadium that it was never found.[20] Back in the big leagues, Beauchamp again struggled, going 4-for-28 in 10 games. The highlight was a 2-for-5 day against the San Francisco Giants in Candlestick Park on September 29. After a line-drive single to left in the second, Beauchamp hit a home run in the top of the eighth off Giants starter Dick Estelle to tie the score at 3-3 in a game the Colt .45s lost 5-4 in 11 innings.[21] For the season Beauchamp appeared in 23 games and batted only .164.

In spite of his major-league struggles in 1964, Beauchamp made the renamed Houston Astros in 1965 and was their Opening Day right fielder in a 2-0 loss to Chris Short and the Philadelphia Phillies. The right-handed hitter continued to get starts against southpaw starters and by early May had raised his average to .308. But he slumped again in part-time duty and by May 22 was down to .189 when the Astros pulled the plug and traded him and pitcher Ken Johnson to the Milwaukee Braves for outfielder Lee Maye.

The Braves immediately sent Beauchamp to their Atlanta Crackers farm club in the International League. There he batted .259 in 88 games, with 13 home runs. That was enough to earn him a mid-September call-up where he saw spot duty at first base and went 0-for-3 with a walk in four plate appearances.

Beauchamp was back in the International League in 1966 in Richmond, where the Braves had moved their top farm club. He was having a banner year there, heading to a potential triple crown, when with about a month left in the season he broke his wrist tagging a runner while playing first base.[22] He was through for the year, finishing with a .319 batting average in 115 games with 25 homers and 77 runs batted in.

He made the now Atlanta Braves out of spring training in 1967 as a reserve first baseman and pinch-hitter, but was sent back to Richmond in early May after only four plate appearances. In Richmond, Jim became a teammate of Bobby Cox, and when they discovered that they were both born in Oklahoma, a close friendship followed that would last over 40 years, as they later worked closely together in both the Toronto Blue Jays and the Atlanta Braves organizations.

Down on the farm, Beauchamp continued to hit for power, slugging 25 home runs in 96 games, although his batting average slipped to .233. After the season, the Braves traded him to the Cincinnati Reds along with outfielder Mack Jones and pitcher Jay Ritchie for third baseman Deron Johnson.

Still only 28 years old, Beauchamp began the 1968 season with the Indianapolis Indians, the Reds' top minor-league affiliate. He played well there, hitting .291 in 80 games, earning a July call-up to the Reds. With Cincinnati he saw spot duty in center field against left-handed pitching and as a pinch-hitter, batting .263 in 31 games and 62 plate appearances. His two home runs both came against the Phillies' ace left-hander Chris Short.

Although Beauchamp stuck with the Reds for the entire 1969 season, he was used sparingly, appearing in 43 games and batting .250 in 60 at-bats. After the season he was traded back to the Houston Astros for pitchers Pat House and Dooley Womack. With the Astros in 1970, he was used almost exclusively as a right-handed bat off the bench. After hitting .192 in 29 plate appearances, he was on the move again, going to the St.

Louis Cardinals on June 13 with utilityman Leon McFadden in a deal for pitcher George Culver. With the Cardinals he hit .259 for the remainder of the year, also mostly as a pinch-hitter.

Beauchamp remained with St. Louis in 1971 and batted .235 in 77 games. After the season on October 21, his hometown of Grove, Oklahoma, had a day for him and named the high-school baseball field after the then 32-year-old. Beauchamp viewed that day as his greatest thrill in baseball.[23]

Two days earlier, Beauchamp had been traded again, this time to the New York Mets in an eight-player swap.[24] The Mets would be his seventh and last stop in the major leagues as a player.[25] He played sparingly for the 1972 Mets, who finished in third place in the National League's East Division, batting .242 in 131 plate appearances. He showed that he still had some pop, however, hitting five home runs, a career high, and driving in 19 runs off the bench.

Beauchamp hit three of those home runs in a two-game span on August 21 and 22 against his old team, the Astros. On the 21st, he homered in the seventh against Jerry Reuss to put the Mets up 2-1. Then in the bottom of the ninth after the Astros had tied the score, Beauchamp slammed a walk-off two-run homer off Jim Ray to win for Jon Matlack and the Mets, 4-2. The next evening he went 3-for-4 off Dave Roberts with a home run, driving in all four runs in another 4-2 Mets victory. He again had the game-winning blow, a two-out, two-run single in the eighth inning to break a 2-2 tie and complete his best two days in the major leagues.[26]

Beauchamp was back with the Mets in 1973 in what proved to be a memorable year for the team as it won the East Division with a mediocre 82-79 record before defeating the heavily favored Cincinnati Reds in the National League Championship Series three games to two to sweep into the World Series against the Oakland A's. Beauchamp was again a little-used bench player, batting .279 in 61 at-bats, with his best game against the Pirates on May 13 when he drove in four runs in a 6-4 Mets win. He did not appear in the NL Championship Series, but manager Yogi Berra called on him to pinch-hit four times in the World Series where he failed to get a hit as the Mets lost in seven games. His last major-league at-bat was as a pinch-hitter in the fifth inning of Game Seven. With the Mets already down 4-0, Beauchamp took a third strike looking against Ken Holtzman for the third out of the inning.[27]

Beauchamp went to spring training with the Mets in 1974, hoping for another year, but was released on March 27. At 35, he was not quite ready to hang up his spikes and signed a minor-league deal with the St. Louis Cardinals, who assigned him to be a player-coach back with Tulsa, a Triple-A team in the American Association. In 73 games and 266 plate appearances, Beauchamp hit only .216 for the Drillers, who nonetheless won the American Association West Division. His last hurrah, however, was an important one. In the playoffs against the Indianapolis Indians Beauchamp slugged a home run in the 15th inning of the sixth game to lead to a win.[28] The Oilers also won Game Seven to claim the league championship. After the season, Beauchamp retired as a player.

Beset by injuries and might-have-beens, Beauchamp played all or parts of 10 seasons in the major leagues, hitting .231. In what amounted to a little more than a full season of play altogether with 661 at-bats, he hit 14 home runs and drove in 90 runs for his career.

Beauchamp, however, was far from through with baseball after 1974. St. Louis Cardinals general manager Bing Devine had pegged Jim as someone who would be an effective coach or manager, and with all the time he spent on the bench, he became a student of the game.[29] After his coaching gig in Tulsa, which Devine had arranged, it didn't take him long to nab a minor-league managing job because by the next season the Astros had called and asked him to manage their Double-A farm club in Columbus,

Georgia. The following year, 1976, Beauchamp moved up to Triple A, managing the Memphis Blues in the International League to a third-place finish.

In 1977 the Astros moved their Triple-A club to Charleston, West Virginia, still in the International League, and Beauchamp moved with them. He led the Charlies to a second-place regular-season finish, two games out of first. In the playoffs, however, Charleston defeated the Tidewater Tides three games to one and then in the finals swept the Pawtucket Red Sox with four straight wins to claim the league championship. In 1978 Beauchamp led Charleston to the regular-season championship with an 85-55 record and was named Manager of the Year of the International League. The Charlies, however, lost in the league playoffs to the Richmond Braves.

The following year the Charlies slipped to sixth place and after the season, one year after his being named Manager of the Year, the Astros released him so that he could "pursue other opportunities."[30] That opportunity came in the Cincinnati Reds organization, which hired Beauchamp to manage their Indianapolis Indians Triple-A club in the American Association. After two sub-.500 years in Indianapolis, Beauchamp was hired by the Toronto Blue Jays to manage the Triple-A Syracuse Chiefs in the International League for 1982. He managed the Chiefs for three seasons, finishing well under .500 each year. After his first season, in which the team finished sixth, he guaranteed a playoff team the next year or said he wouldn't return.[31] The team finished seventh in 1983 and he did return, without making any promises. In 1984 the Chiefs finished seventh again. He could take solace, however, because he had helped develop players like George Bell, Tony Fernandez, Fred McGriff, and Kelly Gruber, the core of outstanding Blue Jays teams in the '80s and early '90s.

Beauchamp's reputation in player development led him back to the Braves organization where he managed their Double-A franchise in Greenville, North Carolina, for three years. In 1988 the Braves moved him back to Triple A with Richmond in the International League for what turned out to be another three-year stint. His 1989 squad was the regular-season champion of the league's West Division and then defeated the Syracuse Chiefs in the playoffs to claim the league championship.

Beauchamp had the unusual distinction of managing his son in 1989. Kash Beauchamp had been selected by the Toronto Blue Jays as the overall number-one pick in the January 1982 draft and was a 26-year-old in this eighth season of professional baseball.[32] The elder Beauchamp was known as a hard-nosed, old-school manager, and there is evidence that he was harder on his son than anyone else.[33]

After 16 years as a minor-league manager, the 52-year-old Beauchamp returned to the major leagues in 1991 with the Atlanta Braves as the bench coach for manager Bobby Cox. He became a fixture with the successful Braves teams of the '90s, serving as Cox's right-hand man. Along the way he won a World Series ring in 1995 as the Braves defeated the Cleveland Indians in six games. Even as coach, however, he couldn't avoid the injury bugaboo. In 1992 he slipped getting off the team bus in New York and had to have knee surgery.[34] Then in 1993 he suffered a serious eye injury when struck by a line drive off the bat of Bill Pecota in batting practice in St. Louis, crushing his cheekbone, breaking his orbital bone, and causing bleeding inside his eye.[35]

In 1998, after the Braves were eliminated in the NCLS, the team juggled the coaching staff and Beauchamp was reassigned as the organization's minor-league outfield coordinator.[36] He served in that position until spring training in 2007. It was his 50th consecutive spring training, but he began not feeling well and was shortly diagnosed with leukemia.[37] He died from the disease later that year on Christmas day. He was 68 years old. Braves manager Bobby Cox, former general manager John Schuerholz, and outfielder Jeff Francoeur, whom Beauchamp had mentored as a young minor leaguer, all gave eulogies at the funeral.[38]

The Braves wore a memorial patch with "Beach" on the left sleeve of their jerseys in 2008 to honor his memory.[39]

Beauchamp was survived by his wife, Pam, and five children, three with his first wife, Judy (Kash, Tim, and Ann Rene), and two with Pam (Shanna and Lauren).[40]

Jim Beauchamp spent his life in baseball and was considered an old-school coach and manager who expected his players to give all-out effort all the time. If they didn't, they would quickly hear about it in colorful language. He also had a soft side, and according to his son Kash his motto was put God first, family second, and one's job third and everything will fall into place.[41]

Notes

1. Jeffrey Lutz, "Baseball Was the Beauchamps' Link," *Wichita Eagle*, July 6, 2008.
2. Chris Vivlamore, "Beauchamp, Ex-Braves Player and Coach, Dies," *Atlanta Constitution*, December 28, 2007: D3.
3. "Word from the Dugout," *Atlanta Constitution*, September 8, 1997: 25; Jamie M. Wise, "Diamond Jim," *Atlanta Journal-Constitution*, September 19, 1991: 186.
4. The baseball coach was also the football coach and thought track was a much better conditioner for football than baseball, and so scheduled few games. John Cronley, "Once Over Lightly," *Daily Oklahoman* (Oklahoma City), May 21, 1964: 27.
5. Clark Nealon, "Jim Brings Big Bat, No Arm in Sling," *Houston Post*, March 1, 1964.
6. Cronley.
7. David King and Tom Kayser, *The Texas League Almanac* (Charleston, South Carolina: The History Press, 2014).
8. While in the hospital, Beauchamp's head was "sandbagged" so that he could not move it at all. Wilt Browning, "Beauchamp Hits End of Trail?" *Atlanta Journal*, May 8, 1967; Wayne Minshew, "Gomez' Arm Okay, Hopes to Help Phils," *Atlanta Constitution*, March 27, 1967: 17.
9. Bill O'Neal, *The Texas League 1888-1987 – A Century of Baseball* (Austin: The Eakin Press, 1987), 314.
10. The game was played on July 28 with Tulsa losing 12-5. Wayne McCombs, "*Let's Gooooooo Tulsa*" – *The History and Record Book of Professional Baseball in Tulsa, Oklahoma – 1905-1989* (Self-published, 1990), 453.
11. In the middle of spring training, Hemus was quoted as saying, "If this kid makes it, we go all the way. And from what I've seen so far, he's ready." Barney Kremenko, "Rookie Center Is Both Fleet and Powerful," *New York Journal-American*, March 11, 1961.
12. Cronley. Another source indicates he separated his shoulder while chasing a fly ball and running into a wall in Tulsa. Hal Hayes, "Lady Luck Frowns on Jim Beauchamp," *Atlanta Constitution*, April 11, 1967.
13. McCombs, "*Let's Gooooooo Tulsa*," 140. He led the team in every offensive category except stolen bases, where he was second on the team.
14. King and Kayser, 74.
15. King and Kayser, 134.
16. Clark Nealon, "Craft Pleased With Card Trade, And Zesty About Colt Training," *Houston Post*, February 18, 1964; Mickey Herskowitz, ".45s Get Beauchamp, Taylor for Warwick," *Houston Post*, February 18, 1964; King and Kayser, 152.
17. Matt Gleason, "You're Out at the Old Ball Game," *Tulsa World*, May 17, 2010.
18. Volney Meece, "34 HRs Ex-89er's No. 1 Memory," *Daily Oklahoman*, July 4, 1969: 27.
19. Nealon; Herskowitz.
20. The ball was hit to center field at twilight and no one ever saw it come down. And no one could find the ball beyond the fence. Bob Burke, *Baseball in Oklahoma City* (Charleston, South Carolina: Arcadia Publishing, 2003), 61; see also Meece.
21. Masanori Murakami, the first Japanese to play in the major leagues, was the winning pitcher for his first big-league victory with three innings of one-hit relief.
22. Wayne Minshew, "For Jim Beauchamp, 1967 Is the Year of Decision," *Atlanta Constitution*, March 3, 1967: 57; Hayes.
23. Unidentified and undated clipping from the Jim Beauchamp clippings file, National Baseball Library.
24. Beauchamp was traded with pitchers Chuck Taylor and Harry Parker and infielder Chip Coulter for outfielder Art Shamsky and pitchers Jim Bibby, Rich Folkers, and Charlie Hudson. Joe Trimble, "Mets Swap Shamsky and 3 for Cards' Quartet," *New York Daily News*, October 19, 1971: 74.
25. The number is eight if one counts the Milwaukee Braves' move to Atlanta in 1966 while Beauchamp was a member of the Braves organization.
26. On October 4, the last day of the season, Beauchamp again had the winning hit, a two-run homer off Balor Moore of the Montreal Expos in the sixth inning. The blow broke a 1-1 tie and proved decisive in a 3-1 Mets victory.
27. Beauchamp also popped out to second baseman Dick Green in the ninth inning in Game One, reached on an error by pitcher Darold Knowles in Game Two, and, batting for Tom Seaver, lined out to left fielder Joe Rudi against Knowles in Game Three.
28. Wayne McCombs, *Baseball in Tulsa* (Charleston, South Carolina: Arcadia Publishing, 2003), 48.
29. Meece.
30. Unidentified clipping dated October 20, 1979, from the Jim Beauchamp clippings file, National Baseball Library.
31. Bob Hill, "Beauchamp Has Sense of Satisfaction Despite Sad Season," *Syracuse Herald American*, July 22, 1984.

32 Kash Beauchamp played all or parts of 14 years in the minor leagues and managed in independent ball. He was having an outstanding year with Knoxville and then Syracuse in 1986 when he suffered a broken scapula on a collision at home plate, which put him out for the season. He later learned that he was to be promoted to the Toronto Blue Jays the following day. He never played in the major leagues. Lutz.

33 Lutz; Volney Meece, untitled article, *Daily Oklahoman*, July 2, 1989.

34 "Beauchamp Injured," *Atlanta Constitution*, August 31, 1992: 30.

35 Mitch Sneed, "Beauchamp Had Little Reaction Time for Foul Ball," *Atlanta Constitution*, July 15, 1993: 151.

36 Thomas Stinson, "Shake-Up: Jones, Beauchamp Out as Braves Juggle Coaching Staff," unidentified and undated article from the Jim Beauchamp clippings file, National Baseball Library.

37 Carroll Rogers, "Beauchamp Beloved in Braves Family – Coach Being Treated for Acute Myelogenous Leukemia." *Atlanta Constitution*, April 19, 2007.

38 Lutz.

39 "Patch on Sleeve Salutes Beauchamp," *Atlanta Constitution*, April 1, 2008: D5.

40 Vivlamore.

41 Ibid.

Pat Corrales

BY JAMES RAY

Pat Corrales

Pat Corrales spent more than 50 years in professional baseball as a player, coach, and manager. Although he will never be confused with a slugging catcher like Mike Piazza, Corrales was an excellent defensive catcher and a student of the game who parlayed his knowledge and experience into a long and successful career as a major-league coach and manager. Respected by his peers and his players, Corrales, a true baseball lifer who began his major-league career with two at-bats for the 1964 Phillies, was still gainfully employed in the big leagues in his 70s.

But baseball didn't seem to be his destiny as a youngster. Corrales' first love was football. As a 6-foot-tall, 184-pound pulling guard and linebacker on the Fresno High School team, Corrales was named to the All-City team, and was chosen by the *Fresno Bee* newspaper as the high-school lineman of the year. He was selected to play in the Shrine Game, held in Los Angeles, which pitted the best scholastic players from Northern California against the best from the Southern part of the state. But before the game took place Corrales was injured.[1] Fearing that college scouts had lost interest in him as a football player, he signed a baseball contract instead with Philadelphia Phillies scout Babe Herman for a reported $40,000 bonus.

Patrick Corrales was born in Los Angeles on March 20, 1941, to David and Josefina (Rivera) Corrales, the fifth of six children. Pat's siblings were Elizabeth, Olga, Peggy, Gabriel, and Evelyn (1943-1949). His father worked as a truck driver in Los Angeles before finding a job as a grinder in an iron foundry in Fresno, California, where the family relocated.

The catcher on the Fresno High baseball team, Corrales acquired the nickname Ike, perhaps after the comic strip character Ozark Ike, who was brawny and who, like Pat, had a plodding gait. At Fresno High he caught future major-league pitchers Jim Maloney and Dick Ellsworth. Future major leaguer Bobby Cox attended a rival high school (Selma), and though Corrales' team routinely beat Cox's squad, the two became colleagues, competitors, and friends.

Corrales signed with Herman and the Phillies on June 26, 1959. Fresh out of high school and barely 18 years old, he was sent to the Johnson City (Tennessee) Phillies of the Class-D Appalachian League, where he hit .243 with 13 RBIs in 23 games. Late in the season he was promoted to the Bakersfield Bears of the Class-C California League, where he went hitless in five at-bats.

Corrales was back in Class D for the 1960 season with the Tampa Tarpons of the Florida State League, where he hit only .246 but led the team with 18 doubles. After the season, on September 24, he married Sharon Ann Grimes in Fresno. The union produced four children, Rene, twins Patricia and Michele, and Jason. Pat climbed through the minors slowly but very steadily. In 1961, he was in Class-B ball and hit an impressive .309 with the Des Moines Demons. By 1964 he was the star catcher for the Arkansas Travelers of the Triple-A Pacific Coast League. In the most competitive league in the minors, Corrales' star shined brightly. In 101 games and 372 plate appearances, he hit .364 with 9 home runs and 48 RBIs. Impressed by the 23-year-old rising star, the Phillies called Corrales up in August, and he made his major-league debut on August 2 before a crowd of 18,000 at Connie Mack Stadium in a game against the Los Angeles Dodgers. In the bottom of the fifth inning, with the Phillies trailing 3-1, manager Gene Mauch sent Corrales up to hit for pitcher Ed Roebuck and he grounded out against left-handed pitcher Larry Miller. Corrales' only other plate appearance with the Phillies that season came on August 11 against the Cubs, when he drew a base on balls from his high-school teammate Dick Ellsworth, a left-hander, and then scored on a grand slam by Johnny Callison. From then on it was watching as the Phillies, who appeared to be headed for the pennant, were undone by a stunning ten-game losing streak in September.

In 1964 Mauch platooned catchers Clay Dalrymple and Gus Triandos. In 1965 Triandos got off to a slow start and was sold to Houston in June. Corrales took his place in the platoon. He played in the most games (63) and had the most at-bats (174) in a season in his nine-year major-league career. Corrales hit .224 with two home runs and 15 RBIs. He also drew 25 walks, which helped him to a .323 on-base percentage. He was named to the Topps All-Rookie team.

Corrales was involved in a memorable collision at home plate on July 10. In the first inning of a game at Connie Mack Stadium, the San Francisco Giants' Willie Mays slid into Corrales, who was blocking the plate, knocking Corrales out and gashing Corrales' neck with his spikes. "Mays was the only guy I've ever seen who seemed to be faster sliding than running," said Giants broadcaster Lon Simmons. "That was in Philadelphia and the fans are pretty rough there. Willie stayed down on the ground. He pretended he was hurt, too, so the fans wouldn't get on his case so bad."[2] Corrales was removed from the game, and Mays, hurt or not, did not take the field for the bottom of the inning. Corrales was back in action five days later, starting a game at Cincinnati and going 3-for-3.

After the 1965 season the Phillies traded Corrales, outfielder Alex Johnson, and pitcher Art Mahaffey to the St. Louis Cardinals for first baseman Bill White, shortstop Dick Groat, and another light-hitting catcher, Bob Uecker. Corrales played in only 28 games in 1966 as a backup to All-Star Tim McCarver and hit just .181. He spent 1967, with the Cardinals' Triple-A team at Tulsa and hit well enough (.274 with 10 home runs and 55 RBIs) to draw interest from the Cincinnati Reds, who sent catcher Johnny Edwards to the Cardinals for Corrales and infielder Jimy Williams. For the next 4½ years, with the exception of a half-season at Indianapolis in 1968, Corrales was the backup to future Hall of Fame catcher Johnny Bench. Bench's production, defense, and durability limited Corrales to just 134 games during his stint in the Queen City.

During the All-Star break in 1969, Sharon Corrales was delivering the couple's fourth child, son Jason, when she developed a blood clot and died on July 22 in Christ Hospital, Cincinnati, seven hours after the child was born. Pat's teammates and the Cincinnati fans were very helpful and sympathetic to Pat's plight. Other major-league teams helped, too, notably the [Baltimore] Orioles' Wives, who held a bake sale and donated the proceeds to the Sharon Corrales Scholarship Fund for Pat and Sharon's children.

During his five years playing for the Reds (1968- June 11, 1972), Corrales hit .231 with two homers and 27 RBIs in 365 plate appearances. He had one at-bat in the 1970 World Series. It was against Mike Cuellar — a pinch-hit groundout to Baltimore third baseman Brooks Robinson that ended Game Five and clinched the World Series for the Orioles. During his time with the Reds, Corrales married Heidy Davis in 1970. They divorced in 1982.

The Reds traded Corrales to San Diego on June 11, 1972, for catcher Bob Barton. With the Padres, Corrales backed up Fred Kendall. He played with the Padres through the end of the 1973 season. Corrales spent the next year in the minor leagues with the Hawaii Islanders, and in 1975 he managed and played two games with the Alexandria Aces of the Double-A Texas League before calling it quits as a player.

Corrales became the third-base coach for the Texas Rangers in 1976 and quickly moved into a bench-coach role for manager Billy Hunter. Hunter was fired with one game left in the 1978 season and Corrales was named to replace him, becoming the first Mexican-American manager in the major leagues. (In his debut the Rangers beat the Seattle Mariners, 9-4.) Corrales continued as manager in 1979. At the halfway mark, the Rangers were 47-34 and tied for first place in the American League West with the California Angels. The second half of the season wasn't so kind. From July 15 to August 3, the team lost ten of its 15 games. In August the Rangers won only nine of 31 games and fell to fourth place, eight games behind first-place California. Despite a strong finish (19-8) in September, the Rangers were unable to dig themselves out of the hole they had created in July and August and finished 83-79 and in third place in the AL West. In 1980 the Rangers took a step back, finishing 76-85 and in fourth place. Corrales was fired at the end of the season.

In 1982 the Phillies hired Corrales to succeed Dallas Green as manager in Philadelphia. Just two years removed from the team's first World Series title, and coming off a playoff appearance in 1981, Corrales headed a team led by future Hall of Famers Steve Carlton, Mike Schmidt, and, as most thought at the time, Pete Rose. The Phillies were in the race from after the All-Star Game until September 13, when they held a half-game lead over St. Louis. But they finished 9-10 down the stretch and the Cardinals won 13 of their last 20 to finish three games ahead of Philadelphia. The Cardinals went on to win the World Series over the Brewers in seven games.

The year 1983 was a strange season indeed for Corrales. On a high note, Pat married Donna Ardene Myers on March 7, while in Clearwater, Florida for the Phillies' spring training. At the All-Star break the Phillies were in first place by .001 over the Cardinals, but were just 43-42. To most everyone's surprise, the Phillies general manager, Paul "The Pope" Owens, fired Corrales and replaced Pat with himself. Corrales became the first (and as of 2019 was still the only) manager to be sacked when his team was in first place. Owens led the Phillies to the division title and National League pennant before losing the World Series in five games to the Baltimore Orioles.

Corrales wasn't unemployed for long. Just two weeks after he was fired, the Cleveland Indians, who had struggled to a 40-60 record, fired manager Mike Ferraro and hired Corrales. Corrales led the Indians to a respectable 30-32 record in the second half of the season, good enough for the Tribe to bring him back in 1984. The team struggled to sub-.500 records in 1984 and '85, but in 1986, they showed promise by finishing 84-78.

On July 1, 1986, Corrales was involved in one of the more bizarre episodes in baseball history. Playing the Oakland A's, the Indians were leading 7-0 in the seventh inning when Tony Bernazard homered to lead off the seventh inning. A's pitcher Dave "Smoke" Stewart responded by throwing a so-called "purpose pitch" that almost hit the

Indians' Julio Franco. Corrales demanded that the umpire eject Stewart, but the umpire instead issued warnings to both dugouts. Corrales began screaming at Stewart, who challenged him to come out to the mound. Corrales did, and he launched a kick that hit Stewart but didn't do much damage. Stewart then knocked Corrales down with a punch. A ten-minute bench-clearing brawl ensued, after which Corrales and Stewart were thrown out of the game. The two made peace after Corrales' "karate fight" at the mound.

The 1986 Indians won 84 games in a very tough American League East division. The young team featured up-and-coming stars Joe Carter, Julio Franco, Mel Hall, and Cory Snyder. After their good finish in 1986, expectations were high for 1987. The April 6, 1987, edition of *Sports Illustrated* featured Snyder and Carter on its cover with the headline "Best Team in the Majors?" But the season didn't pan out as hoped, and Corrales was fired on July 13 after leading the team to a 31-56 record, and was replaced by Doc Edwards. The team finished 61-101, the worst in the majors.

Corrales managed the Toledo Mud Hens, the Detroit Tigers' Triple-A affiliate, to a 58-84 last-place finish in 1988. He spent 1989 as a New York Yankees coach under managers Dallas Green and Bucky Dent.

In 1990 his old high-school rival Bobby Cox hired Corrales as first-base coach of the Atlanta Braves. Corrales was promoted to bench coach in 1999 and stayed with the Braves through the 2006 season, enjoying unprecedented success along the way in the form of 14 division titles, five National League pennants, and one World Series trophy. It was long rumored that Corrales would eventually replace Cox as manager, but he didn't wait. Instead, after the 2006 season, he joined the Washington Nationals' new manager, Manny Acta, as his bench coach.

In 2008 the Nationals finished with the worst record in baseball (59-102), and Acta fired five of his coaches, including Corrales. But Pat returned as bench coach in July 2009 after Acta was fired and replaced by Jim Riggleman. Corrales didn't return to Washington in 2010 but was once again appointed Nationals bench coach in June 2011 by new manager Davey Johnson. Corrales replaced John McLaren, who was reassigned to scouting duty. Johnson let Corrales go at the end of 2011. "I love him to death and he did a great job," said Johnson.[3]

In 2012, Corrales was officially listed as Senior Assistant, Player Development for the Nationals. He served as interim manager of the Nats' Double-A affiliate, the Harrisburg Senators, for about a week in May, filling in for manager Matt LeCroy, who left on paternity leave after his wife gave birth to twins. After the season he was hired by the Los Angeles Dodgers' new President Stan Kasten, who knew him well from their days together with the Braves and Nationals. Pat came onboard as a special assistant to general manager Ned Colletti. "We are happy to have Pat join us," Colletti said on the day of the signing, November 12. "His vast experience, especially from his years in Atlanta and Washington, will be a great strength to our organization. ... I have known Pat for a long time, and some of my early mentors, whom I respect very much, have worked side by side with him."[4]

At the age of 71, Corrales became part of a historic organization whose new ownership was dedicated to winning, and which spent enough money to field a championship-caliber squad. This boded well for Corrales, who as of 2019 was still working with the Dodgers and didn't seem eager to retire any time soon.

Sources

In addition to the sources cited in the Notes, the author also consulted:

Hafner, Dan. "Stewart Lands Punch to Manager Corrales, But Indians Knock Out A's," *Los Angeles Times*, July 2, 1986.

Jaffe, Chris. "Silver Anniversary of the Corrales-Stewart Karate Fight," *Hardball Times*, July 1, 2011.

Morrow, Jeff. "Pat Corrales, answer to a famous baseball trivia question, is temporarily managing the Harrisburg Senators," *Harrisburg Patriot News*, April 29, 2012.

Reddington, Patrick. "Get to Know Your Nationals, Coaching Edition, Pat Corrales," Federal Baseball.com, November 2, 2007, accessed November 25, 2012.

"Indians Fire Manager Corrales and Promote Edwards," *Los Angeles Times*, July 17, 1987.

Also consulted were Baseball Almanac, BaseballLibrary.com, Baseball-Reference.com, Factlookup.com, fanbase.com/Pat-Corrales, Baseballthinkfactory.org, and Pennlive.com.

This biography, originally written in 2013, was updated by Tom Hufford in 2019.

Notes

1. http://fresnoahof.org/pdf/80/PatCorrales_80, pdf accessed December 8, 2012.
2. Tom FitzGerald, "OPEN SEASON / When Runners Attack: the Duel for the Plate," www.sgfate.com, July 26, 2002. https://www.sfgate.com/sports/article/OPEN-SEASON-When-runners-attack-the-duel-for-2818602.php
3. Associated Press, "Nats Keep Davey Johnson As Manager," www.espn.com, October 31, 2011. https://www.espn.com/mlb/story/_/id/7173605/washington-nationals-keep-davey-johnson-manager-2012
4. "Pat Corrales Named Special Assistant to the General Manager," mlb.com, November 5, 2012. https://www.mlb.com/news/pat-corrales-named-special-assistant-to-the-general-manager/c-40173934

Clarence Jones

BY STEVEN SCHMITT

Clarence Jones

Long before launch angles, exit velocities, infield shifts, and OPS calculations, Clarence Jones taught the basics of hitting to some of the greatest players in Atlanta Braves history. Jones played 19 seasons of professional baseball as an outfielder-first baseman. Though his major-league career totaled 58 games with the Chicago Cubs, Jones won two US minor-league home-run titles and two more in Japan. In 1984 home-run king Henry Aaron, Atlanta's director of minor-league player development, hired Jones to groom hitters who helped produce the 1995 World Series victory, three National League pennants, and seven division championships from 1991 to 1998.

Jones emphasized patience, positive attitude, and mental preparation. "Stay back and be patient," he told the likes of Ron Gant, David Justice, Mark Lemke, and Jeff Blauser as he shepherded them as a hitting instructor from Class A to the major leagues. Gant needed to concentrate, work harder in the batting cage, and stop trying to pull every pitch out of the park, Jones recalled in 2019.[1] In 1991 Gant became the Braves' first 30-home-run, 30-stolen-base player since Dale Murphy, whose trade to the Phillies made room for Justice. "I made him get up on the plate," Jones said. "They would try to sneak the ball inside and jam him and he would kill it."[2] Justice hit 23 home runs after the 1990 All-Star break and won Rookie of the Year honors. Jones called Lemke and Blauser the best situation hitters on the 1995 team.[3]

Jones also stressed a positive approach. He told his pupils, "You've got two more" if they missed pitches or took a questionable strike. Teaching hitters to control their swing and hit to all fields produced confidence and results throughout Jones's Atlanta coaching tenure. After Jones told him to cut down on his swing, Dale Murphy socked eight homer runs over a two week-stretch in 1989.[4] Catcher Greg Olson became a 1990 All-Star after Jones advised him to hit to right field more often.[5] Center fielder Otis Nixon practiced putting the ball on the ground and hitting line drives up the middle every day ("If he hit it in the air, he came out of the cage," Jones said) and became a dangerous leadoff hitter.[6]

Mental preparation was the main thrust of Jones's coaching philosophy: Learn what pitchers throw in tight spots and be ready to hit with authority. "Most pitchers have command of one side of the plate," Jones said. "They go to that strength when they are in trouble. Once you learn that, you've figured out a lot of pitchers. If you're thinking too much, you don't see the ball. If you don't see the ball, you swing through it."[7]

Clarence Woodrow Jones was born in Mobile, Alabama, to Henry and Anna Pearl Jones on November 7, 1940.[8] He grew up in Zanesville, Ohio, the fourth of 10 children – six boys and four girls.[9] His father managed night clubs in Zanesville and Coshocton, Ohio, after working for the Zanesville sanitation department. His mother was a homemaker and worked part-time at an egg-processing plant. Clarence played football, basketball, and baseball at Zanesville High School with the goal of becoming a professional athlete. A fullback as a sophomore, Jones played tight end and linebacker in his junior and senior seasons, earning all-conference defensive honors in 1958, twice making a touchdown catch and an interception in the same game.[10] He set a school record of 28 consecutive extra points and boomed kickoffs into the end zone.[11] In his junior season, Zanesville's defending state champion basketball team lost in the semifinals in a battle of 24-0 teams.[12]

Jones's varsity baseball career featured a grand slam on May 1, 1958, at New Concord in a 14-0 victory.[13] The Blue Devils lost in the Central Ohio League tourney finals, 3-0, Jones hitting a triple.[14] That summer the Zanesville American Legion team won the 11th District Legion tournament. "PeeWee" Jones went 3-for-5 with three runs scored and an RBI triple. A week later, Jones homered in a first-round loss in the junior American Legion state tournament, played at Ohio State University. On a 1961 minor-league questionnaire, Jones typed, "I was proud to be part of a team that went to the State in baseball."[15]

After Jones graduated in 1959, a Philadelphia Phillies scout who had seen him in the Legion tournament signed him for $5,000. After playing three games for Class-D Johnson City (Tennessee) of the Appalachian League, Jones quit because of the discrimination in the Deep South. "I was the only black on the team; I couldn't go to theaters or hotels with the guys or eat with them in restaurants."[16] Zanesville High School was 80 percent white and the students did everything together, Jones remembered. The ZHS Boys' Club Jones belonged to emphasized Christian living and good fellowship.[17]

In the fall of 1959, Jones enrolled at Santa Ana (California) College at the recommendation of Southern California head football coach Don Clark and played football and basketball, still hoping to make the pros. Jones studied criminology for two years and worked part-time at Sears Roebuck.[18] In October 1960 Jones married Lorene Miller, whom he met on campus. Soon after, some friends encouraged him to try out for the Dodger Rookies, a team of high-school and college prospects. Jones met Dodgers hitting coach and manager of the Dodger Rookies Kenny Myers the Monday before the season opened. "He put me in the batter's box and I hit several line drives," Jones said. Myers told him he made the team. "In a week, he wanted to sign me (to a Dodgers contract)," Jones recalled. Jones wanted to finish the basketball season but the Dodgers gave him money and a new car. Jones dropped out of Santa Ana and played for the Rookies, then joined Myers at Vero Beach for Los Angeles Dodgers spring training.[19]

Jones said Myers taught players to use their hands and not try to pull every pitch. "He could show you and he could do it," Jones said of Myers, a 13-year minor leaguer who also batted left-handed. As the Braves' hitting coach, Jones adopted Myers' "show, don't tell" approach. "I could still do it and I would show them how to do it."[20]

Jones gained a power-hitting reputation at Class-D Kokomo of the Midwest League in 1961. Three of his eight home runs were grand slams against the Decatur Commodores. *Decatur Herald and Review* sports editor Forrest Kyle advised that Jones be walked with the bases loaded from then on.[21] Later that season, Jones moved to Artesia, New Mexico, and hit nine homers in 36 games for

Spider Jorgensen's Class-A Sophomore League team.[22]

In 1962 the Dodgers promoted Jones to the Great Falls Electrics of the Class-C Pioneer League. On April 23 his grand slam beat Billings 7-4 and won him a $75 suit and $5 in cash. On May 1 Jones hit a three-run homer off Clay Carroll to beat Boise. On July 1, Jones's grand slam against Idaho Falls traveled an estimated 515 feet at Legion Park. Jones set a new team home-run mark with his 21st on August 26, getting a handshake from the previous record-holder, right fielder Eddie Reed.[23] In his first full season, Jones jolted 25 homers, drove in 89 runs and batted .280. He was determined to make it to the majors. "If you're a kid and you like what you're doing, after some time you get better and better," Jones said. "You have to want it and I wanted it." Jones called the Dodgers organization a "great family." Players helped each other and did everything together. "Naturally, you want to be like them," Jones said. "That made me want to be a major-league player."[24] Jones's ambition was to play first base for the Los Angeles Dodgers.[25]

The Dodgers had other plans. Jones played left field for the Class-A Santa Barbara Rancheros of the California League in 1963 while teammate Wes Parker played first base. Jones hit 20 homers and batted .270, then joined Albuquerque of the Double-A Texas League for 12 games and hit two more homers. In 1964 Jones had an MVP season for the Salem (Oregon) Dodgers of the Class-A Northwest League, batting .344 with 33 home runs and a league-leading 120 RBIs. He also led the league with 114 runs scored, 168 hits, and 307 total bases. Topps Chewing Gum Co. chose Jones as one of 15 Minor League Players of the Year. He started in left field for the Class A West All-Stars and was voted the Northwest League all-star left fielder.[26] On August 25 the man the local press called "Big Luke" set a new league record with his 31st home run. "Clarence Jones now ranks as the most productive slugger ever to wear a Salem uniform," the Salem Capital Journal crowed.[27] The Dodgers and the Yakima Braves were .006 apart for the second-half title on September 3 but Salem's regular-season pennant winners missed the playoffs with a 7-6 loss to the Eugene Emeralds, Jones suffering an ankle injury stealing second base.[28]

Jones spent the fall of '64 with the Dodgers' Arizona Instructional League team, then joined Albuquerque for the 1965 season. He beat out future Cubs teammate John Boccabella for selection as the Texas League All-Star first baseman but lost a cow-milking contest to his Dallas-Fort Worth rival three weeks earlier. Afterward, Jones said the closest he got to a cow growing up in Zanesville was watching them from a car.[29] Jones contributed 18 home runs, 79 RBIs, and a .281 average as the Dukes won the Texas League title.[30]

On November 29, 1965, the Chicago Cubs selected Jones in the Rule 5 draft. He played 26 games for Tacoma of the Triple-A Pacific Coast League before torn knee ligaments sidelined him for a month.[31] In mid-June, Jones reported to Dallas-Fort Worth of the Texas League and hit 13 homers with 43 RBIs in 82 games. On July 5 Jones hit a tape-measure blast off Wayne Granger.[32] Eleven days later, his two-run homer off Frank Funk spoiled a shutout and won the game.[33] Jones repeated the trick against Danny Coombs on September 2.[34]

In the fall 1966 Arizona Instructional League, Jones played first base and drove in 28 runs for the Cubs, six more than Bobby Bonds of the Giants.[35] In a March 8 intrasquad game, Jones homered off southpaw Bob Hendley and was hit in the helmet his next time up.[36] On March 22 he homered off Gaylord Perry.[37] After getting two hits against the California Angels, Jones said, "If the man (Cubs manager Leo Durocher) puts me at first base, I'll stay there."[38] Durocher said, "The young man reminds me of Bill White in the field and I like the way he swings a bat," adding that Jones would platoon with future Hall of Fame first baseman Ernie Banks.[39] Then Jones pulled a leg muscle and Banks got his job back.

Jones made the Opening Day roster and moved in with left fielder and future Hall of Famer Billy Williams, who called Jones "C." Jones recalled talking hitting with Williams nonstop from the house to the ballpark. Jones learned from Williams to take four pitches to see if he was over striding, dropping his hands, pulling his head, or not seeing the ball. On April 25 Jones got his first major-league hit, off Mets rookie Tom Seaver. On May 7 he hit a pinch-hit double with two outs in the bottom of the ninth off St. Louis ace Bob Gibson and scored the winning run on Don Kessinger's single. But a 4-for-22 start earned Jones a ticket back to Tacoma. He returned two months later and twice drove in Ron Santo in a 4-3 win at San Francisco. In late July, Jones went 7-for-20 on a road trip to St. Louis and Cincinnati as the Cubs fought to stay in pennant contention. He hit his first major-league home run on July 30, a two-run shot off the Reds' Gary Nolan.[40]

Defensively, Jones struggled as a right fielder in Wrigley Field, with its fierce afternoon sun angle and the wind off Lake Michigan. On August 1 he made a leaping grab of St. Louis catcher Tim McCarver's drive against the ivy in right-center but misjudged two fly balls that cost the Cubs a game against the Phillies. "He's willing to work and has the desire to play," said coach Pete Reiser, who hit countless fungoes to Jones every day. Reiser said Jones may have been afraid of having the ball hit to him. "You can't do that," Reiser said. "You've got to do the opposite – hope they hit everything your way and feel confident that you'll catch it." Jones sometimes flipped his glasses down too soon instead of shading his eyes with his glove until the ball got below the level of the sun. "I know you're not supposed to be thinking about anything else when you're at bat (but) I can't help it sometimes," Jones told a sportswriter.[41] In 53 games Jones logged two home runs, 16 RBIs, and a .252 average. He said Durocher gave him "every opportunity in the world" to become a good major-league player, and "If I had been a good right fielder, I probably could have stayed there."[42]

In 1968 there was no room for Jones on the Cubs roster. Former Dodgers Lou Johnson and Jim Hickman and veteran Al Spangler roamed right field and Dick Nen backed Banks at first base. Jones responded with a league-leading 24 home runs for Tacoma. "You don't belong here," manager Whitey Lockman told him. "I'll do everything I can to get you out of here."[43] Jones rejoined the Cubs in September and played his final major-league game on September 26, 1968, drawing a walk as a pinch-hitter against the Dodgers.

On January 9, 1969, the Cubs traded Jones, catcher Bill Plummer, and pitcher Ken Myette to the Cincinnati Reds for submarine-ball relief specialist Ted Abernathy, a two-time winner of the NL Fireman of the Year award. The Reds sent Jones to Indianapolis of the Triple-A American Association, where manager Vern Rapp told him he had to beat out Jim Beauchamp, who later coached with Jones in Atlanta. Jones hit 21 homers, tying Bernie Carbo for the team lead, Twelve circuit blasts occurred from July 7 to July 30 but Jones never got called to help Cincinnati in a five-team title chase in the NL West. "He didn't like me," Jones said of Rapp, who he said would not recommend him, though the Reds lacked left-handed power off the bench.

Jones once described himself as "one of baseball's real gypsies," estimating that he played professional baseball in 250 to 275 cities in his first 15 years, including eight minor-league stops, and eight seasons in Japan, where he won two home-run titles in the Pacific League and hit 246 home runs.[44] Former major-league second baseman Don Blasingame, a player and then a scout for the Japan leagues, recruited Jones for the Nankai Hawks of Osaka. Former major-league outfielder George Altman – who filled in for Jones on the 1967 Cubs during his two-month demotion – let Jones stay in his house and gave him sound advice in dealing with Japanese umpires, who had wide strike zones. "The more you argue and complain, the worse they get," Altman told Jones. "They start calling you out on everything." Instead of arguing, Jones quit looking for inside pitches to pull over the right-field fence and started hitting to all fields, with excellent results. "Once you learn that," he said, "you come out on top."[45]

Jones estimated that half of his homers in Japan went to center or left field. In four seasons with the Hawks, he hit 132 home runs – never less than 32 in a season – but his best years were ahead. A salary squabble with Nankai led Jones to sign with the Kintetsu Buffaloes of Osaka in 1974. He became the first American to win a Japanese home-run title, pacing the Pacific League with 38, playing in all 130 games. He was a surprise All-Star selection because of his .226 average. Jones dropped to 29 homers in 1975 (his only season below 30 in Japan) but took another Pacific League home-run title in 1976 with 36 in 114 games. On May 31 Jones hit the 206th home run of his Japan career, breaking Altman's record of 205 (1968-1975).[46]

After an injury-plagued 1977 season with Kintetsu, Jones returned to California and became a booking agent for Redd Foxx Productions. (Former LA teammate Willie Crawford's wife was the firm's president.) Foxx hired Jones to serve as concierge, make hotel and travel arrangements, review scripts for the *Sanford and Son* television show, and book acts for Foxx and the company's 28-member troupe of entertainers. That included Foxx's Las Vegas nightclub shows. "Dean Martin, Frank Sinatra and Sammy Davis Jr. rented the Playboy Club for their parties," Jones recalled. In an interview published in the July 28, 1991, *Los Angeles Times,* Jones said the job "wasn't me. I had to wear a suit and tie (and) go to luncheons and parties." The job lasted six months and Jones left to play for the Aguascalientes Raileros in the Mexican League, with Willie Crawford as a teammate. They helped the Raileros ("railroad workers") win the 1978 league championship. Jones and Crawford homered off Cordoba's Diego Segui in game five of the second-round playoff series that the Raileros won in six games. They defeated the Union Laguna Algodoneros in the finals.

Jones chose not to return to Redd Foxx Productions ("He got mad when I quit"), but painful knees ended his playing career. Jones looked for jobs while enduring a custody battle with his first wife, Lorene, whom he divorced in July 1979. "She got the kids," said Jones, who spent summers with Clarence Jr. and Richard.

Jones got his dream job when the Braves hired him as a roving minor-league hitting instructor in 1984. In the middle of the 1985 season, he joined Atlanta to help manager Eddie Haas revive the offense. When the Braves fired Haas at the end of the season and hired Chuck Tanner, Jones was back in the minors, a move that would pay off in the future. Jones coached Ron Gant for three minor-league seasons in Class A, emphasizing hard work, concentration, and patience at the plate. In 1986 Gant logged 31 doubles, 10 triples, 26 homers, 102 RBIs, and 35 stolen bases as starting second baseman for the Durham Bulls of the Class-A Carolina League. "He had more ability than anybody we had," Jones recalled. "Big power, he could run, and he was fearless."[47] Gant joined the Braves in September 1987 and placed fourth in the National League Rookie of the Year voting in 1988. Mark Lemke and David Justice spent 1986 at Sumter (Class-A South Atlantic League) in 1986 while shortstop Jeff Blauser batted .286 with 13 homers and 52 RBIs as Gant's keystone mate at Durham.[48]

On May 22, 1988, Atlanta general manager Bobby Cox fired Tanner – who had hired Jones as hitting instructor to improve the National League's worst offense– and four coaches. Cox, a Dodger signee and a teammate of Jones at Tacoma in 1966, named Russ Nixon manager, Jones as hitting instructor and first-base coach, and future Atlanta manager Brian Snitker as bullpen coach.[49] Jones could show the players what he wanted. He threw at least 100 pitches of batting practice every day and wanted the ball hit right back at him. "You need to learn a lot of things on your own,"

Jones said. "They've got to get in the batter's box and learn to control their nerves. The ones who do that are successful." Jones said 90 percent of hitters in the minors are fastball hitters. "Once they start changing speeds (in the majors), that starts them thinking. If you think a little bit, the ball is by you. You have to know what you want to do."[50]

When Gant had a dismal 1989 season, Jones said, "He has enough power where he shouldn't be going up there looking to hit home runs. They'll come." The following season, Gant hit 32 home runs and stole 33 bases and batted .303. "He prepares himself mentally for every game now," Jones said. "He's learned that when you come up to the big leagues you have to work just as hard as or harder than you had to work to get here."[51]

Justice was "quick enough to hit anything," Jones said, "either the hard stuff or breaking pitches." Justice hit 21 homers in 1991, despite missing two months with back injuries. In 1993 his 40 homers led Atlanta to a franchise-record 104 victories. Lemke hit .450 in the first five games of the '91 World Series and became a folk hero.[52] "He was just waiting to bust out with the whole world watching," Jones said.[53] Blauser learned to use his hands and quick wrists and to attack the baseball. Patience helped Javy Lopez and Ryan Klesko become .300 hitters.[54] Even the pitchers led off batting practice every day. "They could hit and bunt," Jones said. "Our pitchers played a big part in winning games, on the mound or in the batter's box."[55]

Jones let some players excel with what got them to the majors. "The kind of player who comes along once every 100 years," Jones said of 2018 Hall of Famer Chipper Jones, "he always hit the ball hard in the gaps." When struggling at the plate, Jones recalled, Chipper would call his father for help when in a slump. "If his dad can help him more than me," the coach told Cox when asked if the calls bothered him, "I take my hat off to him."[56] Fred McGriff "could hit good pitching," Jones said. "He never got too excited." In 1996 the Braves may have gotten the entire package in center fielder Andruw Jones. "Andruw was a young player who really did understand what he was doing," Jones said. Andruw was a great high-ball hitter, Jones recalled, but was later told to lay off those pitches. "When you get into major-league baseball and take away what they do best," Jones said in 2019, "you're in trouble."[57]

At the end of the 1998 season, Braves general manager John Schuerholz asked Jones to return to Triple-A Richmond as hitting instructor. "It was not in my best interest to do that," Jones said. "I would die there, too." Don Baylor took over in Atlanta and Jones went to Cleveland, reunited with David Justice and coaching Manny Ramirez and Jim Thome. "He'd be the first one at the ballpark and the last one to leave," Jones said of Ramirez. Both worked hard and had time for the kids seeking autographs.[58] Thome slugged 49 homers in Jones's final year as Cleveland hitting instructor and was inducted into the Hall of Fame in 2018.

After retiring from baseball, Jones traveled the world from Alaska to Rome, Europe to the Caribbean. He had two hip replacements, knee surgery, and surgery to remove a stomach tumor. Still in good health, Jones and his second wife, Daphne Galloway Jones, live in Greensboro, Georgia. They met in Richmond in 1988 when Braves coach Willie Stargell introduced them on a double date. They married in September 1989 with Stargell as best man.

In 2019 Jones expressed gratitude for his baseball life. "I loved being a hitting instructor," he said. "I had good people around me and people who tried to help me."[59] His hitting philosophy could be a handbook of life lessons: Be patient. Be positive. Be prepared. Have fun and enjoy what you're doing. Anyone could buy into that.

Clarence Jones's two sons have traveled different paths and had successful careers. Clarence Jr., born December 2, 1965, in Orange County, California, played basketball for Oral Roberts University (1983-86) and Hawaii Pacific University (1986-88), earning first-team all-conference honors at both schools. After playing in Japan (1988-89) and Australia (1989-92), Jones tried out for Lenny Wilkens's Atlanta Hawks in 1993 and 1994. He coached high-school basketball six seasons in California. As of 2019, he coached high-school basketball at Lake Dallas, Texas, a few miles north of Dallas, and taught middle-school social studies.[60]

Richard chose Tuskegee Institute, later pursuing an acting career. Born in Kobe, Japan, on January 16, 1972, he has had roles in dozens of television series since 1993, starring in *Judging Amy* (1999-2005) and playing recurring or supporting roles in *Girlfriends* (2007) and *The Rookie* (2019). He is best known for his leading movie roles in *The Wood* (1999) and *Why Did I Get Married?* (2007).[61]

Sources

In addition to the sources cited in the Notes, the author consulted Baseball-Reference.com and Ancestry.com.

Notes

1. Author interview with Clarence Jones on June 20, 2019.
2. Author interview with Clarence Jones on June 24, 2019.
3. Joe Strauss, "Point of the Order," *Atlanta Constitution*, September 19, 1995: E5.
4. Joe Strauss, "Murphy Power Surge: 5 Homers in 9 Games," *Atlanta Constitution*, July 28, 1989: F5.
5. Mark Bradley, "Olson's Selection an All-Star Story," *Atlanta Constitution*, July 6, 1990: E1.
6. Jones interview July 29, 2019.
7. Jones interview June 24, 2019.
8. Jones's passport issued in 2015 says he was born in Alabama on November 7, 1940. In an interview, Jones confirmed that he was born in Mobile.
9. Jones interview June 20, 2019.
10. "Wildcats Clinch Vital Tilt in Last Seconds," *Zanesville (Ohio) Times-Recorder*, October 18, 1958: 9; "ZHS Trips Lancaster by 35-0," *Times-Recorder*, November 1, 1958: 11; "4 Blue Devils On All-COL Team," *Times-Recorder*, November 22, 1958: 9.
11. Jones interview July 29, 2019.
12. "Tech Ousts ZHS, 53-47; North Tops Middletown," *Times-Recorder*, March 22, 1958: 1.
13. "1 Hitter for Steele; Philo Rolls," *Times-Recorder*, May 2, 1958: 29.
14. Zanesville Blanked in Finals," *Times-Recorder*, May 21, 1958: 13.
15. Z-Legion Captures Tourney," *Times-Recorder*, August 5, 1958: 11; "Local Legion Handed 4-1 Loss in Opening Game of State Tourney," *Times-Recorder*, August 12, 1958: 16; William J. Weiss, Baseball Statistics – Publicity, Pacific Coast League, Western League, Northwest League, California League, Pioneer League, Sophomore League, Arizona Instructional League, Questionnaire, January 27, 1961; Ancestry.com., Clarence W. Jones in U.S. Baseball Questionnaires, 1945-2005. search.ancestry.com/cgi-bin/sse.dll?indiv=1&dbid=61599&h=33917&tid=&pid=&useP-UB=true&_phsrc=VrV59&_phstart=successSource; https://search.ancestry.com/cgi-bin/sse.dll?dbid=61599&h=69077&indiv=try&o_vc=Record:OtherRecord&rhSource=61599.
16. Jones interview June 20, 2019.
17. Jones interview, June 20, 2019; "Boys' Clubs Instill Christian Living and Recognize Good Fellowship," *ZHS 1957 Yearbook*: 62-63.
18. Jones interview June 20, 2019; Weiss questionnaire.
19. Jones interview June 20, 2019.
20. Jones interview June 20, 2019.
21. "Minor League Highlights, Class D," *The Sporting News*, June 14, 1961: 39.
22. baseball-reference.com/register/player.fcgi?id=jones-001cla. Accessed August 11, 2019.
23. "Clarence Jones Blasts Terrific Grand Slam," *Great Falls (Montana) Tribune*, April 24, 1962: 10; "Jones Assures Victory With Three-Run Homer," *Great Falls Tribune*, May 2, 1962: 14; "Jones Hits Four-Run Homer 515 Feet to Pace Sparkies," *Great Falls Tribune*, July 2, 1962: 16; "Elects Lose 8-4 to League-Leading Billings in Weird Contest Here," *Great Falls Tribune*, July 31, 1962: 11; "Jones Sets New Club Homer Mark as Electrics Sweep Doubleheader," *Great Falls Tribune*," August 27, 1962: 13.
24. Jones interview June 20, 2019.
25. Weiss questionnaire.
26. "NYP Nabs Seven Spots on Class A Eastern All-Stars," *The Sporting News*, December 5, 1964: 43; "Minors' Standouts as Saluted by Topps," *The Sporting News*, December 5, 1964: 41.
27. "Dodgers Blast Broncs," *Salem (Oregon) Capital Journal*, August 26, 1964: 25.
28. "Title Hopes Shot," *Salem (Oregon) Statesman Journal*, September 7, 1964: 9.
29. "Spurs and Braves Land 4 All-Star Berths Apiece," *The Sporting News*, July 17, 1965: 47; "Quartet of Austin Players Named All-Stars," *The Sporting News*, September 18, 1965:

29; "Boccabella Milking Champ," *The Sporting News,* July 10, 1965: 35.

30 Carlos Salazar, "Albuquerque Ends 11-Season Drouth – Texas Loop Champ," *The Sporting News,* September 25, 1965: 33.

31 "Coast Clippings," *The Sporting News,* April 30, 1966: 36.

32 "Texas Twinklers," *The Sporting News*, July 23, 1966: 48.

33 "Spurs Wreck Funk's Bid," *The Sporting News,* July 30, 1966: 38.

34 "Texas League," *The Sporting News,* September 17, 1966: 40.

35 "Arizona Instructional League" and "Cactus Cuties" (Final Unofficial Averages)," *The Sporting News,* December 17, 1966: 41.

36 Edward Prell, "Charlie Metro Says Cubs Won't Finish 10th," *Chicago Tribune,* March 9, 1967: 15.

37 Prell, "Holtzman Routed as Gigon Comes Up a Hero," *Chicago Tribune,* March 22, 1967: 56.

38 Prell, "Cubs Jolted, 5-2, for 6th Loss in Row," *Chicago Tribune,* March 23, 1967: 88.

39 Prell, "The Lip Shows Patience with Cubs' Phillips," *Chicago Tribune,* April 1, 1967: 46.

40 Prell, "Cubs Win 8-4; Drop 2d Game to Reds, 3-2," *Chicago Tribune,* July 31, 1967: 58.

41 Robert Markus, "Clarence Jones Flees Cubs' Coffin Corner," *Chicago Tribune,* August 15, 1967: 51.

42 Jones interview June 20, 2019.

43 Jones interview June 20, 2019.

44 Robert Obojski, "12 Million Watched Japanese Baseball in '74," *The Sporting News,* January 4, 1975: 46.

45 Jones interview June 24, 2019.

46 "Names in the News," *Los Angeles Times,* June 1, 1976: 34.

47 Jones interview June 24, 2019.

48 baseball-reference.com/register/player.fcgi?id=blauseoo1jef. Accessed August 20, 2019.

49 "Notebook N.L. West," *The Sporting News,* May 2, 1988: 15; Gerry Fraley, "Tanner Fired; Nixon's the One," *The Sporting News,* May 30, 1988: 28.

50 Jones interview June 24, 2019.

51 Raad Cawthon, "The Return of Ron Gant," *Atlanta Constitution,* July 12, 1990: E1.

52 baseball-reference.com/players/gl.fcgi?id=lemkema01&t=b&year=0&post=1#8-12-sum:batting_gamelogs_post. Accessed August 20, 2019.

53 Thomas Stinson, "Lemke Fights Tooth and Nail to Pinnacle," *Atlanta Constitution,* October 26, 1991: D14.

54 I.J. Rosenberg, "Total Recall: Former Braves Hitting Coach Clarence Jones," AJC, Atlanta.News.Now, September 2, 2015, ajc.com/sports/baseball/total-recall-former-braves-hitting-coach-clarence-jones/X7rvAIybJkWkvWmWdxonFI/. Accessed August 14, 2019.

55 Rosenberg, "Total Recall: Former Braves Hitting Coach Clarence Jones," AJC, Atlanta.News.Now, September 2, 2015.

56 Jones interview June 24, 2019.

57 Jones interview June 24, 2019.

58 Jones interview June 24, 2019.

59 Jones interview June 20, 2019.

60 Author interview with Clarence Jones Jr. on August 2, 2019.

61 thefamouspeople.com/profiles/richard-t-jones-44619.php. Accessed August 11, 2019.

Leo Mazzone

BY BILL PEARCH

Leo Mazzone

With two minor-league seasons under his belt and the 1969 Midwest League campaign rapidly approaching, Leo Mazzone, then a starting pitcher with the Decatur Commodores, sought clarity about his short-term pitching prospects. The young hurler split his first two seasons in the San Francisco Giants system, a total of 56 appearances, between the Medford Giants of the Northwest League and Decatur. Of the 56 games in which he pitched, only 21 were as a starter. Mazzone, a 20-year-old left-hander tapped for a prominent role in the Commodores' plans, turned to an unconventional source of enlightenment. Whoever or whatever he conjured on the opposite end of that Ouija board delivered a message the youngster was elated to receive. The prediction stated that he would earn 15 wins during the coming season.[1] "The one year I remember," Mazzone said, recalling the apex of his minor-league tenure, "was 1969 in Class A in Decatur, Illinois."[2] Having only 11 career wins through 1968, a 15-win season seemed like a pipe dream. Reflecting upon his pitching career, Mazzone admitted that his pitching skills were solid but would have benefited from a different approach. "I would have changed speeds a lot more," he said, "instead of trying to pound my way through."[3]

As the Commodores approached the halfway mark of the 1969 campaign, Mazzone compiled a 5-6 record with a 2.47 ERA. "I've given up worrying about my record anymore," he said. "All I can do is try to keep my ERA down and just hope for the best."[4] Then something clicked. With the season drawing to a close, Mazzone toed the rubber against the Cedar Rapids Cardinals. In enemy territory on Sunday, August 31, he fanned 11 batters and pitched a complete game. He allowed two runs on seven hits to earn his 15th win of the season.[5] Mazzone finished the season with 17 complete games, but he was slated to start during the final game of the regular season. "My teammates flooded the field because we were out of the pennant race and they didn't want to play," he said. He confessed to hurling invective at his fellow Commodores as they departed the ballpark. "I was really mad."[6]

Mazzone was rewarded with a promotion to Double A the following season, but he failed to parlay his success into a major-league career as a pitcher. During his 10 years as a minor-league pitcher, he continued honing his craft. That bore fruit and led to coaching.

"Baseball was always my sport," Mazzone said, reminiscing how the game was, and endured as a household tradition.[7] Anthony "Tony" Mazzone and his wife, Maxine, welcomed their son, Leo David Mazzone, on October 16, 1948, in Keyser, West Virginia, a city across the Potomac River from Maryland. Mazzone's father was a World War II veteran and worked at a local paper mill for nearly half a century. The elder Mazzone was a baseball enthusiast and an accomplished coach and manager. That passion for the game proved significant during Mazzone's earliest baseball instruction.[8] His father, who was a former catcher, piloted his teams to 14 league championships during an 18-year tenure as a manager in Westernport's Bi-State Pony League.[9]

The Mazzone household was strict. Leo admitted that he and his younger sister, Mary Frances, were the products of a traditional household that prioritized Catholic education and daily attendance at Mass.[10] In addition to learning fundamentals in the classroom, Mazzone, with assistance from his father, concentrated on pitching mechanics. Following painstaking days at work – and never missing a day in the process – the elder Mazzone would travel with his son to a neighborhood park to convey pitching essentials.[11]

"He would catch for me as long as I wanted to throw," Mazzone said. "We would spend hours playing."[12] Looking back, he said, "I pitched a long time in my life without walking too many guys."[13] But these pitching sessions were not always scripted and regimented. Mazzone found time for fun, too. "I'd go out and mimic the deliveries of the great pitchers like Whitey Ford and Warren Spahn," he said.[14] That list of imitations also included the likes of two Dodgers legends, Koufax and Don Drysdale. "I loved Sandy Koufax," he said. "I had all their deliveries down when I was a kid."[15]

While Mazzone exhausted his spare daylight hours on the diamond, his time away from the park was filled with baseball, too. A fan of the New York Yankees, he followed their stars and kept a scrapbook chronicling the team and his favorite players like Ford and Mickey Mantle.[16] "I would listen to any ballgame I could get on the radio," Mazzone said, reminiscing about his old transistor radio that was firmly hidden beneath his pillow. "I could hear the games, but mom and dad wouldn't know I was still up."[17]

Mazzone's dedication to his craft during his formative years paid dividends as he attracted professional attention at an early age. The hurler initially received accolades as far back as 1963, when he compiled a 10-1 record and guided his Westernport (Maryland) Pony League team to a pennant and a playoff appearance. As a pitcher for his Bruce High School Bulldogs squad in Westernport, Mazzone was touted as the strikeout king of the Alleghany County High School League. During his senior year, he logged a 7-1 record and fanned 129 batters in 62 innings. Just before signing his first professional contract, Mazzone was pitching for Westernport in the Pen-Mar League.[18]

On September 8, 1966, Mazzone was signed to a San Francisco Giants contract by scout Frank "Chick" Genovese.[19] Mazzone's father announced his son's signing and added that the young lefty had enrolled at Allegany Community College for the fall, but would report to spring training for the Giants' farm teams at Casa Grande, Arizona.[20] After signing his $400-a-month contract, Mazzone inquired about a signing bonus. Genovese responded by saying, "You're kinda small. You'll make all your money once you reach the big leagues."[21]

Mazzone's inaugural training camp in the Arizona sun threw the youngster a curveball. Homesick, he left camp for home, but quickly returned. Mazzone captured the eyes of the coaches and was assigned to Medford of the low Class-A Northwest League.[22]

After success with Medford and Decatur (high-A Midwest League), Mazzone was promoted in 1970 to the Amarillo Giants of the Double-A Texas League, where he transitioned from starting to relieving. "When you don't sign for any money, you have to keep making a spot for yourself every year," he said, making note of the politics inherent to the game. "The top guys got all of the attention, and the other guys got ignored."[23]

Mazzone remained on the Amarillo Giants roster throughout the early 1970s before jumping south of the border and playing in the Mexican League. He opened the 1974 season with the Monterrey Sultanes. "It was unbelievable," Mazzone said, remembering his brief but raucous tenure in Monterrey. "The first time I pitched down there I threw a shutout and when I came off the field they were yelling 'Viva Mazzone, viva Mazzone.' I lost the next couple of games and I thought they were going to run me out of town."[24]

Eventually Mazzone accepted the fact that he would not receive a call to join a major-league squad and that he would never throw a pitch in the big leagues. So after leaving the Giants' system and signing with the Oakland Athletics, he started contemplating his post-playing-career options.

The Athletics' farm director, Syd Thrift, saw Mazzone's potential. "I knew very well that he had a great baseball aptitude, that extra sense about how to pitch and how to play," Thrift said. "He was a very astute judge of what was going on in the present."[25] When Oakland initially offered Mazzone a managerial position, he did not respond well and called Thrift many colorful names. The following day, he apologized and inquired about the job.[26] In April 1976 Mazzone was tapped as player-manager of the new Corpus Christi Seagulls of the Gulf States League. "My goal is to get to the big leagues as a manager," Mazzone said. "But my immediate goal is to create a sound, fundamental base for professional baseball in Corpus Christi."[27]

As a player, Mazzone ended the final season of his pitching career with a 7-2 record and a 3.73 ERA, pitching in 14 games. As a manager, the 27-year-old guided the Seagulls to a first-place finish with a 50-27 record. In 1977, Mazzone's first exclusively as a manager, he led the Seagulls, now in the Lone Star League, to another first-place finish. This time, the Atlanta Braves were watching.

The Braves took notice of Mazzone's managerial work ethic in the minor leagues and invited him to the franchise's instructional league in 1979.[28] Henry Aaron, the Braves' slugging legend, had recently joined the organization as director of scouting. "Hank Aaron was one of my idols growing up," Mazzone said, recalling the moment that he was encouraged to join the organization.[29] "I was a nervous wreck," he said. "We got on the plane to fly to Sarasota, and we hit it off right away on the plane."[30]

Shortly after joining the Braves system, Mazzone discovered a mentor: Johnny Sain, who took the green pitching coach under his wing. (Sain, after an 11-year career as a major-league pitcher, had become a successful and well-traveled pitching coach.[31])

"Johnny was a little bit of a rebel," Mazzone said, referring to the owner of 139 major-league wins for the Boston Braves, New York Yankees, and Kansas City Athletics.[32] Sain was searching for a protégé to whom he could impart his baseball knowledge. Sain, who himself had four 20-win seasons, taught the finer points of his craft to nine men who also compiled 20-win seasons: Jim Kaat, Whitey Ford, Mudcat Grant, Denny McLain, Jim Bouton, Al Downing, Jim Perry, Wilbur Wood, and Stan Bahnsen.[33] Mazzone willingly accepted Sain's tutelage.

During their initial spring-training sessions, Mazzone opened his mind and absorbed all of Sain's baseball knowledge. That meant firing up the grill outside Sain's Winnebago RV, enjoying beverages, and discussing the finer points of pitching.[34]

Both Mazzone and Sain understood that the art and science of pitching was changing. The days of the four-man starting rotation were relegated to the past. With five-man rotations, pitchers were throwing fewer innings and fewer times between starts. Mazzone was drawn to Sain's revolutionary approach to the game. "He was ahead of his time," Mazzone said, discussing his mentor's unorthodox approach. "People were very critical. They feared his knowledge."[35]

The consensus among teams dictated that in a five-man rotation, starting pitchers would throw one session off the mound between starts. Mazzone knew that pitchers needed to place a premium on throwing. He adopted Sain's thinking that pitchers needed more work to close the gap. "I wanted to do two," Mazzone said, acknowledging his belief that pitchers remained sharper in a four-man rotation.[36] Mazzone instituted a new pitching regimen. Pitchers would now pitch more often between starts, but with less intensity.

Mazzone received the call he longed for during the 1985 season. He, along with his mentor, would share duties as co-pitching coaches for the Braves. Then, after returning to the minors for a few seasons, he rejoined the Braves on June 22, 1990.

During Mazzone's tenure as pitching coach for manager Bobby Cox, the Braves experienced unequaled success and dominated major-league baseball during the 1990s. That run included winning 14 consecutive division titles, five pennants, and one World Series, in 1995. Players' names and faces changed during that stretch, but the Braves stood in an elite class because of their pitching staff.[37] Mazzone noticed overnight results. Many of the young arms he trained in the minors – pitchers like Tom Glavine, John Smoltz, Steve Avery, Kent Mercker, and Mike Stanton – skyrocketed to the major-league squad.[38] Each would have independently served as the ace of any other major-league rotation. Later, the Braves signed Cy Young Award winner Greg Maddux away from the Chicago Cubs.

Glavine, the future Hall of Fame left-hander and architect of 305 career wins, pitched 17 of his 22 seasons in the majors with the Braves. "He was very instrumental in me learning my mechanics, being able to repeat my mechanics, and most importantly understanding my mechanics so I could make my own adjustments," Glavine said, shining a spotlight on Mazzone for transforming his career and guiding him along his path to Cooperstown. "That and really understanding regardless of how hard you throw, the importance of being able to locate a fastball and pitch off your fastball, regardless of velocity."[39]

After losing 90-plus games annually to close the 1980s, the franchise's fortunes changed immediately in the new decade. The string of consecutive division titles began in 1991. That season the Braves won the pennant and played in the team's first World Series since departing Milwaukee. While the baseball world made note of Mazzone's formidable young arms, it also noticed his interesting habit of rocking in the dugout. "One of the local radio stations did a song called 'Rockin' Leo,'" Mazzone said. "The first time I heard that, I was driving down the interstate to the Chop Shop."[40]

"I've done it since I was a kid," Mazzone said. "My mother said I did it in the high chair. The doctor said when I get excited, I rock."[41] He said that most of the time, he was not aware he was rocking. "When I was pitching, I rocked all the time," he said. "It's a soothing thing. It's what happens when you're in a high-intensity situation. And that's my way of getting through it."[42]

In the 1991 and 1992 World Series, the Braves lost to the Minnesota Twins and Toronto Blue Jays respectively. But in 1995, all of Mazzone's dedication to the craft of pitching was rewarded. The Braves defeated the Cleveland Indians in six games to win the World Series. "Tommy (Glavine) put a stamp on one of the greatest pitching rotations ever," Mazzone said after the Game Six victory.[43] After the game was over, he just sat in the dugout. "I don't go between the lines," he said. "I feel that's for the players. A coach should be in the background."[44]

In 1996 the Braves finished 96-66 and won the pennant again, the team's fourth in six seasons. Their World Series foe was the Yankees. Game One was played at Yankee Stadium on October 22. The Braves throttled the Yankees, 12-1. Mazzone has declared that that was his favorite moment in baseball. "I grew up a Yankees fan," Mazzone said, acknowledging the wave of emotions and boyhood dreams that washed over him before the game. "I always thought as a little boy Yankee Stadium was a cathedral, the most beautiful place in the world."[45] (The Yankees overcame the loss and won the Series in six games.)

Despite continually reaching the postseason, the Braves reached the World Series only once more with Mazzone as pitching coach, in 1999. They suffered a four-game sweep at the hands of the Yankees.

After the 2005 season, Mazzone parted ways with the Braves and joined the Baltimore Orioles. He signed a three-year contract that reunited him with manager Sam Perlozzo, his longtime friend and the best man at his wedding.[46] "He enjoyed beating you," Perlozzo said, remembering their childhood competitions. "Winning and striking you out meant the world to him."[47]

Mazzone was unable to match his track record of pitching excellence with the Orioles. After two seasons of his three-year contract, he was fired. "At the time it was a great move, but now I regret it," Mazzone said. "I got a chance to go back to my home state."[48] Perlozzo, who had been fired during the 2007 season, admitted that the Baltimore teams suffered in comparison with Mazzone's Braves. "Good baseball people know that Leo didn't have much to work with there, and we had plenty of injuries on top of that," Perlozzo said. "He's still one of the best out there. I am very confident he will get a job, maybe even this year."[49]

But there were no major-league opportunities. In 2016, confident that he still possessed valuable pitching advice, Mazzone accepted an offer to become a special adviser to Brett Harker, Furman University's head baseball coach.[50] "He doesn't directly coach our pitchers," Harker said, stating that Mazzone would coach him on methods to train the team's young arms.[51] Harker added that Mazzone reminded him that pitching must be simplified. "You hear it from the best pitching coach of all time," he said. "That makes you feel better as a coach, but it also carries some weight from the players."[52]

"Leo really enjoys being on the field," Perlozzo said. "It's kind of like all he's ever done."[53]

Sources

In addition to the sources cited in the Notes, the author accessed Retrosheet.org, Baseball-Reference.com, and SABR.org.

Notes

1 Joe Cook, "Ouija Board Betrays Mazzone." *Decatur* (Illinois) *Herald,* June 24, 1969: 14.

2 Leo Mazzone and Scott Freeman, *Tales from the Braves Mound* (Champaign, Illinois: Sports Publishing, LLC, 2003), 9.

3 Mazzone and Freeman, 197.

4 Cook.

5 "Commodores' Mazzone Wins 15th," *Decatur Herald and Review,* September 1, 1969.

6 Mazzone and Freeman, 9.

7 Mazzone and Freeman, 7.

8 Mazzone and Freeman, 7.

9 "Obituary," Boal Funeral Home (boalfh.com/notices/AnthonyTony-Mazzone), Anthony "Tony" Mazzone, died January 12, 2015.

10 Steve Rosenbloom, "Leo Mazzone," *Chicago Tribune,* August 23, 2005.

11 Mazzone and Freeman, 8.

12 "They Call Him 'Rockin' Leo,'" *Albany* (Georgia) *Herald,* May 31, 2015.

13 Mazzone and Freeman, 8..

14 Mazzone and Freeman, 8.

15 Rosenbloom.

16 Cook.

17 Tony Rehagen, "Down & Away Undefined." *SB Nation,* May 13, 2015.

18 "Westernport's Leo Mazzone Is Signed by San Francisco," *Cumberland* (Maryland) *News,* September 9, 1966: 16.

19 "Chronology of Sporting Events in Cumberland and the Tri-State Area for Year 1966," *Cumberland News,* January 7, 1967: 6.

20 "Westernport's Leo Mazzone Is Signed by San Francisco."

21 Mazzone and Freeman, 9.

22 J. Suter Kegg, "Tapping the Kegg: Leo Mazzone Looks Forward to 1968," *Cumberland* (Maryland) *Evening Times,*

    September 12, 1967: 10. Mazzone is shown as 5-feet-10 and weighing 180 pounds.
23 Mazzone and Freeman, 9.
24 Emil Tagliabue, "Creating a Sound Base for Pro Baseball in City Is Mazzone's Goal," *Corpus Christi Caller-Times*, April 9, 1976: 75.
25 Rehagen.
26 Rehagen.
27 Tagliabue.
28 Mazzone and Freeman, 11.
29 "They Call Him 'Rockin' Leo.'"
30 Mazzone and Freeman, 11.
31 J.C. Bradbury, *The Baseball Economist: The Real Game Exposed* (New York: Plume, 2008), 55.
32 Graham Womack, "Baseball Dismissed Leo Mazzone and Johnny Sain – the Hall of Fame Doesn't Have To," *The Sporting News*, June 8, 2017.
33 Tyler Kepner, *K: A History of Baseball in Ten Pitches* (New York: Doubleday, 2019), 8.
34 Rehagen.
35 Rehagen.
36 Mazzone and Freeman, 14.
37 Bradbury, 56.
38 Rehagen.
39 Myron Hosea, "Furman Gets Big-League Boost from Leo Mazzone," *Greenville* (South Carolina) *News*, February 13, 2017: C1.
40 Mazzone and Freeman, 173.
41 Jack Curry, "Atlanta's Pitching Wizard Takes His Magic to Baltimore," *New York Times*, February 20, 2006.
42 Mazzone and Freeman, 172.
43 "At Last!," *Atlanta Constitution*, October 30, 1995: 51.
44 Mazzone and Freeman, 81-82.
45 Rosebloom.
46 Albert Chen, "Off His Rocker: Does Pitching Coach Leo Mazzone's Move Mean That Atlanta's NL East Dynasty Is Near Its End?, *Sports Illustrated*, October 31, 2005: 28
47 Rehagen.
48 "Bored and Restless, Leo Mazzone Wants Back into Baseball," *East Valley Tribune* (Mesa, Arizona), May 10, 2008.
49 "Bored and Restless, Leo Mazzone Wants Back into Baseball."
50 "Leo Mazzone: Special Advisor," Furman University Athletics (furmanpaladins.com/sports/baseball/roster/coaches/leo-mazzone/5).
51 Hosea.
52 Hosea.
53 "Bored and Restless, Leo Mazzone Wants Back into Baseball."

Jimy Williams

BY BILL NOWLIN

Jimy Williams

"No one, and I mean no one knows the game better than Jimy," said Hall of Fame executive Pat Gillick.[1]

Jimy Williams became a baseball lifer, signed to his first professional contract by the Boston Red Sox. After a brief big-league playing career, he won a world championship ring as the third-base coach for the 1995 Atlanta Braves and then – after returning to the Red Sox as field manager – was named American League Manager of the Year in 1999. He worked 12 years as a major-league manager, for the Blue Jays, Red Sox, and Astros. He worked another 15 years as a coach, 13 as third-base coach for the Jays and Braves and two as bench coach for the Philadelphia Phillies.

Williams began as an infielder, signed in 1964 by the Red Sox. He was right-handed, listed at 170 pounds and standing 5-feet-10.

Born as James Francis Williams on October 4, 1943, in Santa Maria, California, a town on the Central California coast 65 miles north of Santa Barbara. Williams and his sister grew up 18 miles away in nearby Arroyo Grande, a beach community of 3,200 residents.

"He grew up poor," wrote Richard Justice, "one of seven children born to an Irish mother who taught in a one-room schoolhouse and an Irish father who tried to make a living as a cattle rancher on the central California coast."

"He learned to ride a horse shortly after he could walk. He showed cattle at 4-H shows. He decided he wanted to be a ballplayer, and a high school teammate remembers him spending hours in the batting cage, then playing in a midnight basketball league."[2]

His father died when he was a teenager.

Williams graduated from Arroyo Grande High School in 1961. He had run cross-country as well as playing baseball and basketball. During his senior year, Williams created a distinction that would stick with him for the rest of his life. For his first 17 years, Williams had spelled his first name with two m's. As a prank he signed a term paper "Jimy" to see if he could get by. He did and it remained. "I guess I could make up a better and more dramatic story. But that's all there is to it," he explained to Jerome Holtzman of the *Chicago Sun Times* in 1987.[3]

In addition to giving his name a unique spelling, Williams began to write headlines with his play on the baseball diamond. His performance at shortstop drew praise. On the advice of his high-school coach, Williams joined the powerhouse program at nearby Fresno State. The Bulldogs had finished third in the College World Series in 1959 and won league titles in 1961 and 1962. They were coached by a future ABCA Hall of Famer, Pete Beiden, who instilled a high regard for fundamentals and teaching skills in Williams.

The one sport he played at Fresno State was baseball. His play in the 1963 and 1964 seasons earned him selection to the all-California Collegiate Conference team. He graduated from Fresno State with a BA degree in agribusiness. He played one summer for Sturgis in the Basin League. During the summer of 1964 Williams played shortstop and batted leadoff on the Alaska Goldpanners, a summer collegiate league team that sported future major leaguers Tom Seaver, Graig Nettles, Gary Sutherland, and Curt Motton. The Goldpanners were ranked as high as second in the National Baseball Congress during the season.

Williams enjoyed hunting and fishing in his spare time.[4]

After signing with the Red Sox, credited to scouts Glenn Wright and Bobby Doerr, Williams's first assignment was to Iowa where he played 115 games for the Waterloo Hawks in the Class-A Midwest League. As a young shortstop, he hit for a .287 batting average (.354 on-base percentage), with 2 homers and 31 runs batted in. His 125 base hits ranked second in the league.

It was his only year in the Red Sox system. They did not protect him and in November 1965 he was selected by the St. Louis Cardinals in the Rule 5 draft.

The Cardinals had Williams in the major leagues the very next year, and his big-league debut came on April 26 against the Dodgers in Los Angeles. After 5½ innings, the Dodgers had a 4-0 lead and manager Red Schoendienst had Williams take over at shortstop. His one at-bat came in the top of the eighth. He was facing Dodgers starter Sandy Koufax. He struck out.

Williams pinch-ran in another game, and came in for defensive purposes in a third game. On May 7, in a home game against the San Francisco Giants, who took a 13-0 lead in the top of the third inning, Williams pinch-hit for Tracy Stallard. He was facing another future Hall of Famer in Juan Marichal; this time he grounded out, shortstop to first. But he stayed in the game, and when he faced Marichal again in the bottom of the fifth, there was nobody out and the bases were loaded. He singled to center field for his first hit in the majors and his first run batted in. Facing reliever Ron Herbel in the eighth inning, he singled to center again. He was 2-for-3 in the game, but the Giants won 15-2.

Williams was given his first start the next afternoon and he singled his first time up and walked his next time up in four plate appearances. He appeared in three June games and four in July, but July 17 was his last game. He and a couple of other Cardinals began tours of duty with the Army Reserve.[5] Williams did his initial two weeks, then went off to Fort Campbell and Fort Leonard Wood for a six-month tour of duty.[6]

Years later, looking back at his debut, Williams said, "I can remember my first big-league hit, but when you only get three you can remember them all."[7] He was 3-for-13 at the plate, for a .231 average.

In 1967 Williams spent most of the year splitting his time between Double A (Arkansas Travelers, Texas League, batting .208 in 28 games) and Triple A (Tulsa Oilers, Pacific Coast League, batting .226 in 61 games.) He was called up in September but appeared in only one game – a start on September 21 against Atlanta. He grounded into a double play and struck out, and Tim McCarver pinch-hit for him in the bottom of the seventh, singling in a run that tied the game, 2-2. The Braves won the game, 4-2. He was, however, a member of the Cardinals team that won the 1967 World Series against the Impossible Dream Boston Red Sox.

In his major-league stint, Williams was flawless in the field, handling 14 chances without an error.

On February 8, 1968, he and Pat Corrales were traded to the Cincinnati Reds for Johnny Edwards.

In 1968 Williams played in 129 games for the Triple-A Indianapolis Indians (Pacific Coast League), batting .226 with 2 homers and 34 RBIs. That October he was drafted by the Montreal Expos as the 32nd pick in the 1968 expansion draft.

In 1969 Williams played for the Vancouver Mounties but appeared in only 35 games. He hit .258. Over the wintertime, he had suffered a shoulder injury moving furniture and it hampered his shoulder throughout 1969, resulting in an early return home to California for treatment and rest. In 1970 he began the season with Buffalo and moved to Winnipeg when the team relocated there in mid-June. In 109 games, he hit .230.

Williams started 1971 with Winnipeg but was traded to the New York Mets on June 16 for minor-leaguer Tony Canzano. He played in 62 games for the Tidewater Tides in Norfolk. Statistics are not readily available. Justice described how he left the game as a shortstop. "His playing career ended after he injured his shoulder in a freak accident, flinging a Styrofoam cup so hard he could hear the tendons in his shoulder rip."[8]

Williams spent the next two years working at the Short Way, a convenience store in St. Louis. "When a Fresno State teammate offered him a job as a minor-league manager, he grabbed it and began his climb up baseball's ladder."[9]

He spent six seasons as a minor-league manager and arrived in the big leagues for good when Bobby Cox hired him to coach third base for the Blue Jays in 1980.

He was working for the California Angels in his first minor-league slot, managing in Single A for the 1974 Quad Cities Angels in Davenport, Iowa. The team finished in first place in the Midwest League South standings, but won just one game in the best-of-three playoffs.

In 1975 Williams was moved up to Double A, managing the El Paso Diablos (Texas League). That team finished 62-71. He played in six games, his last as a player. He was 2-for-17 (.118) with a pair of RBIs.

His next four seasons were all in Triple A. In 1976 and 1977 Williams managed the Salt Lake City Gulls, his first year being the youngest manager at that level in baseball. A minor-league manager can only try to make the best of it, given the players he's accorded. In 1976 the Gulls were 90-54. They lost in the playoffs but Williams was named the All-Star manager. In 1977 they finished second. Over the wintertime after the 1976 season, he managed Obregon in Mexican League baseball.

When Williams married Peggy Sallee, his best man was Gene "Peewee" Fraser, his high-school baseball coach, who had become a second father to him after Williams's own father died.[10]

Williams and Peggy welcomed their first child, Monica, in 1978. Her birth was followed a year later by a brother, Brady. The family later grew with the addition of son Shawn and daughter Jenna.

Jimy Williams spent 1978 in the Cardinals system, and managed the Springfield Redbirds to a third-place finish. His stay in the Cardinals organization was brief. Art Teece, owner of the Salt Lake City Gulls, lobbied new Angels executives to bring Williams back to the organization. "Bringing Jimy back was a key in my resuming a working agreement with the Angels," Teece explained.[11]

Back with the Angels and Salt Lake City in 1979, the Gulls finished in second place but swept both Albuquerque and Hawaii in the two rounds of playoffs. Williams was once again the Manager of the Year.

Williams returned to the majors as Bobby Mattick's third-base coach, working for the 1980 Toronto Blue Jays. He spent the six seasons (1980 through 1985) handling the hot corner. Jimy and Bobby Cox joined forces when Cox arrived in Toronto in 1982.

Cox was named general manager of the Atlanta Braves for 1986. Jimy Williams was named field manager of the Blue Jays. For three years he led the Jays to winning seasons. The 1987 team finished with 96 wins and in second place. Toronto had led the division by 3½ games with seven games remaining on the schedule. Injuries to Ernie Whitt and Tony Fernandez contributed to the team losing every one of the final seven games of the season and they fell short, just two games behind the Tigers in the AL East.

The Blue Jays finished only two games out in 1988 as well, though in a tightly-bunched field that saw them tied for third place. They won nine of their last 10 games, and 15 of their last 18.

After a 12-24 start in 1989, and following a spring-training controversy with outfielder George Bell, Williams was let go and replaced by Cito Gaston.[12]

Williams joined the Braves in 1990 for the first of seven seasons as third-base coach, once again working under Bobby Cox. He developed a solid reputation for working closely with his players. He took some pride in helping keep sharp those who weren't on the starting nine. "The one thing I always tried to do as a coach is talk to players that aren't starting," he said. "Telling them you have to play your nine innings before the game. That way if you get your opportunity, you're prepared. The only way to do it is to play your nine innings during practice. Develop a good work ethic – so you're not just out there doing things, but you're doing them properly. So that realistically, when you get into a game, the game is easier than what you've been practicing."[13]

After three consecutive sixth-place (last place) finishes from 1988 through 1990 and not having finished above fifth place since 1984, the Braves became dominant in the NL East, finishing first for every one of the next 15 seasons (1991 through 2005), save for a second-place slot in the strike-shortened year of 1994. Had the teams played out the final 58 games of the year, there was plenty of opportunity for the Braves to have claimed first place that year, too. The one year they won the World Series was 1995, beating the Cleveland Indians in six games.

One of the most unforgettable moments with the Braves (how often does one have a US president run onto the field after a game and make a beeline to congratulate a third-base coach?) was at the end of Game Seven of the National League Championship Series in 1992. The Braves and Pirates battled it out for six games. Game Seven was in Atlanta and the Braves were losing, 2-0, heading into the bottom of the ninth. The Braves got one run and loaded the bases, but there were two outs. Pinch-hitter Francisco Cabrera singled to left field, the ball fielded by Barry Bonds. Instead of settling for the game being tied, Williams waved baserunner (and first baseman) Sid Bream all the way home from second base. As told by Richard Justice, "President Jimmy Carter leaped from his box seat and ran across the field at Atlanta-Fulton County Stadium. Instead of joining the wild celebration, Carter jogged down the third-base line and shook hands with Braves third-base coach Jimy Williams, congratulating him on the decision to send the slow-footed Bream home on the pinch-hit off the bat of Francisco Cabrera. Williams had challenged the strong arm of a left fielder named Barry Bonds by waving Bream home, and in the aftermath of that trip to the World Series, Cabrera became something of a folk hero in the South while Williams was an all-but-forgotten subplot of the story."[14]

After the 1996 season, Williams was hired by the Boston Red Sox as their field manager. Kevin Kennedy was out after a third-place finish. The Red Sox did distinctly worse, falling to a fourth-place finish, 20 games out of first, in 1997, but they made the wild card in both 1998 and 1999. Each time they lost. In 2000 the Red Sox finished second in the AL East, only 2½ games behind the Yankees, but they didn't win the wild card. Williams didn't make it through a full fifth year with Boston. He had once disciplined superstar Pedro Martinez for showing up late, removing him as starter for that day's game and replacing him with Bryce Florie.[15] He had begun to wear through his relationship with GM Dan Duquette, and was undercut when the GM took center fielder Carl Everett's side in a controversy when Duquette clearly should have backed his manager as a matter of course.[16] He also confounded the local media at times, with folksy-sounding sayings. As Chad Finn wrote in 2016, looking back at Red Sox managers over the prior 40 years, "He spoke in bewildering aphorisms ('If a frog had wings, it wouldn't bump its booty'), wore a flat-brimmed hat before it was in style, and didn't play patty-cake with the media. He seemed uncool. You had to pay attention – or recognize that he was competing with some mighty Yankees teams with a roster of Nomar, Pedro, 20 role players, and three sore-armed former aces – to realize that he was savvy and sly in all the right ways. He's probably the most underrated manager in recent Red Sox lore."[17]

Williams was not one who sought the limelight. "The game is about the players," he would say, and not about him. Richard Justice later wrote that he would dodge even innocuous questions such as why he wore number 3 with Houston. Justice added, "Williams would rather run down Texas Avenue with his hair on fire than discuss himself."[18]

The Sox had been in first place throughout June but went 14-17 after the All-Star break. After 118 games Williams was relieved of his duties and pitching coach Joe Kerrigan served out the rest of the season as manager.[19] Mike Port served as interim GM in 2002 and the Red Sox team was sold to a new ownership group.

At the end of 2001, Williams quickly found a new job and was hired as manager of the Houston Astros. Braves GM John Schuerholz looked back on Williams's time with Atlanta. "I always believed that when we had Jimy, we were the most fortunate team in major-league baseball. Every time I watched him work, whether it was on a bunt defense or infield play or defensive positioning, he was a consummate, hard, exacting worker. He has an enthusiasm and a passion for the game of baseball, for having it played right and the fundamentals executed properly. I think the world of him. He's a top-notch guy."[20]

Succeeding the popular Larry Dierker, Williams began his tenure as Astros manager with the 2002 season. In each of the first two seasons, Houston finished second in the NL Central Division, winning 84 games in 2002 and 87 games in 2003, a frustrating one game behind the division-leading Chicago Cubs. In 2004 he lasted only half a season, replaced the day after the All-Star Game (which was hosted by Houston that year) by Phil Garner. The Astros also fired their pitching coach and hitting coach on the same day. Houston placed second again, a full 13 games behind the St. Louis Cardinals, but were the wild-card team, won the division and took the Cardinals to Game Seven in the NLCS. The Cardinals were then swept in the 2004 World Series by the Boston Red Sox. In 2005 Garner's Astros made it to the World Series, but lost out to the Chicago White Sox.

Jimy Williams worked the 2005 and 2006 seasons as a roving instructor for the Tampa Bay Devil Rays. A photo caption in the *Bluefield Daily Telegraph* read "Home, to Jimy, is a baseball stadium. ..."[21]

In 2007 and 2008, Williams was the bench coach for the Philadelphia Phillies under manager Charlie Manuel. The Phillies won the NL East in 2007 but were swept by the Colorado Rockies in the Division Series. The Rockies were swept by the Red Sox in the 2007 World Series.

In 2008 the Phillies went all the way. They won the NL East, won the Division Series over the Brewers and the NLCS over the Dodgers, losing only one game in each round, and then they won the World Series – again losing only once – from the Tampa Bay Rays.

Williams apparently decided to go out on top, with another world championship ring. He elected not to return for 2009. It appears that the Phillies had not wanted to meet his asking price for salary.[22]

Retired after 44 seasons in professional baseball, Williams and his wife, Peggy, reside in Palm Harbor, Florida. They have two sons and two daughters:

THE 1995 WORLD CHAMPION ATLANTA BRAVES

Monica Jean (b. 1978), Brady Charles (b. 1979), Shawn Thomas (b. 1983), and Jenna Marie (b. 1985).

Monica was an All-America swimmer at Texas A&M and won two gold medals at the World University Games.

Their sons have followed in their father's footsteps. They grew up around baseball. Both sons were ballboys for the National League in the 1993 All-Star Game. Brady played seven seasons of minor-league and independent baseball. Likewise, Shawn put in seven seasons.

In 2019 Brady Williams was manager of the Tampa Bay Rays' Triple-A affiliate Durham Bulls. Shawn managed the 2019 Reading Phils, the Philadelphia Phillies' Double-A minor-league affiliate.[23]

Sources

In addition to the sources cited in the Notes, the author consulted Baseball-Reference.com, Retrosheet.org, and the Jimy Williams player file at the National Baseball Hall of Fame. Thanks for research assistance to Tom Hufford, FX Flinn, and Carl Riechers

Notes

1. Richard Justice, "Ex-Astro Boss Jimy Williams Talks a Good Game," *Houston Chronicle*, October 24, 2008. chron.com/sports/justice/article/Justice-Ex-Astros-boss-Jimy-Williams-talks-good-1785445.php.

2. Richard Justice, "Astros' New Manager Takes Low-Key Approach, Sets High Standards," *Houston Chronicle*, November 2, 2011. chron.com/sports/astros/article/Astros-new-manager-takes-low-key-approach-sets-2015374.php.

3. Jerome Holtzman, "Jays' Williams: He Fits the Mold," *Chicago Sun Times*, August 4, 1987.

4. William J. Weiss questionnaire, dated January 4, 1965, by Weiss.

5. "Don Dennis May Make First Start," *St. Louis Post Dispatch*, July 20, 1966: 4B.

6. "Allen's Drive Hit Guard, Says Red," *St. Louis Post-Dispatch*, August 11, 1966: 4E.

7. Richard Justice, "Astros' New Manager Takes Low-Key Approach, Sets High Standards." He remembered getting the hit off Marichal, but mistakenly recalled it as being the next-to-last game of the season rather than a game in April.

8. Richard Justice, "Astros' New Manager Takes Low-Key Approach, Sets High Standards."

9. Richard Justice, "Astros' New Manager Takes Low-Key Approach, Sets High Standards."

10. Richard Justice, "Astros' New Manager Takes Low-Key Approach, Sets High Standards."

11. "Caught on the Fly," *The Sporting News*. October 28, 1978.

12. Williams had wanted Bell (the AL MVP in 1987) to convert to DH and Bell did not want to. Bell won out and had a good year. In both 1989 and 1991, the Jays finished first in the AL East. In 1992 and 1993, they won the World Series with Gaston as manager. For more of the details, see Neil MacCarl, "Bell vs. Williams; No Gift Exchange," *The Sporting News*, August 8, 1988: 19.

13. Richard Justice, "Astros' New Manager Takes Low-Key Approach, Sets High Standards."

14. Williams said it was "Bream and Cabrera who had made the play, or maybe Damon Berryhill, who drew the walk that put Bream in scoring position. Jimy Williams? Forget it. Just another guy lucky to be wearing the uniform and making a living. To some of the people who know Jimy Williams best, that story speaks volumes about the man. … In that one moment, he had done his job perfectly, yet he had gotten almost no credit. And when someone attempted to shine a spotlight on him, he deflected the attention to others." Richard Justice, "Astros' New Manager Takes Low-Key Approach, Sets High Standards." In another article, Justice quoted Williams: "George Kissell, a great baseball man with the Cardinals, taught me that a good third base coach should do a windshield wiper before every pitch. You go back and forth with your eyes across the outfield before every pitch to see if the defense has changed." Williams had noticed that Bonds had taken two or three steps to his left; he felt that Bonds would need an extra second or two to get into throwing position. See Richard Justice, "Ex-Astro Boss Jimy Williams Talks a Good Game," *Houston Chronicle*, October 24, 2008.

15. Tom Yantz, "Pedro a Late Arrival for Sox," *Hartford Courant*, August 15, 1999. courant.com/news/connecticut/hc-xpm-1999-08-15-9908150156-story.html.

16. For a good summary of the controversy, see Gordon Edes, "Everett Blasts Off Again," *Boston Globe*, September 22, 2000. Everett also needed to be separated from his teammate Darren Lewis.

17. Chad Finn, "Here's Where John Farrell Ranks Among the Best and Worst Red Sox Managers since the '70s," Boston.com, August 18, 2016. boston.com/sports/boston-red-sox/2016/08/18/heres-where-john-farrell-ranks-among-the-best-and-worst-red-sox-managers-since-the-70s.

18. Richard Justice, "Man Pulling Astros' Strings Prefers Anonymity," *Houston Chronicle*, April 4, 2004. On the same

19   theme, see the earlier article by Dan Shaughnessy, "Williams Shows No Appetite for Self-Promotion," *Boston Globe*: D1.

19   The team was 17-26 under Kerrigan.

20   Richard Justice, "Astros' New Manager Takes Low-Key Approach, Sets High Standards."

21   Brian Woodson, "Williams' Baseball Life Continues in Minors," *Bluefield* (West Virginia) *Daily Telegraph*, July 30, 2006: 8.

22   Randy Miller, "Phillies," *Intelligencer* (Doylestown, Pennsylvania), November 2, 2010: C4. See also Sam Donellen, "Phillies Manager Manuel Has Utmost Respect for Departing Bench Coach Williams," *Philadelphia Daily News*, January 22, 2009.

23   A lengthy 2015 article in the *Montgomery* (Alabama) *Advertiser* quoted both sons and their father about aspects of their working lives. Duane Rankin, "Like Father, Like Son: Williams Brothers Follow Dad's Manager Footsteps," *Montgomery Advertiser*, June 20, 2015. montgomeryadvertiser.com/story/sports/baseball/montgomery-biscuits/2015/06/20/jimy-williams-sons-follow-baseball-footsteps/29050643/.

Ned Yost

BY KEN CARRANO

Ned Yost

A major-league ballplayer gets called a lot of things during his career, and a manager probably more so. In the case of Edgar Frederick Yost III, some of those things include taxidermist, catcher, grinder, idiot, app developer, survivor, twitter hashtag (#yosted), clothier, pot scrubber, and hunter. Oh, and one more thing – World Series champion manager.

Ned Yost was born on August 19, 1954, in Eureka, California, the son of Edgar Yost Jr. and Lael (Prindle) Yost. The Yost's divorced while Ned was in elementary school. Yost's father played football at Santa Rosa Junior College where he was named a Little All-American.[1] His mother was a homemaker. In May 1971, when Yost was a junior in high school, his father, a tanker-truck driver for the Arco petroleum company, was killed when a car cut his truck off. "Right after you get drafted, and then you work your way up, the first day you make it in the big leagues, you're thinking, 'Man, I wish he could have seen this,'" Yost said in 2014. "And then in '82, when we made it to the World Series (as a player with Milwaukee), it was, 'Man, I wish he could have seen this.'"[2]

Around the time of his father's death, Yost's family had moved to Dublin, California, where Yost joined the high-school baseball team, with little to no effect. "I went a whole year in high school without getting a hit, 0-36 my sophomore year."[3] Yost would improve, thanks to a summer job. "I went to work at Kentucky Fried Chicken. I was a pot scrubber. I'd sit there and scrub pots all summer long and my arms got strong."[4] Yost's improved strength translated to the field as he earned all-league status as a senior, but didn't translate to any college scholarship offers, so he decided to walk on at Chabot Junior College in Hayward, California.

Chabot had produced several major-league players, including Dick Tidrow and Von Joshua, but coach Gene Wellman didn't think too much of Yost's chances after he was drafted seventh by the New York Mets in the first round of 1974 June Secondary Phase Draft. After deciding to sign with the Mets, Wellman told Yost to take care of himself for the next week. Wellman then told him why a just a week – "Because that's how long you're going to last, son. You're going to be back on the first bus. You think you're a professional player? You ain't going to make it. Good luck. See you later."[5]

Yost went to Batavia of the New York-Penn League in the summer of 1974 to try to prove Wellman wrong. He played in 44 games and hit

.252, splitting time behind the plate and struggling with his defense, allowing six passed balls and 11 errors. Still, his performance gained him promotion to Wausau of the Midwest League for the 1975 season. Yost's hitting was more challenged at the higher level; he hit only .192 while handing most of the catching duties for the Mets' Single-A club. In spite of these troubles, Yost advanced to Double-A ball in 1976, with the Jackson (Mississippi) Mets of the Texas League. In Jackson, Yost improved his defense enough to catch most of the team's games even though he hit only .199 in 83 games.

While with Jackson Yost opened a taxidermy studio during the offseason, behind his uncle's bowling alley. "And that was my winter job. We'd go deer hunting and we'd do taxidermy in the back of the bowling alley back there. It was a lot of fun."[6] Yost would list taxidermy as his current occupation on the National Baseball Hall of Fame questionnaire that players complete when they make the major leagues.

The 1977 season changed the direction of Yost's life. After a great start with Jackson, he was promoted to Tidewater of the Triple-A International League. He continued his good play, hitting 12 home runs in 60 games while batting .291. Once the season ended, he married the former Deborah Ann Ferrell in September 1977. And finally, the Milwaukee Brewers acquired Yost in the Rule 5 draft during the winter meetings. Yost performed well with the Brewers' Triple-A affiliates in Spokane (1978) and Vancouver (1979), earning an invitation to the Brewers 1980 spring-training camp. Yost had confidence that he would make the major-league roster, whatever it would take, telling Brewers coach Larry Haney, "I'll warm up the pitchers, I'll wash the uniforms. I'll scrub out the clubhouse; anything."[7]

Yost made the team as the Brewers' third catcher behind Charlie Moore and Buck Martinez, and made his major-league debut on April 12, 1980, in the first game of a doubleheader against Boston. "We were blowing them out big, 14-0, 15-1, something like that, in the seventh inning and they put me in," Yost recalled. "The first hitter was Carl Yastrzemski. I remember just staring at his face, thinking that I can't believe this is happening."[8] After three appearances without a hit, Yost was sent back to Vancouver in May. His performance there (.309/2/41) earned him a trip back to Milwaukee in September. In his first at-bat back in the big leagues, Yost got his first major-league hit, off Albert Williams in a 15-2 drubbing of the Brewers at the hands of the Minnesota Twins. Yost wound up the season hitting .161 without a home run or RBI.

In December 1980 the Brewers acquired Ted Simmons from the St. Louis Cardinals, seemingly burying Yost deep in the Brewers roster. However, the Brewers traded Martinez in May, and Moore spent time on the disabled list and in the outfield, giving Yost an opportunity to learn from the experienced Simmons. Simmons wanted to pass on what he had learned in the majors, and found Yost a willing, if not skeptical, student. Simmons told Yost that he would have something for him every day to learn. Yost thought, "Yeah, right. And then for the next two and a half years, Simmons had something for me every day."[9] Yost got only 30 plate appearances in 1981 but experienced postseason baseball for the first time as the Brewers won the second half of the strike-shortened 1981 season, losing the Division Series to the New York Yankees.

Yost served as Simmons's primary backup behind the plate during the Brewers' 1982 campaign that took them to Game Seven of the World Series. Yost saw limited action, playing in 40 games with 107 plate appearances. He hit only one home run during the season, but it was one of the most important homers in the Brewers' season. They had taken over first place at the end of July and led the Baltimore Orioles in the AL East by three games with six to play going into their game at Boston on September 29. Yost entered the game in the bottom of the eighth and came up with two on and two out in the top of the ninth inning after Cecil Cooper was intentionally walked. Yost's home run gave the Brewers the 6-3 win and a four-game lead with five games to go over the Orioles. He was so sure he wouldn't be playing on the road trip that he had not packed a bat for the road trip, using Moore's bat to hit the game-winner. "It's a dream come true. You think about it, then you saw 'Naw. That would never happen.'"[10] The Brewers lost their next four, allowing the Orioles to tie for the division lead going into the last game of the season, in Baltimore. Milwaukee defeated the Orioles in game 162 to win the division flag. Yost did not play in the League Championship Series against the California Angels, and walked in his only appearance (in Game Six) of the World Series against the Cardinals.

The home run against Boston was the pinnacle of Yost's playing days. In 1983 he started 57 games behind the plate for the Brewers, 30 more than in 1982. He added six home runs in 1983, but his average dropped to .224 and he continued to struggle throwing runners out, nailing only 8 of 65 would be stealers for a 12 percent rate (the league average was 33 percent). The Brewers decided to move on from Yost, trading him to the Texas Rangers for veteran catcher Jim Sundberg.

Rangers manager Doug Rader thought Yost would be his starter for the 1984 season. "I believe Yost will be a top catcher," Rader said. "But because of the situation in Milwaukee – where Ted Simmons had a lock on the job – he has not been able to prove it. He will get that opportunity with the Rangers."[11] For his part, Yost was excited about the chance to be a number-one catcher. "I'm happy as heck about it," Yost said. "From everything I've heard, I think it's going to be fun."[12] Yost was the Opening Day catcher in 1984, but did not take advantage of the opportunity, hitting only .182 in 80 games. His hitting woes and continued difficulty with baserunners saw him lose time to Donnie Scott, and in April of 1985 he was released by the Rangers, catching on later that month with Montreal, who sent him to their Indianapolis affiliate for the season. Yost's numbers came up a bit at the Triple-A level, and he was called up to Montreal to finish the season and his major-league career. Yost signed with the Braves organization, where he bounced between Triple-A Richmond and Double-A Greenville for the next two seasons.

Knowing his playing days were over, Yost wondered what his next move would be when the Braves asked if he would work with the young players on their minor-league team in Sumter, South Carolina. He wound up being appointed manager in Sumter, and worked with some of the Braves that would go on to success at the major-league level, including Ryan Klesko, Ron Gant, and Mark Wohlers. After three years working in the South Atlantic League, Yost was again promoted to the big leagues, this time as the bullpen coach in Atlanta. "I was in the right place at the right time," he said. "It was just pure luck."[13] Phil Niekro had been the bullpen coach and was named the manager at Richmond, opening up the bullpen-coach job for Yost, working for manager Bobby Cox.

Yost joined Atlanta at the start of one of the most remarkable team runs in sports history. In every year Yost with the Braves (save the strike-shortened 1994 season), they won the National League East title. Yost spent eight years in the Braves bullpen and then moved to the third-base coach's box in 1999. Bobby Dews, who had been the third-base coach, was moved to the bullpen by Cox after the 1998 season.

Yost didn't spend all of his time in Atlanta studying box scores. In May 1993 he opened a clothing store, Major League Image, whose customers were helped to match their wardrobes using a dress-by-the-numbers strategy. The store had evolved from a computer program that Yost and local retailer Mac McLemore had developed. Yost used the system himself – "Hey, my wife can't travel with me everywhere," Yost once joked.[14] He also spent time outdoors with friends, including NASCAR legend Dale Earnhardt. The two were introduced by a mutual friend, Jody Davis. "We hit it off. Hunted together every year," said Yost.[15] Yost even worked on Earnhardt's pit crew during the 1994 baseball strike. Earnhardt was a huge Braves fan, and often pestered Yost to help him get into the Braves dugout so he could help manage. Earnhardt died in a crash near the end of the Daytona 500 in 2001. "There'd be times when we'd have an exciting play on the field and I'd think, 'Boy, I bet that fired Dale up.' I'm gonna miss knowing he's there watching us do our thing. There's a lot to miss when a man like him's not around anymore."[16] Yost began to wear uniform number 3 as a tribute to Earnhardt after his death.

The Brewers were looking for a new manager after the 2002 season. Jerry Royster had been fired after leading the team to a 106-loss season that saw attendance at Miller Park drop by nearly a million. The Brewers had looked at a number of candidates, and had offered the job to Ken Macha, who turned them down to take the Oakland A's open position. Brewers general manager Doug Melvin had not considered Yost until Yost's agent, Alan Hendricks, spoke with him. Melvin also spoke with Cox and Braves general manager John Schuerholz and gave Yost an interview. After he made the hire, Melvin said that Yost's "work ethic, energy and enthusiasm" set him apart from the other candidates.[17] Brewers fans would have been expected to wonder if a guy with no major-league managerial experience was ready for this job, but Yost believed that he was. "I don't have any apprehension about being a major-league manager," he said. "I don't have much experience managing but I've been around a Hall of Fame manager (Cox) for 11 years."[18]

The 2003 Brewers showed improvement in Yost's first year, improving to 68-94. Melvin was pleased with the team's improved play. "I guarantee you he talked our team into 15 or 20 wins last year just by telling the players they were better than they actually were. They believed him and went out and did it," Melvin said.[19] The Brewers continued to improve under Yost, and their record of 81-81 in 2005 was the first time since 1992 that the team did not have a losing record. After a slight step back in 2006, the Brewers rebuild was in full form for the 2007 season. They started the season 16-9 in April and by mid-May had an eight-game lead in a weak National League Central Division. They kept the lead until mid-August when a five-game losing streak knocked them to second place. The Brewers stayed in the hunt and moved into a tie for first on September 18. But the heat of the pennant race seemed to take its toll on Yost and the players. Yost was ejected from three games during a four-game stretch and served a one-game suspension on September 27 for retaliation in a game against the Cardinals. Yost was defiant, stating, "What happened in the past doesn't really concern me right now, but to answer your question, no, I wouldn't do a thing differently."[20] GM Melvin supported Yost, but admitted, "This is a situation we haven't been in before, and it's a situation Ned hasn't been in before as a manager. We handle all these things together as a team."[21] Brewers fans had been filling the sports airwaves and message boards looking for Yost's removal after the team lost an 8½-game lead in June, but Brewers owner Mark Attanasio confirmed Yost's status when he said, "Ned is fine."[22]

The 2008 version of the Brewers played better than they did in 2007 but found the division race more challenging with the improved play of the Chicago Cubs. Still, the Brewers were in the hunt for the playoffs after going 20-7 in August, finishing the month with a record of 80-56 and a 5½-game lead for the wild card over the Philadelphia Phillies. A poor homestand to start September saw the wild-card lead shrink to four games with a key four-game set coming in Philadelphia. The series was a disaster for the Brewers, who lost all four games and their wild-card lead. Attanasio and Melvin had seen enough after the Phillies series, and decided to fire Yost with 12 games left in the season. "When we talked to (Ned), he didn't have all of the answers to what's gone on the last two weeks," Melvin said.[23] Yost said he did not see the move coming, stating, "The timing of it surprised me. It's the nature of the business, but it's gotten a little strange. Two bad weeks (and you get fired)."[24] Yost's bench coach, Dale Sveum, took over the team, and while the results improved only slightly (7-5 over the final 12 games), it was enough for the Brewers to end their postseason drought and claim the wild card. The Brewers were eliminated by the Phillies (who had overcome the New York Mets to win the NL East) three games to one in the Division Series.

Yost spent 2009 on his 210-acre farm in Georgia but was not out of baseball long. In early 2010, Kansas City Royals general manager Dayton Moore hired him as a special assistant to baseball operations. Many saw it as an insurance policy for the Royals, whose manager, Trey Hillman, had taken a lot of criticism after a 97-loss season in 2009. "That's not the motive," said Moore. The motive is hiring good people to impact the organization. Trey was as much on board bringing in Ned as I was."[25] It didn't take long for the insurance policy to be cashed in, as Moore fired Hillman on May 12, 2010, and replaced him with Yost. "Ned has been through what we're going through (in terms of building a club). He has a lot of similarities to Trey, actually as far as their energy and relationship skills with people."[26] Yost later said that managing in the big leagues is mostly about three things: You must manage the personalities of the players, the games, and the media. Thinking he did okay with the first two while in Milwaukee, he decided that he wouldn't read, listen, or watch any coverage of the Royals. Some of the decisions he would make as the Royals returned to respectability would challenge this.

The Royals whom Yost inherited were in many ways like the Brewers in 2003, or even the Braves in 1991. After an 83-win season in 2003, they had three straight 100-loss seasons. Hillman was able to get them out of the AL Central cellar in 2008 with a 75-87 campaign. A promising 18-11 start in 2009 fell apart as the Royals crashed to a 65-97 final record in 2009, setting the table for Hillman's demise. But the poor record translated into high draft choices, and Moore and his staff made some good choices in these years, including first-round picks Alex Gordon (2005), Mike Moustakas (2007), and Eric Hosmer (2008). This infusion of young talent and a manager experienced in growing young talent led to improvements in the standings, from 67 wins in 2010 (Yost was 55-72) to 71 in 2011 and 72 (and a third-place finish in the division) in 2012.

Offseason moves to add pitchers James Shields and Wade Davis lifted expectations for the 2013 season, and *The Sporting News* predicted a second-place finish for the Royals and Manager of the Year honors for Yost. Yost shrugged off the pressure of these expectations, saying, "There's pressure with everything that you do, there really is, whether it's expectation and pressure. But there are so many variables. You can't get too carried away, because there are a lot of things that have got to happen right."[27] The season got off to a fair start, but by the end of May the Royals were 22-30 and in last in the division again. Speculation began to rise regarding Yost's job security, but Moore came to his defense, stating that Yost "was the least of the club's problems.[28] The team responded to Moore's defense of their skipper, going 64-46 the rest of the season to finish in third place with a winning record for the first time since 2003 and a contract extension for Yost, setting up several very exciting years of baseball in Kansas City.

Yost realized by the start of the 2014 season that the strict boundaries he had learned from Cox in Atlanta needed to be adjusted for the player of today. "I've gotten much better results than just coming in and trying to be the tough guy," he said. "The authoritarian. Yelling, screaming. That doesn't work with kids nowadays."[29] Billy Butler noticed the change in Yost. "He's been easier to talk to," Butler said.[30]

The Royals got off to another slow start in 2014, and in early June were three games under .500, bringing up discussion of Yost's job again. But just as in 2013, the young Royals found their form in the summer. They stayed in race for the division crown as well as the wild card. They could not catch the Detroit Tigers for the AL Central, but clinched a spot in the wild-card game after beating the Chicago White Sox on September 26.

The wild-card game cemented Yost's growing reputation as a manager who would manage his way, and not how convention would have him manage. In the top of the sixth inning, the Royals clung to a 3-2 lead, but starter Shields put the first two hitters on. Convention said that Yost should bring in Kelvin Herrera, as he usually did in the seventh inning, but instead he chose Yordano Ventura, a starter who had pitched two days earlier. Ventura promptly gave up a three-run home run and the lead. Fans in Kansas City had taken to Twitter to express their displeasure in similar Yost moves with the hashtag/verb #yosted, describing what happens when a choice goes horribly wrong. When Yost pulled Ventura three hitters later for Herrera, the Royals fans gave Yost rousing disapproval of the moves. "I'd never in my life heard anything like it,' said broadcaster Ryan Lefebvre.[31] "It didn't bother me. I still felt like we were going to win the game. I had no doubt that we would," Yost said.[32] They did, coming from behind with three runs in the eight and one in the ninth to tie, and then with two runs in the 12th after the A's scored one in the top of the frame. So inspired were the Royals after this multiple come-from-behind win that they swept the Los Angeles Angels in the Division Series and then the Baltimore Orioles in the AL Championship Series.

Suddenly the guy who couldn't handle the pressure of pennant race in Milwaukee and had nearly thrown away the Royals' first playoff appearance since 1985 became the first manager in history to start a postseason 8-0. "I've been called a dunce (*Wall Street Journal*), an idiot (*Chicago Tribune*) and everything else. It just doesn't bother me. I'm really comfortable with who I am. I know who I am," said Yost after the season.[33] The Royals faced Yost's favorite team growing up, the San Francisco Giants, in the World Series and came as close as you could to winning, leaving the tying run on third base in the bottom of the ninth inning in Game Seven. Yost spent time during the offseason doing exactly what one would never think he would do – develop an app for iPhone and Android. Ned Yost's Baseball Academics was launched at the American Baseball Coaches Association conference, where it won best in show. "It just teaches kids to think, teaches them to think quick and where to properly throw the ball. Even college coaches said, 'I would make my kids do that,'" Yost said.[34]

The 2015 Royals would not leave anything to chance. Avoiding the slow start that plagued the previous two seasons, they jumped out to a 15-7 record by the end of April, took over the Central Division lead for good on June 9, and won the division by a comfortable 12 games. Yost became the Royals' all-time winning manager on June 18 with his 411th victory. The Division Series against the Houston Astros went the distance, but trade-deadline pickup Johnny Cueto pitched a gem to win the series for the Royals. The Toronto Blue Jays were the opponent in the ALCS, and were dispatched in six games, leaving the Royals in the World Series in consecutive years for the first time. In the 1985 Series, the Royals had to battle back from a 3-1 deficit to claim the title. The 2015 Royals avoided this drama, winning the Series over the New York Mets in five games when they scored two runs in the top of the ninth inning to tie Game Five, then five more in the 12th to win the series.

Yost and the Royals perhaps used up all of their magic in their 2015 run to the title and could not replicate it in 2016. This version of the Royals briefly flirted with first place in May but fell to third in the division with a record of 81-81. The 2017 version was no better, finishing with an 80-82 record. Perhaps the most excitement that 2017 provided Yost nearly cost him his life. On November 4, while in a tree stand on his property in Georgia, Yost fell 20 feet when the stand collapsed as he was trying to attach a safety strap. He broke his pelvis and severed his iliac artery. The trauma doctor told him that he was lucky to be alive, as this type of injury has a 25 to 30 percent mortality rate. "I had my cell phone in my pocket, which was my key to the whole thing and being in a spot on my farm that had service was key," Yost said.[35]

After two mediocre seasons, the Royals decided to rebuild in 2018, and their record fell to 58-104, their second-worst performance in franchise history. Moore hired former Cardinals manager Mike Matheny as a special adviser in November 2018, perhaps as another insurance policy, especially with Yost under contract for only one more season. The 2019 season was more of the same, with the Royals posting a 59-103 record. On September 25, 2019, Yost announced his retirement. Yost may have preferred to simply walk away at the end of the season, but he wanted to thank the Royals fans. "That's what's really important to me," he said at his retirement ceremony on September 27. "I've thoroughly enjoyed my 10 years here, and I've got a world of memories from them 10 years, but what makes them special is you," Yost said gesturing to the crowd.[36] He retired as the winningest manager in Royals history (746-839), and the second-winningest manager in Brewers history (457-502). His 1,203 total wins as a manager rank him 45th in major league baseball history as of the end of the 2019 season.

In May 1983, after hitting home runs in consecutive games in Oakland, Yost saw his old coach Wellman for the first time since he left Chabot. "I was dead wrong about you," Yost recalled him saying. "The one thing I didn't take into account is that you can't keep a good man down."[37] Yost has been called many things during his career, some not fit for print. But he helped build one of the great teams in baseball history, then transformed two small-market losers into winners. Perhaps the best thing said about Yost came from a man who both hired and fired him, Doug Melvin: "He took a franchise that had not been to the playoffs in 25 years, built it up and got it to the playoffs. Then he took a franchise in Kansas City that hadn't been to the playoffs in 30 years and did the same thing. I don't care what anyone says about him. How many managers have done that?"[38]

Sources

In addition to the sources listed in the Notes, the author accessed Retrosheet.org and Baseball-Reference.com.

Notes

1. Vahe Gregorian, "Ned Yost Has Been Making 'Most of What He Has' Since Growing Up a Giants Fan," *Kansas City Star*, October 20, 2014, kansascity.com/sports/spt-columns-blogs/vahe-gregorian/article3185608.html.
2. Ibid.
3. Dick Kaegel, "Yost Recalls Hitless Season in High School," MLB.com, April 22, 2014 mlb.com/royals/news/royals-manager-ned-yost-recalls-hitless-season-in-high-school/c-72993074.
4. Gregorian.
5. Ibid
6. Chris Fickett, "Yes, Royals Manager Ned Yost Was a Taxidermist," *Kansas City Star*, October 27, 2015.
7. Tom Flaherty, "Kid Yost Mentally Ready, So Are Brewers," *The Sporting News*, April 26, 1980: 18.
8. Chuck Greenwood, "'82 World Series Yost's Career Highlight," *Sports Collectors Digest*, July 18, 1997: 60
9. Gregorian.
10. Tom Flaherty, "AL East Notes – Yost an Unlikely Brewers Hero," *The Sporting News*, October 11, 1982: 33.
11. Jim Reeves, "Deals for Ward, Yost Please Rader," *The Sporting News*, December 19, 1983: 42.
12. Jim Reeves, "Yost Promises Plenty of Hustle," *The Sporting News*, December 26, 1983: 47.
13. Greenwood.
14. I.J. Rosenberg, "Getting Dressed by the Numbers," *Atlanta Journal-Constitution*, February 18, 1993: E2.
15. Bruce Schoenfeld, "How Ned Yost Made the Kansas City Royals Unstoppable," *New York Times Magazine*, October 1, 2015.
16. Steve Hummer, "When NASCAR Lost an Icon, Yost and Others Lost a Friend," *Atlanta Journal-Constitution*, February 20, 2001: F5.

17　Michael Cunningham, "Yost Gets Two Years to Show Brewers He's the Man for the Job," *Milwaukee Journal Sentinel*, October 30, 2002: 1C.

18　Drew Olson, "Yost Looks to Catch On in Milwaukee," *Milwaukee Journal Sentinel*, October 29 2002.

19　Tom Haudricourt, "Yost Offers Brewers a Fresh Approach," *Milwaukee Journal Sentinel*, February 22, 2004.

20　Gary D'Amato, "Tumultous Week Finally Ends for Yost," *Milwaukee Journal Sentinel*, September 29, 2007: C1.

21　Ibid.

22　Rick Braun, "Players Not Surprised Yost Returning," *Milwaukee Journal Sentinel*, September 27, 2007: C5.

23　Tom Haudricourt, "Brewers Fire Manager Yost," *Milwaukee Journal Sentinel*, September 15, 2008.

24　Ibid.

25　Sam Mellinger, "Royals Hire Ex-Brewers Manager Yost as Special Advisor," *Kansas City Star*, January 13, 2010.

26　Bob Dutton, "Royals Fire Hillman, Select Yost as Replacement," *Kansas City Star*, May 13, 2010.

27　Pete Grathoff, "Ned Yost, Manager of the Year," *Kansas City Star*, February 6, 2013.

28　Bob Dutton, "Royals' Yost Says He 'Doesn't Listen' to Speculation Regarding His Job Security," *Kansas City Star*, May 29, 2013.

29　Andy McCullough, "Royals Manager Ned Yost Loosens the Reins as He Adjusts to a New Generation of Players," *Kansas City Star*, March 1, 2014.

30　Ibid.

31　Schoenfeld.

32　Ibid.

33　Joe Strauss, Royals' Yost Shrugs Off the Critics," *St. Louis Post Dispatch*, December 9, 2014.

34　Pete Grathoff, "Royals Manager Ned Yost Developed App to Teach Baseball Strategy," *Kansas City Star*, February 4, 2015.

35　Pete Grathoff and Rustin Dodd, "Royals Manager Ned Yost Says He Nearly Died as a Result of Fall from Tree," *Kansas City Star*, November 13, 2017.

36　Lynn Worthy, "Royals Ned Yost Thankful for 10-year Ride," *Kansas City Star*, September 27, 2019.

37　Gregorian.

38　Schoenfeld.

EXECUTIVES

Ted Turner

BY J. SCOTT SHAFFER AND MILLARD FISHER

Ted Turner

Anyone who has met a Braves fan in Boise, Idaho, has Ted Turner to credit. After purchasing the Atlanta Braves, Turner's satellite television superstations offered the first nationwide sports telecast and made Braves fans out of people all over the United States, while setting a model for sports broadcasting in the twenty-first century.

Robert Edward Turner III ("Ted") was born on November 19, 1938, in Cincinnati. He grew up in an affluent family: His father, Edward Turner, owned a billboard advertising company. Young Turner's childhood was filled with loneliness that would eventually translate into youth rebellion.[1] Still, out of tragedy, Turner took over his father's small company and transformed it into a multi-billion-dollar television empire.

Turner spent most of childhood growing up alone. Having lived with his grandparents for most of his adolescence while his father served in the military during World War II, his parents sent Ted to boarding school at the age of 6. While Ted was never close with his mother Florence, the family reunited in Cincinnati after the war while Ed established his billboard advertising company. Facing increased competition for advertising in the Ohio market, Ed moved the family to Georgia, where he had seen poorly designed billboards during the war.[2] After the move, Ted was shipped off again, this time to the Georgia Military Academy. The young Northerner failed to fit in with the rest of the students and antagonized his peers. In one instance, he called Robert E. Lee a "traitor" and faced torment by his angry peers.[3] During the summers, Ted worked at his father's thriving advertising company. In 1950, as he entered the sixth grade, his father enrolled him at the McCallie School, the top prep school in the area. He continued his mischievous behavior resulting in a long disciplinary record and an average academic performance.[4]

Regardless of his C average, Turner gained acceptance into Brown University in 1956. Unlike McCallie or the Georgia Military Academy, Turner was not bound by strict institutional rules, but he stayed out of trouble despite his habit for partying.[5] He also found a passion for the sea. In his spare time at the university, Ted sailed with his college friends. Additionally, he joined the Coast Guard Reserve. But Turner's time at Brown was limited as he broke one of the university's few rules (the one prohibiting women from staying in male students' rooms). Brown expelled him and subsequently Turner rejoined his Coast Guard Reserve unit for the remainder of his duty before accepting a managerial position at his father's company.

Through his service in the Coast Guard, Turner met his first wife, Judy Nye. He asked her to join him as he competed in the National Flyer sailing competition. Ted won the National Flyer, his first major sailing championship, and married Judy two weeks after the competition, on June 23, 1960, in Chicago. Returning to work at his father's company, Turner excelled in the advertising business. He credited his ancestry for his success in saying, "[I got] my work ethic from the Germans, and my colorfulness from the French and the British. My judgment and conservatism from the Dutch."[6] Most importantly, despite his rebellious youthful behavior, Turner desired to please his father.[7]

However, tragedy struck in 1963. Ed Turner's recent acquisition of General Outdoor Advertising Co. left him with a significant amount of debt. The burden of the financial challenges facing the company proved too much for Ed and he committed suicide six months after the acquisition.[8] While his father had reservations about handing the company over to his relatively inexperienced son, his will gave Ted the company.[9]

Turner led the company through the financial challenges and established a sense of urgency within the organization to look for new business opportunities.[10] The cash flow each month was enough to cover the debts, but instead of reinvesting the money into billboards, Turner invested in his future ventures in radio and television.[11] While he remained focused on the business, the stress of his father's suicide and relationship with his wife deteriorated. Judy and Ted divorced in 1964. Turner and Jane Shirley Smith, a Delta Airlines stewardess whom he met at a Young Republicans gathering, were married on June 2, 1964.[12] Turner also began aggressively pursuing his passion for sailing. He competed at the Savannah Yacht Club and even entered in the Olympic trials that year. Balancing his life between sailing and managing the company, by 1970 he had paid off most of the company's debts and it remained profitable.[13]

Two years earlier in 1968, facing bankruptcy, the Atlanta-based Rice Broadcasting Inc. sought to sell its local TV station, WJRJ-TV.[14] The station used UHF signals to broadcast, which at the time could only reach about five percent of area TV viewers.[15] However, UHF broadcasting was on the rise and in 1970 Turner hopped on the opportunity to purchase the company. Seeing television as the future of advertising, he used his billboards to advertise for the station.[16] In the first year, the station lost nearly a million dollars, surviving on the revenues generated by billboards.[17] In 1972 Turner hired a consultant, Kent Burkhart, to find ways to increase viewership of television. Burkhardt advised taking advantage of the launch of Satcom I, a communications satellite, into space.[18] Satellites transmit TV signals into remote and rural areas, are not affected by weather, and remained cheaper to use than installing equipment to support the current cable infrastructure. HBO became the first company to use satellites to broadcast its signal, and by 1976 Turner's WTCG followed. In just two years, WTCG reached nearly two million households and increased the value of the station to $40 million.[19]

With his expanded footprint in American homes, Turner saw a great business opportunity to expand sports. Turner had previously worked out a deal with the Braves to broadcast games on WTCG. He then resold the broadcasting rights in 24 other states, creating a network for Braves baseball across the South, the largest such network in the country.[20] With a monopoly on the media rights for the team and plunging attendance, Turner purchased the ballclub along with the Atlanta Hawks basketball team. With his ability to broadcast anywhere in the country after the satellite purchase, the Braves received increased national attention. Locally, Turner gained publicity with bold comments including, "I don't want to see any more 'Loserville' headlines in the paper. ... Getting into the World Series within the next five years is my objective."[21]

Turner proved to be an owner unlike any other baseball had seen, though he knew little about the game before purchasing the team.[22] Sports pundits wondered aloud about who got the worst deal when the Braves fell to sixth place in Turner's first year, and the owner himself sparked more media interest than the players. According to Braves player Phil Niekro, "There's never been an owner like him. He enjoys it more than anyone in the ballpark. He'd really like to put on a uniform and play in the game."[23] Turner started his inaugural year in 1976 by rankling fellow owners with his signing of hurler Andy Messersmith. The Dodgers ace and Orioles pitcher Dave McNally had won free agency through a legal challenge to Organized Baseball's reserve clause. While other owners reeled from the stunning legal decision, Turner penned Messersmith to a multiyear deal worth more than $1 million, a huge salary increase for a player considered one of the top pitchers in the league.[24] In midseason Turner unveiled plans for a new television "superstation," WTBS TV 17, to be broadcast via satellite from Atlanta, with Braves games at the core of its programing. The maverick owner then gave Messersmith uniform number 17 and the nickname "Channel" which was sewn above his uniform number. National League President Chub Feeney chastised the brash millionaire for his advertising ploy, but Turner gained national exposure for his team, increasing viewership and game attendance.[25]

The following year, in 1977, Turner tried to finesse baseball's free agency again by agreeing to a deal with San Francisco outfielder Gary Matthews before Matthews' contract with the Giants had expired. Already looked down upon by Commissioner Bowie Kuhn and the other club owners, Kuhn suspended Turner for a year and fined him for contract tampering.[26] Turner fought the decision in court and remained in control of the team. On May 11, 1977, with the Braves already in a losing streak, Turner further complicated the controversy when he appointed himself manager of the failing Braves. He relieved manager Dave Bristol and stepped into the dugout himself in full uniform. He presented his move as an attempt to get closer to his investment so he could see what the managerial job entailed before choosing Bristol's replacement.[27] The next day, the National League disallowed the move, reinstating Bristol. Later in the year, the league denied Turner's appeal regarding his suspension and his sentence began. After Bristol finished the 1977 season, the Braves hired New York Yankees coach Bobby Cox as manager to help rebuild the team.

After Turner was reinstated with the Braves, he continued to balance a hectic schedule between growing his media empire, sailing in the America's Cup competition, and serving an active role with the baseball team. With Cox selecting players, the owner invested heavily in promising talent, though the strategy did not pay off in the standings. Despite Turner's victory in the America's Cup in 1977, the Braves on the field did not replicate his seagoing success. In 1978, the team finished last in the standings, but attendance had doubled since Turner purchased the team and television viewership continued to increase, all contributing to the Securities and Exchange Commission's market valuation of Turner's company at over $50 million.[28]

With the success of his superstations, Turner saw another opportunity for the future of television. Just has he had brought baseball to more people by increasing broadcasting; he applied the same model to round-the-clock broadcasting of news. In the 1980s, Turner rebranded his WTBS-TV to Cable News Network (CNN), capable of reaching nearly 26 million households and placing the network on a par audiencewide with ABC News.[29]

After the 1981 season, Bobby Cox left the team to manage the Toronto Blue Jays. The talent that Turner and Cox had assembled synched well with new skipper Joe Torre in 1982. The Braves started the season with 13 straight wins for the best start in league history. Midway into the season the team looked as if it had the pennant already clinched. Instead, the Braves slumped in the worst imaginable way, losing 19 of 21 games and plummeting as the Giants and Dodgers gained ground. The three-way pennant race went down to the last week and then the final day, as the Braves led the Dodgers by one game. Inexperienced and cracking under pressure, the Braves lost their final game. But the Dodgers also lost and the Braves won the division title. Discounting the team's ouster in the NLCS by the St. Louis Cardinals, their success reinforced Turner's growing influence as a national media king and proved that the boisterous Southern businessman could not only sway public opinion but could also run a baseball team.

After 1982, the Braves slowly sank back down in the standings. In 1985, Turner rehired Bobby Cox from the Blue Jays as general manager, placed Chuck Tanner in the dugout, and quietly set to work rebuilding his team. Despite amassing the most promising talent available, the Braves finished last or next to last in every season from 1985 through 1990. Throughout the 1980s Turner slowly took a less active role in the Braves organization as he managed the growth of CNN, founded the Olympic-like Goodwill Games, and expanded his acquisitions further in purchasing MGM/US Entertainment studios (including the Metro Goldwyn Mayer's library of more than 4,000 films).[30] He also created the World Championship Wrestling, which began competing with Vince McMahon's World Wrestling Federation on Monday nights. The league survived until March 2001, when Turner sold it to his competition. The late 1980s saw the end to his second marriage as he and Jane divorced.

By 1991, cable television had spread to every corner of the United States. More than half of American homes now subscribed. Suddenly, Turner's baseball plans were developing as nicely as his other business ventures. The Braves climbed back to the top of the National League, becoming the first National League team to go from worst to first in a single season. As one of the nation's most eligible bachelors, Turner wooed and married controversial movie star Jane Fonda, and the pair were often seen together at games rooting for his Braves. Although they lost the 1991 World Series to the Minnesota Twins, the Atlanta organization had a strong young team featuring the best pitching staff Turner's money could buy. Atlanta was back on top in the National League in 1992, but the Braves lost the World Series to the Toronto Blue Jays. They continued winning throughout the decade. They won the division title in every season from 1991 to 1999 (excluding the 1994 strike year), and not missing a beat when the franchise was switched from the NL West to the NL East. The Braves won the World Series in 1995, but lost twice to the New York Yankees in 1996 and 1999. As the club prospered, Ted Turner seemed to mellow, looking more settled and relaxed in his box seat than did the loud and ambitious man who once took over the team himself.[31] During the 1991 playoffs, cameras even caught him dozing off once.[32]

In business, Turner continued to expand his footprint in the 1990s with the creation of the Cartoon Network in 1992 and Turner Movie Classics in 1994. He oversaw the purchase of two movie production companies, New Line Cinema and Castle Rock Entertainment. In 1996, Time Warner and Turner Broadcasting announced a $7.5 billion acquisition deal.[33] As part of the agreement, Turner became a vice chairman of Time Warner and headed all the merged company's cable TV networks. When Time Warner merged with AOL in 2001, Turner became vice chairman and senior adviser of AOL Time Warner Inc. He continued to work until 2003, when he resigned as vice chairman of the company.

After his marriage to Jane Fonda, Turner became a devoted philanthropist and environmentalist. He donated one billion dollars to establish the United Nations Foundation and created the Nuclear Threat Initiative, which sought to prevent the use of weapons of mass destruction. He provided extensive funding to conservation efforts through his Turner Foundation.[34] He also co-created and co-wrote the animated children's series *Captain Planet and the Planeteers*, which centers on teenage environmental activists.[35] Turner became America's largest private landowner: 2 million acres, more than the land area of Delaware and Rhode Island combined. Many of his ranches got involved in sustainability and ecotourism. He built up the largest private bison herd in the world, with 50,000 head. In hopes of increasing demand for bison, Turner co-founded Ted's Montana Grill, a restaurant chain specializing in burgers and other entrees made from fresh bison meat.[36]

Turner's philanthropy gained him numerous honors. He was inducted into the America's Cup Hall of Fame in 1993, received the Peabody Award in 1997, was awarded an honorary doctorate by Trinity College in 2001, and was inducted into the Advertising Hall of Fame in 2004. On April 7, 2004, he received a star on the Hollywood Walk of Fame. In 2006, he received the Bower Award for Business Leadership from the Franklin Institute's premier science and technology education and development center in Philadelphia. A year later, Turner was the recipient of the Junior Achievement Award, from the organization that provides hands-on business training programs to youth throughout the world. Also in 2007, Turner was inducted into the United States Business Hall of Fame.

Sources

In addition to the sources cited in the Notes, the authors consulted Baseball-Reference.com.

Notes

1. Porter Bibb, *Ted Turner: It Ain't as Easy as It Looks* (Boulder, Colorado: Johnson Books, 1997), 10-11.
2. Bibb, 11.
3. Bibb, 11-12.
4. Bibb, 24.
5. Bibb, 24-25.
6. Bibb, 6.
7. Bibb, 48.
8. R.S. Denisoff, "Ted Turner's Crusade: Economics v. Morals," *Journal of Popular Culture* 21, no. 1 (Summer, 1987): 27, 30.
9. Bibb, 48.
10. Bibb, 51.
11. Bibb, 52.
12. Bibb, 53.
13. Denisoff, 30.
14. Bibb, 71.
15. Bibb, 71-72.
16. Bibb, 65.
17. Denisoff, 30.
18. Denisoff, 30.
19. Denisoff, 30.
20. Bibb, 80.
21. Bibb, 109.
22. Bibb, 110.
23. Eric Golanty, "Andy Messersmith," SABR Biography Project, sabr.org/bioproj/person/caef6d23.
24. Bob Warja, "Come to Think of It: The Day That Changed Major League Baseball Forever," Bleacher Report, April 10, 2009, bleacherreport.com/articles/154265-come-to-think-of-it-the-day-that-changed-major-league-baseball-forever. See also Robert Goldberg and Gerald Jay Goldberg, *Citizen Turner: The Wild Rise of an American Tycoon* (New York: Harcourt, 1995).
25. Paul Lukas, "Uni Watch's Friday Flashback: What's in a Nickname?" ABC News, May 13, 2016, abcnews.go.com/Sports/uni-watchs-friday-flashback-nickname/story?id=39088122
26. Bibb, 117.
27. Bibb, 117.
28. Bibb, 136.
29. Denisoff, 31.
30. Bibb, 297-299.
31. Bibb, 367.
32. Bibb, 404.
33. Jeff Pelline, "Time Warner Closes Deal for Turner" *San Francisco Chronicle*, September 23, 1995. sfgate.com/news/article/PAGE-ONE-Time-Warner-Closes-Deal-For-Turner-3023794.php.
34. Tim Gray, "Giving as Good as He Gets," Business Insights: Global, August 6, 2012.
35. Gray.
36. Bibb, 384-388.

Stan Kasten

BY BOB WEBSTER

Stan Kasten

For over four decades, Stan Kasten has been a highly respected sports figure who developed a reputation for creating winning franchises by relying on three pillars – scouting and player development, enhancing the fan experience, and community outreach – to establish franchises built for long-term success on and off the field.[1]

This strategy has apparently worked. With Kasten as team president, the Atlanta Braves won the National League division title for 12 consecutive years from 1991 through 2003, with the exception of the strike-shortened 1994 season. During this time, the Braves average attendance was 37,794. The NBA Atlanta Hawks won 50 or more games in four consecutive seasons during the late 1980s and made the playoffs seven consecutive seasons with Kasten as president in the '90s.[2] Since he took over as the Los Angeles Dodgers president and CEO in April 2012, the Dodgers have finished in first place in the NL West and advanced to postseason play seven consecutive years beginning with 2013 while leading the major leagues in attendance in each of those years.

Stanley H. Kasten was born in Lakewood Township, New Jersey, on February 1, 1952, to Nathan and Sylvia Kasten.[3] Kasten, his younger brother, Mitchell, and his younger sister, Mimi, were raised about 100 miles north of Lakewood Township in Farmingdale, New Jersey. Kasten grew up in a world of Holocaust survivors, including his Polish parents.[4] "My dad spent World War II in camps and my mother was on the run," said Kasten, adding that the couple met in a displaced persons camp in 1946, came to the United States in 1949, and married in 1950, two years before Stan was born.[5] "I grew up with Jewish study from grade school to high school," he recalled. "It was wall-to-wall, 24-7." Kasten decided in high school to commit to an Orthodox lifestyle, even though his parents were less observant.[6] Kasten attended the Ner Israel Rabbinical College in Baltimore, then graduated from the Yeshiva University High School for Boys in 1969.[7]

At the age of 19 in 1939, Nathan Kasten was taken from his home in Poland during the Holocaust and given a death sentence that he was able to avoid because of his age and his strength. He was moved from prison camp to prison camp because he was strong enough to shovel the dead bodies into the ovens or pile them into giant graves. After many terrifying experiences in his five years in prison camps, Nathan was sent to a displaced persons camp where he spent two years before finding his way to America, but not before meeting his future wife, Sylvia, who survived a prison camp in Poland by posing as a Gentile. All 53 of Nathan Kasten's living relatives were killed in the camps.[8] Sylvia's family met the same demise. Thirty close family members, including her two brothers and four of her seven sisters, were also murdered during the Holocaust, not because of anything they had done, but because they were born Jewish.[9] After Nathan Kasten was finally out of the camps, he was confronted by a German soldier taunting him with Holocaust photos. Kasten pummeled the soldier and took the photos, which he has shown his children to remind them of their great fortune.[10] Sylvia Kasten, Stan's mother, said her children were not constantly reminded of the Holocaust experience, although she noted, "My children know where we come from."[11]

Nathan and Sylvia moved to America where they knew nobody, didn't speak the language, and had nothing. Upon arriving in America, Nathan became a tailor and they raised their three children on a chicken farm that they eventually turned into a hotel-restaurant in Farmingdale. There is an interesting story about how they transitioned from a chicken farm to a hotel-restaurant. There was an amusement park behind the chicken coop. Stan Kasten recalled, "They had rodeos and simulated Indian raids, and at 4 o'clock the bad guy would get shot. The constant sound of gunfire drove the chickens nuts and they literally had heart attacks, thousands of them." Nathan Kasten received money as settlement from the amusement park and remodeled the chicken coop into a motel and built a family restaurant (The Charcoal Flame) next door.[12]

It was at the hotel-restaurant that Stan learned a valuable lesson. One afternoon he was walking across the parking lot from the motel to the restaurant when a trash can blew over behind him, scattering garbage everywhere. Stan saw it, but just kept walking. His father saw this from a restaurant window and when Stan came through the door, his father jumped all over him. Kasten recalled: "He looked at me and said, 'You are the laziest thing I have ever seen.' That never left me. That stuck with me forever. I am a fundamentally lazy person, but I combat it every day when I think about the trash can," said Kasten.[13]

That was not the most important lesson Stan learned as a child. The lesson learned in their household from his parents' prison camp experience was the insanity of discrimination. "It's a mental illness. It's a disease," said Kasten.[14]

Kasten loved baseball, but his parents didn't understand it. Since Stan loved it, they let him play. Nathan never went to one of his youth-league games. "After all they had been through, they just wanted us to be happy and productive," said Stan's sister, Mimi Werbler.[15]

"My father's life taught me that you can never forget how incredibly lucky you are to live in a country where you can be whatever you want to be," Kasten said. "How I live my life is built on that belief."[16]

"The best man I ever met"? Kasten said. "My father was also the best role model I've ever met."[17]

Nathan died from complications of diabetes in 1996 at age 75 and Stan's mother, Sylvia, died in 2009.[18]

Kasten earned a degree in psychology from New York University in 1973 and a law degree from Columbia University in 1976.

In 1977 Kasten married Helen Weisz. They met while attending the same Jewish day school and they attended the same temple in New Jersey. Their parents traveled similar paths. Helen's father was from Hungary and survived Nazi concentration camps, and her mother, a Pole, escaped by hiding.[19] The Kastens have four children; Alana, Corey, Sherry, and Jay.[20]

After law school, Kasten and his wife were touring ballparks across the country when he met Ted Turner. Kasten spotted Turner leaving Busch Stadium in St. Louis after a Braves-Cardinals game. "I meet a lot of people and most of them ask me for jobs," Turner recalled. "Stan said that he'd work for nothing. That was an offer even I couldn't refuse."[21] Kasten said, "I liked him, he liked me and so he gave me a job as legal counsel" in Turner's sports empire.²²

In that capacity, Kasten went to work for Turner in 1977 with Turner's Atlanta Hawks NBA franchise. In 1979, at age 27, Kasten became the youngest general manager in NBA history when he was promoted to that position. On September 2, 1982, Kasten traded John Drew and Freeman Williams to the Utah Jazz for Dominic Wilkins, before Wilkins ever played an NBA game.²³ Kasten built his team around the nine-time All-Star and the Hawks became a perennial contender, with four consecutive 50-victory seasons and seven consecutive playoff appearances in the 1990s. In addition to being the general manager, Kasten took on the role of team president in 1986 and became the first NBA executive to win back-to-back Executive of the Year awards, in 1986 and 1987.²⁴

In 1986 Kasten also became president of the Braves. In an interview at the SABR Analytics Conference in March 2013, in Phoenix, Arizona, Kasten explained how that happened: "By the time Ted asked me to take over the team, we were a last-place team with the highest payroll in baseball. Which is almost hard to do if you're trying to do it on purpose! That's a bad situation. I didn't want to do it ... Ted said, 'Do it in addition to the Hawks. You'll be the only guy running two teams.' I said, 'Ted, that's such a bad idea.' But Ted had and I had an understanding, when we disagreed on something, we just did things his way. And that's how I took over."²⁵

The mounting pressure of trying to win 244 regular-season games a year (162 for the Braves and 82 for the Hawks) was immense. Kasten had six television sets at home and his wife once said, "He's waiting for a TV to come out that has four different screens at the same time."²⁶ The double duties took some getting used to. Kasten's secretary once typed a Braves-related letter on Hawks stationery, so Kasten taped a reminder on her typewriter: "Is what I'm about to type Hawks or Braves?"²⁷

After the 1985 season, former Braves manager Bobby Cox returned to Atlanta as the general manager. After a few lean years of finishing in last place or next to last, in the summer of 1990 Kasten mentioned to John Schuerholz, then the GM in Kansas City, that he planned to move Cox back to the dugout and bring in a new GM. He asked Schuerholz if he had any suggestions for a new GM. Schuerholz told Kasten that he was interested. In October of that year, Schuerholz became the new GM of the Braves and Kasten gave him and Cox full authority over baseball decisions.

By 1990 the Braves had a trio of outstanding young pitchers, John Smoltz, Tom Glavine, and Steve Avery. After winning 65 games in 1990, the Braves won 94 in 1991 and finished in first place in the NL East. Great defense played a huge part in their success, helping the three young pitchers have outstanding years. Glavine won 20 games, Avery won 18, and Smoltz won 14. Veteran Charlie Leibrandt provided 15 wins. The Braves defeated the Pirates in the NLCS but lost to the Minnesota Twins in seven games in the World Series.

From 1991 through 2003, with Kasten as president, Schuerholz as general manager, and Cox as manager, the Braves won 12 consecutive division titles (excluding the 1994 strike year), five National League pennants, and the 1995 World Series.²⁸

In addition to running an NBA and an MLB team, Kasten was involved in a few remodels and construction of sports facilities. He helped get a deal worked out with the Atlanta Olympic Committee to convert the Olympic Stadium to a major-league ballpark to be called Turner Field. The Braves played their final game at Atlanta-Fulton County Stadium in 1996 and moved into Turner Field in 1997. Kasten was also in charge of the construction of Philips Arena, the new home of the Atlanta Hawks and the new NHL Atlanta Thrashers in 1999. Kasten became president of the Thrashers, making him the only person who was president of three sports teams at once. He held all three positions until 2003, when the Hawks and Thrashers were sold.²⁹

The Montreal Expos relocated to Washington to become the Nationals after the 2005 season. Major League Baseball, which owned the team during the relocation, sold it to a group led by Washington area real-estate developer Ted Lerner and including Kasten. Kasten became the public face of the group and announced that the focus of the team would be pitching and developing young players.[30]

The Nationals finished in or near last place in the NL East during their first few seasons and struggled to be competitive. The Nationals' struggles and the owners' reluctance to spend for top-notch free agents while waiting for the young players to develop may have been high on Kasten's list of reasons to leave the Nationals after the 2010 season.[31]

Kasten became part of the Guggenheim Baseball Management Team, which bought the Dodgers from Frank McCourt in 2012. Kasten became the club's president and CEO. The ownership group also included Mark Walter, CEO of Guggenheim Partners, and ex-NBA star Earvin "Magic" Johnson.[32]

Under Kasten's oversight, the Dodgers have won the NL West championship every year through 2019 while leading the major leagues in attendance each year. The Dodgers have also maintained one of the top-rated farm systems. In 2017 they were named *Baseball America*'s Organization of the Year.[33]

Kasten acquired a reputation as a builder. Besides getting a deal worked out with the Atlanta Olympic organizing committee to convert the Olympic facility to Turner Field[34] and to oversee the construction of Philips Arena, as president of the Washington Nationals, Kasten oversaw the construction of Nationals Park.

Kasten led a remodel of Dodger Stadium in time for the 2014 season and a $100 million renovation that was to be ready in time for the 2020 season, when the Dodgers were to host the All-Star Game.[35]

Kasten has been on numerous MLB, NBA, and NHL ownership committees, including NBA committees on marketing, player pensions, and expansion, and the NBA Board of Governors, the MLB owners' negotiating committee, and the NHL's Board of Governors and its executive committee. He is a former trustee of the Naismith Basketball Hall of Fame.[36] Kasten, the Los Angeles Sports Council's 2013 Executive of the Year, is on the board of directors for the LA84 Foundation as well as LA2028, the group organizing the 2028 LA Olympics and Paralympic Games.[37]

Sources

In addition to the sources cited in the Notes, the author consulted Baseball-Reference.com.

Notes

1. mlb.com/dodgers/team/front-office/stan-kasten.
2. basketball-reference.com/executives/kastest99x.html.
3. jewishvirtuallibrary.org/stan-kasten.
4. Bill Plaschke, "Dodgers' Stan Kasten Shaped by His Father's Unforgettable Lessons," *Los Angeles Times*, June 15, 2013. latimes.com/sports/la-xpm-2013-jun-15-la-sp-0616-plaschke-20130616-story.html.
5. Robert Nebel, "Stan the Man," *Atlanta Jewish Life Magazine*, Fall 2001; bobnebel.tripod.com/kastenprofile.html.
6. Nebel.
7. jewishvirtuallibrary.org/stan-kasten.
8. Plaschke.
9. Gary Pomerantz, "I Told Ted I Didn't Think It Could Be Done," *Atlanta Constitution*, February 19, 1989: 18C.
10. Plaschke.
11. Pomerantz.
12. Pomerantz.
13. Plaschke.
14. Plaschke.
15. Plaschke.
16. Plaschke.
17. Plaschke.
18. Plaschke.
19. Pomerantz.

20 I.J. Rosenberg, "Whatever Happened to … Stan Kasten," *Atlanta Journal Constitution*, February 19, 1989, ajc.com/sports/whatever-happened-stan-kasten/kQw9QVZIiGsT-3frOkR1DrI/.

21 Rosenberg.

22 Pomerantz.

23 basketball-reference.com/executives/kastest99x.html.

24 basketball-reference.com/executives/kastest99x.html.

25 sabr.org/latest/2013-sabr-analytics-highlights-stan-kasten.

26 Pomerantz.

27 Pomerantz.

28 sloansportsconference.com/people/stan-kasten/.

29 Nebel.

30 Jim Lovino, "Stan Kasten Says Goodbye to Nats," NBCWashington, September 23, 2010, nbcwashington.com/news/sports/stan-kasten-says-goodbye-to-nats/1839492/.

31 Lovino.

32 si.com/mlb/2017/10/31/who-owns-los-angeles-dodgers.

33 mlb.com/dodgers/team/front-office/stan-kasten.

34 Rosenberg.

35 Bill Plunkett, "Dodger Stadium to Undergo $100-Million Renovation During Offseason," *Orange County Register* (Anaheim, California), July 23, 2019. ocregister.com/2019/07/23/dodgers-announce-100m-plan-for-major-stadium-renovations/.

36 sloansportsconference.com/people/stan-kasten/.

37 mlb.com/dodgers/team/front-office/stan-kasten.

John Schuerholz

BY DAN LEVITT AND MARK ARMOUR

John Schuerholz

John Schuerholz spent 26 seasons as a big-league GM, winning 16 division titles, six pennants, and two World Series. In Kansas City he oversaw that franchise's first World Series. After moving to Atlanta, he took over a team that had lost more than 90 games four consecutive years and won the next 14 division titles (excepting the truncated 1994 strike season) and five pennants. Schuerholz displayed an uncanny knack for re-tooling his team, knowing which holes could be filled by integrating prospects and which needed outside solutions. In recognition of his front office accomplishments, Schuerholz was unanimously voted into the Baseball of Fame in 2016 by the Today's Game Era Committee.

John Boland Schuerholz was born on October 1, 1940, into one of Baltimore's most famous athletic families.[1] His parents, John, Sr. and Maryne (Rinny) Schuerholz, brought him up among some great athletes and coaches. His grandfather William Schuerholz coached at Loyola College in Baltimore from 1912 to 1926 and had 10 children; he occasionally put together a basketball team with his sons as the players. John's uncle Gilbert (his godfather) was an All-American soccer goalie and member of the US Olympic team; his uncle Wilson was a football star at East Carolina Teachers College; and uncle Don was a captain of the University of Maryland basketball team right after World War II. John Sr. was also a great basketball player and manned second base in the Class-D minor leagues in the years leading up to WWII.[2]

Though relatively small, John was also a stellar athlete. He starred at Baltimore City College High and then at Towson State University in Maryland, where he played soccer and baseball all four years. Schuerholz was all-conference in both sports, and in 1962, his senior season, he was named the school's athlete of the year. In 1974 he was inducted into the Towson Athletics Hall of Fame.[3]

After graduation Schuerholz took a job at North Point Junior High in Baltimore teaching eighth grade English and world geography. He also went back to school to earn a Master's degree in Administration and Supervision of Secondary Schools. Nevertheless, just two courses short of his master's, Schuerholz remained drawn by baseball, and on a whim sent a letter to Baltimore Orioles owner Jerry Hoffberger asking about an entry-level position in their front office. Hoffberger passed the request along to executive vice president Frank Cashen, who had once been a Baltimore sportswriter. Cashen recognized the Schuerholz name and called the young schoolteacher in for an interview, where he met with Cashen, GM Harry Dalton, and farm director Lou Gorman. Gorman and Dalton liked Schuerholz, and they hired him as Dalton's administrative assistant.[4]

Two years later, in 1968, Gorman joined the front office of the expansion Kansas City Royals, taking Schuerholz along with him. In Kansas City, GM Cedric Tallis assembled a strong front office that, over the first several years, included several other future general managers, notably Gorman, Syd Thrift, and Herk Robinson. Once again Schuerholz started in an administrative assistant position, but he slowly worked his way up.

In the mid 1970s Tallis, now in the Yankees front office, courted Schuerholz with a promotion to farm director. When Schuerholz informed the Royals he was joining the Yankees, Royals GM Joe Burke counter-offered with an expanded role (also farm director) and presumably more money. Schuerholz decided to stay in Kansas City. "Cedric was irate," Schuerholz recalled, telling him, "'I can't believe you would go against your word.'" Although Schuerholz felt he had made the right decision, he never managed to rebuild his relationship with Tallis.[5] In 1979 the Royals promoted him to vice president of player personnel; in October 1981 they named him GM, elevating incumbent Joe Burke to president.

When Schuerholz left Baltimore the O's were just embarking on a historically notable run of success. One of the keys to the Orioles' success was the refinement of the Oriole Way, a systematic approach throughout the organization to the team on and off the field—items such as scouting, teaching of baseball skills, approach to talent acquision, management of the farm system, player evaluation, and how players were expected to behave off the field. Gorman and Schuerholz brought this discipline to Kansas City where it eventually evolved into the Royals Way.

And the Royals Way helped Kansas City become successful more quickly than any other pre-free agency-era expansion franchise. The team won its first division title in 1976, winning again in 1977 and 1978. The Kansas City team eventually broke through to the World Series, winning the AL pennant in 1980, but slipping back below .500 in the strike-shortened 1981 season.

As Kansas City GM in the fall of 1981, Schuerholz inherited a talented manager in Dick Howser. "Dick had a great ability to appreciate how hard it is to play the game of baseball," Schuerholz said. "He knew how hard you had to work and how you had to prepare. He also knew what it took to be a member of a winning team."[6]

Schuerholz felt his squad was relatively close—despite their overall fourth-place finish in 1981, the Royals made the expanded playoffs by winning the division over the second half of the split season. In one of his first moves, Schuerholz hoped to fill a couple of needs for his mostly veteran team by swapping several young players for Vida Blue and outfielder Jerry Martin. While no longer the pitcher he had been in the early 1970s, Blue was still one of baseball's top pitchers, and the team rebounded to 90 wins in 1982. But cocaine was becoming a problem in baseball in the early 1980s, and Blue and Martin proved a distraction in 1983, as a cocaine investigation dogged them and other players. Moreover, Schuerholz later wrote that, according to the federal drug investigation, it was Blue that introduced the drug to the Royals.[7] After the season Blue and Martin, along with star center fielder Willie Wilson and first baseman Willie Mays Aikens, pleaded guilty and were each sentenced to three months in prison.

Despite the lost 1983 season, the Royals still had a strong nucleus, particularly of position players. Along with Wilson, the team had George Brett at third, Frank White at second, Hal McRae at DH, plus fireman Dan Quisenberry in the bullpen. Rather than try to rebuild his aging rotation with veterans, Schuerholz promoted a trio of young starters in 1984: Bret Saberhagen (20),

Mark Gubicza (21), and Danny Jackson (22). For 1985, he acquired veteran catcher Jim Sundberg to help his young staff acclimate. A couple of great trades, landing first baseman Steve Balboni in late 1983, and left fielder Lonnie Smith in May 1985, further augmented his roster. In 1985 the revamped Royals won the franchise's first World Series. In recognition of the Royals season, *The Sporting News* named Schuerholz Executive of the Year.

Over the remainder of the 1980s, the Royals sat on the fringes of the division race but could not capture another title. The team made some astute draft picks, such as outfielder and football star Bo Jackson, but Schuerholz also made what he considered his worst deal--swapping pitcher David Cone for catcher Ed Hearn--and some suspect free agent signings, such as reliever Mark Davis, towards the end of the decade.

By this time the Royals' executive suite was becoming a little unwieldy: In 1983 longtime owner Ewing Kauffman had brought in a partner, real estate mogul Avron Fogelman. The latter had been trying to put his stamp on operations, principally by leaning on Schuerholz to act as his proxy within the front office, which led to some friction. Moreover, by 1990, the value of Fogelman's real estate investment portfolio was crumbling in the wider commercial real estate crisis, and he was looking to use his half of the franchise as loan collateral. In this uncertain environment, Kauffman was considering selling the team altogether.[8]

In the summer of 1990, Schuerholz happened to be talking to Atlanta president Stan Kasten, who mentioned that the team was planning to move incumbent GM Bobby Cox back to manager and bring in a new GM. Kasten asked Schuerholz if he had any recommendations. Schuerholz, after contemplating the shifting sands within the Royals' front office, let Kasten know that he would be interested. Kasten quickly agreed, and in October 1990, Schuerholz joined the Atlanta Braves as GM with full authority over baseball operations. Schuerholz also received a pay raise, reportedly to $400,000 per year under a five-year contact, up from $180,000 (plus some shares in real estate investments through Fogelman) in Kansas City.[9] As he had in Kansas City, Schuerholz also inherited a great manager in Atlanta. A Hall of Famer in his own right, Bobby Cox in the dugout gave Schuerholz a leg up as he refashioned his ballclub.

Schuerholz took control of a franchise coming off a last-place finish that had not been relevant for some time, having lost at least 97 games in each of the past three seasons. Nevertheless, the team had a solid core of young pitchers in John Smoltz, Tom Glavine, and Steve Avery, plus outfielders Ron Gant and David Justice. As he had back in Kansas City, Schuerholz went to work to support his young hurlers, acquiring four solid defensive players: first baseman Sid Bream, shortstop Rafael Belliard, third baseman Terry Pendleton, and centerfielder Otis Nixon. In 1991 Pendleton also turned in a great hitting season, winning the league MVP, and the Braves won their first pennant since 1958, before losing in the World Series. For this historic single-season turnaround, Schuerholz received the Executive of the Year award from United Press International.

At spring training in 1992, Schuerholz worked out a deal with Pirates GM Ted Simmons for Barry Bonds, with one year left on his contract, in exchange for pitcher Alejandro Pena, outfielder Keith Mitchell, and a player to be named later. Unfortunately for the Braves, Simmons was overruled internally, and the trade fell through.[10] The Braves returned with pretty much the same lineup as the previous season, and the team once more captured the league flag, but again fell short in the World Series.

Schuerholz was not typically a participant in the big-name free agent auctions, but prior to the 1993 season, the Braves rocked the baseball world by signing free-agent Greg Maddux, the 26-year-old ace of the Chicago Cubs, to bolster a pitching staff that was already the envy of the league. Maddux responded with the second of his four straight Cy Young awards, but the team fell to the Phillies in the NLDS.

After his quick success in Atlanta, other teams pursued Schuerholz to oversee their baseball operations. Baltimore reportedly reached out to him in late 1993 regarding a chief executive position, and the Cubs contacted him for a similar role late in the 1994 season before hiring Andy MacPhail for the job. The Braves, responding to the market demand for their GM, extended Schuerholz's contract through 1999. In early 1998 they extended his contract again, this time though 2003 with a club option for 2004.[11]

The Braves could not have maintained their success for a decade without a continual influx of talent. The team that won the World Series in 1995 was much different than the one that had lost four years earlier: five of the eight position players, two starting pitchers, most of the bench and all of the bullpen had turned over. When the Braves lost the World Series in 1999, five of the eight position players, two starters, and all of the bench and bullpen were different from the champions of 1995.

Most importantly, Schuerholz continually addressed aging and ineffective players with internal solutions (if available) as opposed trading his prospects for more aging veterans. Good teams are often reluctant to give significant roles to untested players. The Braves of the early 1990s had several veteran journeymen that needed replacing within a few years. What set the Braves apart from other great teams of the past generation was their willingness to give regular roles to the jewels of their farm system. When Terry Pendleton or Ron Gant needed replacing, Schuerholz did not trade his young talent for veteran solutions. In 1994 the Braves gave starting positions to Javy Lopez and Ryan Klesko, and within two years both Chipper Jones and Andruw Jones were key players. Later still, Rafael Furcal, Marcus Giles, and Adam LaRoche claimed jobs.

Schuerholz also made several impressive trades to keep his team competitive. During his first two years Schuerholz made a couple of minor late-season trades that bolstered the Braves for the stretch run and playoffs, picking up reliever Alejandro Pena in 1991 and Jeff Reardon in 1992, though the latter struggled in the World Series after a stellar September. In perhaps his best and most timely deal, Schuerholz landed Fred McGriff from San Diego for prospects in July 1993. The Braves went 51–17 after the acquisition to capture their third straight division title.

Whether on trades or free agent signings, Schuerholz and his staff generally displayed sound judgement in identifying veteran solutions, often securing very good players for a reasonable return. For 1998 he added still-productive first baseman Andrés Galarraga, and the next season he brought in outfielder Brian Jordan and second baseman Bret Boone. In 2002 he landed Gary Sheffield, and when the outfielder bolted as a free agent two years later after finishing third in the MVP voting, Schuerholz traded for J.D. Drew to replace him. Drew finished sixth in the MVP voting, and he, too, then departed as a free agent. In retrospect, the inclusion of then-prospect Adam Wainwright in the swap makes it seem less advantageous. Regarding moves that received criticism, Schuerholz often defended them by highlighting the need to manage to a budget, though he also maintained that ownership rarely forced him to cut payroll.

On the pitching side of the equation, Jaret Wright may have represented Schuerholz and the Braves organization at its most astute. Wright had been the tenth overall pick in the 1994 draft but was often injured and from 2000 through 2002 had pitched only sparingly; when he had been on the mound, he threw poorly. Nevertheless, when Wright was available on waivers late in the 2003 season, Schuerholz claimed him on the advice of his scouts, and Cox and renowned pitching coach Leo Mazzone helped Wright turn in a great 2004 season.[12] Unfortunately, Wright jumped to the Yankees after the season for an impressive free agent contract.

One of the reasons the Braves' magnificent run eventually ended was because the farm system could not continue to produce stars the way it had in the mid-1990s, putting additional pressure on Schuerholz's trades and free agent signings. Nevertheless, even in 2002 and 2003, 12 years after Schuerholz's first division title, the team was still winning 101 games in both years.

Schuerholz often liked to note that the Braves on average turned over ten players on their roster every year. "One of the key responsibilities we have as general managers is managing change effectively," he said. "I think it's true in any business. We exist in an environment where change occurs in a bizarre fashion at a bizarre pace. We have to keep our antennas up and keep our minds open. We have to understand that change is inevitable, especially in our business, where we rely on human beings to perform physically, and we have to be able to manage the changes that are required in an effective manner."[13]

Schuerholz was forced to handle several controversies during his tenure in Atlanta, though none rose to level of legal consequences of the early 1980s drug trials, including Cox's arrest for allegedly striking his wife in 1995, *Sports Illustrated's* infamous profile of John Rocker in December 1999 in which the reliever callously demeaned a whole host of minorities and ethnic groups, and Furcal's DUI arrest in 2004 (his second).

After the 2007 season the 67-year-old Schuerholz intended to retire from the front lines of baseball operations, but the Braves asked him to stay on as team president and he happily agreed. To direct the front office, he promoted his longtime assistant Frank Wren to GM. After a few mediocre years, the Braves returned to the postseason in 2010, followed by appearances in 2012 and 2013. But after missing the playoffs in 2014, Schuerholz dismissed Wren and brought in veteran GM John Hart to oversee baseball operations. More recently, he and Hart promoted John Coppolella to GM, and Schuerholz was elevated to Vice Chairman.

In 2013 the Braves announced their intention to leave Fulton County's Turner Field and move to Cobb County. Though Schuerholz was not the driving force behind the move or the development of the new stadium itself, as team president he was highly supportive and involved. "We wanted to [develop and control the commercial space] in the area surrounding Turner Field," Schuerholz said. "When we found out that that was impossible, we were told that it would not happen, that we had no choice. But the concept of building a major league ballpark and mixed-use development, we believed was valid."[14] The new stadium, SunTrust Park, opens in 2017.[15]

Schuerholz and his wife Karen live in Atlanta where the couple moved when John accepted the Atlanta GM job. The two have been married over 35 years and have two children, Jonathan and Gina. Jonathan played for several years as a second baseman in the Braves organization, peaking at AAA and an invitation to major league spring training. After his playing career ended, he followed in his father's footsteps, taking a job in the Braves organization in 2014. He is currently an assistant director of player development.

Along with baseball and teaching, Schuerholz had two other loves: clothes and music. He dates his interest in dressing well to a pair of "electric blue" pants with "saddle stitching down the side, [and] a matching belt," that his uncle gave him. Much of his musical taste dates to his formative years, and "with my apologies to Beethoven," Schuerholz contends that "Come and Go with Me" by the Del-Vikings is the greatest song of all time.[16]

The Atlanta Braves from 1991 to 2005 enjoyed one of the most impressive runs of success by a franchise in sports history. The team has been underrated because it navigated through the post-season unscathed only once, in 1995, but Schuerholz's maneuvering that kept this team at the top for 14 years is truly remarkable. When added to his legacy in Kansas City, Schuerholz clearly merits a ranking among the best general managers ever.

Notes

1. www.wbal.com/article/209758?title=brett-hollander-talks-to-baseball-legend-and-baltimore-native-john-schuerholz.

2. articles.baltimoresun.com/2009-05-11/news/0905100079_1_university-of-maryland-schuerholz-maryland-basketball-team; www.wbal.com/article/209758?title=brett-hollander-talks-to-baseball-legend-and-baltimore-native-john-schuerholz; www.legacy.com/obituaries/baltimoresun/obituary.aspx?n=maryne-schuerholz-rinny&pid=98287943&fhid=4134.

3. www.towsontigers.com/news/2016/12/5/schuerholz-inducted-into-baseball-hall-of-fame.aspx; *1984 Kansas City Royals Media Guide*, 5; www.wbal.com/article/209758?title=brett-hollander-talks-to-baseball-legend-and-baltimore-native-john-schuerholz; www.towson.edu/news/2016/schuerholz_hof.html.

4. www.wbal.com/article/209758?title=brett-hollander-talks-to-baseball-legend-and-baltimore-native-john-schuerholz.

5. John Schuerholz, *Built to Win: Inside Stories and Leadership Strategies from Baseball's Winningest GM* (New York: Warner Books, 2006), 127-28.

6. Richard Justice, "Schuerholz a Baseball Institution after Almost 50 Years," MLB.com, December 1, 2014.

7. Schuerholz, *Built to Win*, 239.

8. Joe Strauss, "New GM Schuerholz Likes to Think Positive but Faces a Major Task," *Atlanta Journal*, November 4, 1990; Schuerholz, *Built to Win*, 123-24.

9. Strauss.

10. Schuerholz, *Built to Win*, 1-4.

11. Joseph A. Reeves, "Twins' MacPhail in Line To Replace Cubs' Cook 'Down the Line,'" chicagotribune.com, September 4, 1994; John Steadman, "Schuerholz Puts Stamp on Game after Chance Letter," *Baltimore Sun*, September 23, 1994; Rod Beaton, "NL Alters Method to Pick Chiefs for Umpiring Crews," *USA Today*, March 5, 1998.

12. Schuerholz, *Built to Win*, 42-44.

13. Russell Adams, "The Culture of Winning," WSJ.com, October 5, 2005.

14. Joe Mock, baseballparks.com/2016/09/26/turning-the-page-on-turner-field/

15. I. J. Rosenberg, "Whatever Happened to...Jonathan Schuerholz," ajc.com, February 27, 2016; I. J. Rosenberg, "Looking Back: John Schuerholz," ajc.com, March 31, 2016.

16. Thomas Stinson, "Model for Success," *Atlanta Journal Constitution*, April 2, 2000.

Chuck LaMar

BY JUSTIN KRUEGER

Chuck LaMar

Chuck LaMar once commented, "I'm a baseball guy and my heart lies with the people out in the field. … I was one of those and I started out in professional baseball as an area scout and I drove 50,000 miles a year away from the wife and those kiddos as much as anybody so I can truly relate to those people out in the field."[1]

With a career in baseball that stretches over 40 years, another of his quotes that also appropriately describes his efforts is: "The guys who work the hardest have the chance to be the luckiest."[2]

LaMar was born in Twin Falls, Idaho, on July 22, 1956. His family moved in 1964 to Houston, Texas, where he would became a multisport star at Madison High School. He played college baseball at Texas Christian University in Fort Worth, part of the time as team captain. His younger brother, Danny, was a first-round pick of the Cincinnati Reds in the 1979 amateur draft. His father and grandfather played baseball in the minor leagues. LaMar's father, Charles William LaMar, was an office manager at Alloys of Texas and his mother, Sarah Charlotte "Sally" LaMar, was employed at Texas State Optical.

After college LaMar began what became a lifetime of working in baseball. After graduating from TCU in 1978 he taught and coached at St. Thomas Catholic High School in Houston. Eventually he followed Texas Wesleyan University head baseball coach Larry Smith to his new post at the University of Indiana. LaMar was one of Smith's assistant coaches. In 1984 he made his way back to Texas when he was hired as the head baseball coach at Mary Hardin-Baylor University. In his one year there, LaMar proved a tireless recruiter and developer of young players. He recruited pitcher Buddy Groom, who later pitched 14 seasons in the major leagues. Another player on his team was future major leaguer Brett Gideon.[3] LaMar left Hardin-Baylor after one year, in January 1985, to become the scouting supervisor for the Cincinnati Reds. In 1988 he joined the Pittsburgh Pirates as the director of minor-league operations. Two years later he joined the Atlanta Braves as the director of scouting and player development. The Braves had the top minor-league organization in 1991, 1992, and 1993. LaMar quipped about his "real good timing" in heading these efforts.[4] In 1993 he was promoted to assistant general manager of player personnel.

The perception of a gruff and/or aggressive personality and a lack of people skills began early in LaMar's career and continued to follow him. Braves executive Scott Proefrock recalled their time together in the '90s: "There's no bull---- with him. He's right to the point."[5] Not shockingly, some felt LaMar was too impersonal and cold.

Still, LaMar was understood to be a true baseball man. He understood organizational operations, was a talented scout, and believed strongly in player development. LaMar's collection of baseball experiences went hand-in-hand with his strong work ethic.

His time in Atlanta coincided with an exceptional run of success by the Braves. Asked about the possibility of leaving to go to another organization, LaMar replied, "I wanted to do the best job I could with the job at hand. If someone wanted me they knew where I was. I was in no hurry to leave the Atlanta Braves."[6]

In 1994 Lamar interviewed for GM positions with the St. Louis Cardinals and the Texas Rangers. He did not get either job. However, it was not long until he was named GM of a major-league club. On July 19, 1995, LaMar was hired by Tampa Bay Devil Rays owner Vince Naimoli as the vice president of baseball operations and general manager of the expansion club. The hire brought high hopes.

Naimoli said, "I like the guys who have dirty fingernails, guys down in the trenches who work their way up. ... Chuck has had every job on the ladder, high school, college, a scout. ... He has been with three very successful organizations. He's a very good scouting and development guy. That's the way we want to build this franchise."[7]

LaMar was chosen over 27 original candidates, including the other finalist Frank Wren, assistant GM of the Florida Marlins.[8]

LaMar referred to the GM position as "a dream job, to start from scratch with an expansion franchise, and doing it the right way."[9] The right way in his mind was following the examples of John Schuerholz in Atlanta and Pat Gillick in Toronto by building a top-notch scouting department and having a deep farm system. LaMar was a scout at his core, and believed player development was the way to build a winner in Tampa Bay.[10]

It was a full 2½ years before the Devil Rays would field their first major-league team but LaMar was busy building the organization. His hiring was widely lauded in baseball circles. Pirates GM Cam Bonifay commented, "He has tremendous instincts for the game and for people and for player evaluation and player movement. ... It's a perfect match."[11] Scott Proefrock said, "He leaves no stone unturned to make an organization better. ... He's always looking for ways to get better, to innovate, to beat the competition. Fire in the belly is a good way to describe that." Similar comments were heard throughout the major leagues.

Early on in his tenure as GM, LaMar said, "We have a chance to build one of the finest organizations in baseball."[12] And for the next decade LaMar tried hard to do so. There were definite successes. He built an organization from the ground up, streamlined their minor-league system, and pushed an organizational emphasis on player development.

Building the Rays (formerly the Devil Rays) from the ground up was a monumental task. One reason LaMar put such a premium on scouting was to get a competitive edge over big-spending teams like the Yankees and Red Sox. There was no way the Devil Rays could compete financially with them. A year into the job, LaMar noted that he had hoped for a more hands-on approach in the scouting and development of players in the organization, but that the great number of responsibilities of a GM did not allow for the role he had first imagined for himself. In his new position, he learned about the need to delegate responsibilities.

In the two-plus years from his appointment as GM to when the Devil Rays played their first game in 1998, LaMar was busy building the organization. He put together a geographically aligned minor-league system from rookie ball up through Triple-A. He also helped establish a minority internship program that was similar to the one he had overseen while with the Atlanta Braves.

It was a program that was at the center of a 1999 issue involving Hank Aaron and LaMar. The controversy centered on the Braves' minority program when LaMar was still in their employ. Aaron said LaMar had taken credit for the minority initiative program with the Braves and remarked, "All of that is a lie. ... I can't sit here and have him take credit for it."[13] LaMar responded that he was merely the caretaker of the program, but that "there are four people who started this initiative within baseball operations ... Rubye Lucas, Henry Aaron, John Schuerholz, and Stan Kasten."[14] LaMar noted that he used the Braves' program as an exemplar for a similar program he started with the Devil Rays.

After the 1997 season LaMar was given a new five-year contract. Naimoli commented, "He's done a great job. ... He knows exactly what he wants to get done and he implements the plan. He's the hardest worker I've ever seen. He's so precisely organized. And he's got an answer to everything. He's been there and done that. He knows all the nuances."[15]

Prior to the Devil Rays inaugural play on the field, LaMar commented, "Our dress rehearsal has been very good ... but we're fixing to get to the dance."[16] To be sure, there were grand dreams that the Devil Rays would mirror the success of two of LaMar's mentors, Pat Gillick in Toronto and John Schuerholz in Atlanta.

But, as LaMar also noted, "We are going to enter a period starting in 1998 and beyond where there are going to be some questions asked. There is going to be some criticism laid toward us. There are going to be some ups and downs that every major-league organization goes through."[17]

As it turned out, the game on the field proved infinitely more difficult as the Devil Rays struggled to be competitive.

The desire to be competitive from the beginning required the successful melding of veterans, young players, and other teams' castoffs. LaMar's initial foray into signing major-league veterans included Wilson Alvarez, Dave Martinez, and Roberto Hernandez. Inaugural game starter Alvarez posted a 17-26 record in three seasons with a 4.62 ERA. In a little more than two seasons before being traded to the Chicago Cubs, Martinez batted .272 and hit 10 home runs with 98 RBIs. Hernandez had a 3.43 ERA and 101 saves in his years. Wade Boggs also returned to his hometown and finished out the last two seasons of his Hall of Fame career. He got his 3,000th hit with the Devil Rays in 1999. Fred McGriff also added much needed offense during the early seasons. Despite the moves, things did not go according to plan and the Devil Rays remained cellar dwellers.

The Devil Rays began with three straight last-place finishes in the American League East. In their inaugural season of 1998 they were 63-99 and finished 51 games behind the eventual World Series champion New York Yankees. The 1999 season saw a six-game improvement to 69-93. In both seasons they ranked near the bottom in runs scored.

LaMar's best effort to generate more offense in Tampa Bay was "The Hit Show" of McGriff, Jose Canseco, Greg Vaughn, and Vinny Castilla during the 2000 season. At the time, LaMar commented, "You go Canseco, McGriff, Vaughn, Castilla, in whatever order from 3 to 6. If you look at the averages, the hits, the RBIs, the homers, it's comparable to anyone in baseball."[18] If healthy, maybe so. But that was never the case as injuries and downturns in production took their toll on the aging sluggers. In 2000 the Devil Rays finished 69-92, last again.

After three straight last-place finishes, it was believed that manager Larry Rothschild would likely be fired. To the surprise of many, Rothschild kept his job until 14 games into the 2001 season when he was finally sacked. At the time the Devil Rays' record was 4-10. Asked about the timing of firing Rothschild, LaMar remarked, "It was a feeling in my gut," and that "the true sadness for me is not in making the decision. That was tough. But it's the knowledge that some of the personnel decisions I made handcuffed the organization and his ability."[19] Hal McRae took over as manager and finished with a record of 58-90. The Devil Rays tied the Pittsburgh Pirates for the season's worst record at 62-100. The 2002 season was even worse. They finished at 55-106, tying the Detroit Tigers for the worst record (the Milwaukee Brewers finished a half-game better at 56-106). When McRae was fired after the season, LaMar noted, "I'm not making him a scapegoat. ... I'm responsible for the personnel. I think he could've won more games with better talent."[20]

In the offseason LaMar hired the hometown candidate, Lou Piniella. Piniella had asked out of the final year of his contract managing the Seattle Mariners, a team he led to 116 victories in 2001, to come to Tampa Bay. Despite the Devil Rays' losing nearly 300 games over the previous three years, there was optimism in the organization. Through the continued losing, Naimoli still held fast to LaMar's vision for the Devil Rays. Nevertheless, the 2003 season, even with a new manager, turned out similar to the previous seasons. With a record of 63-99, the Rays finished last in the American League East for the sixth season in a row.

Even so, prior to the 2004 season LaMar was given a two-year contract extension. Owner Naimoli commented, "If you look at the design of the team, the fact that we have the fruition of our farm system coming, which is Chuck's doing, as well as his very skilled blending of veteran players at reasonable prices this year, operating within a payroll we can afford, I think it's been great work, frankly."[21] In 2004 the Devil Rays climbed out of the AL East cellar for the first time, finishing in fourth place at 70-91, three games up on the Toronto Blue Jays.

In 2005 the Devil Rays fell back to 67-95 and finished last in the American League East for the seventh time in eight years. There was also a switch in Devil Rays ownership from Vince Naimoli to new principal owner Stuart Sternberg. The change spelled the end of LaMar's tenure in Tampa Bay.

He was relieved of his duties in October 2005 (as was manager Lou Piniella).

The Devil Rays compiled a record of 518-775 with LaMar as GM. Despite his best efforts, LaMar and the Devil Rays were not able to re-create the magic of the Atlanta Braves under GM John Schuerholz. LaMar's time in Tampa Bay was ultimately marked by the failure to win enough games.

After his firing, LaMar said, "I take full responsibility for this organization not winning during the eight major-league seasons that I've been here. ... It's the general manager's responsibility, no matter what the circumstances are, to find a way to put a winning product on the field."[22]

LaMar also said, "I don't think this organization has ever been stronger on the field. It's obvious to everybody. I've been saying it for years and years. It's finally good to actually see the wins instead of my rhetoric."[23] The Rays had finished the second half of the 2005 season at 39-34, their first-ever winning half.[24]

Another time he said, "I was one of the first employees they ever hired and was there 10 years, which is an awfully long run in today's baseball. ... I gave my heart and soul to them."[25]

His tenure in Tampa Bay might be best remembered for the number of veterans the Devil Rays brought in during the tail-end of their careers. Some worked out well on team-friendly deals, including Wade Boggs, Fred McGriff, Tino Martinez, Jose Canseco, and Greg Vaughn. Other signings that did not work out so well included Wilson Alvarez and Vinny Castilla. Juan Guzman was a particularly bad signing. Guzman signed for $6 million and gave the Devil Rays one start of 1⅔ innings. He allowed seven hits and eight runs. It was the last time he pitched in the major leagues.

There were other moves that turned out shockingly bad. The signing of the elite high-school pitcher Matt White to a $10.2 million contract did not pay dividends as White suffered shoulder problems that led to three surgeries. He never played in the major leagues. The trading of Bobby Abreu for Kevin Stocker was a straight stinker. Abreu went on to hit 288 home runs in the major leagues, while Stocker played parts of three seasons with the Devil Rays, hitting .250 with 9 home runs and 60 RBIs. The third pick of the 2000 draft, right-handed starting pitcher Dewon Brazelton, was bad; the pitcher out of Middle Tennessee State University compiled a won-lost record of 8-23 with the Devil Rays and a 5.98 ERA before being shipped to the San Diego Padres. The $34 million contract to Greg Vaughn was not a complete loss, but did not pay the dividends the cash-strapped organization had hoped for. In his first two seasons with the team, 2001 and 2001, he hit a total of 52 home runs and drove in 156 runs. His last season in Tampa Bay included 69 games played, 8 home runs, and 29 RBIs.

The strength of the Devil Rays minor-league system under LaMar's leadership was evident in the drafting and development of prospects such as Carl Crawford, Rocco Baldelli, B.J. Upton, and Josh Hamilton.

In 2007 LaMar was a special assistant to Washington Nationals GM Jim Bowden. He worked as a national cross-checker for draft prospects. After the 2007 season LaMar joined the Philadelphia Phillies as their director of professional scouting. It was a position the team created just for him and his skill set.

Phillies assistant GM Ruben Amaro Jr. expressed his pleasure with the hiring of LaMar: "To have that kind of experience, to have his knowledge base, to have that kind of baseball person in our organization is a tremendous addition." Fellow assistant GM Mike Arbuckle added, "He's an excellent evaluator … and that's at any level."[26]

Asked during spring training in 2008, about his time with the Devil Rays, LaMar said, "I think this year and next year people in baseball are going to realize what a good job of scouting we did."[27] His comments proved correct as the newly named Rays finished in first place in the American League East with a record of 97-65. Under the leadership of senior vice president Gerry Hunsicker and general manager Andrew Friedman, the Rays made the playoffs and reached the World Series for the first time in their history.

They lost the Series to the Phillies in five games. At the time, LaMar was the Phillies assistant GM of player development and scouting. Before the Series, LaMar reflected on his role with the Devil Rays:

"Sitting here, to have had some impact on both teams in the Series, it's really overwhelming. When you look at the group of players, not only still with this team tonight, but all the players that they traded to get the pieces that they needed, you're talking about a very significant group. But I take much more pride in the big picture of having started this organization on a foundation of scouting and player development, and the staff that was hired then."[28]

LaMar resigned as Phillies assistant GM of player development and scouting in September 2011. It was reported that he was dissatisfied with how the Phillies organization was investing in the amateur draft and player development. The sustained success of the Phillies brought with it lower draft picks which in turn had taken a toll on the quality of their farm system. It amounted to more difficulty in developing players.[29] Two months later LaMar joined the Toronto Blue Jays as a special-assignment amateur scout. Andrew Tinnish, the Blue Jays director of amateur scouting, declared, "[W]ith over 25 years of experience, we welcome Chuck's insight and expertise."[30]

In 2018 LaMar took a position as a scout with the San Diego Padres.

Sources

In addition to the sources cited in the Notes, information was gathered from LaMar's Hall of Fame clippings file, Baseball-Reference.com. Baseball-Almanac.com, and Retrosheet.org.

Notes

1 Marc Topkin, "Baseball Team, Baseball Man," *St. Petersburg Times*, July 20, 1995.

"Braves Win! Braves Win! Braves Win!"

2 Bill Chastain, "LaMar Talking Brave; The Devil Rays GM Will Follow Atlanta's Recipe for Success in the Draft," *Tampa Tribune*, June 2, 1996.

3 Jerry Prickett, "Take Him Out to the Ballgame: Former UMHB Coach Has Ties to Rays, Phillies," *Temple* (Texas) *Daily Telegram*, October 22, 2008. tdtnews.com/archive/article_aa235ab0-4586-526b-8553-2b398d2df4e2.html

4 Prickett.

5 Topkin, 1995.

6 Topkin, 1995.

7 Rod Beaton, "Devil Rays Hire LaMar as First GM," *USA Today*, July 20, 1995.

8 Hubert Mizell, "GM Choice Gives Fans Ray of Hope," *St. Petersburg Times*, July 20, 1995.

9 Mizell.

10 Chastain.

11 Topkin, 1995.

12 Topkin, 1995

13 Roger Mills, "Aaron Criticizes LaMar," *St. Petersburg Times*, December 16, 1999.

14 Mills.

15 Marc Topkin, "Rays Reward LaMar," *St. Petersburg Times*, January 14, 1998.

16 Chastain.

17 Topkin, 1998.

18 Associated Press, "Vaughn Boosts D-Rays' Power," ESPN Baseball, December 13, 1999. a.espncdn.com/mlb/news/1999/1213/231875.html.

19 Gary Shelton, "LaMar's Gut Check: Firing Rothschild," *St. Petersburg Times*, April 19, 2001.

20 Associated Press, "Baseball Roundup; Devil Rays Fire McRae; Tigers Dismiss Pujols," *New York Times*, October 1, 2002. nytimes.com/2002/10/01/sports/baseball-roundup-devil-rays-fire-mcrae-tigers-dismiss-pujols.html.

21 Marc Topkin, "LaMar Gets Contract Extension," *St. Petersburg Times*, March 29, 2004.

22 Damian Cristodero, Dave Scheiber, and Marc Topkin, "LaMar Issues Apology to Fans," *St. Petersburg Times*, October 7, 2005.

23 Scott Carter, "Several Moves Backfired on Rays' Only GM," Tampa Bay Online, October 6, 2005. Newspaper clipping found in LaMar's file at the National Baseball Hall of Fame.

24 Carter.

25 David Murphy, "Phillies Scout LaMar Knows Tampa Bay Rays Well," *Philadelphia Inquirer*, March 6, 2008. inquirer.com/philly/hp/sports/20080306_Phillies_scout_LaMar_knows_Tampa_Bay_Rays_well.html.

26 Murphy.

27 Murphy.

28 Tyler Kepner, "Now With the Phillies, an Ex-General Manager Left His Mark on the Rays," *New York Times*, October 23, 2008. nytimes.com/2008/10/24/sports/baseball/24lamar.html.

29 Craig Calcaterra, "Report: Chuck LaMar Quit Because He Questioned the Phillies' Commitment to Player Development," NBC Sports.com, September 9, 2011. mlb.nbcsports.com/2011/09/09/report-chuck-lamar-quit-because-he-questioned-the-phillies-commitment-to-player-development/.

30 Associated Press, "Blue Jays Add Chuck LaMar," MLB.com, November 4, 2011. toronto.bluejays.mlb.com/content/printer_friendly/tor/y2011/m11/d04/c25899142.jsp.

Paul Snyder

BY LEE LOWENFISH

Paul Snyder

Paul Snyder was the indispensable man behind the scenes of the Atlanta Braves' success. If anyone has said a bad word about him, it has not been recorded in the hothouse world of baseball. A baseball lifer since he started his career as a Braves minor-league outfielder-first baseman in 1958, Snyder is a rarity in that he has spent his whole life with one organization. He has worn many hats – minor-league player, minor-league player-manager and manager, area scout, director of player development, director of amateur scouting, and special assistant to the general manager. He has experienced his share of triumphs and setbacks but he has carried on with an unmatched work ethic and a relentlessly positive attitude. In his career-long search for talent for the Braves, Snyder's travels have led him, in the words of author Charles Fountain, from "Central American homes with dirt floors and no plumbing ... [to] suburban mansions."[1]

Snyder has been called the Braves' Branch Rickey because his knowledge of baseball from A to Z is so encyclopedic. Though he is never one to blow his own horn, his peers have recognized him numerous times: the 2004 Roland Hemond Award given to someone "who has demonstrated a lifetime commitment to professional baseball scouts and scouting, and player development history"; election to the Braves Hall of Fame in 2005, and the prestigious "King of Baseball" title bestowed at the 2006 minor leagues' winter meetings. When *Baseball America* celebrated its 20th anniversary in 2001 and 25th anniversary in 2006, Snyder made both lists of the 20 and 25 most notable baseball people during those two timespans.

Paul Luther Snyder was born on June 11, 1935, in the small central Pennsylvania town of Dallastown, about eight miles northwest of York.[2] He fell in love with baseball early on. By the age of 15 he was making a local name for himself by competing against older players in area semi-pro twilight leagues. A scout for the Brooklyn Dodgers was interested in signing the outfielder-first baseman after high school, but Snyder's parents insisted that he start college because neither one had done so. Turning down a baseball scholarship to Penn State, Paul accepted a football scholarship to Lebanon Valley College in nearby Annville; it was a school sponsored by the Church of the Brethren, to which his mother belonged. A back injury on the football field and a lack of interest in academics led Snyder to leave college after only one year. He returned home to help his father in the plumbing and heating contracting business, and he resumed playing baseball in a top-notch twilight league run in nearby Red Lion.[3]

Sterling Arnold, a bird-dog scout for the Washington Senators, expressed interest in signing him, but the amateur free-agent draft was still eight years away so Snyder could entertain more offers. Milwaukee Braves scout John Ogden, who had made a prominent name for himself as a scout for Connie Mack's Philadelphia Athletics and later as an executive with the minor-league Baltimore Orioles, convinced Snyder that the Braves were a more stable and prosperous organization than the penny-pitching Senators. The Braves were in their heyday in Milwaukee – they would win the World Series in 1957, lose a rematch to the Yankees in 1958, and lose two straight in the National League playoff to the Dodgers in 1959. Ogden didn't need a hard sell to get Snyder to ink a Braves minor-league contract that would pay him $2,500 if he made the roster of a minor-league team in his first season.[4]

In 1958 Snyder enjoyed an outstanding rookie year for Midland, Texas in the Class-D Sophomore League – .350 BA, .574 SLG, with 15 HR and 106 RBIs. (It was a new, short-lived league that folded in 1961.) He felt that playing semipro ball back home with older men had prepared him very well for pro ball. In 1959 Snyder was promoted to Cedar Rapids in the Class-B Three-I League (Illinois, Indiana, Iowa), but a roster crunch forced him down to the Eau Claire Braves in the Class-C Northern League. He wound up hitting over .300 in both stops, but his back flared up again while he was traveling on the rickety team bus to a road game in Winnipeg, Canada. He amassed only 326 AB, 120 fewer than during his rookie season. His balky back would require spinal surgery, and it became a chronic problem during his playing career.

The 1960 season found Snyder demoted to the Class-D Wellsville Braves of the New York-Penn League. Still plagued by the bad back, he hit .241 in only 101 at-bats for the franchise in western New York State. But Snyder always found a silver lining whatever his circumstances. He developed a lifelong friendship with Wellsville player-manager Harry Minor. Minor, a native of Long Beach, California, was at the end of a 12-year minor-league playing career that never reached the majors. Minor would start a scouting career the next season for the Braves, and in 1968 joined the Mets where he enjoyed a 44-year career, being instrumental in signing such future stars on the 1986 world champions as Darryl Strawberry, Lennie Dykstra, Kevin Elster, and Kevin Mitchell.[5]

Minor took an immediate liking to Snyder, who was seven years his junior. It wasn't just Snyder's batting tools, his line-drive stroke, and his ability to wait on the pitch. He liked even more Snyder's aptitude for the mental side of game, noticing that he was an attentive listener and observer and was looked up to by younger teammates. Minor shared with Snyder a lot of his accumulated baseball knowledge, some of it delivered while driving the team bus. Among the lessons Snyder learned was never to criticize any individual in front of the team. After a game, whether a win or a loss, Minor just asked the players to sit in silence for about 15 minutes thinking about the day's events. He then told them to flush the experience and prepare for tomorrow.

In 1961 Snyder's back issues abated and he enjoyed a stellar season. Assigned again to Class-B Cedar Rapids, he led the Three-I League in hits and compiled the impressive line of .310 BA, 14 HRs, 76 RBIs, and .450 SLG. In 1962 the strapping 6-foot-2, 200-pound Snyder enjoyed his best year as a player, hitting .312, slugging .495 with 19 HR and 113 RBIs for the Austin Senators in the Double-A Texas League.

For 1963 he was promoted to the Denver Bears, the Braves' Triple-A Pacific Coast League franchise. His elation at arriving one step from the majors was quickly doused when his back flared up again. After one game early in the season, Denver manager Jack Tighe called him in for a heart-to-heart discussion. The former skipper of the Detroit Tigers noted Snyder's declining mobility. "You have only one tool now, line-drive power," Tighe bluntly told him, adding that at nearly the age of 28 he wasn't getting any younger.[6] Yet like others in the Braves organization, Tighe didn't want to lose Snyder's services. He told him that a player-manager job was open at Greenville, South Carolina, in the Class-A Western Carolinas League, and he knew that farm director John Mullen wanted to hire him.

The death of a dream is never easy for any player, but after letting the bad news sink in, Snyder thought about his future. His wife was due with their first child, and he knew he had to make a living to support his family. He didn't want to leave baseball, so he quickly accepted the offer and headed to his first assignment as player-manager. As the years passed, Snyder never failed to credit Jack Tighe for his frank evaluation and for kick-starting him toward his new career. "Never lie to a player" is the lesson from Tighe that Snyder always kept in mind.

At Greenville, Snyder took over for Jim Fanning, who was a rising star in the Braves' player-development system. (By the end of the decade Fanning would become a key member of the Montreal Expos expansion franchise.) "He was like a big brother to me," Snyder remembered in an October 2019 phone interview. "You could take any problem to Fanning and he would always suggest a sensible solution." In the same interview Snyder also lavished praise on Roland Hemond, who was another vital early influence before he left to join the expansion California Angels. "Roland taught me to always call players by their first names," Snyder recalled.[7]

Snyder's managerial career started auspiciously as the Greenville Braves won the 1963 Western Carolina League playoffs. Snyder took over 263 at-bats in his last semi-regular year as a player, hitting .316. (His career average rested at .318.) The following season of 1964 started with Snyder working as a co-manager with Andy Pafko for the Binghamton Triplets in the Class-A New York-Penn League. On the staff with Pafko, the former Cubs-Brooklyn Dodgers-Milwaukee Braves slugger, was Walter "Boom Boom" Beck, the pre-World War II Phillies hurler who had gotten his nickname for giving up line drives that loudly caromed off the tin wall at cozy Baker Bowl.

It was during the 1964 season that the future "Braves Branch Rickey" had his first and only encounter with Branch Rickey himself, who was in his last season as a consultant with the Cardinals. (He died late the next year at age 83.) Snyder was part of a Braves contingent that traveled to a meeting in Sarasota where the Braves, Cardinals, White Sox, and Yankees were finalizing plans for a new cooperative league to be called the Sarasota Rookie League. Snyder vividly remembered Rickey arriving in a Chrysler limousine and holding forth for most of the day on the fundamentals of running, throwing, sliding, and baserunning. He recalled that Rickey stressed the importance of using games in this cooperative league as lessons in player development.[8]

Snyder managed the Sarasota Braves to a 1964 pennant with a 36-23 record. In 1965 he returned to Florida to manage again, this time in West Palm Beach, where the Braves had moved their franchise in what was now called the Florida Rookie League. (In 1966 the name was changed again to the Florida Gulf Coast League.) Snyder led the team to a strong second-place finish; one of his young players was Wayne Garrett, who four years later was a platoon third baseman on the World Series champion New York Mets.

Meanwhile, the parent franchise was facing a serious problem as it prepared to set up shop in Atlanta for the 1966 season. There was evidently nobody in the organization who knew anything about stadium operations. Already seen as a good company man, Snyder was asked by Braves president John McHale to fill the void although he knew nothing about hiring and organizing grounds crews, arranging stadium cleaning contracts, and other business issues. The workload was so heavy that at times, Snyder told author

Bill Shanks, "I slept in the first aid room."[9] The stadium operations job became the only job in Snyder's baseball career that he did not enjoy because he was far removed from working with and evaluating players.

After the season, he was rescued from the administrative side when he learned that Jack Tighe, who had turned from managing to scouting, was leaving the organization. Snyder asked Braves general manager Paul Richards for Tighe's job and his wish was granted. Always a sponge for picking up lessons from his elders, Snyder learned a lot about baseball strategy and techniques from Richards, who encouraged talking the game with players – in practices and before and after games. Snyder picked up many durable insights from Richards' fertile baseball brain without developing the oversized ego of the well-traveled manager.

Snyder started his career as a Braves scout in 1967 and immediately fell in love with the profession. He loved being out in the field doing hands-on development work with aspiring players. The good company man did return to manage in the lower minors four more times in the early 1970s, and led each team to a winning record: in 1970, the Magic Valley Cowboys in Twin Falls, Idaho, in the Pioneer League; in 1971 and 1973, Wytheville, Virginia, in the Appalachian League; and in 1972, Greenwood, South Carolina, in the Western Carolinas League. But his commitment to building lasting organizational success through scouting and player development became permanent when the Braves named Snyder's former Austin Senators teammate Bill Lucas scouting director in 1972. The men shared a mutual admiration society because Lucas immediately named Snyder his assistant scouting director.

William DeVaughn Lucas was a rarity in the baseball business, an African-American who worked his way up the ladder to a prominent front-office position. Born January 25, 1936, in Jacksonville, Florida, Bill Lucas, like Paul Snyder, got the baseball bug early on. He broke in as a peanut vendor for the local Braves affiliate in the Class-A South Atlantic League, rose to team batboy, and in high school became a star shortstop. At the historically black Florida A&M University in nearby Daytona Beach, he earned All-American honors from the NAIA (National Association of Intercollegiate Athletics). A six-year minor-league career ensued, interrupted at times by military service. Paul Snyder is convinced that Lucas would have made the majors had he not suffered a knee injury when they were teammates in 1962. Lucas retired two years later and briefly tried teaching school, but the siren call of baseball was too strong.[10]

In 1965, the last year of the minor-league Triple-A Atlanta Crackers' existence, Lucas served as the team's public-relations director. The year 1966 began with Lucas working in the mailroom of the newly minted Atlanta Braves, but he quickly was tapped to start a community-relations department aimed at building interest in the Braves in the black community. In 1967 Lucas became assistant to farm director Eddie Robinson, the former Indians and Yankees first baseman. When Robinson was promoted in 1972 to vice president in charge of baseball operations, Lucas was named his successor as farm director. It did not hurt Lucas's rise in the organization that his sister, Barbara, was married at the time to the Braves' reigning superstar, Hank Aaron. But there was no doubt that the Braves had found a man blessed with the rare combination of passion, compassion, and dispassion. As Eddie Robinson later wrote in his memoir *Lucky Me*, Lucas was "a talented fellow" and a "forward thinker."[11]

Paul Snyder found in Bill Lucas a soul baseball brother. He once described Lucas as a rare teammate who read books on the team bus "that had no pictures."[12] For his part, Lucas never forgot that during their season as teammates in Austin, Paul had been heartsick that his friend had to endure segregated second-class living conditions, often sleeping in a rundown apartment building with no windows. Yet Lucas never complained and always came to the ballpark ready to work and compete.

Bill Lucas understood intuitively that for Paul Snyder color did not exist. What only mattered were the answers to two basic questions: Could the farmhands play the game? And how could we make them better players?

Lucas took special pains to ease the transition into pro baseball of the many players of color the Braves were bringing into the organization. One of those players was Johnnie B. "Dusty" Baker Jr., who was drafted in the 25th round in 1967 out of high school in Carmichael, California, near Sacramento. Baker still glows with the memory of how Lucas cushioned him from the worst aspects of racism in the South that Baker had never experienced so directly in California. Lucas took such an interest in Baker's advancement as a person as well as a player that when Dusty graduated with honors from the Dress Blue program in his Marine Reserve training camp program a few years later, Lucas attended the ceremony. The idea that the Braves organization was a family that took care of each other was not lost on Baker, who made it a point to pick up his African-American teammate Ralph Garr in Louisiana on his annual cross-country automobile trip to Florida for spring training. (Garr himself felt the warm vibes from Lucas and was thrilled when he was hired as a Braves scout in 1984, a position he still held in 2020.)[13]

As the Braves scouting and philosophy program took hold under Lucas and Snyder, certain principles became obvious. There was a shared belief that high-school players with high ceilings were the preferred athletes to draft and develop under the care of veteran coaches. They especially encouraged the scouting of high-school pitchers, or at most community college pitchers, who hadn't been ruined by overuse and could be trained by pro coaches to throw correctly. They might take two or three extra years to develop, but Lucas and Snyder firmly believed that the patience was worth the end result. Hiring good pitching coaches and hitting coaches and instructors for the minor leagues became paramount. Soon former major-league hurlers Bruce Del Canton, Bill Fischer, and Eddie Watt would be hired by the system for their teaching abilities.

As Snyder's career blossomed, he was especially grateful to Lucas for introducing him to one of the Braves' most respected area scouts, Bill Wight. "What a gift Bill Lucas gave me by assigning me to two weeks on the road with Bill Wight," Snyder told me in our phone interview. Although the southpaw's career record of 77-99 doesn't look impressive, Wight lasted 12 years in the majors after being traded in 1948 from the Yankees in the deal for fellow southpaw (and future scout) Eddie Lopat. Wight earned industrywide respect from his peers for the intensity and guile in which he approached his craft. Pitchers were particularly awed at his move to first base. Shortly after retiring, Wight turned to scouting, first with the expansion Houston Colt .45s, for whom he signed future Hall of Famer Joe Morgan.

From 1967 through 1994 Wight served the Braves as a California area scout who played a very influential role in meetings before the amateur draft. He would be central to the signing of such future Braves stars as Dale Murphy, Bob Horner, Ron Gant, Brian Hunter, David Justice, and Dusty Baker. (Baker remembered Wight as a thoughtful, caring person who was instrumental in persuading him to sign with the Braves and turn down college baseball, basketball, and track scholarship offers.) What fascinated Paul Snyder about Bill Wight's scouting acumen was that he was more expert at appraising hitters than pitchers. He surmised that Wight's keen evaluation of hitters had to come from his awareness that he didn't have overpowering stuff as a pitcher so he had to understand hitters' weaknesses to survive. "At times I'd scout with him and he'd ask about my radar gun, 'Whatdya get? Whatdya get?'" Snyder remembered with a chuckle.[14]

Before the arrival of Bill Lucas at the helm of the farm system in 1972, the Braves did not have great success with the amateur free-agent draft. However, on the horizon in Portland, Oregon, was

Dale Murphy, a gifted athlete who as early as the ninth grade was attracting the attention of legendary Ohio State football coach Woody Hayes. The strong consensus of the Braves scouting staff was that Murphy should be a first-round draft pick, and he was indeed taken at that level in 1974. He did not excel immediately in the minors, and a knee injury would ultimately force his switch from catcher to the outfield. Yet the compassionate understanding that was the watchword under Lucas and Snyder worked wonders with Murphy. He never forgot the Braves' insistence that he accept a bonus for his production in his mediocre minor-league season of 1976 even though he didn't reach the requisite numbers.[15]

Paul Snyder always liked to cite the old adage that you needed to draft 10 pitchers for every one who truly had a career. So in addition to signing Dale Murphy in the first round of the June 1974 draft, the Braves selected southpaw Larry McWilliams in the first round of the January draft (for those players who had not finished at least three years of college by June) – McWilliams, a Paris, Texas, junior-college hurler, went on to a 13-year major-league career. Picked in June out of small colleges were two future longtime Braves hurlers, Rick Camp in the seventh round and lefty Mickey Mahler in the 10th round. With the trade of Hank Aaron back to Milwaukee at the end of the 1974 season, the organization's youth movement seemed to be accelerating.

On the major-league level, however, ownership was in flux. The whirlwind known as Ted Turner arrived on the scene in 1973 as a part-owner eager to use Braves' games as programming for his WCTG TV station in Atlanta. The station was still showing mostly old movies with his emphasis on news still a ways off. "I hate the news. News is evil. It makes people feel bad," he said at the time.[16] When rumors were flying that the Braves might be sold and moved to another city, Turner bought full ownership in the team after the 1975 season.

The Braves were competing in the tough NL West Division dominated by the Cincinnati Reds and the Los Angeles Dodgers. Yet in 1976, the first season with Turner as full owner,

attendance picked up by 53 percent. Braves games became carnivals with pregame ostrich races, contests in pushing a baseball with one's nose between first base and home plate in which Turner occasionally took part, and scantily-clad damsels cavorting around the field. He relished the publicity of being of an owner. He even managed one game after he sent incumbent skipper Dave Bristol on a "scouting vacation" during a long losing streak. The Braves lost in Turner's one-game turn at the helm, and afterward the baseball establishment came down hard on him for making a "mockery of the game." National League President Chub Feeney dug up an obscure rule that prevented an owner from managing a game without special permission from the commissioner, and Commissioner Bowie Kuhn refused to grant a waiver.[17]

Paul Snyder admired Ted Turner's energy and showmanship, but he sensed early on that Turner did not understand how to develop baseball players. Out in the field evaluating amateur talent and minor leaguers, Snyder stayed out of Turner's way, feeling confident that Bill Lucas had earned the respect of the owner. Indeed, Lucas was promoted in 1976 to vice president of player development, becoming the first black general manager. (He was not given the GM title, something Turner kept for himself.) Unfortunately, the indefatigable Paul Snyder was allowing danger warnings about his health go unheeded. In the fall of 1975, he went on a hunting trip with two of his favorite players, pitchers Joe and Phil Niekro. Snyder's doctor warned him that a serious heart condition must be monitored, but when he returned from the trip, he thrust himself back into work. There were drafts to prepare for – the January draft of players not eligible in June and then the big June one.[18]

The 1976 draft would be a fruitful one –in the fifth round the Braves picked University of

Nebraska-Omaha catcher Bruce Benedict, who would play 12 years in the majors and later become a coach. Then, the night after the June draft, while watching the Johnny Carson *Tonight Show* and planning to stay awake for the rebroadcast of a Braves game on TBS, Paul Snyder felt all the lights go out. He had suffered a major stroke. He was rushed to a hospital in Atlanta where he stayed for two weeks. Only 40 years old, Snyder lost almost all feeling in his right side. Once back at home, his wife, who usually doubled as his radar gun assistant, took on an even more crucial role as his main physical therapist. He slowly began to feel better, but he told author Bill Shanks that he may have lost two years of memory during his ordeal. Bill Lucas stood firmly beside his ailing friend, insisting that Snyder must be kept on the payroll and everything must be done to nurse him back to health. When some in the organization thought about cutting ties with Paul, Lucas responded, "I could do that, but you'd have to replace me, too."[19]

By the next season in 1977, as Snyder was back to full-time work, the baseball world had gone through revolutionary changes. As a result of impartial arbitrator Peter Seitz's decision just before Christmas in 1975, veteran pitchers Andy Messermith and Dave McNally were freed from the constraints of the perpetual reserve system. The Players Association had worked out a new basic agreement with the owners that created a professional free-agent draft after the 1976 season in which all players with six or more years of major-league service could be free to sell themselves to the highest bidder. Not surprisingly, Ted Turner immediately barged into the free-agent market by signing Andy Messersmith. He was not allowed, however, to attire Andy with the number 17 and the word "Channel" above it on the back. Commissioner Bowie Kuhn nixed that bald advertising ploy for Turner's TV station. Turner also incurred the wrath of Kuhn for declaring publicly that he wanted to sign outfielder Gary Matthews away from the Giants before the free-agent draft even started. He was slapped with a year's suspension although it wasn't fully enforced.[20]

Messersmith never regained 20-game-winning form with the Braves and was gone after two seasons. Matthews did become a Brave for four seasons but his defensive liabilities negated his relatively adequate offense. The 1977 and 1978 Braves plummeted to the NL West basement, but organizationally there were some promising signs in scouting and player development. After a fallow 1977 draft, the Braves were far more productive in 1978. The draft produced three future major leaguers in the first three rounds. Slugging third baseman Bob Horner in the first round, who was rushed to the majors from Arizona State University without any minor-league seasoning as Ted Turner salivated at the prospect of a big bopper to pair with the slowly-emerging Dale Murphy in the lineup. Catcher Matt Sinatro came aboard in the second round from a West Hartford, Connecticut, high school; he would enjoy a 10-year major-league career. Steve Bedrosian was nabbed in the third round, another player from a cold-weather area, the University of New Haven in Connecticut. Paul Snyder had a special affinity for players from the Northeast who dealt with chilly if not frigid conditions and emerged as major leaguers. (Bedrosian did enjoy greater success with other teams, winning the 1987 Cy Young Award as a Phillies reliever and later pitched for the Giants and Twins.)

Then on May 1, 1979, tragedy hit the Braves organization. The hard-working Bill Lucas had just finished watching on TV Phil Niekro's 200th win over the Pirates in Pittsburgh when he suffered a brain aneurysm. He died two days later. Bill Lucas was only 43. At the funeral in Atlanta, an overflow crowd of mourners extolled the baseball pioneer. Renowned Florida A&M football coach Jake Gaither said that he had never met a finer leader than Bill Lucas and called him "one of God's great men." (Bob Lucas, Bill's younger brother, would later coach baseball at Florida A&M and also scout for the Braves.) Flamboyant Ted Turner said that Lucas was now the general manager on a team in heaven with Ty Cobb, Babe Ruth, and Lou Gehrig. Dale Murphy struck a more subdued genuine note when he remembered how Lucas had greeted him warmly at the airport when he first came to Atlanta as a raw amateur. Murphy called it "a sacred honor to fulfill his dream" of a Braves pennant.[21]

When the Braves moved to Sun Trust Park in 2018, they memorialized Bill Lucas in several ways. The main street was named Bill Lucas Way, a Bill Lucas Conference Room was created, and a Bill Lucas Diversity Apprenticeship was established. It is a fitting honor for Lucas, who made it a point to try to hire an African-American for every white person he brought into the organization. Longtime Braves publicist Bob Hope never forgot how Lucas had demonstrated his belief in gender equality when he escorted Hope's wife to a sports dinner where no women had ever been invited. When Lucas was elected to the Braves Hall of Fame in 2006, Paul Snyder said simply, "He planted a seed, and we just carried through with it."[22]

John Mullen, who had started his front-office career with the Boston Braves and offered Snyder his first managing job, returned from the Houston Astros to become Lucas's replacement with the title of general manager. Yet the Braves continued to be also-rans and often basement dwellers in the tough NL West division dominated by the Dodgers and the Reds with the Giants also becoming contenders. Though the Braves finished one game over .500 in 1980 during Bobby Cox's first tenure as Braves manager, a 1981 slip to fifth place in the division led Ted Turner to replace him with Joe Torre.

Titles never meant anything to Paul Snyder but with the loss of Bill Lucas, he was now named the Braves scouting director and poised to start the most brilliant decade of his service to the Braves. He kept most of Lucas's talented scouts like Bill Wight and added some key ones of his own. Rod Gilbreath, a third-round 1970 middle-infield draft choice from a Laurel, Mississippi, high school, was named a West Coast scout. Snyder had managed Gilbreath at Magic Valley in the Pioneer League in 1970 and a paternal relationship quickly developed. Gilbreath was amazed at the depth of Snyder's evaluating skills and his ability to be frank without being insensitive. He knew how "to recognize players who could play, and what to do with players who couldn't play," Gilbreath told Bill Shanks.[23]

In 1980 Snyder hired Harold "Hep" Cronin as a full-time Midwestern area scout who later became a national cross-checker. The father of UCLA basketball coach Mick Cronin, Hep in 1969, while coaching high-school baseball in Cincinnati, had been hired as a Braves associate scout. Though the focus and demands of coaching and scouting were obviously different – coaching focused on immediate wins and scouting emphasizing long-range development – the Braves Way that Bill Lucas started and Paul Snyder was continuing looked at the whole player, his mental makeup and not just his tools or his statistics. Cronin loved working for a boss like Snyder who always listened intently to his area scouts' opinions. Paul never pulled rank, Cronin told Bill Shanks, because "he'd rather migrate to talk to the area scout from Tennessee or something."[24]

One of the older scouts that Snyder brought into the fold was indeed from Tennessee – Lou Fitzgerald from Cleveland, Tennessee. He had been one of Paul Richards' right-hand men in Richards' prior jobs with the White Sox, Orioles, Colt .45s/Astros, and Braves. From the White Sox, Snyder picked up another savvy evaluator, Fred Schaffer, who specialized in pitching. Back in the mid-1950s he had signed future American League All-Star southpaw Gary Peters, and in 1988, as we shall soon see, Fitzgerald would be one of the biggest advocates for signing Michigan high-school southpaw Steve Avery.

Though Bill Lucas did not live to see the June 1979 draft, he was pleased with the January 1979 results when Milt Thompson became a Brave.

He was signed out of a Gaithersburg, Maryland, high school in the second round and would enjoy a 13-year major-league career, mainly as a utility outfielder. Ventura, California, high-school outfielder Brook Jacoby was a genuine diamond in the rough, picked in the seventh round in January. The June 1979 draft brought into the fold first-rounder Brad Komminsk from a Lima, Ohio, high school; Jacksonville University shortstop Paul Runge in the ninth round (who would have an eight-year major-league career); and a steal in the 23rd round, Southeastern Oklahoma State outfielder Brett Butler. Of course, neither Paul Snyder nor any of the player-development staff had much input when Ted Turner okayed the 1983 trade of Butler and Jacoby to the Indians for Len "No Hit" Barker that turned out disastrously for the Braves. (As for Komminsk's failure to live up to his billing as a "can't miss" prospect, Snyder remained baffled. Except for average running speed, Komminsk seemed to possess all the tools, Snyder reflected in our phone interview. He probably lost confidence and listened to too many suggestions.)

In 1980 the Braves hit pay dirt in the first round of both drafts. Right-hander Craig McMurtry from McLennan (Texas) Community College was picked in January and southpaw Ken Dayley from the University of Portland was the June first-rounder. Another serviceable future utility fielder came in the 15th round when Stanford University's Paul Zuvella was selected. Though Dayley wound up enjoying a fruitful career as a relief pitcher, mainly for the Cardinals, Snyder regretted that he never became a core Braves starter. "He should have lasted a long time with us," Snyder told Bill Shanks. "His psyche was beaten down."[25]

That the draft can be a very unpredictable procedure was proven when the 1981 and 1982 drafts produced no future major-league Braves. They did select Livermore, California, high-school southpaw Randy Johnson in the fourth round, but he chose college at UCLA and later was picked by the Expos before starting to show his Hall of Fame form with the Mariners. The 1983 draft was much more fruitful. Two gems were found, one relatively high and one far lower in the draft. Shortstop Ron Gant from a Victoria, Texas, high school wasn't even in the registry of the Major League Baseball Scouting Bureau. The bureau had been established in 1974 to streamline information for all the clubs (though not every organization joined it). Gant was known more for his football and basketball skills but when tipped off by a local source, influential Bill Wight made a trip to Texas. When he filed a glowing report on Gant's promising athletic tools, Gant shot up the Braves' draft lists and they nabbed him in the fourth round.

The lower-round find in the 1983 draft was unheralded future starting second baseman Mark Lemke, picked in the 27th round out of Notre Dame High School in Whitesboro, New York. He epitomized the Lucas-Snyder belief that a team cannot win without grinders who may lack glitz and glamour but care only about winning. Listed at 5-feet-10 and 167 pounds, Lemke played in the spirit of his predecessor Glenn Hubbard, who had been drafted in the 20th round in 1975 and played 10 seasons for the Braves. Lemke's offensive stats were not gaudy but they would increase noticeably in the postseason. He was a peerless defender, the kind of fielder you wanted the ball hit to. When Lemke tried a comeback as a knuckleballer in an independent league in 1999, he told *New York Times* writer Dan Barry, "To be honest with you, I enjoy playing the game of baseball."[26] (The Braves also selected in 1983 outfielder Jay Buhner in the ninth round out of McLennan Community College in Texas but he did not sign – the Pirates drafted Buhner later, the Yankees picked him up in a trade, and he became a star when traded to the Mariners for Ken Phelps – a transaction that drew the scorn of George Constanza in a memorable *Seinfeld* episode.)

The 1984 draft turned out to be crucial to the Braves' future success. Future Hall of Famer Tom Glavine came aboard in the second round, and Lemke's future double-play partner Jeff Blauser was picked in the first round of the January secondary draft. Blauser's signing was uneventful, but the wooing of Glavine from a possible hockey career was more complicated. It provides a prime example of how the Braves Way, started under Bill Lucas and continued under Paul Snyder, was beginning to function smoothly and successfully.

Newly appointed Braves Northeastern area scout Tony DeMacio knew what kind of athletic talent Glavine possessed. He was the star of both his hockey and baseball teams at Billerica High School, a few miles northwest of Boston, where his father, Fred, had been a star football player. The Braves knew that the senior Glavine had discouraged Tom from playing football because of the chance of permanent injury. Yet they weren't sure how deep was Glavine's love of hockey. He had been offered a four-year hockey scholarship at the University of Massachusetts-Lowell and was also drafted in the fourth round by the Los Angeles Kings of the National Hockey League. With the Red Sox the only team in town since 1953, DeMacio wanted to downplay his interest in Glavine lest the newspapers got wind of it and pressured the Red Sox to get in on the bidding. To add to the complications, longtime Braves Northeastern scouting supervisor Bob Turzilli wasn't that high on Glavine as a baseball player.[27]

By the time of Tom's senior year, most internal doubts within the Braves brass had been eliminated about his baseball abilities. He had a sensational season both on the mound and playing center field on days he wasn't pitching. Billerica High made the Eastern Massachusetts high school state finals against Brockton with Glavine pitching nine scoreless innings and then throwing out from center field a potential winning run in the bottom of the 10th. (The victim happened to be a nephew of late heavyweight champion Rocky Marciano.) To cap off his great day, Glavine started the winning rally in the 13th inning.

When it was time for Snyder, DeMacio, and Turzilli to meet with Glavine and his father shortly before the draft, they were all impressed by Tom's maturity. He, not his father, took charge of the meeting, asking good questions about what minor-league life would be like and how fast he could expect promotion. The Braves contingent left the room, convinced that Glavine wanted to play baseball and would turn down the hockey scholarship offer. When draft day came, the Braves breathed a sigh of relief when he was still available in the second round; according to *Baseball America's Ultimate Draft Book*, the Blue Jays would have picked him next.[28]

In 1985 the Braves made another unconventional selection by choosing in the fourth round David Justice from tiny Thomas More College in Crestview Hills, Kentucky. Justice was another player that scouting's conventional wisdom branded as too raw and undisciplined to develop in baseball; after all, he started college on a basketball scholarship before he became bored with all the running. Scout Lou Fitzgerald loved Justice's athleticism and felt confident that the Braves' growing stable of coaches and instructors would bring out the baseball player in him. He saw Justice as a genuine diamond in the rough who had finished high school at the age of 15 and was only 18 when he left Thomas More after his junior year because of its weak noncompetitive baseball program.[29] (There were other future major leaguers selected in the 1985 draft. The first-rounder was right-hander Tommy Greene from Whiteville [North Carolina] High School, who wound up having an eight-year major-league career though injuries curtailed what might have led to greater success. The eighth-round pick in 1985, West Covina, California, high-school outfielder-first baseman Al Martin, who stayed in the majors for most of 11 seasons.)

Atlanta's 1986 first-round June pick turned out to be southpaw Kent Mercker, who entered the organization out of Dublin, Ohio, High School. He never emerged as a star with the Braves so there is a "what-if" quality to the 1986 Braves draft because they selected three high schoolers who did not sign until later with other teams. Southern

Illinois University outfielder Steve Finley in the 11th round and Louisiana high-school pitcher Ben McDonald in the 27th round – both later were signed by the Orioles with McDonald 1990's number one pick in the country. Also drafted in the 18th round but unsigned by the Braves in 1987 was Phoenix high-school outfielder Tim Salmon, the future Angels star right fielder.

If 1986's draft was not very productive, the year still goes down as a vital one in Braves history because Bobby Cox returned as general manager, and Stan Kasten was promoted to team president. Kasten had worked for Ted Turner since 1977, becoming at age 27 the youthful general manager of Turner's Atlanta Hawks in the National Basketball Association. He had long spurned Turner's request to take on the top position in both sports, but now he felt ready and willing. Kasten, Cox, and Paul Snyder were all on the same page about the importance of investing in scouting and player development. When Kasten expressed the hope that tryout camps could be established in every state where of course TBS was already airing, Snyder and Cox positively beamed. Where previously the Dodgers had more than four times as many scouts on their payroll as the Braves, Kasten with Ted Turner's blessing rapidly closed the gap, raising the number of full-time scouts from five to eighteen and also hiring many more minor-league coaches and instructors.[30]

Starting in 1987 there was only one amateur free-agent draft, in June, and the Braves picked two important contributors to the future 1995 champions – infielder-outfielder Brian Hunter was selected in the eighth round out of Cerritos College in California (nine-year major-league career) and lefty short reliever Mike Stanton came in the 13rd round out of Alvin (Texas) CC (19-year major-league career). Number-one draft pick southpaw Derek Lilliquist was signed out of the University of Georgia and would enjoy an eight-year major-league career as a pitcher and later a long tenure as major-league pitching coach for various teams.

In 1988 Taylor, Michigan, high-school southpaw Steve Avery was the Braves' number-one selection. On the scholastic level, Avery had been virtually unhittable. Scout Fred Schaffer, Paul Snyder's top pitching adviser, drooled over Avery's arsenal of velocity and movement that was rare in someone so young. Snyder loved to tell the story that in one game the plate umpire gave Steve Avery a gift strike call. "Mr. Ump, this guy don't need no help," the overmatched batter wailed to the plate umpire."[31] The 1988 draft also brought to the Braves in the eighth round future closer Mark Wohlers, picked out of high school in Holyoke, Massachusetts. Enjoying his first full season in the Braves organization in 1988 was youthful future Hall of Famer John Smoltz, whom the Braves had pilfered from the Detroit Tigers for veteran pitcher Doyle Alexander during the 1987 pennant race. Alexander did help the Bengals win the AL East but he retired two years later. In picking Glavine earlier, and now Wohlers and Smoltz, another pitcher hardened by a cold-weather upbringing in Michigan, the Braves were beginning to see the fruits of their strong commitment to youthful pitching.

The Braves were not so fortunate in the first round of the 1989 draft, when they selected catcher Tyler Houston from a Las Vegas high school. Houston did last in the majors for eight years without shining. Far more successful was fifth-round selection Ryan Klesko, from high school in Westminster, California, who was drafted as both an outfielder and left-handed pitcher.

A nagging elbow injury curtailed his development as a minor-league pitcher, and though his potent bat brought him soon to the majors, the arm ailment led to his ultimate switch from the outfield to first base. Klesko would be a key contributor to the 1995 champions and last for 16 seasons in the majors.

The last great coup of Snyder's fruitful decade as Braves director of amateur scouting came with the selection of Larry Wayne "Chipper" Jones Jr. in the 1990 draft. The Braves hierarchy was split between choosing the switch-hitting Jacksonville, Florida, prep-school shortstop and the Arlington, Texas, high-school right-hander Todd Van Poppel. Scout Red Murff, who had nurtured and signed Nolan Ryan for the Mets out of an Alvin, Texas, high school, was very high on Van Poppel. In fact, he had already developed a friendship with the prospect's father and publicly compared the youngster to Ryan. Murff admitted in his memoir, *The Scout*, written with Mike Capps, that he probably had driven up the price the Braves would have to pay.[32]

Young Todd Van Poppel had several bargaining chips: a baseball scholarship offer from the University of Texas; a reported desire to pitch for the 1992 USA Olympic team; and representation by rising player agent Scott Boras. General manager Bobby Cox and Paul Snyder flew to Texas shortly before the draft to meet with the prospective draft pick. "There were no negotiations at all with the young man," Snyder later told *Baseball America*. "We talked to his mother and father, but never to him."[33] He even spurned meeting with Red Murff, his biggest advocate among the scouts. It led Murff and other people to believe that Van Poppel and Boras had already made a deal with the reigning World Series champion Oakland Athletics, who would pick him sixth in the draft and provide a contract reportedly worth $1.2 million.[34]

The Braves quickly turned to gauge the interest of Chipper Jones in becoming a Brave. Paul Snyder sent scouts Tony DeMacio and Dean Jongewaard to meet with Jones and his family at their home in Pierson, Florida. The Jones family greeted the Braves emissaries far more warmly than the Van Poppels had. They had seen DeMacio, Snyder, Hep Cronin, and Bill Wight at Chipper's games because he was a hot prospect. Veteran Reds scout George Zuraw had gifted Chipper with a bunch of wooden bats while he was still in the eighth grade because he was sure that he would need to get used to them after high school. By the age of 14 Chipper was already playing in American Legion tournaments. He was also a top-notch wide receiver in football, leading all Florida high schools in catches.[35]

As much as Jones's physical talents tantalized the Braves hierarchy, his background and makeup attracted them even more. Chipper's mother was an expert equestrienne, specializing in dressage, which Chipper described in his autobiography, *Ballplayer*, as "ballet for horses." Larry Sr. was a schoolteacher and his only child's longtime baseball coach. After the ninth grade, Chipper's parents sent him to the Bolles School in Jacksonville for better schooling, good athletic competition, and more discipline. Chipper tells the story in *Ballplayer* that his parents told Bolles coach Charles Edwards, "If he steps out of line, you jerk a knot in his tail." It turned out that Edwards, an African American and former star wide receiver at Vanderbilt, became one of Chipper's biggest boosters and friends.[36]

It did not take long for an agreement to be reached. DeMacio and Jongewaard saw immediately that Chipper wanted to turn pro and turn down a baseball scholarship offer from the University of Miami. Chipper had interviewed Scott Boras as a possible agent, but he was turned off by the agent's aggressiveness and his willingness to threaten enrollment at Miami as a bargaining ploy to raise the ante. Jones wound up accepting less than a $300,000 bonus, approximately one-quarter of Van Poppel's haul. But Jones wanted to be a Brave and enjoyed a far longer career than Van Poppel, and all with one team.[37]

The remainder of the 1990 draft did not produce any future regulars for the Braves, and the varsity was still having trouble winning at the major-league level. A 1990 dip into the free-agent market to sign first baseman Nick Esasky backfired when Esasky developed vertigo early in the season and had to abruptly retire. With the team struggling in midseason, manager Russ Nixon was fired and Bobby Cox returned to the dugout. After the season, John Schuerholz was lured from Kansas City to become general manager. Wanting to bring in his own people, Schuerholz replaced Snyder as scouting director with Chuck LaMar, and Snyder was given the title of special assistant to the general manager.

Snyder was always one of those people who believed that the success of an organization comes when people are not concerned about getting the credit. If he was miffed at having his scouting directorship taken away, he kept quiet, good company man that he always was. He still saw the Braves' future as bright. "Omigod, we had so much talent coming," Snyder remembered in our phone interview. So Snyder continued to work in the field with scouts and player developers as the Braves startled the baseball world by rising from the 1990 basement to the 1991 NL East title, their first in their remarkable run of 14 straight division titles. The signing of free-agent third baseman Terry Pendleton gave the Braves a good run-producer, defender, and, maybe most of all, a leader.

John Schuerholz also believed in scouting and player development as the key to any successful organization, but he was willing if necessary to sign a key free agent. Especially if his trusted scouts told him that Pendleton would recover from injuries that had hampered his production in St. Louis. Paul Snyder reflected later on Schuerholz's tenure with the Braves, "He taught us how to win," adding, "He'll talk at our organizational meetings in January, and those scouts can't wait to get out of that room, and get their radar guns and get to work."[38] Meanwhile, the organization was continuing to hire new scouting blood with Snyder's input always valued. Dayton Moore, the general manager of the Kansas City Royals who oversaw their World Series teams of 2014-2015, was hired as a Mid-Atlantic scout in 1994. He said of Snyder, "You go away from your interaction with Paul knowing that he had listened to everything you said."[39]

In the summer of 1995 Chuck LaMar left the Braves to become general manager of the expansion Tampa Bay Devil Rays. Snyder was asked to take over the duties of director of player development starting the next season. Always willing to help the company in any way, he gladly accepted the new assignment. In the meantime, he started to advance-scout the possible opponents for the Braves in the 1995 playoffs. When the Braves at last won the World Series in 1995, he rejoiced quietly with the rest of the staff, who voiced their appreciation for his steady work over the decades. Snyder found it especially satisfying that Tom Glavine won the clinching game. He thought back with pleasure to 11 years earlier when he first brought into the organization the gifted hard-working teenager who, like the scout himself in his younger days, did not mind working in construction to keep himself fit and active during the offseason.

Snyder served as player development director through 1998, and then answered the call in 1999 to resume his job as scouting director. In 2001 he was again given the title of assistant to the general manager, where he remained until his retirement in 2006. Yet he has never really left the organization and never will. When enshrined in June 2013 into the Professional Scouts Hall of Fame at the home of the Charleston River Dogs of the South Atlantic League, Snyder explained, "You have to step away from the game before you realize how great it is. ... Guys you work with every day for 30 or 35 years are what matter to me."[40]

Turning 85 in 2020, he expected to be in Braves' spring training for every year as long as he was able. It remains the happiest time of year for a man who has made scouting and player development his life's major work. Without his guidance, keen evaluative skill, and compassion, the Atlanta Braves would never have become the remarkable Beast of the NL East.

Acknowledgments

The writer wants to acknowledge the indispensable help of Baseball-Reference.com and Baseball

America's *Ultimate Draft Book* (no date of publication).

Notes

1. Charles Fountain, *Under the March Sun: The Story of Spring Training* (New York: Oxford University Press, 2009), 152.
2. Warm gratitude to Paul Snyder who patiently explained in phone interviews how his birth year was originally listed as 1936 when he signed as a player but was apparently restored to 1935 when he came closer to pension eligibility.
3. Phone interview with Paul Snyder, September 22, 2019; Paul Snyder interview at Jamestown, New York's Diethrick Field, July 26, 1999, youtube.com/watch?v=Lma5bPA3T2s.
4. Andrew Sharp, "John Mahlon 'Jack' Ogden," SABR Bioproject; YouTube Snyder interview.
5. The Mets Hall of Fame Achievement Award was bestowed upon Harry Minor in 2013.
6. Paul Snyder YouTube Interview.
7. Phone interview with Snyder; Andy Esposito, "In Memory of Harry Minor," *New York Sports Day*, January 19. 2017.
8. Paul Snyder, phone interview; YouTube interview.
9. Bill Shanks, *Scout's Honor: The Bravest Way to Build a Winning Team* (New York: Sterling and Ross Publishers, 2005), 43.
10. Alex Putterman, "The Forgotten Legacy of Bill Lucas," atlantic.com, June 4, 2007.
11. Eddie Robinson with C. Paul Rogers III, *Lucky Me: My Sixty-Years in Baseball* (Dallas: Southern Methodist University Press, 2011), 164.
12. Putterman.
13. Phone interview with Dusty Baker, September 26, 2019; in-person interview with Ralph Garr, New York City, November 9, 2019.
14. Phone interviews with Paul Snyder and Dusty Baker; email from Tony DeMacio, December 16, 2019.
15. Bob Hope, *We Could've Finished Last Without You* (Atlanta: Longstreet Press 1991), 188.
16. Hope, 156.
17. Michael O'Connor, *Ted Turner: A Biography:* (Santa Barbara, California: Greenwood Press, 2010), 72-75.
18. Shanks, 45.
19. Shanks, 46.
20. O'Connor, 74.
21. Lee Walburn "Bill Lucas," *Atlanta Magazine*, May 2011. atlantamagazine.com/great-reads/bill-lucas/.
22. Hope; Putterman.
23. Shanks, 48.
24. Shanks, 43; See also Paul Daugherty, profile of Cronin, cincinnati.com, June 5, 2018. cincinnati.com/story/sports/columnists/paul-daugherty/2018/06/05/mlb-draft-insight-conversation-longtime-atlanta-braves-scout-hep-cronin-mick-cincinnati/673802002/.
25. Shanks, 87.
26. Dan Barry, "Loose Grip on a Ball, Tight Grip on Dream," *New York Times*, August 8, 1999.
27. Tom Glavine, with Nick Cafardo, *None but the Braves: A Pitcher, a Team, a Champion* (New York: Harper Collins, 1996), 22-34; email from Tony DeMacio, December 30, 2019.
28. Allan Simpson, ed., *Baseball America's Ultimate Draft Book* (no publication date), 294.
29. John Ed Bradley, "Justice Prevails," *Sports Illustrated*, June 6, 1994.
30. Shanks, 111; phone interview with Paul Snyder, January 8, 2020.
31. Shanks, 134.
32. Red Murff with Mike Capps, *The Scout: Searching for the Best in Baseball* (Dallas: Word Publishing, 1996), 283.
33. *Ultimate Draft Book*, 377.
34. Murff, 284-85.
35. Email from Tony DeMacio, December 30, 2019; Chipper Jones with Carroll Rogers Walton, *Ballplayer* (New York: Dutton, 2017), 25-6.
36. Jones, 13, 25-26, 30.
37. Jones, 49-61; DeMacio email. Dean Jongewaard, brother of Roger Jongewaard, the renowned scout who insisted the Mariners draft Ken Griffey Jr. as number-one pick in nation, was an expert Braves negotiator. He informed the Jones family that Chipper could have access to a full four-year college scholarship later in his career.
38. Fountain, 152.
39. Shanks, 49.
40. "Braves' Paul Snyder Inducted into Professional Baseball Scouts Hall of Fame," South Atlantic League's Charleston River Dogs news release, June 16, 2013.

Bill Bartholomay

BY ALAN MORRIS

Bill Bartholomay

The man primarily responsible for bringing the Braves to Atlanta in 1966 was William Conrad "Bill" Bartholomay. He was born in the Chicago suburb of Evanston on August 11, 1928, to parents who were fond of baseball, especially his mother. One of his earliest memories is of his mother taking him out of school on Ladies Day to attend a Cubs game at Wrigley Field.[1] His parents, Henry and Virginia Bartholomay, were good friends of the Wrigley family, who owned the Cubs. Bill vividly remembered serving as batboy for the Cubs when he was about 8 years old. He even had the opportunity to play softball with the Wrigley family at their summer home on Lake Geneva, Wisconsin.[2] Bill was also lucky enough to have attended spring training during the war years. Teams were not allowed to travel far for their spring training so the Cubs and White Sox went to French Lick Springs in Indiana. Bill and his family would take the four-hour train ride to see the team practice.

Bartholomay thought he was probably the only individual who had met all 10 commissioners of major-league baseball. "I got on Judge Landis' knee at 2 years old," said Bartholomay. "It was at the Wrigley's place on Lake Geneva. Obviously, I don't remember much about that, but in the course of my work with baseball over the years I've had occasion to know the other nine Commissioners much better."[3]

Virginia Bartholomay drove for the Army Motor Corps in World War I and was active in the Red Cross during World War II.[4] She lived most of her life in Lake Forest, a suburb north of Chicago. In addition to being a baseball fan, she loved to garden and was a lifelong member of the Lake Geneva Garden Club. Henry Bartholomay was an executive at Alexander & Alexander, one of the largest insurance brokerages in the United States.[5] Bill graduated from Lake Forest College, north of Chicago, in 1955. Both he and an older brother, who graduated from Harvard, entered the insurance business after graduation.

Bartholomay's passion for baseball led him to join with business partners to purchase a share of the White Sox in 1962. After less than a year, he learned that the owners of the Milwaukee Braves were willing to sell. The same friends who had joined him in the White Sox venture sold their minority shares and agreed to purchase the Braves. His pursuit of the Braves was not an easy one. In an interview with David Sweet in 2014, Barholomay said, "The only person I stalked in my life was Mr. [Lou] Perini (owner of the

Braves). Finally, his secretary took pity on me."[6] Bartholomay and his group of investors purchased the Braves in November 1963.[7] Bartholomay was made chairman of the board, a title he still held as of his passing in 2020 though it was emeritus.

The story of how the Braves found their way from Milwaukee to Atlanta is well documented in sportswriter Furman Bisher's book *Miracle in Atlanta*. Bartholomay played the central role in this endeavor. Bisher wrote that the new Braves owners did not buy the team intending to move it from Milwaukee but that they soon realized it was not financially feasible to remain in Milwaukee.[8] Atlanta's efforts to become a major-league city coincided with a baseball franchise that was in trouble. After a contentious battle, the deal was sealed and the Milwaukee Braves became the Atlanta Braves on April 12, 1966.

"You have to put the Atlanta move in perspective," said Bartholomay. "The second year in Milwaukee, we weren't drawing well. All the great players – Hank Aaron, Willie Mays, Jackie Robinson – had come from the South. But there were no pro teams playing down there."[9] Reminiscing about the Braves' first game in Atlanta, when they lost in extra innings to the Pirates, Bartholomay recalled every detail of the game and he summed up the event: "It was great, the whole city was electrified."[10]

In August 2003 Bartholomay was appointed vice chairman of Willis Group Holdings, a giant multinational brokerage. As he was introduced, the chairman of the company said, "Bill has distinguished himself as a leader in business, sports, civic and philanthropic organizations. He is a man of unquestionable integrity and forthright leadership; his involvement with a diverse group of concerns speaks volumes about his ability."[11] Bartholomay's sports résumé is lengthy. In addition to his tenure as chairman of the board of directors of the Braves, he has served on Major League Baseball's executive council, chaired the ownership committee, co-chaired the league's equal opportunity committee, and is a trustee of the Major League Baseball Players Pension Plan. He headed the search committee to name a new commissioner of baseball in 1993. In 2002 he was inducted into the Atlanta Braves Hall of Fame.

Of his baseball memories, Bartholomay listed the 1995 World Series, Hank Aaron's 715th home run on April 8, 1974, and the Braves Opening Day on April 12, 1966, as his favorites.[12] "Tommy Glavine pitched that tremendous shutout to win Game Six of the '95 World Series which gave me the first and only World Series ring and my cohorts too. Ted Turner and I were pretty excited about that game."[13] The mention of Ted Turner brought a huge smile to his face. Bartholomay was in Atlanta to attend Ted Turner's 75th birthday party and was eager to talk about his friend. "I'm a member of the Ted Turner fan club," he said.

Regarding Aaron's 715th home run, Bartholomay said, "I was sitting in the front row with Hank's mother and father. There's a place you go beyond adrenaline – I carried his mother above the barrier and onto the field after he hit it."[14]

In an earlier interview, Bartholomay said, "Ted's just a beautiful guy, he's a loyal guy. Players liked him. A lot of people like Ted. I'm number one on that list."[15] An incident detailed in Turner's autobiography relates how the two became friends and eventual business partners. In 1974 Turner's fledgling TV station, WTCG, was looking for programming. Turner had sailing friends who knew Bartholomay and used those connections to arrange a meeting. Turner proposed tripling the amount of money the Braves were getting for broadcasting on the local Cox Broadcasting station (WSB-TV) by offering $600,000 for the rights to 60 road games. Bartholomay and Turner agreed in principle to the deal. Bartholomay asked Turner for time to give WSB a courtesy call before the announcement. When he did, the Cox people were angry and said they would match any deal offered by the "Mickey Mouse UHF station owned by Turner." Bartholomay went back to Turner and asked him if the Braves could walk away from the deal. Turner replied, "Look Bill, a deal's a deal. I've been told that a handshake from you is as good as a signed contract and that's why I agreed to let you talk to Cox before our announcement." Bartholomay was a man of his word, "he stuck by his guns and we got the Braves."[16] Thus began a relationship that led to Turner purchasing the Braves in 1976.

Bartholomay's love affair with baseball began as a child and it was fueled by reading and listening to games on the radio. Asked about those early influences, he recalled the early sportswriters Grantland Rice, Scotty Reston, and Red Smith, who became a good friend.[17] Bartholomay also remembered Waite Hoyt and Ernie Harwell. "I grew up listening to Waite Hoyt," he said. "We were more excited about rain than we were about the baseball because he told great stories."

Bartholomay expressed fond memories of umpires. "My favorite was Jocko Conlan, who always wore a bowtie. I knew Jocko very well and he knew me as a little kid up in Illinois." Other umpires who impressed him along the way were Beans Reardon and George Magerkurth. "Umpires have a tough job to do and they work well together," Bartholomay said. "They are an important part of the game."

The inevitable question of who is your favorite player always comes up when two or more baseball fans talk. This was not an easy question for Bartholomay; he had known many as a fan and team executive over the years. It was no surprise that the first person he mentioned was Hank Aaron: "Hank is the greatest player I've ever seen and had the honor of knowing, and Dale Murphy is one of my very dear friends." He recalled greats from the Milwaukee Braves days: Eddie Mathews and Warren Spahn. He reminisced about Andy Pafko and Gabby Hartnett as well as Stan Hack and Ted Lyons from his Chicago days. And Ernie Johnson: "he was like a tiger between the lines, reminding me of Greg Maddux."

Even at the age of 91 he was still active, attending ballgames, serving on boards of directors and managing the Bill Bartholomay Foundation, which he founded in 1990. The foundation provides funding for education, health, churches, children, and animals. Its two biggest beneficiaries are the Chicago Museum of Science and Industry and the Lincoln Park Zoo.

Bill Bartholomay died March 25, 2020, at the age of 91. He entered New York's Presbyterian Hospital a few weeks after attending spring training at the new Braves facility in North Point, Florida. According to his daughter, Jamie, he was fighting a respiratory infection and had gone to New York to see specialists, "but at 91 years old, I think he just got tired," she said. Perhaps the response from his beloved Braves summed up the many accolades: "Bill Bartholomay was a dear, thoughtful friend who will be missed, his legacy will surely stand the test of time for the Atlanta Braves and all of baseball."[18]

Notes

1. Interview with Bill Bartholomay, November 23, 2013, by the author. Unless otherwise indicated, all direction quotations from Bartholomay come from this interview.
2. Abe Schear, "Bill Bartholomay: The Chairman," *Baseball Digest*, June 2004.
3. David Sweet, "He's On the Ball with America's Pastime," *North Shore Weekend East* (Highwood, Illinois), July 10, 2014.
4. *Chicago Tribune* obituary, August 23, 1993.
5. *Chicago Tribune* obituary, June 6, 1966.
6. David Sweet, "Baseball Continues to Fit the Bill," *North Shore Weekend* (Highwood, Illinois), July 12, 2014.
7. Schear.
8. Furman Bisher, *Miracle in Atlanta* (Cleveland: World Publishing Company, 1966), 55.
9. Sweet.
10. Sweet.
11. Press release, Willis Group, August 6, 2003, willis.com.
12. Interview by author with Bill Bartholomay, November 23, 2013.
13. Glavine pitched eight innings of the shutout.
14. Sweet.
15. Schear.
16. Ted Turner and Bill Burke, *Call Me Ted* (New York: Grand Central Publishing, 2008), 103-5.
17. Interview by author with Bill Bartholomay, November 23, 2013.
18. Tim Tucker, "He Brought Atlanta to the Big Leagues," *Atlanta Journal-Constitution*, March 27, 2020: C1.

 BROADCASTERS

Skip Caray

BY WYNN MONTGOMERY

Skip Caray

"*Braves Win! Braves Win! Braves Win! Braves Win! ... Braves Win!!*"

That call still gives fans of the Atlanta Braves goosebumps.[1] That's how Skip Caray ended his description of the play that sent the 1992 Braves to their second consecutive World Series. He repeated his signature "Braves Win!" line a few times more than usual after Sid Bream barely beat the throw to the plate (a play that will forever be known in Atlanta as "The Slide"), capping a three-run ninth-inning rally in the deciding seventh game of the NLCS.

Three years later, Caray made another memorable call when the Braves clinched their first (and thus far only) World Series championship. Many fans still use a "talking" bottle opener[2] that allows them to savor that moment every time they open their favorite beverage:

... Fly ball deep left center, Grissom *on the run... Yes! Yes! Yes! The Atlanta Braves have given you a championship! Listen to this crowd! A mob scene on the field!*

Both calls reflect one of Caray's trademarks as an announcer. He gave the details of the play and then turned his – and his audience's – attention to the action on the field,[3] saying "Listen to this crowd!" or "Just watch."

Those calls were two of the many that endeared Harry Christopher "Skip" Caray Jr. to most fans of the team that he (with a powerful boost from Superstation TBS) helped to make "America's Team." Caray spent the last 33 years of his distinguished broadcasting career as a member of the Atlanta Braves broadcast team. Perhaps it was inevitable that the son of the legendary Harry Caray would follow in his father's footsteps, as his father hoped that he would.[4] However, that career was not a foregone conclusion. He knew that having a famous father might open job opportunities he might not have gotten otherwise, but he also knew that his every action would be carefully scrutinized and therefore he would "have to be even better."[5] He later said, "I wanted to be judged on my own ability, my own style."[6]

Skip Caray was born in St. Louis on August 12, 1939. His mother was Harry Caray's first wife, Dorothy Kanz. When he was 7 years old, he learned that his parents were splitting up when, as he walked to school, he saw a newspaper headline saying "Caray's Wife Tunes Him Out."[7] He didn't live with his famous father after that, but they stayed close, and he was able to join him in Florida for part of spring training. Once the Cardinals' season started, the young Caray often hung around the ballpark with his father during the early innings before heading home by bedtime.[8] Every night at 8:30, the elder Caray would pause during his broadcast to say, "Goodnight, Skippy."[9] Years later, Skip said that he would never forgive his father for doing that because he was kidded about it all through high school – even by opposing football players.[10]

As a teenager Caray had no interest in broadcasting because "my dad had the corner on that."[11] He earned all-city recognition as a 6-foot, 220-pound linebacker[12] on his high-school football team and aspired to be a professional football player until a knee injury quashed that dream.[13] He also played baseball, but later recalled that his only pitch was a fastball and he was wild, resulting in an 0-2 record as a senior.[14] While in high school, at age 15, he also started his broadcasting career with a once-a-week radio show during which he interviewed young athletes. Harry Caray, who later claimed to have devised a "master plan" to give his son that opportunity,[15] publicly greeted news of that show with a paraphrase of his famous home-run call: "It might be, it could be, it is – another sports announcer coming to haunt me."[16]

After high school Caray enrolled at the University of Missouri, where his journalism major kindled an interest in broadcasting.[17] During the summers he worked at KMOX in St. Louis. He also wrote, produced, and directed a nightly sports show on campus and made his play-by-play debut at the state high-school basketball tournament. He also teamed with his father to broadcast the university's football games[18] and with Jack Buck to call Saint Louis University's basketball games.[19]

Following graduation with honors from Missouri in 1961and a brief tour in the Army, Caray struck out on his own in 1963. He moved away from St. Louis to (at least partially) escape his father's shadow and joined the broadcast team of the Tulsa (Oklahoma) Oilers, a farm team of the major-league Cardinals. *The Sporting News* speculated that it was "the first time that father and son have aired [baseball] games simultaneously."[20] In Tulsa the young Caray had to re-create play-by-play action for road games from the Western Union ticker tape that provided pitch-by-pitch updates. He struck a small piece of balsa wood to simulate the crack of a bat.[21] In midseason he left the Oilers and became the Atlanta Crackers' announcer, a job he held until the minor-league Crackers were displaced by the arrival of the Braves from Milwaukee in 1966.

On November 23, 1963, Caray and his father participated in an event that was believed to make radio history. KMOX offered the first-ever simultaneous radio broadcast of three college football games. Harry Caray did play-by-play for the Illinois-Michigan game while Skip handled Missouri's game at Kansas, and Jack Buck covered Oklahoma at Nebraska.[22] That same month, Caray married Lila Jean Osterkamp in a civil ceremony that was formally blessed in a church ceremony the following April.[23]

Two years later, Caray enjoyed two milestone events. In February Lila gave birth to their first child, Harry Christopher Caray III. They called him Chip, and he would grow up to join his grandfather and his father as a respected member of the sportscasting "fraternity." Then on May 30, 1965, Skip broadcast his first major-league baseball game (Milwaukee Braves vs. Houston Astros in the Astrodome). That year, Atlanta's WSB-TV was whetting the appetites of local fans for the Braves' 1966 relocation by televising some of the Milwaukee games back to Atlanta. The legendary Mel Allen, one of the announcers for those telecasts, was not available for that May game because of a death in his family, and Caray was recruited to take his place. It was believed to be the first time the son of a major-league announcer broadcast major-league play-by-play.[24]

Caray joined the NBA Hawks as broadcaster for their final season (1967-68) in St. Louis. He then turned down an offer to become broadcaster for the NHL St. Louis Blues[25] and moved to Atlanta to remain the "Voice of the Hawks." By this time, a daughter (Cindy) had joined the

Caray household, and – in an eerie echo of his own father's behavior – Skip left his family on what Lila described to the children as "a long road trip"[26] that ended with a divorce in 1970.

Caray soon became an Atlanta institution. Jesse Outlar, the *Atlanta Constitution* sports editor, celebrated the arrival of the "accurate and entertaining basketball announcer" who was "a "welcome addition to the local sports colony."[27] A few months later, Outlar praised Caray as a "personable and talented" announcer whose "knowledgeable broadcasts" had attracted a wide fan base for the Hawks.[28] In 1970 Caray won his first Georgia Sportscaster of the Year Award, an honor that he received again in 1973 and 1974.[29] When Harry Caray, by then broadcasting Chicago White Sox games, won the Illinois version of that award in 1974, the Carays had achieved another "father-son" first (recognition as their state's top sportscaster in the same year).[30]

During those early years in Atlanta, Caray continued to build the Hawks' radio fan base and gained experience covering a team that lost regularly in the postseason.[31] In 1969, when the Hawks added television coverage, Caray moved to TV and turned the radio mic over to Larry Munson, who was well-known to local sports fans because of his play-by-play calls of University of Georgia Bulldogs football games. Caray later admitted that, to make that change, "I had to lie that I had done television before. I never had, but I was afraid it would cost me my job."[32] His on-the-job training obviously was successful.

By 1970 Caray was enough of a local "celebrity" to be featured in the advance billing of the annual July 4 "Salute to America" parade down Peachtree Street with Debbie Reynolds, several Atlanta Braves stars, and *Peanuts*' Snoopy.[33] Caray also hosted a regular weekday radio show and was a frequent emcee at functions hosted by the Hawks Booster Club and the Braves 400 Club, where his sarcastic wit soon earned him a reputation as "the South's Don Rickles."[34] He also found time to support local charities, serving as Georgia Epilepsy chairman[35] and co-hosting a Super Sports Telethon to benefit exceptional children.[36]

In 1971 a comment in the *Atlanta Constitution* that must have warmed Caray's heart reported that the new broadcaster for the Chicago White Sox was Harry Caray and identified him as "the pop of Atlanta Hawks announcer Skip Caray."[37]

In 1973 Caray did play-by-play of a hockey game for the only time in his career. He had to fill in on short notice for longtime friend and colleague Jiggs McDonald, who was the regular broadcaster for the NHL Atlanta Flames, and (as befits a legend) there are varying accounts of his performance. Furman Bisher said that "you never knew the difference except for the accent."[38] However, Bob Neal, who shared the broadcast booth that night, said that Caray did not know the players' names and "just said 'our guy' or 'the bad guys.'"[39] McDonald himself said he listened to the game, and Caray used names for the visiting players. When McDonald asked where he got those names, Caray replied that he used the names of former college classmates.[40]

On June 17 of that same year, Caray and McDonald teamed up for a broadcasting first. They provided commentary for the tape-delayed telecast of a May 3 game between the Atlanta Apollos and the Montreal Olympics of the North American Soccer League. It was the "first indoor soccer game in a major arena"[41] and yet another in the growing list of sports that Caray covered in his career.

In January 1976 Atlanta communications mogul Ted Turner, whose station WTCG (later to become WTBS) carried the telecasts of all of Atlanta's pro sports teams, purchased the Atlanta Braves. Later that month, the Braves announced their new broadcast team. Caray, who had been with WTCG since it acquired broadcast rights to the Hawks' games in 1972, and Pete Van Wieren were the new guys joining longtime Braves announcer Ernie Johnson. That announcement was only the beginning of what would be a watershed year for Skip Caray.

Caray shared the new team owner's "irreverent distaste for stodgy rules"[42] and believed that Turner meant it when he told him to say whatever he wanted. During those early days, when the Braves' baseball was sometime boring, Caray would thumb through *TV Guide* and offer uncomplimentary reviews of whatever was coming up next on TBS.[43] Later, Turner upbraided him for criticizing the team, but backed down when Caray pointed out that the Braves were in last place.[44]

Caray had turned down an opportunity to join his father on the Chicago White Sox broadcast team. He preferred to remain in his new hometown and to continue creating his own image. Although he may not have known it at the time, he had chosen the career path that he would follow for the rest of his life. In February 1976 he entered into another lifelong and life-changing relationship when he remarried. His new wife, Paula Prather, was a widow with an 8-year-old daughter (Shayelyn), whom he adopted.[45] He and Paula were together for the rest of his life, and she became his "best friend."[46]

In July Caray was awarded a new contract to continue as the Hawks' play-by-play announcer with the added responsibilities as director of media sales for the Omni. Coliseum.[47] On a much less serious note, a few days later (on July 26, 1976) he donned racing silks and joined the new Braves owner and others in a pregame ostrich race. Caray later claimed to have won the race despite having a "slow dumb ostrich,"[48] but Bob Hope (not "Old Ski Nose"), the PR "brains" behind that race, said a local sportswriter won.[49]

In December 1976 WTCG became the nation's first "superstation." By 1982 the station (now WTBS) was bringing Braves baseball to more than 21 million subscribers.[50] The voices they heard belonged to the Braves broadcasting trio, who had barely known each other when they stood together for their introductory announcement. They had soon developed an entertaining chemistry that endeared the lackluster[51] Braves to a nationwide audience for 13 years – until Ernie Johnson decided to move exclusively to radio in 1989. According to Furman Bisher, while "sundry others came and went," that trio "became engraved on the hearts of Braves' listeners."[52]

Each member of that trio also earned a place among the top 60 "all-time best announcers" based on the rating system developed by Curt Smith.[53] Any such ranking is subjective and every one of these "mikemen" (except for number one Vin Scully) is sure to have admirers who think they should be rated higher. Smith tried to minimize disputes by ranking each announcer on a scale of 1-10 in each of 10 criteria, but those ratings are subjective and therefore open to disagreement. Atlanta fans might even disagree about Johnson (number 43) being rated higher than Caray (45) and Van Wieren (59). Regardless of how one feels about individual ratings, however, having all three men who shared broadcasts for one major-league team for 13 years appear on this list is unprecedented.

Before that first season together, Caray, who was to do television only, said that he was looking forward to doing baseball again and talked about the differences between broadcasting baseball and basketball. He noted that the slower pace of baseball gives a broadcaster "more time to do your job, which is basically to tell the people who's winning, to educate them about the players, to keep the listeners and viewers in the game."[54] He also observed that working with others was going to be interesting for him because most of his basketball work was solo. Working as a team turned out pretty well; together "good ol' Ernie and funny ol' Skip and the learned Professor [Pete]" were, "in the grand scheme of things, as good as broadcasting ever got."[55] That trio dominated the Georgia Sportscaster of the Year award as one of them was honored in 10 of their 13 years together. Caray earned another four awards (1979-81-84-87) while Johnson (1977-83-86) and Van Wieren (1980-88-89) each claimed three.

During his first 16 years with the Braves, Caray continued as the Atlanta Hawks' primary broadcaster, providing "superb play-by-play coverage … mixed with off-the-wall dry-witted insights."[56] He still found time to take on a few other assignments that further demonstrated his versatility as a play-by-play announcer, and he experienced some significant personal changes.

In 1982 Caray briefly negotiated with the Mets before signing a three-year contract with TBS,[57] and he and Paula became the parents of yet another future sportscaster. Josh Caray would grow up to become the play-by-play announcer for college football and men's basketball (Stony Brook University) and baseball (Yale) and minor league baseball (the Rome [Georgia] Braves, Hudson Valley Renegades and, starting in 2020, the Rocket City [Madison, Alabama] Trash Pandas). When Caray learned that his new son had asthma, he quit smoking "cold turkey," even though he admitted that he had "smoked like a forest fire" until then.[58]

On December 11 of that same year, Caray was in the booth at the Capital Center in Landover, Maryland, to call the ballyhooed basketball matchup between the University of Virginia and Georgetown, featuring Ralph Sampson and Patrick Ewing.[59]

On July 4, 1985, Caray was in the broadcast booth for another memorable game. It received no special hype beforehand, but assumed legendary status – at least in Atlanta. The Mets were in town to start a four-game series, and there was a sellout crowd of 44,947. Rain pushed the game's 7:40 scheduled start time back by 84 minutes and caused a 41-minute interruption in the third inning. The game then went 19 innings (before the Mets prevailed 16-13) and ended at 3:55 A.M. Almost 10,000 hearty souls stuck around for the promised Independence Day fireworks … and got them, starting at 4:01 A.M. Nearby residents thought that the Civil War had returned and the city was again under siege. Caray said, "It's the latest I've ever stayed out doing something I wasn't ashamed of."[60]

In 1985 Caray made his first and only movie with a cameo role in *The Slugger's Wife*, which Caray himself described as "one of the worst movies ever made."[61] His sole foray into the world of publishing came nine years later when he co-authored (with Don Farmer) *Roomies: Tales from the World of TV News and Sports*, which did not become a bestseller,

In 1986 Caray was part of the TNT broadcast team for the inaugural Goodwill Games in Moscow. He covered boxing (paired with Paul Hornung)[62] and motoball, which Atlanta newspapers described variously as a demonstration sport and a novelty sport and as either polo or soccer on motorcycles. Caray admitted that he knew little about the sport[63] and opined that he didn't think he was expected to treat it "like the Second Coming."[64] He did know that the goalies were the only players not on a motorcycle and noted that they would be easy to spot because they would be the "ones with tread-marks all over them."[65] He also admitted that he didn't know the names of any of the players, but could "make up whatever names I want."[66] Years later, Braves CEO Terry McGuirk said he was sure he heard Caray "mention several Russian czars playing that day."[67] Caray was back (to cover baseball) for the 1990 Goodwill Games; motoball did not return. However, it is unlikely that Caray's coverage was the reason the event was dropped from all future Goodwill Games.

Ernie Johnson announced in March 1989 that he planned to retire at the end of the season.[68] A few days later, Skip Caray announced that he had hired an agent and would "explore other possibilities" when his contract expired also at the end of the season.[69] Negotiations with TBS continued during the season, and an agreement was reached shortly after Caray was hospitalized overnight in Los Angeles after suffering shortness of breath, chest pains, and an irregular heartbeat.[70] He was released in time to broadcast a 2:00 P.M. game the next day.

The 1990 Braves finished in last place and were so inept that one LA sportswriter suggested that TBS might stand for "Those Braves Stink."[71] A year later the team surprised everyone by winning the National League pennant, and Skip Caray had a memorable year for personal as well as professional reasons. His oldest son, Chip, had followed him into the "family business" and had experienced much early success. Early in 1991, he joined the Braves broadcast team to work primarily on the radio with Ernie Johnson, but also to replace his father when the elder Caray was doing play-by-play for the NFL Atlanta Falcons. The two Carays were also scheduled to do some Braves games together. The first time that happened (on April 26, 1991), the elder Caray warned his son, "If you don't do a good job, I'll take away your allowance."[72]

Less than a month later, that duo joined Harry Caray for a broadcasting first that may never be replicated. For the first time, three generations from one family broadcast the same major-league baseball game. The date was May 13, 1991, when the Braves visited Wrigley Field. After a press conference at Harry Caray's restaurant, all three Carays did an opening on-field segment. Then Harry went to the WGN booth as usual to call the Cubs game while Skip and Chip (dubbed "A Chip off the Old Blocks" by *The Sporting News*[73]) went to TBS to do the same. They called the same game, but did not do so side-by-side in the same broadcast booth. At the time, Skip downplayed the hoopla, saying, "The game is the story. The Braves are the story. Not us."[74] Later, however, he called that game his "most memorable."[75]

With much less hype, the trio had shared a booth once before – on November 28, 1989. The two younger Carays were doing play-by-play of an NBA game in Miami – Skip for TNT and Chip for the Sunshine Network – and Harry, who was in town for a college football game, dropped by their broadcast booth and made a brief "cameo" appearance.[76]

On August 26, 1991, with the surprising Braves only one game behind the Dodgers in the National League pennant race, Caray carried off a rare broadcasting feat when he "covered" two games simultaneously. He was doing play-by-play of the Expos-Braves game in Atlanta, and the Braves had rallied from a six-run deficit to take the lead. The Dodgers were in Chicago in a close game, which was airing on the press-box TV in Atlanta, Caray started relaying the play-by-play of that game as well as the Braves game.[77]

Caray's work with Braves soon required enough of his time that he had to give up two other major broadcasting jobs. The 1991-92 basketball season was Caray's last as the "Voice of the Hawks" – a role he had played since the team came to Atlanta 24 years earlier. Caray had also done Atlanta Falcons football games in 1990 and 1991, a commitment that caused him to miss 25 Braves games in August and September 1991, when the team surprisingly was in the pennant race. He was relieved of those duties in 1992.

The Braves' 1991 "worst-to-first" season began a string of 14 consecutive postseason appearances and 14 first-place finishes in 15 years, missing only 1994, when the players strike cut the season short and canceled the postseason. Skip Caray and Pete Van Wieren (and Don Sutton, who joined the team in 1989) were there for that entire streak as the "aural chroniclers of one of the best baseball runs ever."[78]

The combination of the Braves' consistently good performance and the wide coverage provided by the superstation created a huge fan base for the team and its broadcasters, and Caray was always the "most colorful and conspicuous"[79] member of that broadcast crew. He was "the one we thought we knew best … the funny one … the snarky one."[80] His "dry wit and humor" made the broadcasts "more fun" without taking away from the action."[81] While those who liked him called him "witty and honest," some found him "sarcastic and opinionated."[82] He was known for his "humor and … wit … and zingers, and also there was nobody better at calling a big moment."[83] His distinctive "nasally voice" and witty (often tongue-in-cheek) delivery[84] were easily recognizable. He was a self-described "wise-ass cynic,"[85] who became for many fans "the sound of summer in the South."[86] Caray told listeners "what was happening and also what [he] thought of what was happening."[87] According to his longtime broadcast mate, he was "brash, cynical, impatient" and "possessed one of the quickest minds … of anyone I've ever been around."[88]

About the importance of mental quickness, Caray once observed, "I've known people who are a lot smarter than me who couldn't do broadcasting because they didn't have the ability to see something and get it out in a short period of time. I guess that's a natural ability that some people have."[89] Caray obviously had that innate ability. Immediately after his memorable Bream call, broadcast partner Joe Simpson congratulated him for his "great call," and Caray's response was. "What did I say? I have no idea what I said."[90]

Caray also possessed a "mysterious way of knowing the home town of fans who caught foul balls in the stands"[91] – a trademark that made gullible listeners wonder how he could possibly know that the lucky fan was "a young fella from Hahira, Georgia." Another oft-repeated line came during lopsided losses; Caray would tell listeners: "It is OK, folks, to go and walk your dog now, if you promise to support our sponsors."[92] He loved to label small crowds "partial sellouts"[93] and to comment during day games on the number of older men who had brought their twentyish granddaughters/nieces to the game.[94]

During the 1990s the Braves continued to win during the regular season and falter in the postseason except for the magical 1995 season. Joe Simpson joined the broadcast team in 1992, and that four-man crew worked together in various combinations as the "Voice of the Braves" until Sutton's departure in 2006. Their tenure was not always smooth, however, as changes in team ownership and increased competition for viewers affected their roles and eventually left Caray feeling estranged.

After losing the World Series in 1991 and 1992 and the NLCS in 1993 and seeing the postseason canceled in 1994, the Braves (the "Team of the Nineties") finally stopped being "bridesmaids"[95] and won the World Series, and it was Skip Caray who captured the moment. After calling the final out (see above), he noted, "It's over. The monkey is off the Braves' back."[96] Turner Sports called its one-hour video highlighting that season "Braves Win … It All." Appropriately, Caray and Van Wieren provided the voiceover.[97]

During spring training in 1996, while broadcasting a game involving Braves reserve infielders, Caray offered the kind of one-liner that made him famous. He commented that a possible double play could go [Ed] Giovanola to [Tony] Graffanino to [Aldo] Pecorilli, which made him "hungry for some pasta."[98]

Caray was in the local newspapers regularly in 1996 primarily because of his pregame call-in show. He was frequently accused of being rude with most of the complaints appearing in "The Vent: Selective Invective," the *Atlanta Journal-Constitution*'s column that published anonymous complaints. Caray admitted that he "might be abrupt, but never purposely rude."[99] While one venter suggested that Caray had been cured ("Vent-ilated"[100]), the complaints continued for the next few years.

In 1997 the Braves had a new ballpark (Turner Field, which had been built for the 1996 Olympics), and Caray and the other broadcasters got to handle interleague games for the first time during the regular season. Caray dubbed this innovation "a healthy thing" because "the fans wanted it," but observed that when you looked at the lineups, "you felt like you were loaded or at spring training."[101]

In 1998 TBS switched from being a superstation to basic cable and announced in February that it would carry fewer Braves games. Later TBS would also change the pairings of the four broadcasters, and Caray would work with Joe Simpson, doing half of each game on radio and half on TV. Before that happened, Caray received word that his father was in critical condition in California. Harry Caray died on February 18 with his son and other family members at his bedside.

That May, during his first trip to Wrigley Field after his father's death, Skip Caray talked about the impact that death and how the response of fans at the funeral had affected him. He said that he had "lost his edge," and hoped to have "more patience" and be "less caustic, less acerbic."[102] The following month, while Caray was recovering from a bruised spinal cord sustained when he fell off a treadmill, Pete Van Wieren filled in for him as host of the pregame show. Afterward, he said he now understood why Caray was sometimes "cranky" on the show.[103]

That pregame show continued to be controversial. In 1999 another local radio station started a competing show called *The Zone,* and used ads that mimicked Caray's snarkiness. Then, in an extensive profile piece,[104] a new, more mellow Skip Caray was introduced. He talked openly about his past and how he had changed. He admitted that while between marriages he had followed in his father's "hard-living footsteps." He chased women and drank heavily. After he remarried, he gave up the first and somewhat moderated the second. He still enjoyed "cocktails and dinner, cocktail and dinner, cocktail and dinner…"[105] and had "heard more last calls than play balls"[106] until finally swearing off alcohol on New Year's Day 2000. Caray attributed his recent makeover to two factors: (1) the continuing criticism of his grouchy persona on the pregame show, where he did not suffer fools, especially those who asked questions that he had answered many times (e,g, slugging percentage and the infield fly rule) and (2) his health. He had said earlier that the concern shown by fans in Chicago during this father's funeral had touched him and given him a new appreciation for his fan base. The "new" Caray was a surprise to many and some said it was too long coming. Bob Wessler, former executive VP for TBS, said that Caray was "the most difficult employee" he ever dealt with.[107]

During that wide-ranging interview, Caray also talked about his philosophy toward calling a game. He said, "I'm always thinking of a guy driving a tractor-trailer rig across the South. … He wants to stop, but he can't; he has to keep going; I try to keep him awake and entertain him."[108]

Caray and Van Wieren celebrated their 25th anniversary as Braves broadcasters in 2000, and Caray may unknowingly have laid the groundwork for a future member of their profession. On May 21 he needed a day off to attend son Josh's high-school graduation and asked John Smoltz, who was recovering from elbow surgery, to fill in for him. Smoltz did the color commentary alongside each of the other Braves broadcasters, perhaps gaining experience that served him well when he entered broadcasting after his Hall of Fame playing career. On July 30 Caray and Van Wieren were honored in pregame ceremonies at Turner Field; they threw out the ceremonial first pitch and received Braves' jerseys bearing their names and the number 25.

At the end of that season, Caray was paired with Joe Morgan on NBC doing the American League Division Series (Yankees vs. A's). It was the first time he had called a major-league game for other than TBS, and initially he showed a few jitters.[109]

In 2001 the Braves announced that all four members of the Braves broadcast team (later dubbed the Gab Four[110]) would take turns hosting the pregame show. There was no reference to earlier criticisms of Caray's handling of this show. A year later, a body scan revealed that Caray had clogged arteries, and he underwent successful angioplasty. Shortly afterward, he was "honored" with his own bobblehead, about which he said, "It doesn't look like me at all."[111]

The success of TBS and other superstations had led to "explosive growth" of regional sports networks, and the Braves were no longer "the only game in town."[112] Things came to a head before the 2003 season. Executives at Entertainment Networks, the multimedia Times-Warner corporation of which TBS was now a part, decided to combat declining cable ratings by aiming for a broader audience. Its telecasts were renamed "MLB on TBS" rather than "Braves on TBS," although the Braves would still appear in all of the games.[113] Key to this re-imaging was the decision to have Don Sutton and Joe Simpson handle the nationally televised games on TBS and to relegate Caray and Van Wieren (who were considered "too biased" toward the Braves[114]) to radio and regional telecasts on Turner South. Local sportswriters and fans were shocked and quickly voiced their disapproval of the move. A nonscientific ajc.com/sports poll that asked, "Do you like the Braves juggling their TV announcers?" attracted 11,147 votes, 89 percent of which declared the decision to be "horrible."[115]

Despite the negative reaction, the change was made, and TBS ratings dropped another 25 percent. While the executives offered other possible reasons for that decline, they soon reversed that decision and returned to the four-man setup after the All-Star break, using a new "mix and match" approach that kept the same pairs on radio and TV for the entire game. The change, which was attributed to "long and loud protests,"[116] was front-page news in Atlanta. Upon his return, the usually crusty Caray was "downright syrupy"[117] as he said that the public support was "humbling."[118] Perhaps he remembered saying after his first season with the Braves, "My job is really in the hands of the fans. If they like me, I work. If they don't, I don't."[119]

A year after that temporary demotion, Caray and Van Wieren were jointly inducted into the Atlanta Braves Hall of Fame, joining longtime partner Ernie Johnson (Class of 2001). During that induction ceremony, Johnson talked of a surprising (to some) side to Caray, saying that he had "a bigger heart than anyone can imagine."[120] Caray was a longtime supporter of Camp Twin Lakes, for children with special needs; he adopted numerous rescue dogs and brought one into the broadcast booth on a "Bark in the Park" Day; he kept in touch with and visited a former Braves player who was in prison in Alabama.

Now that the fans had spoken, Caray and Van Wieren continued to be key members of the Braves broadcast team along with Sutton and Simpson. Chip Caray joined the team in 2005, after a successful lobbying effort by his father,[121] giving the Braves five broadcasters. The Braves' loss to Houston in the NLDS ended the team's postseason streak, and more changes were coming. Early in 2006 Time Warner sold Turner South to Fox Cable Networks, and Fox replaced the TBS broadcast crew with its own people.[122] The Braves also were for sale; Time Warner and Liberty Mutual completed that deal in May 2007.

Skip Caray's heart issues that had surfaced in 1989 did not go away. In 2003, a year after his angioplasty, he received a Pacemaker. Although he had eventually given up cigarettes and alcohol, his high-school weight (210 pounds) had fluctuated in his later years between 230 and 290 pounds while his 6-foot height didn't increase.[123] Early in his career, his weight was often a source of humor, as when he quipped, "The opera isn't over until the fat announcer shuts up."[124] It had become a source of concern. He was suffering from diabetes, congestive heart failure, arrythmia, and reduced kidney and liver function.[125]

Caray rode an emotional roller-coaster in 2007. He started the baseball season with a reduced role, relegated primarily to radio. On April 29 he drove 70 miles to Rome, Georgia, where he shared the broadcast duties with his youngest son, Josh, who was the regular announcer for the Braves' Class-A farm team there.[126] Later that season, TBS announced that it was parting ways with the Braves at the end of the season. In September he was hospitalized and missed several games, but returned to do play-by-play for the final Braves game on TBS on September 30. His partner for that game was his other son, Chip. He summed up that experience saying, "I did the first one and now I'll be doing the last one. The only difference is I'll be doing it with my boy. ... Working with Chip on that last one will be an emotional day, but it'll be great."[127] It was the end of an era, and it ended with a thud as TBS snubbed Skip (and Pete) when choosing its playoff broadcasters – a decision that Caray described as "hurtful" – especially because "nobody gave me a reason."[128] In October, he was in intensive care for three weeks, so close to death that his next of kin were told to stay nearby.[129]

Yet he was back for the 2008 season – for home games, at least – skipping spring training for the first time in his Braves career and accepting a reduced workload on Peachtree TV, the new home of the Braves. He missed a few games because of health issues, and at times "his delivery was a little slower and his speech a little slurry,"[130] but most of the time he seemed to be his old self. On July 31 Caray had one "one of his best broadcasts of the year" as the Braves got their only win in a four-game series against the Cardinals. He was "sharp, alert, quick, funny, opinionated."[131] In short, he was like the Skip Caray of old. It was to be his last broadcast; his trademark signoff line ("So long, everybody.") was never more appropriate.

Everyone was surprised that, after that performance, Caray was not able to come back the next night for the start of a three-game series against Milwaukee. He missed all three of those games, and the Braves left for the West Coast. During their flight – on August 3, 2008 – the team got the word that Skip Caray had died. Paula. his wife of 32 years, had found his body in the back yard of their home where he apparently was refilling the bird feeder.[132] Despite his recent health issues, everyone who knew Caray was shocked by his death, which was front-page news in Atlanta under the headline: "Braves Lose the Voice That Made Us All Fans."[133]

Tributes appeared in newspapers around the country, and fans throughout America shared their memories. One of those fans was former President Jimmy Carter, who said that he "enjoyed … [Caray's] superb commentary on the games."[134] Braves President John Schuerholz declared, «Our baseball community has lost a legend today."[135] Furman Bisher suggested one last "Memorial Wave"[136] for Caray, who had been a vocal and "ardent anti-wave activist."[137]

On August 11, 2008, a huge crowd gathered early at Atlanta's Cathedral of Christ the King "for a two-hour funeral Mass disguised as a celebrity roast."[138] It seemed fitting to many that the service started late because the Braves team bus was delayed by a traffic jam;[139] during his broadcasts, Caray often gave "traffic reports" that belittled Atlanta's seemingly never-ending road work. Once it began, the service was befitting a man with Caray's sense of humor. In that ornate gothic edifice, Caray's closest friends and colleagues remembered him – and regaled the mourners – with stories and remarks that, like Caray himself, were "honest and funny." Even Monsignor Tom Kenny's homily compared Caray's spiritual journey "home" to a play at the plate and paraphrased a familiar call, intoning "Here comes the slide. … Skip's safe. Listen to the crowd of angels and saints. They're going berserk."[140]

The day after the funeral, the Braves had a public tribute at Turner Field, where Georgia's governor, Atlanta's mayor, Braves executives, and fellow broadcasters shared their memories of Skip Caray. Commissioner Bud Selig sent a letter that called Caray "one of the great broadcasters of our era."[141] After that evening's scheduled pregame salute was rained out, it was held the next night before the second game of day/night doubleheader. The band played "Amazing Grace"; highlights of his 33-year career with the Braves were shown on the center-field video board; and the Atlanta Police Department Honor Guard provided a 21-gun salute. The sign indicating that the main television booth was now the "Skip

Caray Broadcast Booth" was unveiled, and the crowd responded with a standing ovation. Six of Caray's seven grandchildren threw the ceremonial first pitch, and the Braves revealed the "SKIP" patch that they would wear on their right uniform sleeves for the rest of the season.[142] Then the Braves were battered by the Cubs just as they had been in the first game, leading Bobby Cox to suggest that "Skip had a better night than the Braves did – much better."[143]

On the first anniversary of Caray's passing, Chipper Jones, who inspired one of Caray's hallmark calls ("a chopper to Chipper), said, "Skip will not be forgotten. He was as much an icon in Atlanta as any ballplayer who ever came through here."[144] Caray continued to be honored after his death. In 2009 he and the recently retired Van Wieren received the Atlanta Sports Council's first Furman Bisher Award for Sports Media Excellence.[145] He was inducted into the Atlanta Sports Hall of Fame later that year and into the Georgia Sports Hall of Fame in 2013, but as of 2020 he had not received the honor that he most wanted. He has not joined his father as a recipient of the Ford C. Frick Award, which is presented to one sportscaster each year by the National Baseball Hall of Fame. The recipient is recognized during the Hall's annual Induction Weekend, but is not an inductee, and therefore technically is not a Hall of Famer. The selection process has changed over the years, and for a few years a fan vote via Facebook chose three of the 10 candidates from whom the selection committee chose the winner. That was the case in 2008, and an article on the newspaper page describing Caray's funeral encouraged fans to vote for him. Although he did not get enough votes to earn a spot on that ballot, Caray was on the 10-man ballot for the 2010 and 2012 awards. The selection committee chose another candidate in each of those years. It would have been fitting for him to win the 2020 award on the 25th anniversary of the Braves' World Series championship, but he was not even among the finalists for that year's award. The fan vote has now been eliminated, but the website (inductskipcaray.com) that Paula Caray started after her husband's death is still online and has several videos of Skip in action.

After his health scare in 2007, Caray said, "Without baseball, there would be a big hole in my life."[146] The converse is true: Without Skip Caray, there is a hole in baseball for fans who knew him as the "Voice of the Braves." His voice is now silent, but the echo remains.

Sources

In addition to the sources cited in the Notes, the author consulted Baseball-Reference.com, Historic Newspaper Archives (newspapers.com), the National Baseball Hall of Fame's Giamatti Research Center, Paper of Record, and the *Sports Illustrated* Vault. He also watched numerous YouTube videos that allowed him to hear Skip Caray and experience once again small doses of his many talents.

Notes

1. Walter Bergeson, "5 Greatest Calls by Atlanta Braves Broadcaster Skip Caray," Rant Sports (rantsports.com/mlb/2014/04/25/5-greatest-calls-by-atlanta-braves-broadcaster-skip-caray/).
2. The bottle opener may be available on eBay (ebay.com). The author used this often while researching and writing this article. Search on "Skip Caray Talking Bottle Opener."
3. Bottle opener.
4. Harry Caray with Bob Verdi, *Holy Cow!* (New York: Villard Books, 1989), 212.
5. Tony Silvia, *Fathers and Sons in Baseball Broadcasting* (Jefferson, North Carolina: McFarland & Company, 2009), 93.
6. Tim Tucker, "Braves Lose the Voice That Made Us All Fans," *Atlanta Journal-Constitution*, August 4, 2008: A-4.
7. Tim Tucker, "Braves Lose the Voice That Made Us All Fans": 92.
8. Caray, 211.
9. Larry Stewart, "Despite Caray-Over, Skip Calls the Game in His Own Glib Way," *Los Angeles Times*, July 29, 1988. (Note: Some sources report that Harry Caray said, "Good Night, Skip.")
10. Stewart.
11. "Skip Caray Has Made It on His Own," *Los Angeles Times*, February 23, 1986. latimes.com/archives/la-xpm-1986-02-23-sp-11097-story.html.

12. Ken Picking, "Skip Caray: Father Did Know Best," *Atlanta Constitution*, December 22, 1979: 4-C.
13. "'93 Broadcasters," Atlanta Braves *FAN Magazine* (Volume 28, Number 1): 60.
14. Bob Wolf, "Carays Set a Big-Time First," *The Sporting News*, June 12, 1965: 27.
15. Picking: 1C; Caray, 212-214.
16. "Tuning In," *The Sporting News*, July 11, 1956: 50.
17. *Los Angeles Times*, February 23, 1986: Archives.
18. Wolf.
19. *Los Angeles Times*, February 23, 1986: Archives.
20. Wolf.
21. Jack Wilkinson, *The Game of My Life* (Champaign, Illinois: Sports Publishing, LLC, 2007), 106.
22. "KMOX Airs Triple-Header: 3 Grid Games at Same Time," *The Sporting News*, November 30, 1963: 32.
23. "Church Ceremonies Bless Marriage of Skip Caray," *The Sporting News*, April 18, 1964: 59.
24. Curt Smith, *Voices of the Game* (South Bend, Indiana: Diamond Communications, Inc., 1987), 481.
25. Picking: 4C.
26. James Joyner, "Fathers Day for the Carays – A Special Day at the Park," Outside the Beltway, June 19, 2005. outsidethebeltway.com/fathers_day_for_the_carays_-_a_special_day_at_the_park.
27. Jesse Outlar, "This and That," *Atlanta Constitution*, November 8, 1968: 2-C.
28. Outlar, "This and That." *Atlanta Constitution*, March 2, 1969: 2-C.
29. nationalsportsmedia.org/awards/state-awards/georgia.
30. Al Thomy, "On the Town," *Atlanta Constitution*, April 24, 1975: 2-E.
31. From 1963 to 1968, the St. Louis Hawks lost six consecutive division finals or semifinals. After moving to Atlanta, the team continued that pattern, losing in the conference finals or semifinals for five years in a row (1969-1973).
32. Picking: 4-C.
33. Ad in *Atlanta Constitution*, June 26, 1970: 19-A.
34. George Cunningham, "Thurmond: Davis Is a Hustler," *Atlanta Constitution*, October 24, 1969: 7-D.
35. "Caray Heads Charity Drive," *Atlanta Constitution*, June 2, 1970: 3-C.
36. "Telethon Aids Kids," *Atlanta Journal and Constitution*, May 21. 1972: 14-D.
37. Wayne Minshew, "Baseball Banter," *Atlanta Constitution*, January 20, 1971: 5-D.
38. Furman Bisher, "Born to Broadcast," *Atlanta Constitution*, August 5, 2008: D-7.
39. "Fans and Colleagues React," *Atlanta Constitution*. August 5, 2008: D-7.
40. Carroll Rogers, "Wit, Calls of Caray Celebrated," *Atlanta Constitution*, August 12, 2008: D-4.
41. "Heavy Rains Stop Apollos," *Atlanta Constitution*, May 3, 1973: 2-D.
42. Eldon L. Ham, *Broadcasting Baseball* (Jefferson, North Carolina: MacFarland and Co., 2011), 193.
43. Jim Cofer, "R.I.P. Skip Caray," (jimcofer.com), August 4, 2008.
44. Tucker, "Braves Lose the Voice That Made Us All Fans," 92.
45. Stewart.
46. Picking: 4-C.
47. "Caray Gets a New Deal with Hawks," *Atlanta Constitution*, July 25, 1976: 4-D.
48. Wilkinson, 106.
49. Bob Hope, *We Could've Finished Last Without You*, quoted in "Q&A on the News," *Atlanta Journal-Constitution*, October 31, 1995: A-2.
50. Curt Smith, *Voices of the Game*, 444.
51. Only three winning seasons in 14 years (1976-1989).
52. Furman Bisher, "Born to Broadcast," *Atlanta Constitution*, August 5, 2008: D-1.
53. Curt Smith, *Voices of Summer* (New York: Carroll & Graf, 2005), 392, 248-252, 348-352, 352-354.
54. Darrell Simmons, "Three on a Mike: Broadcast Team Varies in Style," *Atlanta Constitution*, April 9. 1976: 7-S.
55. Mark Bradley, "2nd Lifelong Voice of Braves Retires," *Atlanta Constitution*, October 22, 2008: D-4.
56. "TV Week," *Atlanta Constitution*, February 15, 1981: 2. (Caray is pictured on the cover.)
57. Tim Tucker, "Braves Acquire Journeyman Moore," *The Sporting News*, February 20, 1982: 42.
58. Furman Bisher, "Caray Versatile and Direct," *Atlanta Constitution*, August 5, 2008: D-4.
59. That game is available in its entirety on YouTube; UVA won 68-63. youtube.com/watch?v=RGiTVTaGq9o.
60. Guy Curtright, "Camp's Longest Hit Lives," *Atlanta Journal-Constitution*, July 4, 1999: D-2.
61. alchetron.com/Skip-Caray.
62. Rosen, "Caray Claims Unique Goodwill 'Duties,'" *Atlanta Journal-Constitution*, June 21, 1986: D-8.
63. Rosen.
64. John Carman, "Can Skip Carry His Weight in Coverage of Motoball?" *Atlanta Constitution*, July 11, 1976: C-1.

65 Carman.

66 Carman.

67 "Caray Tribute," *Atlanta Journal-Constitution*, August 13, 2008: D-8.

68 Prentis Rogers, "Ernie Johnson Will Retire After Season," *Atlanta Constitution*, March 3, 1989: F-1.

69 Rogers, "Inside TV-Radio Sports," *Atlanta Constitution*, March 7, 1989: D-2.

70 Joe Strauss, "Caray Hospitalized, Released Later," *Atlanta Constitution*, September 16, 1989.

71 Mike Downey, "TBS: Is It Short for Those Braves Stink?" *Los Angeles Times*, April 11, 1990.

72 Glenn Sheeley "Sports Scene," *Atlanta Journal-Constitution*, April 27, 1991: C-2.

73 Leslie Gibson, "A Chip Off the Old Blocks," *The Sporting News*, May 13, 1991: 55.

74 I.J. Rosenberg and Prentis Rogers, "Harry, Skip, and Chip Get to Caray on Together," *Atlanta Constitution*, May 14, 1991: E-1.

75 Wilkinson, 106.

76 Jeff Schultz, "A Caray Collision," *Atlanta Journal-Constitution*, May 13, 1991: E-6.

77 Jeff Schultz, "On the Air," *Atlanta Journal-Constitution*, August 27, 1991: F-6.

78 Bradley, "2nd Lifelong Voice of Braves Retires."

79 Curt Smith, *Voices of the Game*, 480

80 Mark Bradley, "Caray Called with Humor and Honesty," *Atlanta Constitution*, August 4, 2008: D-1.

81 "Braves Broadcasts," *FAN*, 1982 (Atlanta Braves Official Scorebook/Vol. 17, No. 4): 35.

82 Tyler Barnes, "Telling It Like It Is," *Braves Illustrated: Official 1988 Yearbook*: 55.

83 Kirk McKnight, *The Voices of Baseball* (Lanham, Maryland: Rowman & Littlefield, 2015), 288.

84 Tucker, "Braves Lose the Voice That Made Us All Fans."

85 Tucker, "Braves Lose the Voice That Made Us All Fans."

86 Tucker, "Braves Lose the Voice That Made Us All Fans."

87 Bradley, "Caray Called with Humor and Honesty."

88 Pete Van Wieren with Jack Wilkinson, *Of Mikes and Men* (Chicago: Triumph Books, 2010), 151.

89 Martha Payne, "Family Business," *FAN '98* (Braves Magazine and Scorecard: Vol. 33, Issue 2): 66.

90 *Atlanta Journal-Constitution*, "Caray Tribute," August 13, 2008: D-8.

91 Mike King, "Skip, TBS Helped Make Atlanta," *Atlanta Journal-Constitution*, October 2, 2007: A-10.

92 ecelebritymirror.com/celebrity-babies/skip-caray-harry-carays-son-dorothy-kanz/.

93 Bob McCoy, "Keeping Score," *The Sporting News*, December 10, 1984: 8. (19,548 capacity; 3,605 attendance).

94 Cofer.

95 Van Wieren, 133.

96 "Braves Broadcaster Skip Caray's Call of the Final Out," *Atlanta Journal-Constitution*, October 30, 1995: C-19.

97 Prentis Rogers, "TV-Radio," *Atlanta Journal-Constitution*, December 16, 1995: E-2.

98 I.J. Rosenberg, "Braves Notebook," *Atlanta Journal-Constitution*, March 24, 1996: E-4.

99 "Peach Buzz," *Atlanta Journal-Constitution* August 29, 1996: G-2.

100 "The Vent," *Atlanta Journal-Constitution* September 3, 1996.

101 Rogers, "TV/Radio," *Atlanta Journal-Constitution*, June 13, 1997: D-2.

102 Wilkinson, "Tough Wrigley Visit for Skip," *Atlanta Journal-Constitution*, May 31, 1998: D-1, D-7.

103 Rogers, "Radio-TV," *Atlanta Journal-Constitution*, June 14, 1998: D-2.

104 Drew Jubera, "A Less Harried Caray," *Atlanta Journal-Constitution*, May 21, 2000: M1, M-3.

105 Christian Boone, "Wit, Calls of Caray Celebrated," *Atlanta Journal-Constitution*, August 12, 2008: D-4.

106 Glenn Sheeley, "Caray Announcers' Youngest Member Isn't Totally a 'Chip Off the old Block,'" *Atlanta Journal-Constitution*, June 8, 1991: D-2.

107 Jubera: M-3.

108 Jubera: M-3.

109 Rogers, "Radio/TV," *Atlanta Journal-Constitution*, September 8, 2000: G-2.

110 Mike Tierney, "Braves Rehire Broadcasters," *Atlanta Journal-Constitution*, November 13, 2002: C-1.

111 Wilkinson, "Doll Has Caray Shaking His Head," *Atlanta Journal-Constitution*, July 20, 2002.

112 Van Wieren, 160.

113 Tucker, "'Too Braves' for TBS," *Atlanta Constitution*, March 27, 2003: E-1.

114 Van Wieren, 160.

115 *Atlanta Constitution*, March 27, 2003: E-1.

116 Tucker, "Skip and Pete Back on Braves Telecasts," *Atlanta Journal-Constitution*, July 8, 2003: A-1.

117 Steve Hummer, "Free Range," *Atlanta Constitution*, July 19, 2003: C-2.

118 Tucker, "Skip and Pete Back on Braves Telecasts."

119 Darrell Simmons, "Caray Not a 'House' Man," *Atlanta Constitution*, October 23, 1976: C-2.

120 Tucker, "Braves Lose the Voice That Made Us All Fans."

121 Van Wieren, 171.

122 Tucker, "Turner South Crew Replaced," *Atlanta Journal-Constitution*, April 29, 2006: D-1.

123 Picking.

124 Picking.

125 Carroll Rogers, "Ailing Caray Will Skip Road," *Atlanta Constitution*, April 1, 2008: D-2.

126 Tucker, "This Is Something I Was Born to Do…," *Atlanta Journal-Constitution*, May 5, 2007: A-1, A-10.

127 Rogers, "Skip Caray Back in Booth," *Atlanta Journal-Constitution*, September 20, 2007: D-5.

128 Tucker, "'Hurt' Caray Off Post-Season Team," *Atlanta Journal-Constitution*, September 27, 2007: D-1.

129 Rogers, "Ailing Caray Will Skip Road."

130 Van Wieren, 185.

131 Van Wieren, 185.

132 Tim Tucker, "Wife, Family Coping with Death," *Atlanta Journal-Constitution*, August 5, 2008: D-1.

133 Tucker, "Braves Lose the Voice That Made Us All Fans."

134 "Fans and Colleagues React," *Atlanta Journal-Constitution*, August 5, 2008: D-7.

135 "Braves Announcer Skip Caray Dies," *Sports Illustrated*, si.com/mlb/2008/08/04/skip-carayobit.

136 Furman Bisher, "Caray Versatile, Direct," *Atlanta Journal-Constitution*, August 5, 2008: D-4.

137 Jack Wilkinson, "The Men in the Booth," *Atlanta Journal-Constitution*, August 7, 1991: E-1.

138 Terence Moore, "The Stories and Jokes of His Life Remembered, "*Atlanta Journal-Constitution*, August 12, 2008: D-1

139 "Only Fitting," *Atlanta Journal-Constitution*, August 12, 2008: D-4.

140 Rogers, "Even the Monsignor Borrows Famous Line," *Atlanta Journal-Constitution*, August 12, 2008: D-1.

141 "Caray Tribute," *Atlanta Constitution*, "August 13, 2008: D-8.

142 David O'Brien, "Braves Report," *Atlanta Journal-Constitution*, August 14, 2008: C-3.

143 O'Brien, "Double the Trouble," *Atlanta Journal-Constitution*, August 14, 2008: C-3.

144 O'Brien, "Skip Caray Still Intensely Missed," *Atlanta Journal-Constitution*, August 4, 2009: C-2.

145 Furman Bisher, "My Opinion," *Atlanta Journal-Constitution*, January 25, 2009: C-2.

146 Rogers, *Atlanta Journal-Constitution*, September 20, 2007.

Joe Simpson

BY CURT SMITH

Joe Simpson

Perhaps Joe Simpson was destined to play and describe a game of pitch and catch and hit. For one thing, the holiday baby was born December 31, 1951, at a time when baseball was the only game in town. Imagining the pastime, hearing it on radio, or watching on television, no one needed slow motion, stop-action, or instant replay: Baseball's presence was enough. For another, Joe was blessed by geography. The decade's titan, Mickey Mantle, hailed from Spavinaw, Oklahoma, only 170 miles from Joe's birthplace in Purcell, speaking to and for Simpson's Baby Boom generation (born between 1946 and 1964). It was mesmerized by the Mick's shock and awe of speed and power. In his 1951 rookie year, Yankees manager Casey Stengel said memorably, "That kid can hit balls over buildings."[1]

When Mantle died in 1995, Bob Costas spoke at a memorial about how he and millions of others idolized number 7 in their youth: "We tried to crease our caps like him; kneel in an imaginary on-deck circle like him; run like him, heads down, elbows up."[2] Simpson understood. Each 1950s baseball morn, Joe and his father inhaled the prior day's box scores: "Dad taught me to read about the Yankees. I mean, they were baseball," Simpson said. "Whitey Ford, Yogi [Berra], [Roger] Maris – the whole club, a national team. But above all, how'd Mick do? Did he homer, go two-for-four? Mantle's how I learned to read."[3]

Simpson shared most of the speed but not the power of the pinstripes' icon – ultimately taller than Mantle (6-feet-3 vs. 5-11), but slimmer (175 vs. 195 pounds). The bat-and-throw-left All-American outfielder-first baseman at the University of Oklahoma was picked by the Dodgers in the third round of the 1973 draft, played for LA, Seattle, and Kansas City, and retired in 1983. He then became a popular 1987-91 Seattle Mariners announcer, since 1992 eclipsing that appeal on Atlanta Braves radio/TV. The German philosopher Friedrich Nietzsche said, "That which does not kill us makes us stronger."[4] Humor has been one Simpson ally; indefatigability, another.

Initially, his need for both seemed dim. In 1970, the Norman, Oklahoma, high-school senior hit .435, made the All-Boomer Conference and All-Oklahoma first team, and led his club to the state Class 4-A title. Next, the college marketing major twice led the Sooners to the NCAA World Series, forging their then-career-best in runs (93), hits (125), and doubles (27). In 1973, the LA draftee debuted for the Pacific Coast League Albuquerque

Dukes by stealing a base, knocking in a run, and throwing out a runner at the plate. Struggling in the PCL – "It was a compliment I was even there," he said – Simpson moved to California League Bakersfield, tying a .304 average, 24 RBIs, and 14 steals, then to 1974 Waterbury, hitting an Eastern League sixth-high .298. His 30 RBIs and 18 stolen bases helped him make its All-Star team.[5]

In 1975 Simpson joined the defending National League titlist Dodgers, playing scattered parts of that and the next three years, never with more than 30 at-bats in more than 29 games. "The farm system was stacked, the Dodgers had a good team, it was hard to break in," he said.[6] On October 1, 1978, the Angelenos, soon to lose a second straight World Series, played at fourth-place San Diego in a game that meant little except for Gaylord Perry, "who wants his 3,000th career strikeout before everybody goes home," starting against LA to coincide with Fan Appreciation Day. By the fifth inning, Joe was playing center field, "giving a Dodgers regular the rest of the day off." In the 10th inning, he hit with two out and Perry at 2,999 K's. Gaylord got two strikes before Simpson fouled off "four super wet spitballs."[7]

Finally, Simpson took a pitch "a foot off the plate. Big Lee Weyer yells, 'Strike three!' me cussing him in vain." The ballpark popped a cork. "Gaylord gets his milestone, the Padres carrying him off the field. At least I've made history: victim 3,000!" Two weeks later, Simpson saw in *The Sporting News* that baseball had somehow miscounted. *Another* strikeout had been number 3,000 two innings earlier. Who was it? "*Me!*" he said, in a rare game with the Dodgers where he actually had two at-bats.[8] "I already *held* the record when in the 10th I *set* the record." In truth, his niche with the Dodgers had become no laughing matter.

Picture Simpson as a 1975-79 jack-in-the-box: pushed down, tearing up the minors' pea patch, then popping up to again ride the big-league bench. In 1975 he stole 30 bases and knocked in 49 runs for Albuquerque. In 1976 he was sent down once more, swiping 40 bases with 60 RBIs. Again, LA ho-hummed, Simpson getting just 30 bigs' ups in 23 games. The Oklahoman was the last player cut in 1977 spring training – "a bitter disappointment."[9] He replied by topping the PCL in average (.370) and triples (10) for the first half, adding 45 RBIs, a league third-best 26 steals, and 13- and 19-game hit streaks – lining to all fields, standing more erect, and working with LA hitting instructor Dixie Walker and ex-Dukes outfielder Paul Ray Powell.[10]

Surely, this would get Simpson noticed – except it didn't. In his view, the Dodgers had become a franchise of Doubting Thomases. Later he said, "I never got a chance,"[11] despite hitting .303 in the 1973-78 Dodgers farm system, and .313, .349, and .309 in 1977-79 spring training. The year that resembled most a burr under his saddle was understandably 1977. After hitting well all spring and in the Freeway Series against the Angels, Joe was released a day before the opener to accommodate Boog Powell, who "was to give the Dodgers insurance against an injury to starter Steve Garvey,"[12] but was himself released.

Despite marauding through Triple A, Simpson watched LA sign or trade for Jimmy Wynn, Dusty Baker, Rick Monday, Vic Davalillo, Derrel Thomas, Gary Thomasson, and Von Joshua. Joe's rationale: "The Dodgers have lost confidence in their farm system"[13] – and therefore in him.

"Ridiculous," Dodgers vice president Al Campanis jibed, noting to *TSN* what he termed "a strong crop of youngsters"[14] in the system. "It's frustrating," Simpson told *TSN*'s Gordon Verrell, "not only for me but for all the young players in the organization."[15] A likelier cause was his paucity of power: at that point, only 15 home runs in six professional years.

Given "a chance," Joe showed occasional embers of the Dodgers' hoped-for punch. In 1976, demoted by Big Blue, Simpson bashed two home runs in three days, crediting LA outfielder-first baseman Bill Buckner: "Bill talked to me and helped me lay the bat more over my shoulder."[16]

Sadly, the power surge became the exception, not rule. Ultimately, Joe retired having gone deep once every 155 at-bats in his nine-year (1975-83) major-league career.

On April 30, 1979, Simpson, signed by Seattle after the Dodgers' adieu, hit a two-run pinch-hit ninth-inning homer, his first, against Baltimore, the O's winning, 8-7, an inning later.[17] That August 27, he became the first Mariner to get five hits in a game, the first four singles. In the 12th inning, he doubled and scored Seattle's sixth run as the newest and "10th … member of the American League's five-high society," read *The Sporting News*, the M's edging Cleveland, 6-5.[18] Simpson's first year in Seattle was his finest in the bigs, hitting .283 in 120 games.

He also found that even in the majors things could even out. On April 25, 1979, Simpson bashed his first big-league dinger, off Boston's Tom Burgmeier. Two years plus one day later, the savvy center fielder made a bonehead play. With one out and runners at first and second, Oakland's Dave McKay hit a drive deep to center field that Joe corralled for an out – number three, he surmised. Ambling toward the dugout, not a care in the world, Simpson belatedly learned the error of his ways, Cliff Johnson scoring from second base: A's win, 9-4.[19]

Increasingly, Simpson also flashed the humor familiar to Braves radio/TV. The Eastern Seaboard is often dubbed unforgiving – witness Bob Uecker's mot, "They have Easter egg hunts in Philadelphia, and if the kids don't find the eggs, they get booed."[20] In 1982, Simpson's last year with the M's, he saw another side of the Seaboard in Fenway Park, not always a pacific place for an enemy center fielder. A bleacher creature yelled, "Okie Joe!" (Recalled Simpson: "This guy had done his homework."[21]) Soon a chant began: "Ok-ie Joe! Ok-ie Joe!" Later the man began singing the title song of the musical *Oklahoma!*, leading "Ok-ie Joe!" to turn around and start conducting. He recalled, "The guy's singing, pals join in, and we converse." Next night, Simpson back in center, the same fan brought photocopies of the words, "passed them around, and soon the *bleachers* are in song! A year later I'm traded to Kansas City, not even playing, and from the stands I hear, 'Where the wind comes sweepin' down the plain.'[22] Amazing. The musical ends, 'Oklahoma! OK!' -- a good word for these fans."[23]

Later that year Simpson coined "Mr. Jello," a "caper" from Jessica Fletcher via Raymond Chandler. The Mariners arrived in Chicago amid an already endless season – Joe, beat writer Tracy Ringolsby, and co-conspirator Richie Zisk determined to shorten or at least enliven it. "Ringolsby is in the bar trying to distract manager Rene Lachemann," said Simpson. "Zisk gets Rene's suite key from traveling secretary Lee Pelekoudas."[24] He, the recently named "Ok-ie Joe!", and Larry Andersen went upstairs, put cherry jello with buckets of ice in the toilet, and suite furniture, including bed, in the bathroom. When the dresser didn't fit, they unpacked Rene's suitcase and stored his clothes. The phone rang, so "we remove the speakers, jimmy the suite door, write disparaging remarks on the mirrors and TV screens with soap, and leave," said Simpson. "Rene enters, is trapped, nowhere to sit, no way to call, jello everywhere, the bathroom so jammed the hotel had to take off the door."

A day later, arriving at Comiskey Park, the conspirators saw a message on the blackboard: "$500 reward for information on Mr. Jello." Rene tried to make them confess by saying his friend, White Sox skipper Tony La Russa, had security people dusting for fingerprints. "Next, he said the hotel was going to charge us for room damages. Scared, we didn't buckle," said Simpson. "In Milwaukee, we put balloons in Rene's office holding up a box of Jello. He calls area balloon shops to find who placed an order – all but hired a private eye."[25] Finally, at the year-end team party, Mr. Jello's offenders confessed. It didn't make the Mariners better – they finished 76-86 –but at least made the season seem shorter.

Simpson finished 1982 with a .257 average, hitting a strong .284 in the second half but not convincing M's President Dan O'Brien. "Generally there was a feeling," he said, "we should get some of our younger players on the roster."[26] Simpson knew the way – shipped if not to San Jose then to the M's Triple-A affiliate at Salt Lake City, admitting to being to "dumbfounded" yet choosing to view it as "a positive thing. I had a good second half, and I'm sure some team can use me."[27] The culprit, as usual, was cash, *The Sporting News* reported, Simpson earning "a reported $100,000 in 1982. ... He could have figured to command at least $120,000 this year," the major-league minimum salary then $35,000.[28] There is no way of knowing if Mr. Jello played a role.

Unflagging, Simpson wrangled a 1983 tryout, then one-year contract, with Kansas City, a franchise culturally at one with the people of his youth. Its Royals (later, Kauffman) Stadium had just turned 11 years old, a paladin of personality. In a *Kansas City Star* story headlined "Royals' New Outfielder Treasures Old-Fangled Ballparks," Simpson revealed that "I somehow wish I could get in a time machine and go back and watch a game at Ebbets Field." He had a turn-of-the-century photograph of the Dodgers' home, prizing big-league parks no longer here. "I love the game, and I love nostalgia," he said, "so I put the two together in a hobby."[29]

In "There Used to Be a Ballpark Right Here,"[30] Frank Sinatra sang tenderly of 14 classic parks built from Shibe Park in 1909 to Yankee Stadium in 1923. Simpson collected photos of each – Forbes Field in Pittsburgh, its vast acreage grown heavy with base hits; the Polo Grounds, its pee-wee foul lines flanking a Sahara of a center field; Tiger Stadium in Detroit, a right-field overhang making the upper deck much closer than the lower to home plate. Joe played in or visited post-1950s big-league parks, including the almost two dozen built since Camden Yards opened in 1992 – each a cathedral of the outdoors, different in length, size, and feel.[31] His favorite: Fenway Park, its left-field wall as seductive to a pull hitter as a beer in Prohibition.[32]

Sadly, Simpson's large love of ballparks did not enlarge his home-run panache. In 1983 he batted .168 in 91 games with no home runs, 20 hits, and 21 strikeouts in 119 at-bats. He also pitched in two games, threw three innings, and allowed one run. Simpson made more pitching than at-bat appearances, two and one, respectively, in the season's last six weeks – not good, if you're an outfielder, which Joe was.[33] After the season, the parent Royals left him unprotected, assigning his contract to their Triple-A club in Omaha – for no big-league team would purchase it for a mere $25,000, as Kansas City had bought Simpson's pact from Seattle a year before, rescuing him from possible reassignment to the minors.

That winter the Royals also acquired Orlando Sanchez, Jorge Orta, and Lynn Jones, vying for his position. "The Royals are talking about a commitment to youth," wrote Ringolsby in the *Kansas City Intelligencer*. A headline read: "Royals' Simpson has work cut for him."[34] On Joe's side were speed, glove work, and likability, skipper Dick Howser saying, "If a manager ever pulls for a guy to make a club, I'm pulling for him," adding that Okie Joe would get "every opportunity to make the club. The thing he has to do is show me he can hit." Simpson said, "I don't care how many bus rides I have to make or how many 'B' [early-morning] games I play in, I just want to get the chances."[35] They would come from elsewhere, and soon.

Four times that offseason his old club, the Mariners, called to offer Joe a job as a TV commentator. Each time he declined, not ready to give up the joy of playing, prophesying Robert Redford as Roy Hobbs in *The Natural*,[36] the story of a veteran in love with baseball, released later in 1984 to spectacular success. "Eventually, I want to get to into broadcasting, and I may never have an opportunity like that fall in my lap," Simpson said. "But I don't want to look back in 10 years and say, 'I know I could play better than I did in 1983.'

I want to prove that now."[37] The Royals cut him. Hired as an Angels coach, he became, as Dizzy Dean often said, a TV "commertater" for Seattle, who each of his five years there (1987-91) finished in the second division of the American League West.

A decade earlier radio/TV's Dave Niehaus had fashioned the then-expansion Mariners' Northwest Opening into states like Idaho, Utah, Montana, Oregon, and up into Alaska. Enormously popular, he won a landslide 2003 *Sports Illustrated* survey that asked Washingtonians, among other things, their favorite announcer: 36 percent said Niehaus; next, football's John Madden, 8 percent.[38] "He was a great man," said Simpson, working closely with Niehaus. "I learned from him how to prepare, to be objective, not to think of yourself as a player anymore, and always to be the people's voice. He taught me so much."[39] Simpson spent his time wisely: learning, analyzing, laughing, numbed only by the Mariners' home Kingdome – to the online book *This Great Game* "a swirling, petrified cupcake bitten into by locals, who quickly disliked [it] once the new stadium smell wore off.[40]" In 1992 he joined a wagon train more pioneering than even the Mariners into the Great Northwest.

Webster's New World College Dictionary defines cable TV as "a television system in which a high antenna and one or more dish antennas receive signals from distant and local stations, electronic satellite relays, etc., and transmit them by direct cable to the receivers of persons subscribing to the system."[41] By the 1970s, newly available satellites forged cable channels that charged a monthly fee to complement free programming. In 1976 Ted Turner changed Atlanta station WTCG's name to WTBS, made it the first television "SuperStation," bought the Braves, and next year made their schedule the outlet's TV program cornerstone, becoming a profound influence on his team specifically and baseball generally. The Braves became the self-styled "America's Team."

Cable swelled baseball's stage; baseball, cable's audience. "TBS was just one offering," said Braves Voice Ernie Johnson Sr. "People weren't aware how it could sell the Braves a world from Georgia."[42] In 1982 Atlanta began the season a big-league record 13-0 – and people were. To Johnson, the streak became "the 'two-by-four' that hit America between the eyes." In Storm Lake, Iowa, a sign read "The Atlanta Braves: Iowa's Team," Ernie said, adding that in Valdez, Alaska, a Braves Fan Club chapter pooled cash, bought a screen, and named its bar "The Braves Lounge."[43] Across the country viewers thanked Turner for bringing TV baseball back to small-town America. SuperStation Voices emerged: Tim McCarver on WOR New York; Harry Caray on WGN Chicago; above all, Caray's son Skip, Pete Van Wieren, and lead Voice Johnson, TBS.

"All during this time," said the *New York Times*'s George Vecsey, "cable led baseball's growth."[44] Picture nightly TV baseball, coast to coast – if not a miracle, as welcome as an open bar. In January 1992 this happy hour welcomed Simpson after Turner Sports TV and WGST Atlanta regional radio spent late 1991 judging Voices to replace Dave O'Brien, leaving for the new Florida Marlins, and Johnson, arguably cable TV's first superstar, retiring.[45] According to Turner executive producer Don McGuire, network execs heard tape from more than 100 broadcasters and talked to Johnny Bench and Jim Palmer – but chose Oklahoma '73 to complement TBS's Caray, Van Wieren, and Don Sutton because of "the style. [It] is similar," said Simpson, 42. "They treat games as games – not life or death,"[46] basic cable by then wiring almost every US home.

In a sense, history heightened irony. Royals general manager John Schuerholz had released Simpson in 1983, effectively ending his playing career. Now Braves GM, he helped nationally launch Okie Joe's new career. McGuire said he was "alarmed at how many [Voices] are vociferous home-team cheerleaders," not thinking "we did that anymore."[47] Simpson's contrast made him the only person offered the position. He likened his new job to a Texas two-step. Step one was to be nice and easy. A second: be honest – more irony, given what happened several decades later. "If you always tell the truth, you won't get in trouble."[48]

Trouble had recently submerged the Braves, including four straight 1987-90 last-place NL West crashes in a row. In 1990 Atlanta braved baseball's worst record: 65-97. A year later the worst-to-firsters led the Dodgers on the last day of the season by a game. "Stretch by [John] Smoltz," Van Wieren said on TBS. "The pitch to Cedeño. A high fly ball to right field! ... Back goes Justice! He's got it! And the magic number for Atlanta is one! The Braves have clinched a tie for first."[49] The Giants then beat LA, Atlanta taking the West for the first time since 1982. Next, it won the League Championship Series and went to the limit against Minnesota in the World Series. Three games went extra innings. Five went one-run. "It was phenomenal," said Van Wieren, "and Game Seven was terrific"[50] – the Twins' Jack Morris beating relief pitcher Alejandro Peña in 10 innings, 1-0.

Next year was as theatric, the '92ers scoring thrice in the ninth inning of NLCS Game Seven to edge the Pirates, Joe briefly airing the World Series on WSB Atlanta.[51] Simpson meshed well, at one with the South's culture, in only his fourth year as a Braves Voice named "Georgia Sports Broadcaster of the Year."[52] His honor lit 1995, after a strike begun in August 1994 curbed each year's schedule, stained the record book, and put a premium on likability – a Simpson forte. It also helped that the Braves routed the NL East, won the Division Series and LCS, then became the first team to win the World Series for three different cities – Boston, Milwaukee, and Atlanta. "Fly ball, deep left-center! [Marquis] Grissom on the run! Yes! Yes! Yes! The Atlanta Braves have given you a championship!"[53] Caray said of World Series Game Six. Van Wieren later said of the Series title: "I keep thinking of '95. We thought that we'd win a bunch more than one."[54]

Atlanta lost other World Series in 1991-92, 1996, and 1999.[55] The Braves coming so close time and again was softened historically by how except for 1994, the player strike and lockout erasing the postseason, they won their division title each year from 1991 to 2005 – a nonpareil 14 straight years.[56] Similarly, the broadcast team began feeling angst *off* air. For a long time, the Braves' 1976-89 trio of Ernie, Skip, and Pete had been thought immutable (to some, doubtless immortal). Johnson's 1991 retirement saddened millions. One weekend in 2000, Simpson found that without the serenity of TBS baseball's Mr. Rogers, things perhaps inadvertently didn't run as unflappably as before.

On Saturday, June 24, TBS superimposed a Friday night video box over the next night's at Atlanta's Turner Field to show that the latter was four-five inches smaller. This backed Brewers manager Davey Lopes's claim that the Braves had been unfairly utilizing the catcher's-box rule to get outside strikes called.[57] The fracas infuriated the Braves, leading them to ban TBS Voices from taking the team charter flight to Montreal. Tuesday morning club President Stan Kasten and Turner Sports President Mark Lazarus met, releasing a statement affirming the Braves-TBS "long-standing, warm relationship."[58] That night manager Bobby Cox met with Simpson and Turner Sports coordinating producer Glenn Diamond before batting practice. TBS Voices boarded the club flight later – the catcher's-box dispute leaving almost as quickly as it came.

In late 2002 Simpson, Caray, Van Wieren, and Sutton each signed a four-year pact with Turner Sports, which then set about breaking up its old gang before another opening pitch. In March 2003 TBS, citing "network research," yanked Skip and Pete from their quarter-century niche, replaced by Simpson and Sutton. Its "logic" was two-fold. Turner wanted a less partisan national tilt. After 27 years, it also felt the pair too closely twinned to the Braves. Overnight, Caray and Van Wieren careened from shore-to-shore video to regional radio and 36-game Fox Sports South TV, seen only in Southeast precincts. Creatures of habit, baseball-watchers turned off the dial.

"TBS just doesn't sound the same," rued the *Miami Herald*'s Barry Jackson. Ratings fell, many missing Pete's studied delivery and Caray's acidic charm. "Neither man's strength," Jackson wrote of Sutton/Simpson, "is play-by-play."[59]

For Okie Joe, much of this mental worry turned problematic in 2004. Soon after turning 52 on New Year's Eve, he felt pain in his midsection that paled after an hour. A month later, as Simpson slept in his Marietta, Georgia, home, it struck again, more intensely. Initial diagnosis at a nearby hospital traced the cause to reaction to medication. Next day, waiting for his dentist's office appointment, he doubled over in enormous pain and was rushed by ambulance to Piedmont Hospital. An infection, coupled with high fever, put him in such peril that daughter Meg, a Villanova law student, and Gabe, an Auburn freshman, were asked to hasten home. "That's how scary it was," Simpson said.[60]

From a hospital bed, Dad brightened to see his two children home from college to lend moral support, not knowing they had been summoned in case there was a funeral to attend – *his*. Simpson would spend more than half of February there, suffering from acute pancreatitis, an inflammation of the pancreas that left him seriously ill and hospitalized for two weeks. Medically, a gallstone had clogged his bile duct, forcing the pancreas to start eating away. "Metaphorically?" wrote the *Atlanta Journal-Constitution*'s Mike Tierney. "He was caught in a rundown, with no certain escape before getting tagged out. Doctors 'didn't know which way it was going to go,'"[61] he wrote, meaning life or death.

Eventually Simpson was released after a 16-day stay, knowing that he must return to have his gall bladder, with its hundreds of stones, removed. He got a blunt reminder 1½ weeks later – a gall-bladder attack. Its location in his body led to more complicated surgery than usual in early March. The Braves announcer's voice, usually familiar, was "barely recognizable," said Tierney. He had lost 30 pounds, "becoming Simpson Lite, resuming regular eating, easy on the fat." Much of 2004 was spent regaining physical health.[62] After a year off for good behavior, Simpson was accosted by an inchoate 2006 that tested his mental equilibrium. "May you live in interesting times" is an old Chinese curse.[63] On occasion the broadcaster must have yearned for tedium. Meantime, many Braves viewers did, for reasons quite apart from health.

In April 2006 the Fox Cable Network acquired the regional network Turner South TV from Time Warner, airing 58 games and changing the booth. Out: the familiar Caray, Van Wieren, Simpson, and Sutton. In: Bob Rathbun and Jeff Torborg. The shakeup left TBS's old foursome calling 70 national games a year – Caray and Van Wieren's fewest since the 1970s – plus Braves radio, a change inviting backlash, which came.[64] "A Braves broadcast simply isn't a Braves broadcast without Skip, Pete, and Don," said Robert Bruce, 30, of Dunwoody, Georgia. "I think this really stinks."[65] Somehow the franchise was trying to bridge the gulf between Ted Turner's original product and a Braves new world.

The most seismic change, once unimaginable, upended 2007, Turner selling the Braves to Liberty Media while also peddling TBS to Time Warner, which, the *Oklahoma City News* noted, had "national ambitions." On September 27, Mel Bracht wrote, "Bye, bye, Braves," in a story headlined "After 30 Years Together, Braves, TBS Parting Ways."[66] He was mourning on behalf of many who had never even set foot near the South. Three days later the Braves bid a sad goodbye to TBS, its regular coverage having linked five American presidents from Jimmy Carter to George W. Bush – Skip Caray and son Chip suitably calling the final game: Houston beating the visiting Braves, 3-0, on Sunday, September 30.[67] The telecast included the "top moments of Braves baseball on TV," as voted by the public.

Coming from the broad interior of America, Simpson was among those who especially grasped what TBS had meant and what its loss might cost. "I think the people who are going to be most disappointed about this are some of the older generation who enjoy watching across the country and have grown to be really attached to them," he said. "The Braves have become their favorite team whether they lived in Montana or Illinois or anyplace else."[68] He – they – recalled how Turner bought, renamed, and promoted TBS as a SuperStation, airing almost each regular-season game, even replaying them in early-A.M. hours, and billing the club as "America's Team" – even as a second-division franchise.

"I don't think that [label] was really a stretch because we still get fan mail from every state," Simpson told Bracht.[69] At peak, TBS's Voices were household names, as well-known as WGN's Harry Caray or even NBC's Vin Scully. By contrast, in 2008 new ownership's "national ambitions" ended daily baseball, aired a big-league first-round playoff series and LCS, and debuted a July-September Sunday *Game of The Week* – hype less than TBS's, despite Ernie Johnson's excellent work as studio host. Simpson did 40 to 45 free Braves games for Peachtree TV and 105 paid for Fox Sports Net (FSN) South.[70] It was a stark change from the SuperStation entering your den nightly.

Easy and relaxed, Simpson practiced what Ronald Reagan said he had learned from airing Cubs radio in the 1930s: "You can have 15 facts and one story, and if the story is told well it's the story the audience recalls."[71] Such a one-size-fit-all style suited regional TV (Turner Field's 1997 debut, replacing Atlanta-Fulton County Stadium, and outside events at Atlanta's 2000 All-Star Game), national video (TBS's 2007 Colorado-San Diego playoff and 2007 and '09 Rockies-Phillies Division Series) and Atlanta's regular season, hopscotching via such variations as Peachtree TV, Turner South, FSN South, and Fox Sports Southeast.

In 2017, the Braves left Turner Field, afterthought to the 1996 Olympics, for a real baseball site, suburban SunTrust Park, nearer their season-ticket base. Execs hoped that it would swell team attendance and postseason buzz, using the franchise's two prior parks as a model for what to mimic and avoid. On January 27, 2018, Okie Joe was inducted into the Atlanta Braves Hall of Fame.[72] On August 8, 2018, the *Atlanta Journal-Constitution*'s Mark Bradley wrote, "As an emcee for official functions, inductee into the ... Braves Hall of Fame, and main TV commentator, in sum he's a big deal, the Braves' leading ambassador."[73]

By then, that status had become clouded – due to criticism, depending on your view, that was legitimate or hyperbolic. Bradley wrote that on July 28 Simpson had criticized the Dodgers for a minute and a half for "wearing T-shirts and pulled-up pants during practice at SunTrust Park," Braves TV showing the garb. "If I were a Dodger fan, I'd be embarrassed," Simpson said, "and I don't know how Major League Baseball allows such attire when the gates are open."[74] He called "an embarrassment what (LA's Chase Utley) had on" – a T-shirt reading "K Cancer," the Atlanta Voice not knowing it meant a charity begun by pitcher Jason Motte, briefly a Brave. Later Simpson privately spoke with Utley to explain.[75]

Ten days later, on August 7, Washington Nationals rookie Juan Soto batted in the first game of a doubleheader at Nationals Park. "If he's 19," Simpson said on-air, "he's certainly got his man's growth,"[76] implying that Soto must be older, as fellow Dominican Danny Almonte had been in 2001, throwing a perfect game for a New York team in the Little League World Series when he was two years too old.

After that fiasco and 9/11's trauma in 2001, foreign visas had become more tightly scrutinized. Even so, the Braves somehow failed to discern Rafael Furcal's real age – 21, not 19 as listed – embarrassing the team when his visa was uncovered before he reported to 2002 spring training.[77] This backdrop preceded Simpson needlessly, mistakenly, tarring Soto. Ken Rosenthal of The Athletic reported that between games of the 2018 twin bill Nats President Mike Rizzo approached the Braves announcer to set the record straight.[78]

In Game Two, Simpson thought he did, saying on-air, "If you were with us in Game One, you might have heard me make a comment off the top of my head about if [Soto is] 19. Well, he is. He's a bona fide 19."[79] It was not enough for those to whom the incident merged politics, age, and even alleged homerism. "The idea that Soto is lying about his age is one that's never been raised before," wrote *USA Today's* Jesse Yomtov, "and there's certainly a racial undertone behind Simpson's remark."[80] Jeff Passan of Yahoo Sports, via Twitter, assigned Joe to "the past, so it's not a surprise that he proffers this sort of garbage."[81] Absent was past context.

Suddenly, ideology seemed a prism for everything Simpson. Once, Milwaukee leading Atlanta at SunTrust, the broadcaster said, "The Braves are getting smoked, they just gave up another run, and the organist is playing songs for the [opposing] team, the guys walking up to the plate ... like everybody's holding hands and singing *Kumbaya*. I don't get it."[82] To Mark Bradley, it showed favoritism, the Atlanta columnist writing, "[Joe] rarely criticizes a Brave, while praise for an opponent seems offered through gritted teeth."[83] Was favoritism a legitimate gripe, or a guise to curb free speech?

That November, Fox Sports South and Fox Sports Southeast jointly announced Simpson's demotion as lead broadcast analyst on their regional networks. The *Atlanta Journal-Constitution*'s Tim Tucker said both would brook an extreme 2019 makeover – and as it happened, beyond. Former Braves first-round draft choice Jeff Francoeur replaced Simpson on each, working about 100 games.[84] Okie Joe shifted more to radio while still having a video presence, albeit reduced. Analyst and former Braves pitcher Tom Glavine upped his number of TV games, filling Simpson's void. Chip Caray remained on play-by-play.

According to Tucker, Simpson was surprised by the joint Braves-Fox decision. "I had proposed cutting back, but my proposal was a lot different than theirs," the broadcaster said. "I was suggesting maybe cutting back to the 120 TV games, hoping to fill in the rest with some radio. But they've cut me back to 20 or 30 TV games with the rest [about 100] being radio," working with Ben Ingram, Jim Powell, and past TV partner Sutton on a rotating basis, "so that came as a surprise."[85]

Team CEO Derek Schiller and Fox Sports South GM Jeff Genthner both insisted that Simpson's "controversial" statements over the past year had not factored into the decision. "Absolutely not," Genthner said. "To emphasize that point, we didn't reprimand Joe, didn't do anything to admonish him in any way."[86] Schiller called the demotion "just coincidence. Remember, he still is going to be a broadcaster for the Braves."[87] A *Journal-Constitution* headline best caught the mood: "Not What the Braves Had in Mind: Joe Simpson, Controversy Magnet."[88]

To Simpson, among others, such criticism missed his intent. "I have a very strong protective instinct on the game and its customs and history and traditions, so my comments [on Dodgers garb] were only intended as a defensive mechanism of the game," he said, noting the Braves "expect[ing] their players to be professional, look professional."[89] Simpson attributed his Soto misstep to a larger issue baseball had mishandled in the past. Read that way, his view was understandable. Others read it differently. Welcome to America today.

Either way, Okie Joe remains a Braves link to the grand troika of Ernie Sr., Skip, and Pete at a time when "America's Team" became baseball's TV linchpin to the land, especially the sprawling rural and small town. That sublime legacy is unlikely to be forgot.

Sources

Grateful appreciation is made to reprint all play-by-play and color radio text courtesy of John Miley's The Miley Collection. In addition to the sources cited in the Notes, most especially the Society for American Baseball Research, the author also consulted Baseball-Reference.com and Retrosheet.org websites for box scores, player, season, and team pages, batting, and pitching logs, and other material relevant to this history. FanGraphs.com provided statistical information. In addition to the sources cited in the Notes, the author also consulted:

Books

Koppett, Leonard. *Koppett's Concise History of Major League Baseball* (Philadelphia: Temple University, 2015).

Smith, Curt. *A Talk in the Park: Nine Decades of Baseball Tales from the Broadcast Booth.* (Washington: Potomac Books, 2012).

___. *Voices of The Game: The Acclaimed History of Baseball Radio and Television Broadcasting* (New York: Simon and Schuster, 1992).

Van Wieren, Pete, with Jack Wilkinson. *Of Mikes and Men: A Lifetime of Braves Baseball* (New York: Random House, 2010).

Whitaker, Lang. *In the Time of Bobby Cox: The Atlanta Braves, Their Manager, My Couch, Two Decades, and Me.* (New York: Scribner, 2011).

Newspapers

The *Atlanta Journal-Constitution* has been a primary source of information about Joe Simpson's career. The *Kansas City Intelligencer, Miami Herald, The Sporting News,* and *USA Today* also were extremely helpful. Other contemporary sources include Associated Press and Yahoo Sports.

Interviews

Ernie Johnson Sr., with author, May 1986 and August 2001.

Ronald Reagan, with author, March 1980.

Joe Simpson, with author, July 2011 and December 2019.

George Vecsey, with author, March 1986.

Pete Van Wieren, with author, March 2008.

Notes

1. stevetheump.com/themick.htm.
2. speakola.com/eulogy/for-micky-mantle-by-bob-costas-1995.
3. Joe Simpson interview with author, December 2019.
4. goodreads.com/author/quotes/1938.Friedrich_Nietzsche.
5. Material in this paragraph, *1975 Los Angeles Dodgers Media Guide.*
6. Simpson December 2019 interview.
7. Simpson July 2011 interview.
8. "Padre Pickups," *The Sporting News,*" December 30, 1978: 37.
9. Simpson December 2019 interview.
10. Carlos Salazar, "Simpson Swinging Torrid Bat in Bid to Join Dodgers," *The Sporting News,* July 16, 1977: 35.
11. Simpson December 2019 interview.
12. sabr.org/bioproj/person/54f3c5fa Joseph Wancho, "Boog Powell," Society for American Baseball Research.
13. Gordon Verrell, "It's Now or Never For Dodger Rookie Simpson," *The Sporting News,* March 24, 1979: 40.
14. Verrell, "It's Now or Never."
15. Verrell, "It's Now or Never."
16. Simpson July 2011 interview.
17. "Mariners Notes," *The Sporting News,* May 19, 1979: 15.
18. "A.L. Five-Hit Clubbers," *The Sporting News,* September 15, 1979: 28.
19. "A.L. Box Scores," *The Sporting News,* May 16, 1981: 20; Simpson September 2016 interview.
20. azquotes.com/author/14917-Bob_Uecker.
21. Simpson July 2011 interview.
22. stlyrics.com/lyrics/oklahoma/oklahoma.htm.
23. stlyrics.com/lyrics/oklahoma/oklahoma.htm – includes all paragraph quotations.
24. Simpson July 2011interview, includes all material in this paragraph.
25. Simpson July 2011 interview.
26. "M's Drop Simpson, Add Rookie Moses," *The Sporting News,* November 22, 1982: 41.
27. "M's Drop Simpson, Add Rookie Moses."
28. "M's Drop Simpson, Add Rookie Moses."
29. Mike McKenzie, "Royals' New Outfielder Treasures Old-Fangled Ballparks," *Kansas City Star,* March 11, 1983: 3C.
30. genius.com/Frank-sinatra-there-used-to-be-a-ballpark-right-here-lyrics.
31. Simpson December 2019 interview.
32. Simpson December 2019 interview.
33. Tracy Ringolsby, "Simpson Faces Adversity, but Buttons Up," *Kansas City Intelligencer,* March 2, 1984: D-1.
34. Ringolsby.
35. Ringolsby.
36. moviefone.com/movie/the-natural/1024701/main/.
37. Ringolsby.
38. Bill Syken, "The Poll Washingtonians Weigh In on Sports," *Sports Illustrated,* November 17, 2003. si.com/vault/2003/11/17/354065/the-poll-washingtonians-weigh-in-on-sports.
39. Simpson December 2019 interview.
40. thisgreatgame.com/ballparks-kingdome.html.
41. *Webster's New World College Dictionary,* Fourth Edition. (New York: Macmillan USA, 1999), 203.

42 Ernie Johnson Sr. interview, with author, May 1986.

43 Ernie Johnson Sr. interview, with author, May 1986.

44 George Vecsey interview, with author, March 1986.

45 "Turner Adds Simpson on Braves Show," *USA Today*, January 23, 1992.

46 "Turner Adds Simpson on Braves Show."

47 "Turner Adds Simpson on Braves Show."

48 "Turner Adds Simpson on Braves Show."

49 Play-by-play courtesy of The Miley Collection.

50 Pete Van Wieren interview, with author, March 2008.

51 Simpson December 2019 interview.

52 "Joe Simpson: Fox Sports South & Fox Sports Southeast. *2018 Atlanta Braves Media Guide,*" 471.

53 Play-by-play courtesy The Miley Collection.

54 Van Wieren March 2008 interview.

55 worldcat.org/title/official-major-league-baseball-fact-book. *Official Major League Baseball Fact Book 2001 Edition* (St. Louis: The Sporting News, 2001), 412.

56 mlb.com/news/braves-14-straight-titles-should-be-cheered-c237410912.

57 Carroll Rogers, "Braves Report: Announcers' Flight Ban Lifted," *AccessAtlanta!,* June 28, 2000.

58 Carroll Rogers.

59 Barry Jackson, "TBS Just Doesn't Sound the Game: Van Wieren, Caray Missed," *Miami Herald,* April 25, 2003.

60 Mike Tierney, "Simpson on the Upswing after Illness," *Atlanta Journal-Constitution.* March 28, 2004.

61 Tierney.

62 Tierney.

63 quoteinvestigator.com/2015/12/18/live.

64 Tim Tucker, "Turner South TV Crew Replaced," *Atlanta Journal-Constitution,* April 29, 2006. ajc.com.

65 Tucker, "Turner South TV Crew Replaced."

66 oklahoman.com/article/3134933/after-30-years-together-braves-tbs-parting-ways.

67 baseball-reference.com/boxes/HOU/HOU200709300.shtml.

68 Simpson December 2019 interview.

69 Simpson December 2019 interview.

70 Simpson December 2019 interview.

71 Ronald Reagan interview with author, March 1980.

72 foxsports.com/south/story/tim-hudson-joe-simpson-braves-hall-of-fame-010418. "Tim Hudson, Joe Simpson to Be Inducted into Braves Hall of Fame," FOXSPORTS.com., January 4, 2018.

73 ajc.com/blog/mark-bradley/not-what-the-braves-had-mind-joe-simpson-controversy-magnet/ZAZAGpQL5xBmjBPBdS6hCN/. Mark Bradley, "Not What the Braves Had in Mind: Joe Simpson, Controversy Magnet," *Atlanta Journal-Constitution*, August 8, 2018.

74 Bradley, "Not What the Braves Had in Mind."

75 Bradley, "Not What the Braves Had in Mind."

76 Bradley, "Not What the Braves Had in Mind."

77 washingtonpost.com/archive/sports/2002/03/02/an-age-old-numbers-game/ee4cc261-9ea5-4ce9-8b63-30a909ec4524/.

78 sportingnews.com/ca/mlb/news/juan-soto-age-joe-simpson-video-nationals-braves-fox-sports-south-southeast/1ktowpz7zrtkh1fcd5fdv95z2q. Tom Gatto, "Joe Simpson Wonders Whether Nats' Juan Sato Telling Truth about Age," *The Sporting News*, August 7, 2018.

79 Gatto.

80 usatoday.com/story/sports/mlb/2018/08/07/juan-soto-joe-simpson-age/930668002/. Jesse Yomtow, "Braves Announcer Joe Simpson Backtracks After Suggesting Juan Soto Is Lying about Age.," *USA Today,* August 8, 2018.

81 awfulannouncing.com/mlb/braves-analyst-joe-simpson-creates-even-more-controversy-with-age-related-comments-about-nationals-star-juan-soto.html. Matt Yoder, "Braves Analyst Joe Simpson Creates Even More Controversy with Age-Related Comments about Nationals Star Juan Soto," *Awful Announcing,* August 8, 2018.

82 Bradley, "Braves Analyst Joe Simpson."

83 Bradley, "Braves Analyst Joe Simpson."

84 ajc.com/sports/ajc-exclusive-changes-coming-braves-broadcast-team/6Fcr7e7lIYrlMKnE21J8iI/?ecmp=braves. Tim Tucker, "Exclusive: Changes Coming to Braves' Broadcast Team: Francoeur Becomes Lead TV Analyst; Simpson Moved Mostly to Radio," *Atlanta Journal-Constitution,* November 29, 2018.

85 Tucker, "Exclusive: Changes Coming to Braves' Broadcast Team."

86 Tucker, "Exclusive: Changes Coming to Braves' Broadcast Team."

87 Tucker, "Exclusive: Changes Coming to Braves' Broadcast Team."

88 Bradley.

89 Tucker, "Exclusive: Changes Coming to Braves' Broadcast Team."

Don Sutton

BY GREGORY H. WOLF

Don Sutton

"I never wanted to be a superstar, or the highest paid player," said Don Sutton. "[A]ll I wanted was to be appreciated for the fact that I was consistent, dependable, and you could count on me."[1] By that measure, Sutton achieved his goal and more, as few pitchers in baseball history were as reliable, and as healthy, for as long as the right-hander. During his 23-year major-league career (1966-1988), Sutton logged as least 200 innings in 20 of his first 21 seasons, a remarkable stretch interrupted only by the strike-shortened campaign of 1981; and fanned at least 100 batters in 21 straight seasons, a feat subsequently duplicated only by Nolan Ryan, Greg Maddux, and Roger Clemens. As of 2019 Sutton ranked tied for 14th in victories (324), 10th in shutouts (58), seventh in innings pitched (5,282⅓) and strikeouts (3,574), and third in games started (756) in major-league history; and given the trends in baseball, his positions seem permanently fixed. Despite those gaudy "counting statistics" that deservedly secured his enshrinement in the Hall of Fame, Sutton wasn't flashy or overpowering and was rarely mentioned among the best pitchers of his era. He received votes for the Cy Young Award in only five separate seasons, all of which came during a five-year period (1972-1976), when he finished in the top five in the NL; and he won 20 or more games in a season just once. Sutton never put together a career-defining season with eye-popping statistics, like his contemporaries – from Sandy Koufax, Tom Seaver, and Bob Gibson, to Jim Palmer, Gaylord Perry, and Ryan – and never authored a no-hitter. More than anything, Sutton was a relentless, fierce, yet enigmatic competitor; to his detractors, he was a compiler and more concerned for himself than his team. "Baseball was a job for me," said the hurler bluntly. "It was not an emotional experience. It was a job that I wanted to keep getting better and better at."[2]

Donald Howard Sutton was born on April 2, 1945, in Clio, Alabama, a small rural farming community in Barbour County in the southeastern part of the state. His parents, Charlie Howard and Lillian (McKnight) Sutton, were just 18 and 15 years old respectively at the time of Don's birth, and subsequently welcomed two more children into the world, Ron and Glenda.[3] The elder Sutton was a sharecropper and eventually relocated his family around 1950 to Molino, in the Florida panhandle, about 25 miles north of Pensacola, where he also worked seasonally in construction. During his baseball career, Don often cited his parents as role models, and it's easy to understand why. They instilled in him uncompromising determination, an unyielding work ethic, and a devout religious conviction, qualities that defined his professional baseball career, too. Despite his grade-school education, Howard Sutton was self-made man, eventually received his high-school equivalency degree in his 40s, and became a concrete specialist. The Suttons were strict Evangelical Christians who expected their children to follow a righteous a path, but also pull their weight by holding down part-time jobs and earning money for their clothes and spending money.

"All I ever wanted to be was a pitcher growing up," said Sutton. "If you asked me where I wanted to play, I'd have said in the middle of the diamond. Whose diamond, I don't care."[4] Those words characterized Sutton's approach to baseball from the time he started playing in pastures and local sandlots to Little League through 24 years of professional baseball. Pitching was always more important for Sutton than the team whose jersey he wore. Abandoning any pretense of playing other positions by the age of 11 to concentrate exclusively on pitching, Sutton fell under the tutelage of his sixth-grade teacher, Henry Roper, who had hurled in the New York Giants organization. Roper taught the pre-teen Sutton how to throw a curveball and tutored him in the basics of mechanics and delivery. "I learned to throw a curve by raising my index finger," remembered Sutton, "and digging the tip into the ball."[5]

Sutton played football, basketball, and baseball at Tate High School, but vacated the hardwood and gridiron after his sophomore year to focus on pitching. Growing up more than 700 miles from the nearest big-league city (St. Louis), Sutton was a self-described New York Yankees fan, who devoured games on his transistor radio. He idolized three pitchers, Dick Donovan for his intensity, Camilo Pascual for his knee-buckling curve, and Whitey Ford for his strategy.[6] Modeling his game on his trio of heroes, the 6-foot-1, yet lanky and thin Sutton posted a 21-7 slate in his three varsity seasons at Tate.[7] In his junior year (1962), he led the Aggies to the Class A state championship, tossing a 13-inning complete-game two-hitter with 11 strikeouts to defeat West Palm Beach Forest Hill in the finals.[8]

Disappointed that he received no professional offers despite his prep success, Sutton pursued his passion. Following graduation in 1963, he was a Connie Mack all-star, and then enrolled at Gulf Coast Community College in Panama City, Florida.[9] That spring he posted a 5-4 slate while fanning 130 in 90 innings, earning an invitation to play for Sioux Falls in the highly competitive, amateur Basin League, which featured some of the best collegiate players in the country.[10] Even more important than his 5-5 record and 118 punchouts in 90 frames was the national exposure Sutton achieved. His summer baseball season concluded with his participation with the Wyoming (Michigan) Colts in the National Baseball Congress Tournament in Wichita, Kansas. Sutton (3-1) was named to the all-tournament team, which also included Seaver, star of the champion Alaska Panhandlers.

By the end of the summer, Sutton had a major decision to make. His bona fides established, Sutton had attracted scouts from at least nine major-league teams. He was especially impressed with Los Angeles Dodger scouts Leon Hamilton, Monty Basgall, and Burt Wells, their honesty and humble attitudes, and the club's long and distinguished tradition of grooming top-notch hurlers. They also informed Sutton that the baseball's inaugural amateur draft would take place the following year, and that he might be able to assert more control over the financial aspects of his signing if he returned to school for another year. In the end the choice was an easy one: Sutton eschewed higher offers and signed with the Dodgers for an estimated $15,000 bonus and stipends for college, in September 1964.[11]

Sutton reported to the Dodgers' minor-league spring camp in Vero Beach, Florida, in spring 1965. Just 19 years old, he quickly emerged as the best prospect in the Dodgers system, eventually packing on some weight to 185. He debuted with Santa Barbara in the Class-A California League, retiring 19 of the first 20 batters he faced in his first game, en route to a complete-game five-hit victory.[12] Two months later, he was the circuit's top twirler (8-1, 1.50), and earned a bump to Albuquerque in the Double-A Texas League. Another auspicious debut, a complete-game, eight-inning three-hitter with 13 strikeouts in the first game of a doubleheader, led to a 15-6 record, culminating with the league championship. Sutton recalled that his first year in pro ball introduced him to two skippers who profoundly impacted his career: his first manager, former Dodgers catcher Norm Sherry, who helped him relax and enjoy the game, and Roy Hartsfield, a stern tactician and student of the game.

Sutton reported to skipper Walter Alston and his first spring training with the Dodgers in 1966. Coming off a dramatic World Series title in seven games over the Minnesota Twins, the club was without Koufax and Don Drysdale, both of whom were holding out. Sutton assumed he'd be demoted once the aces reported [which they did in mid-March] and got into game shape; however, he quickly proved he was big-league-ready. He tossed seven innings of seven-hit ball, yielding three runs, but just two earned and fanned seven in his debut, a 4-2 loss to the Houston Astros on April 14 in Los Angeles. Four days later, he avenged that loss, holding the Astros to three runs in eight frames to notch his first victory, 6-3, in the Astrodome. On May 11 he blanked the Philadelphia Phillies in Connie Mack Stadium to record his first shutout, drawing raves from Phillies star Johnny Callison, who called him the best rookie since Juan Marichal.[13] Dodgers VP Fresco Thompson praised Sutton for his "great natural talent" and his calm demeanor, noting that the rookie was "completely composed, both on and off the diamond."[14] With the Dodgers in a tight three-team pennant race with the Pittsburgh Pirates and San Francisco Giants, "Little D" (as the LA press liked to call Sutton in a nod to Big D Drysdale) pulled a muscle in his right forearm on September 5, endangering the team's pennant aspirations.[15] Plagued by arm pain, Sutton made only four more starts, logging just 14⅓ innings, for the rest of the season, but the Dodgers picked up the slack, moved into first place on September 11 and secured the pennant on the last day of the season. The Dodgers were swept by the Baltimore Orioles in the World Series. Sutton did not play because of his injury, which also prevented him from joining the club on its subsequent goodwill junket and baseball trip to Japan.[16] Despite the injury, the 21-year-old's rookie season was a resounding success. He split his 24 decisions, posted a 2.99 ERA in 225⅔ innings, and fanned 209, seventh most in the NL; however, his excellent control, walking just 52, garnered the most praise from players and coaches.

Noted for his command, Sutton's pitching arsenal consisted of five pitches. He initially relied early in his career on his fastball with good movement and a curve, one of baseball's best benders, which he threw on any count. He eventually added a slider, screwball, and a changeup that improved as he matured. He threw all the pitches with the same delivery and motion, like a fastball, varying only the grip for each pitch, which he hid effectively behind his hip.[17] "My pitching philosophy didn't change from the time I was a kid," quipped Sutton. "I believed in changing speeds, throwing strikes and throwing a curveball for a strike when behind in the count."[18] Never overpowering, despite striking out at least 200 batters in a season five times in his first eight campaigns, Sutton relied on technique, precision, strategy, and his pinpoint accuracy for his success. He challenged hitters up in the strike zone and was prone to the gopher ball, but kept batters guessing. "He emits an air of professionalism," said Burt Hooton about his Dodgers teammate (1975-1980). "He is the same whether he getting his tail kicked or tearing up the joint."[19] Opponents routinely claimed Sutton doctored pitches, scuffing them, which led to umpires checking him for sandpaper or other defilers, though nothing was ever found. Like Gaylord Perry, noted for his occasional wet one, Sutton exploited the opponents' charges of cheating, effectively creating a phantom pitch for them to worry about.

Sutton's progress over the next four seasons (1967-1970) was sporadic as the Dodgers organization underwent changes, including Koufax's retirement after the 1966 season, the end of GM Buzzie Bavasi's era (1950-1968), and the beginning of Al Campanis's tenure. The offensively-challenged Dodgers dropped to 73-89 in 1967, their worst season since 1944, then 76-86 in 1968, marking the first time the club had posted consecutive losing seasons since 1933-1938. Like his team, Sutton slumped; his ERA spiked to 3.95 (fourth highest in the NL) in his sophomore season. The front office entertained ideas of trading the hurler for a much-needed bat in the offseason, which Sutton spent fulfilling military obligation in the US Army Reserve, serving as a private at Fort Gordon, Georgia.[20] Discharged in mid-March, Sutton reported to camp late, struggled, and began the season with Triple-A Spokane (Pacific Coast League) to get in shape. In the "Year of the Pitcher," when the NL batted a collective .243 and teams scored just 3.43 runs per game, Sutton started off slowly and was ultimately demoted to the bullpen after a second consecutive sluggish start, on June 20. Perhaps feeling more empowered in his third season, Sutton was livid, and displayed the sharp tongue that would characterize his career, barking, "Because I'm owned by this team, I'll have to do what I am told or I'm out of baseball."[21] Sutton was too good to rust in the pen, though, and after a five-week exile, returned to the rotation in late July and put together a strong stretch over the final two months of the season (7-7, 2.06 ERA in 109 innings) to finish with his second consecutive 11-15 record, and a 2.60 ERA.

Shortly after the conclusion of the 1968 season, Sutton married Patti, a local Southern Californian whom he had met the previous year.[22] They had two sons, Daron, born in 1969, and Staci, four years later.

The Dodgers entered a new phase of prolonged success beginning in 1969 when major-league baseball expanded to 24 teams, finishing with an 85-77 slate and in fourth place in the newly formed NL West in the first season of realignment. On a staff featuring 20-game winners Claude Osteen and Bill Singer, Sutton was often overlooked. On May 1 he tossed the first of his five career one-hitters, yielding only a one-out eighth-inning double to Jim Davenport to beat the Giants at Candlestick Park, as part of his streak of 27⅓ consecutive scoreless innings, the second longest in the NL that season.[23] Sutton compiled what proved to be his career highs in starts (41) and innings (293⅓), yet produced a losing record for the third straight season (17-18) and an ERA (3.47), when adjusted to consider ballpark factors, was higher than league average.[24] In 1970 the Dodgers finished in a distant second place behind the Big Red Machine of Cincinnati, while Sutton fashioned another similar season, including a worse than league-average adjusted ERA. The highlight of his 15 victories was a stellar 10-inning, five-hit shutout with a career-best 12 punchouts (achieved six times) on July 17 at Dodger Stadium against the New York Mets and Seaver, who hurled nine scoreless on two days' rest after having started and hurled three scoreless innings in the All-Star Game.

After five seasons in the majors, Sutton proved to be a dependable workhorse, logging more innings than any NL hurler except bluebloods Fergie Jenkins, Gibson, Marichal, Perry, and teammate Osteen, yet the Alabaman was far from a star. Sutton had a losing record (66-73) and his ERA (3.45) when adjusted was worse than league average.[25] All of that changed beginning in 1971, when Sutton put together the first of seven consecutive stellar seasons, which coincided with the Dodgers' re-emergence as one of the NL's perennially top teams.

In 1971 the Dodgers engaged the Giants in an exciting pennant race that heated up in September, when Sutton emerged as an ace. However, he had started off the season poorly, and fell to 1-5 (with a 4.60 ERA) on May 22, dropping his career slate to 67-78. Dejected, suffering a crisis of confidence, and plagued by a sore elbow, he consulted an orthopedic doctor, but perhaps more importantly worked with pitching coach Red Adams to refine his mechanics. He switched to a more over-the-top delivery, rather from the three-quarters position, which put stress on his elbow.[26] That change led to Sutton's best season thus far (17-12 and the NL's fifth-lowest ERA, 2.54), highlighted by going 5-1 in his seven starts in September, fanning 57 in 57 innings, walking just seven while posting a 1.74 ERA. With the Dodgers needing a victory and a Giants loss on the last day of the season to force a playoff, Sutton got the start and displayed his humor when he arrived at the park on September 30 with his hand wrapped in gauze, informing teammates and coaches that he had had an accident cooking.[27] The 52,684 in Dodgers Stadium sat quietly as Sutton tossed a six-hitter to beat the Astros, 2-1, emitting their loudest groan in the eighth when it was announced the Marichal and the Giants defeated the hapless San Diego Padres, 5-1.

The 27-year-old Sutton considered 1972 his "best" and "most consistent year," helping the Dodgers to the NL's best team ERA (2.78), but that couldn't overcome a sluggish offense, resulting in a distant second-place finish to the Reds.[28] Named Opening Day starter for the first of seven consecutive seasons, Sutton began his seventh big-league season by winning his first eight decisions, extending his winning streak to 11 games. Included was a stretch of 30⅔ consecutive scoreless innings, 10 of which resulted in a tough-luck no-decision against the Expos in Montreal despite yielding only one hit. He was named to his first All-Star squad, tossing two scoreless frames and fanning two in the NL's 4-3 win in 10 innings. He concluded the season with a sense of déjà vu, winning his last five decisions in September, highlighted by three consecutive shutouts as part of a career-best streak of 36 consecutive scoreless innings, the longest such streak in the NL that season. The second of those whitewashings, an 11-inning three-hitter with 11 punchouts against the Giants at Dodgers Stadium on September 22, was the 100th victory of his career. Arguably the best game of his career, too, it was his career-longest pitching outing, subsequently matched twice, though both resulted in no-decisions. Despite missing several starts due to the first players strike in baseball history, from April 1 to 13, canceling 86 games, Sutton finished with a 19-9 slate, set career highs in complete games (18) and an NL-leading nine shutouts (which as of 2019 was still the Dodgers record for right-handers). He also led the NL in WHIP (0.913) for the first of four times in his career and fewest hits per nine innings (6.1), and finished tied with four others for fifth place in the Cy Young Award which the Phillies Steve Carlton (27 wins) won by garnering all 24 first-place votes.

Sutton posted similar numbers in 1973 (18-10, 2.42 ERA), but the Dodgers finished in second place for the fourth consecutive season. The tide turned in 1974, by which time a cadre of prospects from the club's deep farm system, such as infielders Steve Garvey (who was named NL MVP in '74), Davey Lopes, Bill Russell, and Ron Cey, had gained much-needed experience on the big-league level. Added to the mix were two offseason acquisitions, Jimmy Wynn (32 HRs, 108 RBIs) and rubber-armed, enigmatic reliever Mike Marshall (who set a big-league record by hurling in 106 games and won the Cy Young Award); as well as hard thrower Andy Messersmith (staff-best 20 wins), acquired from the California Angels two years earlier. Sutton got off to a hot start, pitched a shutout on Opening Day and then added two consecutive blankings, including a one-hitter, to improve his record to 6-2 on May 14, before the bottom suddenly and completely unexpectedly fell out.

Sutton fell into a deep slump, going more than two months without winning a start and posting a miserable 5.64 ERA in 14 starts from May 19 through July 20. Remarkably, the Dodgers maintained their first-place standing. Critics claimed the 29-year-old was suddenly washed up, had lost his heater (which was never overwhelming to begin with, topping out at 88 or 89 MPH, according to Sutton[29]); or was tipping his pitches; or maybe hiding an injury. Through it all, Smoky Alston stuck with his longtime hurler. In the era before teams employed mental skills coaches and psychologists, Sutton recognized that baseball was much more than a clash of talents. "[M]ost of us have similar abilities," he said. "The differences are mental and emotional and the big thing is mental preparation. That's where everything starts: the poise, the confidence, the concentration."[30] Sutton also believed his struggles resulted from his mental situation, and not from what his detractors charged. Willing to try anything to end his slump, Sutton contacted LA hypnotist Arthur Ellen, who had helped former teammate Maury Wills, in late June. "I only saw him once," said Sutton, who also revealed his initial skepticism because of his Christian Fundamentalist beliefs. "[B]ut after that I knew I could have a good time doing my job. ... I credit Ellen for giving me back my ability to relax and pitch to my potential."[31] Sutton's slump didn't magically end after the first visit, but when it did, he transformed into one of baseball's best hurlers, going 13-1 with a 2.17 ERA in his last 17 starts. The Dodgers withstood a serious challenge from the Reds in September and took their first NL West crown, in the 161st game of the season, on October 1 in Houston. Fittingly Sutton started the game and hurled five shutout innings before yielding to relievers, to pick up his 19th victory of the season in the NL-most 40th start and secure the Dodgers' first postseason berth since his rookie campaign nine years earlier.

With the best record in baseball (102-60), the Dodgers were overwhelming favorites against the Pirates (88-74) in the NLCS. In Game One in the Steel City, Sutton shut out the Bucs on four hits, fanning six. Longtime LA sportswriter Jim Murray called it a "masterpiece," adding that Sutton is the "most underrated pitcher in the league."[32] Four days later, in Tinsel Town, Sutton stamped the Dodgers ticket to the fall classic by a performance almost as good as his first, holding the Pirates to three hits in eight innings to pick up the win in a 12-1 laugher. Widely predicted to capture their first title since 1965, the Dodgers met their match against the rough-and-tumble Oakland A's, in search of their third straight World Series championship. Sutton yielded just five hits in eight strong innings to win Game Two, 3-2, in LA, to even the Series, but that victory proved to be the Dodgers only one against their postseason-experienced adversaries. The A's took the next three, including Game Five, which Sutton started. (He was removed for a pinch-hitter in the sixth, with the Dodgers trailing 2-0.)

The Dodgers' hold on the NL West crown was short-lived as the Big Red Machine ran roughshod over the entire league in 1975 and 1976 to capture consecutive pennants and then became the first NL team to win consecutive World Series since the New York Giants in 1921-1922. Donning what became his signature man-permed, curly hair, Sutton produced a typical Suttonesque season, going 16-13 in '75, leading the NL in WHIP and strikeout-to-walk ratio for the first of three times in his career; he also hurled two scoreless innings in the All-Star Game. In 1976 he won 21 games (3.06 ERA), which included the most dominant stretch in his big-league career, going 14-1 with a 1.62 ERA from July 7 to September 27. He finished a distant third in voting for the Cy Young Award, behind winner Randy Jones (22-14, 2.74) of the Padres and the Mets' Jerry Koosman (21-10, 2.69). With two games remaining in the '76 season, 64-year-old Alston, feeling pressure from the front office, retired, ending his 23-year tenure as the Dodgers' skipper.

Alston's retirement marked a turning point in Sutton's career, and especially with his relationship with the Dodgers. "Alston was the most secure, best man that I have ever met," said Sutton, who appreciated how his skipper confronted problems behind closed doors instead of airing dirty laundry to the press.[33] Furthermore, Alston's quiet demeanor mirrored Sutton's own introverted personality in some respects, and they formed a mutual trust, indeed respect, for one another.

Sutton was unimpressed when longtime Dodgers coach and scout Tommy Lasorda, who had served as interim skipper for the final two games of the '76 season, was named permanent skipper in 1977. According to Ron Fimrite's feature on Sutton in *Sports Illustrated* in 1982, Sutton mentioned to reporters that spring that he had wanted his former catcher Jeff Torborg as the club's new manager, but knew it had been a foregone conclusion that Lasorda would land that job. The Dodgers' senior member, Sutton was "not an ally" of the new manager, and disdained his "showbiz approach."[34] Lasorda's rah-rah style clashed mightily with Sutton's staid, conservative, indeed introverted approach. The stage was set for some explosives in La-La Land, and Sutton was well beyond the point in his career that he would back down. Years after retiring, Sutton reflected on his relationship with Lasorda, and commented, "One regret I have is that Tommy and I never took a day, just the two of us, and sat down and explained our personalities to each other."[35]

Sutton had a complex personality, to say the least. "Don's the kind of guy you either like or you don't," quipped longtime Dodgers teammate Bill Russell.[36] Reserved with his emotions, Sutton could be icy, blunt, and matter-of-fact with his criticism of teammates. "I am much more comfortable dealing internally with ideas than I am externally with people," said Sutton, who gave the impression of being aloof, disinterested, stubborn, impatient, or cocky; some players objected to his religious convictions, leading to a standoffish attitude.[37] "I don't know that anybody here [with the Dodgers] was ever that close to Don," said Ron Cey.[38] Fimrite might have captured the intricacies and apparent contradictions of Sutton's personality best, opining that the hurler "masks his seriousness about life and obsession with perfection with a blithe manner that the uninitiated might confuse with flippancy. He protects the vulnerable underside of his nature with the quickest wit in baseball."[39] On the other hand, Sutton never forgot his Alabama roots, poor upbringing, or religious grounding, referring to himself as "nothing more than a semipolished hick."[40] His brutal honesty and willingness to speak his mind led occasionally to combustible confrontations in a clubhouse filled with highly competitive, yet easily insulted athletes.

Lasorda led the Dodgers to consecutive NL pennants in 1977 and 1978, losing to the New York Yankees in the World Series each season. Sutton put up similar numbers in both campaigns, going 14-8 and 15-11 and logging about 240 innings; however, the tone of the seasons was drastically different. In the former, Sutton blazed through the first half of the season and was chosen to start his first All-Star Game. The 32-year-old tossed three scoreless innings and earned the victory in the NL's 7-5 triumph at Yankee Stadium. It was his last of four All-Star appearances, during which he yielded just five hits and no runs in eight frames. The Dodgers featured big bats with a quartet of sluggers with at least 30 home runs (Dusty Baker, Cey, Garvey, and Reggie Smith) and the majors' best pitching staff, which led the baseball with a 3.22 team ERA, behind five starters who logged at least 212 innings (Sutton, Hooton, Tommy John, Rick Rhoden, and Doug Rau). After John, who led the staff with 20 wins, was hit hard in the opening-game loss to the Phillies in the NLCS, Sutton came to the rescue in Game Two, tossing a complete-game 7-1 victory. Lasorda took no chances in the highly anticipated World Series with the Yankees, sending the club's longtime stalwart to the mound in Game One in Yankee Stadium. Sutton fulfilled a lifelong dream of pitching in the "House that Ruth Built" in the fall classic, but wasn't overcome with emotions. "I approach play with more emotion than I do work," he quipped. I approach work analytically and logistically, not emotionally. It's a day at the office."[41] Sutton went seven strong innings and was relieved in the top of the eighth after yielding the go-ahead run, 3-2. The Dodgers tied the game in the ninth before losing in the 12th. Called on again in Game Five with the Bombers on the verge of their first title since 1962, Sutton calmly dispatched the Yankees, 10-4, tossing a complete game to win his fifth consecutive postseason decision. The next day, however, Reggie Jackson spanked home runs on three consecutive pitches, and Yankees were back on the top of the baseball world.

Lasorda wanted the Dodgers to project his cheerleader disposition and Hollywood feel-good family vibes, but Sutton never bled Dodger blue. "I never considered the Dodgers family," he quipped in businesslike fashion. "I only have one family."[42] Behind the Dodgers' façade, animosity was stirring, especially between the skipper and Sutton, who Lasorda apparently felt never was in his corner, but also between some of the players. And it wasn't in Sutton's DNA to placate his teammates. The situation came to a head when Sutton was interviewed by sportswriter Thomas Boswell of the *Washington Post*. The hurler expressed his frustration that the baseball world seemed infatuated with "Steve Garvey, the All-American boy"; and bluntly called Smith the club's best player the last two years, noting that he doesn't get the attention because he doesn't "smile all the time" and tells the truth, much like Sutton himself, which alienated people.[43] Garvey confronted Sutton in front of his locker before a game at Shea Stadium in New York on August 20 and a brawl ensued. Sportswriter Milton Richman described it as "concentrated fury amounting to an almost homicidal desire to tear one another apart."[44] Players and coaches finally separated the two who emerged with scratches on their face and a red eye for Garvey, the result on a finger poke.[45] That ugly episode aside, the Dodgers weren't belting each other like the early 1970s A's or even the champion Yankees. The Dodgers continued to roll, and once again led the NL in home runs and lowest team ERA in 1978. Their postseason results repeated the script from the previous year: They defeated the Phillies in four games in the NLCS and lost to the Yankees in six in the World Series. One major difference was Sutton, who was clobbered in all three of his postseason starts. Charged with the loss in each, he surrendered 17 runs (14 earned) and 24 hits in 17⅔ innings.

Over the next two seasons Sutton chipped away at Dodgers pitching records as the club slumped to a sub-.500-seaon in 1979 and then squandered a September lead to finish runner-up to the Houston Astros in 1980. En route to a 12-15 slate in '79, Sutton labored through eight innings, yielding nine hits and four runs (three earned) against the Reds at Riverfront Stadium on May 20 to record his 210th victory, thus breaking Drysdale's cherished mark. The following season, the 35-year-old pitched his best and most consistent ball in five years, posting a 13-5 slate, leading the majors in ERA (2.20) and WHIP (0.989), and ranking second in the NL by allowing just 6.9 hits per nine innings.

Granted free agency after the 1980 season, Sutton signed a four-year pact with the Astros. "It was kind of exciting," he said about the challenge of a new team. "I think I reached a stage with the Dodgers where they really didn't appreciate what I was delivering for them, and I didn't appreciate how nice it was to play there."[46] Sutton left his mark on the Dodgers, setting team records for wins (233), starts (533), innings pitched (3,816⅓), strikeouts (2,696), and shutouts (52), all of which still stood as of 2019.

After 15 years of stability in Dodger blue, Sutton was often on the move in his last eight seasons (1981-1988), playing for four different teams, plus the Dodgers again, and was involved in two late-season trades to clubs needing an extra arm for a postseason push. Sutton's stint with the Astros lasted less than two full seasons, yet they were packed with drama – and not the positive kind. A strike by the players and their union led to the first work stoppage in baseball since 1972 and wiped out approximately one-third of the season. Teaming with another graybeard, Nolan Ryan, Sutton (11-9) fortified baseball's best staff, and led the NL once again in WHIP (1.015). With the Astros just a victory away from clinching the second-half championship (as part of a convoluted attempt to generate interest and extend the postseason), Sutton was hit on the right knee by a pitch from the Dodgers Jerry Reuss at Dodger Stadium on October 2.[47] The result was a fracture and Sutton missed the Division Series, which the Astros lost to the Dodgers.

In the offseason, Sutton gave an interview to longtime *Los Angeles Times* sportswriter Ross Newhan that turned himself into a persona non grata in Houston.[48] Sutton recounted a conversation with Astros GM Al Rosen, expressing his desire to finish his career on the West Coast in order to be with his family, who remained in the LA area, and business interests, and had no desire to live in Texas, though he didn't consider his signing to be a mistake. Once Houston papers picked up the story, Sutton and Rosen, who had prematurely ended his career to spend more time with his family, began verbally sparring, with Sutton apparently going so far as to suggest that he would return a signing bonus in order to be freed from his contract.[49] Sutton was booed loudly by Astros fan in his first start of the season, but the catcalls about a spoiled millionaire soon morphed into cheers when Sutton rolled off seven straight victories after losing his season debut. Sutton (13-8, 3.00 ERA) was back in form, but the Astros struggled, playing under .500 ball. In a salary dump at the trading deadline, the Astros sent the 37-year-old to the Milwaukee Brewers on August 30 for Kevin Bass, Frank DiPino, and Mike Madden.

Landing in the middle of an exciting divisional race, the old graybeard immediately shored up the Brewers' pitching corps, which had been led by Pete Vuckovich and Mike Caldwell, but was without reigning AL Cy Young Award and MVP winner Rollie Fingers, out with an arm injury. The Brewers were a raucous, home-run-smashing team, tabbed Harvey's Wallbangers in honor of skipper Harvey Kuenn, and featured eventual AL 1982 MVP Robin Yount, Cecil Cooper, Gorman Thomas, Ben Oglivie, and Paul Molitor. Sutton went the distance in his first start, losing 4-2 to the Cleveland Indians in the second game of a twin bill on September 2 at County Stadium, then blanked the Detroit Tigers on seven hits for his first AL victory five days later. The outcome of the division crown rested on the last series of the season, with the second-place Orioles in Baltimore. The Brewers lost the first three games, outscored 26-7, creating a tie in the standings and setting up a winner-take-all finale on October 3. In the most important regular-season game of his life, Sutton was at his best, tossing eight strong innings, yielding just two runs, as the Wallbangers bashed their way to a 10-2 victory and the West crown.

The Brewers' struggles returned in the ALCS against the California Angels, who took the first two games of the best-of-five series in the Southern California sun. In another win-or-go-home game, Sutton went 7⅔ innings, yielding all three of his runs in the eighth, but emerged victorious, 5-3, in a courageous outing. "We were shut down for seven innings by one of the cleverest pitchers of the last 15 years," quipped Angels skipper Gene Mauch. "He's capable of taking the straight out of the ball without defacing it. Our players didn't say a word about it. They know what the man is capable of doing with finger dexterity."[50] Reggie Jackson, who faced Sutton in the 1977 and 1978 World Series, agreed. "I've never seen him better. He had control of four pitches. He beat me fair and square. I didn't have one good swing."[51]

The 1982 World Series featured a clash of styles: The Brewers' long ball vs. the St. Louis Cardinals' speed and small ball. In a back-and-forth Series, with plenty of unexpected twists, Sutton fared poorly in both of his starts, both of which took place in the Gateway City, yielding a combined 12 hits and 11 runs (9 earned) in just 10⅓ innings, picking up the loss in Game Six. The Redbirds won the final two contests of the Series to capture their first title since 1967.

In his two full seasons with the Brewers, Sutton went 22-25 while the Brewers finished in fifth and then the cellar of the AL West. Nonetheless Sutton had fond memories and experiences of Beer City, perhaps feeling at home in a gritty, battle-tested, and workmanlike town that reminded him of his own personality. "Milwaukee was the greatest place I ever played," he cooed, praising the locals as sincere, genuine, and authentic. "It's a blue-collar lifestyle and work ethic that is very simple. There's no pretentiousness. I loved pitching in County Stadium."[52]

In December 1984 Sutton was traded to the Oakland A's in a multiplayer transaction. Just 20 victories shy of 300 to begin his 19th season, the 40-year-old proved to be the staff's most effective hurler, notching 13 victories before the A's sent him in a post-trade-deadline waiver deal to the Angels, who were battling the Kansas City Royals for the West crown. Sutton won his first two starts for the Halos, who eventually faded down the stretch, losing eight of their final 13 to finish runner-up to the Royals by one game.

In a quest for what he considered his "inevitable" 300th victory, Sutton began the 1986 campaign with the Angels so poorly that many skeptics wondered if he could win five more games.[53] He lost his first three decisions and posted a staggering 9.12 ERA in his first five starts before winning a game. Number 299 came in dramatic fashion on June 9 when he faced 306-game winner Tom Seaver of the Chicago White Sox and emerged victorious, spinning a two-hitter at Comiskey Park to record what proved to be the final shutout of his career. Nine days later, in front of more than 37,000 raucous fans at the Big A, Anaheim Stadium, the self-described "mechanic" and "unspectacular grinder" became the 19th pitcher in major-league history to win 300 games. Praising Sutton as a "working class hero," L.A. sportswriter Mike Penner wrote that the right-hander "did it his way, shunning the bright lights and sticking to a nose-to-the-grindstone work ethic," in a performance that mirrored the pitcher's personality: a distance-going three-hit, 5-1 win. Yet another historic matchup occurred 10 days later in Anaheim, when Sutton faced a 304-game winner, knuckleballer Phil Niekro of the Indians. The matchup marked the first time 300-game winners had faced one another since Tim Keefe and Pud Galvin on July 21, 1892. Fittingly, Sutton and Niekro pitched to a draw, saddled with no-decisions, though the Alabaman won the statistics contest, going seven strong innings and yielding three runs, while a wild Niekro logged a wobbly 6⅓ innings, also surrendering three runs, but 10 hits and seven walks. Sutton finished his fairy-tale-like season with a 15-11 slate while the Angels cruised to the West title. In the ALCS against the highly favored Boston Red Sox, Sutton got the call in Game Four, dueling eventual 1986 Cy Young Award winner Roger Clemens to a draw, throwing four-hit, one-run ball over 6⅓ innings in an Angels victory in 11 innings in Anaheim. Sutton's second appearance of the series was in Game Seven, in Boston, when he relieved John Candelaria in the fourth, trailing 7-0, tossing 3⅓ innings of mop-up duty, yielding one run.

After a rough season with the Angels in 1987 (11-11, 4.70 ERA) and missing the 200-inning mark for the first time in his career (191⅔) excluding the strike-shortened season, Sutton came full circle in 1988, signing with the Dodgers for his 23rd season. It was obvious that the 43-year-old had no more gas in the tank as he labored through 16 starts, landed on the disabled list with a sprained elbow, for the first and only time in his career, and was released on August 10.[54] "It was a mistake," admitted Sutton about his return. "It ended up being a depressing way to end my relationship with the Dodgers."[55]

Sutton retired with a 324-256 record, plus six more victories in the postseason, and a 3.26 ERA;

his adjusted ERA was 108, or 8% better than league average. He also threw 58 shutouts, 10th most in big-league history; among pitchers who began their career after 1920, only Warren Spahn, Ryan, Seaver, and Bert Blyleven tossed more. Sutton also tossed at least nine scoreless innings on seven other occasions for which he received a no-decision. Never a threat at the plate, Sutton batted a paltry .144 and did not hit a home run in 1,354 lifetime at-bats.

Not expected to be a first-ballot Hall of Famer, Sutton garnered 56.8% in his initial year of eligibility, in 1994 [75% was required for enshrinement]. His totals steadily rose and in 1998 he was elected to the Hall of Fame with 81.6% of the votes, and was the only player elected by the baseball writers that year. [Larry Doby, who integrated the American League in 1947 with the Cleveland Indians, was elected by the Veterans Committee]. The news came after an anxious period in Sutton's life. In November 1996, his daughter with his second wife, Mary, was born four months premature, though gradually she became stronger and was discharged from Piedmont Hospital in Atlanta in March.[56] Sutton's Hall of Fame plaque depicts him with a Dodgers cap; the Dodgers retired his number 20 in 1998.

Sutton made a smooth transition into broadcasting immediately after retiring from baseball. He had begun laying the foundations for his career behind the microphone as early as 1969 when he served as a disc jockey at a radio station in Burbank in the offseason, and had been a television sports commentator periodically in the next decade. After broadcasting Dodgers games in 1989, he began a long and distinguished career doing play-by-play and analysis with the Atlanta Braves in 1990 until 2006. He returned to the club in 2009, after a two-year stint with the Washington Nationals, and as of 2019 called Braves games. In 2015 the Braves inducted Sutton into their Hall of Fame. "Don has been an integral part of the Braves family for decades, and is most deserving of this honor," said Braves President John Schuerholz.

"Generations of Braves fans have been wowed by his knowledge and charmed by his ability to bring life to the broadcast. He is undoubtedly beloved throughout Braves Country."[57]

Sources

In addition to the sources cited in the Notes, the author also accessed Retrosheet.org, Baseball-Reference.com, the SABR Minor Leagues Database, accessed online at Baseball-Reference.com, SABR.org, *The Sporting News* archive via Paper of Record, the player's Hall of Fame file, the on-line archives via Newspaper.com, and Ancestry.com.

Notes

1. Robert S Weider, 'Don Sutton: An Unsung Achiever among Mound Elite," *Baseball Digest*, September 1985: 35.
2. Bill Ballew, "Sutton Eyes Hall after Successful Career," *Sports Collectors Digest*, February 1, 1991: 102.
3. "Don and Patti Sutton Were Striking Out Till They Got Help – And Now They're Safe at Home," *People*, April 5, 1982: 90.
4. Ballew: 102.
5. Ron Fimrite, "'God May Be a Football Fan'," *Sports Illustrated*, July 12, 1982: 71.
6. Kevin Huard, "SCD Interviews 300-Game Winner Don Sutton," *Sports Collectors Digest*, February 1, 1991: 105.
7. Ronnie Joyce, "Former Aggie, Sutton Sign Dodger Contract," *Pensacola News-Journal*, September 13, 1964: 37.
8. Bill Kirby, "Northeast Wins Class AA Title," *Tampa Tribune*, June 15, 1962: C1. Sutton faced Harry Dahl, who also went the distance, fanning 16. Dahl later signed with the Los Angeles Dodgers, on the recommendation of scout Leon Hamilton, in June 1964, presaging Sutton's signing by about three months. See "Dahl Signs with Dodgers for 'Substantial' Bonus," *Palm Beach Post-Times*, June 7, 1964: D1. He went 15-15 in two seasons in the minors.
9. "Connie Mack All-Star Team," *Pensacola News-Journal*, July 31, 1963: 2.
10. All statistics from Sutton's junior-college, Basin League, and NBC participation are from Ronnie Joyce.
11. Frank Finch, "Scouts' Sales Talk Landed Don Sutton." *Los Angeles Times*, July 7, 1966: III: 4.
12. Associated Press, "Santa Barbara Rookie Pitcher Impresses in Cal League Opener," *Reno News-Gazette*, April 15, 1965: 13.
13. Ray Kelly, "Freshman Hurler Earned Starter's Diploma," *Philadelphia Bulletin*, May 12, 1965.
14. Bob Hunter, "L.A.'s New Big D Sutton Death to Foes," *The Sporting News*, May 14, 1966: 3.

15 Frank Finch, "Sutton Hurt as Dodgers Whip Giants," *Los Angeles Times*, September 6, 1966: III, 1.
16 "Don Sutton Skips Trip to Rest Arm," *Los Angeles Times*, October 12, 1966: III, 1.
17 Weider: 32.
18 Huard: 104.
19 Fimrite: 68.
20 Wilt Browning, "Grenade Explodes Sutton's Confidence," *Atlanta Constitution*, December 6, 1967: 2-D.
21 George Lederer, "Sutton Saves Win, but Hates Work," *Independent Press-Telegram* (Long Beach, California), June 23, 1968: S-2.
22 "Don and Patti Sutton Were Striking Out Till They Got Help – And Now They're Safe At Home."
23 Sutton streak of 27⅓ innings (April 23 to May 6) was second to the Chicago Cubs Ken Holtzman's 33⅔ from May 6 to 24.
24 Sutton's adjusted earned-run average (ERA+) in 1969 was 96; league average is 100.
25 His five-year adjusted ERA was 95.
26 Bob Hunter, "No. 20-Win Button in Sutton's Goal," *The Sporting News*, May 13, 1972: 3.
27 Ron Rapoport, "Dodgers Miss Despite Final Triumph," *Los Angeles Times*, October 1, 1971: III, 7.
28 Ballew: 102.
29 Weider: 31.
30 "N.L. Flashes," *The Sporting News*, June 22, 1974: 22.
31 Ross Newhan, "Sutton: 1974 Was Entrancing," *Los Angeles Times*, January 16, 1975: III, 1.
32 Jim Murray, "Sutton's Masterpiece Gets the Quiet Awe It Deserves," *Los Angeles Times*, October 6, 1974: III, 1.
33 Ballew: 101.
34 Fimrite: 72.
35 Ross Newhan, "Little D's Big Day," *Los Angeles Times*, July 26, 1998.
36 Fimrite: 75.
37 Weider: 32.
38 Fimrite: 75.
39 Fimrite: 67.
40 Ibid.
41 United Press Internaional, "Win or Lose, Dodgers' Sutton WILL Have Fun!" *Valley News* (Van Nuys, California), October 11, 1977: 12.
42 Fimrite: 73.
43 An excerpt of Thomas Boswell's article from the *Washington Post* was reprinted in "Morning Briefings," *Los Angeles Times*, August 18, 1978: III, 2.
44 "Morning Briefings," *Los Angeles Times*, August 23, 1978: III, 2.
45 The entire episode and its aftermath were recounted by Scott Ostler, "Suddenly, the Hugging Turns to Punching," *Los Angeles Times*, August 21, 1978: III, 2.
46 Ballew: 102.
47 Mark Heisler, "Astros Lose Sutton, Game," *Los Angeles Times*, October 3, 1981: III, 1.
48 Ross Newhan, "Sutton Talks of Coming Home," *Los Angeles Times*, February 18, 1982: III, 4.
49 Fimrite: 79
50 Ross Newhan, "Sutton Utilizes Twilight Zone to Stall Angels." *Los Angeles Times*, October 9, 1982: III, 1
51 Ibid.
52 Ballew: 102.
53 Mike Penner, "Sutton Is on the Button – 300th Is a 3-Hitter," *Los Angeles Times*, June 19, 1986: III, 1.
54 Sam McManis, "Dodgers Hand Sutton His Walking Papers," *Los Angeles Times*, August 11, 1988: III, 1.
55 Balfour.
56 Jill Lieber, "Baby's Struggle Preoccupies Suttons," *USA Today*, January 5, 1998.
57 Phil W. Hudson, "Braves to Induct Legendary Broadcaster Don Sutton into Hall of Fame," *Atlanta Business Chronicle*, April 20, 2015.

Pete Van Wieren

BY BOB LEMOINE

Pete Van Wieren

Skip and Pete. Two names forever etched in the history of the Atlanta Braves and in the history of baseball on television. Just the mention of their names brings back warm memories and a smile to many baseball fans, and not just those in Atlanta. Rarely is one of them ever mentioned without the other also being mentioned. For 33 years, from abysmal records to a miraculous revival and the formation of a dynasty, the voices of Skip Caray and Pete Van Wieren narrated the story of the Atlanta Braves on radio and television. They had very different styles, but their chemistry resulted in a lifetime of memories. "With his thick glasses and thinning hair, Van Wieren didn't fit the classic television mold," wrote Paul Newberry in the *Rochester Democrat and Chronicle*. "But his soothing voice and ability to come up with obscure statistics in the pre-Internet era paired well with Caray, who was known for his biting sarcasm and witty retorts."[1] With the advent of cable TV, Skip and Pete gained a following of millions of fans around the country who either had no major-league team in their market or could only rarely see their home team on television. The Braves acquired the nickname "Team of the 90s" through this national exposure, and Skip and Pete were the main voices they heard describing this dynasty. Van Wieren was dubbed "The Professor" due to a physical likeness to another with the same nickname, but his thorough study and preparation for each game qualified him to inherit the name on its own.

Peter Dirk Van Wieren was born on October 7, 1944, in Rochester, New York, to Howard and Ruth (Jardine) Van Wieren. He grew up in the nearby blue-collar suburb of Greece in a home owned by his maternal grandparents, Wilbur and Eunice Jardine. "It was a typical *Leave It to Beaver* neighborhood," he recalled, "except folks went to work carrying lunch boxes, not briefcases."[2] His aunt, Helen Jardine, also lived with them.

Baseball was always a part of Pete's life from the very beginning. He grew up a fan of the Rochester Red Wings of the Triple-A International League, a farm club of the St. Louis Cardinals. Van Wieren remembered listening intently on the radio as Jack Buck and others called the Red Wings games on the radio. He also remembered the first professional game he attended, at Rochester on August 13, 1950, when Rochester and Jersey City played a 22-inning marathon before the home team prevailed, 3-2. "That game really got me hooked on the Red Wings," he said. When he was at the ballpark, Pete would often glance up at the men whose voices he heard on the radio, Buck and other announcers, as they made their way to the press box.[3] "The more I watched them," Van Wieren said, "the more I wanted to someday do what they did."[4] Even as a boy, the young "professor" would analyze the Red Wings games, keeping a scrapbook and replaying the play-by-play of games in his driveway as he threw a rubber ball off the garage door. He would skip down to the local pharmacy and grab a copy of *The Sporting News*, which he read cover to cover by first grade.

Van Wieren had a large extended family, which would gather for birthdays and special occasions. The gatherings never included Pete's father, however. Pete had been told that Howard had died in World War II. When Pete applied to Cornell University, he learned of a scholarship for children of deceased veterans. He had to provide basic information about his father which he couldn't answer. He asked his school librarian at Rochester's Charlotte High School for assistance. She pointed him to the public library, where he could look up the directory of World War II casualties. He couldn't find his father's name, so he asked his mother. Pete had uncovered a family secret.

Howard Van Wieren abandoned Ruth when she was pregnant with Pete. He was a truck driver for a Coca-Cola bottling company in Rochester. When he discovered her pregnancy, he disappeared, abandoning his truck and taking the money he had collected that day. A police investigation was unable to find Howard's whereabouts. A couple of weeks after Pete was born, Howard called, asking about the newborn. The family sent him a bus ticket to come and visit young Pete. Ruth waited hours for Howard to arrive, but he never showed and instead sold his ticket for cash. No one in the Van Wieren family heard from Howard again.[5]

Pete enrolled at Cornell in 1961. "I rarely missed a sporting event," he recalled, noting that he did other things in his free time. "I learned which taverns you could get into without proof of age – I was only 16, and the minimum drinking age in New York at that time was 18."[6] He also wrote for the campus newspaper, the *Cornell Daily Sun*, which led to freelance opportunities for the *Baltimore Sun*.[7] Covering a Cornell-Scranton baseball game, Van Wieren met Harry Dorish, a former major-league pitcher now a scout for the Milwaukee Braves. Before the game, the engineer for the student radio station, WVBR, rushed in, exclaiming that his announcer couldn't make it and he needed a replacement. "Go ahead, give it a try," Dorish said to Van Wieren. "You might like it. It's easier than writing."[8] Pete did, and took his first step into broadcasting.

While on campus, Van Wieren also became involved in a band called the Hustlers, named for the popular Paul Newman movie. They opened for Bo Diddley and performed with Chubby Checker, with Pete playing the drums. He also spent time investigating the mystery of his father. Howard's parents, Joseph and Katherine Van Wieren, lived in nearby Buffalo. A visit to them brought only disappointment, however, as they had not heard from Howard in years. They rejected invitations he sent them to visit him at Cornell. "Years later, after both of them had died, we learned that they were both ashamed of what their son had done and fearful that we were seeking their financial help – which we were not," Van Wieren wrote.[9]

With responsibilities at the newspaper and to the band, Van Wieren let his grades slip and he soon dropped out of Cornell. He married his girlfriend, Elaine Rosinus, who was working toward a teaching degree. The newlyweds moved to Washington where Pete's mother was working as an office manager for Senator Kenneth Keating of New York. Pete got a job working for the *Washington Post* in merchandising and promotion. His first flyer promoted the legendary sportswriter Shirley Povich.

Van Wieren still had his dream of being a baseball broadcaster, so an ad he saw in the *Post* for the National Academy of Broadcasting piqued his interest. He began taking night classes at the school, where he learned to operate radio equipment. One class assignment sent him to the press box at Griffith Stadium to record his own broadcast of a Washington Senators-Chicago White Sox game. "I was sitting between the Chicago and Washington radio crews with my little tape recorder and hand mike and I kept thinking, 'This is going to be great. I can see myself doing these things when I get my first job.'"[10]

Pete finished his courses in less than a year and was soon hired at WEER Radio in Warrenton, Virginia. Pete led the morning news and sports, worked as a disc jockey, and did sales as well as commercials. He remembered vividly his first sports assignment. "They told me to go out and cover a horse show," he remembered a few years later. "I didn't know anything about horses then and I don't know much about it now. And to do it on radio! Well, it's hard to talk to a horse. I ended up getting dressed in a nice suit to make a good impression. When I got there, it was raining and everything was covered with mud except all the people at the show who knew enough to wear boots and old clothes."[11] He also did the play-by-play of the Fauquier High School football team.

Van Wieren would be there just a few months, however, as the station manager in Manassas, Virginia, heard Pete's work and offered him a job at radio station WPRW. He did play-by-play for high-school sports, Little League, and American Legion baseball. The press box at the football field would shake when the train rumbled by. "After one game I climbed down the 50 rickety ladder steps and mentioned how shaking the thing was," he recalled. "The old wino who took care of the grounds looked up and said, 'Yup. Couple more trains come by and the whole thing'll go.'"[12] Van Wieren was ready to move on and seek a professional baseball job, which he landed in September of 1966 at WNBF Radio in Binghamton, New York.[13]

The Binghamton Triplets were the Double-A affiliate of the New York Yankees but did not have any broadcasting coverage for lack of sponsors. Pete asked the station manager, "If I could sell them, could I do them?" He agreed, and Pete pulled double duty working on the radio from 3 P.M. to midnight, then would go out knocking on the doors of local businesses the next morning. His hard work paid off as sponsors put the Triplets on the air in 1967.[14]

The broadcasting rights moved to WINR for 1968, so Pete followed the team there. In those days, access to updated player statistics depended on a weekly mailing from the league office. Pete worked out a deal with the *Binghamton Evening Press*, which received daily box scores from wire reports but did not publish them because of space restrictions. Someone at the paper now saved these box scores and hung them on the wall in the sports department under the sign "Pete's Peg." Van Wieren would pick these up and compile statistical notebooks of each team, becoming the go-to information guru who was always up to date.[15]

Binghamton's *Press and Sun Bulletin* advertised Van Wieren's daily radio show on WINR on the same entertainment page that advertised Don Knotts and *Perry Mason*. "Tune to the big winner for Pete Van Wieren," the ad hyped of the 10:30 A.M.-2 P.M. show. "Tune in for the best of all kinds of music … with time and weather checks all tied together with the bright thread of commentary that is Pete's specialty."[16] Van Wieren's duties included a Sunday *Challenge Bowling* program. "The extra $30 a week was well worth it, even if it meant interviewing one champion who had no teeth," Pete joked.[17]

In 1969 the Triplets moved to Connecticut so Van Wieren relied on broadcasting high-school basketball and basketball games for Broome Tech, a local junior college. During a postgame interview at Broome, a janitor turned off the power and the gym lights. "We were stunned for a minute," Pete said, "and I didn't have any way to tell the station what had happened. Luckily, I had battery power to hook up and we got it going in a minute.

The rest of the interview was done in a dark gym by the light of radio tubes."[18]

In 1970 Van Wieren submitted a tape of a broadcast he did to the Yankees. The club was impressed with Pete but instead chose Bill White, the first African-American play-by-play announcer in baseball. The Van Wieren family was growing as sons Jon (1967) and Steven (1970) came along. Pete needed a stable income. He would have to become a weatherman to do it.[19]

Pete's new job in 1972 was for a new ABC-TV affiliate in Toledo, Ohio. The station had such a strapped budget that Pete would have to give the weather forecast in addition to his sports anchor duties. He quickly tired of the double duty. As luck would have it, Van Wieren's eye caught a story on the Associated Press wire. Marty Brennaman, the play-by-play announcer for the Tidewater Tides (Norfolk, Virginia) of the Triple-A International League, was leaving to begin his legendary career with the Cincinnati Reds. Pete immediately interviewed and became the new Tidewater play-by-play announcer for 1974, taking a salary cut from $18,000 to $10,000. He didn't mind it, as now he could concentrate on his love of baseball while finding jobs on the side. He served as the team's beat reporter for away games for the *Norfolk Ledger-Star* and also did play-by-play for the Virginia Red Wings hockey team of Norfolk for two seasons, calling games for the International League pennant winners in 1975.[20]

After the 1975 season, the Atlanta Braves fired announcer Milo Hamilton. Van Wieren applied and heard a life-changing phone call from Braves announcer Ernie Johnson. "How would you like to become part of the Braves' broadcast team?" he asked. "You've got the job. Welcome to the family." The Braves also had another new announcer: Skip Caray. The duo would become lifelong friends and spent the next three decades together in the booth. Caray had been broadcasting Atlanta Hawks basketball games since 1968. Johnson, Caray and Van Wieren covered both television and radio broadcasts. Ted Turner purchased the Braves franchise in January 1976, and baseball on the emerging industry of cable television would never be the same.[21] "Skip was always off the wall," Johnson remembered in 2004. "Took me a while to get used to it. You didn't know quite what to say. I made the adjustment. Pete was very businesslike and talked like a professor, so we started calling him 'The Professor.' And if we ever needed any information, we'd say, 'Go ask Pete.' He kept such great records and stats."[22]

"The whole thing is a dream come true for me," Van Wieren told Larry Bump of the *Rochester Democrat and Chronicle* shortly after the announcement. "I've tried for several jobs and gotten close a couple of times, but finally getting a job like this is something you never expect. I've never had any ambition further than reaching this level. Now, I'd like to keep the job for a while and develop the same kind of respect Vin Scully has among other broadcasters."[23] Van Wieren was starting to get comfortable with his new position, covering the Braves in spring training and into the first month of the season. The "Professor" sobriquet was bestowed on Van Wieren by Johnson because of Pete's resemblance to former Reds pitcher Jim Brosnan, who also had the nickname for his scholarly appearance and the small library he traveled with on the road.[24] Pete was known for his academic, scholarly approach to the game. "One of the things that made game preparation so enjoyable for me is my love of research," he said. "I truly enjoy digging through old box scores, newspaper stories, record books, and magazines, hoping to hit on some interesting fact I never knew before. Whenever I could, I would share those findings with viewers and listeners."[25]

Far from a scholarly approach was the temperamental nature of Ted Turner, the Braves owner. Turner called Van Wieren to his hotel room and asked him if he was accustomed to traveling while at Tidewater. Satisfied with Pete's answers, Turner then called traveling secretary Donald Davidson's room and told him he was fired. Davidson had been with the Braves since their Boston days, beginning as a 10-year-old batboy. Davidson, all of 4 feet and 85 pounds, had become a Braves institution, as pictures with Babe Ruth, Ted Williams, Casey Stengel, and others revealed.[26] "I felt very bad for Donald, who had treated me so well during my first months with the team," Van Wieren wrote.[27] So in addition to broadcasting, Pete would spend the day handling everything from hotels and plane tickets to buses and equipment trucks. He survived his first season with the Braves, who finished a dreadful 67-94, the first of five straight losing seasons. Perhaps the most notable event came in December when Turner made his cable television station, WTCG, available to other cable systems around the country via satellite. In a couple of years, WTCG would become WTBS (Turner Broadcasting System).[28] The Braves would now be a national team.

Van Wieren saw historic and also bizarre moments with the Braves in the late '70s. Turner himself managed the Braves for one game in 1977. In 1978 fans at Atlanta's Fulton County Stadium saw Braves pitchers hold Pete Rose hitless to end his 44-game hitting streak. Van Wieren witnessed Phil Niekro's 200th win and also the shocking death of Braves executive Bill Lucas.[29] Handling two jobs was wearisome, however, and Pete considered leaving the Braves. One day a call came from Boston radio station WITS, which then carried the Red Sox games. Red Sox play-by-play man Ned Martin was moving to the TV booth. Pete considered the possibility, but WITS needed to boost its signal or risk losing the broadcasting rights in 1979.[30] Pete decided to stay in Atlanta, but told Turner he was done being the traveling secretary and could now concentrate solely on broadcasting.

Van Wieren had even more opportunities as Turner's new Cable News Network (CNN) debuted in 1980. Pete filled in on some weekend and late-night sports segments. When the players strike put the 1981 season on hold, Caray and Van Wieren passed the time by broadcasting the games of the Braves Triple-A club in Richmond, Virginia. When play resumed, ratings on TBS soared, and with Joe Torre as the new manager, the Braves became a legitimate contender.[31] The team began the 1982 season 13-0 and went on to win the National League West before being swept by the Cardinals in the NLCS. "Despite the disappointing ending," Van Wieren remembered, "the season was a spectacular success. TBS ratings soared. *Sports Illustrated* did an article on Braves fans in Storm Lake, Iowa; Valdez, Alaska; and Reno, Nevada. Our fan mail was pouring in from all over the world, and Braves fans were showing up in virtually every ballpark on the road."[32]

The Braves success was short-lived, however, as they finished second in 1983 and 1984, then a pitiful fifth (66-96) in 1985. Three games over this time, however, were some of Van Wieren's most memorable moments. The first was an August 12, 1984, game against San Diego that resulted in several brawls and the ejection of 13 players. The second was the July 4, 1985, game in Atlanta against the Mets. That contest went 19 innings and included over three hours of rain delays. In the 18th inning, with the Braves trailing 11-10, Atlanta pitcher Rick Camp hit a home run to keep the Braves alive. The Mets scored five off Camp in the top of the 19th and the Braves fell short, 16-13. The Fourth of July fireworks then began at 4 A.M. on July 5, frightening residents in the neighborhood. Another memorable moment was Bob Horner's four-home-run game in 1986. "He did it! He did it!" the excited Van Wieren exclaimed after the fourth cleared the fence. "He becomes the 11th player in major-league history to hit four homers in one game. His name is in the record books."[33]

TBS decided to add a fourth member to the broadcast booth, so Van Wieren, Caray, and Johnson were joined at times throughout the 1980s by Darrel Chaney, John Sterling, Billy Sample, and Don Sutton. Ernie Johnson retired after the 1989 season.

Bobby Cox, who managed the Braves from 1978 to 1981, returned as general manager, promising it would take five years to rebuild the club. Van

Wieren described the 1986-1990 years as "one long losing season."³⁴ The club finished at or near the bottom of the NL West and averaged 96 losses per season. The team invested in scouting and player development, while acquiring players who would turn the franchise around in the next decade. Cox would return to the dugout and be a part of that remarkable era, which included names now synonymous with the Braves: John Smoltz, Tom Glavine, Chipper Jones, Mark Lemke, David Justice, Ron Gant, and others. The 1990s would be the decade of the Braves.

The 1991 season was remarkable as two teams, the Twins and Braves, went from worst the year before to best, facing each other in the World Series. This was the first of 14 consecutive seasons in which the Braves would win their division title. The Braves-Twins World Series was an instant classic, going all seven games and finishing with a 1-0 Minnesota victory in 10 innings. Van Wieren summed up the series from the radio booth: "The Minnesota Twins have won the World Series and may be the world champions, but the Atlanta Braves have won the hearts of baseball fans all over America."³⁵ Skip, Pete, and Sutton were included in the Braves' parade after the Series before a crowd of 750,000. "We weren't treated like we lost," Van Wieren said. "It could not have been any better."³⁶

The 1992 Braves returned to the World Series in memorable fashion. The improbable Francisco Cabrera singled home a lumbering Sid Bream to beat the Pirates in the ninth inning of Game Seven of the NLCS, a classic moment of baseball history. Skip and Pete again covered the World Series on radio. The Braves lost again, this time to Toronto.

The addition of Greg Maddux on the mound and Fred McGriff at first propelled the Braves to 104 wins in 1993, the most in franchise history. Both the Braves and San Francisco (103-59) had hot seasons, with the Braves narrowly beating out the Giants for the division crown. But they weren't any hotter than the night smoke started billowing out of the Atlanta Fulton-County Stadium press box, two booths from where Van Wieren and Caray had been preparing for the broadcast. Everyone was evacuated onto the field after an explosion. "Once on the field, we couldn't believe what we were seeing," Van Wieren wrote. "The radio booth that we had been sitting in 10 minutes earlier was entirely engulfed in flames. So was most of the adjoining press box. The fire apparently had started when a breeze blew part of a paper tablecloth into one of the Sterno burners. Once the flames reached the drop ceiling, which was shared by all of the booths on that level, the fire quickly spread. The boom that Skip and I heard was a steel beam above the drop ceiling exploding from the intense heat."³⁷

The Braves lost to the Phillies in the NLCS. The 1994 players strike ended that season's pennant race. "It was agonizing watching millionaires and billionaires bicker over dollars," Van Wieren wrote.³⁸ Pete had a void during August and September, the time of year when he was used to the edge-of-your-seat pennant race. The time off became a period of personal reflection on his life. By chance, new information had been discovered about his father.

A cousin had called and said some old photographs of Ruth and Howard from the 1940s had been discovered. Donald Dykstra, Howard's cousin, told Ruth that Howard lived as a derelict on the streets of New York and died in 1971. He was buried in the potters field on Hart Island, off Manhattan, where unclaimed bodies are buried. Howard's father was notified of his son's death but refused to claim the body, wanting nothing to do with him. Pete still wanted some sense of closure and decided to visit his father's grave. The graves were unmarked, and there was no joy in his discovery. "I also learned that the simple coffins are stacked five-deep in numbered sections three rows by ten rows," he said. "It's just a dump, is what it is. Knowing what I do about his life, this seems like an appropriate final resting place."³⁹

The extra time for Van Wieren in 1994 led into his usually busy winter. He had been broadcasting Atlanta Hawks basketball for TBS or the later Turner Network Television (TNT) since 1976, originally handling the radio coverage while Caray handled television. As the popularity of TBS grew in the 1980s, its basketball coverage grew and so did Pete's exposure in the hard-court world. He worked beside basketball gurus such as Doug Collins, Rick Barry, Steve Jones, and Hubie Brown. Turner also acquired the rights to the Atlanta Falcons preseason football games in 1977. Van Wieren also called college football games for TBS and later University of Florida football on Sportschannel Florida.[40]

The 1995 season for the Braves began with replacement players in spring training, as the strike continued, but ended with a World Series championship, the first since the franchise moved to Atlanta in 1966. The Braves won the NL East by 21 games. This was their new division following realignment and the addition of a wild-card playoff team. Television coverage had also changed with the new Baseball Network, a joint venture of ABC and NBC. The networks would broadcast every game on the Monday night schedule and include a broadcaster from each team. Van Wieren was chosen as the Braves announcer and his assignments also included the National League Division Series between the Braves and Colorado Rockies, the first NL wild-card team. Pete worked alongside Larry Dierker. "Working that series with Dierker established a friendship and mutual respect," Van Wieren said. "We truly enjoyed the experience."[41] The Braves won the series, then swept Cincinnati in the NLCS.

The World Series was a matchup between the powerful Cleveland lineup and the Braves' pinpoint-control pitching. In Game Six, Tom Glavine pitched a masterful eight innings of one-hit shutout baseball, and the Braves won the Series with a 1-0 victory. The longtime Braves broadcasting duo called the game on radio and both were standing in the booth as Skip called the final out. "Yes! Yes! Yes! The Atlanta Braves have given you a championship! Listen to this crowd!"[42]

The Braves returned to the World Series in 1996, falling to the New York Yankees, while the 1997 club lost in the NLCS to the Florida Marlins. This pattern of regular-season success and failure in the playoffs would become the reputation of the Braves through the rest of the century and beyond. They lost the 1998 NLCS to San Diego, and the World Series to the Yankees in 1999. From 2000 to 2002, the Braves failed to advance beyond the NLCS despite high expectations.

Baseball on television had changed by 2003. Regional sports networks were available throughout the country, meaning TBS was not the only game in town. Ratings had dropped, and TBS executive producer Mike Pearl decided the TV booth needed a shakeup. Skip and Pete were being moved to strictly radio broadcasting. The outcry from the fans was fast and furious, and Skip and Pete were now the focus of media coverage. TBS lost ratings, and the four-man TV-radio rotation returned after the All-Star break. Both veteran broadcasters were humbled by the outpouring of support from the fans.[43]

The broadcasting duo was back on TBS as the Braves again lost in the NLDS, to the Cubs in 2003 and to the Astros in 2004. In 2004 Skip and Pete were inducted into the Braves Hall of Fame. In his induction speech, Van Wieren made a subtle comment over the actions of TBS management in the previous year. "I would like to thank Ted Turner and Terry McGuirk (the current Braves chairman) for their leadership, their friendship, and their loyalty. I have worked for 11 different executive producers over the years. I would like to thank 10 of them."[44]

The Braves won their 14th straight division title in 2005 and again were bumped early in the playoffs. This was the end of an era in many ways, as the 2006 team failed to return to the playoffs. Turner Broadcasting and Time Warner merged, with Time Warner taking control of the team. Ted Turner was gone from the picture. TBS was broadcasting fewer Braves games and agreed to a partnership with MLB to broadcast other games, including the postseason.[45] Liberty Media purchased the club in 2007 from Time Warner, and the Braves' 30-year affiliation with TBS came to an end. Skip and Pete continued to broadcast games on the radio. The Braves missed the postseason again, then fell to 72-90 in 2008.

In August of that year the Braves longtime broadcasting duo came to an end after 33 years. After suffering with health issues related to diabetes, Skip died suddenly. Pete spoke at his funeral. "Every day we'll hear that voice. Every day we'll remember that wit, that humor. Every day we'll recall that attitude. So, instead of saying goodbye, I'm just going to say thank you. Thank you, Skip, for letting us be a part of your life."[46]

Van Wieren announced his retirement at the end of the 2008 season, his 43rd year in broadcasting and 33rd with the Braves. "Losing Skip was certainly a tough thing," Van Wieren noted, "but that didn't affect my decision. If anything, it reinforced my decision. I didn't want to keep on working until I couldn't do it anymore. I really did another whole year of postseason games when you add it up," he said, referring to the decade-plus of Braves playoff appearances. There were so many great wins, so many great come-from-behind wins, all those great pitching performances. It's hard to single anything out."[47] Stan Kasten, the Braves' longtime president, said, "Before there was an internet, Pete was our 'human internet.' He collected stats and anecdotes so that he could always be prepared to talk about any player on both teams and really bring the game into the fans' minds."[48]

On April 10, 2009, the Braves honored Pete at the new Turner Field. There were gifts and a video tribute presented, and the radio booth was renamed the Pete Van Wieren Broadcast Booth.[49] In 2010 Pete wrote his autobiography, *Of Mikes and Men: A Lifetime of Braves Baseball* with Jack Wilkinson. Almost exactly a year after retiring, Van Wieren was diagnosed with cutaneous B-cell lymphoma and began chemotherapy and radiation treatment. "This is certainly not what I planned to do when I retired," he said, noting that he planned to travel the world with Elaine and spend time with their grandchildren.[50] The experience redefined for him what a true "hero" was. "My heroes used to be the ballplayers," he told students at the University of Georgia's Terry College of Business in March of 2014. "My heroes now are cancer doctors, oncologists and nurses and the people who work in those facilities, because of the dedication that they show."[51]

The Van Wierens celebrated their 50th wedding anniversary on June 13, 2014, with a trip to the Bahamas. That was Pete's last "good day" as his health deteriorated, according to his son Steve in an online memorial. Pete Van Wieren died on August 2, 2014, at the age of 69.

"He lived a tremendous life," Steve said of his father, "one of which many would dream to live. He lived life to the fullest. But he was more than a broadcaster."[52]

Sources

In addition to the sources listed in the Notes, the author was assisted by:

Baseball-reference.com

Cassidy Lent, A. Bartlett Giamatti Research Center, Cooperstown, New York, who provided Pete Van Wieren's file.

Notes

1. Paul Newberry (Associated Press), "Broadcaster Pete Van Wieren Dies," *Rochester Democrat and Chronicle*, August 3, 2014: D4.
2. Pete Van Wieren and Jack Wilkinson, *Of Mikes and Men: A Lifetime of Braves Baseball* (Chicago: Triumph Books, 2010), 11 (Hereafter cited as *Biography*).
3. *Biography*, 12-13.
4. *Biography*, 14.
5. *Biography*, 15-16.
6. *Biography*, 17.
7. By then the Red Wings were a farm team of the Baltimore Orioles.
8. *Biography*, 18.

9   *Biography*, 90.
10 Bill Dowd, *Binghamton Press and Sun Bulletin*, January 24, 1969: 15.
11 Dowd.
12 Dowd.
13 *Biography*, 21-22.
14 The quote is from a speech Van Wieren gave to students at the University of Georgia Terry College of Business, March 2014. youtube.com/watch?v=gvWMGgNk_vQ. Retrieved May 19, 2019.
15 *Biography*, 23-24.
16 *Binghamton Press and Sun Bulletin*, October 14, 1967: 23.
17 *Biography*, 25.
18 Dowd.
19 *Biography*, 25-27.
20 *Biography*, 27-29.
21 *Biography*, 29-32.
22 Jack Wilkinson, "Skip & Pete, Whatta Team, Whatta Show," *Atlanta Journal-Constitution*, August 11, 2004 (online).
23 Larry Bump, "Van Wieren Moving Up," *Rochester Democrat and Chronicle*, December 3, 1975: 69.
24 *Biography*, 150-151; Mark Armour, "Jim Brosnan," SABR BioProject, sabr.org/bioproj/person/b15e9d74. Retrieved May 18, 2019.
25 *Biography*, 204.
26 "Donald Davidson," *New York Times*, March 30, 1990: D17; Richard Luna (United Press Internaional), "Baseball's Biggest Man, Donald Davidson, Is Fighting for his Life," October 8, 1986. upi.com/5423425. Retrieved May 14, 2019.
27 *Biography*, 33.
28 Sam Hopkins, "TV-17 Cable Net Opens Friday," *Atlanta Journal Constitution*, December 17, 1976: 92; Richard Zoglin, "WTCG to Become WTBS on Aug. 27," *Atlanta Journal Constitution*, August 8, 1979: 29.
29 *Biography*, 39.
30 *Biography*.
31 *Biography*, 39-44.
32 *Biography*, 47.
33 Transcript taken from a YouTube video of the game originally played July 6, 1986. youtube.com/watch?v=aODckrL9fVk. Retrieved May 15, 2019.
34 *Biography*, 49.
35 *Biography*, 73.
36 *Biography*, 76.
37 *Biography*, 85.
38 *Biography*, 89.
39 *Biography*, 92.
40 *Biography*, 119-128.
41 *Biography*, 101.
42 *Biography*, 105.
43 *Biography*, 161-166.
44 *Biography*, 169.
45 *Biography*, 171-172.
46 *Biography*, 188.
47 "Braves Radio-TV Announcer Van Wieren Retires After 33 Seasons," SI.com, October 22, 2008.
48 Associated Press, "Longtime Braves Broadcaster Van Wieren Dies at 69," August 2, 2014.
49 "Braves Radio-TV Announcer."
50 Mark Bowman, MLB.com, "For Pete's Sake." Undated article in Van Wieren's Hall of Fame file.
51 youtube.com/watch?v=gvWMGgNk_vQ.
52 "Peter Dirk Van Wieren," Dignity Memorial. dignitymemorial.com/obituaries/roswell-ga/peter-vanwieren-6070806. Retrieved May 19, 2019.

Ernie Johnson Sr.

BY DANA SPRAGUE

Ernie Johnson Sr.

A right-handed relief pitcher whose major-league career spanned the entire decade of the 1950s, Ernie Johnson retired with a lifetime record of 40-23 and an ERA of 3.77 in 273 games. "Maybe not the stuff of Cooperstown," remembered Hall of Famer Eddie Mathews, a former teammate, "but damn it, the man could pitch."[1] Johnson's even greater claim to fame, however, was as a television broadcaster for the Atlanta Braves. His 52-year association with the Braves was the longest of any person in the organization.

The youngest of three children, Ernest Thorwald Johnson was born in Brattleboro, Vermont, on June 16, 1924. His father, Thorwald, and his mother, Alina "Inkie" Ingeborg, had emigrated from Sweden in the early 1900s. They were lured to Brattleboro by the Estey Organ Company, a world-famous manufacturer of pipe organs. With many Swedes among its 300 employees, Estey was one of the biggest employers in Vermont around the turn of the century, and the neighborhood where Ernie Johnson grew up, close to the Estey factory, was known as Esteyville. Ernie's father worked at Estey for 45 years, and also delivered newspapers on Sundays during the Great Depression.

Johnson recalled that he sometimes went along on those delivery runs "just to be with my father and read the sports page."[2] The children of Esteyville were crazy for sports, and Ernie's first paying job was caddying at the local golf course. "A caddie received 35 cents for nine holes and 60 cents for eighteen," he remembered. He occasionally played a round when he was not caddying, but for the most part his free time was spent in neighborhood games of baseball, football, or basketball, depending on the season. "We played pickup baseball games over on the hospital grounds and neighborhood teams at Oak Grove School," Johnson remembered. "We also played baseball and basketball teams at Austine School for the Deaf. I became friends with several of the deaf students" Growing up in Vermont, Johnson never played Little League baseball; in fact, the Little League field in Brattleboro was not built until 1952, ten years after he made his professional debut. Ernie's first taste of organized sports came in high school. He always had above-average size and was a good all-around athlete, but most felt that his best sport was basketball. His father installed a hoop outside their house, and Johnson recalled that he and his friends played even in the snow.

Yale University was interested in Ernie as a basketball player. Even after he chose baseball as his profession, Ernie stayed in shape during winters by playing semipro basketball in Vermont and professional basketball in Connecticut.

According to most accounts, Johnson was merely an average baseball player until 1942, his senior year at Brattleboro High School. He actually lost his first game that season, 8-1 to a strong team from Greenfield, Massachusetts, but only one of the runs was earned. Ernie bounced back with a win in his next start, taking a shutout two outs into the ninth inning before yielding a two-run homer.

Johnson's next three games comprise one of the most unusual pitching streaks in the history of high-school baseball in Vermont. On May 8 he pitched a one-hit shutout against Springfield. In his next game, against Bellows Falls on May 13, he pitched another one-hitter, this time taking a no-hitter into the ninth inning before giving up a single. Then on May 20 he took another no-hitter into the ninth inning in a game against Deerfield, Massachusetts. Again his no-hit bid was spoiled, this time by a pair of hits with one out, but he also struck out 20 in what was probably the best game of his high-school career.

For the 1942 season, Johnson pitched all but two of Brattleboro's games, averaging 12 strikeouts, compiling a 6-3 record, a 1.09 earned-run average, and a .409 batting average, and leading the team with 13 RBIs. At the time, though, almost nobody thought he was a potential major leaguer. When asked about it years later, one of Johnson's former teammates replied, "It never entered my mind or any of our other teammates' minds. Baseball players from Brattleboro, Vermont, just don't make it to the major leagues."[3] One man, however, thought differently. Ray Draghetti, Johnson's coach at Brattleboro High School, believed his 6-foot-4, 180-pound pitcher had the size and talent to make the majors. After graduation, Draghetti took him to Boston for a couple of tryouts, as described in Bob Dubuque's article in the June 19, 1942, edition of the *Brattleboro Reformer*:

"We haven't been asleep, but just careful in not reporting that Ernie Johnson was down in Boston for a few days trying out with the Red Sox. It got pretty well noised around, but we wanted to wait until the kid got home again to find out what the story was.

"Ray Draghetti, who took Ernie to Boston yesterday to work out with the Braves, said the [Red] Sox were interested in the Brattleboro High School star and let him read the fine print on a contract, which he did not sign. The [Red] Sox wanted Ernie to stay home and put on some beef this summer and go south with them on a farm team in the winter. However, it would appear to be a summer wasted here since there is little prospect of semipro ball. That's the story to date."

One week after the tryouts, Casey Stengel's Boston Braves gave Ernie the choice of traveling with the big-league team and throwing batting practice or signing a contract and reporting directly to the minors. He chose the former, and within ten days he was 100 miles from home, pitching batting practice to a team that included future Hall of Famers Paul Waner and Ernie Lombardi. Before his tryout with the Red Sox, Ernie had never been to a major-league game.

After 2½ weeks of traveling with the Braves, Johnson signed a minor-league contract, receiving $125 per month and a signing bonus of $100. The Braves sent him to Hartford of the Class-A Eastern League, for whom he made his professional debut on August 9, 1942. Johnson pitched in only eight games that summer, posting a 2-2 record and a 2.84 ERA, but one of them stood out in his memory: "My mom was a homemaker, a great mom. She went to Hartford once to watch me pitch and I gave up a three-run homer. The fans started booing. She turned to some of them and proudly said, 'That's my boy.' They slumped down in their seats quietly."

Before the 1943 season Johnson was drafted into the U.S. Marine Corps. He participated in the Okinawa invasion and was discharged as a staff sergeant in February 1946. His family liked to joke that America was losing the war when he entered the service and had won by the time he was discharged.

Johnson returned to Brattleboro in 1946. That winter, while attending a high-school basketball game, he first noticed Lois Denhard, a cheerleader. They were married a year later. "When we first met, she asked me what I did. I said, 'Play baseball,' and she said, 'No, really, what do you do for a living?' After she saw my first minor-league check, she asked again." The next several years were like a roller-coaster ride for the Johnsons. After only one inning of work with Hartford in 1946, Ernie was demoted to Pawtucket of the Class-B New England League. Although he pitched adequately, as attested by his 3.95 ERA, Johnson was 4-7, one of only two losing records in his 14 years as a professional pitcher. He returned to Hartford and posted winning records in 1947 and 1948, and in 1949 he earned a promotion to the Braves' Triple-A affiliate, the Milwaukee Brewers of the American Association. After only 11 innings, however, the Braves demoted him to Class-A Denver. Undaunted, Johnson became one of the best pitchers in the Western League, and his 15-5 record and 2.37 ERA earned him a place on the all-star team.

The Boston Braves invited Johnson to spring training as a non-roster player in 1950. After giving up a home run to Ted Williams in an exhibition game, Johnson remembered manager Billy Southworth saying, "Don't worry, kid, he's hit 'em off better pitchers than you." The resilient Vermonter surprised everyone by breaking camp with the big-league club. For the first time he was earning what he describes as "real money" – $5,000 a year.

Johnson made his major-league debut in Philadelphia on April 28, 1950, becoming the only player from Brattleboro ever to play in the majors. Although he pitched in only 16 games, he managed to hang on with the Braves for most of the season. Johnson was 2-0, but his 6.97 ERA probably accounts for his late-season demotion to Hartford.

The Braves sent Johnson to the minors again in 1951, this time to Milwaukee, but he refused to become discouraged. He went 15-4, led the American Association in ERA (2.62) and winning percentage (.789), and pitched the Brewers to the Governors' Cup and a Junior World Series victory over the Montreal Royals. Including his five postseason victories, Johnson was a 20-game winner in 1951.

Johnson started the 1952 season with Boston, and this time he was in the majors to stay. Bothered by a sore arm, Ernie pitched mostly in relief and went 6-3 for the Braves. He also received 10 starting assignments and pitched a shutout in one of them – one of only three complete games he pitched in the major leagues.

For the rest of his career Johnson pitched almost exclusively in relief, which was surprising because as a starter his worst inning was usually the first. Also surprising for a reliever was that his best pitch was his palmball, which was designed to induce groundballs, not strikeouts. "He made my job a lot easier," Eddie Mathews remembered. "His palmball would sink and it kept me busy."

Before the 1953 season, the Braves left Boston, where they were always less popular than the Red Sox, and headed west for Milwaukee, where Johnson had played minor-league ball just two years earlier. It was the first change of cities for a major-league franchise in half a century, and the Braves' success in Milwaukee guaranteed that it would not be the last. From 1953 to 1957, in the major-league city with the smallest population, the Braves averaged 2.1 million in attendance, almost doubling their nearest competitor.

Johnson remembered the euphoria of those early years in Milwaukee: "I've been in baseball for more than three decades, and I've never seen anything remotely close to Milwaukee in the '50s. They were wild, incredible years. Nobody cared in Boston whether we lived or died. Then, in

Milwaukee, the town went bananas. We couldn't buy a thing – fans would give us everything free. The players were treated like royalty. Every day was a feast.

"The news of the shift had come in spring training down in Bradenton. When we went north to Milwaukee, they had a huge parade and we went downtown. When we got there, I'll never forget how the people put up a Christmas tree – in April – inside the Schroeder Hotel. They were so beautiful. They said that since we'd missed Christmas with them, they wanted to celebrate it with us now. So there were hundreds of presents under the tree – shaving kits, toiletries, radios, appliances. Just ga-ga from the first day.

"It was like a small town. Some of us lived five minutes from the park. In those first few years we'd go around town, and even when we tried, we couldn't pay for what we bought – the sponsors wouldn't let us." Johnson himself got off to a poor start to the 1953 season – so poor, in fact, that he thought he might be headed back to the minors. But things turned around, and in one stretch of seven days he received credit for three victories. He became a mainstay in the bullpen of a great Milwaukee pitching staff. His 35 relief appearances led the team, and his 2.67 ERA was second on the staff to Warren Spahn's league-leading 2.10.

Johnson followed up that performance in 1954 by posting a 2.81 ERA in 40 games, establishing himself as one of the premier relief pitchers in baseball. Toward the end of that season the citizens of Brattleboro planned a special day in his honor which was recounted in Vic Harrison's article "Toast for a Great Guy" in the *Brattleboro Reformer*.

Though the New York Yankees were the dominant team of the 1950s, the Braves, with future Hall of Famers like Mathews, Spahn, and Henry Aaron, more than held their own. The Braves won the pennant in 1957 and met the New York Yankees in the World Series. Johnson remembered the thrill of pitching in Yankee Stadium: "I remember walking to the mound and all I could think of was, 'Son, you've made it. You've finally made it.' God, I was so happy. I was walking with the ghosts of Ruth and Gehrig – me, just a kid who had lived and died baseball all his life."

The Braves won the 1957 World Series in seven games, and Johnson played a major role. Pitching in Games One, Three, and Six, he gave up only two hits and one run in seven innings, striking out eight and walking one. The only run he gave up was a homer off the foul pole by Hank Bauer that proved to be the winning run in Game Six, but when asked if he thought it was a cheap shot, Johnson replied with characteristic modesty: "There was nothing cheap about that home run. He hit it so hard it may have bent the pole."

After the World Series, Johnson returned to Brattleboro for a welcome-home dinner. He was billed as "Brattleboro's Own World Series Hero," and family, friends, and local dignitaries attended.[4] Among them was Bill Jackowski, a National League umpire from nearby North Walpole, New Hampshire. A story has it that in one game Ernie complained to Bill about his calls on ball and strikes. Jackowski took off his mask and said, "This isn't the West River Valley League in Vermont. Stop complaining and just throw the ball." "That [story] may be true," Johnson said, "but we both had great respect for each other. Billy once told me we were friends off the field, but on the field I don't know you and it was understood that we both had jobs to do."

The 1958 season was be Johnson's last as a player in Milwaukee. Pitching in only 15 games, he once again had a winning record (3-1), but his ERA ballooned to 8.10. Before the season was over, the Braves, who were on their way to another World Series matchup against the Yankees, placed the 34-year-old Johnson on waivers. He remembered it distinctly:

"When the Braves got waivers on me in August, I guess the race was pretty well settled and nobody wanted to pay the $20,000 to claim me along with the salary. Then the Braves were very decent with me and let it be known that I could make my deal or stay with their chain, as I pleased. I know there were stories that I tried to land with the Giants and other National League clubs, but that isn't so. The first man to call me when I was free was [Paul] Richards and I didn't look further."

Richards managed the Baltimore Orioles. Johnson spent his final year in the major leagues with Baltimore in 1959. He pitched respectably, compiling a 4-1 record and a 4.11 ERA, but the Orioles released him after the season. He signed with Cleveland, but arm troubles plagued him in the spring of 1960, and although he appeared on a baseball card that year with Cleveland, he never threw a pitch for the Indians. "They offered to send me to the minors to work things out, but I knew it was time to call it quits."

Johnson returned to Milwaukee and hosted a television show called *Play Ball*, in which he and a guest sat around talking baseball and drinking milk. One of his first guests was Joe Garagiola. When Johnson told the affable catcher that he was nervous appearing on television, Garagiola told him to "just be yourself." It was advice that worked well over the years for Johnson.

For a year Johnson handled the commentary on 20 Braves telecasts and also did some speaking on the banquet circuit, but his main job was selling life insurance for Northwestern Mutual. "I thought I'd be selling insurance the rest of my life," he recalled. But in 1962 the Braves offered him a full-time job in the front office as an administrative assistant to team president John McHale, and Ernie accepted. "Being in the front office had always been my ambition," he said. "From the time I broke into baseball, that was what I wanted to do rather than managing or coaching."

Johnson's job eventually evolved into that of a full-time broadcaster. He moved with the club to Atlanta after the 1965 season and was named Georgia Broadcaster of the Year in 1977, 1983, and 1986. He received three television Emmys. He retired as a full-time announcer at the end of the 1989 season.

Johnson's popularity with Braves fans was never more evident than on September 2, 1989, when the Braves held Ernie Johnson Day. The attendance exceeded 42,000, the largest crowd for a Braves home game that entire season. During the pregame ceremony, Johnson received a television set from his fellow broadcasters, a satellite dish and annual use of a condominium in Florida from TBS, and an automobile from the Braves. He also received proclamations from the Brattleboro selectmen and the governors of Vermont and Georgia. "It was fabulous," Johnson exuded. "… It was the greatest day I have ever had and it is something Lois and the whole family will never forget."[5]

By 2000 Johnson was semiretired, living in Alpharetta, Georgia, and spending lots of time with his wife, three children (daughters Dawn and Chris are teachers, and Ernie Jr., following in his father's footsteps, was a sportscaster for WTBS and on network sports), and seven grandchildren). He still called about 30 games a year on Sports South Network and substituted occasionally on TBS. Over his 32 years in broadcasting, Johnson worked more than 4,100 games, and through it all maintained his grace and gentle humor. For all of the home runs hit by Hank Aaron and knuckleballs thrown by Phil Niekro, nobody spread more goodwill for the Braves than Johnson. "I love baseball," he once said, "and I think it shows."

Johnson was inducted into five Halls of Fame: the Braves Hall of Fame, the Atlanta Sports Hall of Fame, the Georgia Radio Hall of Fame, the Georgia TV Hall of Fame, and the Georgia Sports Hall of Fame.

After an extended battle with congestive heart failure, Johnson died on August 12, 2011, in Cumming, Georgia. While going through the many passages from the online tributes Braves fans had posted about his father, Ernie Jr. read one that buckled his knees. It said, "When you heard Ernie Johnson do a game, it was like summertime would never end."[6]

Sources

A version of this biography originally appeared in *Green Mountain Boys of Summer: Vermonters in the Major Leagues 1882-1993*, edited by Tom Simon (New England Press, 2000).

In researching this article, the author made use of Johnson's file at the National Baseball Hall of Fame Library, the Tom Shea Collection, the archives at the University of Vermont, and several local newspapers.

Notes

1. Atlanta Braves public relations department, no date. Johnson's file at the National Baseball Hall of Fame Library.
2. All quotations, unless otherwise noted, are from the author's interview with Ernie Johnson in 1993.
3. Author's interview with high-school teammate Bob Ratti in 1993.
4. Vic Harrison, *Brattleboro* (Vermont) *Reformer*, no date, no page. Player's file at the National Baseball Hall of Fame Library.
5. Ken Campbell, *Brattleboro* (Vermont) *Reformer*, September 5, 1989: 15.
6. Carroll Rogers, "Ernie Johnson, Jr., emotional, grateful, proud following death of his father," Atlanta Braves with David O'Brien, http://blogs.ajc.com/atlanta-braves-blog/2011/08/13/ernie-johnson-jr-emotional-grateful-proud-following-death-of-his-father.

Ernie Johnson Jr.

BY CURT SMITH

Ernie Johnson Jr.

In 1957 the Milwaukee Braves seized that city's sole major-league baseball title, beating the New York Yankees in a memorable seven-game fall classic. It capped an odyssey begun when the National League franchise moved from Boston shortly before the 1953 season – the first big-league club to change sites since 1903.[1] The Braves' stunning success ensured that other clubs would one day pick up stakes and leave.

Through 1958, baseball's smallest market yearly led its league in attendance, peaking at 2,215,404 in 1957. "Rush for tickets," read *Sports Illustrated*, "rivaled only by [Broadway's then-runaway hit] *My Fair Lady*."[2] The team's river of handclapping ran through the Upper Midwest – and beyond. "We'd go into Crosley Field – the Reds were crummy – and there'd be 30,000," said 1950 and 1952-58 Braves starting and relief pitcher Ernie Johnson.[3] For a few years – so brief they seem almost fictive – the Braves seemed baseball's Brigadoon.

Raised in rural Vermont, Johnson had spent most of his youth throwing baseballs at a blanket hanging from a tree limb or swatting apples with a broom. Similarly, son Ernie Johnson Jr. spent his childhood in Milwaukee during the Braves 1950s bonanza "hitting and catching a plastic baseball," John Hays wrote in the *Atlanta Constitution*.[4] "By himself. Announcing every play to an imaginary audience." Jr.'s sole regret was that "I could've been older so I could've gone to the [1957] World Series," known he was there, "and watched my father pitch. That would have been great."[5] Sadly, he was one year old when Dad pitched brilliantly, the Braves edging the mighty Bombers.

Through 1959, Milwaukee won two pennants, barely missed two more, and became baseball's capital. "Dad liked to self-deprecatingly joke about his career," Jr. said, "but Ernie Johnson was a pretty darn good relief pitcher."[6] Senior was a 1957 regular-season 7-3, then had a 1.29 World Series ERA: "Dad's [Series] line score … in the scrapbook my mom, Lois, put together – three games, seven innings, one run, two hits, one walk, eight K's," still recalled with pride.[7] From Milwaukee to Atlanta, from Jr. "hang[ing] around the batting cage" as a boy to later hailing Dad by keeping next to his scorebook a 1954 plastic-encased baseball card that he had bought one day at a card store – one Johnson absorbed the other.[8]

Junior's only memory of Sr. as a big-league player is of him walking out the door in 1960 spring training in Tucson, Arizona, and telling wife Lois, "I've gotta go get a *Sporting News*." The son thought he said *Sporty News*.[9] By then, Ernie Sr. had already been put on waivers by the Braves in late 1958, joined Baltimore, been released after the 1959 season, and signed by the Indians, only to brook arm trouble. Luckily, Jr. was old enough to see Sr. return to Milwaukee in 1960 and host a post-retirement TV show called *Play Ball*, "where I'd talk baseball and drink our sponsor, milk,"[10] said Ernie Sr., to become Jr.'s role model: as a man and, ultimately, a Voice.

Then and looking back, the child of the late 1950s and early '60s sensed the "world's greatest childhood. I used to … have Hank Aaron ask me how my Little League team was doing," Jr. said.[11] As Sr. became WJMJ-TV analyst and postgame host, Jr. sat in the back of the booth watching him "do his job. And not just watching how he did his job, but how he interacted with" and regarded people. "He felt very blessed, very lucky to be doing this. And he always told me, 'Ernie, this game's not about me. It's about the people on the field. Don't ever let the game be about you.'" The same creed applied to "not yapping over pictures that are conveying the [park's] electricity … I don't have to say, 'Boy, listen to this crowd.' You're listening to it.[12]

Increasingly, the main sound at Milwaukee County Stadium was foul balls banging off empty seats. By 1963, tepid clubs and absentee owners plunged attendance to 773,018.[13] In 1964 the franchise disclosed it would move to Atlanta, a judicial fiat delaying the shift. In that strange interregnum of 1965 – the Braves still Wisconsin's, but one foot out the door – Sr. aired "a tease for next year," he said, "when the ballclub came south,"[14] calling 17 TV and 53 radio games on Atlanta station WSB. A year later he, Milo Hamilton, and Larry Munson did each game on WSB's 36-outlet radio network and 18 TV road games on its baseball-largest 19-affiliate TV arrangement in Alabama, Florida, Georgia, North and South Carolina, and Tennessee.[15]

A decade later Johnson replaced Hamilton as lead Voice, invoking pops "that bring rain" and "give that one a blue star."[16] His new stage, WTBS Atlanta, became a superstation, bulging baseball's and cable's clientele, Ernie almost universally beloved. From the start his son wanted to be like the son of Swedish immigrants who served in World War II, and had already begun to sire for the Braves the same kind of oneness with the South that they had once forged in Wisconsin, and from whom he would learn lessons to meet challenges greater than any to be found on the field.

At 18, Dad had signed with NL Boston, then entered the Marines, his immediate future clear. At that age Ernie Jr. made the 1974 University of Georgia team as a freshman without a scholarship – but was cut by a new coach in fall 1975:[17] Like untold players before and since, a fine fielder (here, infielder) but unable in any way to secure first base. "I walked on as a freshman," he later joked, "but I was told to walk off as a sophomore."[18] Talking to Dad by phone, Jr. said, "Well, I've got to do something else with my life."[19] The English major promptly set upon being a teacher and a baseball coach until one day Braves announcer Skip Caray told Ernie Sr., "Your boy has a better voice than you and I put together."[20]

Hoping that Skip was right, Johnson decided to follow his father into the big leagues of radio/TV, knowing that he would need a different kind of résumé. In 1977 the still-student joined campus radio station WAGQ-FM as news and sports director. Next year he graduated from Georgia with a BA in journalism, summa cum laude, to become a late-night TV news anchor at WMAZ-TV in Macon, Georgia. One evening proud Papa drove just close enough to viewing scrutiny to watch his newscast at a hotel. "I told them I needed a room for just a half-hour," Sr. later said.[21] It is possible that the hotel operator had heard that request before.

In 1981 the young man who was easy even then to like in an often callous field moved to Spartanburg, South Carolina, as WSPA-TV news reporter. Next, Jr. went where Dad had gone before – WSB, the Atlanta institution founded in 1922, call letters denoting "Welcome South, Brother," the first radio station to broadcast in the South.[22] Johnson joined it as general-assignment news reporter. In 1983 he aired news coverage of a Braves-Dodgers series. Seeing him, the news director urged Jr. to audition for weekend sports anchor/reporter. Junior did, staying till 1989. In 1984, nominated for a state Emmy award in sports reporting, he said he would like to win for his Dad and Mom "for all the support they've given me and the time they've spent talking to me."[23] He got the chance again.

For some time, Ernie Jr. himself had begun to fashion a distinctive niche as husband and future dad. In 1979, anchoring news in Macon, the 23-year-old spotted a drive-in teller at the bank where he took his checks. Able to behold Cheryl DeLuca only from the waist up, Jr., in his burgundy Chevrolet Monza, was still smitten, saying, "She says we met through seven inches of bulletproof glass."[24] Ernie and Cheryl married in 1981. The depth of Jr.'s love for his dad lit the wedding rehearsal – the elder Johnson's first absence from a Braves game in his 15 years behind their mic. The rehearsal mug was engraved: *My Best Man. My Best Friend.*[25] The younger man was would soon be OK on his own.

In 1989 Johnson Jr. left WSB for Sr.'s Turner Sports to host and call a slew of gigs, including play-by-play, a pregame, halftime, and noted post-twin-bill studio show, *Inside the NBA,* on TNT, pro basketball and the popular *Fan Night* on NBA-TV. Junior bolstered Turner's and CBS's joint NCAA postseason hoops, voiced PGA tour shot-by-shot coverage, co-hosted college football in studio – and also did TNT's FIF World Cup, the Championships, Wimbledon, the NFL, and sports at the Goodwill Games and Olympics.[26] Such success at an early age – Ernie's 30s and early 40s – has caused others to lose their compass. By contrast, Johnson fixed the familial and familiar: first, building a family; and second, unexpectedly, working with his father. His core rested on *faith,* the kindly light that led – and *example*, absorbing Dad's stability in a field where disorder is often the order of the day.

A licensed professional counselor, Cheryl gave birth to two biological children, son Eric and daughter Maggie, in the 1980s.[27] By 1991, moved by the plight of Romanian orphans as Eastern Europe came undone in the wake of the Soviet Union's collapse, she told her husband she felt compelled to travel there to try to act. While Johnson attended to his work, Cheryl, Eric, and Maggie traveled to Bucharest on an adoption trip "in search of a girl under a year in age with no permanent handicap." She was introduced "instead to a three-year-old boy with special needs, including a clubfoot and inability to speak."[28]

The boy "was the first child they brought out of the orphanage," Ernie Jr. said. "It was obvious he … had a lot of developmental delays and he couldn't walk. My wife's a gem and called … and said, 'I saw a child today, and he's so much more than we can handle. But I can't go through the rest of my life wondering whatever happened to that kid.'"[29] Straightaway he told her to bring the boy, Michael, home to their house in Braselton, Georgia, just outside Atlanta – where a year later, he was diagnosed with muscular dystrophy, confined to a wheelchair and artificial respirator then, but whose survival Johnson would call "a blessing"[30] – a miracle of life.

"It's not all seashells and balloons and everyone's happy," Cheryl said two decades later. "It's not. You're dealing with a lot of baggage that you're trying to unpack."[31] Care was extensive, expensive. Daughter Maggie had become a special-education teacher. The Johnsons had adopted three more children: daughter Carmen, an infant girl from Paraguay, and, more recently, daughters Ashley and Allison, adopted domestically through foster care in Cleveland. "Most of us will be tested at some point by ailing children or aging parents," Tim Sullivan wrote in the *Courier-Journal*. "Fewer of us seek out strenuous situations beyond our immediate family. Fewer still have gone as many extra miles as have Cheryl and Ernie Johnson." To

Jr., such goodwill was "rooted in our ... Christian faith. We're instructed to care for orphans and widows. ... We're getting a heck of a lot more out of it than they are" – caring for the ill and vulnerable, not seeking klieg lights or applause.[32] Tested, he would continue to pass.

Even as the Johnsons increasingly did good, "America's Team," as owner Ted Turner termed it, increasingly did well, forging popularity akin to the 1950s Braves – and a dynasty to exceed them. Senior often warmly recalled the club's 1953 arrival in Milwaukee. "They had a huge downtown parade ending at the Schroeder Hotel, where they'd put up a huge Christmas tree, saying that since we'd missed Christmas let's celebrate it now in April! – and we did!" Burghers gave players free beer and milk. Hundreds of presents circled the tree – "radios, appliances, shaving kits, gaga from day one." Yearly the Braves got cars from dealers rent-free. "[Warren] Spahn already *had* a car. So, fans gave him another – for his family."[33]

Each year seemed to eclipse the next. Boston's 1952 Braves played to 281,278. The second-place '53ers drew a National League record 1,826,397. 1954: The Braves became the first NL club to draw 2 million. 1955: Milwaukee hosted the All-Star Game. 1956: It staged a manic pennant race with Brooklyn and Cincinnati, ending in second place, a game behind Brooklyn. Johnson relieved in 36 games, was 4-3, and had a 3.71 ERA. On August 7, Jr.'s date of birth, 26,049 at Milwaukee County Stadium saw the Braves beat the Cubs, 6-1, to remain in first place by 1½ games. "Who would have thought," Ernie Sr. said, "that years later Ernie [Jr.] would join me on air in Atlanta" to retrieve the age's magic?[34]

After the 1991 season, Senior retired as *the* Braves superstation presence. In the 1992 Series, Skip Caray asked him to call three innings on Braves radio. "Nothing like completing the résumé," Johnson said then and later, wryly turning humor on himself.[35] During the first half of the 1990s, with no Series title, the Braves sought to finally complete *their* postseason résumé. 1991:

Trading worst for first, they took the NL West on the next to last day and the LCS in Game Seven – Atlanta's first pennant. In 1992 Francisco Cabrera's pinch-hit single capped a Game Seven rally to give the Braves an NL-winning LCS victory.[36] Few will forget Jimmy Carter leaving his seat as Sid Bream scored the decisive run, then sprinting to clear the rail, dodge police, reach the plate, and hug skipper Bobby Cox, the players, and Cabrera like a teammate – memorable, *indelible*.[37]

1993: The Braves drew a franchise-best 3,884,720, then lost the LCS. 1995: Good things come to those. The club finally took a World Series, their first since 1957 – the first franchise south of the Mason-Dixon Line. The 1996 season became a postscript: The Braves closed Atlanta-Fulton County Stadium. The Braves made the postseason every year from 1991 to 2005 – a player lockout canceled 1994's – 14 straight times. They won their division a sublime 11 straight years from 1995 to 2005, and in 2013 becoming a region's cult. "We rarely miss a game [watching] mostly on television," President Carter wrote in 2004 of his family from Plains, Georgia, "and my general well-being is strangely affected by the latest performance of the Braves."[38]

Paul Simon sang, "Mother and Child Reunion."[39] From 1993 to 1996, the South's leading father-and-son reunion watched and described much of the Braves dynasty, Atlanta regional cable outlet SportsSouth (a.k.a. Sports Net South or FSN South) having sagely asked Jr. to work with a man, his father, who was a legend and who had already allegedly called it quits. The *Atlanta Constitution*'s Carroll Rogers was among those to whom the younger Ernie confessed that "no matter what happens in his broadcasting career, the highlight will always be the time he spent broadcasting Braves games with his father on Wednesday nights on SportsSouth in the 1990s" – something, he added, that Dad had long known.[40]

Until then, Chip Caray, Skip's son, aired the middle three innings and Ernie Sr. the first and last three. Each Johnson followed roughly the same road, to their and viewers' pleasure. Ernie's lack of prior play-by-play experience didn't trouble the junior partner: "If you can do rowing, you can do baseball because in rowing there's not much to do when all you've got are eight guys sitting in a shell for seven minutes."[41] He felt able to convey baseball for having followed it, spun baseball cards, sensed the game since youth, known what A. Bartlett Giamatti caught in his lyric essay *The Green Fields of the Mind*.[42] In 2010, when Ernie Jr. began TBS TV play-by-play, the *New York Times*'s Stuart Miller wrote incisively, "[He] may be best known as a basketball guy … but he has always held baseball closest to his heart."[43] Doing 1990s baseball with Sr. "rekindled that love in me," Jr. said, "indescribable having him as my partner."[44]

For four years, father and son announced a sport they loved with a person they cherished. Then, in 1999, Ernie Sr., 75, finally did his last game, his voice still falling lightly on the ear. Senior kept it casual, as always focusing on the Braves, ending with a farewell from the three-time Georgia Broadcaster of the Year, Emmy honoree, and future 2001 inductee into the Braves Hall of Fame. He then retired for good to his Crabapple, Georgia, farm, near Atlanta, where a US Marine Corps' flag – "Next to family, there's nothing I'm prouder of" – flew proudly from a pole in the front yard.[45] Thereafter, Ernie Jr., a.k.a. "E.J." "Mr. Smooth," and "Elevator Ernie," "would picture him and my mom in front of their [TV] set" when doing a telecast.[46] For a time when the Braves won a local telecast he used his signoff – "and on this winning night, so long everybody" – borrowed without Dad's permission, said Ernie Jr., "but with," Johnson added, "his blessing and my love."[47]

Increasingly, the younger Johnson seemed to buoy, if not bless, any sport he did. In 2002 the TNTer was nominated for the first time for an Emmy for "Outstanding Sports Personality, Studio Host," sharing the award with NBC and HBO's Bob Costas. In 2006 Johnson took the award by himself. (In 2015, he won again, giving the award to the daughters of the late ESPN sportscaster Stuart Scott, who died that January.) Studio basketball and shot-by-shot golf largely defined him, *Inside The NBA* winning an additional two Emmys. Ernie Jr. called his NBA studio work a "free-for-all" and hosting the PGA Championship "caption writing."[48]

When in February 2006 Johnson disclosed that he had cancer, he told TNT *Inside the NBA* co-hosts Charles Barkley and Kenny Smith that it was still all right for them to call him a nerd. Ray Glier of the *Atlanta Constitution* then rightly noted that the "nerd" was also a "traffic cop" who had "kept the show running smoothly,"[49] balancing Smith's insight and Charles Barkley's otherworldly bluster. Cancer made Johnson miss TNT's British Open and PGA Championships in 2006, the patient returning to *Inside the NBA* that year while chemotherapy treatment continued. In October it ended, putting cancer in remission, Johnson, 50, relying on "faith and family."[50]

Then, in 2007, TBS, citing "national ambitions," traded its three-decade-long daily Braves identity for a national regular-season Sunday afternoon *Game of the Week* – actually, 13 games a year after NBA playoffs ended – plus postseason baseball. Suddenly, the network became a different country, like neutral Belgium. As part of the pact, Johnson also began airing 40 Braves games locally on sister channel Peachtree TV. "When I did games with Dad, and when I did them with Smoltzie [John Smoltz] on Peachtree TV [in 2010], we knew it was the Braves network, and we'd cater the broadcasts that way," he said.[51] National partners have included Smoltz, Ron Darling, Buck Martinez, and David Wells. Always present: Johnson's 1954 baseball card of his Dad. Cost: $7.50, Jr. said.[52] Value: Priceless.

Under TBS's new big-league pact, Junior at first filled the same niche that he did on the network's pro basketball coverage: studio host. In July, hoops season over, Johnson traded one born-in-America sport for another,[53] kibitzing into October about a lifetime love. For a time

Ernie worked with Cal Ripken, Jr, play-by-play reverting to Chip Caray, who became "an object of ridicule, fired after [the 2009 playoffs]," wrote the *Dallas Morning News*'s Barry Horn. In early 2010, Horn added: "Ladies and gentlemen, meet Ernie Johnson, a relatively soft-spoken broadcaster in a business of ... decades of cable's Turner Sports has made him the signature voice of TBS and TNT."[54] Jr. became head ball and striker," leaping at the chance because "baseball has been in my blood for a long, long time."[55]

In 2010 Ernie did play-by-play of all seven national Sunday sets and the postseason Division Series (here, Yankees-Twins). Many had seen Ernie gild other sports before the pinstriped DS sweep. Still, that did not ensure a sure transition to the high-wire world of prime-time hits, runs, and (broadcast) errors. It did suggest that he learned quickly – and like Dad, in a radio/TV world of cosmic egos, worked well with others. Reviews were boffo. Bayed the *Denver Post*: "Ernie Johnson Jr. makes slick transition to baseball."[56] Jr.'s "easy-going but animated play-by-play translated well," said the *Baltimore Sun*'s David Zurawik, "never ... forcing himself on the action. Instead ... the game c[a]me to him at its own speed, especially in a playoff game."[57]

His approach was intentional, said Ernie: "Less is always more in a playoff game."[58] On, say, a June afternoon, "well, you lay out [say nothing at the mic] and you can hear a popcorn vendor. But ... in a playoff game, it lends itself to saying less." It was also personal. "I've done this as a baseball fan all my life watching a game on TV, and I'm saying [to a Voice], 'Hey, take a breath. You don't need to talk all game. I don't need to hear you.'"[59] If Johnson needed to draw a picture or explain stratagem, he never fantasized about getting paid by the word. Above all, he respected the game's past and pace, inherited from Pop. According to writer John Hays, the largest baseball picture on the den wall at Ernie Sr.'s farm had showed a "small boy pulling on the pants leg of a large man."[60] Both were wearing baseball uniforms. "The man, a onetime major leaguer, is not showing a boy how to hold a bat or how to throw a curveball. Instead, he is simply close by, a companion whom the boy can reach for if he chooses."[61] It seemed a metaphor for each's life.

As Shakespeare writes in *Hamlet*, Act 4, Scene 5, however: "When sorrows come, they come not single spies. But in battalions."[62] The first came soon after Ernie regularly adopted his Dad's farewell, in 2010 using it on WPCH, Peachtree TV, with Joe Simpson and Smoltz, saying, "'So for Joe and John, this is Ernie Johnson and on this winning night, so long everybody.'"[63] On August 12, 2011, Senior died of congestive heart failure worsened at 87. Junior had just finished a broadcast at the PGA Championship when he learned of his father's passing. He and Cheryl had sat by his bedside to read online passages posted by Braves fans, many of whom "consider Johnson Sr. the original voice of the Braves, even if he shirked that kind of adulation," wrote the *Constitution*'s Carroll Rogers.[64]

His son loved reading them. "Some of these things just hit you so strongly. It was stories about having dad sign something for a six-year-old or just sneaking transistor radios into your shirt to listen to Braves games." He read a passage shortly after his father's death "that puts it so simply that that it just buckled my knees. It said, 'When you heard Ernie Johnson do a game, it was like ...'" Jr. paused, overcome with emotion, then "... summertime would never end."[65]

"Life is a blink," said the son. "It really is, it zips right past you" – perhaps Dad's favorite verb. Inevitably, he would say a game was "zipping along," no matter how slow or fast its rhythm.

"We treasure having him for 87 years or as old as we are. He had a great life. He impacted a lot of people and just taught us all a lot – not by preaching, but just by watching him on a daily basis," how he acted with players, with "fans, how he took time for everybody."

"My dad would always say, 'Well, Ernie only had one problem with the game of baseball and that was the pitched ball,'" Johnson said, laughing. "I couldn't hit a lick."⁶⁶

Ernie's Everest will always be the symmetry of his airing Braves games with Dad on

Wednesday nights on SportsSouth in the 1990s – just as Shakespeare would have appreciated the irony of the location of his first game after Dad's death. By coincidence, Jr. was assigned to a September 11 Brewers-Phillies set in Milwaukee, place of his birth and youth. He "went to his neighborhood when his father worked for the Braves," wrote *USA Today*'s Mike Lopresti. "He parked at his grammar school and jogged through the memories."⁶⁷

The next month Jr. would have aired the NLCS, also in Milwaukee, Ernie looking forward to the postseason. That day the phone rang. Wife Cheryl called from an Atlanta hospital, giving the phone to a doctor asking permission to put a tube down the throat of their 23-year-old special-needs son Michael, fighting to breathe with pneumonia and muscular dystrophy. It was, the doctor said, a matter of life and death. Johnson's baseball season ended that night.

Instead of airing the postseason, Jr. adopted a routine. Arrive at the hospital by 2 P.M., relieve Cheryl, and stay till next morning in a seat next to Michael. "It's very important for him when he wakes up in the middle of the night that he sees me or my wife or one of our kids," Johnson said.⁶⁸ He followed, like clockwork, day after day.

"Sometimes, it's all you can do," he said. "Those nights where you're in the hospital and you're sitting bedside. Michael really doesn't really care about baseball. He's not a big sports fan," loving cars and asking people what they drive. He would fall asleep. Johnson would "sit there and watch the games and eventually get some sleep in those very comfortable folding chairs that always provide restful nights."⁶⁹ Occasionally, Michael would awake and whisper. Dad was there in the dark to respond. That," he said, "is why you're here."

"Looking back, 2011 had "really been a trust-God year"⁷⁰ – Ernie Jr.'s faith tested as it had not been since 2006, when, non-Hodgkin's lymphoma having been diagnosed in 2003, Ernie began chemotherapy treatment. As it continued, the Christian since 1997 worked regularly with the Fellowship of Christian Athletes and Samaritan's Feet, a nonprofit organization dedicated to putting 10 million pairs of shoes on children's feet in the next 10 years. One step after another seemed a sane way to live, as Jr. found a decade later. In 2018 he missed the NLCS because doctors forbade flying after finding blood clots in each leg. "They gave me blood thinners," Ernie said, "and told me to stay grounded."⁷¹ In 2019 Milwaukee declared May 17 "Ernie Johnson Jr. Day," the well-grounded honoree revisiting the home in suburban Brookfield where the Johnsons had left in 1964.⁷²

When the Braves won the 1957 Series, Ernie Sr. got a ring that Jr. now wears. In 1958, losing the Series, they "got National League champion cufflinks." After Sr. died, Lois gave their son "these [links] for Christmas [2011]," said Ernie, wearing them each time he called a game, baseball or not.⁷³ His Dad having aired more than *four thousand* Braves games, many on TBS as "America's Team," Ernie Jr. did the 2013 Braves-Dodgers Division Series, then the NLCS. For him, Turner Field meant meeting the points of his past. "I got here early just so I could go out to the Braves Hall of Fame. I heard his [recorded] voice on the train car out here."⁷⁴

"Braves games," wrote Atlanta columnist Jeff Tucker, "have not been shown regularly on TBS since 2007," when, as noted, "the Atlanta-based network ended the team's three-decade run as national programming."⁷⁵ For many, finding the club on the network of their youth again meant a wistful trip back to a Braves old world. A Midwesterner tweeted: "I used to watch Braves games on TBS when I was a kid. Loved Dale Murphy and the old stadium cause the Royals were not on here." Losing, 6-1, to LA, a Braviac wrote, "Well, at least it's nice to see the #Braves back on Superstation WTBS, where they belong."⁷⁶

Ernie Johnson Sr., like TBS, was a tough act to follow, but the son has never minded being Ernie Jr. "I'd introduce him and some people would call him Ernie Sr.," Johnson said. "I just say, 'This is classic Ernie and I'm just Ernie.'" [77]

Self-deprecatory and easy-listening, Senior loved a story that is evocative of the son. Prior to 1953 the Braves and Red Sox staged a preseason Boston City Series. In 1950 Ernie, a rookie, faced Red Sox legend Ted Williams.

Johnson began by curving the future Hall of Famer. "Great decision," Ernie said. "In seconds it's rolling to the Hotel Kenmore." Braves manager Billy Southworth consoled the young pitcher: "Don't worry," he told Sr. "He's hit them off better pitchers than you."

In 1952 veteran Vern Bickford faced Ted at the Braves' training camp in Bradenton. Bickford retired Williams his first at-bat. "Ted's up this inning," Vern told mates later. "Let's see how far that donkey can hit one."

"What are you gonna do?" said Johnson. "Lay it in there three-quarter speed and see what happens," Vern said. Williams promptly hit the right-center-field light tower.

"We're roaring as the inning ends," said Ernie. Bickford comes back, shakes his head, and says, "Well, at least I got my answer.'"[78]

Each time Ernie Jr. does a game, a baseball viewer gets his answer. This Johnson calls the hardest sport to broadcast as well as did – his Dad.

Sources

Grateful appreciation is made to reprint all play-by-play and color radio text courtesy of John Miley's The Miley Collection. In addition to the sources cited in the Notes, most especially the Society for American Baseball Research, the author also consulted the Baseball-Reference.com and Retrosheet.org websites' box scores, player, season, and team pages, batting, and pitching logs, and other relevant material. FanGraphs.com provided statistical information. In addition to the sources cited in the Notes, the author also consulted:

Books

Koppett, Leonard. *Koppett's Concise History of Major League Baseball* (Philadelphia: Temple University, 2015).

Smith, Curt. *A Talk in the Park: Nine Decades of Baseball Tales from the Broadcast Booth*. (Washington: Potomac Books, 2012).

___. *Voices of The Game: The Acclaimed History of Baseball Radio and Television Broadcasting* (New York: Simon and Schuster, 1992).

Van Wieren, Pete, with Jack Wilkinson. *Of Mikes and Men: A Lifetime of Braves Baseball* (New York: Random House, 2010).

Whitaker, Lang. *In the Time of Bobby Cox: The Atlanta Braves, Their Manager, My Couch, Two Decades, and Me*. (New York: Scribner, 2011).

Newspapers

The *Atlanta Journal-Constitution* has been a primary source of information about Ernie Johnson Jr.'s career. The *Kansas City Intelligencer*, *Miami Herald*, *The Sporting News*, and *USA Today* also were extremely helpful. Other contemporary sources include Associated Press and Yahoo Sports.

Social Media

YouTube has been a source of information about several recent events in Ernie Johnson Jr.'s life.

Interviews

Ernie Johnson Jr. with author, May 2010

Ernie Johnson Sr. with author, May 1986 and August 2001.

Ronald Reagan with author, March 1980.

Pete Van Wieren with author, March 2008.

Notes

1 Jason Reed/Fansided via Call to the Pen, "MLB History: Looking Back at MLB Teams That Relocated," FoxSports.com, June 30, 2017. foxsports.com/mlb/story/mlb-history-looking-back-at-mlb-teams-that-relocated-012017.

2 "Analysis of This Year's Braves: Spectator's Guide," *Sports Illustrated*, April 15, 1957: 71.

3 Ernie Johnson Sr. interview with author, May 1986.

4 John Hays, "The Johnsons: Two of the Boys of Summer," *Atlanta Constitution*, June 15, 1984: 31.

5 Hays, 31.

6 Ernie Johnson Jr. interview with author, May 2010.

7 Johnson Jr. interview.

8 Johnson Jr. interview.

9 Hays, 31.

10 Johnson Sr. interview with author, August 2001.

11 David Zurawik, "Ernie Johnson on Sportscasting: 'Don't Call It Work,'" *Baltimore Sun*, October 12, 2014.

12 Zurawik.

13 milwaukeebraves.info/attendance.htm.

14 Johnson Sr. August 2001 interview.

15 "Log of Play-by-Play Broadcasts and Telecasts," *The Sporting News*, April 16, 1966: 29.

16 Johnson Sr. May 1986 interview.

17 Hays, 38.

18 Stuart Miller, "30 Seconds With Ernie Johnson: From Hardwood to the Diamond," *New York Times*, May 2, 2010: SP10.

19 Hays, 38.

20 Hays, 38.

21 Hays, 38.

22 gpb.org/georgiastories/stories/voice_of_the_south.

23 Hays, 38.

24 Tim Sullivan, "TNT's Ernie Johnson Mixes Talk, Action," *Louisville Courier-Journal*, August 7, 2014: K3.

25 Hays, 38.

26 Premiere Speakers Bureau, Ernie Johnson bio. premierespeakers.com/christian/ernie-johnson/bio.

27 Mike Lopresti, "TBS' Ernie Johnson Spends October Bedside, Not in the South," *USA Today.com*. Updated October 10, 2011.

28 Sullivan.

29 Lopresti.

30 Lopresti.

31 Sullivan.

32 Sullivan.

33 Johnson Sr. May 1986 interview.

34 Johnson Sr. August 2001 interview.

35 Johnson Sr. August 2001 interview.

36 Baseball Almanac Francisco Cabrera stats. baseball-almanac.com/players/awards.php?p=cabrefr01.

37 mlb.com/news/best-playoff-hits-in-baseball-history-c296323348. Richard Justice, "These Are the Best 25 Postseason Hits," mlb.com, September 27, 2018.

38 Jimmy Carter, *Sharing Good Times* (New York: Simon & Schuster, 2004), 11.

39 genius.com/Paul-simon-mother-and-child-reunion-lyrics.

40 Carroll Rogers, "A Lifetime of Admiration," *Atlanta Constitution*, August 14, 2011: C3.

41 Prentis Rogers, "Johnson Father-Son Team Starts Braves Work Today," *Atlanta Constitution*, March 6, 1993: 46.

42 A. Bartlett Giamatti, "The Green Fields of the Mind," *Yale Alumni Magazine*. yalealumnimagazine.com/articles/3864.

43 Miller.

44 Miller.

45 Johnson Sr. August 2001 interview.

46 Miller.

47 Johnson Jr. May 2010 interview.

48 Sullivan.

49 Ray Glier, 'Traffic Cop' Ernie Johnson Jr. Keeps the Show Running Smoothly at TNT," *Atlanta Constitution*, February 11, 2007: T5.

50 Glier.

51 Tim Tucker, "Ernie Jr. Honors His Dad," *Atlanta Constitution*, October 5, 2013: C8.

52 Johnson Jr. May 2010 interview.

53 springfield.edu/where-basketball-was-invented-the-birthplace-of-basketball.

54 Barry Horn, "TBS Baseball Voice Ernie Johnson Knows He Won't Be Loved by Rangers Fans," *Dallas Morning News*, October 15, 2010.

55 Horn.

56 Dusty Saunders, "Ernie Johnson Jr. Makes Slick Transition to Baseball," *Denver Post*, October 11, 2010.

57 Zurawik.

58 Zurawik.

59 Zurawik.

60 Hays, 31.

61 Hays, 31.

62 sparknotes.com/nofear/shakespeare/hamlet/page_240/. Act 4, Scene 5, *Hamlet*.

63 Carroll Rogers, "A Lifetime of Admiration," *Atlanta Constitution*, August 14, 2011: C3.

64 Carroll Rogers.

65 Carroll Rogers.

66 Carroll Rogers.

67 Lopresti.

68 Lopresti.

69 Lopresti.

70 Lopresti.

71 youtube.com/watch?time_continue=10&v=4VQFQSWjzOo&feature=emb_title.

72 facebook.com/NBAfromBR/videos/376120559913106/.

73 Tucker.

74 Tucker.

75 Tucker.

76 Tucker.

77 Carroll Rogers.

78 Johnson Sr. May 1986 interview.

BALLPARK

Atlanta-Fulton County Stadium

BY SCOTT MCCLELLAN AND BOB BARRIER

Atlanta-Fulton County Stadium

From its beginning, as a plank in Ivan Allen's campaign platform for mayor, to its end, hosting the Olympic baseball competition and a World Series in its final year of existence, Atlanta Stadium was a major part of the push to make Atlanta a world-class city. The stadium succeeded in attracting teams from major-league baseball, the National Football League, and even the North American Soccer League. But the teams vacated the premises of 521 Capitol Avenue SE for alternate local venues, one by one, until the stadium was demolished on August 2, 1997, to make room for a parking lot to serve the Braves' new home.

While Braves fans were celebrating their World Series championship in 1995, it was very clear that the end was in sight for Atlanta-Fulton County Stadium. For at least 10 years there were suggestions and plans to renovate the stadium or move the Braves somewhere else. From a venue that was celebrated as sparkling and amazing in 1965 to a site enclosing the doldrums and non-sports-like hijinks of the dismal '80s to the astonishing, almost magical resurrection of the "Worst to First" Braves of 1991 and their sudden power of the mid-'90s, the 31-year story of the stadium needs to be retold, as it is fading from sports memory in contrast to new playing fields, a Hall of Fame cast of pitchers and manager, and 14 consecutive playoff appearances.

Soon after his 1962 inauguration, Allen was told by *Atlanta Journal* sports editor Furman Bisher that the Kansas City Athletics' owner, Charlie Finley, was coming to Atlanta to look for potential stadium sites. Allen and Bisher showed Finley four sites; when he saw the last, at the junction of I- 75/85 and I-20 a mile south of downtown, he told them, "This is the greatest site for a stadium I've ever seen. If you build it, I'll bring the Athletics here as soon as it's finished." The American League declined to approve this deal, but when the Milwaukee Braves were induced to move to Atlanta instead, plans for the stadium swiftly took shape.

Having developed a strong friendship with local architect and civic leader Cecil Alexander, Mayor Allen wanted his firm to design the facility. The head of the stadium authority preferred another firm, so the architects were compelled to form a joint venture, Finch-Heery Architects, which went on to design many other ballparks. Alexander did on-site research at Yankee Stadium, Shea Stadium, Busch Memorial Stadium, and D.C. Stadium (later renamed RFK Stadium). He gave his notes to his partner Bill Finch, who designed a circular stadium, with playing dimensions 325 feet down the lines and 402 feet to straightaway center, built in 51 weeks at a cost of $18 million.

The Stadium: A Functional Arena or a "Concrete Doughnut"

Twenty years after the closing of the stadium, a baseball and art critic remembered the architectural design of the stadium. Both of the architects "embraced a modern quasi-minimalistic 'international style,' ... that prioritized function over form, certainty over décor. Shunning traditional Southern esthetics, Atlanta Stadium (as it was called from 1966 to 1975) was like many of the other multipurpose stadiums that would be built in the 1960s – contemporary but sterile, practical but domesticated, bureaucratically formed to appease both football and baseball sensitivities within the same space."

More simply and critically, "one sports writer derided Atlanta Stadium and the other stadiums constructed in this era as 'concrete doughnuts.'" Such constant criticism irritated Atlanta sportswriter Jim Minter, whose exuberant reporting of that first opening weekend had reached high enthusiasm: "Atlanta Stadium is in the right place. It is precisely the right place. Anywhere else would be poor business and an abandonment of the 'undaunted, unconquerable, unsurpassed Atlanta spirit,' which was alive and well a short two decades ago. ... The real problem with major league sports in Atlanta is not the stadium, but rather the consistently disappointing performances of the teams playing there."

In the words of the baseball/art critic mentioned above, "sky-blue hues echoed throughout the otherwise white stadium, from the 50,000 plus wooden seats across three decks (including a petite second level partly reserved for media) to its upper deck overhang rim with horizontal Latin banks rather than the tall towers of electric lamps used in older facilities. In 1977 the stadium was remodeled with plastic seats, light blue on the field level and orange in the upper deck.

Atlanta Stadium: The Early Years

Although the Braves originally planned to move to Atlanta for the 1965 season, an antitrust suit filed by the City of Milwaukee against the Braves postponed the move for a year, so Atlanta Stadium hosted the last season of the International League's Atlanta Crackers in 1965. The first game at the stadium, however, was an exhibition game between Milwaukee and Detroit on April 9, 1965. Milwaukee won the game, 6-3, in front of 27,232 fans. Tommie Aaron hit the first home run there, a three-run shot in the first inning. Although traffic and parking problems delayed the start of the game, and long lines at the unfinished concession stands caused some irritation for fans, Atlanta Stadium's inauguration was generally viewed as a huge success for the city. On April 17 the Crackers opened their 1965 season with a victory over the Rochester Red Wings and then proceeded to sweep the three-game weekend series, just as the parent club had done to Detroit the previous weekend. The Crackers finished their only season in Atlanta Stadium in second place with a record of 83-64 and drew slightly more than 150,000 for the season.

The Braves opted to proceed with the move in 1966 despite the lawsuit, which was eventually decided in favor of the team. The Atlanta Braves debuted in their new home at 8:11 P.M. on April 12, 1966, before a capacity crowd of 50,671 fans, losing 3-2 to the Pirates. Joe Torre hit the first regular-season major-league home run in the ballpark in the fifth inning and added another in the bottom of the 13th. Although the Braves won a couple of division championships (1969, 1982) prior to their unprecedented title run beginning in 1991, Atlanta Stadium was, for the most part, the home of long stretches of bad baseball and paltry attendance for much of the 1970s and 1980s.

The Launching Pad

The stadium is best known as the site of Hank Aaron's 715th home run, launched into the Braves' bullpen just beyond the left-center-field fence on April 8, 1974. As Aaron circled the bases, the team's Native American mascot, "Chief Noc-a-homa," emerged from his tepee in the left-field stands to celebrate the home run with his customary war dance.

After moving to Atlanta, Aaron changed his stance, bringing his hands closer to his body. He made himself into a pull hitter and became one of the few players to see his home-run totals increase after the age of 35, helped by the 1,050-foot elevation of a new home park that became known as "The Launching Pad."

The stadium seemed to have left its mark on the Braves, who continued to base their offense around the home run even after moving into the more pitcher-friendly Turner Field.

The "Launching Pad" reputation was born in early 1966 when the team bus was returning from a road trip and the new pitchers stood up to get their first look at the stadium: "Veteran pitcher Pat Jarvis told them, 'There it is, boys. Welcome to the Launching Pad. You might as well get used to it. The ball really jumps outta there.' That was it. Atlanta Stadium was forever nicknamed for the pitchers of the National League."

The longest home run hit at the stadium was 475 feet by the Cubs' Willie Smith, June 10, 1969. During the 1996 Summer Olympics Cuba's Orestes Kindelan hit a ball 521 feet. After Aaron: The Doldrums of the 70s and 80s

After Ted Turner purchased the Braves in 1976, Atlanta Stadium hosted weddings at home plate, Fourth of July fireworks, and ostrich races around the warning track in an attempt to boost dwindling attendance. The ostriches weren't always confined to the warning track: Skip Caray recalled steering his bird directly from center field to home plate to steal a win.

Nor were the fireworks necessarily confined to July Fourth: the 1985 fireworks show started at 4:01 A.M. on July 5 after a 19-inning defeat and caused many of the stadium's neighbors, awakened by the noise, to fear that the area around the park had become a war zone. The City of Atlanta soon made it illegal to start fireworks shows after midnight. Responsibility for caring for the playing surface was transferred from the Atlanta municipal street-maintenance crew to a full-time groundskeeper in 1989. When John Schuerholz became general manager in 1990, Ed Mangan came with him from Kansas City and greatly improved the field conditions.

The New Miracle Braves

The teams that took the field also improved greatly under Schuerholz. The Braves went from "worst to first" in the NL West in 1991, losing to the Minnesota Twins in a riveting World Series that fall. In 1993 the Braves drew a franchise-record season attendance of 3,884,720. The Braves were nine games behind the Giants in the NL

West standings on July 20, 1993, when a pregame fire in the press box coincided with the arrival of first baseman Fred McGriff, who had been acquired in a trade with the San Diego Padres. Together, the press box conflagration and McGriff lit a fire underneath the Braves, who went 50-17 over the remainder of the season to secure the NL West flag.

Two of the stadium's most enduring moments came in the postseason during the club's resurrection in the 1990s: Francisco Cabrera's ninth-inning, two-out pinch-hit single in Game Seven of the 1992 NL Championship Series, culminating in Sid Bream's dramatic slide into home with the game-winning run, clinched the Braves second consecutive NL title; and when center fielder Marquis Grissom caught a fly ball to complete a combined one-hit shutout by Tom Glavine and Mark Wohlers on October 28, 1995 in Game Six of that year's World Series, the stadium finally hosted its first (and only) major-league championship. But by then the Braves were already looking forward to taking over Atlanta's 1996 Olympic Stadium, built on an adjoining lot, which would be reconfigured for baseball before the 1997 season and renamed Turner Field. The Braves played their last game in Atlanta Stadium on October 24, 1996, a 1-0 loss to the New York Yankees in the fifth game of the 1996 World Series.

That 1996 Series was indeed a bitter loss, for the team that year was an especially gifted one: It won a franchise record 56 games at home, hit .270, and homered 197 times (third-best ever for the team during the Atlanta-Fulton County Stadium years). The stellar pitching staff was one of the best in baseball, with John Smoltz (24-8 with 2.94 ERA), Greg Maddux, 15-11 with a 2.72 ERA, and Mark Wohlers saving 39 games. They swept the Dodgers in three games and rallied from a three-games-to-one deficit to beat the St. Louis Cardinals in the best-of-seven NLCS. In the World Series they beat the Yankees the first two games in Yankee Stadium, and appeared well on the way to consecutive World Series titles.

However, because of bad luck and bad playing in the field, they lost the next four games. The fourth game was the turning point. After the Braves led 6-0 into the sixth inning, the Yankees scored three runs on a misplayed pop foul and a two-run, two-base error, and then tied the game in the eighth on an infield hit, a force out on what should have been an inning-ending double-play ball, and a three-run homer. In the 10th, a two-out walk, an infield single, and an intentional walk followed by another walk, and a misplayed infield fly resulted in the two runs for the final score: Yankees 8, Braves 6. After this disaster and another error-causing loss, 1-0, in the fifth game, the collapse was completed with a 3-2 loss back in New York.

Other Sports and Events at the Stadium

Like the Braves, the Atlanta Falcons, a newly created National Football League team, played their first season in 1966, and they remained at Atlanta-Fulton County Stadium until the Georgia Dome opened in 1992. The Falcons opened on September 11, 1966, losing to the Los Angeles Rams 19-14. They finished that first season 3-11. Though the Braves had occasional pennant winners and one World Series championship, in their 26 years at the stadium the Falcons played in only six postseason games, advancing to the second round only twice. Only six of those 26 years were winning seasons, with the low point in attendance a game against Green Bay drawing only 10,000 fans. The Falcons' regular-season record over 26 years was 144 wins, 235 losses, and 5 ties, a .380 winning percentage, and a little better at home: 85-105-2, .438. If these generally mediocre years did not greatly appeal to the fan, the layout of the football field at the stadium was even more unsatisfactory: it was turned so that anyone sitting on the 50-yard line was 50 yards away from viewing.

College football soon came to the Atlanta-Fulton County Stadium in the form of the newly established Peach Bowl. The games were usually between teams from the Atlantic Coast Conference and the Southeastern Conference, with occasionally teams from the Big Ten and the Midwest. From 1968 through 1971 the game was played at Georgia Tech's Grant Field, and the most noteworthy aspect of the first four games was respectively the bad weather: cold wind, driving rain, swirling snow, and rain and mud. From 1971 through 1992, the Peach Bowl game was played at Atlanta-Fulton County Stadium, 21 games in all, including 11 teams in the Top 20, the highest ranked being the last one, New Year's Day 1992, with number 12 East Carolina defeating its intrastate rivals number 21 NC State 37-34. With the Georgia Dome opening in 1992, the games found a warm, dry, and impressive venue, thereby becoming eventually one of the top six postseason bowl games.

During the summer of 1996 – and in the middle of the baseball season and while the Braves were on an extended road trip – the baseball games on the 1996 Summer Olympics were held at Atlanta-Fulton County Stadium from July 20 through August 2. Eight nations participated (Cuba, Japan, the United States, Nicaragua, Netherlands, Italy, Australia, and South Korea), playing each other in 28 preliminary games and the top four moving on to the semifinals and final. Cuba, which was undefeated in the preliminary rounds, defeated Nicaragua 8-1 and Japan defeated the United States 11-2. The United States won the bronze Medal 10-3 over Nicaragua, and Cuba finished undefeated, winning the Gold 13-9 over Japan.

Summary – and an Image of the Past

In their time at the Atlanta-Fulton County Stadium, the Braves won 1,265 games and lost 1,166, 99 more wins although being outscored by 126 more runs. Overall, the Braves record was 2,388 won and 2,493 lost, a .489 average. The team batting average was .254, with 4,293 home runs, 19,053 RBIs, 20,350 runs, and 42,044 hits.

A small section of Atlanta-Fulton County Stadium's left-field wall, the site of Aaron's 715th home run, was left standing when the area was transformed into a parking lot next to Turner Field. Late in 2013, the Braves announced that they would leave the latter park behind as well and move to the northern suburbs. Beginning in 2017 the Braves played at SunTrust Field in Cobb County.

When the Braves abandoned Turner Field for SunTrust Park, Georgia State University purchased the facility and made it into a more oval-shaped football stadium with a memory of Atlanta Fulton County Stadium: "[T]he outfield wall will fuse in the memorial remnant of Aaron's 715 home run. Thus, anyone who attends the Georgia State baseball game in the near future can relax, kick back, and imagine the stadium that once surrounded the field and helped introduce Atlanta into the big leagues."[25]

Acknowledgment

This article represents a revised and expanded version of an earlier article by Scott McClellan, which appeared as part of SABR's BioProject.

Sources

In addition to the sources cited in the Notes, the author consulted Baseball-Reference.com, Pro Football-Reference.com, homeofthebraves.com, and Reidenbaugh, Lowell. *Take Me Out to the Ball Park* (St. Louis: The Sporting News Publishing Co., 1986).

Notes

1. The stadium was originally referred to as "Atlanta Stadium." The names "Atlanta-Fulton County Stadium" or just "Fulton County Stadium" saw common usage starting a few years later. It is unclear exactly when any given name became the "official" title.
2. The stretch of Capitol Avenue near the site of Atlanta Stadium and its successor, Turner Field, was renamed "Hank Aaron Drive" in 1997.
3. Cecil A. Alexander, *Crossing the Line* (Atlanta: W&C Publishing, 2012), 141.
4. Alexander, 142.
5. Philip J. Lowry, *Green Cathedrals* (New York: Walker & Company, 2006), 9.
6. Eric Gouldsberry, "The Ballparks: Parks of the Past, Atlanta-Fulton County Stadium," *This Great Game*. Accessed 27 January 2020. thisgreatgame.com/ballparks-atlanta-fulton-county-stadium.html.
7. Quoted in Kenneth R. Fenster, "Atlanta-Fulton County Stadium," in *New Georgia Encyclopedia*, December 10, 2019.

8 Jim Minter, "Clean Up Atlanta Stadium and Leave It Where It Is," *Atlanta Constitution*, March 3, 1985: 94.

9 Gouldsberry.

10 Marion Gaines, "37,232 Watch Braves Cage Tigers, 6-3, in Rousing Debut of Stadium," *Atlanta Constitution*, April 10, 1965: 1. The Braves swept the three-game exhibition series from the Tigers, which drew 106,000 fans.

11 Lloyd Johnson and Miles Wolff, eds., *The Encyclopedia of Minor League Baseball* (Durham, North Carolina: Baseball America, Inc., 2007). The Crackers were relocated to Richmond, Virginia, for the 1967 season, and renamed the Richmond Braves.

12 Bob Klapisch and Pete Van Wieren, *The World Champion Braves: 125 Years of America's Team* (Atlanta: Turner Publishing Inc., 1996), 134-135.

13 Ira Rosen, *Blue Skies, Green Fields* (New York: Clarkson Potter/Publishers, 2001), 24. Stadium capacity was typically cited as 52,000 in the local media.

14 Rosen.

15 Jack Wilkinson, *Game of My Life* (Champaign, Illinois: Sports Publishing, LLC, 2007), 106.

16 Bill James, *The Bill James Historical Abstract* (New York: Villard Books, 1988), 416.

17 Ed Hinton, "Science Can't Explain Stadium's 'Missiles,'" *Atlanta Journal and Constitution*, April 5, 1981: 9C. This article includes a table showing the home runs hit in the National League ballparks from 1976 to 1980, with Atlanta-Fulton County Stadium having for that period more than 100 over the nearest competitor (799 over Wrigley Field's 690). The article interviews scientists as well as Braves sluggers Dale Murphy and Bob Horner in an unsuccessful attempt to explain the "Launching Pad." However, an analysis of total home runs from Baseball-Reference.com reveals that in the 31-year-period of the stadium, 4,617 home runs were hit there (the Braves hitting 2,385); whereas for the same period of years, Fenway Park had 4,625 and Wrigley Field 4,621. So Atlanta-Fulton County Stadium, during the period in question, is third in number of total home runs hit, averaging 148.9 per season in contrast to the overall 31-year period of 153.9. Interestingly, for the 20 years that the Braves occupied Turner Field, the average was almost the same, 150.4. The real "Launching Pad" might be SunTrust Park, in which for three years the home run average was 182.7. These are all total home runs, Braves and opposing teams.

18 Charley Roberts, "Smith HR Equal to Poncey Pokes," *Atlanta Constitution*, June 17, 1969: 39.

19 Tom Whitfield and Joe Strauss, "Day 5: Baseball Atlanta-Fulton County Stadium," *Atlanta Constitution*, July 23, 1996: 85.

20 John Pastier, *Ballparks, Yesterday and Today* (Edison, New Jersey: Chartwell Books, Inc., 2007), 98.

21 Wilkinson, 130.

22 Lowry, 9.

23 Eric Pastore, *500 Ballparks* (San Diego: Thunder Bay Press, 2011), 41.

24 Jay Jaffe, "The 1996 Yankees and the Epic Comeback That Started Baseball's Last Dynasty," *Sports Illustrated*, August 26, 2016. si.com/mlb/2016/08/1996-yankees-reunion-world-series.

25 Gouldsberry.

NOTABLE GAMES

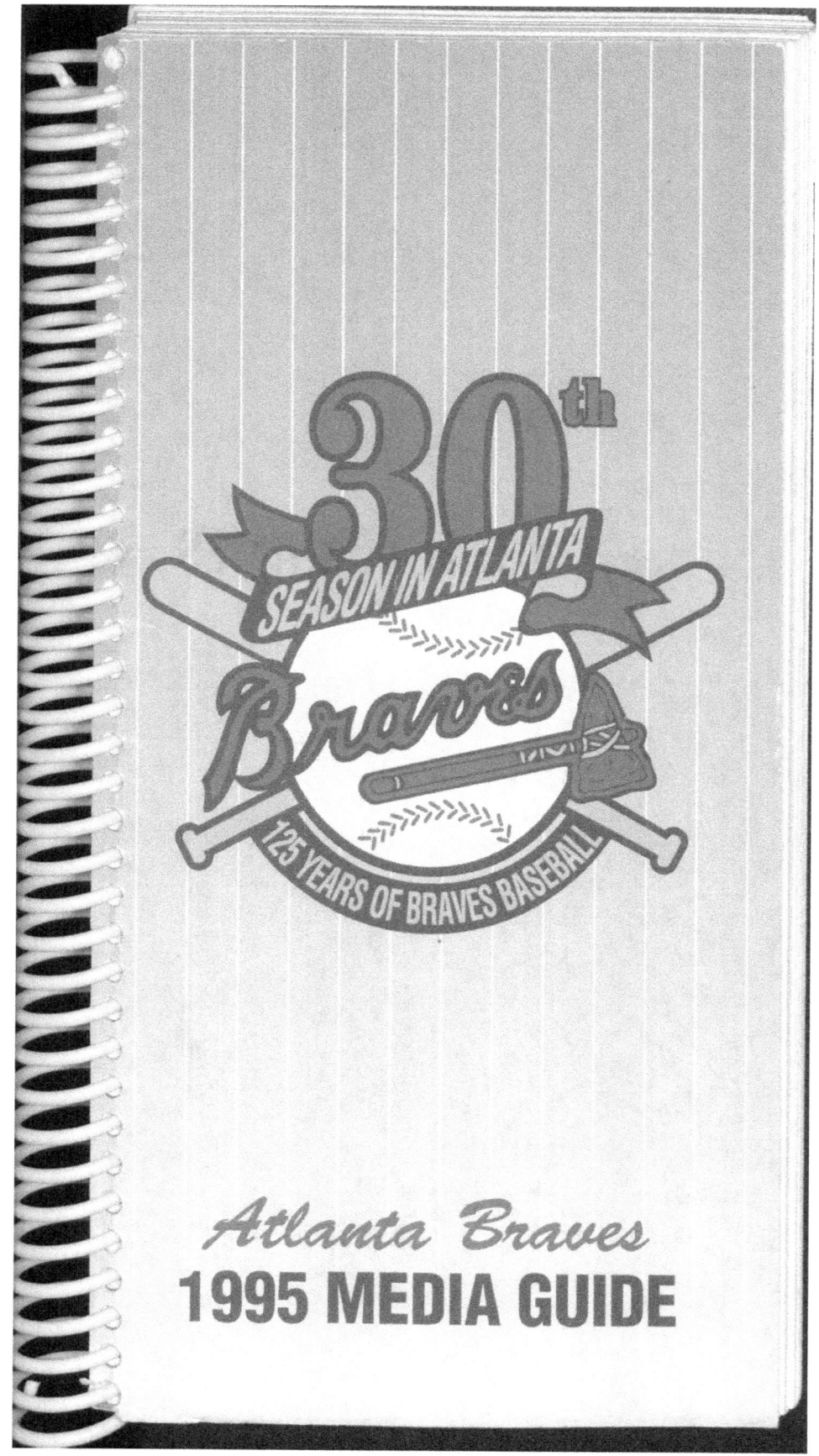

Opening Day

APRIL 26, 1995: ATLANTA BRAVES 12, SAN FRANCISCO GIANTS 5, AT ATLANTA-FULTON COUNTY STADIUM, ATLANTA

BY CHRIS JONES

While most teams enter a new season with a sense of optimism, few have faced the level of expectations placed on the 1995 Atlanta Braves. After acquiring center fielder and leadoff man Marquis Grissom from the Expos before the season, general manager John Schuerholz went so far as to say, "We're the first team to ever win the World Series in April."[1] While the statement was undoubtedly made tongue-in-cheek, and Schuerholz would also make the somewhat contradictory statement that "we have high expectations, but no pressure," there was no disputing that the Braves were the class of the National League heading into the season.[2]

Typically, such lofty expectations are accompanied by an increase in attendance. But 1995 was not a typical year for major-league baseball; the prior season had been cut short due to the players strike and fans across the country were reluctant to return. Even the New York Yankees coming to town for the final exhibition game of the spring resulted in only "between 8,000 and 9,000" actually in attendance (though the team announced a crowd of 25,309).[3]

The sparse crowd did not go unnoticed by the players. Outfielder David Justice said, "There's nobody here. The fans are upset at what's gone on. [T]hey're showing it by not showing up. I can't blame them."[4] Player representative Tom Glavine was more optimistic, attributing the sparse crowd to a number of factors: "It's cold. [I]t's an exhibition, and it's a school night."[5] Glavine added, "I think it's foolish or naïve to think that everyone who wasn't here stayed away because of the strike' … [But] every time there's a low crowd, people are going to blame the strike."[6]

Whatever the reason for the low turnout for the exhibition game, the Braves hoped for a livelier crowd for Opening Day, April 26. A 4:05 P.M. start time on a Wednesday did not help matters, though, and only 24,091 showed up at Atlanta-Fulton County Stadium to see the Braves open the season against the San Francisco Giants.[7] One local writer opined that such an attendance figure was "the sort of crowd once reserved for Sunday afternoons in the '80s."[8] The team was even "greeted by scattered boos" to start the game.[9] On the field, however, the Braves wasted little time giving those who did show up something to cheer about.

Three-time Cy Young Award winner Greg Maddux, who had made only one spring-training start due to a bout with chickenpox,[10] got the season off on the right foot by setting down the Giants in order in the top of the first. In the Braves' first, the newly acquired Grissom got an early start toward endearing himself to Atlanta fans as he led off with a double. Five consecutive singles followed, by Jeff Blauser, Chipper Jones, Fred McGriff, Justice, and Javy Lopez, and the Braves took an early 4-0 lead.

After the game, Giants manager Dusty Baker lamented his club's poor start. "Maddux is the premier pitcher in baseball," and if you "spot him four runs it's just about over," he said.[11] That was just about right, as Maddux did not allow a hit until J.R. Phillips connected for a solo home run with one out in the fifth inning. By that time, even Maddux himself had a hit, having led off the second inning with an infield single. Maddux scored on a throwing error as the Giants tried to turn a double play to get out of the inning, and McGriff singled home another run to make the score 6-0 after two innings.

The score remained the same until the fourth inning, when McGriff tallied his third hit, a solo home run to right field. McGriff, in the last year of the contract he had signed with the San Diego Padres before being traded to Atlanta, showed that a slow spring training, in which he hit only .240 with one home run, was nothing to worry about. Manager Bobby Cox said he never had any doubt that McGriff would be ready to go at the opening bell. Cox said McGriff "starts out slow, but he's always working on things. Everything he does builds up to Opening Day."12

Phillips's home run in the fifth put the Giants on the board, and accounted for the first run Maddux had surrendered in three previous Opening Day starts, over a span of 20⅔ innings.13 The Giants added two more runs in the sixth with an RBI single and groundout from Robby Thompson and Matt Williams, respectively. An RBI single by Brad Woodall in the seventh pushed Atlanta's lead to 8-3, but the Giants continued to pull closer in the eighth, when a single by John Patterson and a home run by Robby Thompson made the score 8-5.

But the Braves would not be overtaken on this day. Jeff Blauser doubled to lead off the bottom of the eighth. Chipper Jones, making the first Opening Day start, followed with an RBI single to center field. Jones had actually won the Braves' shortstop job in the spring of 1994, but a knee injury sidelined him for the year and he re-emerged in 1995 as the team's third baseman for the foreseeable future.14 Following Jones was McGriff, who continued to have a memorable day by blasting his second home run, giving himself five RBIs for the game. David Justice capped the scoring with a solo home run, and the Braves had a 12-5 lead. Brad Clontz closed out the game for the Braves with a 1-2-3 ninth inning.

The Braves' 12 Opening Day runs were their third highest total in 1995, surpassed only by outbursts of 15 and 17 against the Rockies and Cubs, respectively. The victory was also part of the team's fast start, as they won seven of their first eight games on their way to 90 wins and the National League East crown. That title would of course later be overshadowed when the Braves topped the Cleveland Indians to win the 1995 World Series, proving general manager Schuerholz's April prediction correct.

Sources

In addition to the sources noted in the Notes, the author accessed Retrosheet.org and Baseball-Reference.com.

Notes

1. "NL East: The Best, Braves, Just Got Better," *Cincinnati Enquirer*, April 26, 1995: 61.
2. "Astros, Padres Test Value of Big Trade," *Daily Advertiser* (Lafayette, Louisiana), April 26, 1995: 25.
3. Tom Saladino, "Braves Searching for Fan Support at Home," *Daily World* (Opelousas, Louisiana), April 25, 1995: 7.
4. Saladino.
5. Saladino.
6. Mark Bradley, "Braves Fans Reveal Remaining Ill Will by Their Absence," *Atlanta Constitution* April 27, 1995: 50.
7. Rand Cawthon, "24,091 Respond to National Pastime's Lure," *Atlanta Constitution*, April 25,1995: 50. The announced attendance for the game was 32,045, but actual attendance in the "half-filled" ballpark seemed to belie that figure. Mark Bradley's accompanying article cited the same "actual attendance" figure of 24,091.
8. Bradley.
9. "Braves Start Fast, Rout Giants, 12-5," *Santa Cruz* (California) *Sentinel*, April 27, 1995: 13.
10. Denise N. Maloof, "McGriff Quickly Resumes Role as Braves' Main Power Source," *Atlanta Constitution*, April 27, 1995: 50.
11. "McGriff Crushes 2 HRs, Braves Rip Giants 12-5," *Florida Today* (Cocoa, Florida), April 27, 1995: 25.
12. "McGriff Quickly Resumes Role as Braves' Main Power Source."
13. "Braves Beat Giants 12-5," *Selma* (Alabama) *Times-Journal*, April 27, 1995: 9.
14. "Atlanta Braves," *New York Daily News*, April 23, 1995: 15C.

Chipper Jones Belts First Career Home Run

MAY 9, 1995: ATLANTA BRAVES 3, NEW YORK METS 2, AT SHEA STADIUM, QUEENS, NEW YORK

BY PAUL HOFMANN

The early-season Tuesday evening game was the first of a three-game series between the Atlanta Braves and the homestanding New York Mets.[1] Tied for second with the Montreal Expos, the Braves were coming off a rare four-game sweep at the hands of the Philadelphia Phillies in Atlanta. They entered the Mets game with a record of 7-5, 1½ games behind the Phillies. The Mets had already suffered four agonizing walk-off defeats in the season's first two weeks and were 4-7, four games off the pace.

The game drew an announced crowd of 14,882 to see an intriguing pitching matchup that pitted two of the National League's more notable pitchers against each other. Neither pitcher had distinguished himself in his first two starts of the season.

Left-handed change-of-speed artist Steve Avery was the starter for the Braves. The two-time 18-game winner entered the game with a record of 0-1 and a 5.19 ERA. The Mets countered with two-time American League Cy Young Award winner Bret Saberhagen. The Mets right-hander also entered the game with a 0-1 record and an elevated 7.50 ERA.

The game-time temperature was a seasonally cool 62 degrees and conditions were dry when Saberhagen delivered the game's first pitch at 7:35 P.M. Saberhagen and Avery traded 1-2-3 innings in the first before the Braves scored first in the top of the second. Dwight Smith drew a one-out walk off Saberhagen, the only walk he would yield in the game, before Charlie O'Brien lined a home run deep into the bleachers down the left-field line. After an inning and a half, the score stood at Braves 2, Mets 0.

For a while it seemed as though "the 25th career home run of eternally light-hitting former Met backup catcher O'Brien"[2] might be the difference as the two starters engaged in a classic pitching duel. Avery kept the Mets off the board until the bottom of the sixth, when the home team scored a run. Saberhagen led off the inning with a double to left. Brett Butler laid down a sacrifice bunt to third, moving Saberhagen to third. Edgardo Alfonzo followed with a fly to deep right-center to score Saberhagen and make the score 2-1.

Greg McMichael replaced Avery in the bottom of the seventh. The move was part of a double switch that sent Mike Kelly into right. McMichael, who was the Braves' closer a year earlier and was now a right-handed setup man, pitched a scoreless seventh.

Josias Manzanillo relieved Saberhagen in the top of the eighth. The right-hander from the Dominican Republic entered the game with a record of 0-0 and and 11.12 ERA. Manzanillo retired the Braves to keep the Mets within a run.

McMichael returned to the mound for a second inning in the bottom of the eighth. After retiring Brett Butler on a grounder to second and getting Alfonzo to fly out to right, McMichael appeared headed for an easy inning as Mets second baseman Jeff Kent came to the plate. Kent, who was mired in an early-season slump (.167 with one home run and three RBIs), deposited an 0-and-1 offering from McMichael into the left-field bullpen, tying tie the game.

Braves rookie left fielder Chipper Jones led off the top of the ninth. The switch-hitting Jones, who entered the game hitting .233, was playing because regular outfielders David Justice and Ryan Klesko were injured. With the count 2-and-0, Jones, who was batting left-handed, crushed a fastball into the right-field loge seats off Manzanillo.[3] Jones's first major-league home run gave the Braves a 3-2 lead and put McMichael in a position to earn the victory. After the game, Jones told reporters, "I can't tell you the feeling I had when I was rounding first base. It is really a weight off my shoulders."[4]

Right-handed rookie Brad Clontz, who had saved three of the Braves' first seven victories but faltered in his previous outing, came on in the bottom of the ninth to preserve the victory for McMichael. Clontz hit leadoff batter Todd Hundley and Carl Everett sacrificed the Mets catcher to second. Clontz then retired Ricky Otero and David Segui on fly balls to end the game. Acknowledging his failure to hold a one-run lead two days earlier, Clontz said afterward, "I wanted to get back out there in a one-run game and finish it out."[5]

McMichael earned the victory and moved his record to 2-0. Clontz earned his fourth and final save of the season. He blew a save opportunity in his next outing and relinquished the closer role to right-hander Mark Wohlers. Manzanillo, who less than a month later was claimed off waivers by the pitching-starved New York Yankees, suffered the loss for the Mets. The time of the game was 2:21.

The victory was the Braves' sixth in seven on the road. Manager Bobby Cox put the victory in context after the game: "After losing four straight at home and coming in here to face one of the best pitchers of the last 15 years, I'd say that was a great win for the Braves."[6]

Jones's first major-league home run was a long time coming for the future Hall of Famer, who was ticketed for superstardom after being selected number one in the 1990 amateur draft out of the Bolles School in Jacksonville, Florida. He played in eight games with the Braves when the rosters expanded in September of 1993 and was slated to start the 1994 season as the team's left fielder. This all changed on March 19, 1994, in an exhibition game against the Yankees at Fort Lauderdale, Florida. In the top of the fifth inning, Jones hit a groundball to shortstop, but the throw pulled Yankees first baseman Jim Leyritz off the bag. In an effort to avoid the tag, the rookie angled his body awkwardly and then crumpled to the ground.[7] Jones missed the entire 1994 season.

Over the years, the Braves-Mets rivalry brought out the best in Jones. In 245 games against the Mets, he hit .309 with 49 home runs and 159 RBIs. As the rivalry heated up, New York fans increasingly focused their wrath on Jones, serenading the Braves star with chants of "Lar-ry, Lar-ry" – after pitcher Orel Hershiser mentioned in an interview that the Braves' star hated being called by his given name.[8]

Jones finished the season with a batting average of .265 with 23 home runs and 86 RBIs, numbers that in many years would have earned him Rookie of the Year honors. However, in a controversial vote, Jones finished runner-up to Japanese phenom Hideo Nomo of the Los Angeles Dodgers. The 26-year-old Nomo had pitched for five years before coming to the Dodgers as a free agent and leading the National League in strikeouts in his first season.[9]

Jones went on to have a legendary career with the Atlanta Braves and finished his Hall of Fame career with a .303 average, 468 home runs, and 1,623 RBIs. Along the way he won the 1999 NL MVP Award, captured the 2008 NL batting title, and thrilled baseball fans everywhere.

Sources

In addition to the sources cited in the Notes, the author relied on Baseball-reference.com and Retrosheet.org.

Notes

1. The start of the 1995 season was delayed as a consequence of the 1994-95 players strike. The season did not open until April 26.

2   Howard Blatt, "Not Feeling Chipper: Jones' HR in 9th Beats Josias," *New York Daily News,* May 10, 1995: 52.

3   Blatt.

4   I.J. Rosenberg, "And Then Along Came Jones in the 9th," *Atlanta Constitution*, May 10, 1995: 21.

5   Rosenberg.

6   Rosenberg.

7   William Juliano, "Remembering a Not So Chipper Start to Future Hall of Famer's Career," The Captains Blog, March 22, 2012. Retrieved from captainsblog.info/2012/03/22/remembering-a-not-so-chipper-start-to-future-hall-of-famers-career/13990/.

8   John Romano, "Braves-Mets: War of the Words," *Tampa Bay Times*, October 12, 1999: 10C, as cited by Jacob Pomrenke in "Chipper Jones," SABR BioProject. Retrieved from sabr.org/bioproj/person/b7c916e5.

9   Pomrenke.

Klesko and Jones Lead Braves' Biggest Offensive Show of the Season

JUNE 6, 1995: ATLANTA BRAVES 17, CHICAGO CUBS 3 AT ATLANTA-FULTON COUNTY STADIUM

BY RICHARD CUICCHI

The Atlanta Braves were the prohibitive favorites to get to the World Series in 1995. The prior season had been shortened by the players strike and consequently there were no playoffs. But in the three seasons before that, the Braves showed dominance in the National League with appearances in a League Championship Series and two World Series. The Braves ultimately wound up marching to the World Series again, largely on the strength of their pitching. But a game in early June showed that they could also hit with power with the best of teams.

The 32,402 fans attending the June 6 contest against the Chicago Cubs in Atlanta witnessed the team's best offensive performance of the season. The game was marked by the Braves' 20 hits and five home runs, led by left fielder Ryan Klesko and rookie third baseman Chipper Jones, who together drove in 10 of the runs. The rout was highlighted by eight Braves runs in the fourth inning, their most in one inning since 1991.

The day before, the Cubs had fallen out of first place in the NL Central Division for the first time in the season after losing to the Braves. The Cubs' pitching staff had the best ERA in the league coming into this game.[1] Right-hander Steve Trachsel, who hadn't recorded a winning decision in his last three starts, took the hill in his first-ever appearance against the Braves.

The Braves were in a battle with Montreal for second place in the East Division, which Philadelphia led by three games. On a mound staff that included future Hall of Famers Tom Glavine, Greg Maddux, and John Smoltz, 27-year-old left-hander Kent Mercker took his turn in the rotation. Now in his seventh season with the Braves, he had been converted into a full-time starter in 1994.

After the Cubs scored a run in the top of the first on a single, a balk by Mercker, and two groundouts, Atlanta started its onslaught in the bottom half. Marquis Grissom and Chipper Jones singled (his first of four hits in the game) and Fred McGriff hit a sacrifice fly. Klesko then hit a two-run blast, his first homer of the season. He had been a slump, batting .211 with only three extra-base hits coming into the game.

The Braves scored again in the second, when Mark Lemke hit a leadoff single, took second on Mercker's sacrifice, and scored on Grissom's second single of the night. Grissom, who had recently lost his leadoff role to rookie Brian Kowitz because of poor hitting, seemed to be adjusting well to the number-two slot in the batting order.

After a scoreless third, the Braves had their huge inning in the fourth. Javier Lopez led off with his sixth homer of the season. After walking Lemke and Kowitz, Trachsel was replaced by Willie Banks, who had been struggling with a 10.45 ERA and was reportedly on the trading block. Banks walked Grissom, loading the bases. Jones followed with two-run single. After McGriff was intentionally walked, loading the bases again, Klesko cleared them with his first major-league grand slam. (He would go on to hit 10 during his 16-year career.) Jeff Blauser added to Banks's grief with a back-to-back solo home run to make the score 12-1.

Perhaps relaxed by his comfortable lead, Mercker gave up a leadoff triple to Shawon Dunston and a run-scoring single to Jose Hernandez in the top of the fifth. The Braves retaliated in the bottom of the inning with a two-run homer by Jones, his eighth of the season. Blauser added a run-scoring single.

The Cubs scored their last run of the game in the sixth, with Mercker yielding a single, a double, and an RBI groundout by Todd Pratt.

Turk Wendell, who had relieved Banks in the fifth, finished the game for Cubs. He allowed two more Braves runs in the seventh inning, on a two-run single by Lopez.

Braves relievers Brad Clontz, Pedro Borbon Jr., and Steve Bedrosian succeeded Mercker and closed out the game without allowing any baserunners.

Klesko finished the day going 4-for-5 including his two round-trippers, with six RBIs and three runs scored. He avoided the sophomore jinx stigma (he was third in NL Rookie of the Year voting in 1994) when he finished the season with 23 home runs, 70 RBIs, and a slash line of .310/.396/.608. Klesko seemed relieved after the game, saying, "I'm here to drive in runs and I finally did my job."[2]

Jones was also 4-for-5, with four runs scored and four RBIs. As the runner-up for Rookie of the Year in 1995, the switch-hitter collected 23 home runs and 86 RBIs for the season. Braves manager Bobby Cox gushed about Jones's potential after the game, saying, "I'm going to get his uniform after the season and get him to autograph it. It will be worth more [than two of his baseball cards]."[3]

The Braves' five home runs were their most in a game in 1995. The franchise record was eight, hit on August 30, 1953, against Pittsburgh. Grissom, Blauser, and Lopez each collected three hits. The Braves' 20 hits matched their total on May 16 when they defeated Colorado, 15-3.

Mercker gave up five hits and struck out five during his six innings. He claimed his third win. Trachsel yielded seven earned runs in 3⅓ innings, with his ERA increasing from 2.86 to 3.99. Banks, who gave up eight runs, was traded to the Los Angeles Dodgers two weeks later.

The Cubs seemed to take the loss in stride, even though it was their fourth in six games, all on the road. Manager Jim Riggleman said, "We just got whipped. They just pounded the ball and beat us."[4] Cubs outfielder Brian McRae echoed Riggleman's sentiments: "We got our butts whipped."[5] The Cubs failed to regroup and get back into first place again.

A month later the Braves took hold of first place and never relinquished it. They wound up with the best record (90-54) in the NL, carried largely by their pitching staff, which led the league in ERA and WHIP. While the Braves were second in the league in home runs, they finished second lowest in batting average and fifth lowest in on-base percentage.

Atlanta fulfilled the preseason prediction of a World Series appearance. The Braves lost only one game to the Colorado Rockies in the NLDS and then swept the Cincinnati Reds in the ALCS. Their defeat of the Cleveland Indians in the World Series was their only World Series championship from 1991 to 2005, when they won consecutive division titles (except for the strike year). Altogether they won five pennants in the 1990s. As such, they became known as the Team of the '90s.

Sources

In addition to the sources listed in the Notes, the author consulted Baseball-Reference.com, Retrosheet.org, and the *1996 Atlanta Braves Media Guide*.

Notes

1. Joseph A. Reaves. "June Not Kind to Cubs' NL-Best Pitching Staff," *Chicago Tribune*, June 7, 1995: Section 4, 3.
2. I.J. Rosenberg. "Braves Crank Up Power 17-3," *Atlanta Constitution*, June 7, 1995: D1.
3. Rosenberg.
4. Reaves.
5. Reaves.

Braves Retake NL East Division Lead

JULY 4, 1995: ATLANTA BRAVES 3, LOS ANGELES DODGERS 2, AT ATLANTA-FULTON COUNTY STADIUM, ATLANTA

BY JACK ZERBY

American Independence Day, July 4, roughly marking the middle of the baseball season, is also significant in the venerable history of the Boston-Milwaukee-Atlanta Braves franchise. On July 4, 1914, the Boston Braves lost both ends of a home doubleheader to the Brooklyn Robins to further embed themselves in the National League cellar with a 26-40 record. But under manager George Stallings, those Braves then caught fire, finished 94-59, and won the pennant by a comfortable 10½ games. By then both Stallings and his team had earned the appellation "Miracle."[1] The club topped things off by sweeping the 1914 World Series from Connie Mack's formidable Philadelphia A's.

The Milwaukee Braves stood in third place, 42-32 and a game and a half out when play finished on July 3, 1957. They finished 95-59, eight games ahead, to win the National League pennant then beat the New York Yankees in the World Series.[2]

By the end of the 1990 season, the ebb and flow of mediocrity that had plagued the Braves since their move from Milwaukee to Atlanta left the team at with a 65-97 record in last place in the National League West Division. There was no place to go but up – and the 1991 Braves did just that, with a rejuvenating mix of veteran and young players. That team was 38-37 and 8½ games out at the close of play on July 3 before charging to a 94-68 record under reinstalled manager Bobby Cox to win the NL West divisional pennant by one game.[3] They went on to nip the Pittsburgh Pirates four games to three in the NLCS, then fall to the Minnesota Twins by the same count in a World Series that many still count among the most exciting in baseball history.

The suddenly relevant Braves repeated as West Division champions in 1992 and 1993. But whatever the 1994 standings might have been will forever be an unsolvable mystery, as player-management discord resulted in a strike that stopped play after the August 11 games, wiped out the postseason, and extended into 1995 spring training.[4]

Baseball initially struggled through a farce of spring training with what ownership termed "replacement players" before the strike was settled by court injunction on March 31. Traditional spring training got a late start, which delayed the start of the 1995 regular season.[5]

Striving for a fourth straight divisional title, the 1995 Braves, now in the reconfigured National League East, initially had trouble getting traction.[6] Yet they never fell below third place, and by June 25 had climbed back to second, but were still 4½ games behind the Philadelphia Phillies. But by June 29, an offday on which the Phillies lost, Atlanta was 2½ games back after a walk-off win at home against Montreal the night before. The Braves rolled into Philadelphia on Friday, June 30, for a four-game set that could set the tone for the rest of the divisional race.

The Braves' division deficit was back to 3½ games when the Phillies' Tyler Green outdueled John Smoltz on Friday night, 3-1. Then, the dominance of the Braves' starting pitching asserted itself as Greg Maddux, Tom Glavine, and Steve Avery paced Atlanta to wins in the next three games. After Avery's 10-4 win on July 3, the Braves were 38-25, had cut the margin to a half-game, and were on their way back home to meet the Los Angeles Dodgers on Tuesday night, July 4.

The Phillies had an afternoon game that day in Pittsburgh. Despite Philadelphia's heritage as the home of the Liberty Bell, they absorbed some cracks of their own, losing 7-0 to their cross-state rival Pirates. That evened the National League standings, giving the Braves an opportunity to move back into first place for the first time since May 7, when the Phillies had slipped past them.

On the Fourth, 49,104 fans filled Atlanta-Fulton County Stadium for traditional holiday fireworks and to greet their team after the success in Philadelphia. The Dodgers were in their own pennant race; the Rockies had increased their lead in the NL West to one game with a win on Monday while the Dodgers were idle.

Dodgers manager Tom Lasorda tabbed 21-year-old righty Ismael Valdez, a second-year man, as his starter. Valdez sported a 2.53 ERA and had won five straight starts in June before losing his last outing, against the San Diego Padres on June 28. The fifth starter in Atlanta's rotation, lefty Kent Mercker, was Bobby Cox's choice. On paper the Dodgers appeared to have the best of it – Mercker's ERA over 12 starts through June 28 was a pedestrian 4.68 on a starting staff featuring three future Hall of Famers in Maddux, Glavine, and Smoltz, along with 1991 National League Championship Series MVP Avery.

The pitchers dominated both halves of the first inning, getting all six outs on a total of 14 pitches. Valdez was especially effective, retiring the Braves on five, with an outfield assist by right fielder Raul Mondesi thwarting Chipper Jones's attempt to stretch a single into a double. Mercker's first-inning success evaporated in the second. Eric Karros ripped his first pitch into left field for a double, went to third base on Roberto Kelly's sharp single up the middle, then scored on Mondesi's sacrifice fly to center fielder Marquis Grissom. Mercker got some help when Kelly strayed far enough off first base for Grissom to double him up there as he tried to scramble back. That out saved a run when the next batter, Tim Wallach, homered to left to make it 2-0, Dodgers. Mercker then fanned Billy Ashley to escape further damage. The Braves responded, getting one run back in their half of the second on a solo home run down the right-field line by David Justice.

Los Angeles got runners as far as third base in each of the third and fourth innings, while Valdez kept the Braves in check until Ryan Klesko's solo homer on an 0-and-2 pitch tied the game with two outs in the Atlanta seventh. Then, after Greg McMichael, who had replaced Mercker to open the seventh inning, and Brad Clontz, who replaced McMichael for the final two outs in the Dodgers' eighth, kept the score knotted, Cox pulled managerial magic as the Braves batted in the their eighth. He used Dwight Smith to pinch-hit for number-eight hitter Rafael Belliard, who had done nothing with Valdez.

Smith worked a six-pitch walk. Pinch-hitter Mike Mordecai bunted him to second on the first pitch. Lasorda elected to intentionally walk Grissom to pitch to Jeff Blauser, who was in the midst of a prolonged slump.[7] This time, Blauser got to a 3-and-2 count and broke his bat on Valdez's seventh pitch, but managed to bloop the ball just out of reach of shortstop Jose Offerman as Smith roared home with the lead run. "I'll take it. Texas Leaguers aren't too bad. The past few days I hit a few balls hard and they didn't fall in," Blauser told writers.[8]

That run was enough to move the Braves into first place, as closer Mark Wohlers polished off Mondesi, Wallach, and pinch-hitter Dave Hansen on nine pitches to seal the win for Clontz.

It had indeed been another significant July 4 for the Braves franchise. Atlanta went on to win eight of their next nine games. By July 15 they were 21 games over .500 and led second-place Philadelphia by 6½ games in the division. The Braves cruised in first place the rest of the way, finished 90-54 with the shortened schedule, and won the 1995 NL East crown – their fourth straight – by a tidy 21-game margin. With that kind of dominance and the playoffs looming, another miracle might be in the offing.

Sources

In addition to the sources cited in the Notes, the author used the Baseball-Reference.com and Retrosheet.org websites for box scores, team and player pages, and game and season logs.

Notes

1. "Braves Ready to Fight for World Honors," *Boston Globe*, October 4, 1914: 53.

2. The Boston Braves moved to Milwaukee for the 1953 season. The franchise left Milwaukee for Atlanta after the 1965 season.

3. Cox, who had managed the Braves from 1978 through the 1981 season, took over from Russ Nixon on June 23, 1990.

4. The 1994 Braves stood 68-46 and in second place, six games behind the Montreal Expos in the new NL East, when the strike stopped play.

5. Gershon Rabinowitz, "Revisiting Replacement Players," blog at Baseball Essential.com, posted March 15, 2015, accessed June 10, 2019. Major-league schedules were shortened to 144 games for 1995. The Braves didn't open their regular season until April 26.

6. Beginning with the 1994 season, the National League reconfigured its divisional alignment with a new Central Division. Before the 1994 realignment, the East and West Divisions had seven teams each; as realigned, the East and new Central Divisions had five teams each, and the West had four. The Braves and Dodgers, former rivals in the West Division, were now in different divisions.

7. In the preceding Philadelphia series, Blauser had been 1-for-19. Jack Wilkinson, "Blauser Breaks Bat, Slump, Dodgers," *Atlanta Constitution*, July 5, 1995: 25. He was hitting .222 going into this game, but had managed a single in the fourth inning. The hit was a nonfactor when Blauser was promptly erased on Jones's double-play ball.

8. Wilkinson.

Braves Win Ninth Consecutive Game on McGriff's Home Run

JULY 9, 1995: ATLANTA BRAVES 3, SAN FRANCISCO GIANTS 2, AT ATLANTA-FULTON COUNTY STADIUM, ATLANTA

BY THOMAS J. BROWN JR.

The Atlanta Braves started July 1995 on a tear, winning eight games in eight days. They started the streak 2½ games behind the Phillies. After their eighth consecutive win, they had moved into first place, 3½ games ahead of Philadelphia.

San Francisco arrived in Atlanta after splitting six games to start July. The Giants started the month just 1½ games behind the first place Colorado Rockies in the National League West Division. After losing the first two games of the series in Atlanta, the Giants had fallen to five games behind the Rockies. The Giants were hitting just .251, last in the National League.

Giants general manager Bob Quinn was trying to find a way to get the team back on track. He was preparing to attend the coming All-Star Game as part of his search for another pitcher to help a pitching staff that had been racked by injuries. "We've scored enough runs to win our share of games, but as is so often the case in baseball, our pitching hasn't always caught up with our hitting," Quinn said.[1]

Kent Mercker started the July 9 game for Atlanta. Mercker joined the Braves in 1990 and by 1995 he was the fifth pitcher in a rotation that included Tom Glavine, John Smoltz, and Greg Maddux. He entered the game with a 4-4 record. He had thrown well in his previous two starts but failed to pick up a win.

Mercker pitched solidly for the first four innings. He surrendered just one hit, a single to Mark Carreon in the second. The Giants reached base again in the fifth when Royce Clayton singled. Clayton put himself in scoring position when he stole second, but Mercker struck out Giants starting pitcher Terry Mulholland to end the threat.

Mulholland had won his first two starts in May but had struggled recently. He entered the game with a 2-7 record, having lost six times in his previous seven starts. His ERA over that time was 7.41.

Mulholland started shakily, giving up consecutive singles to Chipper Jones and Fred McGriff with two outs in the first. After walking David Justice to load the bases, Mulholland struck out Javy Lopez to end the inning.

After the first, Mulholland settled down and seemed to shake the mound struggles he had suffered over the past two months. He gave up just two more hits, groundball singles, over the next five innings while striking out six Braves. One of the hits was a second single by McGriff with two outs in the sixth. When Mulholland threw a wild pitch to Justice, the ball hit the backstop and bounced straight back to the catcher, who threw a dart to second to get McGriff and end the inning.

"That was probably the best that I've thrown in two years," Mulholland said after the game. "My arm felt great, I had a good curve, fastball, slider, and I felt like I could pitch the ball where I wanted to. I actually had fun out there for six innings.[2] Giants general manager Quinn was likely encouraged by his performance as well.

With the game scoreless, Mulholland was taken out for a pinch-hitter in the seventh when a walk and single put a Giant at third. Mercker gave up a single to Kirt Manwaring and walked Mike Benjamin. Giants manager Dusty Baker sent right-handed batter Rikkert Faneyte to hit for Mulholland against the lefty Mercker. Mercker struck him out on three pitches and then got Darren Lewis to fly out to center field to keep the game scoreless.

Braves skipper Bobby Cox replaced Mercker with Greg McMichael in the top of the eighth. Mercker had given up only four hits in one of his best performances of the season.

McMichael got the first two batters out. Glenallen Hill then singled through a hole in the left side of the infield. The next batter, Carreon, on a 3-and-1 count, hit a home run over the left-field wall to give the Giants a 2-0 lead.

Shawn Barton who had replaced Mulholland in the seventh, pitched two perfect innings. With two outs in the Giants' ninth, Barton was removed for pinch-hitter John Patterson as the Giants tried to build on their lead. Patterson singled and went to third when Lewis singled. Lewis stole second, but Braves reliever Mark Wohlers struck out Robby Thompson to end the threat.

In the bottom of the inning, Rod Beck came in to close out the game for the Giants. Beck walked leadoff batter Jeff Blauser. Jones then ripped the ball to center for a single. It was hit so hard that it looked for a moment that Lewis might catch it. This brought up McGriff. Beck threw him two splitters in the dirt and McGriff swung at them, missing by a wide margin.

Beck threw the next pitch higher, figuring that McGriff would be looking for another low pitch. McGriff was not and he connected on the pitch, sending it over the wall in dead center for a walk-off home run. "The pitch worked; it went down. He was waiting on it; he knew it was coming," said Beck afterward.[3]

The walk-off homer was McGriff's first round-tripper since June 21. "I was trying to push the runners over. The way that Lewis was going back, I thought that he had plenty of room. [The home run] is something to build on for the second half of the season. I haven't had a great start so far," McGriff said.

McGriff also noted that it was only his 11th home run of the season. "It hasn't been a great year for me homer-wise," he said. "It's one of those things. Beck's a great pitcher. If this was a month ago, this was a fly ball. Right now everything we do is working."[4]

It was the first blown save for Beck since May 23. "I figured that I'd throw one for a strike, he figured that I'd throw one for a strike and he hit it out of the ballpark. It didn't work out very well," Beck said.[5]

The win made it nine in a row for the Braves. "That team over there, they believe they can't lose any more," Giants first baseman Carreon said.[6] The win put the Braves up by four games over the Phillies. "We're up four and that's pretty good for this club," said Cox, understating his team's accomplishment.[7]

Blauser, the Braves shortstop, was more emphatic: "You never feel like you are out of it. That is a pretty good feeling to have."[8]

As the Braves celebrated their victory and prepared for a few days off for the All-Star break, Baker shared his disappointment with the loss. It was the Giants' 13th loss in 19 games. "This was a big game because we could have started the second half one game under .500 instead of three," Baker commented. "It hurts you when you lose three games in three days. This is something that we'll have to use as a source of hunger when we get back home."[9]

The Braves lost when play resumed after the All-Star break, falling to the Pirates 2-1 in a makeup game in Pittsburgh. But they quickly put that loss behind them and won the first three games of a series against the Padres. The Braves finished July with a 20-7 record and an eight-game division lead over the Phillies.

Sources

In addition to the sources cited in the Notes, the author used Baseball-Reference.com and Retrosheet.org for box-score, player, team, and season information as well as pitching and batting game logs, and other pertinent material.

Notes

1 Henry Schulman, "Giants Gone Fishing for Pitching," *San Francisco Examiner*, July 10, 1995: 41.
2 Ibid.
3 I.J. Rosenberg, "McGriff HR in 9th Saves Braves," *Atlanta Constitution*, July 10, 1995: 17.
4 Henry Schulman, "Giants Beat," *San Francisco Examiner*, July 10, 1995: 45. McGriff finished the season with 27 home runs.
5 Ibid.
6 Ibid.
7 Rosenberg.
8 Ibid.
9 Schulman, "Giants Gone Fishing."

Maddux Tosses 2-hitter While Throwing Only 88 Pitches in 1-0 Win

AUGUST 20, 1995: ATLANTA BRAVES 1, ST. LOUIS CARDINALS 0, AT BUSCH STADIUM, ST. LOUIS

BY MIKE HUBER

On a warm Sunday August evening,[1] the hot first-place Atlanta Braves (66-39) were visiting the last-place St. Louis Cardinals (42-63)[2] in the final game of a three-game series that pitted two close friends as mound opponents. The strike-delayed start to the 1995 season meant that each team had played only 105 games to this point and each had fewer than 40 games left to play in the season.

A crowd of 24,613 turned out at Busch Stadium to see their beloved Cardinals, sporting what many considered the worst offense in baseball, take on the game's stingiest pitcher, Greg Maddux. Before this series, the Cardinals had lost 16 of 19 games, dating back to July 27. In that stretch, they had scored more than four runs only twice, and they had been shut out four times. Atlanta had fared much better, winning 11 of 15 contests before visiting Busch Stadium, and although they weren't scoring many runs, their pitching was holding opponents to even fewer tallies. Braves skipper Bobby Cox handed the ball to Maddux (12-2) to try to win the third game and stop the mini-skid. Maddux "had extra incentive as he took the mound."[3] In what could be termed bragging rights, he was facing his boyhood friend and Las Vegas neighbor,[4] Cardinals starter Mike Morgan (4-6).

Maddux was hands-down the best pitcher in baseball. The ace of the Atlanta staff, he had won the last three Cy Young Awards in the National League. However, the right-hander had not pitched in 10 days, having missed his last start in Atlanta with a bad case of the flu. Morgan, on the other hand, was not having a great year. He had started the season with the Chicago Cubs, and came to St. Louis with minor leaguers Paul Torres and Francisco Morales in a June 16 trade for Todd Zeile and cash. Coming into this game, Morgan had lost his last three starts.

Maddux faced his toughest batter when Bernard Gilkey led off the bottom of the first. Gilkey worked a full count and fouled off a few more before flying out to right on the eighth pitch of the at-bat. Maddux then threw just three more pitches to retire both Ozzie Smith and John Mabry.

Morgan had allowed a two-out single to Chipper Jones in the first and then a single to Charlie O'Brien and a walk to Mark Lemke in the second, before working out of the jam. The Braves broke onto the scoreboard in the top of the third. Marquis Grissom led off with a double and went to third base on Jeff Blauser's sacrifice bunt. Jones came through with an RBI groundout to second, bringing Grissom home. In the fourth, Morgan gave up back-to-back singles to David Justice and Ryan Klesko to start the frame, but two grounders led to a double play and the third out, and the score remained 1-0 in favor of Atlanta.

No St. Louis batter reached until Maddux allowed a leadoff single up the middle to Brian Jordan to start the bottom of the fifth. Jordan stole second base, but Maddux stranded him there, striking out Ray Lankford and getting David Bell and Scott Cooper. A leadoff double by Danny Sheaffer opened the bottom of the sixth, but Maddux turned him into an LOB statistic by retiring the next three Cardinals hitters. He had thrown 64 pitches through the first six innings.

Morgan and Maddux sent opposing batters back to the respective dugouts. According to the *Atlanta Constitution*, "The Braves needed a shutout, considering how they were shut down by Cardinals right-hander Mike Morgan."[5] Despite a rocky start, Morgan faced the minimum in the fifth, seventh, and eighth innings. Maddux finished the game stronger than how he began. He sent the first 12 batters he faced back to the dugout, "as well as the last dozen."[6]

Tony Fossas relieved Morgan to pitch the ninth and Fred McGriff greeted him with a double to center. Justice then launched a fly to deep left for the first out. McGriff tried to advance after the catch, but Gilkey threw a strike to Cooper at third, who tagged out the sliding McGriff for a double play. Klesko grounded out and the Cardinals were down to their last inning. It took Maddux just seven pitches (the third such inning in which he economically used only seven pitches) to get his three foes, and the game was over. Atlanta had prevailed, 1-0.

Morgan got 18 groundball outs in his eight innings of work. When asked after the game about his competition with Maddux, Morgan kept it all in perspective. "I wasn't pitching against Maddux, I was pitching against the Atlanta Braves. I kept my club in the game and gave us a chance to win. I did my job. That's the best I can do."[7] Cardinals interim manager Mike Jorgensen praised his starter, Morgan, saying, "Gutsy performance all the way. He did a heck of a job, just got bested by a little bit."[8] The Cardinals suffered their 15th shutout of the season. The next day, Cincinnati came to St. Louis and the Cardinals won in walk-off fashion, starting a stretch in which they won six of seven games, rising out of the bottom of the standings. Another six-game win streak in September put them in fourth place to stay.

After the game, Maddux told reporters, "That is as good as I can pitch. It's nice to be able to say that. Usually there's something that could have been better."[9] Only two Cardinals batters had full counts. Regarding his missed start, Maddux said, "I think the time off did me a lot of good. I felt strong. I felt like spring training."[10] Cox's Braves used Maddux's victory as confidence to reel off six more victories, but although they had won seven in a row, they gained only a game and a half in the standings. A strong September helped the Braves finish the season with a record of 90-54.

Jorgensen had praise for Maddux, too, saying, "When he gets in a jam, he pitches better, which is unbelievable."[11] He added, "He's a master, he puts every pitch almost exactly where he wants to. That's one tough guy to go up against."[12]

The 1-hour, 50-minute game was the shortest in the majors to this point of the season. In earning his 13th victory of the year, Maddux threw just 88 pitches, 66 for strikes. Maddux tied Cincinnati Reds hurler Pete Schourek for the NL lead in victories. Since May 23, Maddux was 11-1 with a 1.53 earned-run average. More amazingly, in his last 16 road starts (dating back to the 1994 season), Maddux's record was 15-0 with a sub-one (0.96) ERA.

Maddux made such quick work of the Cardinals that the team had to wait in the locker room before heading out of St. Louis. According to the *Springfield News-Leader*, "the Atlanta Braves' team plane was in another city when (Maddux) got the last out."[13] The plane had been delayed by thunderstorms in Atlanta.

Maddux had seven more starts in the 1995 season. He went 6-0, raising his record to 19-2 and lowering his earned-run average to 1.63, the best in baseball. His 19 wins (and .905 winning percentage) were also tops in baseball,[14] and his 209⅔ innings pitched, 10 complete games, and three shutouts led the senior circuit.[15] He was rewarded at the end of the season by a unanimous selection for his fourth consecutive Cy Young Award. (He received all 28 first-place votes.) Schourek finished a distant second in the voting for the league's best pitcher.

THE 1995 WORLD CHAMPION ATLANTA BRAVES

Sources

In addition to the sources mentioned in the Notes, the author consulted baseball-reference.com and retrosheet.org.

Notes

1. The game-time temperature was 87 degrees Fahrenheit.
2. Atlanta was in the National League East Division, while St. Louis was in the NL Central Division.
3. Dan O'Neill, "Maddux Doesn't Take Long to Short-circuit Cards 1-0," *St. Louis Post-Dispatch*, August 21, 1995: 15.
4. O'Neill.
5. I.J. Rosenberg, "Get Well (vs.) Cards: 2-Hitter for Maddux," *Atlanta Constitution*, August 21, 1995: 27.
6. Rosenberg.
7. O'Neill.
8. "Maddux Masterful in St. Louis," *Springfield* (Missouri) *News-Leader,* August 21, 1995: 27.
9. Rosenberg.
10. Rosenberg.
11. Rosenberg.
12. "Maddux Masterful in St. Louis."
13. "Maddux Masterful in St. Louis."
14. Baltimore's Mike Mussina also had 19 wins in 1995.
15. Dodgers rookie Hideo Nomo also recorded three shutouts in 1995.

Chipper Jones Hits Two Home Runs in 1995 NLDS Game One

OCTOBER 3, 1995: ATLANTA BRAVES 5, COLORADO ROCKIES 4, AT COORS FIELD, DENVER

BY LAURA H. PEEBLES

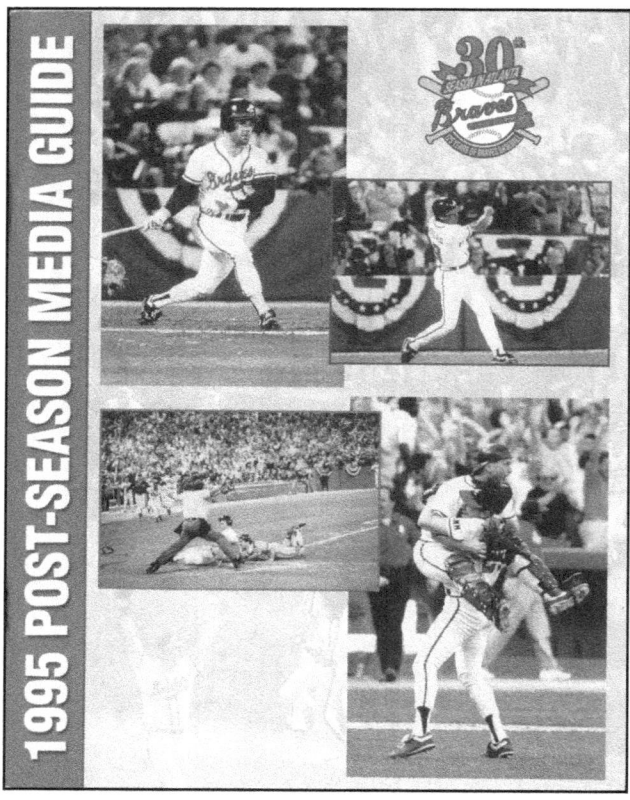

The first National League Division Series in major-league history got underway in Denver on October 3, 1995. Unlike the Conference Series and the World Series, the NLDS was a five-game series.[1] The Rockies, in just their third year of existence, were hosting the Braves. Colorado had played hard to the end of the season, finishing the year at 77-67, just one game behind the Dodgers in the NL West. The Braves had coasted to the end of the season. They clinched the NL East Division on September 13, finishing with a 90-54 record, 21 games ahead of the Mets.

Greg Maddux pitched for the Braves. He had not pitched in Denver in 1995 although he had pitched there in 1993 and 1994. Pitching in Denver is challenging since pitches move (or don't move) differently in the mile-high air. Maddux finished the regular season with a major-league-leading 19-2 record and 1.63 ERA. However, one of those losses was his only game against the Rockies (May 17), one of his worst games of the year.

The Rockies sent Kevin Ritz to the mound. His regular-season stats were pedestrian: 11-11 record, 4.21 ERA. However, he had pitched four perfect relief innings against the Braves on September 12.

The game started with Marquis Grissom fouling off several pitches, then grounding out to the shortstop. Mark Lemke lined into right for a single. Chipper Jones, the Atlanta rookie third baseman, was up next. Unlike the other regulars, Atlanta manager Bobby Cox had kept Chipper playing after September 13 to keep him sharp. This was his first postseason appearance. It was not particularly impressive: He grounded into a double play to end the top of the first.

Maddux had little trouble with the Rockies: Eric Young grounded out, then Joe Girardi singled into center. But that was all for the Rockies: Dante Bichette and Larry Walker grounded out.

The top of the second started normally enough: Fred McGriff grounded out to third, then David Justice singled into center. Ryan Klesko hit a dribbler toward the pitcher. Ritz's throw went by first baseman Andrés Galarraga as Klesko ran past first. Galarraga retrieved the ball and tagged Klesko, who was called out by first-base umpire Jerry Layne. Klesko had not made an obvious turn toward second: He had barely kicked up some chalk dust running past the bag. Cox came out to "state his case" to Layne rather vociferously, but avoided getting tossed. Justice had advanced to third on the bad throw but was left there when Charlie O'Brien grounded out.

The bottom of the second was over on seven pitches. Galarraga grounded out, then Ellis Burks singled but was erased when Vinny Castilla grounded into a double play.

The Braves got on the board first: After Jeff Blauser and Maddux grounded out, Grissom hit a hanging slider just over the fence in center, 415 feet from home plate. Lemke flied out with the score 1-0, Atlanta.

Walt Weiss opened the bottom of the third by tapping back to Maddux, who bobbled the ball but got the out at first. Ritz (.188 BA) hit a slow roller toward second, almost beating the throw. Young hit a standup double into center past the diving center fielder. O'Brien paid a visit to the mound, perhaps just to give his pitcher a break: Maddux hadn't had a strikeout yet, unusual for a pitcher with a 7.8K/9 ratio in the regular season. Girardi battled but grounded to first to end the inning.

The Braves threatened again in the top of the fourth. Chipper lined out, but a single by McGriff and a walk to Justice put two on with one out. But Ritz struck out Klesko and O'Brien to end the threat.

The Rockies took the lead in the bottom of the fourth. Bichette grounded out, Walker walked. Galarraga's single sent Walker to third, then Burks's sacrifice fly brought him home (although he had to jump over the catcher after touching home plate to avoid a collision). Castilla then homered: 3-1, Rockies. Weiss flied out to end the inning.

Blauser opened the fifth with a strikeout. Maddux's hit deflected off third baseman Castilla's glove – right to shortstop Weiss, who made the throw in time for the out. Grissom grounded to Castilla, who couldn't handle the ball: He didn't even try a throw. Ritz tried several times to pick Grissom off but to no avail: Grissom probably had second stolen, but Lemke was caught looking for the third out. In the bottom of the fifth, Maddux allowed a single to Young, who was then erased on a double play.

Chipper hit Ritz's first pitch in the sixth for a home run. After McGriff flied out, Justice walked. Klesko singled and Burks misplayed the ball, allowing Justice to take third. With Ritz at 102 pitches, Rockies manager Don Baylor changed pitchers to side-arming Steve Reed. Luis Polonia hit a groundball toward third: The Rockies got the force out at second but couldn't turn a double play as the ball was hit too slowly. With Blauser batting, Polonia stole second, then took third on a bad throw by Girardi. After two more pitches, the Rockies intentionally walked Blauser to pitch to Maddux. The strategy worked as he struck out with the score tied, 3-3.

In the bottom of the sixth, the Rockies got two singles, but one was erased on a double play and the other was left on base when Burks grounded out.

Reed continued pitching the seventh. Grissom was credited with a double when center fielder Burks dived but couldn't hold the ball. Lemke bunted up the third-base line. Reed grabbed the ball and got the out at third. That was all for Reed. He gave way to Bruce Ruffin, who got Chipper to ground into another double play

Castilla also opened the home half of the seventh by doubling into center. He was replaced by pinch-runner Trent Hubbard. Maddux hit Weis with the first pitch. Pinch-hitter Jason Bates was ruled not to have been hit by the pitch while bunting, although the slow-motion replay showed the ball hitting his hand. He grounded out, advancing the runners. Atlanta intentionally walked Young.

Pinch-hitter John Vander Wal tapped back to the mound: Atlanta was able to get a "home and first" double play to end the inning and keep the score tied. That ended Maddux's night at 85 pitches with no strikeouts, somewhat unusual for him. During the last two innings the Colorado mascot, Dinger, had been bouncing up and down behind home plate doing his best (worst?) to distract the pitcher.

Mike Munoz took over the pitching for Colorado in the top of the eighth. He got McGriff and Justice out, but then was replaced by Darren Holmes after Klesko singled. Javy López and pinch-hitter Dwight Smith both singled as well, scoring Klesko: 4-3, Atlanta. Another pinch-hitter, Mike Devereaux, flied out to center.

Atlanta's new pitcher, Greg McMichael, started by walking Bichette. Walker singled to right. Bichette took third when right fielder Justice bobbled the ball. Galarraga's hit down the third-base line was grabbed by a diving Chipper, who got the force out at second. Atlanta's next pitcher, Alejandro Peña, gave up a double to Burks on the first pitch, tying the game at 4-4. After Jayhawk Owens struck out, Weiss was intentionally walked to load the bases. Bates battled but flied out to end the eighth with the score still tied.

Curtis Leskanic started out well in the top of the ninth, getting Grissom and Lemke to ground out. Chipper took two balls, then hit his second homer of the game. McGriff struck out but the damage had been done: Atlanta led, 5-4.

Mark Wohlers, with his 100-MPH-plus pitches, took the mound for Atlanta. Young grounded out, then Mike Kingery and Bichette singled. Walker walked to load the bases. Galarraga struck out (not surprising since he led the league in strikeouts). With all the pitching changes and double switches, Colorado found itself out of bench players so sent Lance Painter,[2] a relief pitcher, to the plate. As might be expected from a player with four strikeouts in nine at-bats for the year, he struck out to end the game.

Chipper Jones, just beginning his Hall of Fame career, was the hero of the night for Atlanta on both offense and defense despite grounding into two double plays. Greg Maddux, even without having his usual swing-and-miss stuff in this game, went on to postseason success[3] -- and the Hall of Fame.

The Rockies' postseason ended quickly: they won only one NLDS game, in Atlanta. Atlanta went on to beat the Cleveland Indians in the World Series in six games.

Sources

In addition to the source cited in the Notes, the author consulted the recorded game on YouTube: youtube.com/watch?v=JymlAJarzB8, as well as Baseball-Reference.com and Retrosheet.org.

Notes

1. Not everyone was a fan of the shorter series format. Braves GM John Schuerholz and manager Bobby Cox both wanted a seven-game series. Tim Tucker, "Baseball is better suited to a best-of-seven playoffs," *Atlanta Constitution*, October 4, 1995: D5.

2. Painter had one previous pinch-hit appearance, May 6, 1995. He walked. His career BA was .175 in 51 PA.

3. He pitched two games in the 1995 World Series with a 1-1 record.

Avery and Devereaux Shine as Braves Complete 1995 NLCS Sweep

OCTOBER 14, 1995: ATLANTA BRAVES 6, CINCINNATI REDS 0, AT ATLANTA-FULTON COUNTY STADIUM

GAME FOUR OF THE NATIONAL LEAGUE CHAMPIONSHIP SERIES

BY RICHARD CUICCHI

After winning their fourth division title in 1995, the Atlanta Braves were on a quest for their first World Series championship, having captured three division titles but losing two World Series in the first half of the decade. Their chances were looking optimistic after they defeated the Colorado Rockies in four games in the Division Series and winning the first three games of the Championship Series against the Cincinnati Reds. Then they completed the sweep of the Reds largely through the efforts of Steve Avery and Mike Devereaux, who weren't the usual headliners of the team.

During the first three wins against the Reds, the Braves managed to limit the strengths of the Reds' offense: the ability to hit home runs (third in the NL) and steal bases (first). Future Hall of Fame starting pitchers Tom Glavine, John Smoltz, and Greg Maddux, aided by relievers Greg McMichael, Alejandro Pena, and Mark Wohlers, had held the Reds to five runs. The Reds hadn't hit a home run in the series and were prevented from stealing bases in two of the games.

With his team down three games to none, including two extra-inning games the Reds could have won, manager Davey Johnson expressed concern before the fourth game that the players had been pressing too hard.[1] They had finished second in the league in runs scored and slugging percentage, so they weren't accustomed to being held to meager offensive production.

While Braves manager Bobby Cox considered starting Glavine again in Game Four, he settled on left-hander Avery, who had just completed the worst season (7-13, 4.67 ERA) since his rookie year in 1990. Although he had shown improvement in his last three regular-season starts, Avery was still dropped from the rotation for the NLDS against Colorado. He made two brief relief appearances. However, Avery was no stranger to the playoffs, having been named the MVP of the 1991 NLCS against Pittsburgh and having started four World Series games in 1991 and 1992. Before the fourth contest against the Reds, Avery said, "I really wanted to pitch in this series. I've been throwing the ball well for the last couple of weeks and I feel I am ready."[2]

Devereaux, who had been acquired from the Chicago White Sox six weeks before to serve as a platoon player, got the start in right field in place of David Justice, who had reinjured his knee in batting practice. Devereaux had also gotten starts in left field in Games Two and Three in order to get another righty (instead of Ryan Klesko) in the lineup against Reds lefties.

Left-hander Pete Schourek got the start for the Reds. He had pitched well against the Braves in Game One, yielding only one run on six hits in 8⅓ innings, while striking out eight in a no-decision. He had been 18-7 with a 3.22 ERA during the regular season and would finish as runner-up for the Cy Young Award.

Steve Bedrosian, the Braves relief pitcher who had been released in August, returned to the Atlanta stadium to throw out the ceremonial first pitch. A favorite of Braves fans, he had two stints with them during his 14-year career, 1981-1985 and 1993-1995.

Avery and Schourek were locked in a duel for the first six innings. The only score came in the bottom of the third when Mark Lemke drove in the Braves' first run with a single that scored Rafael Belliard. Lemke's hit came at an opportune time, considering that he had gotten only six hits in 34 plate appearances in the previous playoff games. The run would turn out to be the only one the Braves needed.

Schourek gave up eight hits, but had only one other difficult inning, the fifth, when he worked out of a bases-loaded jam.

Avery demonstrated that he was indeed ready for the Reds as he predicted. He struck out six and gave up only two hits and three walks in his six innings. He allowed only one runner past first base.

McMichael replaced Avery in the top of the seventh with his third relief appearance and retired the side in order. The reliever had already picked up a save and a win in the two extra-inning games.

Michael Jackson relieved Schourek in the seventh and immediately ran into trouble. Grissom led off with a triple and scored on a passed ball with Fred McGriff at bat. Devereaux came through with a three-run homer to widen the lead to 5-0. His excitable sprint around the bases didn't give Braves fans much time to savor the moment.[3] The Braves' final score came on Luis Polonia's infield single off Dave Burba that scored Lopez.

Pena and Wohlers closed out the eighth and ninth innings for the Braves to complete the shutout and clinch the National League pennant for the fourth time in five seasons.

The Braves' pitching staff had led the league in ERA and WHIP during the regular season. They were again outstanding throughout the series as they recorded a 1.15 ERA and 1.026 WHIP. Atlanta turned eight double plays in the series, including three in the final game.

Devereaux's performance earned him the Championship Series MVP Award. It was the only time he was recognized with such an honor during his 12-year major-league career.

Reds first baseman Hal Morris offered his explanation of the rout of his usually powerful team: "They're definitely a cut above anyone else in our league and probably in baseball. I'm just amazed we didn't score more runs. Some of it was bad luck, but the majority of it was the excellent job their pitching staff did."[4]

The Braves were the first team to sweep a Championship Series since the best-of-seven format began in 1985. The *Atlanta Constitution* referred to Cincinnati as the "Big Dead Machine" for being swept.[5] This was a takeoff of the Big Red Machine label they earned during their dynasty seasons in the 1970s.

Reds manager Johnson had high praise for his opponent, saying, "This is the strongest team they've had in the last few years. It is the best bullpen they've had since I can remember. Everybody knows about their starting pitchers and they are pitching better than they have ever pitched. They've held a very explosive club under two runs per game."[6] Johnson, whom the Reds' front office planned to replace as manager by Ray Knight the next season, called his team "the best bunch of guys I've ever had to manage." He added, "The future looks bright for Cincinnati, with or without me."[7]

In a raucous clubhouse after the game, Braves owner Ted Turner celebrated as champagne was poured over his head while his players danced around him.[8] The celebration wouldn't end there. The Braves went on to win the World Series in six games against the Cleveland Indians. The only two previous Braves franchise World Series championships had come when the team was located in Boston in 1914 and Milwaukee in 1957.

THE 1995 WORLD CHAMPION ATLANTA BRAVES

Sources

In addition to the sources cited in the Notes, the author consulted Baseball-Reference.com, Retrosheet.org, and the following:

Glyer, Ray. "Devereaux Trades Bench for MVP," *Cincinnati Enquirer*, October 15, 1995: C2.

Tucker, Tim. "These Braves Better than Teams of '91, '92," *Atlanta Constitution*, October 15, 1995: E5.

Notes

1 Thomas Stinson. "'Nervous' Reds Went Into Offensive Doldrums at Wrong Time," *Atlanta Constitution*, October 15, 1995: E6.

2 Jack Nicholson. "Tradition Continues: Avery Shines in NLCS," *Atlanta Constitution*, October 15, 1995: E4.

3 Allene Voisine. "Devereaux Latest Hero in Braves Playoff Lore," *Atlanta Constitution*, October 15, 1995: E5.

4 Chris Haft. "No Runs, Three hits, Goodbye," *Cincinnati Enquirer*, October 15, 1995: C1.

5 I.J. Rosenberg. "Avery, Devereaux Shine in 6-0 Finale," *Atlanta Constitution*, October 15, 1995: E1.

6 Stinson.

7 Rory Glynn. "Shut Out, Sent Home," *Cincinnati Enquirer*, October 15, 1995: A1.

8 Rosenberg.

Greg Maddux's Gem Spoils Indians' Return to World Series

OCTOBER 21, 1995: ATLANTA BRAVES 3, CLEVELAND INDIANS 2, AT ATLANTA-FULTON COUNTY STADIUM

BY JACOB POMRENKE

For Atlanta Braves ace Greg Maddux, his long-awaited World Series debut was a chance to shake off a reputation of playoff futility for himself and his team. For the Cleveland Indians, it was a chance to shake off the rust from a 41-year postseason drought. For major-league baseball, it was a welcome respite from the painful memories of the previous October, when the World Series was not played at all due to a labor dispute between the owners and players.

When Maddux took the mound on October 21, 1995, at Atlanta-Fulton County Stadium, it had been 728 days since the last World Series game. The players' strike and subsequent owners' lockout had canceled the 1994 World Series and delayed the start of the 1995 regular season, alienating many fans in the process. The raucous crowds that greeted the Braves and brought Atlanta to a standstill during their first two World Series trips in 1991 and '92 were nowhere to be found; the city greeted its third National League pennant with skeptical restraint.[1]

In Cleveland the mood was much more festive as 50,000 fans gathered for a pep rally downtown[2] before the World Series opener. The Indians' 100-win season and their first American League pennant since 1954 captivated a fan base that had waited a long time for success. The last time the Indians had won it all, back in 1948, the Braves played their home games in Boston.

All eyes were on Maddux, baseball's best pitcher, who was soon to win his fourth consecutive NL Cy Young Award after posting a dominant 19-2 record with a 1.63 ERA. His 260 ERA+, which compares his ERA relative to the league average, ranks as the fifth-best in major-league history. But after signing with the Braves as a free agent in 1993, Maddux had struggled in October, bringing a 5.57 career postseason ERA into Game One.[3]

No one questioned Maddux's counterpart on the mound when it came to postseason pedigree. Orel Hershiser had never lost a game in the playoffs (7-0, 1.47 ERA) and was coming off a dominant ALCS against the Seattle Mariners in which he captured MVP honors. When asked how he was able to raise his game in October, the 37-year-old right-hander said, "It's that nervousness, that little extra edge, like little butterflies. It's always a constant reminder that something special is going on."[4]

The Indians also brought one of the most potent offenses in baseball history to Atlanta. Powered by Albert Belle, Jim Thome, Manny Ramirez, and Eddie Murray, the Tribe led all major-league teams in hits, runs, home runs, slugging, and on-base percentage in 1995. With seven .300 hitters in the Indians' lineup for Game One, they were so loaded that future Hall of Famer Dave Winfield – who had driven in the World Series-winning run for the Toronto Blue Jays against the Braves in 1992 – was left off the postseason roster.

Within minutes of Maddux's first pitch, Kenny Lofton, Cleveland's speedy leadoff hitter, manufactured the first run of the World Series by reaching on an error, stealing second and third base, and scoring on a groundout by Carlos Baerga.

The Braves got the run back on Fred McGriff's long home run, 436 feet deep into the right-center-field seats, to lead off the second inning. Then the game settled into a tight pitching duel between the two aces.

The Indians broke up Maddux's no-hitter on a single by Thome with one out in the fifth inning, but they could not break the 1-1 tie. Meanwhile, the Braves could not break through against Hershiser, either. Only one Atlanta baserunner had advanced into scoring position, back in the first inning, but shortstop Omar Vizquel made a diving stop of Chipper Jones's line drive to start a double play and end the threat. Through six innings, Hershiser had allowed three hits and Maddux only one. But Vizquel's Gold Glove-winning hands failed him in the game's most critical moment.

After walking the first two hitters in the seventh, a frustrated Hershiser took himself out of the game after 101 pitches. "Orel was pitching well," Indians manager Mike Hargrove said. "There was no indication he had run out of gas. … He caught us off-guard, he caught us by surprise."[5]

Reliever Paul Assenmacher's control wasn't much better, as he loaded the bases with a walk to Mike Devereaux. Julian Tavarez came on to face pinch-hitter Luis Polonia, who hit a soft grounder up the middle that was misplayed by Vizquel. He was still juggling the baseball when he stepped on second base to force out Devereaux, but McGriff came home with the go-ahead run to give the Braves a 2-1 lead. Manager Bobby Cox argued with umpire Bruce Froemming to overturn the call at second base, hoping to keep the bases loaded and play for a big inning. When Cox returned to the dugout, he called for a small-ball strategy instead. Rafael Belliard perfectly executed a squeeze bunt, bringing home David Justice with the Braves' third run. Not a single ball left the infield in the entire inning.

Maddux mowed down the heart of the Indians' order in the eighth, dispatching Thome and Ramirez on easy groundballs and inducing Sandy Alomar Jr. to pop out to first base. In the ninth, the Indians threatened briefly – thanks again to the speed of Kenny Lofton. With one out, he sliced a single to left field for the Indians' second hit of the game. He boldly tried to advance to third base on Vizquel's groundout and scored when McGriff's throw across the diamond skipped past Chipper Jones. But Maddux retired Baerga on a foul popup to Jones to end the game and give the Braves a 3-2 win.

Maddux threw 95 pitches, 63 for strikes. It was only the third recorded instance in World Series history that a pitcher threw a complete game in fewer than 100 pitches.[6] He allowed just four balls to reach the outfield and faced three batters over the minimum.

"I don't think you will ever see anyone pitch better than you saw Greg Maddux pitch tonight," Hargrove said. "He just dominated that game."[7]

Maddux's teammate, John Smoltz, called it a "masterpiece," adding, "One thing [is] for sure: He put to rest the tag that he can't pitch in the postseason. I don't think he'll ever have to hear that again."[8]

Sources

In addition to the sources cited in the Notes, the author consulted box scores and play-by-play at Baseball-Reference.com and Retrosheet.org.

Notes

1. Charmagne Helton, "No Clean-Up or Festivities for Downtown," *Atlanta Journal-Constitution*, October 22, 1995: E9; Bill Torpy, "City Begins to Don a Series Game Face," *Atlanta Journal-Constitution*, October 22, 1995: E11.

2. Jim Auchmutey, "Baseball's Old Maid," *Atlanta Journal-Constitution*, October 21, 1995: D10.

3. Greg Maddux, Postseason Pitching Game Log, Baseball-Reference.com, baseball-reference.com/players/gl.fcgi?id=maddugr01&t=p&year=0&post=1. Two of Maddux's seven postseason starts were with the Chicago Cubs in 1989.

4. David Falkner, "Postseason Traumatic Shock Syndrome," *The Sporting News*, October 23, 1995: 17.

5. Ross Newhan, "Hershiser Walks Out on Indians at Crucial Moment," *Los Angeles Times*, October 22, 1995: C12.

6   Stan Coveleski for the 1925 Senators and Bret Saberhagen for the 1985 Royals were the others. See Baseball-Reference.com Play Index: baseball-reference.com/tiny/lHuwA.

7   I.J. Rosenberg, "Game 1's a Maddux 2-hitter," *Atlanta Journal-Constitution*, October 22, 1995: E1.

8   Phil Sheridan, "Maddux Weaves Some Game 1 Magic," *Philadelphia Inquirer*, October 22, 1995: D1.

Glavine, Justice Win Back the Fans and Bring a World Series to Atlanta

OCTOBER 28, 1995: ATLANTA BRAVES 1, CLEVELAND INDIANS 0, ATATLANTA-FULTON COUNTY STADIUM, ATLANTA

BY JACOB POMRENKE

It was only fitting that Tom Glavine was on the mound for the Atlanta Braves in Game Six of the 1995 World Series.

After all, he was on the mound during the franchise's leanest years, leading the National League in losses in 1988. He was on the mound for the Braves' dramatic turnaround in 1991, winning the NL's Cy Young Award for the first time. And he was on the mound in 1995 when major-league players returned to the field after a costly labor dispute that had canceled the previous year's World Series. Throughout the season, Glavine was booed by the hometown fans for his outspoken role as a representative for the players union.

As the longest tenured player on the Braves World Series roster,[1] Glavine had seen it all. On their shared car ride to the ballpark the previous day, teammate Greg Maddux told him "how glad he was that I was getting a chance to win it, that I deserved it, the fact that I had been here longer than anybody. … A lot of people have come up to me and said this is the perfect game for me to pitch. Certainly, this is a unique opportunity," Glavine said.[2]

If all eyes were on the Braves' starting pitcher, their fans' *ears* were all tuned in to David Justice. The star right fielder made headlines on the morning of Game Six with a controversial rant about the lack of support from Atlanta's home crowds during the fall classic:

"What happens if we don't win? When's the parade then? They'll run us out of Atlanta. … If we don't win, they'll probably burn our houses down. … If we get down 1-0 tonight, they will probably boo us out of the stadium. You have to do something great to get them out of their seats. … I'm the only guy that will sit here and say it, but there are a lot of people that feel this way."[3]

Glavine was far more diplomatic, pointing out that Indians fans in Cleveland were giddy about snapping their 41-year World Series drought and that Braves fans had been just as enthusiastic a few years earlier: "I don't think it's fair to expect our fans to be the same as in 1991. … You can't recapture that," he said.[4]

If Justice's intention was to fire up the sellout crowd of 51,875 at Atlanta-Fulton County Stadium, he certainly accomplished his goal. He was loudly booed during player introductions and one fan behind home plate held up a sign that read, "Justice, hope your bat is as big as your mouth!"

The biggest bats in baseball belonged to the Cleveland Indians, who led the major leagues in nearly every offensive category during the regular season. Their .291 batting average was the highest by any team since the 1950 Boston Red Sox. After beating Maddux in Game Five, the Indians returned to Atlanta with a confident outlook. Glavine took it personally when some Cleveland players said they had already beaten the Braves' best pitcher.[5]

On a crisp 56-degree night, Glavine coolly dispatched the Indians from the moment he took the mound in Game Six, holding the Tribe hitters helpless with his trademark circle changeup.

Through the first five innings, he didn't allow a hit at all. His only blemishes were two walks to Albert Belle, Cleveland's powerful cleanup hitter.

Home-plate umpire Joe Brinkman, who had never called a Glavine start during the regular season,[6] said the Braves left-hander lived up to his reputation for making hitters chase outside pitches.

"Tommy had a lot of pop on the outside corner," Brinkman said. "He just kept popping guys, outside, outside, outside. … He can lull you to sleep out there and finally, as an umpire, you have to say, 'Okay, that's as much as you're going to get out there.' … It was the most masterful performance."[7]

Tony Peña finally ended Glavine's bid for a no-hitter to lead off the sixth inning, poking a soft single to right-center field. But Glavine worked around the base hit to keep the game scoreless.

Meanwhile, the Braves could do little damage against Indians starter Dennis Martínez. The 41-year-old right-hander from Nicaragua flirted with danger, allowing four hits and five walks in 4⅔ innings, but Atlanta could not push any runs across. Justice began a two-out rally in the fourth inning with a double to left-center and the Braves quickly loaded the bases, but weak-hitting Rafael Belliard flied out to end the rally.

Justice had been virtually invisible in the postseason, with no extra-base hits and just five RBIs entering Game Six. As he stepped up to the plate to lead off the sixth inning, Braves fans were ready to forgive him for his critical pregame statements if he could help deliver the city's first World Series championship.

Facing a tough left-handed reliever in Jim Poole – who had played college baseball just a few miles north at Georgia Tech – Justice drove a 1-and-1 fastball deep into the right-field seats. The ballpark erupted in a pent-up display of emotion and fans showered love on their outspoken outfielder. On NBC's television broadcast, Baseball Hall of Famer Joe Morgan quipped, "It's okay to talk the talk if you can walk the walk."[8]

"I have never felt that much pressure in any game I've played in my life," Justice said. "Nor do I think I ever will again."[9]

With a 1-0 lead, Glavine looked nearly invincible. He cruised through the seventh and eighth innings, allowing just three walks and the single to Peña on 109 pitches. But his shoulder stiffened up when the Braves' offense spent a long time at the plate in the seventh (again failing to score after loading the bases). When manager Bobby Cox and pitching coach Leo Mazzone asked Glavine how he felt before the ninth inning, he told them he was tired and getting away with a lot of mistakes. Cox decided to bring in fireballing closer Mark Wohlers to finish the game.

"It says a lot for the relationship we have with Tommy, that he would be able to come to us in that spot and tell us the truth," Cox said. "So many other pitchers would have said nothing. … Those who weren't true to themselves in a situation like that, how would they be able to stomach it if they'd blown it?"[10]

After struggling to connect with Glavine's changing speeds for eight innings, the Indians had little chance against Wohlers' 100-mph fastballs. Wohlers had emerged as a reliable stopper out of the bullpen, which had long been the Braves' biggest downfall in their disappointing postseason runs since 1991. He set down Kenny Lofton, Paul Sorrento, and Carlos Baerga in order in the ninth. When center fielder Marquis Grissom ran down Baerga's fly ball and squeezed it in his glove for the final out, Atlanta could finally celebrate its long-awaited championship.

No one was happier than the left-handed pitcher who had been with the Braves since the beginning, through the last-place seasons of the 1980s, two heartbreaking World Series defeats, and the player strike that turned some hometown fans against him.

"It's the best feeling in the world," said Glavine, who was honored as the World Series MVP after throwing the first one-hitter in a World Series game since Boston's Jim Lonborg in 1967.

"The first time we saw Glavine I wondered how this guy had won so many games. Now I know," Baerga said.[11]

Sources

In addition to the sources cited in the Notes, the author relied on Baseball-Reference.com and Retrosheet.org.

Notes

1 Jeff Blauser, like Glavine, made his debut with the Braves in 1987 but he did not play in the 1995 World Series due to a leg injury suffered in a collision with the Reds' Hal Morris during the NLCS.

2 I.J. Rosenberg, "It's Glavine's Turn for the Clincher," *Atlanta Journal-Constitution*, October 28, 1995: D4.

3 I.J. Rosenberg, "Justice Takes a Rip at Braves Fans," *Atlanta Journal-Constitution*, October 28, 1995: D1.

4 Rosenberg, "Justice Takes a Rip at Braves Fans."

5 Gordon Edes, "Bravo for Braves – Finally," *South Florida Sun-Sentinel* (Fort Lauderdale), October 29, 1995: 4C.

6 As an American League umpire, Brinkman's only prior experience calling Glavine's pitches was in the 1991 All-Star Game in Toronto.

7 Tom Glavine with Nick Cafardo, *None But the Braves: A Pitcher, A Team, A Champion* (New York: HarperCollins, 1996), 8.

8 Prentis Rogers, "Justice Stole the Show with Controversy, Bat," *Atlanta Journal-Constitution*, October 29, 1995: E7.

9 Jayson Stark, "A Deciding Game That Lived Up to Its Predecessors," *Philadelphia Inquirer*, October 29, 1995: C4.

10 Glavine, 2.

11 Paul Hoynes, "Oh, So Close," *Cleveland Plain Dealer*, October 29, 1995, accessed online at cleveland.com/tribe/2015/10/1995_world_series_game_6_atlan.html on December 29, 2019.

CONTRIBUTORS

Contributors

Mark Armour is a researcher and writer who lives with his family in Oregon's Willamette Valley.

Jesse Asbury joined SABR in 2017 and is a fixture at the Oklahoma Chapter's meetings. He grew up in southeastern Tennessee, where he spent many a night in the 1990s watching the Braves on TBS and taking family trips to Atlanta-Fulton County Stadium and Turner Field. He is still patiently waiting for Dale Murphy and Fred McGriff to get into the Hall of Fame. An IT analyst working for the University of Oklahoma, he lives in Norman, Oklahoma, with his wife, Tristianne.

Bob Barrier taught composition and literature at Kennesaw State University for 37 years, and also directed the university writing center. His interests in baseball include media (especially re-created baseball broadcasts and the rhetoric of newspaper accounts of games), early baseball history, and the minor leagues. He has published and presented on Atlanta Braves broadcasters, the art and rhetoric of radio baseball re-creations (profiles and presentations of Nat Allbright, Dodgers broadcaster in the 1950s); the heyday of minor-league baseball after World War II; the Selma Christians of the Southern Association; young-adult baseball literature as well as Southern literature; and the American ghost story. His earliest memories of Atlanta Stadium are seeing Sandy Koufax beat the Braves 2-1 in June 1966 and watching Hank Aaron win the All-Star Game in 1972. Unfortunately, he could not get tickets for the 1995 World Series.

Matt Bloss is an attorney residing in the Syracuse, New York, area. A SABR member, he is a diehard baseball fan who also has an interest in muscle cars, reading, traveling, and spending time with his niece and three nephews.

Richard S. (Scott) Brimer was born and raised in Atlanta and has been a Braves fan since they arrived in Atlanta in 1966. He has been a member of SABR since 2008 and has a keen interest in baseball history. He retired from active duty in the US Air Force and is now a budget analyst for the Air Force. He lives in Panama City, Florida, with his wife, Josefina.

Thomas J. Brown Jr. is a lifelong Mets fan who became a Durham Bulls fan after moving to North Carolina in the early 1980s. He was a national-board-certified high-school science teacher for 34 years before retiring in 2016. Tom still volunteers with the ELL students at his former high school, serving as a mentor to those students and the teachers who are now working with them. He also provides support and guidance for his former ELL students when they embark on different career paths after graduation. Tom has been a member of SABR since 1995, when he learned about the organization during a visit to Cooperstown on his honeymoon. He has become active in the organization since his retirement and has written numerous biographies and game stories, mostly about the New York Mets. Tom also enjoys traveling as much as possible with his wife and has visited major-league and minor-league ballparks across the country on his many trips. He also loves to cook and makes all the meals at his house while writing about those meals on his blog, Cooking and My Family.

A lifelong White Sox fan surrounded by Cubs fans in the northern suburbs of Chicago, **Ken Carrano** works as a chief financial officer for a large landscaping firm and as a soccer referee. Ken and his Brewers' fan wife, Ann, share two children, two golden retrievers, and a mutual distain for the blue side of Chicago.

Alan Cohen has been a SABR member since 2010. He serves as vice president-treasurer of the Connecticut Smoky Joe Wood Chapter and is datacaster (MiLB First Pitch stringer) for the Hartford Yard Goats, the Double-A affiliate of the Colorado Rockies. His biographies, game stories and essays have appeared in more than 40 SABR publications. Since his first *Baseball*

Research Journal article appeared in 2013, Alan has continued to expand his research into the Hearst Sandlot Classic (1946-1965), which launched the careers of 88 major leaguers. He has four children and eight grandchildren and resides in Connecticut with wife Frances, their cats, Morty, Ava, and Zoe, and their dog, Buddy.

Warren Corbett is the author of *The Wizard of Waxahachie* and a contributor to SABR's BioProject. He lives at Pawleys Island, South Carolina.

Joe Cox has written or contributed to 10 sports books. His most recent solo offering, *A Fine Team Man: Jackie Robinson and the Lives He Touched*, was published by Lyons Press in 2019. Joe also practices law, and lives with his family near Bowling Green, Kentucky, where you might find him rooting on the Class-A Bowling Green Hot Rods.

Richard Cuicchi joined SABR in 1983 and is an active member of the Schott-Pelican Chapter. Since his retirement as an information technology executive, Richard authored *Family Ties: A Comprehensive Collection of Facts and Trivia about Baseball's Relatives*. He has contributed to numerous SABR BioProject and Games publications. He does freelance writing and blogging about a variety of baseball topics on his website, TheTenthInning.com. Richard lives in New Orleans with his wife, Mary.

Tim Deale is chairman of the Larry Doby Chapter of SABR. A native of Deale, Maryland, and now residing in South Carolina, Tim is a contributor to BioProject and a member of the Nineteenth Century Research Committee. A former sports talk show host in Annapolis, Maryland, he is currently writing books about baseball. Among the things he enjoys are researching statistics, old-time baseball, and making lists of the top players and pitchers in various categories. He learned about baseball at an early age listening to Baltimore Orioles games on the radio with his grandmother, and now wants to help preserve baseball history and pass it on to other generations. He would like to write/make a baseball documentary.

Kyle Eaton, a lifelong Atlanta Braves fan, is a nonprofit professional residing in Memphis, Tennessee, with his wife, son, and two dogs. He spends his free time running, watching baseball, volunteering for an animal rescue group, advocating for children's literacy, and faking this whole fatherhood thing until he can hopefully figure it all out. He admittedly owns more bobbleheads than any grown man should own, but he is at peace with this for now. His brief biography of Javy López was his first foray into baseball history.

Dr. Millard Fisher is a devout baseball fan who reads extensively all types of baseball material, and particularly enjoys biographies and the history of the game. He is an avid and loyal Braves fan. When not cheering for them, he speaks internationally on health issues and medicine, and has had numerous research presentations on those subjects. He was on the president's committee that formulated guidelines targeting health implications for tobacco usage. In addition, he is a consultant for several national and international organizations such as the World Future Society, the Centers for Disease Control, and the National Institutes of Health. He has given more than a dozen presentations at SABR conventions. Dr. Fisher is past president of the Magnolia SABR Chapter in Georgia, and a frequent speaker at the National Baseball Hall of Fame in Cooperstown. He resides in Stone Mountain, Georgia.

Sam Gazdziak has been a trade journalist for 20 years and writes about music and baseball whenever he can. In 2018 he decided to combine his two loves of baseball and cemetery exploration into the website RIP Baseball, which features stories about the baseball graves he's found. He's visited more than 500 graves so far in more than 20 states and has almost been locked in cemeteries twice. He also writes obituaries for recently deceased ballplayers and other interesting bits of baseball history that he comes across. Sam lives in the Atlanta area but was born in Chicago and remains a diehard Cubs fan. For more information visit ripbaseball.com.

Peter M. Gordon is a longtime member of SABR who›s written articles for over 18 of our published books, including the history of the Tampa Bay Rays› first year for 2018›s *Time for Expansion Baseball*. He's an award-winning poet with more than 100 poems published, including his best-selling chapbook of baseball poems, *Let's Play Two*. After a 40-year career creating and curating content for platforms from live theater to digital video, he lives in Orlando, Florida, and teaches business of film in Full Sail University's Film Production MFA program.

Paul Hofmann, a SABR member since 2002, is the associate vice president for international affairs at Sacramento State University and a frequent contributor to SABR publications. Paul is a native of Detroit and a lifelong Detroit Tigers fan. He currently resides in Folsom, California.

Mike Huber is a 25-year SABR member who is currently chair of SABR's Games Project Committee. He enjoys researching and writing about players who have hit for the cycle. As a professor of mathematics at Muhlenberg College, Mike involves students in simulations and predictions of different parts of the national pastime. He has been rooting for the same American League East team since there has been an American League East Division.

Tom Hufford was one of the 16 Founding Members of SABR at Cooperstown, New York, in 1971, and served one year as secretary and nine years on the SABR Board of Directors. He was president of the Braves 400 Club in 1991 and 1992, and received the club's Ivan Allen Jr. "Mr. Baseball" Award, presented annually to the "person who has contributed significantly to the promotion of baseball in the Atlanta area," in 2017. An architect/engineer by profession, he was a consultant to the Atlanta Braves during the design and construction of Turner Field.

William H. "Bill" Johnson is the author of a full-length biography, *Hal Trosky: A Baseball Biography* (McFarland & Co., 2017), along with over two dozen essays for the Society for American Baseball Research's BioProject. He retired from the US Navy in 2006 after a 24-year career in naval aviation. In addition, he has presented papers at several baseball-history conferences. He graduated from the University of California (Berkeley) with a degree in rhetoric, and has subsequently earned a master of arts in military history from Norwich University and a master's in aeronautical science from Embry-Riddle Aeronautical University. He currently teaches unmanned aviation at Embry-Riddle.

Chris Jones is an attorney at Phelps Dunbar, where he practices in the area of commercial litigation, with a focus on property rights, eminent domain, real-estate disputes, and contract disputes. He is a lifelong baseball fan and a member of SABR since 2015. The highlight of his playing days was being drafted by the Toronto Blue Jays in the 2001 amateur draft. He resides in the Dallas/Fort Worth area with his wife and four children. For firm information, visit phelpsdunbar.com, or contact Chris directly at chris.jones@phelps.com.

Greg King, a historian and environmental planner by profession, is a resident of Martinez, California, the town where Joe DiMaggio was born, and conservationist John Muir passed away, both in 1914. Greg co-founded the Dusty Baker-Sacramento Chapter of SABR in 1994. His primary baseball research interests focus on the Dodgers.

Justin Krueger enjoys playing baseball with his wife and kids out in the pasture at the family farm. He also likes that everyone in his family has a different favorite major-league team. His daughter, Katherine, loves the Blue Jays, his son, Coupland, roots for the Cubs, and his wife, Emily, is a lifelong fan of the Houston Astros. Justin is currently a doctoral candidate at the University of Texas at Austin in social studies education, and a fan of the Texas Rangers.

Bob LeMoine grew up in Maine and has lived and died with the Red Sox for most of his life. He joined SABR in 2013 and has contributed to several SABR book projects. Having a love for both history and baseball, he usually contributes to most SABR book projects. Bob lives in Rochester, New Hampshire, and works as a high school librarian and adjunct professor.

Len Levin is retired after a long career as a newspaper editor in New England. Currently he is the grammarian for the Rhode Island Supreme Court and copyedits their decisions. He also copyedits many of SABR's books, including this one.

Dan Levitt is the author of several baseball books and numerous essays. He is a longtime SABR member and a recipient of the Davids Award and the Chadwick Award. His books have won the Larry Ritter Book Award and the Sporting News-SABR Baseball Research Award, and have twice been finalists for the Seymour Medal.

Lee Lowenfish, a member of SABR since 1976, is the author of *Branch Rickey: Baseball's Ferocious Gentleman*, which won the 2008 Seymour Medal for best book in baseball history in 2007. After he met Tony Lupien, the former Red Sox first baseman and Dartmouth College baseball coach, at the 1978 SABR national convention in Paramus, New Jersey, they collaborated on *The Imperfect Diamond: The Story of Baseball's Reserve System and The Men Who Fought to Change It* (Stein and Day, 1980). In 2010 the University of Nebraska Press, publisher of the Rickey biography, released a third edition of *The Imperfect Diamond* with the new subtitle, "A History of Baseball's Labor Wars." In 1984 he wrote for Tom Seaver *The Art of Pitching* (William Morrow). After schooling at Columbia and the University of Wisconsin, Lee started his college teaching career in Baltimore, where he became an ardent Orioles fan. It is a good thing he loves baseball history because the Orioles' past sure looks more enticing than its future.

Scott McClellan joined SABR back in 1988. He once said of himself that he worked as a land-title examiner when not attending Braves games.

Wynn Montgomery is a retired bureaucrat and educator and a recovering workaholic. He has been a SABR member since 1983. As a member of the Magnolia Chapter in Atlanta, Wynn served as co-editor of SABR's 2010 Atlanta convention journal. Since moving to Colorado in 2011, he has become a Rockies fan while continuing to follow the Braves from afar. His baseball interests include the art and history of the game, minor-league and college baseball, and the Negro Leagues. With two other SABRites, he takes an annual "B-4" Road Trip that feeds his passion for Baseball, Battlefields (mostly Civil War), Burial Grounds (historic cemeteries), and Barbecue. He has seen every major-league team play a home game and has visited more than 100 minor-league and college ballparks.

Alan Morris is a native Atlantan and lifelong Braves fan. He witnessed their first game in Atlanta in 1966 and was a season-ticket holder for 25 years. He currently serves on the Board of Directors for the Atlanta 400 Braves Fan Club and is a longtime SABR member. Alan takes an annual baseball road trip and has seen games in all of the current major-league ballparks. After a career working with and for people with disabilities, he combined his love of baseball and Atlanta history to become a tour guide at Atlanta's historic Oakland Cemetery. He researched the history of baseball in the city and created a "Boys of Summer" tour describing Atlanta's first baseball contest in the spring of 1866. Seven of the participants in that game are buried on the cemetery grounds. Alan is married to his childhood sweetheart, Nancy, and has two children and one grandchild, who attends Braves games with him. Her name is Alice but he calls her "Peanut."

Bill Nowlin wishes he'd been to even one Boston Braves game in his lifetime. No such luck. But he's been to something over 1,000 Red Sox games. After nearly 50 years in the music business as a co-founder of Rounder Records, he started writing books about the Red Sox, and then editing and writing articles and books about all sorts of baseball subjects for SABR.

Tony S Oliver is a native of Puerto Rico currently living in Sacramento, California, with his wife and daughter. While he works as a Six Sigma professional, his true love is baseball and he cheers for both the Red Sox and whoever happens to be playing the Yankees. He is fascinated by baseball cards and is currently researching the evolution of baseball tickets. He believes there is no prettier color than the vibrant green of freshly mown grass on a baseball field.

Bill Pearch is a lifelong Chicago Cubs fan in spite of pressure from his hard-core extended White Sox family. He is now happily married to a Milwaukee Brewers fan. He is a marketing communication manager with experience working for park districts, philanthropic organizations, and civil engineering firms. He has attended at least one game in 40 different major-league parks and writes about his travels on his blog at billpearch.com. He serves as Chicago's Emil Rothe Chapter newsletter editor and recently contributed to the SABR publication *Comiskey Park: The Base Ball Palace of the World*.

Laura Peebles is a retired CPA, still writing and editing tax materials part-time for Bloomberg. She brings her writing and editing skills to SABR as an associate editor for the Games Project. Her other baseball project is writing rhyming game summaries of Washington Nationals games. She lives with her wife, two cats, and an ever-growing collection of baseballs in Arlington, Virginia.

Jacob Pomrenke is SABR's director of editorial content, chair of the Black Sox Scandal Research Committee, and editor of *Scandal on the South Side: The 1919 Chicago White Sox*. Growing up in Atlanta in the 1990s, he lived and died with the Braves dynasty during those years. Thanks to Tom Glavine, he became perhaps the first 9-year-old pitcher with a circle changeup. He now lives in Scottsdale, Arizona, with his wife, Tracy Greer, and their cats, Nixey Callahan and Bones Ely.

James Lincoln Ray is a Philadelphia lawyer whose dream is to someday be the best baseball historian in the country. He is a featured baseball writer for Suite101.com, and has published more than 400 articles about the national pastime since 2006. His work has been quoted and referenced in numerous national publications, including the *Wall Street Journal* and the *New York Times*.

Carl Riechers retired from United Parcel Service in 2012 after 35 years of service. With more free time, he became a SABR member that same year. Born and raised in the suburbs of St. Louis, he became a big fan of the Cardinals. He and his wife, Janet, have three children and he is the proud grandpa of two.

Joel Rippel, a Minnesota native and graduate of the University of Minnesota, is the author or co-author of 10 books on Minnesota sports history and has contributed as a writer to several books published by SABR.

Paul Rogers is president of the Ernie Banks-Bobby Bragan (Dallas-Fort Worth) SABR Chapter and the co-author of four baseball books, including *The Whiz Kids and the 1950 Pennant*, written with his boyhood hero Robin Roberts, and *Lucky Me: My 65 Years in Baseball*, authored with Eddie Robinson. He was the co-editor of recent SABR team histories of the 1951 New York Giants and the 1950 Philadelphia Phillies and is a frequent contributor to the SABR BioProject and Games Projects. His real job is as a law professor at SMU, where he was dean of the law school for nine years and has served as the university's faculty athletic representative for 33 years.

Steven D. Schmitt is the award-winning author of *A History of Badger Baseball – The Rise and Fall of America's Pastime at the University of Wisconsin* (UW Press, 2017). He has been a SABR member since 2010 and has written articles for SABR books and for the SABR BioProject. He is a graduate of the University of Wisconsin-Madison with bachelor's and master's degrees in journalism and mass communication and a member of the Wisconsin Alumni Association.

J. Scott Shaffer is a systems analyst with the Department of the Navy, a university teaching associate, and an officer in the Navy Reserve. His work can be found in numerous publications covering political science, naval history, and baseball. Currently living in Southern California, Scott is an avid Angels fan and recently published an article in SABR's Games Project on Shohei Ohtani's hitting for the cycle.

Curt Smith grew up in Upstate New York cheering the Yankees vs. the Braves in 1958, the first World Series he recalls. Later, he sought atonement by writing extensively about Braves Voices from Fred Hoey and Jim Britt to Earl Gillespie, Milo Hamilton, and beyond. Smith's 17th book is *The Presidents and the Pastime: The History of Baseball and the White House*. Prior books include *Voices of the Game*, *The Voice*, and *Pull Up a Chair: The Vin Scully Story*. He is senior lecturer of English at the University of Rochester, a GateHouse Media columnist, and past host or keynote at the Great Fenway Writers Series, Cooperstown Symposium on Baseball and American Culture, the NINE Conference, and numerous Smithsonian Institution series.

The former President of North Country Natural, Inc., a natural-food distributorship, **Dana Sprague** may own Vermont's finest collection of baseball memorabilia. A sixth-generation Vermonter, Dana has written for the *Green Mountain Boys of Summer*, the *Rutland Herald*, and the *Brattleboro Reformer*. Dana is owner/founder of the Vermont Baseball Museum and currently lives in Brattleboro, Vermont.

Creg Stephenson has written about sports, mostly college football, for a variety of print and online publications since 1994. He lives in Mobile, Alabama, birthplace of five Baseball Hall of Famers and many "Hall of Very Gooders." After years of procrastination, he finally joined SABR in 2019.

Mark S. Sternman followed the Montreal Expos ardently from 1979 to 2004. In addition to profiling Mike Mordecai, Sternman has written biographies of Mike Stenhouse and Jose Vidro for other SABR books. He remembers the 1996 Braves with particular fondness because he won a beer from a colleague after betting that New York would top Atlanta in the World Series.

John Struth has been a member of SABR for 20-plus years. He fell for baseball at an early age and that blossomed to love during the Miracle Mets championship in 1969. He has contributed several bios for SABR publications and has presented at the Jerry Malloy Conference.

Sean Teters is a recent college graduate from the University of West Georgia and currently works as a baseball analytics and advanced scouting assistant for Kennesaw State University Baseball. He was born exactly one week prior to the demolition of old Atlanta Fulton County Stadium, home of the 1995 World Series champion Atlanta Braves. The lifelong love of Atlanta Braves baseball drives his career in baseball.

Stew Thornley is humbled and honored to have been a SABR member since

1979 and to have rubbed shoulders in the comfort station with five Hall of Famers.

Clayton Trutor, Ph.D., teaches history at Norwich University and is the chair of SABR's Vermont chapter. He is a frequent contributor to the BioProject and the author of *"Loserville": How Atlanta Remade Professional Sports and Professional Sports Remade Atlanta* (University of Nebraska Press, 2021). He'd love to hear from you on Twitter: @ClaytonTrutor.

Cosme Vivanco is a Chicago-based writer who received his master of fine arts in creative writing from Columbia College in 2010. As a child, he developed an incredible passion for baseball history. His other areas of interest are politics and music. He has run in the Chicago Marathon four times and hopes to do it again in 2021. His biography of Steve Carlton was included in SABR's *20 Game Losers*. He also contributed to *Met-rospectives: A Collection of the Greatest Games in New York Mets History*.

Nick Waddell has been a SABR member since 2006, and has authored bios for books on the Tigers, Mets, Red Sox, and Padres. He is a lifelong Detroit Tigers fan, and currently resides on the Upper Peninsula of Michigan.

Joseph Wancho has been a SABR member since 2005. He serves as the vice chair of the Baseball Index Project and occasionally contributes to the BioProject as well as the Games Project.

Darin Watson lives in Hot Springs Village, Arkansas, with his wife, Michelle, and four pets, including a cat named after Alex Gordon. Darin both joined SABR and relocated to Arkansas from the Kansas City area in 2018; it was a busy year. This is his third contribution to a SABR book so far and he is excited to add to that list. He grew up in Topeka, Kansas, learning to love the Royals, and still considers himself lucky that he is old enough to remember the 1985 World Series. He works for a media company and blogs about Royals history at ulstoothpick.com.

Bob Webster grew up in northwest Indiana and has been a Cubs fan since 1963. Now living in Portland, Oregon, Bob spends his time working on baseball research and writing and is a contributor to quite a few SABR projects. He worked as a stats stringer on the MLB Gameday app for three years and is a member of the Pacific Northwest Chapter of SABR and on the Board of Directors of the Old-Timers Baseball Association of Portland.

Steve West is a freelance writer in Texas. He has written a number of articles for the BioProject, and was co-editor of the SABR book on the 1972 Texas Rangers, *The Team That Couldn't Hit*.

Gregory H. Wolf was born in Pittsburgh, but now resides in the Chicagoland area with his wife, Margaret, and daughter, Gabriela. A professor of German studies and holder of the Dennis and Jean Bauman Endowed Chair in the Humanities at North Central College in Naperville, Illinois, he has edited a dozen books for SABR. He is currently working on projects about Shibe Park in Philadelphia and Ebbets Field in Brooklyn. Since January 2017 he has been co-director of SABR's BioProject, which you can follow on Facebook and Twitter.

Jack Zerby has been a follower of Braves baseball since a move to southwest Florida in 1980 left him well removed from western Pennsylvania and broadcasts of the Pirates, the team of his early fandom. Ted Turner's WTBS and Skip Caray filled the gap left by KDKA and Bob Prince. The ups and downs of the Braves have filled Jack's springs, summers, and falls ever since and have inspired much of his SABR writing, especially for the Games Project. Jack and his wife, Diana, live in Brevard, North Carolina. He is a retired attorney and estates/trusts administrator. He joined SABR in 1994.

Friends of SABR

You can become a Friend of SABR by giving as little as $10 per month or by making a one-time gift of $1,000 or more. When you do so, you will be inducted into a community of passionate baseball fans dedicated to supporting SABR's work.

Friends of SABR receive the following benefits:
- ✓ Annual Friends of SABR Commemorative Lapel Pin
- ✓ Recognition in This Week in SABR, SABR.org, and the SABR Annual Report
- ✓ Access to the SABR Annual Convention VIP donor event
- ✓ Invitations to exclusive Friends of SABR events

SABR On-Deck Circle - $10/month, $30/month, $50/month

Get in the SABR On-Deck Circle, and help SABR become the essential community for the world of baseball. Your support will build capacity around all things SABR, including publications, website content, podcast development, and community growth.

A monthly gift is deducted from your bank account or charged to a credit card until you tell us to stop. No more email, mail, or phone reminders.

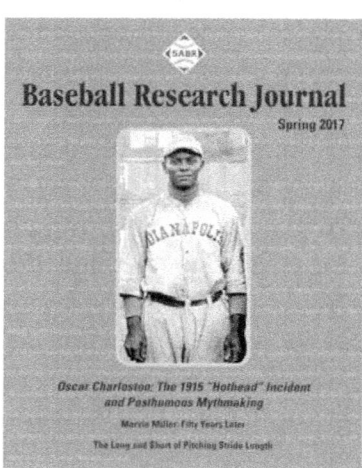
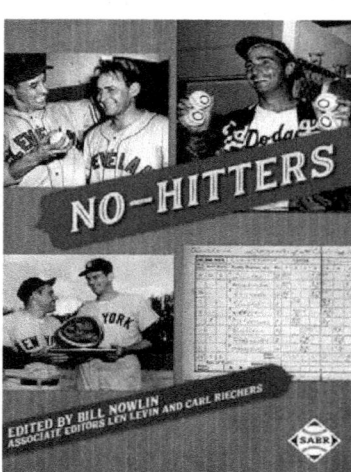

Join the SABR On-Deck Circle

Payment Info: _____ Visa _____ Mastercard

Name on Card: _____

Card #: _____

Exp. Date: _____ Security Code: _____

Signature: _____

- ○ $10/month
- ○ $30/month
- ○ $50/month
- ○ Other amount _____

Go to sabr.org/donate to make your gift online

Society for American Baseball Research

Cronkite School at ASU
555 N. Central Ave. #416, Phoenix, AZ 85004
602.496.1460 (phone)
SABR.org

Become a SABR member today!

If you're interested in baseball — writing about it, reading about it, talking about it — there's a place for you in the Society for American Baseball Research.

SABR memberships are available on annual, multi-year, or monthly subscription basis. Annual and monthly subscription memberships auto-renew for your convenience. Young Professional memberships are for ages 30 and under. Senior memberships are for ages 65 and older. Student memberships are available to currently enrolled middle/high school or full-time college/university students. Monthly subscription members receive SABR publications electronically and are eligible for SABR event discounts after 12 months.

Here's a list of some of the key benefits you'll receive as a SABR member:

- Receive two editions (spring and fall) of the *Baseball Research Journal*, our flagship publication
- Receive expanded e-book edition of *The National Pastime*, our annual convention journal
- 8-10 new e-books published by the SABR Digital Library, all FREE to members
- "This Week in SABR" e-newsletter, sent to members every Friday
- Join dozens of research committees, from Statistical Analysis to Women in Baseball.
- Join one of 70+ regional chapters in the U.S., Canada, Latin America, and abroad
- Participate in online discussion groups
- Ask and answer baseball research questions on the SABR-L e-mail listserv
- Complete archives of *The Sporting News* dating back to 1886 and other research resources
- Promote your research in "This Week in SABR"
- Diamond Dollars Case Competition
- Yoseloff Scholarships

- Discounts on SABR national conferences, including the SABR National Convention, the SABR Analytics Conference, Jerry Malloy Negro League Conference, Frederick Ivor-Campbell 19th Century Conference, and the Arizona Fall League Experience
- Publish your research in peer-reviewed SABR journals
- Collaborate with SABR researchers and experts
- Contribute to Baseball Biography Project or the SABR Games Project
- List your new book in the SABR Bookshelf
- Lead a SABR research committee or chapter
- Networking opportunities at SABR Analytics Conference
- Meet baseball authors and historians at SABR events and chapter meetings
- 50% discounts on paperback versions of SABR e-books
- Discounts with other partners in the baseball community
- SABR research awards

We hope you'll join the most passionate international community of baseball fans at SABR! Check us out online at SABR.org/join.

SABR MEMBERSHIP FORM

	Standard	Senior	Young Pro.	Student
Annual:	☐ $65	☐ $45	☐ $45	☐ $25
3 Year:	☐ $175	☐ $129	☐ $129	
5 Year:	☐ $249			
Monthly:	☐ $6.95	☐ $4.95	☐ $4.95	

(*International members wishing to be mailed the Baseball Research Journal should add $10/yr for Canada/Mexico or $19/yr for overseas locations.*)

Name _____

E-mail* _____

Address _____

City _____ ST _____ ZIP _____

Phone _____ Birthday _____

* Your e-mail address on file ensures you will receive the most recent SABR news.

Participate in Our Donor Program!

Support the preservation of baseball research. Designate your gift toward:
☐ General Fund ☐ Endowment Fund ☐ Research Resources ☐ _____
☐ I want to maximize the impact of my gift; do not send any donor premiums
☐ I would like this gift to remain anonymous.

Note: Any donation not designated will be placed in the General Fund.
SABR is a 501 (c) (3) not-for-profit organization & donations are tax-deductible to the extent allowed by law.

Dues $ _____

Donation $ _____

Amount Enclosed $ _____

Do you work for a matching grant corporation? Call (602) 496-1460 for details.

If you wish to pay by credit card, please contact the SABR office at (602) 496-1460 or sign up securely online at SABR.org/join. We accept Visa, Mastercard & Discover.

Do you wish to receive the *Baseball Research Journal* electronically? ☐ Yes ☐ No
Our e-books are available in PDF, Kindle, or EPUB (iBooks, iPad, Nook) formats.

Mail to: SABR, Cronkite School at ASU, 555 N. Central Ave. #416, Phoenix, AZ 85004

SABR BioProject Team Books

In 2002, the Society for American Baseball Research launched an effort to write and publish biographies of every player, manager, and individual who has made a contribution to baseball. Over the past decade, the BioProject Committee has produced over 6,000 biographical articles. Many have been part of efforts to create theme- or team-oriented books, spearheaded by chapters or other committees of SABR.

THE 1986 BOSTON RED SOX:
THERE WAS MORE THAN GAME SIX
One of a two-book series on the rivals that met in the 1986 World Series, the Boston Red Sox and the New York Mets, including biographies of every player, coach, broadcaster, and other important figures in the top organizations in baseball that year. .
Edited by Leslie Heaphy and Bill Nowlin
$19.95 paperback (ISBN 978-1-943816-19-4)
$9.99 ebook (ISBN 978-1-943816-18-7)
8.5"X11", 420 pages, over 200 photos

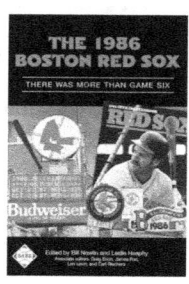

THE 1986 NEW YORK METS:
THERE WAS MORE THAN GAME SIX
The other book in the "rivalry" set from the 1986 World Series. This book re-tells the story of that year's classic World Series and this is the story of each of the players, coaches, managers, and broadcasters, their lives in baseball and the way the 1986 season fit into their lives.
Edited by Leslie Heaphy and Bill Nowlin
$19.95 paperback (ISBN 978-1-943816-13-2)
$9.99 ebook (ISBN 978-1-943816-12-5)
8.5"X11", 392 pages, over 100 photos

SCANDAL ON THE SOUTH SIDE:
THE 1919 CHICAGO WHITE SOX
The Black Sox Scandal isn't the only story worth telling about the 1919 Chicago White Sox. The team roster included three future Hall of Famers, a 20-year-old spitballer who would win 300 games in the minors, and even a batboy who later became a celebrity with the "Murderers' Row" New York Yankees. All of their stories are included in Scandal on the South Side with a timeline of the 1919 season.
Edited by Jacob Pomrenke
$19.95 paperback (ISBN 978-1-933599-95-3)
$9.99 ebook (ISBN 978-1-933599-94-6)
8.5"x11", 324 pages, 55 historic photos

WINNING ON THE NORTH SIDE
THE 1929 CHICAGO CUBS
Celebrate the 1929 Chicago Cubs, one of the most exciting teams in baseball history. Future Hall of Famers Hack Wilson, '29 NL MVP Rogers Hornsby, and Kiki Cuyler, along with Riggs Stephenson formed one of the most potent quartets in baseball history. The magical season came to an ignominious end in the World Series and helped craft the future "lovable loser" image of the team.
Edited by Gregory H. Wolf
$19.95 paperback (ISBN 978-1-933599-89-2)
$9.99 ebook (ISBN 978-1-933599-88-5)
8.5"x11", 314 pages, 59 photos

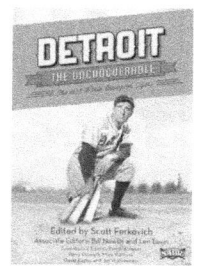

DETROIT THE UNCONQUERABLE:
THE 1935 WORLD CHAMPION TIGERS
Biographies of every player, coach, and broadcaster involved with the 1935 World Champion Detroit Tigers baseball team, written by members of the Society for American Baseball Research. Also includes a season in review and other articles about the 1935 team. Hank Greenberg, Mickey Cochrane, Charlie Gehringer, Schoolboy Rowe, and more.
Edited by Scott Ferkovich
$19.95 paperback (ISBN 9978-1-933599-78-6)
$9.99 ebook (ISBN 978-1-933599-79-3)
8.5"X11", 230 pages, 52 photos

THE TEAM THAT TIME WON'T FORGET:
THE 1951 NEW YORK GIANTS
Because of Bobby Thomson's dramatic "Shot Heard 'Round the World" in the bottom of the ninth of the decisive playoff game against the Brooklyn Dodgers, the team will forever be in baseball public's consciousness. Includes a foreword by Giants outfielder Monte Irvin.
Edited by Bill Nowlin and C. Paul Rogers III
$19.95 paperback (ISBN 978-1-933599-99-1)
$9.99 ebook (ISBN 978-1-933599-98-4)
8.5"X11", 282 pages, 47 photos

A PENNANT FOR THE TWIN CITIES:
THE 1965 MINNESOTA TWINS
This volume celebrates the 1965 Minnesota Twins, who captured the American League pennant in just their fifth season in the Twin Cities. Led by an All-Star cast, from Harmon Killebrew, Tony Oliva, Zoilo Versalles, and Mudcat Grant to Bob Allison, Jim Kaat, Earl Battey, and Jim Perry, the Twins won 102 games, but bowed to the Los Angeles Dodgers and Sandy Koufax in Game Seven
Edited by Gregory H. Wolf
$19.95 paperback (ISBN 978-1-943816-09-5)
$9.99 ebook (ISBN 978-1-943816-08-8)
8.5"X11", 405 pages, over 80 photos

MUSTACHES AND MAYHEM: CHARLIE O'S THREE TIME CHAMPIONS:
THE OAKLAND ATHLETICS: 1972-74
The Oakland Athletics captured major league baseball's crown each year from 1972 through 1974. Led by future Hall of Famers Reggie Jackson, Catfish Hunter and Rollie Fingers, the Athletics were a largely homegrown group who came of age together. Biographies of every player, coach, manager, and broadcaster (and mascot) from 1972 through 1974 are included, along with season recaps.
Edited by Chip Greene
$29.95 paperback (ISBN 978-1-943816-07-1)
$9.99 ebook (ISBN 978-1-943816-06-4)
8.5"X11", 600 pages, almost 100 photos

SABR Members can purchase each book at a significant discount (often 50% off) and receive the ebook edtions free as a member benefit. Each book is available in a trade paperback edition as well as ebooks suitable for reading on a home computer or Nook, Kindle, or iPad/tablet.
To learn more about becoming a member of SABR, visit the website: sabr.org/join

THE SABR DIGITAL LIBRARY

The Society for American Baseball Research, the top baseball research organization in the world, disseminates some of the best in baseball history, analysis, and biography through our publishing programs. The SABR Digital Library contains a mix of books old and new, and focuses on a tandem program of paperback and ebook publication, making these materials widely available for both on digital devices and as traditional printed books.

GREATEST GAMES BOOKS

TIGERS BY THE TALE:
GREAT GAMES AT MICHIGAN AND TRUMBULL
For over 100 years, Michigan and Trumbull was the scene of some of the most exciting baseball ever. This book portrays 50 classic games at the corner, spanning the earliest days of Bennett Park until Tiger Stadium's final closing act. From Ty Cobb to Mickey Cochrane, Hank Greenberg to Al Kaline, and Willie Horton to Alan Trammell.
Edited by Scott Ferkovich
$12.95 paperback (ISBN 978-1-943816-21-7)
$6.99 ebook (ISBN 978-1-943816-20-0)
8.5"x11", 160 pages, 22 photos

FROM THE BRAVES TO THE BREWERS: GREAT GAMES AND HISTORY AT MILWAUKEE'S COUNTY STADIUM
The National Pastime provides in-depth articles focused on the geographic region where the national SABR convention is taking place annually. The SABR 45 convention took place in Chicago, and here are 45 articles on baseball in and around the bat-and-ball crazed Windy City: 25 that appeared in the souvenir book of the convention plus another 20 articles available in ebook only.
Edited by Gregory H. Wolf
$19.95 paperback (ISBN 978-1-943816-23-1)
$9.99 ebook (ISBN 978-1-943816-22-4)
8.5"X11", 290 pages, 58 photos

BRAVES FIELD:
MEMORABLE MOMENTS AT BOSTON'S LOST DIAMOND
From its opening on August 18, 1915, to the sudden departure of the Boston Braves to Milwaukee before the 1953 baseball season, Braves Field was home to Boston's National League baseball club and also hosted many other events: from NFL football to championship boxing. The most memorable moments to occur in Braves Field history are portrayed here.
Edited by Bill Nowlin and Bob Brady
$19.95 paperback (ISBN 978-1-933599-93-9)
$9.99 ebook (ISBN 978-1-933599-92-2)
8.5"X11", 282 pages, 182 photos

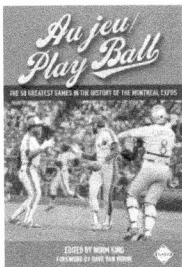

AU JEU/PLAY BALL: THE 50 GREATEST GAMES IN THE HISTORY OF THE MONTREAL EXPOS
The 50 greatest games in Montreal Expos history. The games described here recount the exploits of the many great players who wore Expos uniforms over the years—Bill Stoneman, Gary Carter, Andre Dawson, Steve Rogers, Pedro Martinez, from the earliest days of the franchise, to the glory years of 1979-1981, the what-might-have-been years of the early 1990s, and the sad, final days.and others.
Edited by Norm King
$12.95 paperback (ISBN 978-1-943816-15-6)
$5.99 ebook (ISBN978-1-943816-14-9)
8.5"x11", 162 pages, 50 photos

ORIGINAL SABR RESEARCH

CALLING THE GAME:
BASEBALL BROADCASTING FROM 1920 TO THE PRESENT
An exhaustive, meticulously researched history of bringing the national pastime out of the ballparks and into living rooms via the airwaves. Every play-by-play announcer, color commentator, and ex-ballplayer, every broadcast deal, radio station, and TV network. Plus a foreword by "Voice of the Chicago Cubs" Pat Hughes, and an afterword by Jacques Doucet, the "Voice of the Montreal Expos" 1972-2004.
by Stuart Shea
$24.95 paperback (ISBN 978-1-933599-40-3)
$9.99 ebook (ISBN 978-1-933599-41-0)
7"X10", 712 pages, 40 photos

BIOPROJECT BOOKS

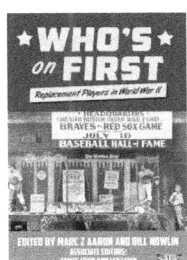

WHO'S ON FIRST:
REPLACEMENT PLAYERS IN WORLD WAR II
During World War II, 533 players made the major league debuts. More than 60% of the players in the 1941 Opening Day lineups departed for the service and were replaced by first-times and oldsters. Hod Lisenbee was 46. POW Bert Shepard had an artificial leg, and Pete Gray had only one arm. The 1944 St. Louis Browns had 13 players classified 4-F. These are their stories.
Edited by Marc Z Aaron and Bill Nowlin
$19.95 paperback (ISBN 978-1-933599-91-5)
$9.99 ebook (ISBN 978-1-933599-90-8)
8.5"X11", 422 pages, 67 photos

VAN LINGLE MUNGO:
THE MAN, THE SONG, THE PLAYERS
40 baseball players with intriguing names have been named in renditions of Dave Frishberg's classic 1969 song, Van Lingle Mungo. This book presents biographies of all 40 players and additional information about one of the greatest baseball novelty songs of all time.
Edited by Bill Nowlin
$19.95 paperback (ISBN 978-1-933599-76-2)
$9.99 ebook (ISBN 978-1-933599-77-9)
8.5"X11", 278 pages, 46 photos

NUCLEAR POWERED BASEBALL
Nuclear Powered Baseball tells the stories of each player—past and present—featured in the classic Simpsons episode "Homer at the Bat." Wade Boggs, Ken Griffey Jr., Ozzie Smith, Nap Lajoie, Don Mattingly, and many more. We've also included a few very entertaining takes on the now-famous episode from prominent baseball writers Jonah Keri, Joe Posnanski, Erik Malinowski, and Bradley Woodrum.
Edited by Emily Hawks and Bill Nowlin
$19.95 paperback (ISBN 978-1-943816-11-8)
$9.99 ebook (ISBN 978-1-943816-10-1)
8.5"X11", 250 pages

SABR Members can purchase each book at a significant discount (often 50% off) and receive the ebook edtions free as a member benefit. Each book is available in a trade paperback edition as well as ebooks suitable for reading on a home computer or Nook, Kindle, or iPad/tablet.
To learn more about becoming a member of SABR, visit the website: sabr.org/join

SABR BioProject Books

In 2002, the Society for American Baseball Research launched an effort to write and publish biographies of every player, manager, and individual who has made a contribution to baseball. Over the past decade, the BioProject Committee has produced over 2,200 biographical articles. Many have been part of efforts to create theme- or team-oriented books, spearheaded by chapters or other committees of SABR.

THE YEAR OF THE BLUE SNOW:
THE 1964 PHILADELPHIA PHILLIES
Catcher Gus Triandos dubbed the Philadelphia Phillies' 1964 season "the year of the blue snow," a rare thing that happens once in a great while. This book sheds light on lingering questions about the 1964 season—but any book about a team is really about the players. This work offers life stories of all the players and others (managers, coaches, owners, and broadcasters) associated with this star-crossed team, as well as essays of analysis and history.
Edited by Mel Marmer and Bill Nowlin
$19.95 paperback (ISBN 978-1-933599-51-9)
$9.99 ebook (ISBN 978-1-933599-52-6)
8.5"X11", 356 PAGES, over 70 photos

DETROIT TIGERS 1984:
WHAT A START! WHAT A FINISH!
The 1984 Detroit tigers roared out of the gate, winning their first nine games of the season and compiling an eye-popping 35-5 record after the campaign's first 40 games—still the best start ever for any team in major league history. This book brings together biographical profiles of every Tiger from that magical season, plus those of field management, top executives, the broadcasters—even venerable Tiger Stadium and the city itself.
Edited by Mark Pattison and David Raglin
$19.95 paperback (ISBN 978-1-933599-44-1)
$9.99 ebook (ISBN 978-1-933599-45-8)
8.5"x11", 250 pages (Over 230,000 words!)

SWEET '60: THE 1960 PITTSBURGH PIRATES
A portrait of the 1960 team which pulled off one of the biggest upsets of the last 60 years. When Bill Mazeroski's home run left the park to win in Game Seven of the World Series, beating the New York Yankees, David had toppled Goliath. It was a blow that awakened a generation, one that millions of people saw on television, one of TV's first iconic World Series moments.
Edited by Clifton Blue Parker and Bill Nowlin
$19.95 paperback (ISBN 978-1-933599-48-9)
$9.99 ebook (ISBN 978-1-933599-49-6)
8.5"X11", 340 pages, 75 photos

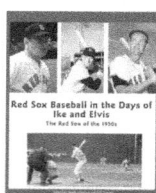

RED SOX BASEBALL IN THE DAYS OF IKE AND ELVIS: THE RED SOX OF THE 1950S
Although the Red Sox spent most of the 1950s far out of contention, the team was filled with fascinating players who captured the heart of their fans. In *Red Sox Baseball*, members of SABR present 46 biographies on players such as Ted Williams and Pumpsie Green as well as season-by-season recaps.
Edited by Mark Armour and Bill Nowlin
$19.95 paperback (ISBN 978-1-933599-24-3)
$9.99 ebook (ISBN 978-1-933599-34-2)
8.5"X11", 372 PAGES, over 100 photos

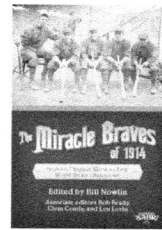

THE MIRACLE BRAVES OF 1914
BOSTON'S ORIGINAL WORST-TO-FIRST CHAMPIONS
Long before the Red Sox "Impossible Dream" season, Boston's now nearly forgotten "other" team, the 1914 Boston Braves, performed a baseball "miracle" that resounds to this very day. The "Miracle Braves" were Boston's first "worst-to-first" winners of the World Series. Refusing to throw in the towel at the midseason mark, George Stallings engineered a remarkable second-half climb in the standings all the way to first place.
Edited by Bill Nowlin
$19.95 paperback (ISBN 978-1-933599-69-4)
$9.99 ebook (ISBN 978-1-933599-70-0)
8.5"X11", 392 PAGES, over 100 photos

THAR'S JOY IN BRAVELAND!
THE 1957 MILWAUKEE BRAVES
Few teams in baseball history have captured the hearts of their fans like the Milwaukee Braves of the 1950s. During the Braves' 13-year tenure in Milwaukee (1953-1965), they had a winning record every season, won two consecutive NL pennants (1957 and 1958), lost two more in the final week of the season (1956 and 1959), and set big-league attendance records along the way.
Edited by Gregory H. Wolf
$19.95 paperback (ISBN 978-1-933599-71-7)
$9.99 ebook (ISBN 978-1-933599-72-4)
8.5"x11", 330 pages, over 60 photos

NEW CENTURY, NEW TEAM:
THE 1901 BOSTON AMERICANS
The team now known as the Boston Red Sox played its first season in 1901. Boston had a well-established National League team, but the American League went head-to-head with the N.L. in Chicago, Philadelphia, and Boston. Chicago won the American League pennant and Boston finished second, only four games behind.
Edited by Bill Nowlin
$19.95 paperback (ISBN 978-1-933599-58-8)
$9.99 ebook (ISBN 978-1-933599-59-5)
8.5"X11", 268 pages, over 125 photos

CAN HE PLAY?
A LOOK AT BASEBALL SCOUTS AND THEIR PROFESSION
They dig through tons of coal to find a single diamond. Here in the world of scouts, we meet the "King of Weeds," a Ph.D. we call "Baseball's Renaissance Man," a husband-and-wife team, pioneering Latin scouts, and a Japanese-American interned during World War II who became a successful scout—and many, many more.
Edited by Jim Sandoval and Bill Nowlin
$19.95 paperback (ISBN 978-1-933599-23-6)
$9.99 ebook (ISBN 978-1-933599-25-0)
8.5"X11", 200 PAGES, over 100 photos

SABR Members can purchase each book at a significant discount (often 50% off) and receive the ebook editions free as a member benefit. Each book is available in a trade paperback edition as well as ebooks suitable for reading on a home computer or Nook, Kindle, or iPad/tablet.
To learn more about becoming a member of SABR, visit the website: sabr.org/join